CULL

CHOOSING WELL

BRAD LANCASTER

Library of Congress Cataloguing in Publication Data:
Lancaster, Brad.
Cull: Choosing Well/Brad Lancaster
Includes bibliographical reference and index

ISBN 978-0-9986435-0-2

Published by:
　　　　Saint George's Hill Press
　　　　17503 10th Avenue N.E.
　　　　Shoreline, Washington 98155

First Printing: 2017

This book is printed in Times New Roman font.

Printed in the United States of America for
St. George's Hill Press, Shoreline, Washington.

For Kate, Shelby, and Ryan

CONTENTS

CULL: CHOOSING WELL

(THE CORE ARGUMENT IN ONE VOLUME)

Contents of the Companion Volume

Cull: Epitomes

(Companion Volume to *Cull: Choosing Well*).

PREFACE

"Man needs a rule for his will,
and will invent one if one be not given him."

William James
The Sentiment of Rationality
1905

Once, for several years, I supplemented the educations of three precocious middle schoolers: Ryan, Kate, and Shelby. A forty-eight inch oak table nestles at the front windows of my home. It was our diminutive campus. We read cosmology, human history and prehistory, great minds east and west, religious canons, classic novels, physics, and sundry materials that snatched attention. We laughed and examined and criticized and giggled. Those many days were, for me, an idyll of childhood revisited.

Snow fell outside on a December afternoon. I belabored the importance of making good decisions. Kate asked, "*How* do you make good decisions?" I trotted out the LEARN mnemonic I stole somewhere: Look for need, Evaluate options, Act, Reassess, then make a New attempt. Kate squinted, "That was easy." I shook my head and frowned. "Not so much. All sorts of factors and ideas affect choosing well. Let me think about it." So, I did.

Ludwig Wittgenstein said, of his *Philosophical Investigations,* which examines meaning, understanding, logic, mathematics, and consciousness, that his efforts convinced him he would never succeed. Failure etched the implacable granite of his subjects. So too, *Cull.* Answering Kate leads one from the early Pleistocene epoch, to brain evolution, to the nature of consciousness, to goodness and evil, to meaningful community, to childlessness and nurture, to nonviolence, to anarchy and coercion and kithdom, to a shelf of priceless books, and thirty thousand years hence. Human conduct taxes the reader. It taxed this writer--more, in fact, than his purse of talent could bear.

This book deliberates choosing well.[1] How does humanity need to change its habits of thought? To whom should we be listening for moral guidance, and what habits should we inculcate? What choices should we make about our to-

---

[1] Epictetus said, "What, then, shall we do?—This is a subject of enquiry for the man who truly philosophizes and is in travail of thought." Epictetus, *Discourses,* 145 (Book I, Section 22.18).

getherness, and how shall we make those decisions? How do we peer deep
enough into our future to do ourselves, and our progeny, any good?   The book
offers rules for one's will. It dishes up fodder for rumination. It bores a peep-
hole into the sanctum of the finest minds that have deliberated these issues by
means of epitomes[2] of core works. The book addresses not only making good
decisions, but also offers thoughts on what constitutes goodness, a conversation
liberally spiced with approaches alternative to those with which you may be familiar. Behind William James's concern about finding a "rule for the will" lurks
the suspicion that most people gulp their preferences whole from fractured pots
of family and peer stews, most often making themselves drunk upon religious or
ideological orthodoxies.[3] Failing that, as James says, one creates. This book is
of the latter sort—invented, syncretistic,[4] and ultimately idiosyncratic. I mean
that the writer is in the answer. My chaff could not be winnowed from this
grain.[5] *Caveat lector.* Still, this book is neither a personal pastiche nor, as
Wittgenstein criticized his *Investigations*, an album. It is not autobiography, but
neither does it pretend objectivity. One hopes the book helps.

As to what I say, you will disagree with me occasionally or often. That is
as it should be. Gandhi taught that *seeking* truth matters. Our errors grow rapid-

---

[2] An "epitome" is a summary of a written work, a brief version which could also be called an abstract or abridgement. See *Webster's Third New International Dictionary*, s.v. "epitome."   As I
epitomize a work, I attempt to focus on that work's core argument, to the neglect of digressions, examples, illustrations, tables, worksheets, and other useful, but voluminous, explanatory tools. Generally, my epitomes capture twenty to forty pages of original material per epitomized page. Especially dense work may have a ratio of one epitomized page to ten pages of original text. The point of
epitomizing these works is to grant access to the core argument of difficult books without poring
over thousands of pages of occasionally opaque materials. This latter effort would exceed the free
time available to most working people. Epicurus epitomized his own work. He argues that, for
those unable to examine his longer works, capturing an outline of thoughts is better than nothing.
Epicurus, *Letter to Herodotus* in *The Essential Epicurus*, 19.

[3] Some friendly editors have urged me to drop my frankness about religion and ideology. I personally have been religious. I have been drunk on orthodoxy (and may still be so in ways I do not comprehend.) Nevertheless, religious and ideological orthodoxies appear for most a refuge from thinking. If thought forms were groceries, religio-ideological enthusiasts buy from the prepared-foods
counter. *Cull* offers different fare.

[4] "Syncretism" blends ideas, sometimes contradictory, from diverse schools of (often religious)
thought, not infrequently with insufficient attention to the consistency of the wedding. See *Webster's Third New International Dictionary*, s.v. "syncretism."

[5] John Paul Lederach argues that the academic penchant for avoiding personal reference is misguided, pretending to an objectivity in the writer that is in fact absent. Lederach says: "When we attempt to eliminate the personal, we lose sight of ourselves, our deeper intuition, and the sources of
our understandings—*who we are* and *how we are in the world*. In so doing we arrive at a paradoxi-
cal destination: We believe in the knowledge we generate but not in the inherently messy and personal process by which we acquired it." Lederach, *The Moral Imagination*, viii.

ly irrelevant, because the world dwells in its Objectivity, after which we infrequently grasp. Gandhi believed that what gods there are instruct those who grapple, no matter how wrongheaded they begin. I cannot follow Gandhi in his sacred asceticism. Theological ethics, in which enterprise one imagines that gods tell men how to behave, suffers senescence.[6] Its grip has slipped, at least as to me. This book grounds human morality in the stuff of this earth and the tangle of hominin neurons. The work does not rely upon theodiction,[7] though, as one can gather from the epitomized works contained at Volume II, much of interest emerges from those who make theodictic claims.

If the sentiment nestles in you that all is well with the human world, that men should tweak here and prod there, to get matters just about right, then you will want to put this book down now. Mine are painful solutions. Much of human existence lingers, in my view, senselessly near the border of the horrid. I hope for more and better. I encourage you to so hope as well, Kate. Ours is an era of intense specialization. This book swims against that tide. I presume to assess the human moral circumstance generally (which is the great value and great flaw of this book). What emerges from these pages is a prescription, a tonic for collapsed meaning.

Beneath all the words of this book hunkers a conviction: humans must imagine better futures. We need this bread-of-the-heart, just as our bodies need daily sustenance. Absent visions of a preferable future, we perish, like malnourished babies. Yet, among men, few agree that humanity needs rudimentary redirection of imagination. Most prefer nits and half-measures, praying that the hurtling highway of history holds no sharp turns that demand deceleration and consulting a map. The well seek no remedy.

Odd that I find myself compelled to ask whether you really want to read this book. But I do ask.[8]

---

[6] "Senescence" means aging or withering, and often includes the connotation that the senescent suffers diminished mental powers. See *Webster's Third New International Dictionary*, s.v. "senescence" and "senesce."

Alasdair MacIntyre argues that contemporary moral dialogue has grown nonsensical, for the world from which our moral terminology derives has been lost to modernity. So, our moral discussions find no end and reach no conclusions. We converse in a non-conversant manner, believing that moral goodness amounts to nothing more than one's approval for the object of claimed good. To escape our conundrum, MacIntyre believes we need to recover the lost world of moral discursus and virtue story-telling. For that recovery, MacIntyre looks to Aristotle, Aquinas, and Catholic theology. MacIntyre, *After Virtue*, 2-12, 22, 121, 256-263.

[7] I coin the terms "theodiction" and "theodictic" (mash-ups of Greek for "god" and Latin for "utter" or "speak") to specify experiences after which one asserts a god has spoken to or through him. I view myself as an undomesticated theist with a much-trammeled, but nevertheless persistent, blunt streak. *Mea culpa.*

[8] This is a book of many words. The Hindu *Upanishads* warn that wordiness is weariness. *Upanishads*, 142 (*Brihadaranyaka Upanishad* 4.3-4). The biblical Preacher of wisdom asserts that making

So, Kate, walk with me, if you will.[9] These two volumes, if read with a bit of care, proffer an education in morality. I have culled the best of the many books you might read, if time permitted. Time does not permit. I offer the guts of those books by way of epitomes. I chew them, savoring some, spitting out others. I make suggestions that satisfy a few readers, mostly people inclined to make their relationships intense and intentional. Some others gag on my words, deeming me one more yammerer in a world crammed with ceaseless yammer.

If you will, Kate, survey these convened fragments. Work your puzzles. In the end, expand your view of Kate, she who culls. That changes everything.[10]

---

books and persistent study exhaust one endlessly. *Ecclesiastes* 12:12. Rousseau warns that too much reading makes one a presumptuous ignoramus. Rousseau, *Emile*, 450. Edmund Burke complains of his *Reflections*: "This letter is grown to a great length, though it is indeed short with regard to the infinite extent of the subject." Burke, *Reflections on the Revolution in France*, 167. All may be right.

[9] This book offers a walk, which is a process. *Cull* does not offer a structure (despite frequent passages the could be interpreted as such), which would be a destination or utopia. Gary Bloom accuses me of unconscionably "burying my lede" in the last pages of *Cull*. So, I repent. *Cull* describes a *process* of human dialogue, a big action-oriented conversation about meaningful togetherness. Such talking, if made habitual, might result in widespread meaningful human community. I go so far as to offer ideas about where such conversation might take us as a global community.

[10]*Cull* contains many footnotes. For the author, the tastiest flavors of any book lie in its footnotes. For others, footnotes annoy or distract; hence, the growing publication practice (which I find lamentable) of relegating footnotes to the text's end (making them endnotes). **If *Cull's* footnotes bother you, please do not read them.** But then, you ask, how should one know to avoid these footnotes without reading this footnote? I have no answer.

INTRODUCTION

For fifty millennia, humankind has expanded.

Humans erupted from the horn of Africa, rimmed the Indian Ocean, and guttered in Tasmania. We flowed up the Pacific Rim and back across Asia. We spread across the fertile crescent and occupied Europe. We crossed Beringia[11] and peopled the New World. Numbers grew, with occasional setbacks. Lately, we settled in our expanding billions, filling every nook, feeding ourselves from every readily arable inch. We probed our moon, and launched robotic surrogates to the system's planets. Life off-planet appears harsher than hoped. Humans glut the earth, crowding one another, crowding out other species. Human spreading has foundered, not for failure of inclination, but for absence of opportunity. Newcomers cling to cliffs, tempting gravity, and people floodplains, disbelieving rain. So, mankind reaches transition. Humanity passes its tumultuous adolescence, pondering what adulthood may hold.[12]

What will be the shape of our transition? What does the next 30,000 years of human life look like? What will humans make of themselves, now that expansive nomadism is dead? Once, when we argued, petulant families pulled up stakes and moved to an adjacent unoccupied valley. Every valley is now claimed by someone. Again, when resources thinned, people moved to greener pastures. No unclaimed resources remain.[13] Always, when scowling neighbors intruded, we feared them, and they us. Perhaps we fought, as pillaging became a detestable alternative to foraging. For the foreseeable future, no violent insularity will prove profitable. Humanity's most fundamental life solutions are being recast. How will we soothe conflicts? How will we consume only what can be replaced or reused? How will humans shackle violent territoriality? Ultimately,

---

[11] Beringia was a large land connection (now inundated, but repeatedly exposed during Pleistocene periods of intense glaciation and lowered sea levels) that linked extreme eastern Siberia with extreme western Alaska.

[12] Perhaps sentient species, as well as the members who comprise them, dwell in a maturational schema. Might our collectivity adopt stable patterns and steady progress of a communal adulthood, leaving behind the streaky and risk-laden approaches that appeal to ego-centric teenagers? Tolstoy argued: "What is now happening to the people of the East as of the West is like what happens to every individual when he passes from childhood to adolescence and from youth to manhood. He loses what had hitherto guided his life and lives without direction, not having found a new standard suitable to his age, and so he invents all sorts of occupations, cares, distractions, and stupefactions to divert his attention from the misery and senselessness of his life. Such a condition may last a long time." Tolstoy, *Letter to a Hindu*, 16-17.

[13] Except perhaps in the open ocean. But, then, men are not fish.

how will we stanch our penchant to overpopulate? How can man learn to peer beyond his next full belly, greener pasture, or fortuitous sexual encounter?[14]

Nature will solve these problems if humankind cannot. Starvation, war, and pestilence have, and may again, thin our numbers. Perhaps we should now add to that grave afflictive list our inane persistence in failed solutions. Generally, the human deliberative consensus has been that nature's winnowers are forces to be resisted. Mankind devotes vast energies to blunting the impact of natural depredation. Our best motives urge us to preserve life, to accommodate others, to open doors to tomorrow. What alternatives exist, now that our past has passed?

The solutions this book proposes are old. They emerge from this writer's concatenation of ancient insights and saws, as well as those of a few moderns. The core among these sources I have epitomized, hoping to entice you to explore those you fancy. I trust such snippets help. The solutions I proffer also incorporate recent insights unavailable to thinkers born earlier, insights about human evolution and prehistory, evolutionary neurology, neuroaffective brain systems, cooperation, sociology, and post-theological analysis. I select simple rules for conduct proffered by history's wisest moralists. I frame a political theory, kithdom, which describes communities of friends choosing better futures. Ultimately, the book is a mélange culled from writers brighter than me, but perhaps less dogged. *Cull* proffers a revised structure for human living, one that bears the possibility of enduring into our indefinite future. Any such construction, and the particular rules that govern it, are an iteration of justice.[15] Every morality adjudicates individual interest and communal interest, balancing one against the other, and specifying what forms of expression for each drive are permissible. This balance, however, is no zero-sum game. Kithdom acknowledges that, in practice, individual and collective interests commingle and conjoin. The resulting flux may be excessively wondrous and abundant (or not). One gets what she wants from flourishing life with communal others. A community flourishes by well-addressing the needs of its several members. Meaningful community is a fire to which every member contributes a stick, and around which all huddle to warm themselves.

---

[14] John Paul Lederach says of conflict resolution that the work requires moral imagination, which he defines as "the capacity to imagine something rooted in the challenges of the real world yet capable of giving birth to that which does not yet exist." Lederach, *The Moral Imagination*, ix. Such imagination is required for the task of building meaningful community as well.

[15] Jessica Flack indicates that Garret Hardin styles justice as a way of living that can endure far into the unknown future. Flack, "Any Animal Whatever," 3.

Some books offer truth. Despite the hundreds of unequivocal assertions in this work, I lack confidence I reach much truth. Morality, as a topic, is slippery, maze-riddled, and awash in the neuroscience tsunami. Xenophanes argued that if one happened to stumble across the truth, he would not recognize it, for our limited thoughts consist in nothing more than aggregated human discoveries; our theories, on a good day, weave a web of guesses.[16] Schopenhauer notes that truth in morality bristles with difficulties; on it "all philosophers in every age and land have blunted their wits."[17] Truth proves slippery, except where gods speak. In theodiction, metaphysics[18] intrude, never all that welcome, bearing mysterious antinomies[19] and jocular contradictions. Some books toss a brick of truth on the reader's table. This book lands lightly, with barely a thud. It proposes not god-following, but *a process of action-oriented exploratory conversation.* I suggest a planetary future replete with deliberation and cautious action and experimental social revisions in human-sized communities. I invite dissent and careful listening.

We should talk. We should care.

We can make better decisions.

---

[16] Xenophanes, *Fragments* 34 and 35, relying on the translation of Karl Popper, *Conjectures and Refutations*, 152-153. Xenophanes was a sixth century B.C. pre-Socratic Greek philosopher, whose entire corpus has been lost. His thought is represented in snippets cited by later authors in their own works; its extent is forty-five brief fragments. J. H. Lesher disputes Popper's translation of Xenophanes Fragments 34 and 35. Lesher offers extensive commentary and dishes up six alternative interpretations of Xenophanes's intent in Fragments 34 and 35. Lesher, *Xenophanes of Colophon*, 155-176. In my view, Lesher's own view ends up not deeply differentiated from Popper's. See Lesher at page 186.

[17] Schopenhauer, *The Basis of Morality*, 3. Many pulped forests and torrents of ink have collided furiously expressing ethical deliberations of philosophers and philophasters. (A "philophaster" dabbles in philosophy, among whose number I count myself.)

[18]"Metaphysics" is a branch of philosophy that addresses the questions "what exists?" and "what is what exists like?" In metaphysics, a distinction is often made between what can be sensed (*phenomena*), and what underlies those sense perceptions (*noumena*). So, a metaphysician conjures what he believes lies beneath and behind what we sense. Metaphysics done well amounts to disciplined imagining. Metaphysics done poorly amounts to circular reasoning, in which desired results are quietly injected into premises. Schopenhauer finds a metaphysical structure essential to every scheme of moral philosophy. But then, Schopenhauer has little patience for moral philosophy. Schopenhauer, *The Basis of Morality*, 4, 74-75.

[19] An "antinomy" is a paradox, or a contradiction between two views, each of which is in itself reasonable. See *Webster's Third New International Dictionary*, s.v. "antinomy."

I. CULL[20]

Think, Kate, *about decision-making, yours and humanity's.   Examine its flow and eddies.   We choose well or poorly, alone and together.   Have we erred?   Almost all would answer that we have chosen poorly, though for diverse reasons.*[21]   *Let us converse about character, that is, our aloneness with ourselves and our togetherness with friends, acquaintances, and strangers.   Let us deliberate what augments or erodes meaningful community.   Let us contemplate human flourishing.   Taste ethics I adopt or reject; weigh objections and replies.   Pull together fragments that fix in mind what humans are: evolved moral and social animal brains-in-bodies, riven by jostling subconscious drives and emotions, frequently conscious but fitfully rational.*[22]   *You have complained that I, as a teacher, suffer comic incapacity in expressing myself.   You are undoubtedly correct.   Bear with me.   A little slack in my tether, please.   Scoff, Kate, when appropriate.   Like chili pepper in one's sleepy oatmeal, friends jolt.   Let us mull strenuous topics.   Let us cull.   Together.*

    1.   **Choosing.**   To act, one culls.[23]   One sorts for and adopts good; one identifies and ejects evil.[24]   One hopes, by culling, to undertake actions that por-

---

[20] "Cull" means: a) select the best from among others (as in gathering), or b) to remove the defective from among others (as in winnowing). See *Webster's Third New International Dictionary,* s.v. "cull." For example, one culls excellent essays in creating an anthology, and one culls sick animals from a healthy herd.

For the reader's convenience, I have epitomized **Cull** *(see pages 431-455).*

Throughout the text, the symbol |♪| indicates that the work that follows the symbol is epitomized for the reader's convenience in the companion volume, **Cull: Epitomes,** *where succinct summaries of critical ethical works are presented alphabetically by author's last name.   In my view, one's ethical literacy profits by familiarity with the works I have epitomized, which works also provide deep texture to the arguments I make in* **Cull: Choosing Well.** *My words here are too subtle: if you know little or nothing of a work I have epitomized, take the time to read my epitome in Volume II.   I joke not.   Do it.   You will be glad you did.*

[21] Gregory Bateson styles the way we think as a "maze of hallucinations." Bateson, *Steps to An Ecology of Mind,* 483. The Dalai Lama advises: "Analyze. Think, think, think. When you do you will recognize that our ordinary way of life is almost meaningless." Dalai Lama, *How To Practice,* 37.

[22] Some readers lament my resistance to including the "soul" as a fundamental component of any description of humanity. I resist because not all share that view of mankind, but all acknowledge humans are animals with brains. I offer several thoughts on the mind-body problem in the course of this text, not all of which evidence reserve about expressions of human spirituality.

[23] William Godwin, in 1793, argued (in a fit of eighteenth century irrepressible optimism) that human nature is perfectible, and one approaches such perfection by means of comparison of one idea

tend worthy outcomes. One aspires, by culling, to avoid actions that threaten ill results.[25] Moral action begins when one recognizes good acts and evil acts amid life's hurtle, and adopts a stance concerning these events.[26] Conduct-culling fashions, to the extent they are plastic, the member and her community. What sort of person are you? What sort of person do you want to become? What sort of social world issues from people possessing the character you hope takes root in you?[27]

---

or course of action with others, which leads one to a preference. Preference among competing options leads to action. [♪] Godwin, *Political Justice*, Vol. I, 43, 169-170 (Book I, Chapter VI). Michael Tomasello argues that instrumental rationality is nothing other than imagining likely outcomes of possible actions and choosing among them for maximum benefit. Tomasello, *A Natural History of Human Thinking*, 14.

[24] Plato argues that wickedness is more to be feared than death, because moral evil is harder to avoid. [♪] Plato, *Apologia, §39A*, 137. I do not employ the words "good" and "evil" in their solely moral sense. Impulses of attraction and repulsion drive the behavior of all living things, and establish the ancient and biological basis of our conscious dichotomy "good and evil." The Chinese philosopher, Mo (5th century A.D.) advocated an ethical system of propagating what benefits and eschewing what harms. [♪] *Mozi*, 41 (Part III, §16). In the Buddhist tradition, King Milinda asked sage Nagasena the nature of virtue. Nagasena replied that one pursues dharmas, some of which are wholesome and others unwholesome. The virtue of mindfulness draws attention to helpful dharmas, to the detriment and neglect of injurious dharmas. [♪] Conze, *Buddhist Scriptures*, 152 (citing *Milindapañha*). But within the Buddhist tradition, Seng-ts'an disagrees. He asserts that preferring one state of affairs over another diseases the mind. Peace pervades those who find perfect emptiness of mind, an absence of preferences. Seeking right and wrong confuses, and jeopardizes emptiness. [♪] Conze, *Buddhist Scriptures*, 171-172 (citing Seng-ts'an, "On Believing in Mind.") Again, in the Pali Buddhist tradition, wise men transcend assessments of good and evil. [♪] *Dhammapada*, 39, 267. But, elsewhere, a Buddhist seeker abstains from what hurts and seeks what helps, in the process, purifying the mind. [♪] *Dhammapada*, 183, 268-269. The *Qur'an* teaches that good acts positively repel evil. [♪] Muhammad, *Qur'an* 28:54. Ethical culling, that is, sorting good from evil, proves to be the foundational meta-scheme of most systems of ethics. Plato takes this question, whether one trends toward goodness or badness, to be the great test of men. One must not let money or acclaim or influencing others tempt one from becoming a person of justice and virtue. [♪] Plato, *Republic*, 330 (§608b).

[25] And yet, Master Zhuang warns that the Great Man "knows no line can be drawn between right and wrong, no border can be fixed between great and small. *Zhuangzi*, 101 (Autumn Floods, Section 17).

[26] This task may not prove so simple as it may sound. Richard Weaver asserts that getting real people to make real decisions about their own lives by sorting what is better from what is worse proves widely problematical. He suspects that modern man has grown morally moronic. Weaver, *Ideas Have Consequences*, 1. William Godwin believes men always choose what they deem preferable, and never knowingly adopt what they deem evil, nor return to evils previously abandoned. [♪] Godwin, *Political Justice*, Vol. I, 70-71 (Book I, Chapter VI). I wish Godwin were right. Godwin wildly underestimates cultural momentum, which induces men to persevere in patently dysfunctional behaviors despite their misgivings. Our age butts bluntly against the brick wall of failed imagination. Aristotle asserts that where such deliberative culling is well-done, it constitutes practical wisdom, which seeks the best among possible alternative goods. [♪] Aristotle, *Nichomachean Ethics*, 110 (§1141b). Michael Shermer, surveying the arc of human history, concludes that *homo sapiens* grows more and more moral. Shermer, *The Moral Arc*, 3.

[27] John Dewey identifies the core issue, in deliberations of any sort, the kind of person that issues from such a decision, and the sort of world the decision will fashion. [♪] Dewey, *Human Nature and Conduct*, 217. Dewey argued that progress means that one increases the present meaning of choices of conduct. [♪] Dewey, *Human Nature and Conduct*, 280, 282. David Hume finds that human in-

Good acts build meaningful human community.[28] Evil acts injure meaningful community. Humans nourish themselves and nurture one another in meaningful community. Meaningful community distributes human necessities, such
as food, drink, shelter, clothing, rest, membership, security, money, political office, political power, professional office, professional power, kinds of work, leisure, education, kinship, friendship, love, divine approbation, honor and recognition, and sex.[29] Of greater importance, human community provides a framework for investing these necessities with import within the cooperation of a human group.[30] For humans, meaning outweighs happiness.[31] Humans, with great

---

stincts do not govern, but rather the core concept is public utility of this or that rule. We ask, What
world emerges from this rule? What features of common life will be hobbled by that rule? Hume,
Enquiry Concerning the Principles of Morals, 97 (Chapter 3, Section 47).

[28] Aristotle opines that the best lives emerge from living in a community that well-governs life in a
manner that is as good as it can be under the circumstance. Members are happy to the extent their
acts accord with wisdom and excellence, provided they have enough external goods to undertake
good acts. [♪] Aristotle, *Politics*, 166-168 (1323a.18 and 1323b.22, 39). Robert Owen concurs. A
member's happiness emerges from conduct that promotes her community's happiness. Owen, *A
New View of Society*, 14. Pregnantly, Jaak Panksepp argues that humans are heirs to a mammalian
motherload of meaning encoded in our emotional lives. He calls humans "inheritors of ancient biological values that constitute the very ground of meaning within our minds." Panksepp and Biven,
The Archaeology of Mind, 494. Meaning is a pervasive affective state that tinges all of consciousness, provided we do not live and think in a manner that precludes its psychological tinting. Hannah
Arendt argues: "Action, as distinguished from fabrication, is never possible in isolation; to be isolated is to be deprived of the capacity to act. Action and speech need the surrounding presence of
others no less than fabrication needs the surrounding presence of nature for its material, and of a
world in which to place the finished product." Arendt, *The Human Condition*, 188. When we act,
for good or ill, we act within a human community. We act to affect that community.

[29] Michael Walzer argues that human society, as a whole, distributes social goods to its members.
Doing so well, without the domination of one sort of social good over others, constitutes complex
equality. Each good has its own sphere, and ought not be translated into another, or dominated by
another. Walzer takes complex equality to be the essence of a good society. Walzer, *Spheres of Justice*, 3-20.

[30] Muhammad urges Islamic communities to avoid dissension. Successful communities urge what is
good and forbid what is wrong, acting as brothers, because God brought them together. [♪] Muhammad, *Qur'an*, Sura 3:103-104.

[31] "Happiness" denotes a human emotional state characterized by various degrees of pleasant affect;
one seeks to perpetuate such states. See *Webster's Third New International Dictionary*, s.v. "happiness." "Meaningful existence" connotes welcomed integration into the purposive activity of an intentional human community. Thinkers disagree about the role of happiness in human motivation.
Aristotle argues that the goal of human activity is *eudaemonia*, which may be translated a "flourishing life in the company of friends" or, less adequately, "happiness." [♪] Aristotle, *Nichomachean
Ethics*, 193-199 (1176b-1179a). Sigmund Freud argues that humans are never happy, but cannot
stop seeking happiness. Freud, *Civilization and Its Discontents*, 27-28 (Section 2). Bentham changes
the focus to outcomes. Bentham advocates a cost-benefit scheme for evaluating human actions. An
act is measured by its social consequences. Bentham's scheme is sometimes called "consequentialism" or, his own preferred term, "the principle of utility." Bentham argues that act is best which
promotes the greatest happiness of the largest number of individuals. [♪] Bentham, *The Principles
of Morals and Legislation*. Peter Berger changes the focus from happiness to meaning. Berger argues that human communities fabricate a psychological universe in which members of the community find their meaning and place. [♪] Berger, *Sacred Canopy*. Panksepp augments Berger (and con-

regularity, sacrifice happiness to purchase meaning. We suffer, even die, to promote group action, real or imagined, when we believe our acts nurture those whom we love and with whom we identify.[32] Absent meaningful community, humans sicken and perish.[33]

The good in human existence is meaningful participation in a meaning-laden community.[34] What conduct[35] might one undertake to create such a community?

---

tradicts him) by asserting that much of human meaning is inherited from mammalian evolution, and lies implicit in our mostly-subconscious affective lives. Panksepp and Biven, *The Archaeology of Mind*, 494. Victor Frankl argues that mankind searches not for happiness, but for meaningful existence, the acquisition of which is the primary goal of human life. Frankl, *Man's Search for Meaning*, 99. In Sessan Amakuki, *On Hakuin's Zazen Wasan*, a Zen Buddhist argues that by meditating, one discovers that everyday life gleams with personal meaning. [♪] Conze, *Buddhist Scriptures*, 137. Epictetus, the Stoic slave, asserted that the good for humans is moral purpose. Epictetus, *Discourses*, 63 (Book I, Section 8.16). Schopenhauer styles our desire for happiness an "inborn error." We cannot but long for happiness, but soon learn that the world trends against us. Hence, suffering is inherent in experience. Schopenhauer's thought tails into Brahmanist and Buddhist concepts, recapitulating themes of those metaphysical systems. Schopenhauer, *The World As Will and Representation*, Volume II, 638.

[32] Such meaning-aimed action is most evident in soldiers on missions, but also in parents rearing well-attended children. We see sacrifice of happiness for common weal when politicians adopt unpopular, but necessary, stances; when firemen rush into smoking houses; when obese people prune food choices or fast-food lovers munch broccoli; when one reads difficult books; when congregations welcome smelly or surly people; when food banks are flush; when electorates vote to tax themselves for meritorious purposes unlikely to personally benefit them. That for which we sacrifice a good is a superior good. Meaning exceeds happiness.

[33] Watzlawick calls the mental structure within which people find their sense of meaning a "third order" perception. First order perceptions are raw sense data. Second order perceptions are those data constructed into useful concepts. Watzlawick calls this second order perception "knowledge about knowledge" or "meta-knowledge." The aggregate pattern of one's experiences, which melds into one's worldview in which one is socially embedded, is the third order perception (meta-perception of one's meta-knowledge). Man perishes in despair where his third order perceptions prove less-than-compelling to him. Watzlawick, Bavelas, and Jackson, *Pragmatics of Human Communication*, 248-249. Tolstoy laments his dearth of meaning, despite a well-heeled, relationally-rich, aristocratic, and morally-exemplary life. He recounts the intellectual and spiritual tale of how he found some meaning. [♪] Tolstoy, *A Confession*. Sebastian Junger argues: "Humans don't mind hardship, in fact they thrive on it; what they mind is not feeling necessary. Modern society has perfected the art of making people not feel necessary." Junger, *Tribe*, xvii.

[34] Martin Buber calls genuine community among persons the preeminent aspiration of history. Anything less than a sociality rooted in the actual relation of one man with another is counterfeit. Buber, *Paths in Utopia*, 133. Sarah Blaffer Hrdy notes that human babies gauge how older others around them evaluate objects of shared attention, looking to those elders for keys to meaning. Hrdy, *Mothers and Others*, 115. Stirner acknowledges that a human's natural state is togetherness, but urges all to seek self above all, and to subjugate any person or thing which one might fancy. Stirner, *The Ego and Its Own*, 271, 275. I suspect we all know a Stirnerite or two, and wish we did not.

[35] "Conduct" denotes deliberated activity, especially insofar as the choice of activity reflects moral conviction. The term may be distinguished from mere "behavior," which is human activity that may emerge without conscious choice. See *Webster's Third New International Dictionary*, s.v. "conduct" at §3c. Aristotle argues that choice concerns matters potentially within one's control, and not matters such as fate, nature's laws, and randomness. One deliberates a choice by selecting among alternatives by some process of rationalization. One deliberates when outcomes are uncertain. With

As used in this book, a "**community**" aggregates a number (say, ten) of constituent social groups, which are called "**circles**," themselves each number-ing around 150 members.[36]   Families and their supportive mentors and alloparents, small groups of collaborating colleagues, or small associations of in-timates (friends), called "**cadres**," identify themselves with a circle, or among various circles in a community.[37]   A community's ten or so allied and overlap-ping circles share an economic organization and social ethos, which its members select and manage.   Communities are, for the purposes of this book, the basic building block of the human world,[38] each having a voice, both directly by tech-nological means, and representatively, through chosen speakers, in the "**Com-**

---

human choice comes responsibility for means and outcomes, though deliberation primarily addresses means, in Aristotle's view.   One bears responsibility where acts are voluntary, meaning that the agent originates the act under a known set of circumstances.   Where acts derive from forces outside oneself and one makes no contribution to the act, the outcome is involuntary, and one bears no re-sponsibility.   [♪] Aristotle, *Nichomachean Ethics*, 117-141 (Book III, §§i.1-iii.19).

[36] The particular community size recommended in this work emerges from Zhou, "Social Group Size Organization," 440.   The research underlying Zhou's estimate of the maximum number of active so-cial connections the human cortex can manage derives from the work of Robin Dunbar.   Dunbar, *How Many Friends Does One Person Need?*, 21-34.   The estimate of 150 as the maximum number of human social connections is sometimes called the "Dunbar Number."   Zhou estimates the usual tribal population at 1,000-2,000.   Henri Bergson notes: "Man was designed for very small societies. . . . The original state of mind survives, hidden away beneath the habits without which indeed there would be no civilization.   Driven inwards, powerless, it yet lives on in the depths of consciousness." And a bit farther along, Bergson says, "Humanity must set about simplifying its existence with as much frenzy as it devoted to complicating it."   Bergson, *The Two Sources of Morality and Religion*, 275, 307.

[37] Maoist ideology employs the term "cadre" to identify a party official.   [♪] Mao, *Little Red Book*, 109 (Chapter 10).   I use the term in its English sense of a core group of persons or trainers.   See *Webster's Third New International Dictionary*, s.v. "cadre," definition 2a.   Aristotle argues that friendship and genuine community are coextensive.   Friendship requires community.   Communities without friendship are hollow shells.   [♪] Aristotle, *Nichomachean Ethics*, 154, Book VIII, Chapter 9 (1159b-1160a).   Robin Dunbar notes the hierarchy of threes in friendship.   One has three to five in-timates, people with whom one shares everything.   The next level comprises about fifteen members, sometimes called the "sympathy group."   The subsequent level involves thirty to fifty or so mem-bers.   An intermediate grouping includes about 500 members.   The tribal grouping includes 1,500 people.   So, there exists a rough increase by factors of three: 5, 15, 50, 150, 500, 1500.   Dunbar says no one knows what these numbers correspond to in real life.   We tend to have contact with the smallest circle at least once weekly, at least once a month with the circle of fifteen, and at least once yearly with the circle of 150.   Dunbar, *How Many Friends Does One Person Need?*, 32-33.

[38] Leidloff, speculating on revising our shared Western culture, contemplates just such a diminution in social scope from millions to tens.   We need groups of tribal size and comprehensible expanse. Leidloff, *The Continuum Concept*, 141.   Aristotle finds that ten people do not constitute a polis, but that a hundred thousand cannot constitute a polis, since the polis is the seedbed of friendship.   [♪] Aristotle, *Nichomachean Ethics*, 180 (1170b).   Aristotle goes so far as to say that friendship is com-munity, and that our social relations mirror our relationship to ourselves.   [♪] Aristotle, *Nichomachean Ethics*, 182 (1171b).   Thomas Jefferson, reflecting on what he had learned from ob-serving how the American Constitution functioned, advised that we form "wards" in which every man is engaged in making choices about his most local and pressing concerns.   "[T]he whole is ce-mented by giving to every citizen, personally, a part in the administration of public affairs."   Jeffer-son, *Writings*, 1400 (*Letter to Samuel Kercheval*, July 12, 1816).

mons," the global community of communities.[39]   This concentric "cadre-circle-community-commons" structure constitutes a "Quad sociality."[40]   This form of consensual, friendship-laden society is called "kithdom."[41]

This book offers no vision of ideal human existence. Quad sociality is no utopia.[42] It, rather, suggests a process for choosing meaningful forms of living,

---

[39] The word "community" serves several uses in this text. First, it denotes approximately ten circles of around 150 members each, thereby organizing mankind in tribe-sized communities of 1,500-2,000. Second, the term identifies the global Commons, the worldwide community of communities, which this author anticipates might, at some point in the distant future, supplant the national governments that plague humanity presently. Finally, the word "community" enshrines not only a social structure, but also a qualitative aspiration and goal, that every person should matter deeply to some particular group of people more broadly construed than those from whom he is genetically derived. In this latter sense, persons who share my concerns might "build community" or "advocate community." Buber argues that every viable commonwealth is a "community of communities." Buber, *Paths in Utopia*, 136-137. The details of what I define as "human community" will be expanded at length in what follows.

[40]The term "quad" derives from the Latin word *quattuor*, meaning "four." Quad tallies the first letter of each of the four components of *Cull's* sociality: cadre, circle, community, and commons. Each level of human relating (the four Cs) catalyzes companion levels robustly. I advocate Quad sociality to attempt to redress depersonalization of member existence that plagues most Western cultures. First-world persons have traded being known for the pseudo-efficiency of semi-personal existence: citizenship, identification numbers, or unitization. Quad sociality is equivocal. When better evidence indicates a more appropriate size or shape for human social organization, that better theory should be adopted. My point is this: meaningful human existence is never impersonal; regimes that treat human relations impersonally should be abandoned, minimized, or allowed to crumble under the weight of their own misdirected fragility. I employ a diagnostic criterion: when a community must coerce its members to participate in their own well-being, that community should discorporate itself and seek a fresh approach to meaningful life.

[41] Aristotle asserted that such a structure to social life is a natural phenomenon. He hypothesized that the relations of men, women, and slaves gave rise to families, which aggregated into villages, which aggregate into towns (the *polis*). Towns exist, according to Aristotle, to create for members a good life. Man participates naturally in town-sized social groups. Such towns are voluntary associations of intermarrying families, a community of friends whose association aims to create for all in a town the good life. [♪] Aristotle, *Politics*, 12-13 (1251.25-1253.1), 74-75 (1280.30-1231.1).

[42] Jan Oppermann calls kithdom a "pragmatic utopia," meaning that kithdom presents a social structural opportunity that does not, but could, actually exist, either in discourse about political choices, or possibly even in praxis. The problem with all pragmatic utopias, Oppermann argues, is history. How does any people step past its bitternesses, prejudices, and stubbornness in sufficient measure to step into kithdom? Oppermann urges that answers lie in the potency of education. Jan Oppermann, personal correspondence with the author, dated October 14, 2015. Robert Nozick, in contemplating the application of utopian theories to actual living, presents a framework for utopian endeavors that closely tracks that proposed in *Cull*. (In my view, when Nozick abandons utopian theories and speaks of actual application to human society, he has left utopian thought behind in favor of a process of living and improving communities.) Given the diversity of people, no one sort of community might suffice for all. Rather, utopia, as actually lived, is meta-utopia, the framework within which utopian experiments are welcomed, and members pursue their highest visions of the good life. All those who aspire to better societies will welcome the framework, except those of totalitarian sentiments. [♪] Nozick, *Anarchy, State, and Utopia*, 307-320. Nozick calls his framework of diverse community experiments a "utopian process" rather than a utopian state. [♪] Nozick, *Anarchy, State, and Utopia*, 332. Some bloggers (such as Heather Schlegel and Kevin Kelly) have coined the term "protopia" for views of the future that are neither pessimistic (dystopian) or perfectionist (utopia). Rather, protopian views present a positive take on the human future, without claiming to solve every problem or achieve all humans might desire or imagine. The process, which *Cull* describes, of cull-

and for ridding oneself and one's community of forms from which vitality has leaked or forms that were misguided from inception.[43] By this process, communities may move together toward troves of meaning that are now, in our benighted stumbling, hardly recognized and seldom seized. This process of sorting is a core concept: "finely-elaborated culling of conduct."[44]

In culling conduct, one assesses purposeful actions or inactions for their moral outcome. One puts squarely in mind competing courses of action, and rehearses the likely sequels of each.[45] On a turbulent moral sea, one seeks purpose(s) by which to rudder action. The human twilit morass does not readily resolve itself into dichotomies of day and night, that is, of good and evil. We wallow in half-light, never certainly knowing, when we make choices, if the light we see waxes toward dawn or wanes toward nightfall.[46] The human actor, as she chooses, must act or abstain. Moral dichotomy, you see, ultimately impresses us into its service.[47] Life is choice; to cower in hand-wringing indecision is

---

ing conduct in Quad communities in a global kithdom may well be styled "protopian." The process is incremental. Michael Shermer offers a similar emphasis on improved decision-making and step-by-step modifications of the human cultural norm. Shermer, *The Moral Arc*, 398.

[43] Jonathan Haidt suggests that, apart from theodiction, no answer exists for the question: What is the purpose *of* life? Such a question presupposes the existence of a designer, who dwells, for the agnostic, in an epistemological black hole. Haidt answers, instead, the question: What is human purpose *within* life? Haidt answers that happiness exceeds grabbing what we want. We bring portions of happiness with us. We receive portions of it from others. And we participate in happiness by embracing purposes larger than ourselves. Haidt, *The Happiness Hypothesis*, 238-239.

[44] Bateson argues that we need not determine what is best to do under existing rules, but rather determine what other rules might better serve us. Bateson, *Steps To An Ecology of Mind*, 484-485. *Cull* asks readers to change the rules by which we govern ourselves. Sextus Empiricus disposes of all of ethics simply with his skeptical razor: "There can be no expertise in living either. If there is such an expertise, it has to do with the study of good, bad and indifferent things. So since these are unreal, expertise in living is unreal." Sextus Empiricus, *Outlines of Scepticism*, 205 (Book III, Section xxv).

[45] [♪] Dewey, *Human Nature and Conduct*, 190. Aristotle calls such thinking "practical wisdom," by which one chooses what creates the good life as a whole. [♪] Aristotle, *Nichomachean Ethics*, 107 (§1140A). Herbert Spencer argues that conduct includes "all adjustments of acts to ends." A good act is one well-adjusted to its end; a bad act is ill-adapted. A good act is a "highly evolved" act. Spencer considers moral phenomena to be evolutionary phenomena. Spencer, *The Principles of Ethics*, Vol. I, p. 39, 58, 78, 96. Hence, Spencer is often criticized for a doctrine of social Darwinism, which theory plainly distorts Darwin's Darwinism.

[46] Normal people are certain; the sage explores tentatively. [♪] Lao Tzu, *Tao Te Ching*, 64 (20). Life is little more than a long struggle in the dark, so feeble is reason. Lucretius, *De Rerum Natura*, 59 (Book Two, Line 54).

[47] Jaak Panksepp warns that dichotomous schemes (such as good-evil) are tempting, but are not supported by neurobiological research. Panksepp, *Prosocial Brain*, 151. He opts instead for seven foundational emotional neurological subsystems: FEAR, RAGE, SEEKING, LUST, CARE, PANIC, and PLAY. Panksepp, *Prosocial Brain*, 146. Panksepp capitalizes the systems to indicate his technical use of the words. These systems interact in complex, non-dualistic fashion. I argue, *contra* Panksepp, that culling is the most basic of biological impulses, that of approach and withdrawal. Panksepp's neurological subsystems issue drives and motivations that play in moral choice. I argue,

itself a moral choice. None evades moral culling.[48] One chooses well or poor-ly.[49] The point of making decisions well is to fashion for oneself and for one's fellows a flourishing life.[50] One who embraces careful culling improves her chances of establishing a robust, flourishing life for herself and her companions. Perhaps one even renders planetary weal[51] more likely.

One expects some outcomes if the changes proposed by this book come to pass. The human focus migrates from financial capital to social capital.[52] And the means of enforcing rules jags from formality (laws, crimes, judges, police) to informality (mores, intervening friends, raised eyebrows, smiles, consensus). One envisions plummeting coercion. The human social interface grows less fearsome and intricately amicable.[53] David Brooks would call this transition a

---

contra Panksepp, that culling underlies all the impulse and affect systems of the human organism. Culling expresses the urge to homeostasis, to preserve one's life, to maintain equilibrium. Our propensity to cull unconsciously impels us toward life's sweet spot, silently sidesteps life's poisons. I argue that rudimentary ethical culling characterizes all non-pathological human neuroanatomy.

[48] The Buddha taught that one should make his conduct competent and friendly. [♪] *Dhammapada*, 376. Hrdy reports human one year olds find joy or shame in the attitudes of others toward them. Hrdy links this essential moral propensity in human children to our long evolutionary journey during which sensing the intentions of others aided survival. She calls these perceptions "intersubjective involvement." Hrdy, *Mothers and Others*, 117. Henri Bergson says, "Mankind lies groaning, half crushed beneath the weight of its own progress. Men do not sufficiently realize that their future is in their own hands." Bergson, *The Two Sources of Morality and Religion*, 317.

[49] James cites Fitz James Stephen to the following effect: Human decisions are stabs in the dark. We choose, never knowing with certainty the outcome. It is as though we were blind, freezing, lost, standing at a crossroads. To choose a path may lead to death. To choose no path guarantees death by hypothermia. So we choose, knowing our uncertainty. We elect courage and hope. If we choose the wrong path, we die, but we die well. [♪] James, *Will to Believe*, 62.

[50] Kwame Appiah so styles Aristotle's concept of *eudaemonia*. See Appiah, *Experiments in Ethics*, 202ff. Rousseau, in contrarian acerbity, finds self-improvement the root of all evils. Rousseau, "A Discourse on the Origin of Inequality," 60. Oppermann argues that Rousseau intends here, not a rip at self-improvement so much as historical pessimism about human consciousness itself. The more human we become, the unhappier we get. Oppermann believes that Rousseau countered this grim assessment in later works such as [♪] *The Social Contract* and *Emile* and *Reveries of the Solitary Walker*. Jan Oppermann, in correspondence with the author, dated October 14, 2015.

[51] "Weal" designates a state of sound, healthy prosperity. See *Webster's Third New International Dictionary*, s.v. "weal."

[52] Robert Putnam identifies indicators of high social capital. People in high social capital areas are more likely to serve on committees or as officers of a club, and join civic organizations and attend them. Citizens form more clubs. They vote and attend government or school meetings. People visit friends and invite them to their homes. They trust people, are honest with them, and anticipate that others will treat them in like manner. Putnam, *Bowling Alone*, 291.

[53] According to Christopher Boehm, conflict-suppressed egalitarianism is the human norm for (illiterate) small groups. Members actively tamp down individual spectacles of egoism and emotion (which Boehm styles "upstartism"), securing for all (male) tribal members rough political equality. Leaders are hidden, and lead mostly by generosity, and direct groups by indirection. The preemptive suppression of upstarts seeks to utilize them by cooling their hearts and making them gentle. Boehm, *Hierarchy in the Forest*, 45, 55, 65.

change in "moral ecology." Moral ecologies are communal patterns of behavior, beliefs, and habits. These ultimately issue revised institutions, which encourage members to adopt characters that nestle well in those institutions.[54]

Human feelings are, according to Jaak Panksepp, evolutionary memories. Emotions about the prospective weal or woe of choices are genetic ciphers for encouraging adaptive choices or discouraging catastrophic ones.[55] Good choices are emotionally compelling; our thoughts about emotions rein in those affects that exceed what circumstances warrant. A well-deliberated choice expresses a basal urge, diverted by an affective preference, and supported by reasonable review and practiced examination. Colloquially, we aim to desire, feel, think, and only then, in light of experience, act. Our moral impulses consist in ancient priorities bred into the human line, emotive predilections all. In culling, we carefully edit and choose among their diverse thoughtless directives. To cull is to edit mammalian priorities thoughtfully.[56] Where culling is done well, that culling is "finely-elaborated."[57]

One seeks self-knowledge. Just who is the culler in your skin, Kate? Life, absent moral deliberation, is hardly worth the bother.[58] Prudent decision-makers

---

[54] Brooks, *The Road to Character*, 261. I am less hopeful about the utility of societal institutions than Brooks. But I believe every human group's persistent actions issues some form of institution after a time. Brooks argues for a return to the crooked-timber school of thought, a view of man plagued in his inmost recesses by sin and called to acts of self-denial and thoughtful reshaping. Brooks finds that people, recovering a now-lost moral realism, should seek holiness (which sounds in his usage very much like "meaningful existence"), recognize character flaws side by side with one's amazing capacities. He finds humility needful, and pride blinding. Moral struggle defines the good life, which aims at generation-spanning goals and commitments. The good person requires help from her community, tolerates setbacks resiliently, shepherds an inner quiet, knows when she does not know or cannot know, works at needful occupations, seeks incremental change in herself and her community, avoids debacles, and perseveres in seeking what is better. Brooks, *The Road to Character*, 262-267. Much recommends Brooks's effort, in *The Road To Character*, to cultivate a strong character and wise heart, and to save his own soul, as he puts it (at page xiii).

[55] According to Jaak Panksepp, emotions are odd memories, because one need not be able to recall them and comprehend their purposes. Good-or-bad is an evolutionary shorthand for the survival import of choices. Panksepp, *Prosocial Brain*, 150-51.

[56] De Waal calls this a bottom-up morality, since it is not given to mankind by gods or reason. Rather, he argues, human moral priorities are primordial. De Waal, *The Bonobo and the Atheist*, 228.

[57] Epictetus argued that the right use of a human mind is to ferret the true from the false, and to forestall decision when a matter is doubtful. Epictetus, *Discourses*, 51 (Book I, Section 7.5).

[58] [♪] Plato, *Apologia*, 38A. "[T]he unexamined life is not worth living." I depart somewhat from the Socratic formulation. Rebecca Goldstein summarizes the Greek view: "One must *exert* oneself in order to achieve a life that matters. If you don't exert yourself, or if your exertions don't amount to much of anything, then you might as well not have bothered to have shown up for your existence at all." Goldstein, *Plato at the Googleplex*, 8. Dewey notes that the culling enterprise befuddles most men, who desire to be good buddies rather than good human beings. [♪] Dewey, *Human Nature and Conduct*, 5. The Buddha sees moral deliberation as a temporary expedient. When one rises above *samsara*, the perpetual rebirth to suffering, his mind awake and blossoming, ethical distinctions seem childish and are abandoned. [♪] *Dhammapada*, 39. I question Buddha's metaphysics.

cast conceptual nets broadly in their struggle to recognize and elect goodness. The culler sweeps away intellectual detritus, making room for fresh comprehension. The careful decision-maker's far-flung haul includes our evolutionary origins, human eusocial animality, the social genesis of culture in niche construction, the tangled trajectory of fitness guiding the jumbled evolution of human consciousness, our essential sociality and the role of members in it, humanity's predilection for certain conceptual errors, the wisdom of history's finest moralists, withering scrutiny of coercions and violence and governments, exploration of irenism and quasi-anarchist kithdoms, and humanity's efforts in culling a course toward a deliberated human future, to spy the farsight horizon.[59]

On this journey, if you will join me, you will encounter terms, such as: finely-elaborated culling, meaningful community, chatter, Quad sociality, theodiction, socio-neural homeostasis, interpenetration, the coppice of consciousness, neurotypicality, thanatoid transgenerational deliberation, neurodiverse savantism, hominins, niche construction, periconsciousness, hypostatization, simple rules, militant irenism, martials, alloparenting, exponential consensus, wanton members, ultra-minimal coercion, generational reserve, thick and thin, acephalous anarchy, the thousand generations, farsight horizon, and kithdom. These terms were fashioned or purloined or invested with odd or revised connotations in the effort to express thoughts on culling without laboring solely in worn ruts.[60] Neologisms help because one can hardly expect conceptual fluids to settle in altered configurations when poured into shopworn vessels of common use.[61]

Section I (*Cull*) introduces concepts and gives overview of irenic Quad kithdom. Section II (*Culling Foundations*) rummages thoughts on the human animal, our evolution, animal morality, and the structure of consciousness. Unhelpful, or atrophied, or downright dangerous ideas are swept away. Section III (*Member Culling*) aggregates a broad swath of human wisdom, sorting for gen-

---

Rousseau, consistent with his penchant for being entertaining but wrong, opines that when men commenced studying virtue they lost theirs. Rousseau, "A Discourse on the Arts and Sciences," 12. Max Stirner dissents utterly. Morality is to States what faith is to churches. Moral thought keeps all a State's sheep safely within its fences. There is nothing, according to Stirner, sacred enough to rule over man the individual. Stirner, *The Ego and Its Own*, 200. Isocrates argues that the best thing in a man is his good judgment. Isocrates, *To Demonicus*, 25. Hobbes argues that men deliberate when they allow desires and aversions, hopes and fears to attach to the same object or purpose, so that in one moment one desires the outcome, in another flees the outcome, and in choosing we terminate our liberty to vacillate. [♪] Hobbes, *Leviathan*, 44 (Chapter 6).

[59] Albert Schweitzer, in his autobiography, call such thinking "elemental." Elemental thinking examines fundamental human relations, meaning in human lives, and the nature of goodness in human behavior. Schweitzer, *Out of My Life and Thought*, 224.

[60] What makes for a bad habit is fixity upon an old rut while ignoring present possibilities. [♪] Dewey, *Human Nature and Conduct*, 66.

[61] Recall Jesus' proverb about new wine faring disastrously in old wineskins. *Matthew* 9:17.

erally-applicable simple rules for living that might guide most people in the attitudes and actions of intimate friendship in kithdoms, regardless what structure a particular community adopts. Section IV (*Community Culling*) describes some features of Quad sociality kithdom, dependent as these are upon the wild ideation of neurodiverse savants, the retirement of ossified social structures, and the Commons conversational wisdom in thanatoid transgenerational deliberation. Militant irenism and, with sigh and frown, ultra-minimal coercion of wanton actors and communities are also discussed. Section V (*Culling Futures*) recapitulates emphases from ideas in the previous four sections, by way of concluding, in envisioning the distant human future and heartening the sympathetic reader.

One need not read this book from beginning to end, though, in my view, for readers of reasonable endurance, the book is best read in that manner. Most readers may want to pause to read some epitomes of critical ethical works, contained in the second volume, where those works pique the reader's interest or are utterly unfamiliar. Section I (*Cull*) introduces ideas on which all the remaining sections lean. Perhaps you should read it first for orientation. If you relish critique, Section II (*Culling Foundations*) tackles philosophical and historical ideas that should be elaborated or tweaked, and others that should be hawked from one's mental throat into the spittoon of boondoggles. If your concerns lie primarily in personal morality, you might proceed to Section III (*Member Culling*). If your attentions bend toward political philosophy, you could skip to Section IV (*Community Culling*). If your interests lie with the attitudes circling possible futures, you could peek at the short final section, Section V (*Culling Futures*). For those readers who prefer cutting to the chase, the text offers an epitome of *Cull* at the end of Volume I. This epitome may rescue those who despise the text's style and many footnotes from pointless tedium. The epitome offers a gist where time is insufficient for patient chewing.

Culling appears, at first blush, a narrow-minded, self-centered mistress. The culler asks, What may help *me*? What might harm *me*? Subsequent sections of this work relieve the cull's harsh, unhewn lines by convening the far-flung considerations mentioned above. These blur boundaries between individuals and elevate communal life to its due pre-eminence. These considerations also make of friendship, rather than anonymity, the template for all human relating.[62] Such diverse considerations elaborate and inform our culling, refining its

---

[62] I intend nothing obscure by the term "friendship." A. C. Grayling describes friendship nicely: "[W]e meet someone and take a liking to him or her which is reciprocated, and thereafter we enjoy each other's company, laugh together, share interest and views, and over time come to feel that we are part of the fabric of each other's worlds, a valuable part, so that we develop a mutual sense of obligations owed and trust given, and meet each other's needs for boon companionship, comfort, confidences and sharing." Grayling, *Friendship*, 1-2.

rude simplicity. *Good decision-making consists in finely-elaborated culling of conduct.*[63]

Guidance is the best for which one can hope. Every particular circumstance beggars our decision-making capabilities.[64] In every case, it remains for you, dear Kate, to worry together the particular pieces of your personal and communal moral puzzles. Most of virtue consists in the commitment to cull well.[65]

> ***Objection 1: Good and Evil:*** *Some demur that ethical schemes premised on good and evil drag theological baggage into serious discussion of human choice. We have no need for a divine Israeli sorting sheep from goats. We can*

---

[63] Aristotle asserts that good deliberation calculates and inquires, leading to correctness of thought. [♪] Aristotle, *Nichomachean Ethics*, 112 (§1142b). B. F. Skinner denies the possibility of moral thought and the importance of entertaining any. All that matters, in Skinner's view, is moving on from morality to a viable technology of behavior. [♪] Skinner, *Beyond Freedom and Dignity*, 1-25. Jean Jacques Rousseau argues that people's opinions shape their morality. To improve morality, renovate human decision-making. [♪] Rousseau, *The Social Contract*, 174 (Book IV, Chapter 7). Anthony Shaftesbury argues that the human moral sense is inborn, and our opinions and beliefs can under no circumstances dislodge it. Shaftesbury, *Characteristicks*, 25 (Volume II, Part III, Section I).

[64] That a task exceeds us does not recommend forsaking it. Lao Tzu called the Way and the sage-devoted-to-the-Way an "uncarved block" (or "unhewn log"). [♪] Lao Tzu, *Tao Te Ching*, §72 of the Ma-wang-tui manuscript, or §28 of the now-superseded standard text. These Chinese masters acknowledge that the unhewn log, which is the Way, may be sawn or cut, and doing so serves human purposes. But they admonish that the skillful master receives the Way just as it comes to him, without cutting. Nevertheless, analysis and comprehension plague some, especially the philosophical few.

Systematic treatment of all factors involved in finely-elaborated conduct culling may exceed human grasp. Upon careful deliberation, ethical thought frequently devolves into quandaries. Recent philosophical ethics, in which trolley problems and various competition games command an inordinate share of philosophical attention, slides into this conceptual eddy. One must avoid the "quandary quandary," as Appiah terms the conundrum in his *Experiments in Ethics* (page 193ff). Meaningful life exists not to untangle moral birds' nests, but to be lived. Game quandaries and meta-ethical conversation call to mind garage chatter among mechanics debating fuel injectors. It is shop talk, scarcely benefitting those put to the task of driving. Of the Prisoner's Dilemma (criminal partners are offered deals to implicate the other; if neither informs, both go free; if one informs, the informer goes free, but his hapless partner serves eight years; if both inform, each serves five years. Shall one inform?), one can say only that acting in self interest, according to the dilemma, is less desirable than cooperating. See discussion in Singer, *The Expanding Circle*, 47.

Moral puzzles often reflect the competing impulses of neural programs that derive from the human evolutionary past. Quandaries illuminate too little of life to provide useful guidance. To expand Appiah's simile, reliance upon ethical quandary deliberation can be likened to finding one's way through benighted woods with a laser pointer (Appiah, *Experiments in Ethics*, 194). If it proves true that the modularity of our moral cognitive capabilities creates our ethical conundra, then any adequate ethics will prove neurologically eclectic, picking and choosing among available behavioral impulses as deliberated circumstances recommend. Our several moral voices generate cognitive cross-talk. One's inner moral sanctum rings with a din akin to that of a classroom of expectant second-graders.

[65] The biggest obstacle in any task is finding the will to commence it. So too, is one waylaid in becoming a good man. Seneca, *Epistles 1-65*, XXXIV, 3. John Stuart Mill asserts that people have a duty to assist one another in sorting good from evil choices, and having distinguished, to muster motivation to elect the good. [♪] Mill, *On Liberty*, 73.

do without pharaohs' Anubian scales weighing human hearts against feathers of justice. Find some other language. "Good and evil" have grown so heavily freighted as to be immovably useless. "Good and evil" is the dichotomy preferred by tepid minds locked in pointless conflicts. Choose instead "adaptive and maladaptive" from evolutionary biology, or "useful and lacking utility" from utilitarianism, or "weal and woe" from Schopenhauers' skeptical ethics.[66] Why start a challenging conversation with hackneyed dichotomies?

Response: One purpose of this book is to establish a basis for ethical deliberation other than deduction from theological edicts (which prescriptions I call "theodiction").[67] "Good and evil" packs some theological baggage, which I jettison.[68] "Good and evil" also transports the dual connotations I seek. First, "good and evil" describes the human anticipation of an outcome from action. We need words that leave the human actor with her emotional expectancies in the loop, as many quasi-scientific nomenclatures do not. Second, "good and

---

[66] Schopenhauer, *The Basis of Morality*, 84. Schopenhauer's ethical meditation proves, in the end, to be little more than an anthem to selfishness, though he grants that our egos may become commingled with those of others (albeit only slightly). Hence, compassion is possible. Schopenhauer makes of compassion the lone source of bona fide morality. Schopenhauer, *The Basis of Morality*, 85-86.

[67] Theodiction, in its usual format, commences from a sacred text, deemed to be spoken by god(s) or authoritative with respect to the opinions of a god or gods, which text is axiomatic for subsequent moral propositions. One learns from that text what "god" thinks, and deduces what humans "ought" to choose and do, considering those axioms. What human is positioned to gainsay divine edicts? The critical epistemological motion is from god(s) to man. *Cull* prefers, as have most post-Enlightenment rationalisms, an epistemological path that trends from man toward god(s), though *Cull* denies that men comprehend gods. *Cull* seeks a humaniform morality. E. O. Wilson argues that one lives best by seeking to live at liberty from one's religious preferences. [♪] Wilson, *The Meaning of Human Existence*, 158. For a theodictic treatment of the common good, see Maritain, *The Person and the Common Good*, or the [♪] *Torah*, or the [♪] *Qu'ran*. De Waal, a primatologist, calls theodiction "top-down morality," and argues instead for "bottom-up morality." De Waal, *The Bonobo and the Atheist*, 240, 228. Schopenhauer argues that "the conception of ought, in other words, the imperative form of Ethics, is valid only in theological morals, outside of which it loses all sense and meaning." Schopenhauer seeks an empirical ethics, rooted in the actual discovery of pure justice, compassion, and nobility (which, of course, never exist unalloyed in the human breast). Nor can such virtues be examined, locked as they are in the human skull. Schopenhauer, *The Basis of Morality*, 74-75, 81. If Schopenhauer is right about the theological linkage of ethics and gods, *Cull* hunts chimeras. (A "chimera" is something that exists only in imagination and is impossible in reality.)

[68] "Evil," when approached from a theological perspective, generates the problem of theodicy. Susan Nieman puts the problem of theodicy neatly: "The problem of evil occurs when you try to maintain three propositions that don't fit together. 1. Evil exists. 2. God is benevolent. 3. God is omnipotent. Bend and maul and move them as you will, they cannot be held in union. One of them has to go." Nieman, *Evil in Modern Thought*, 119. If humans lack knowledge of things divine, two premises of theodicy vanish (numbers 2 and 3). The problem of evil becomes, why does evil exist? I argue that "evil" is a human perception of human action and inaction, not a metaphysical reality. Evil springs from human ignorance, miscomprehension, ill-deliberation, lethargy, panic, and a few congenital brain deformities. The result of human evil is suffering. So, the question of evil becomes an inquiry into the recognition and truncation of avoidable sentient suffering. See Isabel Cabrera, "*Is God Evil?*", 18. Philip Zimbardo defines: "Evil consists in intentionally behaving in ways that harm, abuse, demean, dehumanize, or destroy innocent others–or using one's authority and systemic power to encourage or permit others to do so on your behalf." Zimbardo, *The Lucifer Effect*, 5 (which text contains details of the Stanford Prison Experiment and Abu Ghraib tortures). Zimbardo seeks to grasp those processes that transform normal people into those who do evil acts.

evil" corresponds neatly to the dance of approach and withdrawal that characterizes all animal response to changing environments.[69] I argue that the urge for
homeostasis (that is, welcoming circumstances that portend weal and evading
those that threaten injury, in repetitive approximations of optimal outcomes)
provides a foundation for human ethical choice, when juxtaposed with other
neuro-affective facts about human cognition.[70] "Adaptive/maladaptive" describes animals in the jaws of evolution's dynamo. Choice is missing. "Use-
ful/useless" turns the focus away from choice to outcome. Consequentialism
(utilitarianism) neglects the moral import of means. Percy Bysshe Shelley said,
"I never will do ill that good may come."[71] No strict utilitarian embraces Shelley's sentiment. "Weal and woe" are acceptable to me, but seem to differ from
"good and evil" only in familiarity. These alternative word-pairs have uses, and
I employ them at several junctures in the book. I recur to good-and-evil because
of that dichotomy's adequacy and familiarity.[72] Critically, good-and-evil recapitulates a dichotomy deeply embedded in human subconsciousness. All we encounter, even before the experience rises to a conscious level, is labeled good or
bad.[73] We are, before we recognize it is happening, launched by deep con-

---

[69] Thomas Hobbes makes these same points in the psychology with which he prefaces his political
philosophy. [♪] Hobbes, *Leviathan*, 39-40. See also pages 110-111.

[70] David Hume agrees. He argues that if we had no prejudices favoring good outcomes, we would
be altogether incapable of making decisions, caught, as we would then be, between one choice and
another in a state of utter indifference. In Hume's words, we choose "between what is useful, and
what is pernicious," and such choices are what we mean by "moral distinctions." [♪] Hume, *An Enquiry Concerning the Principles of Morals*, 120 (Chapter 6, Sections 4-5).

[71] Shelley, "Letter to Elizabeth Hitchener, January 7, 1812," 175. If only the world were so simple
as Shelley imagines. Every person regularly faces circumstances of moral import to which no singu-
larly good response is possible (pay your taxes, though some funds support wars; contribute to one
cause, thereby expending resources that could be given to another; learn of something important to
the neglect of other, potentially more important, matters).

[72] Bernard Gert also recurs to the terms "good and evil." Evil is a decision to inflict harm, which no
reasonable person would choose. What is good is that which no person would avoid except for reasons. Good, in Gert's view, is much more diverse than evil. Gert's moral rules are: a) Don't cause
death, b) Don't cause pain, c) Don't cause disability, d) Don't cause loss of freedom or opportunity,
e) Don't cause loss of pleasure, f) Don't lie, g) Keep your promises, h) Don't cheat, j) Obey the law,
and k) Do your duty.   As to every rule, one should obey except when one would publicly advocate
violating the rule. Moral ideals guide people to higher, but extremely diverse, goals. The moral
rules keep people from doing terrible harms to one another. In Gert's view, morality pertains to
rules all should obey, regardless what sort of life they may wish to create. Gert, *The Moral Rules*,
46-47, 72, 86, 125, 142, 149.

[73] Paul Bloom argues, in the good company of Thomas Jefferson, that good and evil are natural categories of human thought and feeling, as characteristic of the squalling newborn as the most erudite
philosopher. Bloom, *Just Babies*, 4. Richard Kraut cites Thomas Aquinas for the proposition that
"good is to be done and pursued, and bad is to be avoided," which Aquinas takes to be the root of
natural law. The dichotomy "good-bad" forms the basis of practical reflection. Kraut, *What Is Good
and Why*, 271. Carefully scrutinized culling of good options from bad alternatives is the essence of
morality.

sciousness down a path toward approach or withdrawal. Conscious reflection on these dispositions arrives late or never.[74]

Objection 2: Urban Trajectory: Another protests that the inexorable trend in human sociality over the last 50,000 years has been toward cities. The World Health Organization reports that more than half the planet lives in urban centers. Further, these city-denizens are mobile; their lives are fungible from one location to another. The human population is irretrievably committed to massive urbanity and relentless mobility. An urge to wander tickles most young souls, and curiosity drives many to sometimes aimless quests. Quad sociality proposes an impossible lunge backward. Society cannot recur to halcyon days of small town ruralism. Gone are neighborly neighbors. Cities exist because people, well-equipped with abundant social capital, abandoned their hamlets for the ruckus and facelessness of cities. If need for one another lies in the human soul, so too does the dream of freedom from meddling matrons. The author of Cull *offers nothing but metastasis of cloying nostalgia. The book dishes up a much-overcooked omelet of communitarian hash.*

Response: Population density improves community creativity. Living closely together limits human environmental impact. Humans should live in close quarters for their own well-being and to maximize efficiency in transportation and interpersonal communications.

Extant cities are emergency interventions addressing the chronic Sisyphean crisis of human overpopulation. Most migrants move to cities to avoid death by starvation, but then languish, though fed, in lonely anonymity and meaning-starved subsistence. Sheer numbers obstruct much personal relating. Cities overwhelm us. Teeming thousands swamp our limited social capabilities (which peaks around 150 persons). Mobility further injures intimacy with one's companions. Why build an intimacy over decades if your friend might just haul camp and debark from your life? Death is bad enough. When one adds impulsive translocation to the calculus of human relating, friendship appears a poorly-sheltered harbor.[75] These factors cumulate. Humans, deprived of meaningful life, fabricate sad substitutes, or, in a few cases, simply go berserk. Robin Dunbar, a primatologist with a philosophical bent, argues in this manner: Human minds "are not infinitely flexible, whose cognitive predispositions are designed to handle the kinds of small-scale societies that have characterized all but the last minutes of our evolutionary history. . . . It is simply something we have to work with, something we have to adjust our social practices to take account of rather than fight against. . . . The future of our species will be determined by our ability to recognize where those limitations lie and how we can circumvent them, if necessary by recreating the kinds of social environments in which we

---

[74] Bargh, "Our Unconscious Mind," 37.

[75] Robert Putnam argues that mobility is not the cause of the collapse of community in America during the last half of the twentieth century. He asserts that both long- and short-distance mobility have declined (slightly) from 1950 to 1990. He does, however, note that mobility erodes social capital. Highly mobile communities have weaker community ties and less vital civic participation. Commuters are less likely to participate in community organizations. Putnam, *Bowling Alone*, 204-205.

work best. If we can achieve that, the modern world may seem less alienating and become less destructive."[76]

Quad sociality does not douse curiosity, but rather encourages it. The curious should explore, but they should do so from a secure base of friends less prone to sometimes dangerous adventures. The curious should leave home to explore, but then return to their community, full of insights. Of youthful wanderlust, one seeks its source. Does wandering emerge from some inherent predilection of the human spirit? Or does wanderlust express an inarticulate sense that what is being offered in one's home community starves one's youthful hunger for meaning? Juvenile wanderlust may be a beacon illuminating needed change in a community.[77] Would young people drift from their community if that group's exploration of its own world were both vital and adaptive? Certainly, the young need to explore. They should enjoy their excursions. Communities must adapt. The alternative is death.

Quad sociality proposes that mankind shed its overpopulation over the course of centuries by means to be determined in global deliberation of those issues and technical challenges. We could start by telling women the social and personal facts of child-bearing, and asking if they really must bear children. Quad sociality proposes that our infrastructure should emphasize human relations (social capital) over production, transport, and acquisition of goods (financial capital).[78] Quad sociality advocates that we refashion ourselves into small communities comprising ten or so circles, each encompassing around 150 members, living closely together, growing food and fabricating goods in the immediate area surrounding the community, which agriculture and industrial zones serve as buffers between communities and serve as habitat for non-human creatures. Human communities should bunch themselves. Extensive fallow wilds should intervene between bunched communities, where opportunity presents itself. As population falls, humankind should remove and recycle the metals and oil products contained in the previous, now-uninhabited structures. Cities should be de-constructed, and the material used to fashion better-deliberated alternative communities. Each community should choose its own organization in economics, culture, and governance. Having 500,000 or more communities, all enmeshed in a communications grid, collaborating and benefiting from one another, experimenting in cultural and economic productivity, will vastly increase the creativity and opportunities of humankind.

---

[76] Dunbar, *Grooming, Gossip and the Evolution of Language*, 207.

[77] Robert Putnam, in analyzing Americans involvement in civic institutions and organization, notes that Americans have, for the last three decades of the twentieth century, been dropping out and/or failing to attend both political and civic life. Putnam, *Bowling Alone*, 64. Many lament this change. I ask if the horde of leavers are not perceptive? Do the leavers rightly suspect that these hallowed institutions offer no path to meaningful existence? Putnam never really considers this possibility.

[78] Martin Luther King Jr. called America to rapidly transform its values from thing-orientation to person-orientation. We have failed to heed him. [♪] King, *Autobiography*, 340.

I do not propose revolution. Nor do I propose government programs or pogroms.[79] No human should be coerced into altered sociality. The only door opening to Quad sociality is choice. The choice is not, however, mere individual choice, but choices deliberated together in communities. I contend that Quad sociality expresses the longing of every human heart, relieved of the distortions that population pressure, scarcity, and habitual coercive interactions impose upon that longing.

Humans, when adequately nurtured, want to live in social structures that support, rather than inhibit or demolish, their relationships. For most, urban life or rural life is all they know. Alternatives seem far-fetched. When Quad communities grow numerous, a third alternative dawns. Quad sociality resuscitates a version of the life-structure that enlivened humanity for all of its approximately 200,000 years, except the last 5,000.[80] That tail suffers blinding technological leaps, engulfing wars, and sordid, shriveled sociality. Quad sociality names what is wrong with mass, anonymous culture that now grips earth-bound[81] mankind. Quad sociality is inherently persuasive; its structure grows from what lies within people. Build Quad communities. Persuade by doing.[82]

Quad sociality is a culled course toward a deliberated future. Quad sociality addresses and modifies the tangled trajectory of human evolution by cultural choice. Elections of this sort have occupied humanity throughout its 200,000 year history. Humans need no permission to organize themselves differently, to

---

[79] To enforce its one-child policy, the People's Republic of China demanded that pregnant mothers who already had one child must seek abortion. If the woman refused abortion, the government persuaded. It destroyed the family residence, confiscated appliances, or jailed the woman's parents. Eventually, pregnant mothers got abortions. Weisman, *Countdown*, 167. The other side of this coin follows: if all families adopted a one-child policy today, the earth's population in 2100 would be 1.6 billion people, not the ten to fourteen billion presently projected. Weisman, *Countdown*, 415.

[80] James C. Scott says: "Until shortly before the common era, the very last 1 percent of human history, the social landscape consisted of elementary, self-governing, kinship units that might, occasionally, cooperate in hunting, feasting, skirmishing, trading, and peacemaking. It did not contain anything one could call a state. In other words, living in the absence of state structures has been the standard human condition." Scott, *The Art of Not Being Governed*, 3.

[81] E. O. Wilson argues persuasively that humans can never populate distant planets with divergent life forms. As a raw biological proposition, that living community would be fatal to us, and we to them. We must, he argues, make our own planet habitable for the duration of our species' existence. [♪] Wilson, *The Meaning of Human Existence*, 121-122.

[82] The most potent of arguments is live demonstration. I wish to strongly dissociate Quad sociality and "persuasion by doing" from the fascination with violence of some anarchist writers who romanticized anarchistic "propaganda by deed." These "propaganda by deed" acts were simple terrorism, especially to disciples of Michael Bakunin or Johann Most. (Most wrote a pamphlet detailing how to manufacture explosives and demolish buildings. Most, *Science of Revolutionary Warfare*, 1884.) For the more radical among anarchists, teaching by doing meant to rob a bank or assassinate someone powerful. See Woodcock, *Anarchism*, 165, 176, 395-396. Sorel, in his diatribe on Marxist violence, asserts: "It is to violence that Socialism owes those high ethical values by means of which it brings salvation to the modern world." Sorel, *Reflections on Violence*, 295. Violence brings not revolution, but repression. Violence convinces normal people of the inadequacy of the violent man's views. Violent acts corrupt the actor, twisting his moral self into just the sort of person he imagined violence might thwart. Violence is the strategic *cul de sac* in which radical anarchism traveled its long journey to nowhere.

choose life structures that better facilitate deliberated values. People presently possess all powers necessary to intentionally form circles that incorporate their cadres and convene communities where they presently dwell in the bosom of urban Westernism or industrial farming. Cadres can ally themselves into communities *within* their current social environments, using those ill-adapted environments as a chrysalis within which the pupa of Quad sociality may mature.[83]

Do not overthrow what exists. Foment no revolutions. Revolutions are ineffectual spasms of collective impatience. The hegemony of world uniformity and social violence deteriorates of its own accord, and will perish in its time. In the mean time, Quad sociality tests its legs within the floundering culture's shade. So, Kate, think otherwise than this objector. Step up now to what comes next. I do not propose return to simpler times. Quad sociality chooses a new, but deeply human, structure for living. Quad sociality is not fixation upon one fragment of human existence. It is not wild communitarianism. Quad sociality is mankind choosing to be itself, abandoning its predecessors' many errors.

It may be long before wide swaths of humanity elect the social structure of human maturity. Centuries of deliberation and incremental change may yawn before us. Quad sociality proceeds not by throwing off the horrid yoke of coercive institutions, but by opening the hearts of your friends in your circle. We progress one person at a time. Humanity tumbled into modernist urbanity over fifty thousand years by mishap, terror of coercion, and failure of procreative foresight.[84] Recorded history resembles a global social pratfall. Humans can choose Quad sociality as we depart the adolescent folly of thoughtless breeding and violence in favor of a carefully crafted future of cooperation and socially responsible deliberated action.[85] We do so incrementally. Take what steps lie open. Make your world more flagrantly personal. Avoid mere functioning. Get small and irenic. Sidestep life in institutions, corporations, governments. Glide gently toward kithdom. Demand a flourishing life, replete with meaning, for you, for your loved ones, for humankind.[86]

---

[83] I adapt this concept from the preamble to the constitution of the International Workers of the World (the "Wobblies"), who urged that labor establish its new economic society within the shell of the passing society. I adopt the concept without its communist baggage: economic fixation and reveling in violence. See http://www.iww.org/en/culture/official/preamble.shtml.

[84] Sebastian Junger notes: "[H]umans have dragged a body with a long hominid history into an overfed, malnourished, sedentary, sunlight-deficient, sleep-deprived, competitive, inequitable, and socially-isolating environment with dire consequences." Junger, *Tribe*, 23, citing Brandon Hidaka, "Depression as a Disease of Modernity," *Journal of Affective Disorders* 140 (2012): 205-214.

[85] Immanuel Kant tells of his disgust at human corruption in world politics. All details are worked out. Yet, the final result, in broad strokes, is a cloth in which some threads are stupid, other vain, and many vicious and wantonly destructive. Where, in all this, lies man's "superiority"? [♪] Kant, *Universal History with Cosmopolitan Intent*, 119-120.

[86] Michael Shermer defines moral progress as improvement in the survival rate and flourishing life of sentient beings. Shermer, *The Moral Arc*, 12. Richard Kraut argues that any desirable theory of well-being should rise from a foundational idea that is "obvious, widely recognized, and rich in implications." Flourishing is, he notes, just such an idea. Kraut, *What Is Good and Why*, 131.

Objection 3: Putrescence of Communism: *Yet another remonstrates that the terminology of Quad sociality imports unsavory flavors of communism. Communism, whatever good intentions may have moved its creators, served no political purpose other than to sate the bloodlust of last century's foulest dictators. Stalin, Lenin, Mao, Pol Pot: these misguided few, and their numerous minions, define mass murder. They embody coercion's bane. Surely, some happier language can be coined. Terminology that has failed less badly could be seized.*

Response: Some terms of Quad sociality were used in communist theory. Communists abused, but do not own, the language of collectivity.[87] Quad sociality is not revisionist communism, but rather a moderately-conservative mutualist social structure that restores collectivity to its due preeminence. Some Quad communities might choose to explore communist forms of self-government, though I suspect most communities would choose approaches with less ghastly histories. All, if I persuade, will avoid coercion as social policy. Communism advocated dialectical materialism. Quad sociality rejects Leninist dialectical materialism, and promotes dynamic social mutuality. Communism wed itself to violent revolution.[88] Quad sociality promotes irenism (pacifism), consensual governance, and long, slow change vetted by thanatoid transgenerational deliberation. Communism theorized a withering state, but in fact fashioned hard-edged hierarchical bureaucracies committed to totalitarian control. Anarchists, some of whom had communist leanings, offer cogent thoughts on collective existence and the defective rationale for coercive governments. Quad sociality abandons both hierarchical bureaucracy and classical liberal democracy, with their attendant hyper-individualism and coercive majorities, in favor of community consensus[89] in an utterly decentralized welter of lo-

---

[87] The Communist League, which issued [♪] Marx's *Communist Manifesto*, was organized into communes (3-20 members) which aggregated in circles, which was coordinated by a leading circle that acted as a central committee. See Bender, "Historical and Theoretical Backgrounds of the Communist Manifesto," at page 13, which essay serves as the introductory essay to [♪] Marx, *The Communist Manifesto.*

[88] See Lenin, *The State and Revolution,* and [♪] Marx, *The Communist Manifesto.* There exist significant strands of socialist theory that are vehemently pacifist and incrementalist, as are the proposals of *Cull.* See Considerant, *Principles of Socialism,* or Fourier, *The Theory of the Four Movements,* or [♪] Godwin, *Political Justice.* Marxist theorists persist in lionizing revolutionary violence. See Fanon, *Concerning Violence,* for example. Franz Fanon argues that only by violence can Third World natives find equal footing in countering their similarly violent colonial oppressors. From the conflagration of revolutionary murder rises the new communist native man, so Fanon argues. For the purposes of *Cull,* "revolution" describes cultural and political change that is rapid, bloody, and ill-deliberate. Revolution changes mostly personnel. We Americans like *our* Revolution. Yankee doodle--my favorite holiday is July Fourth. But more than two hundred years after the conflict on our American eastern seaboard, we have no king, but a president whose powers far exceed those of any British monarch, and no Parliament, but a Congress as hobbled as any legislative body that ever sat near the Thames.

[89] Some call consensus theory of governance of human affairs "sociocracy." The term means that a group of companions or friends, when acting as a social unit, make decisions for themselves. As practiced by Quaker societies, long adherents of irenism, decisions were made in meetings, run by children, called "talkovers." The governing principles of talkovers were: 1) decision-making by consent only when there are no reasoned or substantial objections (consent is therefore not unanimity, but give and take among friends in the face of differing values), and 2) members are organized in-

cal creativity cross-pollinating through a virtual Commons.[90] Communism mistakes economic reality as humanity's core rationale.[91] Quad sociality dissents. Human dynamic mutuality (that is, friendship) lies at the core of meaningful existence. Quad sociality concurs with Marxist conviction that there must exist some happier way to organize human social relations than classist individualism wedded to profit frenzy. Marx himself took pains to point out that theories such as that proposed in *Cull* are not communist, but utopian socialism. Marx argued that such views as mine are doomed to failure by pacifistic miscomprehension of the historical inevitability of worker violence that lies at the heart of every truly communist scheme.[92] I, obviously, dissent.

Quad sociality is not communism resurrected, dusted off, or splashed with a fresh coat of paint.[93] Quad sociality embraces a collectivist ethic and mutualist anthropology. Quad sociality pries open a door to a desirable future for maturing humanity. Quad sociality is politically conservative, and politically liberal, and both and neither. Quad sociality offers theory to underpin the burgeoning, but incipient, wave of ecovillages, cohousing endeavors, kibbutzim,[94] com-

---

to circles which are linked to higher hierarchical circles by not less than two common members, and 3) decisions should be simple and clear enough for children to grasp. See http://www.quakers.org.au.

[90] John Stuart Mill warns of the tyranny of majoritarian coercion, driving all to conform to the preferences of putative rulers. Mill exhibits the classical hyper-individualistic view of members and collectives. The individual possesses rights over against a potentially coercive majority's dictates. Collective coercion does not extend to that private sphere in which the individual deliberates his sentiments, determines the shape of his life, or associations of consenting adults, provided no acts in these spheres harm non-consenting others. Mill puts the matter: "The only freedom which deserves the name, is that of pursuing our own good in our own way, so long as we do not attempt to deprive others of theirs, or impede their efforts to obtain it. Each is the proper guardian of his own health, whether bodily, or mental and spiritual. Mankind are greater gainers by suffering each other to live as seems good to themselves, than by compelling each to life as seems good to the rest." [♪] Mill, *On Liberty*, 8, 15. I concur with Mill, but only to the extent one perseveres under the thumb of mass impersonal state authorities. Different rules apply within Quad communities, which are small collectives deliberating consensual conscience.

[91] "Economy is the basis, and politics are the concentrated expression of economy." Mao, *On New Democracy*, 3.

[92] [♪] Marx, *The Communist Manifesto*, 82-85. The prime goal of Marxist revolution is, theoretically, to give every worker access to the fruits of his or her labor. Marx goes farther, advocating differential distribution of economic weal according to the needs of the people. "From each according to his ability, to each according to his needs!" Marx, "Critique of the Gotha Programme," 242. Robert Nozick, a libertarian with deep confidence in contractual relations, frames the human economic regime differently: From each according to his choices, to each according to what he makes or receives freely from others. [♪] Nozick, *Anarchy, State, and Utopia*, 160.

[93] Nor is Quad sociality a cryptic version of compulsory relocation and enforced villagizations, such that those attempted in China, the Soviet Union, Ethiopia, or Tanzania. See Scott, *Seeing Like A State*, 223-261 (Chapter 7).

[94] A kibbutz is an egalitarian Israeli residential community, of which more than two hundred exist in Palestine and Israel. The fundamental values of kibbutzim are: 1) physical labor has a moral and redeeming character, 2) all property produced by a community belongs to the community, 3) all members are socially and economically equal, 4) members give according to their abilities, and receive according to their needs, 5) the community may not inhibit individual choices in opinion or influences, 6) the group and its processes are ends in themselves, 7) all member relations should be

munes, urban non-residential fellowships,[95] and intentional communities of various flavors, all of which find the western pattern of urban living a dreadful detour into immiseration.[96] Quad sociality portends the nurture of every person in irenic kithdoms of friends. Allow me to rescue the words "community," "circle," "cadre," and "commons" from their long communist exile.

Objection 4:   Identifiable Evil: Still another deprecates culling of conduct because evil (and, for that matter, good) is banal.[97]   Men doing evil do not sport little tattoos on their foreheads.   They present just as do other men.   None can reliably distinguish between a Nazi railway conductor seating people for a trip to Vienna, and another settling families for travel to Auschwitz.   The evil men do is, for the most part, not diabolical, but rather acquiescence in failed imagina-

---

characterized by mutual concern and intimacy, and 8) such living will redeem Jews of the diaspora from the injurious effects of hundreds of years absent from the land. This description derives from Melford Spiro's analysis of an unnamed Israeli kibbutz in 1951, which Spiro names *Kiryat Yedidim*. Spiro, *Kibbutz*, 10-37. This kibbutz was socialist, even communist, in its economics. There existed no private property and individual ownership was, at least at the beginning, discouraged. The community had an ascetic tendency that well-fitted the shortages that plagued Israel of that time. All decisions were made in town meetings by consensus. Law had little force, but public opinion was potent. Spiro, *Kibbutz*, 98. Formal proceedings were reserved for misdeeds that might result in expulsion. Spiro, *Kibbutz*, 101-102. Members expressed interpersonal aggression as gossip, pettiness, quarrels, and complaining. Problematical persons and behaviors were lampooned in public skits. Spiro, *Kibbutz*, 105. Outsiders were viewed with great suspicion, especially non-Jewish foreigners. Spiro, *Kibbutz*, 107-109. Prestige in work replaced money as social currency. Spiro, *Kibbutz*, 85-89. Universal provision of all needs by the community alleviated much insecurity among members. Spiro, *Kibbutz*, 86-88. Israel's kibbutz movement has moved toward private ownership, commercial sophistication, and some permitted individualism in the last half-century, which events are much lamented by some anarchist commentators. See Horrox, *Living Revolution: Anarchism in the Kibbutz Movement.*

[95] McKnight and Block offer a rationale for urban community and concrete suggestions about how to turn an anonymous American neighborhood into an urban non-residential fellowship, including a description of how one neighborhood accomplished the transition. McKnight and Block, *The Abundant Community*, 145-148.

[96] To experience a taste of groups seeking to resurrect existence in human communities, one may explore them through useful umbrella organizations: the Fellowship of Intentional Communities (http://www.ic.org/) and the Federation of Egalitarian Communities (http://www.thefec.org/). One may wish to consider the long collective lives of Acorn Community and Twin Oaks Community, both located in Virginia, the East Wind Community and Sandhill Community and Skyhouse Community, located in Missouri, and the Emma Goldman Finishing School, located in the Beacon Hill neighborhood of Seattle, Washington. You may also conduct an internet search under the specific type of community that interests you, or get a more general sample by searching "cooperative housing." The Songaia intentional community, located in Bothell, Washington, has written a highly personal account of its first twenty-five years of existence. The book gives a feel for the joys and trouble of intentional living. Lanphear, *Songaia*.

[97] Both good and evil hide in plain sight. They defy words, and frequently evade even careful thinkers, so common is their raiment. Adolf Eichmann, who kept Hitler's trains to Auschwitz running timely and full of enemies of the state, stated, as his Israeli executioner's noose snugged around his neck, that he did not believe in life after death, and that he would see them all again soon enough. Human evil defies logic, nestling in platitudes and habits that lack sense. Arendt, *Eichmann in Jerusalem*, 252. Susan Nieman said of the Nazi regime: "At every level, the Nazis produced more evil, with less malice, than civilization had previously known." Nieman, *Evil in Modern Thought*, 271.

tion, or refusal to entertain certain nettlesome questions, or assertion of the faith of fathers without reappraisal. Evil lurks in the cracks of normalcy. One cannot reliably ferret evil from the swirling cacophony of human clamor. Most evil action is a choking vine that sprouts from a root of pedestrian insensibility or compliant rule-following. Humans do not hatch evil; they ingest it as do they breakfast: half-awake, by rote. Evil is no more detectable than feeding bats on moonless nights—sliced air here, an inaudible squeak there. Culling conduct sets humanity to a witch hunt. When humans fear what cannot be detected, they invent identifiable bogies, then burn them. One prefers moral muddle to the stench of Salem's bonfires.

Response: Most evil is banal indeed. Evil has prominences, its Stalins and Bundys and theocides wrapped in explosive vests. Most evil, however, nestles in valleys between those peaks, in the ill-adapted habits and evolutionary *cul de sacs* of millions, of billions. As I argue in what follows, most evil intends no evil. Evils adopt mistaken goods, often propped up by pompous or pious back-slapping. Rare persons do evil contemplating (or worse, relishing) its bane. Everyman just blunders into evil acts, distracted, lethargic, napping.[98]

Much evil derives from failure to finger evil's elements. That ill I attempt to cure. Evil erodes meaningful community. Communities erode in predictable ways. I describe those well-trodden paths, or at least attempt to do so. Humans err; evils ensue. Where conduct culling is finely-elaborated with practical lessons and broad perspective, decision-making improves.[99] The fruit of communal deliberation of the farsight future tastes sweet. The stakes are high; the game deadly serious.

Moral muddle exceeds comfortable indecision. Moral muddle is the bramble in which evil camouflages itself, there knitting its banal cloak. Moral muddle permits throw-away children, war, cultures of coercion, the hegemony of material goods, and the dramatic ill-nurture of billions. Peer from a possible future. Moral muddle, when seen from the vantage of communities of deeply-nurtured adults, themselves the offspring of generations of deeply-nurtured predecessors, comes clear. Moral muddle is insanity. Moral muddle murders. Moral muddle crushes and deadens. Moral muddle aggregates psychosis. Moral muddle is that cage from which mankind scratches fingers to the bone, seeking escape.[100]

---

[98] Kautilya, in his second century A.D. Indian masterwork on the nature and administration of the State, argues that "Vices . . . are the cause of personal adversities. Vices are due to ignorance and indiscipline; an unlearned man does not perceive the injurious consequences of his vices." Kautilya, *Arthashastra*, 114 (8.3.1-3). (Kautilya is also known as Chanakya and Vishnugupta.)

[99]Epictetus notes that opinion is an insufficient foundation for living. One needs more when it comes to core questions of critical significance. It seems, to Epictetus, that such matters cannot possibly lie beyond human competence, undetermined and hidden. So, there exists some standard after which one seeks. And when one discovers it, he embraces it on every occasion. It is the philosopher's job to do the exploration, to discover those bases of human action which exceed mere opinion. Epictetus, *Discourses*, 281 (Book II, Section 11.16-18), 283 (Book II, Section 11, 25).

[100] I call chatterers those whom Heraclitus calls sleepers. See Heraclitus, Jones translation, *On the Universe*, 90, 94, 95, 114. Were the many indeed sleepers, the world would dwell more quietly. Every whim of opinion sets the fool aflutter. Chatter gushes. Heraclitus seems appreciative of his

> CHATTERERS SOW THE WIND.
> WORDS AGGREGATE AND ROT.
> ONE TILLS THIS SOIL.
> A SEED SPROUTS AND FLOURISHES.
> ONE SAYS,
> FIRST SAPLING IN A
> FOREST OF MEANING.

1.1. *Good.* Good acts augment conditions of meaningful community.[101]

1.2. *Evil.* Evil acts erode conditions of meaningful community.[102]

1.3. *Homeostasis.* In culling conduct, human members and communities seek homeostasis, a social and member equilibrium implicit in our mammalian and primate evolutionary heritage.[103] Meaningful community redirects member and communal activity toward human socio-neural homeostasis.[104]

---

sleepers. He says, "We all work together to one end, some wittingly and with understanding, others unconsciously. . . . Even sleepers are workers and co-operators in the things that take place in the world." Heraclitus, *On the Universe*, 499 (Section XC). The contribution of chatterers seems less patent to me.

[101] Cicero argues that only what is morally right merits seeking. Wisdom distinguishes good from evil. [♪] Cicero, *De Officiis*, Book III, Section VII, 33; Book III, Section XVII, 71. John Rawls correctly distinguishes communities from democratic political society. He argues that democratic societies are based on free and equal citizenry, cooperating in a manner all deem to be fair, tolerating one another in a pluralistic welter. Communities share more than mere political equities. They share gods and values and dreams. [♪] Rawls, *Justice as Fairness: A Restatement*, 21(§7), 94 (§26). The State is no community, but rather an agreement among strangers about how to collectively exercise coercive violence and establish widespread cooperation. Rawls's fair society defines the best conditions of anonymous State existence. I deem Rawls's "fair cooperation among equals" a thin gruel, constituting a cruel and senselessly sparse meal. Rawls never seems to question the propriety of democratic States or their coercions. He takes anonymous society and its impersonal depredations to be axiomatic. [♪] Rawls, *Justice as Fairness: A Restatement*, 5-6 (§2), 20 (§7), 27 (§9), 37 (§11). Albert Schweitzer questions whether humans have the capacity to grasp the meaning of events in the world. We see that all life seeks to "live itself out." Schweitzer, *The Philosophy of Civilization*, 300. Lawrence Tancredi argues that the foundation of morality is hardwired in our brain structures, as are the roots of grammar. Tancredi, *Hardwired Behavior*, 29. G. E. Moore argues that the good is indefinable. Moore, *Principia Ethica*, 61. As Moore thinks impossible, I attempt to give goodness some real life context, which makes goodness definable and also identifies evil. I suppose Moore would style my efforts the naturalistic fallacy run amok. I demur.

[102] The Buddha taught that ill action rots one, bringing woes, as rust corrodes iron. [♪] *Dhammapada*, 240. De Waal, the noted primatologist, adopts a similar formulation, styling "meaningful community" as "mutually satisfactory group life." De Waal, *Primates and Philosophers*, 173.

[103] "Homeostasis" is biological self-regulation by which an organism responds to changing environments to create for itself a dynamic equilibrium conducive to survival. Homeostatic regulation maintains marginally uniform life conditions in the face of persistent environmental change. See *Encyclopædia Britannica*, 15th ed., Volume 6, page 24a, *s.v.* "homeostasis."

[104] By the coined mouthful "socio-neural homeostasis," I mean to capture several ideas. First, human communities seek homeostasis, a state in which members and the community as a whole access what they need and avoid what is injurious by means of feedback loops that instruct all. Second, socio-neural homeostatic feedback instructs the social web of the community members as to needed

Our massively-complex social structures maintain balance and function by social rules and member participation. Prosperity emerges from human brains operating together, interacting, generating survival-enhancing ideas and injecting those insights into cultural habit.[105]

One should not misconstrue this homeostatic urge as longing for utopia. Homeostasis eludes humans and human collectives, because circumstances are in constant flux, as are our perceptions of those circumstances. Socio-neural homeostasis identifies the fact that humans constantly adjust activity, after receiving cybernetic feedback from prior action, to address an inner and innate neurotypical standard.[106] Human neurotypicality includes longing for stability juxtaposed with the ability to adjust to frequent change.[107] Humans bring to their urge for socio-neural homeostasis social attitudes, which attitudes function as the system biases.

To explain, using a metaphor from Gregory Bateson: Human sociality has an innate norm, as does a residential climate control system. A climate regulation system keeps the temperature of one's home at a constant, injecting heat when the interior temperature falls below a predetermined mark, and blowing cool air when the interior temperature rises above a certain mark. You set the mark on your thermostat, pursuant to your idiosyncratic preferences. The "mark," in sociality, is the human socio-neural norm. And here is the crucial fact: the mark is dramatically affected by cultural at-

---

action. Third, members are neural entities; the feedback loop ultimately nurtures and protects human members in a community by adjusting their brains and cultures, which are member and group habit development. Some have suggested that the circumstance that undergirds human happiness is relatively stable homeostasis. The term leans upon the suggestion of Beckoff and Pierce, *Animal Justice*, xi.

[105] [♪] Ridley, *The Rational Optimist*, 4. What distinguishes humans from their less successful hominid predecessors is what happens between brains, not within them. Our ideas, according to Ridley, have sex.

[106] "Neurotypical" is a term coined by the autism community to describe normal human brain function of the majority. Narrowly, that is, within the autism community, "neurotypical" means "not on the autism spectrum." The advocacy group coinage creates language to object to the medicalization of autism, and represents a plea for greater openness in society to diverse modes of mental function. As such, the coinage is part of the "neurodiversity movement," which seeks to assert that brain differences should be accepted with the same sort of openness we are developing toward diverse physical variations. See Harmon, "Neurodiversity Forever." As used in this book, "neurotypical" denotes normal mentation, which occurs in relative high-frequency in the population, the term winnowed of its moral and normative connotations. A synonym might be "statistically dominant" or "non-pathological." "Neurodiverse" denotes lower-frequency mentation, including pathological, neurotic, ecstatic, theological, and other odd states of consciousness and perception. I employ the term "neurodiverse" more broadly than its autism-advocates might prefer.

[107] Rousseau finds change so prevalent that he despairs of enduring happiness: circumstances change, we change, our perceptions change. In the end, all dreams prove empty. Rousseau, *Reveries of the Solitary Walker*, 137 (Ninth Walk).

titudes and preferences.[108] Some cultures, to extend the metaphor, prefer their houses hotter than others. The drive for homeostasis is universal, its particular flavors thoroughly local.

1.4. *Architecture of Conduct.* One may cull conduct skillfully or ineptly.[109] Much of culling is determined by the structure of human neurophysiology (which is a specific elaboration of the biological heritage humans share with all life, that of approach or withdrawal), and proceeds with belated cognitive[110] intervention. Skill in culling adds member experience and cortical insights to the subcortical,[111] precognitive core of approach and withdrawal.[112] Skillful culling is finely-elaborated culling. Skillful culling enhances the architecture of conduct for members and communities, often fundamentally redirecting its precognitive impulses. Consider the finely-culled habits represented by non-violence, dietary restraints, consistent altruism, simplified lifestyles, conscientious childlessness, or charitable endeavors. One anticipates elevated coordination, cooperation, and cohesion in meaningful community where communities carefully cull their conduct.[113]

---

[108] A person's or culture's preferences become the bias of a cybernetic system, creating an attitude toward which a feedback system inclines. Bateson, *Steps to an Ecology of Mind*, 478-479.

[109] You have probably noted, and possibly been annoyed by, my use of the word "one" in this text. David Brooks notes that the usage has fallen out of favor as the preferred pronoun of the pompous. Brooks, *The Road to Character*, 39. The word "one" bears a marvelous multiplicity. It means "a single unit," but also suffices as a substitute for the pronoun "I." It means "everybody" without sounding so homely. "One" can mean "someone extraordinary" as well as "everyone ordinary." The word also bears within it connotations of the One godhead, the unique, the person admired and followed, and the mathematical. "One" has flavors of psychological integrity. I like these ambiguities and multiplicities, especially when writing non-prose. The word "I" is specific, but less adaptable. It makes any work sound autobiographical, even when the work is not.

[110] A typology of motivation to action: 1) Cognition means knowledge involving ideas or experiences. See *Webster's Third New International Dictionary*, s.v. "cognition." 2) Affection indicates feelings and emotions in consciousness. See *Webster's Third New International Dictionary*, s.v. "affection" at §4a. 3) Conation denotes consciousness as it undertakes action on its drives and emotions. See *Webster's Third New International Dictionary*, s.v. "conation." Here, we argue that affective states are frequently conative, with cognition serving primarily to divert unserviceable conative acts. Due to its general lack of familiarity, I avoid the term "conative."

[111] In the brain, the neocortex (which is the "cortical region") physically overarches the limbic system and brainstem. Here, the word "subcortical" denotes the limbic and brainstem systems. This book assumes that most neural processing in the subcortical regions of the brain does not emerge into consciousness. This assumption entails the possibility that individuals remain unaware of many of their motivations and feelings. In this text, I treat consciousness as a film floating upon a subconscious ocean of exceptional depth and darkness.

[112] Jaak Panksepp argues our core emotions emerge from subcortical brain activity and are not organized by conscious activity. Panksepp, *Affective Neuroscience*, 26.

[113] Human conduct is a collective enterprise. No action or inaction elicits no response. [♪] Dewey, *Human Nature and Conduct*, 17.

1.5. *Optimism and Pessimism.* Optimism is an emotional state that fosters in members anticipation of future well-being. Good reasons exist for some optimism. Pessimism is an emotional state that fosters in members an expectation of unwanted outcomes. Good reasons exist for some pessimism. Normal human consciousness is emotionally predisposed to optimism.[114] This is not to say that existence warrants our favor for its rosier elements. The careful decision-maker amplifies negative feedback, since she is neurologically predisposed to neglect it, and quiets her conviction that all will be well, because she knows she is prone to sunshine bias. Optimism and pessimism occlude clear recognition of the empirical outcomes of human choice. One strains to hear the quiet voice of evidence murmuring beneath our din of hopes and fears.[115]

1.6. *Choice and Habit.* In culling conduct, one elects among competing attractive impulses and affections, the person's perceived goods. Each choice terminates some possible futures, creates at least one circumstance, and opens possible new futures previously unrecognized.[116] In choices, great and small, one fabricates portions of one's self, for good or ill.[117] Embedded in the interpenetrating community of many selves, members' choices fabricate the human community, for good or ill. Skillful member culling builds meaningful community by persistent election of well-conceived goods. Electing goods becomes habitual, and influences other members and the community to elect goods. Inept member culling erodes meaningful community by persistent election of ill-conceived goods, which prove, after suffering them for a time, to be evils.[118] Electing evils may become habitu-

---

[114] Sharot, "Optimism Bias," 40-43.

[115] Thucydides observes, in Book IV, Chapter 8, of *Peloponnesian Wars*, that humans entrust what they desire to ill-defined hopes, but subject disdained ideas to withering rational scrutiny. One seeks inner calm emerging from careful deliberation of the objects of desire and terror.

[116] De Beauvoir says that the male's effort to control his environment "is not to repeat himself in time: It is to take control of the instant and mold the future." De Beauvoir, *The Second Sex*, 69. Perhaps that is what women do as well.

[117] According to Dewey, character is habit, and desirable character cleaves to what is excellent in human life. [♪] Dewey, *Human Nature and Conduct*, 38, 207.

[118] Mo advocated less elaborate funerary and mourning rituals in sixth century B.C. China, noting that absurdly expensive practices predominate because habit and custom are confused with what is right. Mo cites that the Kaishu ate their first sons to benefit the second, that sons abandoned their mothers when the father died because none wished to live with the wife of a ghost. The Yan ate their deceased. The Yiqu cremated theirs. Mo advocated simple burial and short mourning. [♪] *Mozı*, 79 (Part III, §25).

al, and influences other members and the community to elect evils.[119] The worst habits are those that are neither adaptive nor adaptable. One finds oneself hurtling down a one-way street to nowhere desirable.[120] I call such paths *"cul de sacs."*[121] They are roads leading nowhere; one can only turn around and travel back to the point where the wrong turn was initiated. As a practical matter, human conduct consists in selecting habits, establishing those habits in one's usual activities, and enduring uncertainty that one has chosen well while the acts play themselves out.

1.7. *Character and Human Nature.* A member's character conjoins his habits, good or ill, with the member's physical capabilities in its communal cultural context. Habits of communal conduct culling and the community's physical environment immersed in its members' characters generate a community's culture.[122] Culture and character are not determined once-for-all, but evolve in response to changed circumstances of members and the community. Ultimately, by means of character and culture, humans deflect their personal and collective courses from that outcome determined by genetic traits. Different results become possible. Culture and character interweave, forming the intricate interdependent adaptive matrix that is human community.[123]

Some components of character and culture are given by the biological and social facts of a person or community. Other components transpire without reflection, emerging from the depths of human neural modules (as described by Panksepp below).[124] Still other components are chosen.[125]

---

[119] Buddhist doctrine, addressing the virtue of vigor, identifies four right efforts. A disciple 1) prevents potential evils, 2) forsakes actual evils, 3) pursues potential goods, and 4) supports and encourages existing goods. [♪] Conze, *Buddhist Scriptures*, 183 (citing Ho-shan's *Memorial*).

[120] John Dewey said that bad habits are those stuck in a previous generation's ruts. [♪] Dewey, *Human Nature and Conduct*, 66. Rabindranath Tagore argued that habits are mental economy, and can become a sort of miserliness, in which a person shuts herself off from growing and changing. Habit can become mere laziness. Tagore, *Nationalism*, unpaginated.

[121] French for "butt of the sack." *Cul de sacs* are traffic calming road structures, most frequently called "dead ends."

[122] Hegel would call this reflexive mutual influence a dialectical relationship, initially highlighting the differences between the two antipodes of human existence (the individual and the communal), then synthesizing a wedding of the divergent perspectives.

[123] E.O. Wilson argues that the human capacity for cooperating deeply on the basis of intimate mutual knowledge creates human eusociality, just as pheromones and instinct created ant eusociality. "Eusocial" species rear their young cooperatively across generations, and divide labor with some members sacrificing personal reproductive success in favor of the breeding success of other group members. Natural selection operates to preserve genes in human groups that tend to create cooperative communication and labor, with competition among groups. [♪] Wilson, *The Meaning of Human Existence*, 19, 75.

[124] Michael Gazzaniga concurs that beneath the welter of diverse human moral opinion lie subconscious brain structures that explain the universal components of many human moral responses. A

Beneath human choosing lies an invisible hand. Our preferences derive from evolutionary pressures in the aboriginal human environment in rift Africa. We feel psychological compulsion to choose those paths that would have benefited the human primate 200,000 years ago on African savannahs. We feel these pressures because genes that generate such traits survived African hardships those many millennia ago, and continue to shape consciousness to the present. Competing gene complements died out. From Africa's survival maelstrom, a mind tuned to the feelings and intentions of others arose. After that social mind settled, a cerebral frontal lobe supporting self-perception evolved. With it came critical analysis. Humans became positioned, as are few animals, to perceive and evaluate their behavioral predilections. Man became a creature that does not merely do what comes naturally, but also deviates from natural behavior for adaptive advantage. We adjust, by habit and culture, what for us "comes naturally."[126] For example, we are tropical primates, but live also in harsh, ill-suited temperate, or even polar, environments. Man is given to small groups of 150 or fewer persons, but more than half of us have adjusted to urban anonymity (albeit poorly). Humans travel naturally at about three miles per hour, but tolerate speeds hundreds of times that velocity. We acclimate to the "unnatural."

Granted, heritable African pressures upon consciousness endure, despite our habitual ameliorations. These elective adaptations pit culture and character against the urgencies bequeathed from the human evolutionary past.

---

universal ethics is, for Gazzaniga, possible, not as a list of set rules, but rather as a context-driven, affectively-valent, survival-augmenting background to human decision-making. Gazzaniga, *The Ethical Brain*, 177-178.

[125] Rousseau admits that, despite his reliance in his thinking on his construction of the natural man, it is doubtful such a natural man existed or will exist. The natural stands in admixture of the cultural in man, defying those who would sort its components. Rousseau, "A Discourse on the Origin of Inequality," 44-45. As is so common among philosophers, Rousseau promptly asserts positively that which he has previously deeply doubted. *Ibid.*, 51. Jan Oppermann argues that I miscomprehend Rousseau. Rousseau's natural man is a philosophical (non-historical) construct, never intended to convey any anthropological content. I must acknowledge that Jan is usually right. Oppermann, in private correspondence with the author, dated October 14, 2015.

[126] Some believe that, in adjusting what "comes naturally" we sorely injure ourselves. Jean Leidloff argues that human thinking, especially when indulging just the sort of deliberative culling I advocate, misleads man, bumps him off his natural evolutionary and emotional "continuum." The spawn is a horror of unmet emotional need that unreels forward in time, robbing every subsequent moment of the serene content it would, in a more natural environment, contain. She advocates constant infant skin-to-skin contact with mother, attentive subsequent parenting, infants sleeping with parents, breastfeeding on demand, welcoming children in all adult activities, and for we many who are afflicted by loss of natural serenity, some serious psychological therapy. Leidloff's book is marred by spasms of over-interpretation (for example, homosexuality originates as a broken continuum effect) and some dubious mysticisms (infants have energy fields that leak into their mother's, and vice versa. Failure to bleed off the infant energy field leads infants to masturbate and adults to sexually fixate). Still, in my view, Leidloff offers insights of value. Leidloff, *The Continuum Concept*, 109-136.

Humanity dwells in the stressed space between a mind adapted to circumstances no longer extant, and a mind adaptable to circumstances yet unimagined. This position makes humans ineradicably creatures of choice. Our relatively simple, grisly life on African savannahs is, for mankind, gone. The human task lies in shaping culture and character to produce flourishing life under present circumstances, in a world transformed by our tools, while ever wedded to the human mind's adaptation to a deeply different environment.

Humans, by nature, are neither congenitally good nor bad, but rather harbor the potential by their choices and predilections to marvelously augment or dramatically impair themselves, their neighbors, and the human community at large. Man is an animal of habits, more than thoughts or instincts.[127] Every habit can, potentially, be called to moral scrutiny, but most are seldom examined. One chooses habits to revise that one suspects will, once reconstructed, augment the meaning of one's conduct.[128] It is each member's and every community's charge to encourage member and community choices that augment meaningful community and deter decisions that erode meaningful community.[129] Human flourishing hangs in the balance. The matrix of member habits and communal culture is the womb from which issues both wonders and monstrosities of character.

1.8. *Instability of Stable Character.* Not only is member character mutable, but past wisdom proves no guarantee of future insight. Consciousness is fragmented, driven by its multifarious drives and longings, each of which may prove, under some set of circumstances, necessary to the member's or community's survival. No human drive is essentially good or evil. Each promotes survival under some set of circumstances similar to those survival pressures under which the drive evolved.[130] From a member accustomed to

---

[127] Reason and primal drives take a back seat to human habit. [♪] Dewey, *Human Nature and Conduct*, 125.

[128] Morality is education in meaning, the meaning of our actions and our existence. [♪] Dewey, *Human Nature and Conduct*, 280.

[129] Aurelius taught that what is bad for hives cannot be good for bees. [♪] Aurelius, *To Himself*, Book VI, 54. Pinker argues that human violence has dramatically declined due to our unwitting right action in promoting those of our neural capabilities that engender peace and thwarting those of our neural capabilities that lead us to frenzy and violence. [♪] Pinker, *Better Angels of Our Nature*, 671-696. I suspect that Pinker projects rampant violence onto the prehistorical canvas where it never existed. It appears that prehistorical conflict resolution consisted more in walking away (to the extent of migrating across the entire planet) than in standing one's ground, fists clenched. See Hrdy, *Mothers and Others*, 247.

[130] To consider possible adaptivity of some "evil" conduct, sociopathy may be an adaptive response to the community's need for members capable of efficient conscienceless murder under exigent circumstances, and the sexual predation of martial rape and sexual slavery may have, on Pleistocene

finely-elaborated culling, behaviors ill-deliberated and shockingly inappropriate may emerge, especially when intense stresses test a member. The
same may be said of community decision-making. Members and communities of finely-elaborated culling take a watchful, cautious stance toward human actions, including their own.

> A FELINE SNARL TEARS THE PITCH OF NIGHT, WAKING A GROUP. A CHILD
> CRIES AND IS CLUTCHED BY HIS MOTHER. HEARTS POUND; PANIC ETCHES.
> CATS HAVE KILLED BEFORE. A WOMAN SOOTHES HER FRIEND, AND GATHERS
> CHILDREN. JOZ, THE CRIPPLED GIRL, CRAWLS IN. A GRUFF VOICE URGES,
> "GIVE IT JOZ." SEVERAL GASP AT THE SKILLED HUNTER'S PROPOSAL. A TEEN
> BOY OBJECTS, "JOZ IS MY FRIEND, AND ONE OF US." THE BOY SNATCHES A
> ROCK AND HURLS IT INTO THE NIGHT. OTHERS MIMIC; THE BRUSH SHUDDERS.
> THE PREDATOR MOVES OFF TO EASIER PREY. HUGS AND TOUCHING SOOTHE
> MEMBERS. ONE WOMAN SHUNS THE GRUFF SACRIFICER. AN ELDER TOUCHES
> THE OSTRACIZED HUNTER'S ELBOW, TO DRESS HIS SOCIAL WOUND. GRUFF
> EYES STAB DOWNWARD.

1.9. *Evil and Error.* Members and communities may elect evils in error. An
evil act elects a misperceived good, chosen for supposed benefit in ignorance of its injurious result.[131]   Inept culling, though lamentable, cannot be

---

savannahs, served as a bulwark against tribal inbreeding. This, I find, a plausible, if disgusting, possibility.

[131] Dewey argues that evils are rejected goods. Evils never come forth declaring their deleterious effects. Evils compete with goods, and, for the fortunate, are rejected. [♪] Dewey, *Human Nature and
Conduct*, 278-281.
    Rousseau finds even his charity, under revised circumstances, becomes harmful. Rousseau,
Reveries of the Solitary Walker, Sixth Walk, 95. Muhammad describes man as hasty, deliberating so
poorly that he prays for harms as often as for good. [♪] Muhammad, *Qur'an* 17:11.
    Hume finds man's fundamental amity so pervasive that he imagines no man might prefer the
unhappiness of others, absent distorting events that twist him (anger, purpose of revenge, for example). Disinterested malice has no place in the human heart. Generalized philanthropy is the rule
among humans. [♪] Hume, *An Enquiry Concerning the Principles of Morals*, 114 (Chapter 5, Section 40).
    Epictetus acknowledged that all action commences in human feeling. Those who err misinter-
pret their feelings. Those with better insights should correct, not condemn, errant others. Epictetus,
Discourses, 119-121 (Book I, Sections 18.1-4). Epictetus goes on to say that all perceptions represent things that are and seem so, things that are not and seem not to be, things that are yet do not
seem to be so, and things that are not yet seem to be so. The educated man recognizes each. Men of
impaired judgment fail these distinctions, and should be pitied as one pities the lame or blind. When
one is deluded by perceptions, one hopes for what cannot come to pass, and so sorrows. Epictetus,
Discourses, 169, 171, 177 (Book I, Section 27.1, Section 27.11, Section 28.9).
    Rousseau asserts that no one does evil to achieve an evil end. Rousseau, *Emile*, 243.
    Benedict de Spinoza believes men are largely impotent to restrain action on our indistinct feel-
ings (Preface). We call "good" that which preserves us. We call "evil" what obstructs our existence
(Proposition 8). Our passions regularly disagree with nature (Proposition 32). Men seek nothing but
their own good, but are frequently in error about what will for them be good (Proposition 19). Men
may, however, be guided by reason, in opposition to their affects. Being guided by reason, they
reach concord with one another (Proposition 35). Whatever conduces to harmonious human fellow-

avoided. Inept culling may teach. Inept culling may lead to skillful cull-ing.[132] Inept culling, thoroughly remediated, gives rise to finely-elaborated culling.[133] One never knows with certainty that the perceived good a mem-ber or community elects may not be later recognized as an emergent evil.[134] One takes heart and plunges on, bringing the best of one's deliberative in-sight to bear. Culling well demands ongoing humility and a willingness to learn. Our goods may prove evils.[135]

1.10. *Pathological Evil.* Certain neurodiversities (at least some of which are cognitive pathologies) preclude skillful culling. Consider sociopathy,[136]

---

ship is good. Discord is evil (Proposition 40). Spinoza, *Ethics*, 161-194 (Fourth Part: Of Human Bondage).

Jared Diamond argues that societies choose to fail by making improvident decisions. Those decisions relate to five factors: a) unwitting damage to one's immediate environment, b) changes to climate (not globally, but semi-locally, such as decades-long drought-rainy cycles), c) hostile neigh-bors (and what choices it takes to generate hostile neighbors), d) friendly neighbors (and the choices and trade it takes to make friends of potential enemies), and e) the society's responses to any of these problems once they become prominent enough to be perceived as problems. Diamond, *Collapse*, 11.

[132] Gregory Bateson argues that all purposive decisions create unanticipated outcomes. Human con-sciousness never perceives more than a fraction of the systems in which it is a part, and so by its ac-tions distorts those systems. The result is negative feedback, a circumstantial cybernetic slap on the wrist or fist to the face. Bateson goes so far as to characterize, perhaps tongue-in-cheek, that purpos-ive human behavior is that original sin by which Adam and Eve departed Eden. Bateson, *Steps To An Ecology of Mind*, 439-442.

[133] Mencius argues that progress arrives only in the wake of failure. One innovates from frustration. Others hear a man only when his learning comes from experience, and spills on to the face and into the voice. *Mencius*, 143 (Book VI, Part B, Section 15).

[134] Heraclitus goes so far as to argue that good and evil are indistinguishable. Heraclitus, Jones translation, *On the Universe*, 57.

[135] [♪] Emerson, *Conduct of Life*, VII, 1083-1086: "[T]he first lesson of history is the good of evil. Good is a good doctor, but Bad is sometimes a better. . . . There is a tendency in things to right themselves. . . . [M]ost of the great results of history are brought about by discreditable means. . . . [T]here is no moral deformity, but is a good passion out of place; . . . [T]here is no man who is not at some time indebted to his vices, as no plant that is not fed from manures. We only insist that the man meliorate, and that the plant grow upward, and convert the base into the better nature." Menci-us takes human nature to be essentially good. *Mencius*, Book VI, Part A, Section 2. Calvin finds humankind essentially corrupt. Calvin, *Institutes*, Book II, Chapter 1, Section 6. Freud finds man-kind lazy, inherently destructive, and lacking in native intelligence. No alternatives to coercion ex-ist. [♪] Freud, *Future of an Illusion*, 6-7. Han Fei Tzu finds men, especially young men, reform themselves, not when loved and wisely instructed, but when faced with coercive punishments from a magistrate. Thus, love is not all we need. [♪] Han Fei Tzu, *Basic Writings*, 103 (§49). I doubt hu-mans are good or evil in their essence, though they can learn to develop such habits; I find most peo-ple embroiled in morally-muddled wandering.

[136] Four percent of the human population (three of these four percent are male, one percent is female) suffer sociopathy, which is a dramatic inability to feel the experience of others. Sociopathy entails the absence of conscience. Sociopathy has been called, in times less sensitive than our own, moral imbecility. See Stout, *The Sociopath Next Door*, 6. Sociopathy is sometimes call psychopathy (to be distinguished from psychosis, a state characterized by impaired function and fractured sense of reality) and is identified in the *DSM V Manual* as "anti-social personality disorder." This fluctuating

some psychoses, dementia, dramatic neurotransmitter deficiencies leading to habitual violence or substance abuse, attachment deficits, some personality disorders, and some brain injuries and diseases, for example. Such suffering members may knowingly elect evils, and influence others to follow their misdirection.[137]   One anticipates needless personal suffering in members gripped by such difficulties.[138]

> ONE IS MANY.
> IF ONE SUBTRACTS:
>   PARENTS, HE SHRINKS;
>   SPOUSE, SHE LESSENS;
>   WORKMATES, HE DIMINISHES;
>   FRIENDS, SHE VANISHES.
> ONE, ALONE, IS NONE.

Defective community co-deliberation, which is the collective correlate of member cognitive pathology, may preclude skillful culling. Such hobbled communities may knowingly elect evils, and induce other communities to follow suit. Consider, for example, the culling habits represented by narcissism, theological or tribal genocide, parental neglect, nihilism, torture, misanthropy, slave-holding, war, rape, substance abuse, facile deliberation, and vapid consumerism. One anticipates degenerating coordination and cohesion in communities where members cull poorly.[139]   Thomas Hobbes argued that the human commonwealth could, were some wisdom employed in its construction, endure forever, despite the mortality of society's constituent members. But because we make bad laws, and lack humility and patience, we misconstrue our togetherness.   Governments become crazy

---

terminology sometimes confuses even professionals, about which Robert Hare, a University of British Columbia psychopathy expert, complains. Hare, *Without Conscience*, 24-25.

[137] Roman Emperor Marcus Aurelius reminds himself that no men do evil intentionally. [♪] Aurelius, *To Himself*, Book IV, §1. Would this were so.

[138] Emerson finds mankind divided into good actors and bad actors. The latter predominate. [♪] Emerson, *Conduct of Life*, VII, 1080. I differ as to percentages.

[139] Mencius explains human corruption by the parable of Ox Mountain. Ox Mountain lay beneath a verdant umbrella of trees near a city. Exuberant foliage burst from its slopes. But humans encroached. Men axed trees. Sheep and cattle grazed. Resilient, Ox Mountain sprouted new shoots and grasses. Scythes and herds returned. Then yet more people and flocks. Soon, Ox Mountain grew barren. Still, hordes came. Livestock stomped roots. Men trampled earth. Soil trickled off precipices. Dust blew from corpses of meadows. Only a bare, rocky knuckle remained. Nothing could ever grow. Mencius said all men have moral sensitivity. But when one lets go his integrity, he goes the way of Ox Mountain. Well nourished, there is no man in which moral grandeur will not blossom. Lacking nutriment, goodness withers in any heart. *Mencius*, 127-128 (Book VI, Part A.8).

buildings, destined to crash down upon members' heads or those of their children.[140]

1.11. *Co-Formation and Co-Resistance.* Member and community interpenetrate in co-reaction.[141] Skillful member culling inclines communities to skillful community culling. Inept community culling may preclude the conditions under which member culling grows skillful. Inept member culling may frustrate skillful community culling. Skillful community culling instructs and redirects members toward skillful member culling. Members maintain a compromised independence, neither being able to integrate the breadth of their uniqueness into the community nor enjoying a freedom to abandon life with social others, which reality Kant memorably calls the "unsociable sociability of man."[142] Communities pull members toward contribution and conformity.[143] But members harbor incommensurate oddities in themselves. They contribute and conform to the extent possible. Silently,

---

[140] [♪] Hobbes, *Leviathan*, 221 (Chapter 29).

[141] Rousseau disagrees. He takes self-preservation and sympathy with the pain of others to be the two subconscious and foundational principles of human action. Rousseau expressly excludes human sociality from those motives he deems fundamental. Rousseau, "A Discourse on the Origin of Inequality," 47. One finds well being, if one is able, by departing cultured life in favor of return to the acorns and caves of primordial existence. Most persons, their primal passions corrupted by civilization, cannot undertake that journey, and are doomed to live in human communities. Rousseau, "A Discourse on the Origin of Inequality, Appendix," 124. Jan Oppermann notes that Rousseau moderated his views in later writings, offering in [♪] *The Social Contract* a pattern for collective living that is not primal. Oppermann, in private correspondence with author, dated October 14, 2015. Rousseau is plainly wrong to the extent he abandons primitive social drives. Prosocial impulses (tendencies to freely do acts that benefit companions) are as fundamental as self-preserving impulses. Intersubjectivity is built into human neural architecture. We sense with great accuracy the feelings and intentions of others. Human pro-sociality differentiates man from all other primates. We are given to cooperate. See Hrdy, *Mothers and Others*, 6-7. Aristotle goes so far as to call intimate friendship a plural identity; one's friend is another self. In Aristotle's view, friendship occurs only between good people where they build intimacy by undertaking good acts for the good purpose of fashioning a desirable community. Aristotle, *Nichomachean Ethics*, 169-172 (1166a-1167b).

[142] [♪] Kant, *Universal History*, 122. The psychological mutualism I advocate in this book contrasts sharply with individualism, so cherished in America, and so typical of Western thought. See [♪] Emerson, *Self-Reliance*, and *Fare Lonely as Rhinoceros* in the Buddhist scriptures for conceptions of man the solipsistic individual. [♪] Emerson, *Self-Reliance*. [♪] Conze, *Buddhist Scriptures (Part II, Chapter 1, Section 3)*. Emerson, as life progressed, found greater importance in friendship and mutual reliance. Emerson, *Conduct of Life*, 1093-1094 (Section VII: Considerations by the Way). Epictetus doubts the possibility of friendship as I describe it, for in his view, intimacy is ever riddled with self-interest and, therefore, something of a sham. See Epictetus, *Discourses*, Book II, 22).

[143] Epictetus noted that no man gets what he desires for himself without contributing to the common good. Epictetus, *Discourses*, 131 (Book I, Section 19.13). Rousseau styles human sociability a weakness. Were men self-sufficient, none would seek company. To be genuinely happy is to be alone. Rousseau, *Emile*, 221. As is so often the case, I find Rousseau simply wrong.

however, they succor a conviction of inviolable identity. Members are, in their deepest, often invisible, selves, unique and non-conformable.[144]

ED LOVED ERMA. THE HIGH SCHOOL SWEETHEARTS RAISED THREE FINE CHILDREN. ED AND ERMA LOVED, AND WERE LOVED BY, THEIR FRIENDS. THE COUPLE WORKED PRODUCTIVELY, CHOSE CAREFULLY, AND DOTED ON THEIR TABBY CAT, CHELSEA. ED AND ERMA VOTED, AND PICKED UP THE TRASH OF OTHERS OCCASIONALLY.

ERMA DIED IN HER SLEEP FROM CARDIAC PROBLEMS LIKE THOSE THAT CLAIMED HER MOTHER AND FATHER. ED GRIEVED. AS THE MONTHS PASSED, ED TOOK TO TURNING HIS WEDDING BAND ON HIS FINGER WHEN HE THOUGHT OF ERMA, WHICH WAS MANY TIMES EACH DAY. HE SLOWLY DIVERTED HIS THOUGHTS FROM HER DEATH TO THE MANY JOYS THEY SHARED. THE WEALTH OF ED'S LIFE WITH ERMA OVERBORE THE PAIN OF MAKING HIS WAY WITHOUT HER. STILL, ED SPUN HIS RING.

ONE SUNDAY AFTERNOON, ED PREPARED FISH DINNER FOR HIS CHILDREN'S FAMILIES. HE SPREAD NEWSPAPER ON THE COUNTER BESIDE THE SINK. ED PLACED HIS WEDDING RING ON THE WINDOW SILL ABOVE THE COUNTER. ED GUTTED, GILLED, AND SCALED HIS MORNING'S CATCH. ONE OF THE GRANDCHILDREN TELEPHONED TO TELL ED SHE WOULD BE LATE. CHELSEA THE TABBY LEAPT TO THE COUNTER, SNATCHED A WHITEFISH LIVER, AND SCAMPERED BEHIND THE COUCH. HER TAIL SWEPT ED'S RING INTO THE FISH GUTS. ED WADDED UP THE DAMP NEWSPAPERS, PRESSED THEM INTO THE KITCHEN GARBAGE CAN, THEN TOOK THAT BAG TO THE TRASH BIN OUTSIDE. AFTER DINNER, ED'S ELDEST SON PULLED THE BIN TO THE STREET. ED SLEPT, ENJOYING THE GLOW OF TOO MUCH WINE AND LAUGHTER. THE GARBAGE TRUCK, LONG BEFORE DAWN, EMPTIED ED'S BIN, AND DUMPED ITS LOAD IN THE PROCESSING STATION. THE LOAD WAS SHREDDED, POURED ONTO A BARGE, AND TUGGED OFFSHORE, WHERE IT WAS LAID IN A DEEP OCEAN RAVINE.

AT MONDAY'S LUNCH TABLE, ED REACHED TO TURN HIS WEDDING RING, BUT THE FINGER WAS EMPTY. ED COULD NOT REMEMBER WHEN HE REMOVED THE RING, AND COULD NOT FIND IT, DESPITE REPEATED SEARCHES. IN THE FOLLOWING DAYS, ED OFTEN REACHED TO TURN THE RING, BUT IT WAS GONE. EVENTUALLY, HE REACHED FOR IT LESS OFTEN. YEARS PASSED. ED RECURRED TO MEMORIES OF ERMA LESS OFTEN. HE DID NOT, HOWEVER, NOTICE THE CHANGE. FOR ED WAS HAPPY.

---

[144] Kant laments mankind's "unsociable sociability," inclined as people are to associate even while isolating themselves. We cannot leave others; neither can we put up with them happily. [♪] Kant, *Idea for a Universal History with Cosmopolitan Intent*, 122. Buddhists view my perspective as fundamentally flawed. Persons do not exist, nor selves, except in the confused mental state that accompanies samsara (this pedestrian world), which is the stage on which the sad drama of reincarnation plays. One finds truth, and release from the karmic wheel of birth-suffering-death, when one transcends the individual, even perception itself, to dwell in sublime emptiness, void of self and sense experience and expectation of any sort. Successful meditators leap off the karmic wheel as buddhas. Accompanying this Buddhist mysticism, Buddha entertained ambivalence about the role of friendship. Friends are needful, especially when of such moral character as to be spiritually helpful; but friends also prove a distraction from the sort of necessary meditation best undertaken in solitude. [♪] *Dhammapada*, 330-331.

ED DIED IN HIS CHAIR ON A SPRING DAY, FULL OF YEARS AND MEMORIES.
CHELSEA LICKED HIS FACE, BUT ED DID NOT SCRATCH HER EARS AS WAS ED'S
CUSTOM. HIS ELDEST DAUGHTER COULD NOT FIND ED'S WEDDING RING. SHE
WONDERED ABOUT THAT.
SO VANISHES MEANING,
SAYS ONE.

1.12. *Meaningful Community.*

1.12.1. *Social Construction of Meaningful Community.* Meaningful commu-
nity is constructed by humans as they cull conduct. Because humans necessarily act in the world, they project themselves outward, with effect.
Because humans are social, they do their active projecting collectively.[145]
Human uniqueness lies in our ability to collaborate with others, even
strangers, with shared goals and common intention.[146] In so doing, we establish social relations and agreed approaches to problems, including
ways of thinking and talking about challenges faced. Meaning emerges
when members find themselves the authors of their existence, and feel
some minimal sense of control over their shared destiny.[147] Over time,
repeated actions become routine, and establish themselves in the habits of
members. Communities tell supportive stories about their cultural habits,
which stories become worldviews in the hands of members given to reflection. The members' perception of reality is a social construct of their
community. Social constructs serve to integrate the member meaningfully
into the work of the community, and to reduce the terror of life's uncer-
tainties, such as death, disease, disaster, and all the misfortunes that befall
people of good faith.[148] Where communities are healthy, groups and

---

[145] Viktor Frankl argues that human individuals fashion meaning for themselves by tasks they set
themselves, by meeting people or situations, and by transforming unavoidable suffering. Frankl,
Man's Search for Meaning, 111.

[146] So argues Sara Blaffer Hrdy, citing Michael Tomasello of the Max Planck Institute. Hrdy, *Mothers and Others,* 9.

[147] Royce, *The Philosophy of Loyalty,* 43-44.

[148] Watzlawick argues that we deem certain matters reliable, then assert those "facts" in support of
our description of "reality." Actually, our subconscious need for self-comprehension in a stable universe leads humans to quest for reality, which "reality" we socially construct, latching onto suggestive, but equivocal, elements of experience. Watzlawick, *The Invented Reality,* 10. When some act
or idea pleases us, we credit that aspect of experience as reliable. Some such acts and ideas become
foundational to our view of the world. Yet, these "reliable" ideas are equivocal. Watzlawick imagines a sea captain sailing through an uncharted channel at night without navigational aids. If the ship
wrecks, the captain has learned one, but not all, of the channel's dangerous features. But if the captain sails free into open waters, he has not learned of the channel's safety, but only that on his one
benighted course, he did not sink. Watzlawick, *The Invented Reality,* 15. Like this sea captain's
course are the reliable data undergirding our worldviews.

members retain the knowledge that their social fabric, though persistent, is malleable and evolving.[149]

Where collective memory of the origin of culture and member habit fades, social routine grows deeply entrenched. Its origins in human choice fade from recollection. In religious communities, humanly-fabricated social obligations migrate to the mouths of gods. Servants of god speak on behalf of the pantheon.[150] As members recognize that they have reduced influence over the course and structure of their social world, especially where communities bloat themselves with overpopulation, communities grow rigid and less adaptive. The social construct ossifies. Adaptive change proves difficult or impossible. Meaning wanes.[151]

---

[149] Maturana and Varela posit that humans co-fabricate their world; uncertainty and fluctuation necessarily attend the construct, which is typical of the human experience when examined finely. Certainty is, in such a universe, unlikely and, possibly, unhelpful. The world one sees is a world fashioned by living with others. Seen from within, that world convinces. But, if one lived differently, or with different others, that social structure would issue a different world. It too would be, to its participants, convincing. Maturana and Varela, *Tree of Knowledge*, 241, 245. A community's fabric is malleable, but remains, nevertheless, a fabric. Its malleability is not borderless.

[150] All religious schemas are not theological. Consider Hegel's view of dialectical Absolute Spirit or the State in Marxism. Though Hegel indulges some vapid god-talk, his social objectivation is implicitly secular. Hegel, *Philosophy of Right*. The Marxist version is expressly anti-theological. [♪] Marx and Engels, *Communist Manifesto*. Buddhism also purports to be non-theological; it does not seem to me, as a practical matter, to be such. American consumerism and its capitalist theory seem of religious significance to many. Each religion, whether of theological and secular bent, recommends that one adopt its values, even when scant evidence supports those values, and often despite direct contrary evidence.

[151] Some argue that Western culture has grown more flexible and tolerant as its populations have grown. Gays marry. Millions think that "black lives matter." Most hope that no Islamist will suffer discrimination. Crime flags. Murder falls. Steven Pinker advises well. Do commerce, hear women, enforce laws, increase sympathy (read novels), and promote rationality. Those who credit Pinker hope we careen (perhaps unintentionally) toward rampant peace. [♪] Pinker, *Better Angels of Our Nature*. I am glad for good outcomes, whenever they occur. Pinker is right that violence has, historically, declined. Pinker fails to identify why, given all the effort, violence nevertheless persists. Coercion is effective, but short-sighted. We coerce "improvements," ignoring the backlash and sequels. After compulsion, all but the most timid among us sucks a seed of retaliation, an emotional imperative to do the doer. Such is the nature of insult. Victims bury relational mines where coercers saunter. Detonations maim. Coercers become victims, and lay their own mines. Where does coercion end? Shall we coerce ever more deeply? Shall every person be watched and prodded and punished into wider submissions, each intrusion more intimate than the last? Will not the circle of vendetta lash ever more deeply our culture and children? The dry well of coercion slakes no cooperative thirst. Coercion stanches those springs of activity that would otherwise become collaborations, poisoning trust. Can one compel tolerance? Can one force caring? Compassion blossoms from quiet listening, not rants. Trust is a seedling that roots only in clement weather. *See* our culture. We dwell senselessly near the border of the horrid. Suicide is up. Anomie is up. American mass murders have become pedestrian. Loneliness is a raging plague. Children starve (usually elsewhere). Homelessness swells like a tumor in society's intestines. We seem to have no answer for sociopaths on rampages. We lack words to deter people who breed heedlessly. Antipathy freezes Congress. Presidents dither. The Pentagon lusts after yet one more war. We invoke martial murder with practiced ease, but gape, astonished, when hated by the survivors of our targets. Americans seem no longer to believe in America. Public confidence in our institutions gutters. I suggest a reason for this collapse of confidence: our groundless faith in compulsion. Coercion is an ethical *cul de sac*.

When humans construct their community poorly, or when communities persist in ossified structures, or when well-constructed communities fail to consistently adapt, human community may seem meaningless. A community's members may fail to connect personal meaninglessness with her community's actions. The member's cull of conduct may seem unrelated to, or even opposed to, the community's purposes. Rebellions, large and small, collectively social and psychologically individual, commence. Ossified social structures fracture. These eventually crumble as changes render them antiquated. Their once-useful life solutions prove increasingly maladaptive.[152] Meaningful life is not natural. Human culture departed the "natural" tens of millennia ago. Stressed humans "naturally" murder to acquire territory and sexual privilege. Thoughtless humans "naturally" breed with heedless abandon. Humans "naturally" wander, seeking resources. Threatened humans "naturally" love "us" and excoriate "them." Humanity's tangled natural trajectory emerges from brains fashioned by gene survival pressures in ancestral east Africa. The principal threat to human well-being is the host of once-adaptive, now erosive, "natural" behaviors that grip the human community. These arose as a result of humankind's millennia-long encounter with scarcity attributable to overpopulation. We have fitfully attempted to respond, unsuccessfully. Our circumstance now demands more of humans. Elect behaviors that douse humanity's erosive impulses. Collaborate. Cooperate. These approaches are more deeply engrained in human bone than rapacity and coercion. Elaborate habits that augment meaningful communi-

---

The only way out is to go back to the beginning and take a different path. Pinker missed that. I thank Michael Loges and the Witless Protection Program participants for the conversation, on February 6, 2016, that led to this footnote.

[152] Berger asserts that humans, due to their unusual cognition, are indeterminate. All must make a place for themselves in the universe, since nature provides no sufficient sense of place. In a process of projecting ideas upon the universe, deeming those ideas inherent in the universal fabric, and then drinking in those projections as objective features of the universe, people create "reality." [♪] Berger, *Sacred Canopy*, 4-5. Berger and Luckmann put it more bluntly: "Reality is socially constructed." Berger and Luckmann, *The Social Construction of Reality*, 1.

Also consider Kuhn, *The Structure of Scientific Revolutions*, whose view differs. Kuhn argues that science evolves, not by incremental improvements, but by revolution from below. Young scientists with different paradigms overthrow or outlive their mentors, whereupon science takes a step forward. One wonders what "forward" means in this context.

Paul Feyerabend argues that there is no identifiable "method" to scientific discovery. Someone explores a bothersome question. He finds answers, which are tested. Others follow using different methods, asking different questions. Feyerabend calls his view "professional anarchism." Understanding emerges from activities which probably include elements of playfulness. Feyerabend says: "There is only one principle that can be defended under *all* circumstances and in all stages of human development. It is the principle: *anything goes*." And "I am convinced that humanity and even Science will profit from everyone doing his own thing." Feyerabend argues that science and the State should be as separate as church and State, and for many of the same reasons. Feyerabend, *Against Method*, 12-19, 159, 238.

ty life.   Cull the alternatives.   Experiment with those possibilities that
survive the cut.

1.12.2. *Good: Conditions Augmenting Meaningful Community.*   A finely-
elaborated cull of human conduct leads toward meaningful community.[153]
Aristotle argues that what matters are the facts of our life together.   These
facts we examine and judge.[154]   In meaningful community, collective existence holds for members the promise of successive approximations of a
group's optimal well-being.[155]   Meaningful community is neither ideal
nor utopian.[156]   Meaningful community engages a process utilizing mem-

---

[153] Sam Harris would call this the "good life." His discussion of morality proceeds from two premises that he believes no reasonable person can deny: "(1) some people have better lives than others,
and (2) these differences related, in some lawful and not entirely arbitrary way, to states of the human brain and to states of the world." Harris, *The Moral Landscape*, 15-16. Ronald Dworkin argues: "We must treat our lives as a challenge, one we can perform well or badly. . . . Each of us
bursts with love of life and fear of death: we are alone among animals conscious of that apparently
absurd situation. . . . We must find the value of living—the meaning of life—in living well, just as
we find value in loving or painting or writing or singing or diving well. There is no other enduring
value or meaning in our lives, but that is value and meaning enough. In fact it's wonderful. . . .
People must take their own lives seriously: They must accept that it is objectively important how
they live." Dworkin, *Justice for Hedgehogs*, 13-14.

[154] [♪] Aristotle, *Nichomachean Ethics*, 199 (1179a). Elsewhere, Aristotle argues that every man
must choose an aim upon which to focus life's efforts. "It is therefore most necessary to decide
within oneself, neither hastily nor carelessly, in which of the things that belong to us the good life
consists, and what are the indispensable conditions for men's possessing it." Aristotle, *Eudemian
Ethics*, 203 (Book I, Section II.2). It appears to me that, though every human bears much in common with all humans in all places and times, a great deal of moral choosing is stamped with local
concerns. So, it is best, as in kithdom, to leave a great deal of looseness in the joints of our various
moral systems. We must also recognize that our own minds are multiplex, sending us in search of
various goods at different times. No one good serves every man in every circumstance. Hence,
"meaningful community" is multi-form, dependent upon the needs and situations of individual
communities, if not in its broad outline, then certainly in its community-by-community specifics.
Kithdom also recognizes that people frequently cannot ferret the better from the worse alternative,
but must do the hard experiment and judge its moral and communal results. Thus is wisdom born.
Aristotle styles poor choices failures to distinguish the good from apparent goods. These latter contravene nature and stem from perversion. Aristotle, *Eudemian Ethics*, 299 (Book II. Section 10.26).

[155] Gustav Landauer, in his critique of Marxist Statism, argues that human community fills a basic
need, which the State cannot approximate. Community imbues member life with familial warmth
and a sense of place. Landauer, *For Socialism*, 126.

[156] Callipolis, Plato's beautiful city philosophically mulled in *The Republic*, is a utopia. As Plato
says, it matters not a whit whether Callipolis exists in real life, since its form exists in heaven for any
philosopher to ponder. [♪] Plato, *Republic*, 312 (§592).

Jan Oppermann argues that Plato's Callipolis was never primarily intended, even by Plato, to
describe cities, but rather to explore the possibilities of philosophical thought in a well-ordered human soul (where thought governs emotion and deep-seated drives). Oppermann, private correspondence with the author, dated October 14, 2015.

Meaningful community is not such an ideal or philosophical exploration. It matters only to the
extent that real people experience real relationships as meaningful. Callipolis is fashioned of gossa-
mer, thin stuff indeed. Kithdoms are built of rock and blood, in the thickest core of human sociality.

Jonathan Glover warns of utopias: "Future generations are unlikely to share all our values.
One obvious consequence of this is that we should not plan utopias for them. . . . If the Victorians

ber capabilities for collective benefit.[157] Meaningful community benefits members, present and future, by collective effort.[158] Meaningful community emerges as human groups create cultures in which they may live well. There, humans engage most human primal drives and affections in a manner that, at best, benefits all, or, at worst, injures none.[159] We ask, What are our facts? How might we make our facts better?

We fashion the "new natural," thereby constructing our future.[160] Here are components:

1.12.2.1. *Physical Sustenance.* Meaningful communities harvest water and food, erect shelter, and dispose of wastes for all members in a manner that can be permanently sustained without injury to the global ecosystem of life. Meaningful communities avoid disrupting ecological homeostasis, since it is the source of the Commons' physical life.[161] Relative ease in acquiring life's necessities tamps down members' neurotic acquisitiveness and hoarding.

---

had been able to use genetic engineering, they would have aimed to make us more pious and patriotic." Glover, *What Sort of People Should There Be?*, 149.

[157] Throughout this work, I argue that human rapacity springs from improvident decisions, intellectual chartlessness, parental ill-nurture, unrecognized sociopaths, and the occasional genetic sport. Human evil is, then, eradicable or, at worst, manageable (or so I assert). Bernard Mandeville, however, scoffs. In Mandeville's mind, the goodness of any society springs *from* its evils. "With great Vices, is a vain EUTOPIA seated in the Brain. Fraud, Luxury and Pride must live, While we the Benefits receive: . . . So Vice is beneficial found, When it's by Justice lopt and bound; Nay, where the People would be great, As necessary to the State, as Hunger is to make 'em eat. Bare Virtue can't make Nations live in Splendor." Mandeville, *The Fable of the Bees*, 34-35. I trust Mandeville is wrong.

[158] Dorothy Day, Catholic social activist and anarchist pacifist, said of community that only by living, working, sharing, and loving God and our fellows together can one address the loneliness inherent in human life. One loves God by loving one's community. Day, *The Long Loneliness*, 243.

[159] David Hume argues that no human can be indifferent to the well- or ill-being of his fellows. We seek the common good and avoid common injury, absent biases. These facts lead us to an ethical theory that what injures is undesirable, and what helps is preferred. Our moral sentiments follows these judgments closely. [♪] Hume, *An Enquiry Concerning the Principles of Morals*, 116-117 (Chapter 5, Sections 43).

[160] Michael Gazzaniga believes it possible that humankind might grasp for itself a universal ethics that is contextual, flexible, and bent toward improving our survival. Gazzaniga, *The Ethical Brain*, 177-178.

[161] By the word "Commons," I designate the communication of the global community of communities, as further described below. At a legal level, a "commons" is the opposite of "property." With property, one can use or destroy at will. With commons, one has a right to use but no right to exclude others or destroy the resource. Hyde, *Common as Air*, 27. Every commons has a carrying capacity, beyond which further use deteriorates the jointly-accessed resource. Hardin, "The Tragedy of the Commons." Hardin's pessimism may not pertain to a Commons consisting in ideas alone and information alone. Hyde, *Common as Air*, 46, 75.

1.12.2.2. *Physical Security.*   Meaningful communities address perceived threats to member and community well-being. As a result, members' stresses remain manageable, facilitating peaceful cooperation among members and among communities. Reducing the frequency of fear-inducing and anxiety-provoking social circumstances promotes the capacity for careful deliberation of conduct.[162] Thoughtful construction of social demands by a community may enable the group to fashion an architecture of conduct that emphasizes those capabilities in members that the group wishes to promote. The human community has, by neglecting social engineering possibilities, long stumbled into pointless homicidal frenzies. We have also been designing our way out of these martial conundra with increasing success, although predominantly by fumbling half-measures.[163] Meaningful communities choose habits that promote perceptions of physical security.

1.12.2.3. *Peace.*   Meaningful communities value peace among members and between communities.[164] Peace preserves social assets and physical capital, and wastes neither on destructive enterprises. Meaningful communities invest vast effort in nurturing the pre-conditions of peace by providing for the basic needs of every member and community. Members promote peace by self-restraint, resilient patience, and well-deliberated sacrifices for community benefit. Members promote peace by rejecting coercive and violent solutions to challenges and problems. Members and communities promote peace by maintaining extensive exchanges among communities, and creating economic interdependence among communities through trade of the communities' products. Members and communities promote peace by teaching peace-making skills to members, and establishing conflict reduction regimes between commu-

---

[162] Jaak Panksepp notes that the vast human cortex remains as subject to the affects of lower brain structures as are creatures with lesser cortices. When little stress impinges, human cognitive and emotional capacities interact reciprocally. When distress impinges, the subcortical (limbic and brainstem) influence take over. One may practice cortical control, but is unlikely to establish much certain control over the chaos of whipped emotion. Panksepp, *Affective Neuroscience*, 301.

[163] Steven Pinker believes that human cognition bears impulses toward violence, as well as impulses toward peaceful coexistence. Cultural adaptations over the last tens of thousands of years have encouraged those peaceful impulses and discouraged the bellicose ones, rendering global cultures with increasingly lower per capita instances of violence. [♪] Pinker, *Better Angels of Our Nature*, xxi-xxvi.

[164] Sigmund Freud is convinced that humankind cannot live peacefully. Violence is innate, born of psychic conflicts that plague every person due to the human need for others (for cooperation and sex) and the aggression inherent in the human animal. Freud, *Civilization and Its Discontents*, 102-103 (Section VI).

nities. The Commons promotes persistent peace by succoring a global culture intolerant of war and bellicose posturing.[165]

1.12.2.4. *Consensual Election of Purpose.*   Meaningful communities choose short-term purposes.   By participating in making decisions, members learn these goals and find ways to contribute integrally to those purposes.   Short-term purposes differ among communities as each devotes itself to various needs of the Commons and to expression of the uniqueness of a particular community's members.   The Commons promotes human meaning by electing, over many generations, a course or spectrum of courses for human endeavor.   Members and communities find local meaning in participation in global and transgenerational purposes.   The process of making such elections, if the decision-making process is not to undermine itself, is consensual.   Human communities, where they deserve that name, are small acephalic[166] kithdoms, comprising cadres of intimate friends.   All autocratic, plutocratic, aristocratic,

---

[165] Franklin Delano Roosevelt, no stranger to war, found war to be the blight from which we all suffer senselessly. On the day before he died, in April 1945, FDR wrote a Jefferson Day Speech, never delivered, in which he said: "We seek peace—enduring peace. More than an end to war, we want an end to the beginnings of all wars—yes, an end to this brutal, inhuman, and thoroughly impractical method of settling the differences between governments. The once powerful, malignant Nazi state is crumbling. The Japanese war lords are receiving, in their own homeland, the retribution for which they asked when they attacked Pearl Harbor. But the mere conquest of our enemies is not enough. We must go on to do all in our power to conquer the doubts and the fears, the ignorance and the greed, which made this horror possible. Thomas Jefferson, himself a distinguished scientist, once spoke of 'the brotherly spirit of Science, which unites into one family all its votaries of whatever grade, and however widely dispersed throughout the different quarters of the globe.' Today, science has brought all the different quarters of the globe so close together that it is impossible to isolate them one from another. Today we are faced with the preeminent fact that, if civilization is to survive, we must cultivate the science of human relationships—the ability of all peoples, of all kinds, to live together and work together, in the same world, at peace. Let me assure you that my hand is the steadier for the work that is to be done, that I move more firmly into the task, knowing that you—millions and millions of you—are joined with me in the resolve to make this work endure. The work, my friends, is peace. More than an end of this war —an end to the beginnings of all wars. Yes, an end, forever, to this impractical, unrealistic settlement of the differences between governments by the mass killing of peoples. Today, as we move against the terrible scourge of war–as we go forward toward the greatest contribution that any generation of human beings can make in this world– the contribution of lasting peace, I ask you to keep up your faith. I measure the sound, solid achievement that can be made at this time by the straight edge of your own confidence and your resolve. And to you, and to all Americans who dedicate themselves with us to the making of an abiding peace, I say: The only limit to our realization of tomorrow will be our doubts of today. Let us move forward with strong and active faith." (http://www.presidency.uscb.edu/ws/?pid=1602). Gwynne Dyer argues that, if our moral imagination does not expand to include all mankind in its scope, then the fragility of nation-states and terrible potency of their (especially nuclear) weapons will cause mankind to perish. Dyer, *War: The Lethal Custom*, 445.

[166] "Acephaly" means lacking a head. Here, the reference is to human community's natural collegiality and egalitarianism. No one person leads or chooses. Communities seek consensus among their society of friends. They exercise the human genius for shared intentionality.

and democratic decisional schemes advocate coercions of various shades.[167]

1.12.2.5. *Resilience.*   Meaningful communities meet obstacles to well-being with patient perseverance. Both a community and its members promote resilience in the face of obstacles. Resilience is the ability to embrace needed change without forsaking other critical values. Resilient members endure the pain of adapting. They recognize the pain of adaptation as a needful part of meaningful life. Resilient communities assist members in adapting by education, therapeutic conversation, and training. Prime challenges to resilience are disease and death. The pain of non-productivity in disease and the grief of loss in death present opportunities for community members to provide care and create teams of supportive circle members to address the needs of stricken families, circles, and communities. Care teams are resilience in action.[168]

1.12.2.6. *Integration into Community Purpose.*   The member finds his place in community purposes, with opportunity to make contributions which the member finds fulfilling. Member acquisitiveness and resistance to communal purposes are tolerated as evidence of diversity and possible savantism, each of which is essential to communal weal. All men are not created equal. Some prosper while others falter. Communities, however, cannot allow member inequality or savantism to rend their social fabric. When any prosper, all must prosper, although not equally. When any suffer, all must share that pain, though not all can participate in such pain equally. Some degree of social engineering and wealth redistribution will prove necessary within many communities and among communities as well. A goal of the Commons should be to achieve these adjustments voluntarily, without coercive taxation or compulsion. When members coordinate their activity with one another to reach agreed goals, members find participation meaningful. Where they fail of such cooperation, no matter how critical their activities may be to human weal, the fact of death robs them of the sense of meaning in their actions, which can issue in existential despair.[169]

---

[167] John Locke, in 1689, argued that though all men must consent to join a commonwealth for the mutual protection, once having consented, one is subjected to the will of the majority of the consenters. This coercive majoritarian rule is necessary because, lacking it, the body cannot proceed in a unified direction, causing the disintegration of the political community. [♪] Locke, *Second Treatise of Government*, 176-177 (Chapter VIII, Sections 95-97).

[168] Care teams form where member's needs challenge the limitations of self-care. Care teams form a part of one's own self-care. Gibson and Pigott, *Personal Safety Nets*, xxvii, 5.

[169] Tolstoy found despair in his fear of death, and asked whether inevitable death did not rob life of any possible meaning. [♪] Tolstoy, *A Confession*, Chapters IV and V. Soren Kierkegaard finds despair the universal human condition, a road sign pointing to God which few heed. [♪] Kirekegaard,

1.12.2.7. *Intimacy.* Each member finds human relations with others in which he feels safe, known, accepted, supported, and challenged.[170] Sexual pairing emerges from such friendships. For those persons possessed of parenting skills, the community supports reproduction, within the limits circumscribed by the sustainable carrying-capacity of the planet for human and non-human life. For those with diminished drive to procreate or moral conviction about not bearing children, alloparenting and mentorship afford opportunity to parent. Each member forms cadres of intimates, which friendships give life meaning.[171] Each member finds a circle affiliation for his cadre with approximately 150 others, which number appears to circumscribe the human capacity for acquaintance relationships.[172]

1.12.2.8. *Tolerance of Differentiation and Deviation.* All members differ from one another, some substantially, in genetic, racial, cultural, sexual, mental, physical, historical, moral, territorial, linguistic, and other ways. The spectrum of human differentiation presents great challenges and unimagined opportunities to communities. Meaningful communities tolerate members, no matter their deviations, to the maximum extent consistent with meaningful community life.[173] A core challenge of every

---

Sickness Unto Death, 45 (Part One, Section B). Atul Gawande criticizes our nursing home environments for meeting medical need while neglecting elders' need to participate in caring for others. He describes the Eden Alternative, in which a nursing home was transformed, to the great benefit of its residents, by adding a dog and two cats to each floor, and a pair of parakeets to every room. For the residents, finding meaning (that is, a reason to live other than themselves) improved health, extended life, and, most important, made life better. Gawande cites Josiah Royce for the idea that humans are not individuals, but rather members of communities, which fact gives their eventual deaths meaning. Gawande, *Being Mortal*, 111-128.

[170] Wollstonecraft calls friendship the "most holy band of society." Men and women, in her thought, are made by God for friendship as equals in virtue. [♪] Wollstonecraft, *Vindication of the Rights of Woman*, 99.

[171] The Danes call such social intimacy "hygge" (*hoo-guh*). This concept, which admits no easy translation, entails community building, making places of sanctuary for people, welcoming and inviting physical and emotional closeness, and embracing what makes one feel expansive and life-full. The person experiencing *hygge* celebrates connection with others and the coziness of those encounters.

Stephen Asma argues that egalitarianism is not the only social justice. We also, to be fair, need preferences, beloved persons, and biases that create meaningful existence. He says, "Everything else of value lies contained in that little word "my."" Asma, *Against Fairness*, 170.

[172] Zhou, "Social Group Size Organization," 440.

[173] John Locke, during the English tug-of-war between Protestantism and Catholicism, finds tolerance the essential mark of the church. "Everyone is orthodox to himself," and so should practice virtue in all humility. Locke, *A Letter Concerning Toleration*, 21. Still, welcoming many, Locke reserves odium and intolerance for atheists. These banish God from their thoughts, and in so doing dissolve the bonds of human society. Tolerance is reserved only for the many varieties of theists among us. Locke, *A Letter Concerning Toleration*, 58. Chinese master Chu Hsi says: "There are

meaningful community is to make a place for every member in which that member can make his or her unique contribution to communal well-being.

1.12.2.9. *Prosperity and Specialization.*   Meaningful communities recognize that specialization, with its intrinsic surpluses, and consequent trade relations with others, improves standards of living.   Meaningful communities encourage members to discover tasks each performs with facility and special skill, trading those skills and products for other essentials produced by members with different skills.[174]   Communities themselves may choose a group occupation to supply a specialized need of the Commons.   Specialization lofts the quality of a community's life, increases social capital and physical prosperity, and fosters interdependence and understanding among communities.

Humans produce goods and services according to their various abilities and skills.   Necessarily, some goods and services will be valued more highly in some communities.   Necessarily, some members will produce more goods and services.   Necessarily, some will prosper economically in greater degree than others.   To strip away such differences among members in the name of equality is an unworkable intolerance.   Members should enjoy the fruits of their labors, and should share as they deem wise.   On the other hand, gross economic disparity among members fractures community weal.[175]   To augment meaning, a community must adopt strategies that leave members in roughly similar economic circumstances, and yet allow members to benefit personally from special skill or enterprise.[176]   Some thoughts on maintaining relative economic equality are contained at Section IV below.

1.12.2.10. *Adaptation.*   Meaningful communities welcome the results of thanatoid deliberation (deliberation by those well-reconciled to the fact of their small part and delimited time, due to death, in making decisions bearing upon the human community) to facilitate their long-term adaptation to circumstances.[177]   Members possessing such skill of insight pro-

---

those matters that one ought not to tolerate.   One can't learn to tolerate everything."   Chu Hsi, *Learning to Be a Sage*, 190.

[174] [♪] Ridley, *The Rational Optimist*, 56.   Ridley describes the trading habits of members as "catallaxy," by which he means that specialization amplifies member quality of life, which serves to further amplify specialization and generate well-being.

[175] [♪] Taylor, *Community, Anarchy, and Liberty*, 95.

[176] I shall make some proposals in this regard in Section IV, Community Culling.

[177] For more on thanatoid deliberation, see below at: Section IV, Community Culling.

vide direction, which, when adopted by a community or communities, guides those communities' efforts for a time. Neurodiverse savants capable of thanatoid deliberation offer communities insights less constricted by cultural norms. Neurodiverse savants do not foresee the future or speak for gods. Neurodiverse savants are able, in a way that eludes neurotypical members, to view community circumstances from an altered and unusually robust viewpoint.[178] The insights of neurodiverse savants can become the objects of study and investigation by neurotypical members, leading to proposals for restructuring communities or the Commons for deliberation by all.

1.12.2.11. *Reverence.* Well-nurtured humans revere life and the environment in which it prospers. Meaningful communities value non-human life, for in it we recognize the roots of our own existence. Non-human species find room for their mode of life, to the extent those others are not inimical to human co-existence. Where animals present a danger, our task is to pre-empt their injuries without exterminating the species. Human-centric decisions, when well-deliberated, protect ecological well-being.[179] The attitude of meaning-laden communities transcends mere concern. Some values exceed factoring, becoming sacral. We suspect, numinously woven with the skein of life, invisible threads of ascendancy. We catch at evanescent whispers of eternity, inaudible beneath the din of days. This voice baffles. Sacrality leaks, ever so slight-

---

[178] I am asked who might be neurodiverse savants. I am most aware of such wonders among those whom I read, though I believe such persons exist in other realms of endeavor as well. I know them from their anthems to individuality, in which neurodiverse savants excel. Among neurodiverse savants, I would number Oscar Wilde, whose idiosyncratic acts and opinions led, under withering English scrutiny, to an early death in Paris. [♪] Wilde, *The Soul of Man Under Socialism.* I would also count Ralph Waldo Emerson, who hunkered in the lee of wealthy friends from the bitter winds of society, and Henry David Thoreau, up to his eyeballs in the frog-water of Walden Pond, among neurodiverse savants. [♪] Emerson, *Self-Reliance*, and [♪] Thoreau, *On the Duty of Civil Disobedience.* I also recognize those unknown neurodiverse savants who tamed fire, recognized the utility of the wheel, first wrote language, and first conceived the world as a non-sacral realm. I might, with a little prodding, include Siddhartha, Confucius, Mo, Moses, Jeremiah, Jesus, Luther, Swedenborg, Nietzsche, and Godwin. David Treffert describes savantism as a condition in which an individual exhibits remarkable powers in some narrowly defined area, often accompanied by substantial impairments in social skills or language or other mental capabilities. Treffert, "Accidental Genius," 54. Traumatic brain injury can cause individuals to exhibit savant-like capabilities, which Treffert calls "acquired savantism." He speculates that savantism, whether inherited or acquired, unleashes genetic knowledge that may well reside in all humans, in a suppressed manner. Treffert, "Accidental Genius," 57. What makes the savant a savant is that he or she can access that inherent knowledge. Among savants, who comprise a vanishingly small percentage of the human population (Treffert's worldwide registry of known savants contains only 319 persons), only a small fraction might have social insights useful in transgenerational deliberation. It seems likely that Treffert defines the concept "savant" more narrowly than do I.

[179] Consider the ecological warnings of Rachel Carson about insecticidal and herbicidal agents. Carson, *Silent Spring.* If Carson's warnings now seem hyperbolic, perhaps that is because she issued her warnings to some effect.

ly, into banality.[180] There exists a current in life, gently tugging one toward serenity. The numen makes me smile contentedly. Do gods tickle you, Kate? Yet, words hide.[181]

1.12.2.12. *A Commons of Elegant Hyper-Cooperation.* Human communities, when deliberating well, recognize themselves as a single interdependent humanity, comprising the community of communities.[182] The community of communities is a commons (one that is virtual), dwelling in the habitual ideation of members and, as a result, coursing over their communication nets. The human Commons, the community of communities, seeks coordination of effort for the weal of humankind. The Commons stores the sum of human knowledge and skill. Every variety of community contributes; its products are employed. The panoply creatively merges into a shape of life for the global Commons by insights culled and adapted from the contributions of neurodiverse savants, and tested by communities. Human communal diversity may weave itself into an extraordinary tapestry of elegant hyper-cooperation.[183]

---

[180] Michael Gazzaniga says that human brains seek belief. "We are wired to form beliefs." Gazzaniga, *The Ethical Brain*, xviii. Edmund Burke claims that "man is by his constitution a religious animal." Burke, *Reflections on the Revolution in France*, 95. Mohandas Gandhi said, "Those who say that religion has nothing to do with politics do not know what religion means." Gandhi, *Autobiography*, 504. Blaise Paschal invites all to wager on gods: "Let us weigh the gain and the loss in wagering that God is. Let us estimate these two chances. If you gain, you gain all; if you lose, you lose nothing. Wager, then, without hesitation that He is." Paschal, *Pensées*, 69 (Section 233). Shaftesbury expressed the matter merrily: "It is impossible that any besides an ill-natur'd Man can wish against the Being of a God: for this is wishing against the Publick, and even against one's private Good too, if rightly understood." Shaftesbury, *Characteristicks*, 22 (Volume 1, Section 35).

[181] Wittgenstein avers: "Whereof one cannot speak, thereof one must be silent." Wittgenstein, *Tractatus Logico-Philosophicus*, 108 (Section 7).

[182] Mo argues that recognizing our intimate linkage to others, and acting to benefit all, creates the good community. The benevolent man seeks benefit for all and opposes what harms. The small man is partial to his own, and seeks to harm others not his own. Harm derives from aggression, oppression, overreaching, disparagement, miserliness, bad faith, senseless harshness, ignoring customs, and assaults. Evils emerge from hatred and prejudices. One who criticizes must suggest an alternative. One replaces prejudice with universality by considering the welfare of others as one's own. In a community, people with skills employ them for the benefit of those lacking such skills. [♪] *Mozi*, 41-44 (*Part III, §16*). Christopher Boehm hypothesizes that human cooperation derives, evolutionarily, from the need to share game meat equitably, in order to keep hunting teams well-nourished. Alpha-male hoarders were suppressed by gangs of opponents, leading, ultimately, to egalitarian cooperation. Boehm, *Moral Origins*, 151.

[183] Bateson notes that, when we make the deep structural changes needed to stabilize humanity's role on earth, no one can predict what patterns may emerge from that reformation. He prays wisdom, rather than violence, will govern. Bateson, *Steps To An Ecology of Mind*, 501. Taylor argues that, absent meaningful community, widely-dispersed political participation and minimal concentration of force (which he calls "anarchy") are impossible. [♪] Taylor, *Community, Anarchy, and Liberty*, 2. Curtis Marean argues that our human inclination to cooperate with non-kin persons was the final element of human evolution that launched mankind's planet-wide migration some 70,000 years ago. Marean, "The Most Invasive Species of All," 34-35. Joshua Greene styles cooperation the "central problem of social existence." Cooperation is how one avoids the Hardin-style Tragedy of the Com-

Objection 5: Trivializing Evil: Some demur that behind evil lies something much more sinister than deviant cognition or misperceived goods. Evil exists not only in its momentary instantiations, but also in itself, as a metaphysical proposition. Some even personalize metaphysical evil as Satan. Surely, this Quad cull of conduct scheme trivializes the evils of war, genocide, mass murder, systematic rape, starvation, child abuse, torture, and other horrors. All appear to be something much more sinister than "misperceived goods." One should be afraid, be very afraid, not least because some, such as this author, trivialize the grave corruption of human depravity.[184]

Response: I try not to indulge rabid metaphysics, without diminishing sacrality. To be clear, when we do metaphysical talk, we, by definition, speak of matters about which human knowledge is untenable. Metaphysical speculations, even metaphysical convictions, may be necessary, but metaphysical conclusions never dislodge clinging sands of uncertainty. Metaphysics can be a diverting pastime, like chess or crossword puzzles, which amuse and pose intellectual mazes. Invoking corrupt demi-urges, however, does not improve human decision-making. What evil we observe around us consists in people and groups making decisions while experiencing powerful subliminal drives and potent ideas. In a few cases, evil actors suffer congenital disease (sociopathy) or careening attachment disasters (narcissism). Under common influences affecting normal people, some make ill-deliberate decisions. Of those, a few prove disastrously misguided. Hypostatizing this phenomenon does not move the ethical ball forward.[185] Worse, imagining a personal boogey-man may divert human choice into the backwater eddies of theological sloughs. Supposed Satanic influence is a necessary precondition to the stench of Salem. May we all vent those smokes from our souls. We have enough to fear without hallucinating miscreant super-demons. The gravity of human evil is in no way diminished by

---

mons. Greene believes that our penchant for cooperation serves humanity well in overcoming selfish motives in our own groups (or moral tribe), but helps little when considering groups outside our own (different moral tribes). He seeks to frame a meta-morality (which he takes to be an extremely flexible version of utilitarianism) that helps divergent tribes communicate and cooperate. Greene, *Moral Tribes*, 20, 26, 291. Sam Harris says: "Cooperation is the stuff of which meaningful human lives and viable societies are made." Harris, *The Moral Landscape*, 55.

[184] Hsün Tzu (Chinese sage, third century B.C.) agrees with this objector: "Since man's nature is evil, it must wait for the instructions of a teacher before it can become upright, and for the guidance of ritual principles before it can become orderly." *Hsün Tzu*, 158 (Section 23).

[185] Watzalawick notes the human inclination to fashion unseen friends or antagonists from features of one's environment. We then deem these imagined entities real, and treat them as forces with whom one must engage. Watzlawick, Bavelas, and Jackson, *Pragmatics of Human Communication*, 243.

   Unexpectedly, I find support for my conclusions about the nature of evil in St. Thomas Aquinas. He says: "Evil cannot be a nature. . . . What all beings desire is good. . . . No nature is of itself an evil." Aquinas offers some argumentation for these propositions persuasive to medieval theologians, but hardly so to us. Nevertheless, Aquinas has concluded that evil is not a metaphysical entity, and derives from the human desire for good once that desire has gone awry. Evil is privation of good. Aquinas, *Aquinas's Shorter Summa*, 126-127.

declining to fulminate about shop-worn superstitions.   Look at human evils. Tell me what you *see.*

Objection 6: Diversity of Purposes: *Another protests that flourishing life in meaningful community ill-represents the prime values of many humans. Some want money. Others long for thrills. Yet others thirst for tribal hysterics of sports and war. Still others dream of serial sex with anonymous partners or un- ending isolation or life devoted to knick-knack collecting. Some humans prefer dissolute lives, jammed with psychoactive substances and serial orgies and wel- fare fraud. Some want to wander into the woods, never to emerge. A few prefer violence, relishing bloodshed and cannibal soups. Michael Walzer argues that no unity underlies the multiplicity of what humans call "good," and to search for such a unity, or assert one (as the author of* Cull *has done), is to fundamen- tally miscomprehend people and distributive justice.[186] If one values the Jesuses and Gandhis and Kings and Swedenborgs and Buddhas of life, one must permit Stalins and Hitlers and improvised explosive devices. The latter are the price of the former. All this welter indicates abundant dissent from the Quad sociality premise that meaningful life is the prime motivation among humans. Quad So- ciality constricts the gusher of human desires to a monomaniacal dribble of one.*

Response: Meaningful existence encompasses all human desires, even ill- conceived choices.   The concept "meaningful" is a bag of sufficient elasticity to accommodate all human values, even misguided ones. Humans seek to flourish. We pray to wallow in meaningful events. Often, a woman's choices in reaching this goal are misdirected. Sometimes, a man's efforts achieve the exact opposite of that he imagined. We frequently err in moral deliberation, or neglect it alto- gether. All misdirected miseries are conceived, by their adopters, as paths to a better life. Unfortunately, these "alternative lifestyles" prove to be no life at all, but formulae for difficult deaths. All are evils misperceived as goods.

Culling conduct improves human choosing.   By deliberating more ade- quately, by emphasizing life experimentation in nurturing communities, by mak- ing a habit of evaluating attempts and choices, by assessing life from mortality's viewpoint, one hopes to render improved decision-making more likely. Many exotic values and preferences emerge from the distortions imposed by urbanism, by our habits of coercion and repression, by our failure to nurture most humans responsibly, and by our failure to address fundamental community dysfunctions with persistence and compassion. We have, one and all, been rendered a touch neurotic (or worse) by events of the last 50,000 years. As our aberrations atro- phy, perhaps many will recognize the centrality of choosing meaningful exist- ence conscientiously. If not, this book will be seldom read.[187]

---

[186] Walzer finds that human "goods" include many features of life that are plainly non-material: be- longing, love, grace, ritual purity, power, honor, kinship, knowledge, security, leisure, reward, pun- ishment. The usual material goods count as well: food, shelter, clothing, transportation, medical ac- cess, stuff, and so forth. This welter does not resolve, according to Walzer, to an underlying unity, regardless how much effort might be expended to accomplish such. "Goods" are fundamentally multiple. [♪] Walzer, *Spheres of Justice*, 3-4.

[187] An epitaph both mine and, possibly, theirs.

Ultimately, I welcome such dissent. Perhaps this work errs in emphasizing meaningful existence. Please experiment. I, and millions of others, shall happily endorse your more adequate idea. Sniping is easy; deciding is difficult. As investigators argue truly: data outweigh models.

Objection 7: Existential Death: *Yet another remonstrates that meaning lacks meaning. Consider Leo Tolstoy. He likened his (supremely successful) life to that of a besieged traveler. This unfortunate traveler leaps into a well to avoid a cruel beast, and hangs by a twig protruding from the wall, for the traveler makes out a dragon lurking at the well's bottom. As he weakens, the traveler sees mice gnaw his twig. Yet he spies drops of honey on the twig and licks them, in the face of his certain doom. The traveler discovers that even the honey tastes less sweet than before he found himself dangling in the perilous well. Meaning is delusion. The meaning of life is death. Whatever one does, it leads to abject, eternal dissolution. Even those whose fame is the stuff of myth eventually fade from fabled memory. Man is dust driven before a gale of lethal winds.*[188] *To speak of meaning, to promise fulfilling integration into purposive activity that renders daily choices sensible and flourishing life possible—that is snake oil. Both the purveyor and purchaser delude themselves. Both, in the end, die, horribly empty.*

Response: Death is the last word about member life, but not the only word. Those who disparage death spin metaphysics. Of what follows death, humans know nothing. Of what precedes birth, humans know nothing. We speak meaningfully only when we speak of what we might know. Denigration of death—prattling on about its empty existential horror—is as baseless as death adulation—babbling on about heavens and angels and Elysium. None knows. Knowledge of such matters is categorically unavailable. Some deaths are difficult; others not. What matters more is the life that preceded its death. If one's nihilism, one's denial of the possibility of meaning, leads one to systematic self-centered narcissism, one does, in fact, die meaninglessly.[189] Human communities create meaning, into which human members integrate themselves. If one's communalism fills life with friendships brimming with deep intimacies and purposive activity, death becomes transition of generations in a web of meaning. The fruits of a decedent's efforts persevere within the living community, enriching it. The member dies within the flow of community, having contributed his life blood to many he loves and a host he values. Death brings its unhappy sting, but no crushing blow. That for which he lived endures into a future of indeterminate duration. His was life well spent.

One may yet not welcome one's death. Every task comes to its end. For most, the depredations of chronic illness render death a not-unwelcome haven. For others, for those who die young or full of plans, acquiescence may prove

---

[188] So worries Tolstoy in his quest for religious certitude. [♪] Tolstoy, *A Confession*, Chapter IV.

[189] Simone de Beauvoir says of nihilism: "Conscious of being unable to be anything, man then decides to be nothing. . . . Nihilism is disappointed seriousness which has turned back upon itself." The nihilist has forgotten that his choices justify the world and make him exist validly. de Beauvoir, *The Ethics of Ambiguity*, 52, 57.

elusive. A pervasive conservatism resides in every breast. We examine every change, shooting a scowl before risking a smile. No change speaks with greater finality than death. Every death rends our collective fabric, tearing from it familiar, often beloved, warp and woof. For death, we harbor well-deserved ambivalence, and occasional hard-bitten animosity.

Count Tolstoy's tale gives voice to the dysphoria attending his clinical depression. Tolstoy mistook his brain dysfunction for insight, a commonplace delusion among depressed persons. He, like all those who suffer profound depression, could not seize the joy in joy. He let despair isolate him. Ultimately, Tolstoy's untreated mental illness killed him. He froze to death in 1910, suffering from pneumonia, on an Astapova railway station bench in the middle of the night, to which seat he fled escaping his nagging wife and despised life of aristocratic privilege.

The meaning of meaning is meaning. There is no "meta" beneath that meta-insight. Meaning is the ultimate word, not one among penultimate values. Humans exist to live meaningful lives. That we seek. One cannot pierce that veil. There is no man behind the curtain. To those who inquire as to the meaning of meaning, I say: Not every question is sensical.[190]

Objection 8: Authorial Hubris: *Still another deprecates this work (and its author) for hubris in believing he has something of general applicability to say. Every person is unique. No assertions about human conduct are warranted, for every such statement asserts too much with respect to many and not enough with respect to some. And such a surfeit of words! The proverbial wordy-birdy nests in this author's mostly-vacant cranium. Abandon this project. Acquiesce in the human moral morass, inevitable and ubiquitous. None knows what brings meaning. That includes the author of this work.*

Response*:* Authors, including this one, are arrogant. The thought of putting one's words on paper for the derision and ridicule of unknown and unborn readers daunts. One perhaps overcompensates. I speak with what confidence I

---

[190] Michael A. Bishop inquires as to the nature of well-being. Is the nature of well-being best ferreted by common sense, by philosophy, or by psychology, he asks? Bishop takes the position that we should grant some credibility to our common sense perceptions about well-being, but also take account of philosophical and empirical psychological insights. Bishop finds that this approach yields some contradiction of our common sense perceptions about well-being, and hence causes discomfort to most. Bishop argues for a network theory of well-being. "Positive causal networks" are personal and dynamic homeostatic (self-maintaining and self-reinforcing) balances that exist among positive emotions, attitudes, character traits, and successes. Well-being, thus considered, is objectively valuable. It is more than a state of mind. Bishop, *The Good Life*, 12, 14-19, 211. Bishop notes that positive causal networks characterize not only individuals, but also group interactions. Bishop, *The Good Life*, 101-104. The objector's complaint demands much penetration where little is available. One is reminded of Preacher's response: "Better is a handful of quietness than two hands full of toil and a striving after wind." *Ecclesiastes* 4:6. I argue that the root of ethics lies in neuroscience and sociology, with all of the nattering discords of those disciplines. This rudiment does not satisfy, as might a categorical imperative or Platonic intuition. But it has the merit of being verifiable and non-elitist. Susan Nieman spoke well: "At times the most hopeful gesture we may be able to manage is not to answer whether life is justified but merely to reject the question. Meaning is a human category, and must be won against a background. A life that was inevitably meaningful would defeat itself from the start." Nieman, *Evil in Modern Thought*, 327-328.

feel. That assurance waxes and wanes. I undoubtedly self-delude. As to length, I have sought to keep this book condensed, brief enough to be read by people with jobs, but encompassing enough to open far-ranging conversations.[191] I speak because we need to talk about ourselves and our togetherness. If I see aright, men misconceive both in deeply injurious ways. If my view illumines, a better world waits. Perhaps such possibilities warrant the hubris of assertion.

1.13. *Evil: Conditions Eroding Meaningful Community.* When a community fails to establish meaningful participation, members suffer and the community fabric frays.[192] Members can no longer maintain interest in their actions, real or imagined. General boredom punctuates long gray plains of emotionlessness. The thrall of apathy tends to surrender only to bouts of depression.[193] Ill-conceived purposes cause members and communities to erode their cohesion and chip away their sense of meaning. Most often, members and communities suffering erosion of meaning find scapegoats to blame and substitutes by which to distract members. In the current milieu, communities are frequently vacated of meaning by the stresses of too many members experiencing too many needs of ever-expanding sorts. I take this meaning-erosive hypertrophy of unsated urges to be the engine of Malthusian dystopia.[194]

---

[191] Socrates sought to truncate his discussion of justice, but his cohorts forbade it. They reminded Socrates that the appropriate duration for such conversations is a lifetime. [♪] Plato, *Republic*, 145 (450b). In my experience, I never seem to know when I have said enough, and when I have said too little. Perhaps, this tension about verbal sufficiency cannot be eradicated from the project of addressing others.

[192] Gustav Landauer argues that the human community is an entity that exceeds individuals, imbued with a spirit and attitude, consisting of webs of groups, expressing an organic unity. Where the spirit or community webs deteriorate, there community dies. Landauer, *Revolution*, 168. Gandhi offers a test for indecision: "Recall the face of the poorest and weakest man whom you may have seen, and ask youself if the step you contemplate is going to be of any use to him. Will he gain anything by it? Will it restore him to a control over his own life and destiny?" Gandhi, as cited in Lelyveld, *Great Soul*, 349. Sam Harris would call this the "bad life." Harris, *The Moral Landscape*, 15-16.

[193] Pugh, *Biological Origins of Human Values*, 428.

[194] Malthus, *Essay on the Principle of Population*. Robert Putnam ominously notes that in the last third of the twentieth century, Americans have been separated from one another and our communities have paled. Yet we have hardly noticed. Putnam, *Bowling Alone*, 27. Putnam's sociological analysis lays blame for the erosion of American social capital upon generational change (those who did not live through the bonding of World War II are less socially active than those who did), electronic communications (especially television), work demands, urban sprawl, and other unknown factors. Putnam, *Bowling Alone*, 277-284. Oddly, Putnam seems never to consider that non-participation in producing American social capital may indicate that many people feel that American social capital is not worth producing. Many (expressly or implicitly) may prefer new structures, and opt out of supporting those older frameworks they find vacant of meaning. One speculates that a reason Rome fell is this: when the Visigoths came flooding over the first of Rome's seven hills, few Romans could muster enthusiasm for preserving the corrupt inanity that Rome had become. In the end, Putnam recurs to mere exhortation that Americans should do more of the same, only harder and better (Chapter 24). He imagines that America oscillates between periods of high and low social

1.13.1. *Overpopulation.* Several billion too many humans inhabit the plan-et.[195] Exactly how many too many billions the earth houses should be a subject of intense scientific scrutiny, leading to a prescription for sustain-able human population and a timetable for reduction of the population that does not lead to untenable demographic imbalances as populations de-cline. My sense remains, after long deliberation, that something less than one billion humans suffices for all relevant purposes we might communal-ly conceive. The number is equivocal; that our long term well-being re-quires far fewer humans is not equivocal.

Humans, among primates, produce the slowest-maturing (and hence most expensive) infants. The pinch comes in a correlative fact. Humans, among primates, also reproduce most rapidly.[196]

Population reduction cannot be compelled and should not become a direct purpose of coercive governments.[197] Ossified coercive government *causes* overpopulation by robbing members of meaningful existence in community, by exchanging member identity for anonymous existence, by permitting high infant mortality, by ill-educating women[198] and their men, and by proffering occupations and life-structures to which members are ill-matched. Scarcity, which accompanies overpopulation, etches social innovation and parches well-springs of ingenuity.[199] As kithdom inte-

---

capital, being now at a nadir. Such constructs obscure cultural collapse in a shroud of hopeful ob-fuscation. Putnam styles thoughts of wholesale change "romantic" and regressive. Putnam, *Bowling Alone*, 382. *Cull* offers a more difficult solution, but one that contains promise.

[195] Bateson argues that the preeminent hurdle to a viable human presence on the earth is population stability. Bateson, *Steps To An Ecology of Mind*, 500. When H. G. Wells envisions human utopia, earth's population has been winnowed to 250 million. Wells, *Men Like Gods*, 68. Henri Bergson warns that humanity must rationalize its reproduction or wars shall consume us. "In no other matter [self-reproduction] is it so dangerous to rely on instinct." Bergson, *The Two Sources of Morality and Religion*, 290.

[196] Hrdy, *Mothers and Others*, 101. Unfortunately, humans also seem blind to the fact of our over-reproduction, largely due to our mathematical incompetence. Albert Bartlett, a retired University of Colorado professor, tells a story: "Imagine a species of bacteria that reproduces by dividing in two. Those two become four, the four become eight, and so forth. Let's say we place one bacterium in a bottle at 11:00 a.m., and at noon we observe the bottle to be full. At what point was it half full?" The answer is, At 11:59am. Exponentiality eludes us. Alan Weisman calculates that "every four-and-a-half days there are a million more people on the planet." Weisman, *Countdown*, 35, 39.

[197] The People's Republic of China, long a haven of coercive excesses, has tried legislating family reproduction. Their results are messy and riddled with unintended sequels.

[198] Albert Weisman calls educated, enabled women "the most effective contraceptive of all." Weis-man, *Countdown*, 43.

[199] Cohen, *How Many Humans Can the Earth Support?*, 355.

grates every member into a community, the dysfunctions of overpopulation may lead many to choose childless alloparenting.

Every person needs to parent; not every person needs to breed. Every child needs more than one or two parents. Many childless people should participate in parenting children who are not biologically their own. As parenting opens to many who are childless, every child should enjoy several non-familial parents (alloparents). In this manner, persons meet their parenting needs. As the technology of conception prevention improves and the tide of unwanted babies subsides, every child may have a loving home and multiple supportive adults. Those who desire to parent will not be forced to reproduce to satisfy their need. Parents should not be replaced by committees. One component of fabricating a flourishing life for future generations consists in parents inviting other willing members of their community to join in nurturing their children, emotionally, educationally, and financially. This is the alloparental care team. Families are, and should be recognized to be, larger than genetic donors and their progeny. Ultimately, the concept of a "family" needs to widen to subsist as a species of cadre. Some cadres nurture children. Others are otherwise occupied. Children of a global Commons need more skills, opportunities, and support than any two parents can provide in isolation.

Failing to redress human overpopulation precludes careful deliberation of the human future.[200] Population pressures insure that humankind squanders its vital energies dousing the wars, famines, droughts, deforestations, plagues, species decimations, resource depletion, slums, pollution, and myriad other exigencies created by overpopulation. The responsibility of the Commons to make possible meaningful community for every human member will prove an untenable ideal absent massive population reductions.[201]

Scarcity, which is the sister scourge of overpopulation, breeds genocide and war and neurotic acquisitiveness. Its substance is starvation where foodstuffs are insufficient, and subsequent diminution of intelligence, health, ability to work, and resilience of its sufferers. Overpopula-

---

[200] As long ago as the third century B.C., Chinese philosopher Han Fei Tzu complained that, though in the distant past men lived by what was freely available in abundance and without disputes over scarcities, now they live in quarreling and competition, because every grandfather has five sons and those sons have five sons. The grandfather has replaced himself with a host, and so the world grows crowded and disorderly. [♪] Han Fei Tzu, *Basic Writings*, 97 (§49). One estimate of global population in Han Fei Tzu's time is 100 million.

[201] Hobbes, in 1651, advised that the surplusage of poor commoners should be shipped to British colonies, where, when they have filled the land, they should settle their overpopulation disputes by general war against one another. [♪] Hobbes, *Leviathan*, 239 (Chapter 30). Estimates of the global population in Hobbes's time range around 500 million.

tion makes coercion and violence appear the lesser of many evil options available to panicked communities.   All human futures worth having on our delimited planet address numbers of humans ten to twenty percent of the existing population.[202]

1.13.2. *Emotional Deprivation.*   Scarcity damages infants.   Some starve. Worse, parents, harried by survival demands, may neglect their babies.   In our culture, mothers launch off to work, relegating baby's emotional ne-cessities to under-paid surrogates who, despite best efforts, cannot provide the attentive love-bond mothers muster naturally.   Some mothers lack emotional and financial support; no spouse, no family, no church, no friends attend the mother-infant pair.   The toll of agonizing separations is tremendous on infant and mother.   The infant's secure attachment may be disrupted.   The pain that abandoned infants suffer staggers comprehen-sion.   Wailing pounds the ears.   For the child, stuck in timelessness, each loss of maternal contact lasts an eternity.[203]   In the end, abandoned babies stop wailing.   The infant does not acquiesce.   He despairs.   He abandons summoning the mother his very fiber demands.   He commences a grim as-sessment of emotional availability of those who should care, an expecta-tion of fractured care that rings through the rest of his nascent life.   Evolu-tion placed babies in arms of mother or an alloparent from birth to around age three.   When a culture deviates from that pattern, the culture stresses both mother and infant, and injures each emotionally and, very possibly, irremediably.[204]

1.13.3. *Ignorance.*   Where stressed, communities often succumb to the temp-tation to stint nurture.   Children and adult members, so highly adapted to learning proficiencies, drift in self-education.   Gifted educators are divert-ed to other tasks.   The results dismay.   The wandering many occupy them-selves in counterproductive enterprises, leading to further failures to edu-cate and pessimism about the prospects of nurturing children.   Hyper-cooperation eludes untrained populations.   The Commons must abandon all nurturing processes that fail to produce knowledgeable, well-integrated members.   In no facet of Western culture is institutional ossification more evident than schools.   Where every child is mentored by parents and non-

---

[202] See further discussion of this topic in Section III, Member Culling, at the subtopic "Bear children only if you must."

[203] Leidloff recounts separations from the infant's perspective poignantly.   See Leidloff, *The Contin-uum Concept*, Chapter 3 ("The Beginning of Life"), p. 29-75.

[204] I discuss infant attachment at greater length in Section III: Member Culling.

parental others, ignorance may become an infrequent and unwelcome misfortune.[205]

1.13.4. *Aimlessness.* Where distracted, communities may fail to establish community purposes into which members may integrate themselves. Communities must, by means they choose, provide members with useful ways to occupy time and provide for member sustenance, shelter, medical care, and general well-being. When they fail to do so, meaningful life grows unavailable, and members' sense of well-being plummets. Flourishing life leaks away.[206] Every community differs in its aims, as its members differ from those of any other community. One excellence of Quad sociality consists in its use of communities as adaptative laboratories. Adaptive structures can be communicated and adopted by sister-communities, or even by the Commons as a whole. The warning of failed enterprise can instruct every community.

1.13.5. *Intolerance.* Uneducated, population-stressed, aimless communities find scapegoats for their suffering. Persons who look, talk, think, dance, dress, or value differently are frequent nominees for "cause of the problem." The human "we," which is the global population of mankind, shrinks by excluding the perceived offending few.[207] If miseries persevere, other classifications are added to the ostracized. Intolerance becomes a norm, and after a time, a culture.[208] Meaningful community misconceives itself as a group sustained by excluding others. The alien, who is by definition diverse, becomes a burden upon society, and no longer its lifeblood and seasoning. Aliens become low priorities for education and integration into communal purposes. Ultimately, intolerance damages the member's view of himself, leading, at a minimum, to intermittent self-loathing.

---

[205] It is not my intention to disparage the extraordinary efforts of my many friends and colleagues who struggle within public schools to provide their students with meaningful educations. I mean to say that we can, and should, create contexts for those teachers who are gifted to interact with our young members in a manner that better serves those learners. When institutions fail, say so, dismantle them, and move on to a better idea.

[206] Sartre's protagonist says: "I am bored, that's all. From time to time I yawn so widely that tears roll down my cheek. It is a profound boredom, profound, the profound heart of existence, the very matter I am made of." Sartre, *Nausea*, 157.

[207] Karl Marlantes, in his philosophical confession regarding killing for the United States Marines during the Vietnam War, describes his mental topography when terminating enemies as "pseudospeciation." Marlantes, *What It Is Like To Go To War*, 40. The advancing opponent was, to him, always something less than human.

[208] Consider Nazi Germany. [♪] Hitler, *Mein Kampf.*

1.13.6. *Injustice and Violence.* Perceived scarcity encourages self-interested wrangling.[209] Being intrinsically social, humans take their cues from their fellows. Selfish acts beget themselves, as one snowflake summons another in commencing an avalanche. Neighbors satisfy themselves with less, if their neighbors also have less. Humans reject more if neighbors get, in unjust proportion, even more still.[210] When one seizes what belongs, in the eyes of another, to that other, those who observe question the justice of one's actions. Where members draw conclusions of injustice, the fabric of community frays. If injustice is persistent, social continuity can dissolve altogether.[211] Violence ensues.[212]

1.13.7. *Coercion.* Communities that erode their meaning resort, as that social wealth slips away, to increasingly nonconsensual impositions. Inordinate funds are captured by taxation to deal with the deteriorating situation. Normalcy finds room for coercion. Interpersonal violence, especially when employed to keep the unwanted alien in his place, or the second-class citizen in hers, is tolerated. Finally, war seems normal enough, and the deadliness and impersonality of its methods creep ever closer to abject depersonalization. Jonathan Glover notes that as martial technology advances, warring nations grow ever more tolerant of anonymous long-distance murder.[213]

---

[209] Christopher Boehm notes that, in hunter-gatherer societies accustomed to generous meat-sharing, famine erodes sharing. Not only do non-kin tribe members get less or no sharing, but even relatives suffer during nutritional downturn. Sharing foodstuffs greases cooperation. Lack of sharing increases conflict. Scarcity whittles community. Boehm takes our moral preference for sharing to be flexible in extremity. Starvation, first, terminates altruistic sharing with non-relatives. Further scarcity limits sharing to immediate relatives. Finally, looming starvation renders every person for himself or herself, even to the extent of intra-family cannibalism. Boehm calls these changes the human "parliament of competing instincts." Boehm, *Moral Origins*, 275-277, 290-291. John Horgan denies that scarcity causes humans to war. "Chronic scarcity has no effect whatsoever on warfare frequency," he reports, citing Carol Ember, a Yale anthropologist. Horgan concludes that the root of war is psychological: we war because we are afraid of war. Horgan, *The End of War*, 94, 153.

[210] Capuchin monkeys welcome cucumber slices as rewards, but launch into tantrums if they can see another capuchin receiving grapes (a preferred treat). De Waal, *The Bonobo and the Atheist*, 232.

[211] Cicero argues that unjust action kills human fellowship. One benefits nothing by savaging his neighbors. [♪] Cicero, *De Officiis*, Book III, Section V, 21, 23. The Buddha taught that only hateful people wish their own pleasure at the expense of others' suffering. [♪] *Dhammapada* 291.

[212] The rate of serious crimes is inversely proportional to the density of social capital in any given society. Putnam, *Bowling Alone*, 307-308.

[213] [♪] Glover, *Humanity*, 47-116. Gwynne Dyer asks whether civilization was a wise experiment, commenced by our ancestors those tens of millennia ago. We were situated to have a good run of millions of years. Now we are faced with global nuclear war and ecological devastation consequent to overpopulation. The eradication of humans, as well as thousands of other species, now seems possible. Dyer, War: *The Lethal Custom*, 440.

1.13.8. *Speciesism and Instrumentalism.*   Habits of thought in meaning-withered communities exclude portions of the human community from a place in the Commons.   Such exclusionary cultures paint their shriveled worldview onto the wider canvas of life.   Species other than the human and habitats other than our own count for less than those related to humans.[214]   Relations to the other-than-human world grow starkly instrumental.   Other species exist for our convenience alone.   We lose touch with the fact that humans evolved from that non-human world, are intimately linked to it, and cannot survive apart from it.[215]   Humans have fashioned technologies to transport sub-tropical environments to less hospitable climes through clothing and air conditioning and irrigation canals.   Our adaptive tools will prove of insufficient power if we disrupt the fundamental equations of life on earth.   Human ecological degradation remains a form of suicidal ideation, which, if practiced with sufficient diligence, might achieve self-extinction.

1.13.9. *Atomization.*[216]   Neglected children may survive without necessary human attachments.   They become isolated adults, often incapable of intimacy.   Western "freedoms" support socially-detached existence.[217]   One abandons his sense of place and meaning (that is, endures anomie) in order to preserve a predilection for guns, loose talk, religious dilettantism,

---

[214] Peter Singer argues that human moral thinking has been growing in its inclusiveness and scope. Our altruism can and should now extend to non-human species, at least to those that experience pain and pleasure. This is a new stage in moral thought. The idea may seem surprising until one recognizes that just 300 years ago, many thought it odd to include slaves and women as full members of the ethical community. Singer, *The Expanding Circle*, 120-121. Singer elaborates more fully in an earlier work. Granting equality to others is a moral proposition, not a factual one. Humans are factually unequal, yet we grant to all humans consideration, regardless of their choices and abilities. The critical component in meriting that consideration is not intelligence, or reason, or skin color, or external pudenda. The critical component of moral consideration is the ability to suffer or experience enjoyment, which form the basis of interests. This latter capacity we share with animals. The speciesist argues that the interests of humanity override even more compelling interests in other species. Singer, *Animal Liberation*, 8-9. Singer details with nauseating specificity abuse of animals for experimentation, testing, industrial meat, egg, and milk production, without belaboring the human penchant for killing or mutilating animals for sport and entertainment. Singer, *Animal Liberation*, 25-157.

[215] Wilson argues that humans injure our species by HIPPO impacts: habitat loss, invasive species, pollution, population growth, and overharvesting. No other biosphere supports human life. Human existence relies wholly on the environment in which it evolved for survival. Preserving that environment might mean human survival of indefinite duration. Injuring that environment entails our own suffering. Killing that environment ensures our extinction. [♪] Wilson, *The Meaning of Human Existence*, 127-132.

[216] Buber calls the dissolution of organic communities into anonymous economies an "atomization" of society. Buber, *Paths in Utopia*, 139.

[217] One of Sartre's characters asserts that hell consists in little else than other humans. Sartre, *No Exit*, 45.

social wandering, and bunker mentality. No man is an individual.[218] Neglected childhood nurture and western democracy's insistence on individualism fabricates a society long on loneliness and armed berserkers, and abysmally deprived of intimacy, meaning, social bonding, and cooperation.[219] Our culture, despite its wonders, belches a stench of loneliness, rendering every person an atom rebounding from random collisions with neighboring atoms. No essential relationship governs. No intimacy binds. We flee to ever-shrinking vestiges of community. Centralized anonymity leaks into our bastions, even as it perverts our self-concepts.[220] We not only are treated as atoms. We come to believe we are atoms. Atoms jostling among atoms.

A terrible possibility emerges. Might humankind, by failing to exercise its ancient capability for reading the intentionality of others and bonding in common enterprises, lose the ability to do so? Might "meaningful human community" become a vestigial longing for man, as dolphins dream of legs? The very stuff of our cells evolves to meet the circumstances in which we dwell. Grave dangers lie in the possibility that *homo sapiens* might, as centuries stretch to millennia, accommodate itself and its sensitivities to global atomized sociality.[221]

1.13.10. *Alternatives in Eroded Communities.* Robbed of meaningful community, members seek substitutes. Members find alternatives to the journey of communities in socio-neural homeostasis, and explanations for

---

[218] Gustav Landauer argues that individuals result from cultural decay, and consist in members who have lost their essential organic connections to one another. Landauer, *Revolution*, 133. Landauer suffers some insupportable romanticism about the communal wonders of the Middle Ages. Herbert Spencer finds that human communal life exists to preserve individual life from external aggressions. Once such aggressions cease, the demands of one's community fall away. "Furtherance of individual lives has been the ultimate end" of community. Spencer, *The Principles of Ethics*, Vol. I, 167. Kithdom disputes Spencer. Individuals find meaningful life only in well-structured communities.

[219] Frankl argues that meaninglessness emerges when one has the physical necessities to live well, but nothing specific to live for. Frankl, *Man's Search for Meaning*, 140. Cacioppo and Patrick cite research that indicates twenty percent of Americans at any given moment are so isolated that their solitude is a significant factor in their unhappiness. Cacioppo and Patrick, *Loneliness*, 5. They also criticize the physical structure of suburban living as a "landscape built for disconnection." Cacioppo and Patrick, *Loneliness*, 255.

[220] Buber argues that the grave danger in centralized bureaucracy lies not in that structure displacing communities, but in its apersonal attitudes percolating into communities, perverting their communal ethos into anonymous association. Buber, *Paths in Utopia*, 131. Pugh argues that many core personal and social dysfunctions arise from anonymous urbanity. Humans are poorly constructed to tolerate such impersonality. *Pugh, Biological Origins of Human Values*, 421. Sartre canonizes isolation: "There is no human nature, since there is no god to conceive it. Not only is man what he conceives himself to be, but he is also only what he wills himself to be after this thrust toward existence. Man is nothing else but what he makes of himself." Sartre, *Existentialism*, 15.

[221] For concerns in this vein, see Hrdy, *Mothers and Others*, 273-294.

their forsaken experience. The greater their misery, the weaker their grasp of infirmity.[222] Many circle the septic drain.[223]

1.13.10.1. *Substance Abuse.* One such alternative is chemical adjustment of one's neural substrate. Occasional release from persistent stresses by such means can prove adaptive, especially when local and temporary stresses rise. Habitual release by pharmaceutical intervention leads to psychological or neurological addiction, ultimately making meaningful community seem a superfluous enterprise. Substance abusers assume the aspect of living death. They come to relish "community" with a substance.[224]

1.13.10.2. *Solipsism.* Other stricken members deny their essential sociality. They deem themselves individuals, deny their membership, and disparage communal existence. Often accompanied by misanthropy and nihilism, solipsism represents a collapse of self-knowledge in response to the fear that emotional abandonment is all human existence has to offer. Bertrand Russell asserts that those who imagine they live independently of their community, act as parasites, sucking life without replenishing its supply.[225]

1.13.10.3. *Apocalyptic Hunkering.* In evolutionary adaptation, one prospers expecting the worst and preparing for it. This often-useful penchant in human psychology can run amok, fixing entire communities in relentless anxiety. Such communities await a seemingly unavoidable decimation, which never arrives. Apocalypticism amounts to communal neurosis, a species of group obsessive compulsion. Generally good outcomes fail to douse apocalyptic trembling. Conviction of the end of

---

[222] Seneca, *Epistles 1-65,* LIII, 7.

[223] The Buddha teaches that ill deeds burn those who do them. Evil acts self-immolate. [♪] *Dhammapada,* 136.

[224] Gabor Maté, who works with people suffering addictions in the poorest neighborhoods of Vancouver, British Columbia, argues that addictions are attempts to alleviate pain, physical or emotional, conscious or unconscious. Anesthetics of choice, however, induce, in the end, yet greater pain. Many attempt to avoid thinking, encountering themselves, because they are empty within. Maté believes this psychological emptiness is culturally pervasive. Maté, *In the Realm of Hungry Ghosts,* 35-36, 39.

[225] [♪] Russell, "What I Believe," 360. Jan Oppermann adds that community can be accessed in many modes, even across the divide of death (through writings). Un-sociable savants bring something to community (consider Van Gogh or Beethoven) without which every community would be poorer. One may replenish what one takes from community in a multitude of ways. Oppermann, in personal correspondence with the author, dated October 14, 2015.

days can become for some cultures a particularly ugly form of conceptual ossification.[226]

1.13.10.4. *Maladaptation*.   Some among discouraged members convince themselves that failure to adapt to changing circumstances is a norm to be welcomed. These persons imagine that nothing can be done to address the wrongs and errors of human choices. They echo the grim assessments of Hobbes (human life absent a vicious tyrant is lonely, compassionless, impoverished, retrograde, and invariably brief. With the tyrant, life is somewhat, but not dramatically, improved)[227] or Sartre (hell is knowing your neighbor).[228] Regardless, a belief that one might play a meaningful part in a meaning-filled community is deemed to be, at a minimum, fiction, and, more likely, a plunge into the worst extravagances of religious utopianism. Meaninglessness is said to be the normal human state, and its abolition a pitiless vacuity.

1.13.10.5. *Loneliness*. Many fall short of making a philosophical perspective of their isolation (as in solipsism), but nevertheless suffer its emotional concomitants. Solitude becomes pathological when it lingers long enough to bolster persistently negative loops of thought, feelings of insecurity, and worrisome behaviors.[229] People inherit degrees of need for relating. Once that need, whatever quantum it might be for an individual, is triggered, he grows more sensitive to social cues, but also less able to interpret them. This incapacity for social understanding may result in yet greater loneliness.[230] Loneliness hides danger. It is as likely a predictor of early death as are obesity, failing to exercise, and smoking.[231] Simply put, lonely humans are having a health crisis.

---

[226] Apocalyptic doom-saying is a droning dysfunction of neurotypical human community. The end of civilization as we know it will "undoubtedly" emerge due to children's shortened attention spans related to social media, nascent anarchy, species extinction, genetic corruption by miscegenation, totalitarianism, overwork, destruction of nature, cometary impacts, endocrine disruption, species extinction, cancer, chemical pollution, nuclear power or weapons, famine and overpopulation, natural resource depletion, polluted air, acid rain, genetic modifications, plagues of various sorts, oncoming glaciations, or global warming. One might add to this list Jesus' frequent intention to reappear on various mountaintops, alien abduction, Jewish messianic expectation, Martian invasion, and God's evident intention to execute humanity after the style of the Noahic floods for our evident moral inexactitude. For an entertaining treatment of "apocaholics," see [♪] Ridley, *The Rational Optimist*, 280-311.

[227] [♪] Hobbes, *Leviathan*, 117-121 (Chapter 17).

[228] Sartre, *No Exit*, 42.

[229] Cacioppo and Patrick, *Loneliness*, 7.

[230] Cacioppo and Patrick, *Loneliness*, 37.

[231] Cacioppo and Patrick, *Loneliness*, 93.

1.13.10.6. *Sports and Sex Addictions.* Robbed of meaningful social connections, many turn to wan ciphers for comfort. With droves of strangers, they rally sports teams. Often such "athletic allegiances" are conducted electronically, rendering human congress a spectator event. Others simulate intimacy by sex with strangers, again most often by cyber-connections. Pale phantoms mimic flesh and blood. Wanly, they whet the lips of those who thirst for genuine intimacy, offering nothing but the diet drink of human sexual syrups: attenuated voyeurism.

1.13.10.7. *Self-Sufficiency.* Some assert, all evidence to the contrary, that they walk the earth as imperial individuals, veritable Nietzschean supermen.[232] These intrepid individualists imagine themselves without social needs, superlatively inventive, and a breed set apart from the rest of humanity's ruck. Such solitary persons find solace in the literary fictions such as Rand's Riordan and Taggart,[233] but in the life lived by humans, none. Thoreau and Emerson imagined themselves free-living, independent individuals.[234] Each failed to notice how deeply their iconoclasm leaned upon the succor of friends.[235] No individuals exist. All are members, even if, from a social and philosophical perspective, horribly mutilated.

1.13.10.8. *Parasocial Surrogates.* Suffering a deficiency of human social connection, we manufacture substitutes. We construe quasi-social relationships as real social existence. We make of pets our friends. We imagine ourselves relating to television personalities. We generate a penumbra of personness around valued objects. We have "personal relationships with god."[236] In short, we project our needs into nearby nonhuman components of our worlds.[237]

---

[232] [♪] Nietzsche, *Genealogy of Morals,* and [♪] Nietzsche, *Beyond Good and Evil.*

[233] Rand, *Atlas Shrugged.*

[234] Rousseau found that only the wicked become famous. Good people are stricken from collective memory or made to look ridiculous. Rousseau, *Emile,* 238.

[235] Thoreau was rescued from his quixotic tilting at the Massachusetts poll tax by silent friends who paid his tax and bailed the iconoclast of Walden Pond from his cell. [♪] Thoreau, *On the Duty of Civil Disobedience,* 27-28. Emerson, emerging from a poverty-stricken, though well-connected, family, lived in his dotage in part by the generosity of friends, who provided much for him. They rebuilt his home after fire destroyed it. They supplemented his needs when Emerson could no longer lecture. Information derived from *American National Biography* Online: http://www.anb.org/articles/16/16-00508.html. Later in life, Emerson better appreciated his friends. [♪] Emerson, *Conduct of Life,* 1093 (Section VII: Considerations by the Way).

[236] Cacioppo and Patrick, *Loneliness,* 260.

[237] Cacioppo and Patrick, *Loneliness,* 256ff.

1.13.10.9. *Acquisition Neurosis.* Possessions, for many meaning-deficient members, substitute for human relations. Things replace people, becoming wordless, but reliable, friends. Every member needs sufficient possessions to conduct meaningful life. All excess possessions distract members from meaningful existence.[238] Acquisitiveness remains the most prevalent balm for meaning-starved individuals in extant Western cultures.

1.13.10.10. *Despair.* Many, finding life vacant of meaning, choose hopelessness as a means of coping. They imagine that nothing matters. Their actions confirm their ideas. Suicide, when not produced by heritable neurochemical imbalance or rational deliberation, is a symptom of despair.[239] So too infanticide and senicide (for example, the thalaikoothal of the Indian province of Tamil Nadu) may evolve from a sense of despair in relatives of the victims. Health plummets.[240]

Objection 9: Dominating Species: *Some demur that overpopulation is hardly mankind's core problem. Were resources more justly distributed, there would be few private jets and no starving children. Were no wars fought, funds sufficient to eradicate malaria and polio and cancer would stand ready. Were neurotic consumerism tamped down just a bit, every child could receive basic education. Earth could sustain another ten billion humans, in addition to the seven it now carries. You complain about species decimation. Certainly, non-human species die off. That is what species do. Most species that ever existed have perished. Evolution's engine ran over them, sparing their fleeter cousins. Dominant species—well—dominate. A dominant species changes its environment to service its own needs to the extent of its capabilities. Birds build nests, bees hives, ants tunnels. Of necessity, as does every species, humans alter environments to which other species are adapted. Those niche-less creatures perish at their evictions. Humans seep into their vacuum. One cannot revise Darwin's law. It nestles in the fabric of life. Why would one want to change evolution's calculus? Evolution is what made humans what we are—dominant.*

Response: Better habits in our living billions could improve life for those among us who lack necessities. It is true. Even without additional funds, well-deliberated changes in impoverished communities might create sufficient wealth

---

[238] [♪] Aristotle, *Nichomachean Ethics*, 14-15 (Book I: 1099a-1099b).

[239] Robert Putnam reports that suicide among youths aged fifteen to nineteen in America has risen 400% in the last half of the twentieth century. Suicide among young adults of ages twenty to twenty-four has risen almost 300%. Putnam, *Bowling Alone*, 261.

[240] Putnam argues that people with strong social connections and high social capital have fewer colds, cardiac problems, and strokes, less cancer, depression, and other ailments that lead to early death. High social capital is as potent a predictor of health as are cigarette smoking, obesity, high blood pressure, and inactivity telling indicators of disease risk. Social disconnection is a serious public health challenge. Putnam, *Bowling Alone*, 326-327.

to launch them on a path to sufficiency. With additional funds, such improvements might occur rapidly. It is all true.

It is not, however, an answer to overpopulation. Without changes of attitude and habit, we could shortly have the additional ten billion humans about which the objector speculates. The truth is that we are overpopulated because we do not know what to say to ourselves or our children about having children. Since 1950, surgical vasectomy has been available to men as a means of birth control. Only since 1970, has it been reliably possible for First World women to govern the number of their babies. In most of the Third World, women still lack the insight and technology to control fertility. And men, apparently, are disinclined to terminate their fertility.

We are only just learning about childlessness. How might a lifetime be spent if not lavished in rearing one's replacements? Were we one instead of seven billion, humanity may have mined all the iron, copper, and other ores our species will ever need, provided we recycle all and tear down our unneeded buildings. Were we one billion instead of seven, vast expanses of the planet could be returned to wilderness. We might fabricate our protein needs synthetically. We might rediscover our own connection to the non-human world. We might find ourselves in what we lost along the way millennia ago— communities. I am not arguing for a return to caves or a renaissance of medieval warrens. Humanity should retain its useful technologies and create new ones. But we need not employ our genius for tools to squeeze yet one more meal from tired soil. We could find something better to do with our efforts.

All species die. It is true. The missing correlative truth is that all species are interdependent. Allowing even one to perish may jerk the lynchpin that secures our foothold on this planet. Humanity may drift into oblivion with the millions of species we have ushered into its darkness. I am not an alarmist. Neither am I blind. We may be able to wrangle coercive institutions into a state where most of our seven billion get by with a modicum of dignity. We may even be able, with vast coercive effort, to keep a number of species from extinction. Why would we do so? The problem is scope. Our numbers exceed our survival competences. We can reduce our numbers over a few hundred years. It is likely little more is required than educating neglected women, and exposing everyone to different possibilities of family life than we have imagined to date. Some men, if educated about the topic, would get a clue. We can become a much less prominent species, at least numerically. Humanity can live with this world, rather than against it.

Cull offers a solution to problems in the human equation.[241] The capstone of cultural dysfunction is overpopulation. We can address excessive breeding by educating women and offering contraception. The associated core problem is

---

[241]Jared Diamond identifies twelve problems he believes threaten human well-being: 1) destruction of natural habitats, 2) over-harvest of wild ocean species, 3) loss of biodiversity, 4) topsoil depletion, 5) fossil fuel use, 6) fresh water depletion, 7) squandering earth's photosynthetic capacity, 8) toxic chemical use, 9) introduction of alien species, 10) harmful atmospheric gas releases, 11) human overpopulation, and 12) over-consumption. Diamond finds all these problems linked to one another. Nevertheless, Diamond calls himself "a cautious optimist." Diamond, *Collapse*, 387-496, 521.

over-consumption. *Cull* suggests human life can profit deeply from pursuit of interpersonal riches and step away from material obsessions.

DECISION'S SLACKROPE WOBBLES.

ONE INCHES TOWARD
    CHOCOLATE,
        RUBY SLIPPERS,
            AND NORMANDIES.

        ONE QUAVERS AT
            BRAMBLES,
                MAZES,
                    AND LITTLE BIGHORNS.

            ONE TEETERS:
                TREMULOUS,
                    OPTIMISTIC,
                        EQUIVOCATING.

Objection 10: Immoral Morality. *Another protests that morality is itself immoral. Every moral tenet brims with cryptic coercion. From what source creeps moral prescription? Whose purposes does self-editing conduct serve? Morality is to States what faith is to religions. Morality keeps citizen sheep well-herded, all the unit ducklings neatly in rows. Morality robs persons of freedoms. No morality binds me. I am me. There is no other like me, not now, not in the past, never in the future. I am not a type. I am unique. No categorical rules bind me. No State or god enslaves me. I, being real, banish States and gods and tribes and all their opinions about my goodness and roles among others. No person or thing other than me and mine matters. I am the real. Away with your spooks and apodictic yammer.*[242] *The author of* Cull *has lost himself in the mystic maze of morality. Befuddled, he stammers.*

Response*:* Chosen constraints are not coercions. My choices occur in a social context, not some ideological vacuum of puerile individualism. Others influence me. I affect them. The words of others linger like fog; some fraction becomes my own. So too, my thoughts waft like smoke through the deliberations, collective or individual, of others. Some bring change. All humans care about their social relations. That interest is hardwired in our brains. Those, like this objector, who deny others their say repress a bit of their own essence. Yes, the objector is unique. So too every human. But that is hardly the final word. Ours is a time of stifling bureaucracies, occasional totalitarianisms, and frequent

---

[242] So Max Stirner argues. Stirner, *The Ego and Its Own*, 198-202, 324. "Apodictic" means expressing absolute certainty or self-evident truths. See *Webster's Third New International Dictionary*, s.v. "apodictic."

pedantries. Praise for the individual under such circumstances rings sweet in the ears. Emerson sounds right when he exhorts every man to resistance, to abandon conformity in favor of one's own lights, to neglect consistency in favor of what appears best today, to embrace divine wonder against the battering hurricane of human opinion.[243]

But such individualistic talk neglects critical facts. We live together, being troop primates. Our togetherness will take some shape, though it need not be that shape presently in vogue. Every shape of human relations bears within it a morality, perhaps thoroughly distinct from familiar moralities, but all sharing in their depths the human predilection for welcoming strangers,[244] daring altruistic interventions, intuiting the pain of others and alleviating it, and longing for more equitable ways of conducting ourselves. Each morality makes claims upon every member's conduct and allegiance. The objector imagines himself alone, the imperious individual surveying his majestic solitude. I must then ask: To whom does he write?

As to stammering, *mea culpa.*

1.14. *Member-Culling Dissected.* Dis-integrated, from a member's viewpoint, finely-elaborated culling comprises sequential elements:

One enjoys equanimity,
then one senses some problem,
then checks her feelings,[245]
then one checks her gut,[246]
then one takes a crude look at the whole (CLAW),[247]
then one steps back and gathers further evidence,
then one ponders and questions,
then one consults others,
then one prognosticates likely outcomes of actions,
then one hopes in prognostication,
then one pessimizes in prognostication,

---

[243] [♪] Emerson, "Self-Reliance," 257-282.

[244] Frans de Waal notes that humans have a reflex to trust and help. Only for tangible reasons does one suspect and refuse assistance. De Waal, *The Bonobo and the Atheist,* 49.

[245] "Feelings" are affects, products of the deep brain structures named, collectively, the limbic system. These modules regulate human social relations, creating some of the experiences we call emotions, especially those that relate to social settings. When, by injury or disease, a victim loses the ability to feel their emotions (through damage to the orbitofrontal cortex), decision-making grinds to a halt, and life falls apart for those sufferers. Lehrer, *How We Decide,* 14-18.

[246] Most neural processing occurs at a subconscious level. In this processing, the visceral nervous complex plays a part.

[247] Gell-Mann, *Quark and Jaguar,* 346. Gell-Mann argues that, to deal with overwhelming complexity, it takes courage to step back and take a crude look at the whole of a system. In my view, humans have a substantial capability of assessing circumstance based, not on evidence or analysis, but on intuition of the likely outcome of a circumstance. This process utilizes neural heuristics of which we know little, though we employ them regularly.

then one decides action is not required, or that action is required (in
    which case)
then one chooses an appropriate action,
then one again checks her gut,
then one acts,
then one inquires about the effects of her action,
then one evaluates the effects of her action,
then one adapts her feelings to the effects of action,
then one revises her self-concept,
then one adjusts her habits in choosing actions,
then one begins again.

1.15. *Community-Culling Dissected.*   Dis-integrated, from a community's
viewpoint, finely-elaborated culling comprises sequential elements:

A community enjoys stable group identity,
then member(s) perceive some dysfunction,[248]
then members watch and wait for that dysfunction to pass,
then the dysfunction passes, or fails to pass (in which case),
then members communicate about the dysfunction within the commu-
    nity, including fact-gathering and taking a crude look at the
    whole problem (CLAW),[249]
then disputes between subgroups holding divergent views of dysfunc-
    tion emerge,
then the community invokes irenic practices[250] to resolve subgroup
    conflict with reshaped identity, or community irresolution (in
    which case),
then conflicted subgroups segregate themselves culturally within the
    community, eventually reconciling, or failing to reconcile (in
    which case),
then conflicted subgroups physically segregate themselves, fissioning
    into separate communities, finding eventual inter-community
    reconciliation or acquiescence, or failing to reconcile or acqui-
    esce (in which case),
then new stable group identities emerge with inter-community conflict,
then inter-community conflict subsides, or fails to subside (in which
    case),
then overt conflict destroys or subjugates or exiles one group,

---

[248] In this context, even a new opportunity can be styled a "dysfunction." The possibilities contained in the opportunity illumine deficiencies of the current circumstance of a group.

[249] Gell-Mann, *Quark and Jaguar,* 346.

[250] See more on peacemaking and irenea at *Member Culling* and *Community Culling* at Sections II and III below.

then stable post-conflict group identities emerge,
then communities begin again.[251]

1.16. *Iterative Learning.* To learn by culling is to learn in steps. One grasps an insight, incorporates it, sees how it works, then moves on to a new insight. One never entirely knows if what one learns is reliable, but one tests, one's community explores. Kithdom invites communities to evolve meaningfully, which necessitates that members abandon ruts and carve revised paths.

1.17. *Cul de Sacs.* Not all iterations lead somewhere. Communities and members, as they learn iteratively, will occasionally find they have chosen paths to nowhere desirable. Only frank acknowledgement suffices in *cul de sacs.* One must identify error, backtrack, and start afresh. Only return to the errant starting point, and culling a different path suffices to free one from roads to nowhere.

1.18. *Non-Linearity.* Culling is non-linear and proceeds subjectively by loops or groups of dis-integrated elements. Member- and community-culling processes interact in complex webs. Neither community nor member culling occurs independently. Both express the emotional exigencies of the members and community. Neither transpires by a thoroughly cognitive process. Some countable things matter little; some things that matter much defy counting.[252] The most critical elements of meaningful community are non-quantitative. Further, there exist possibilities which, while desirable, surpass human conception. One easily over-estimates the proper domain of rational deliberation.[253]

1.19. *Non-Dissectability.* Finely-elaborated culling cannot be adequately comprehended by dis-integration into its member and community elements. Culling is a cognitively-inhibited emotive impulse behavioral web.

   1.19.1. *Non-Rational.* Neocortical cognitive processes suggest the dis-integration tactic for decision-making analysis. Subcortical processes, out of which the cortical deliberation emerges, resist rational dissection.[254]

   1.19.2. *Sub-Cortical, Non-Rational Origin.* Culling conduct emerges from subcortical, precognitive brain structures of the limbic and brainstem sys-

---

[251] Note that in both member decision-making and communal decision-making, the essential element is mistakes. Error is education. One improves by taking mis-steps, later recognized as such. "Unless you experience the unpleasant symptoms of being wrong, your brain will never revise its models." Lehrer, *How We Decide*, 51-54.

[252] "Not everything that can be counted counts, and not everything that counts can be counted." Cameron, *Informal Sociology.* 13. This idea is often wrongly attributed to Albert Einstein.

[253] Wilson, *Group-Level Evolutionary Processes*, 53.

[254] Should this book not end abruptly upon this admission? Apparently not.

tems. These ancient structures are inhibited by cognitive processing. The result is serviceable moral decision-making. The modularity of these decisional systems, and their non-integration with one another, undergirds the likelihood that irreconcilable moral demands arise in consciousness. Moral action may prove to be irreducibly non-systematic. Each neural module evolved to promote survival in some manner under Pleistocene circumstances. Some of these generative circumstances may no longer exist in the human environment, or may exist only by analogy. For example, breeding at will no longer serves human weal; violence against unfamiliar persons now proves maladaptive, where it proved prudent on the ancient savannah; capturing every available calorie no longer benefits members, leading rather to obesity.

1.19.3. *Cerebral Inhibition.* When finely-elaborated, culling recognizes or accommodates or inhibits or redirects human drives and emotions. The cerebrum does not, however, dominate the drives and emotions. It, rather, influences them. All action begins in the older, lower brain structures.

1.20. *Culling is Pervasive.* Good acts (community-augmentive culling) and evil acts (community-erosive culling) emerge from the member neurophysiology and culture of every human and every human community.

1.20.1. *Balance.* Every human, when she culls, weighs self-preservation against group-prosperity. Every human community, in community-culling, weighs group prosperity against threats to members and group prosperity of other groups.

1.20.2. *Multi-Lateral Accommodation.* Members sacrifice to benefit their community. Communities modify habits (cultures) to insure that demands on members are not senselessly onerous. Communities modify their cultures to accommodate the needs of other communities.

1.20.3. *Sub-Ethical Neurological Predicates Undergird Culling.* Attraction-repulsion is the neurological template upon which all human schemes of conduct are scribed. Attraction-repulsion is not an ethical scheme itself, but the very impulse of life. In seeking good, members and communities hunt what is perceived to preserve or augment. In fleeing evil, members and communities fly from what is perceived to threaten or undermine. Culling seeks human homeostasis in body, mind, and social relations. Ethical systems deliberate the cognitive element of choice; the attraction-repulsion impulse itself emerges from subcortical limbic and brainstem systems.[255]

---

[255] Peter Singer agrees. He argues that the root of human morality lies in our evolved predilections, now lately interacting with our cognitive abilities. Singer, *The Expanding Circle*, xi (from Singer's 2010 preface to his 1981 volume).

1.20.3.1. *Approach-Withdrawal.* All organisms seek conducive conditions and flee dangerous ones in the self-preservation dance of approach or withdrawal. Paramecia follow temperature and nutrient gradients in their liquid realms. Hummingbirds seek nectars and avoid cats with startling rapidity.

1.20.3.2. *Higher Animals.* Conscious creatures pursue circumstances they trust will serve their prosperity, and evade doubtful alternatives. Perceived utility governs.

> ONE SCRUTINIZES THIS HORIZON AND HORIZONS PAST.
> ONE DAY SHE EXAMINES WELL,
> ANOTHER DAY POORLY.
> ONE LEARNS, YET
>   STUPIDITY,
>   SLEEPLESSNESS,
>   AND INATTENTION DISTRACT.
> ONE PONDERS WHAT LIES BEYOND THE HORIZON,
> FINDING MYSTERY
>   IN TIME,
>   IN SPACE,
>   IN THOUGHT,
>   IN DECISION.
> A CUSP ARRIVES, EMERGENT.
>   ONE DECIDES.
>   FOR GOOD OR ILL,
>   ONE CHOOSES.

1.20.3.3. *Deliberative Animals.* Deliberating creatures, like humans and some higher mammals,[256] choose among alternative perceived goods. Animals with high cortex complexity and cranial capacity may erroneously choose goods that prove to be evils. All cognitive scales are skewed, you see, by the evolutionary history of the mammalian brain. Beneath decision-making lies the relentless evolutionary pressure of fitness. Brain structures become part of general human cognition when they survive to breed. Finely-elaborated culling recognizes the Pleistocene predilections of human thought, and seeks to ameliorate. Therefore, finely-elaborated culling is a progressive learning activity with substantial potential reward. Recognizing mistaken evils may preserve members and communities by redirecting habits and cultures toward changed action and deliberation. Evolution is not a deliberative process.

---

[256] Mammals with high cortex complexity and cranial capacity include, for example, primates, dogs, cats, elephants, and cetaceans. There exists evidence that some reptiles and birds may also exhibit considered choice among alternatives.

Evolution has built into humanity urges that, left unaddressed in our wildly changed circumstances, will decimate humanity. Recognizing mistaken goods and counter-productive inclinations may divert members and communities from self-destructive action.

1.20.4. *Culling Error.* No member or community reliably discerns all apparent good from evil, nor all apparent evil from good. Every member errs. Every community errs. We are frequently heedless. To improve, we inspect unwanted outcomes. It is commonplace for members or communities to hurtle along injurious paths heedless of the damage suffered. It is commonplace for members or communities to fail to recognize desirable outcomes when they occur. Finely-elaborated culling entails a high degree of structural uncertainty, which recommends humility. We know only parts of the systems (physical, psychological, and social) in which we are immersed. The numinous tickles the periphery of consciousness, elusive. We plan good results. But devastating unexpected feedback may surprise us. Caution beckons.

1.20.5. *Addressing Disputed Evils.* When a member or community is perceived to elect evils, members or communities who perceive those elections differently must initiate a process of irenic reconciliation. Such dialogue entails mutual acknowledgement of the possibility of error, creation of a narrative concerning the dispute that encompasses the opposed viewpoints, agreement about how to address debated factual issues, and a commitment to persevere until reconciliation emerges. All disputants should forgo the alternatives of breach of relationship or degeneration into violence.[257] Human thoughts about meanings, ultimate and penultimate, are diverse. There is room in human ethical exploration for many provisional good ways of life that are incompatible with one another.[258] In viable communities, these diversities are tolerated to the extent they do not render community life unworkable.

1.20.6. *Evil Persons.* Diseased members may elect evils knowing them to be injurious.[259] Such members must be constrained by their community until they no longer present the danger of knowingly electing evils. Diseased members should be evaluated for the cause of their deliberative defects, and those causes, when understood, addressed. Diseased members should be educated about the effects of their misdirected actions on others. No personal evil merits treating the erring member with disrespect. Con-

---

[257] [♪] Stone, Patton, Heen, *Difficult Conversations.*

[258] Kelly, "Navigating Past Nihilism," 5.

[259] Bertrand Russell asserts that human malevolence is the prime cause of war, more culpable than all financial and power motives combined. [♪] Russell, "What I Believe," 362.

straint entails limiting the evil actor's freedom to act by the least intrusive means necessary, while absorbing the untoward effects of her actions into the community's life as an act of self-sacrifice for the benefit of the member and the restoration of victims. Suffering observed and/or education may redirect errant members.[260] The effects of the evil actor's deeds should be portrayed not only to the actor, but also to the actor's family and friends, since he is part of them and they part of him. The evil actor's cadre and circle needs to adjust their conduct as well as the errant member. No community should exact compensatory violence against offenders. Compensatory violence breeds further violence. The echo of retaliatory retribution rings through generations as vendettas.

1.20.7. *Evil Communities.* Deliberatively-defective communities may elect evils knowing them to be injurious. Such erring communities must be constrained by the Commons and the erring community's own dissenting members. Local or global associations of communities nonviolently correct errant communities, until such erring communities no longer present the danger of knowingly electing evils. Erring communities should be evaluated for the cause of their deliberative defects, and, where possible, those causes should be addressed. Erring communities should be educated about the effects of misdirected action on members and other communities.[261] If the cause of a community electing evils proves to be ineradicable, all members and communities must peacefully constrain the erring community's acts, while absorbing the effects of the erring community's actions into the Commons' life as an act of self-sacrifice for the benefit and education of the erring community.[262] Neither a community nor the Commons may exact compensatory violence against an erring community. Suffering observed and/or education may redirect errant communities. Retribution breeds retaliatory violence, beckoning the dog of war, which hunts in packs.

---

[260] [♪] Gandhi, *Satyagraha,* 63 (§17, "A Model Prisoner").

[261] Mo argues that communities that foment war are morally confused. When thieves steal or murderers kill, their crimes injure others and demonstrate deficient benevolence. The greater the victim's loss, the more serious the crime. Among injuries to others, offensive warfare is the greatest. Yet, most people do not condemn offensive warfare, but rather praise it. A murderer who kills one man forfeits his own life in punishment. What ought we to do with offensive warriors who kill hundreds? If a person calls a little color black but a lot white, or a little taste bitter but a tremendous taste sweet, one concludes the person does not know the meanings of the words. So, when a person calls offensive warfare right, one concludes that the speaker is morally confused. [♪] Mozi, 53-55 (*Part I, §17*).

[262] Gandhi would reform criminals by becoming their friends, giving them jobs, integrating them into the community, and offering a real alternative to injurious acts. [♪] Gandhi, *Satyagraha,* 350 (§166: The Satyagraha Way with Crime).

1.20.8. *Constraining Evil Members and Evil Communities*. It is a difficult fact, which has dominated human life from its origins 200,000 years ago, that a tiny minority of humans is willing to injure or kill others for personal gain or preference, and many humans will participate in or tolerate the activities of these rapacious few. Hobbes found the effects of these errant violent members and communities so dire that, in his view, they warranted establishment of a counter-force sufficiently potent to deter or vanquish evil-doers.[263] Hobbes's remedy may be worse than the disease it treats.

Irenic members and communities must adopt clear-headed strategies to deal with evil members. The Commons must adopt effective deterrents for communities electing evils. What might these strategies and deterrents be?

Thanatoid deliberation[264] recognizes that coercive solutions to member and community evil breed responsive coercions. No coercive approach to member or community evil portends desirable outcomes. Coercion, indeed, changes things. But coercive responses to evils leave the fundamental problem of coercion and fear of coercion untouched. One cannot coerce one's way to peace. Coercion breeds coercion. All evil acts contain their own seeds of destruction. Evil acts are maladaptive. After time, even those who deliberated an evil choice, recognize their approach does not work. And the evil doer himself is mortal. Time stanches recalcitrant evil. Section III (*Member Culling*) contains specific proposals for member responses to the evils of friends. Section IV (*Community Culling*) makes specific proposals for community responses to member and community evil. In the end, kithdom retains a small capability to coerce those intent upon havoc.

1.21. *Alternative Ethical Schemes*. Most ethical systems offer a rule (or rules) and delineate exceptions to and permitted deviations from that rule. For each, their fundamental rule is either partially or wholly an heuristic,[265] which by its nature is incapable of justification.[266] The cull of conduct ad-

---

[263] [♪] Hobbes, *Leviathan*, 120-121 (Chapter 17).

[264] See below at Section III for a discussion of thanatoid deliberation.

[265] "Heuristic" denotes a concept or practice that helps one sort complex alternatives, but may not itself be rationally justified. See *Webster's Third New International Dictionary*, s.v. "heuristic." One employs an heuristic when applying a rule of thumb, making an educated guess, following an intuition, or relying on common sense.

[266] Peter Singer argues that ethical systems attempt to resolve, at least partially, the tension between our ability to reason morally, which gives us broad perspective, and our biological desires as individuals to preserve and optimize our private circumstances. Singer, *The Expanding Circle*, 147. Singer goes on to argue that moral reasoning creates in us an objective perspective, one in which the needs of others receive the same priority as our own. He concludes that we should give of our finan-

vocated in this work adopts elements of virtue ethics, Epicurean hedonism, acquiescence ethics, utilitarianism, and duty ethics. Quad sociality is, at its root, an extrapolation of Thou ethics, with a markedly diminished emphasis on the divine dyad.[267] Quad ethics opposes implications of psychological hedonism, legal ethics, theological ethics, and ego ethics.

1.21.1. *Virtue Ethics.* Virtue ethics advises that certain traits of character are desirable, and other traits of character are to be despised. Aristotle's treatment of aretic ethics (virtue ethics) locates desirable traits as the mean between extremes, as, for example, liberality nestles between the vices of stinginess and extravagance.[268]

1.21.2. *Psychological Hedonism.* Psychological hedonism aims moral choice at individual pleasure. If one finds pleasure in an action, one should undertake that action, while avoiding associated pains. In the Greek tradition, the Cyrenaic School advocated psychological hedonism; in the Indian tradition, the Carvakan system touted sensual pleasure and pain avoidance.

1.21.3. *Epicurean Hedonism.* Epicurean hedonism agrees that pleasure is the measure of action, but argues for a long view of matters. Pain accompanies pleasure. Today's drinking should factor tomorrow's hangover in its calculus. Epicurean hedonism tends toward monastic continence, where the long view disparages most short term pleasures. The greatest pleasures lie in enduring tranquility and absence of fear, not in indulgence of transient impulse and desire.

1.21.4. *Acquiesence Ethics.* Acquiescence ethics notes that much of life's unpleasantness is unavoidable, and one's disappointments derive from an expectation of better outcomes than those forthcoming. Consequently, one avoids suffering and disappointment by accepting one's destiny with a detached fatalism, and wedding one's heart to nothing. In Aurelius's treatment, the Emperor adopts the Stoic view of the cosmos as a fated animal. The thoughtful ruler conceives himself as a fleeting participant in the world's inexorable history.[269] In the *Bhagavad Gita* (a core Hindu-

---

cial resources to those in need, regardless what their personal relationship to us may be, until they suffer no longer, or we share something like the suffering those others are experiencing. Singer, *The Expanding Circle*, 153. Singer, however, warns against letting abstract reason govern too absolutely in matters of morality. Humans are not, as a moral proposition, infinitely malleable. Singer, *The Expanding Circle*, 155.

[267] See [♪] Buber, *I and Thou.*

[268] [♪] Aristotle, *Nichomachean Ethics,* 60-65 (1119b-1122a). Alasdair MacIntyre argues forcefully for virtue ethics in his book, *After Virtue.*

[269] [♪] Aurelius, *Meditations,* 91 (Book IV, §40-41), 59-60 (Book III, §10-11), 247 (Book IX, §28).

Brahmanist religious text), Siddartha advises Arjuna to engage battle against his opponents, since he is a warrior, despite Arjuna's reservations, given that many in the opposing army are Arjuna's own relatives. One must perform one's appointed duties without undue reservations. When one enters the right mental state, killing one's relatives and friends in battle is not killing at all.[270] Buddha advises adherents to seek perfect emptiness (Buddhist *nirvana*), abandoning all desire. Suffering vanishes when desire departs.[271]

1.21.5. *Consequence Ethics.*   Consequence ethics is societal cost-benefit analysis. In Bentham's treatment, which he calls principle of utility, the rule he would have all apply is: that action is best which portends the greatest good for the greatest number.[272] Mill adds to Bentham's analysis that the individual's needs and viewpoint matter, which essentially unwinds Bentham's rule.[273] Henry Sidgwick defines utilitarianism: "The conduct, which, under any given circumstances, is objectively right, is that which will produce the greatest amount of happiness on the whole; that is taking into account all whose happiness is affected by the conduct."[274] Many philosophers have attempted to rescue consequence ethics from its various shortcomings, in my view, to no avail.

1.21.6. *Thou Ethics.*   Thou ethics argues that our relationships with every living thing, as well as with god, are the ultimate end of existence, and no act that diminishes these relationships can be deemed moral. Men live to relate. Buber insists that god is the ultimate Thou, and our mutualism with every other living and non-living thing imitates the god-and-man dyad.[275]

---

[270] *Bhagavad Gita,* 9-15 (First Discourse, §§22-47), 188 (Eighteenth Discourse, §17),

[271] The Buddhist seeker lacks everything, wants nothing, and transcends time. [♪] *Dhammapada,* 421. [♪] Conze, *Buddhist Scriptures,* 111-113, 162-164 (The Heart Sutra).

[272] [♪] Bentham, *Principles of Morals and Legislation,* 2 (Chapter 1). Aristotle finds that seeking utility demeans the best of men. [♪] Aristotle, *Politics,* 198 (1338b.3-4). Bentham argues that all who defend principles other than utility mislead, and he issues a warning about those opponents who can turn a phrase: "If such a man happens to possess the advantages of style, his book may do a considerable deal of mischief before the nothingness of it is understood." [♪] Bentham, *Principles of Morals and Legislation,* 19.

[273] [♪] Mill, *On Liberty,* 5-14.

[274] Sidgwick, *The Methods of Ethics,* 411. Sidgwick prefers that we should call utilitarianism "universalistic hedonism." In the end, Sidgwick is unable to prefer, on rational grounds, individual hedonism over universalistic hedonism. Sidgwick, *The Methods of Ethics,* 503.

[275] [♪] Buber, *I and Thou,* 143 (Third Part).

1.21.7. *Divine Justice Ethics.* Divine justice ethics portrays the human world as a stage into which god injects his view of matters. Mosaic ethics is simplest. Yahweh commands 613 specifics for human compliance.[276] The Qu'ran concurs in the sentiment, but differs in the details.[277] Jesus alters the Mosaic view by insisting upon much more stringent rules. Jesus calls not merely for obedience but also for heartfelt accord with demands to love god and men, to forgive generously, and to give no thought to tomorrow. Such rigor appears to Jesus possible in light of Jesus' anticipation of his imminent appearance in power as Yahweh's scion.[278] The Brahmanist scheme is more complicated, yet the same in its ethical fundament. The divine has so ordered the universe that human acts are meted perfect justice. One reincarnates up or down the scale of being depending upon one's merit (*karma*). One departs the karmic wheel when one achieves union with Brahman (Hindu *nirvana*), which achievement requires many lifetimes of unwavering devotion.

1.21.8. *Legal Ethics.*[279] Legal ethics demands compliance with rules, but frankly acknowledges that the source of those rules is the messy business of legislatures or other coercive temporal authorities. The rules are mundane, the rewards and punishments pertain to life in this world.

1.21.9. *Ego Ethics.* Ego ethics situates ultimate ethical insight in extraordinary individuals. Nietzsche asserts that gifted supermen among us become laws unto themselves, doing as they please. Societal rules corral human lambs and other herd animals, upon whom the gifted lunch at will.[280] Fascism locates ethical genius in *Il Duce* or *Der Führer*.[281] Aristotle opines that persons far excelling their compatriots should be killed or banished to preserve a town's stability. In the alternative, such a person could be made king.[282]

---

[276] [♪] *Torah,* all.

[277] [♪] Muhammad, *Qu'ran,* all.

[278] *Mark* 14:62.

[279] By "legal ethics," I intend not only those rules by which lawyers self-govern (rules of professional conduct), but also all moral requirements of law generally (such as, pay your taxes or drive the speed limit or do not beat up your neighbors). I thank Thomas Andrews, in conversation with the author, on February 7, 2016.

[280] [♪] Nietzsche, *Genealogy of Morals,* 29 (First Essay, §13), and [♪] Nietzsche, *Beyond Good and Evil,* 204-208 (What is Noble, §260).

[281] [♪] Mussolini, *Doctrine of Fascism,* 12, and [♪] Hitler, *Mein Kampf,* 512 (Volume II: Chapter VIII: The Strong Man Is Mightiest Alone).

[282] [♪] Aristotle, *Politics,* 82 (1284a.14,36-37), 90 (1288a.15-20).

1.21.10. *Duty Ethics.*   Right action conforms to a rule that adequately expresses a rational duty incumbent upon all men.   In Kant's description, which philosophers call deontological ethics, only those rules which can be deemed obligations of all men, regardless of the rule's consequences, are ethically obligatory.   Such are categorical imperatives.[283]   Kant takes the thought that no man should be treated as a means only, but rather always as an end, to be a categorical imperative.[284]

1.21.11. *Evaluation of Heuristic Alternatives.*   Each of history's ethical traditions contains elements of others.   Quad sociality embraces components of several.   Ethical thought is neither monistic nor elementally simple.   Neural modularity, such as the various emotive impulse systems described by Panksepp's research in affective neuroscience (see discussion at Section II), defeats such systematizing efforts.   We bring many intuitions to bear on complex circumstances, which circumstances may permit limited courses of action.   Humans are peppered by inclinations toward competing courses of action, none of which may claim clear superiority.   Ethical insights are heuristics, incapable of ultimate rational justification.   They may help.   They cannot be proved.

---

[283] Schopenhauer disparages (not without cause) Kantian ethics as "merely theological Morals in disguise." Schopenhauer, *The Basis of Morality,* 67.

[284] [♪] Kant, *Fundamental Principles of the Metaphysics of Morals,* 186 (Second Section).

II. CULLING FOUNDATIONS[285]

Think, Kate,[286] *of how we think. Ideas shape thoughts. Thoughts divert drives and emotions. Diverted emotion-laden drives, often repeated, establish habits. Habits, when shared, inter-weave, becoming practices. Practices, aggregated, become cultures. So, ideas leak deep into social existence. Certainly, we are more than our ideas. We are physical creatures, full of flatulence and fluids. We exist to live, not think. Most of what we are rumbles deep, far below recognition, in the subconscious, in the structure of our bodies and brains. This section of* Cull *explores that obscure topography, that hidden structure.[287] Be clear. Ideas are not all. Still, ideas are much.*

What if ideas misdirect? Do misconceptions injure? If we fancy ourselves birds, one might suffer by stepping from a roof. If we deem ourselves quadru-

---

[285] Not everyone has a taste for philosophy. If, in reading Section II of this book, you find yourself puzzled or bored, you might prefer to encounter similar ideas by means of a story. I recommend Frederik Backman's tale of Ove, a taciturn Swedish working man and his inability to bloody kill himself properly. Ove's experience of existence ably mirrors my points in Section II: Culling Foundations. In addition, Backman's gift of story-telling and humor will, for a time, make your life better than it might otherwise have been. Backman, *A Man Called Ove*.

[286] Note that each section of *Cull* begins with an admonition to think. John Dewey said: "Thought affords the sole method of escape from purely impulsive or purely routine action." Dewey, *How We Think*, 14. Ursula LeGuin, in her novel of a capitalist planet and its anarchist rival colony on that planet's habitable moon, says: "With the myth of the State out of the way, the real mutuality and reciprocity of society and individual came clear. . . . Only the individual, the person, had the power of moral choice–the power of change, the essential function of life. The Odonian society was conceived as a permanent revolution, and revolution begins in the thinking mind." LeGuin, *The Dispossessed*, 333. Daniel Bor, in his book on consciousness and meaning, says: "What we need is a way to crank up our conscious levels in a more immersive way. After all, the more conscious we are, the brighter, more vibrant, and more pregnant with opportunities the world appears. . . . We can try to foster more awareness by biasing our minds as far as possible in the direction of innovation and relying at least a little bit less on our bank of deeply grooved habits." Bor, *The Ravenous Brain*, 269. All of Bor's concerns are encapsulated in my admonition to "think."

[287] David Brooks says, "[T]he unconscious parts of the mind are most of the mind—where most of the decisions and many of the most impressive acts of thinking take place." Brooks, *The Social Animal*, x.

peds, might we waste time cobbling shoes for hands? Some ideas, though per-
sistent and well-regarded, mislead us about ourselves. We embrace priests,
dead now thousands of years, to shape psychology, to define life. No ancients
knew what we now know. Still, great crowds ignore evolution. Hosts imagine
morality either pointless or optional.   Millions disbelieve their animality.
Hordes neglect social existence. Most scarcely comprehend how minds work.
Few imagine the intrinsic pitfalls and periodicity that govern consciousness.

> NONE GRASPS.
> ANCIENT FOREST, IMPENETRABLE.
> A SEED FALLS.
> A LEAF FLUTTERS TO THE GROUND,
> NESTLING THE SEED.
>   NONE NOTICES.
> THE SEEDLING WELCOMES SPRING.
> LEAPS THROUGH FLASHING SUMMERS,
> TWENTY, FORTY, NINETY FEET.
>   NONE SEES.
> CENTURIES FLOW PAST.
> SOIL CONTAGION, BRANCHES WITHER.
> A WIND, THE TRUNK FALLS TO THE
> GROUND.
>   NONE HEARS.
> THE GIANT LOG, UNKNOWN, ROTS.
> ROOTS AND BRANCHES, THEN TRUNK.
> SOIL TO SOIL.
>   NONE KNEW.
> A SEED FALLS.
> A LEAF FLUTTERS,
> A SEEDLING…
>   UNHEWN LOG IN THE WAY,
>   SAYS ONE.

To live better lives as members, and to live better lives as communities, we
need better self-comprehension.[288] *We must embrace our origins in the planet's*
primeval muck. We must deeply examine our religious convictions, especially
where rote repetition boasts no excellence other than antiquity. We must fash-
ion better rules of behavior for ourselves, and create a vibrant, adaptive morali-
ty. We must know we are creatures blood and bone with all others that occupy
or once occupied the earth. We share their history, excellences, and shortcom-
ings. We must recognize how we think and feel, and abandon over-reliance on
rationality, which is ever tepid. We humans are driven, conflicted, extraordi-
narily inventive, and a danger to ourselves. Most, we must recognize that we

---

[288] Bernard Mandeville notes: "One of the greatest reasons why so few people understand themselves is that most writers are always teaching men what they should be, and hardly ever trouble
their heads with telling them what they really are." Mandeville, *Fable of the Bees*, 36.

are more we than I.   We are, in our guts, ineradicably social, inextricably linked.

We are slack in culling an upgraded self-concept.   Do otherwise.

We lose, Kate, what a fresh creature man is.   The oldest ancestor identified in the human line is merely nine million years old and extinct.   Creatures looking vaguely like us are four million years old and extinct.   Our cousins commenced less than two million years ago.   All are extinct.   Homo sapiens, those of us who now crowd the earth, started as a group of a few hundred members less than 200,000 years ago.   We did not start to overpopulate until 50,000 years ago, nor build towns until 15,000 years ago.[289]   Life is three billion years brewing.   Earth's complex life spans one billion years.   Man is new, untested, and endangered.   Our lone exuberance, the self-reflective brain, remains an unproved evolutionary gambit.   Evolution's random excursions prove hazards to most fresh species.   Cortical hypertrophy[290] may prove fatal to mankind.   We are the last remaining sprig on one branch of a once prolific, now obsessively-pruned, bush of hominins.   We hold our evolutionary novelty in a limp grip.   Do otherwise.

2.   ***Evolution****.*   The proclivities of human choice evolved in the east African Rift Valley, where humankind's long-extinct hominin[291] predecessors emerged.

   2.1. *Evolution Generally.*   As conceived by Darwin, evolutionary theory hypothesizes that survival threats, either natural or cultural, favor traits of some breeding individuals and groups, with the result that individuals or groups possessing adaptive genes survive to breed and produce more offspring than those individuals and groups who lack equally effective traits.[292]

---

[289] Jared Diamond argues that we developed none of the habits of States and cities until 5,500 years ago (3,400 B.C.).   Diamond, *The World Until Yesterday*, 12.

[290] "Hypertrophy" describes an organ that has grown unusually large.

[291] A "hominid" is a creature like man. *Webster's Third New International Dictionary*, s.v. "hominid."   The term "hominin" is a newer coinage some believe better reflects the genetic evidence of the lineage of bipedal apes.   Changes to the family tree of mankind and his great ape cousins leave all hominids, and hence the new coinage hominin includes only *homo sapiens*, *homo neandertalensis*, *homo erectus* (Asian branch), and *homo floresiensis*.   So, the coinage segregates mankind and his cousins from the great apes and their line.   Hrdy, *Mothers and Others*, 17.   Among anthropologists, this terminology is disputed.   Throughout, I use the word "human" to indicate *Homo sapiens*, anatomically- and behaviorally-modern mankind, and the word "hominin" to indicate all proto-human members of the primate ancestral branch that includes humans.   This genetic bush is complicated, and at present seems unlikely to yield a complete picture of hominin ancestry.   Harmon, "Shattered Ancestry," 49.

[292] E. O. Wilson argues for multi-level selection, by which he means that gene selection occurs at both the level of the individual gene as well as at the level of genes in a population.   He asserts that selfish genes promote replication in individuals, but altruistic genes outperform selfish genes at the group level.   The evolution of social cooperation depends on the benefits of cooperation and self-sacrifice for reproductive success.   [♪] Wilson, *The Meaning of Human Existence*, 61-63.   Frans de Waal dissents from Wilson's confidence in group selection evolutionary processes, because he

Such trait survival and propagation is called "fitness." Over time, adaptive survival traits dominate breeding populations, as the offspring of those lacking the trait perish. Even tiny changes to critical traits can rapidly dominate a species, especially where the species suffers specific or severe survival challenges. Adaptive traits cumulate to issue new species. Most evolutionary theorists believe that all terrestrial life has, by this process in the course of three billion years, derived from very simple ocean organisms.[293]

2.2. *Non-Teleological.* Natural evolution lacks intention. Mutation and genetic drift generate trait variability. Some traits enhance a breeding individual's survival in an ecological niche (the organism's "fitness"); most mutations are fatal or indifferent.[294] Epigenetic influences,[295] derived from the specific circumstances of individuals, may influence the expression of an individual's genetic complement.[296] Evolution puts a name to this fact: tiny changes in an organism, if adaptive, cause the organism and its descendants to proliferate, eventually supplanting those of its brethren lacking the adaptive trait. Life fits itself to changing circumstances and proliferates to exploit previously barren or less-well-utilized or altered ecological niches. Evolutionary pressures tend toward greater complexity and specialization in organisms. Evolution describes factors affecting biological organisms, as gravity describes factors affecting matter. Evolution intends nothing.[297]

---

thinks, at least with primate groups, too much migration between groups occurs to allow creation of the survival pressure needed. De Waal, *Primates and Philosophers*, 16.

[293] The root of these concepts can be reviewed in Darwin, *The Origin of Species by Means of Natural Selection Or the Preservation of Favored Races in the Struggle for Life,* 1859, and Darwin, *The Descent of Man, and Selection in Relation to Sex,* 1871. Darwin summarized succinctly the rule of organic beings: "multiply, vary, let the strongest live and the weakest die." Darwin, *Origin of Species,* 360.

[294] Panksepp, *Affective Neuroscience,* 327.

[295] "Epigenetic influences" are environmental factors that affect the expression of an organism's genetic complement, which in combination generate the observable individual. Panksepp argues, based on identical twin studies, that about half of the variation in human personality is heritable, half attributable to nurture. Panksepp, *Affective Neuroscience,* 16. Sharon Begley cites research by Michael Skinner at Washington State University to the effect that some environmental insults or life experiences turn on and off genetic materials in a manner that is transmissible at least four generations (in rats). Begley, "Sins of the Grandfathers," 48-49.

[296] McElreath, Richard and Joseph Henrich, "Modelling cultural evolution," 576-577. McElreath and Henrich argue that extra-genetic systems (epigenetic systems) function has extra-genomic systems of heritable trait transmission, and are built either on top of the genetic system or from wholly different mechanisms.

[297] In this regard, E.O.Wilson argues that, because humans are evolved creatures, the spawn of a mindless predilection of proteins toward aggregating complexity, man answers only to himself. Gods and mythologies are human inventions, which can be construed as part of the complexity of human evolving. [♪] Wilson, *The Meaning of Human Existence,* 15-16. Gary Bloom, hopeful pes-

2.3. *Non-Cognitive.* Evolution is not a conscious process. No numen, no su-pra-ordinal presence, guides evolution. There stands no "man behind the curtain" of genetic adaptation. Perhaps more important, evolution is invisible to human subjectivity. Our cognitive and affective predilections operate without reference to the cryptic pressures that produced them. We know not whence we came. Metaphorically, mankind is a person surprised in mid-life to learn that he is adopted; his origins are other than previously imagined. The structure of human consciousness derives from responses of hominin genomes to conditions of Pleistocene East Africa. These originating circumstances are sunk deep in the bog of prehistory; we guess, we infer. We observe only their issue, as one marvels at the Grand Canyon and infers eons of erosion.

2.4. *Messiness.* Evolution is messy. The progeny of living organisms with divergent genes, if adaptive, survive to breed in greater numbers. Evolutionary pressures work upon what exists in an organism's genome. Hence, evolutionary solutions are frequently inelegant, emphasizing what evolution has in abundance—time, and working solely with its only substance—existing breeding organisms.

2.5. *Cooperation and Competition.* Darwinian evolution emphasizes competition among members of a species for scarce resources. Individual animals with less adaptive characteristics eventually lose in competition with better-adapted competitors. Cooperation among members of a species, and even between species, also affects evolution. Some species cooperate in a manner that makes their group's genetic complement more likely to survive. Consider family, troop, hive, and flock characteristics, or the interspecies dependency of human-domesticated animal relationships. Even cells within organisms cooperate to control their numbers, preventing cancerous growths. Cooperation stands alongside competition in fundamentally shaping evolutionary change. The evolutionary drama is not only ruthless, but also solicitous. Survival is as much a snuggle as a struggle.[298] Peter Kropotkin, a younger contemporary of Darwin, wrote *Mutual Aid: A Factor in Evolution*, in which book Kropotkin noted that he failed to see in nature the all-consuming competitive struggle to the death that Darwin contemplated. Kropotkin, rather, noted the many affiliative and cooperative behaviors that characterized many species, and most human interactions. He hypothesized

---

simist and gadfly, reports Gregory Bateson's attempt to vacate intentionality from evolution with these words: "Some species last longer than those that last not so long."

[298] Nowak, "Why We Help," *Scientific American*, July 2012, 36. E. O. Wilson seems to disagree, citing only conflict examples of pressure on a genome. He does, however, emphasize that multilevel selection operates to preserve genes that produce cooperative groupings, arguing that altruistic groups outcompete groups with in-fighting. [♪] Wilson, *The Meaning of Human Existence*, 33, 63.

that these cooperations were at least as important as brief outbursts of competitive frenzy in determining which creatures bred successfully.[299] De Waal notes that evolution has no preference for competition or cooperation. Evolutionary pressures favor whatever strategy produces the larger number of reproducing offspring.[300]   Some are aggressive competitors (such as sharks or alligators). Others are empathic cooperators (such as humans or wolves).

2.6. *Mammals.*   Mammals diverged from reptilian predecessors about one hundred million years ago. A cataclysm that decimated large dinosaurs (65 million years ago) vacated a wealth of ecological niches that mammals filled. Primates[301] are mammals.

2.7. *Primates.*   Human primate predecessors diverged from the orangutan and gibbon primate lineage approximately fifteen to twenty million years ago, from the gorilla primate lineage approximately nine million years ago, and from the chimpanzee primate lineage approximately six million years ago, according to genetic evidence.[302]   These dates are subject to revision, and remain topics of an extensive academic literature peppered with debate.[303]

2.8. *Evolution of Consciousness.*   Human consciousness evolved with the human brain. Human psychological traits are survival adaptations to the conditions of Pleistocene east Africa's Rift Valley, where humans evolved.[304] Wade asserts that the first evidence of modern human behavior dates to East Africa approximately 50,000 years ago.[305]   Wade distinguishes between anatomically-modern humans, which form appears in the fossil record about

---

[299] Kropotkin, *Mutual Aid*, vii-viii. The Russian noted that in many places, such as the Siberian expanses he observed, competition lay not between members of a species, but between all species and the harshness of their environment, a competition life often lost. Cooperation was not merely possible, but requisite. Kropotkin says, "Sociability is as much a law of nature as mutual struggle," and "mutual support not mutual struggle—has the leading part" in the ethical progress of man. Kropotkin, *Mutual Aid*, 4, 179.

[300] De Waal, *Primates and Philosophers*, 52-58. Community interest expresses the fundament of evolved human morality.

[301] Primates are a taxonomic order of Eutherian mammals (those nurturing young in a placenta, as opposed to marsupial pouches), possibly descended from shrew-like tree mammals that evolved in the Paleocene. Primates comprise man, apes, monkeys, and lemurs. All share characteristics of highly coordinated binocular vision, brains large for body size, and specialized grasping limbs. See *Webster's Third New International Dictionary*, s.v. "primates."

[302] Panksepp, *Affective Neuroscience*, 325-26, and [♪] Wade, *Before the Dawn*, 14.

[303] Lewin, *Bones of Contention*, 28.

[304] Mameli, *Evolution and Psychology in Philosophical Perspective*, 21.

[305] [♪] Wade, *Before the Dawn*, 1.

200,000 years ago, and behaviorally modern humans,[306] which archeological and genetic evidence dates to just before the human diaspora from Africa.

2.9. *Human-Affected Evolution.* Once heightened capacity for social interaction, concept manipulation, and tool manufacture evolved in proto-hominins, the primate brain influenced its own evolution. Hominin competition and cooperation strongly affected social and demographic patterns of the hominins. Some argue that territorial encounters left human males suffering death rates from homicide estimated around thirty percent.[307] In addition to natural selection, social selection waxed. Others dissent.[308] Human brains interrupt environmental evolutionary selection feedback by ameliorating survival pressures and constructing less-harsh and novel environments. But, in so doing, humans create new evolutionary pressures which have an as-yet-poorly-understood impact upon the human genome.

As we have innovated ourselves beyond the veldt environment in which our species evolved, we face the prospect that collective culture genetically reshapes our substance and capacities. We meet the critical question: In what particulars shall we deflect evolution's tangled trajectory toward a culled course to a deliberated future?[309]

> **Objection 11: Fiat Creation:** *Some demur that evolution is an unproved hypothesis, here asserted with warrantless confidence. Evolution encapsulates a value-system inimical to human well-being, and contrary to divine revelation. Sacred texts describe a divine hand creating humanity; some texts portray man set apart from the animal kingdom, and in dominion over lower creatures. The values that animate evolution erode an exalted view of mankind, and by doing so succor inhumane treatment of human beings and a demeaning promotion of sub-human life. Evolutionary theory nicely wraps a stinking bag of immorality.*
>
> **Response:** Scientific inquiry deems all facts hypotheses for which some measure of evidence exists. In this sense, the hypothesis of evolution amasses substantial supporting data. Evolution is not a value-system, though some scientists do in fact step away from theological ethics, and sometimes

---

[306] [♪] Wade, *Before the Dawn*, 64.

[307] [♪] Wade, *Before the Dawn*, 85.

[308] Sarah Hrdy, for example, believes that human cooperative impulses are the species fundament. See Hrdy, *Mothers and Others*.

[309] Ludwig Wittgenstein says that those who understand his thoughts on analytical philosophy will see that they are senseless and discard them. He likens his work to a ladder which, after one has climbed it, is kicked away. Wittgenstein, *Tractatus Logico-Philosophicus*, 108 (Section 6.54). Perhaps the evolutionary history of human moral sentiments is like that ladder: a place from which to commence, but which is ultimately surpassed. See Joshua Greene, *Moral Tribes*, p. 25.

confuse that preference with their technical work.[310] Confused scientists exist; one says the same of some deemed saints. Of sacred texts, one finds them useful or useless. The authority of Torah or gospel or Qur'an or Rig Veda lies in the utility of the concepts each contains. Their sacrality is not evident, but is, rather, imputed. Gods write no books. Those who argue otherwise tend to have special glasses through which they peruse texts deemed sacred, much at variance from the glasses they employ reading newspapers, novels, or financial reports. I ask such persons to read their sacred texts without bootstrapping goggles. Plain-reading analysis leaves one appreciating, but not worshipping, sacred texts. No text can make of man a creature more exalted, or less exalted, than he, in fact, is. Man is what, upon inspection, he proves to be. Evolution is no moral system, but an attempt to describe the effects of environmental survival pressure on mutating reproductive biological organisms, and to account for the record of life's transformations on earth. One ought not to object to rainbow refraction physics, though Toranic priests put a different spin on the spectrum.[311] So too, evolution.

> ONE WATCHES
> GRIEF-STRICKEN SAVANNAH ELEPHANTS,
> GREETING DOMESTIC DOGS,
> GRIPING AMERICAN CROWS,
> GARRULOUS BLACK SQUIRRELS,
> CHOLERIC HONEY BEES,
> COOPERATIVE GOATFISH,
> CALCULATING JAY BIRDS,
> CROONING COLOSSAL CETACEANS.
> ONE INFERS,
>   HESITANTLY,
>   MORAL CONSCIOUSNESS.

Not only has man evolved, Kate, but man shares a genetic and behavioral history with all life. This book concerns human morality, in both its local and global aspects. One needs no god to lay morality's foundation. Life shares morality because all life acts. Moral action is a life characteristic, as are movement, reproduction, and metabolism. In simple life, morality lurks elementary. Paramecia seek sugars, flee salts, prefer warmth, evade scald and freeze. We share culling with all life. Higher animals, however, exhibit deeper precursors of human morality. Our virtues and vices inhabit them, albeit in sometimes attenuated fashion. We share their sensitivities, only more so. Human morality is a behavioral line one can trace, without interruption, to earth's first slime mold, and may be intrinsic to life itself. Morali-

---

[310] Freud seems to dangle in this direction. He argues science approximates truth and progresses. Its discoveries are important, if not ultimate. Unlike religion, science is non-illusory. Science gives what is unavailable from any other source. Freud, *The Future of an Illusion*, 100-102 (Chapter 10).

[311] *Genesis* 9:11-13.

ty, therefore, studies empirical facts about man. As we might study bird's beaks or the hiss of a cockroach, so we may study human specificity: man's finely-elaborated natural capacity for making choices. We err when we make of man a pinnacle. Man is one among earth's many animals. What is unusual about humankind is **the way** *we cull. Culling itself is universal. We hold our eusocial[312] animality in a flaccid grip. Do otherwise.*

3. *Non-Human Quasi-Moral Behaviors.*[313] Quasi-moral behaviors pervade social mammal communities as well as some non-mammalian social species. Morality is an adaptive strategy for social living that characterizes many animal species; rules that promote tranquility and cooperation predominate.[314] Animal consciousness resembles human consciousness.[315] Many creatures, even some non-vertebrates, exhibit behaviors that can only be fairly described as conscious, including rewarding, punishing, attention, REM sleep, and decision-making.[316] In our moral consciousness and decision-making, humans

---

[312] "Eusocial" describes high level social organization within a species, characterized by cooperative care of young, overlapping generations within the group, and a division of labor between breeding and non-breeding members. See [♪] Wilson, The *Meaning of Human Existence*, 19.

[313] Beckoff and Pierce argue that one should not qualify animal morality. Animal behaviors plainly exhibit the stuff of morality, and should be recognized as such. These thinkers argue that denying animal morality is mere bad habit, one thoughtful people should abandon. Beckoff, *Animal Justice*, 10. Other thinkers disagree. Jesse Prinz, in a chapter entitled "The Limits of Evolutionary Ethics," questions characterizations of animal behaviors by researchers finding morality in animals, and concludes that even the great apes lack "oughtitudes." Prinz, *Emotional Construction of Morals*, 262. See also Silk, "Empathy, Sympathy, and Prosocial Preferences in Primates," 123. Silk concludes, after recounting the various studies and anecdotes supporting primate prosociality, that findings of moral sentiments in primates lack reliable empirical bases. Patricia Churchland argues that nonhuman animals have social values, such as caring for young and others, cooperation, punishment, and reconciliation. Churchland, *Braintrust*, 26.

[314] Beckoff and Pierce, *Animal Justice*, 3,5. Flack and de Waal collect examples of non-human social mammals exhibiting behaviors suggestive of moral capability in an excellent paper. Flack, "Any Animal Whatever," 1-29. Much of humanity doubts animal morality. Francis Wayland (writing in 1835) says, "[The brutes] differ from us chiefly in being destitute of any moral faculty." Wayland, *The Elements of Moral Science*, 364.

[315] The urge to set human existence apart (perhaps more accurate is "far apart") from animal existence Frans de Waal calls "anthropodenial." Some reject, even before any evidence is amassed, that humans are not, and cannot be, animals. De Waal, *Primates and Philosophers*, 65. Epictetus, for example, argues that animals are not of "primary importance," by which he means that animals are not ends in themselves, as are humans. Humans are vessels for a fragment of divinity, which is reason. To that sacred spark all men owe their highest loyalty. When a person cares for herself, she is literally "nourishing God." Epictetus, *Discourses*, 255, 269 (Book II, Sections 8.12 and 10.3). Darwin said that "the difference in mind between man and the higher animals, great as it is, certainly is one of degree and not of kind." Darwin, *Descent of Man*, 126.

[316] I take those who hedge about labeling these animal behaviors "conscious" to be in the grip of a need to preserve uniqueness aplenty for humanity over against earth's other animals, or to be possessed by an overweening concern to avoid making of non-human animals "little defective people" by means of anthropomorphizing speech. These animal behaviors deserve the same nomenclature we employ when we observe similar behaviors in humans. To do otherwise sucks meaning from the language itself.

share, in a heightened manner, a moral heritage common to the mammalian line, and to some social creatures outside the mammalian line, such as birds and octopi.[317]   The section that follows supports only two basic propositions: first, that many animals share capabilities similar to those of humanity that we take, in mankind, to underlie our moral capabilities, and, second, that many animals exhibit behaviors that are expressly moral, that is, behaviors aimed to smooth social tension, express other-attentive emotion, preserve group cohesion, and accomplish collective tasks of import.   I proceed anecdotally.   Systematic investigation of such behaviors is a scientific endeavor far beyond the scope of this work.   My point here is to persuade you, Kate, that human morality shares a family likeness with morality-like behaviors in animals.   Do not mistake morality for a divine benefit crowning human consciousness.   Morality is a widespread behavioral phenomenon that has evolved among many social species.   Morality emerged deep in our evolutionary past, among non-human, possibly even non-mammalian, predecessors.[318]

3.1. *Suggestive Animal Capabilities.*   Humans express unique behaviors.   We split atoms, conduct censuses, and ponder conundra.   Most human behaviors, however, merely intensify behaviors extant in other species, species much older than humanity.   Some human capability intensifications have been misconstrued as human uniqueness.   Quasi-moral behaviors are among the animal behaviors intensified in humans.   Morality-like behaviors exist in non-human, even non-mammalian species.   De Waal calls these underlying capabilities "building blocks" of morality, which rudimentary components are shared by higher primates and humanity alike.[319]

Some prefer to call animal moral behaviors "prosocial," indicating that a behavior promotes a group of animals' well-being, but may do so without what we might call cognition (as in ants or termites or bees).   That is, the prosocial behavior may be instinctive or a rote cultural repetition.   Calling animal moral behaviors "prosocial" helps researchers avoid the uncomfortable fact that many animals behave as though they are moral actors.

---

[317] Such is the gist of *The Cambridge Declaration on Consciousness*, issued by prominent neuroscientists on July 7, 2012.   The Declaration was written by Philip Low.   Editors of the Declaration include Jaak Panksepp, Christof Koch, and others.   Joan Silk doubts such conclusions.   She finds even claims for primate sympathy and empathy rest on doubtful observations.   Silk, "Empathy, sympathy, and prosocial preferences in primates," 123.

[318] Joshua Greene memorably states, "Out of evolutionary dirt grows the flower of human goodness."   Greene, *Moral Tribes*, 65.

[319] De Waal, *Primates and Philosophers*, 167.

Many capabilities some deem prototypically human behaviors characterize non-human species. Human morality emerges within a rich tapestry of behaviors we share with other species.[320]

Some critical abilities some animals share with humans are:

3.1.1. *Sociality.* Many species live in groups, from ants and bees to fish and birds to bonobos and elephants. Many species, including dolphins, black tits, Siamese fighting fish, and fiddler crabs, know the relationship between their group members. These many animals, and others, exhibit prosocial affiliative and helping behaviors, which lie near the root of social existence. Social animals, artificially separated from their normal social form of living, experience depression and stress.[321]

3.1.2. *Cooperation.* Bee and ant societies have long been recognized as eusocial communalisms, with deep specializations. Chimpanzees and bonobos hunt cooperatively, as do lions, dolphins, whales, and harrier hawks. Yellow saddle goatfish of Lake Malawi hunt prey cooperatively, with one fish driving prey and others cutting off escape routes. Groupers and moray eels hunt jointly, employing a signal system groupers use to rouse the normally nocturnal eels. Together, groupers prey on fish in open spaces, while eels consume those hiding from grouper forays in crevices.[322] Ravens have been observed leading wolf packs to an elk carcass, so that the wolves will tear it apart, leaving morsels for the ravens.[323] Most primates live in cooperative, though not necessarily eusocial, communities. Most primate interactions are affiliative (relationship building and affirming).[324] Among social animals generally, cooperation binds members to one another.[325] Their emotions and thought processes predispose them to wide-ranging cooperation.

3.1.3. *Tactical Deception.* Some birds and snow foxes issue false alarm for strategic purposes. Cocks may give a food call, then copulate with approaching hens. Jays and ravens build fake food caches to throw off thieves.

---

[320] Hannah Arendt argues, that, even if this is so, how does that help humans? Recognizing the animality of our many misbehaviors hardly helps us to know how, for example, to reduce violence. The studies that underlie these conclusions about human-animal shared morality may even serve to make us more comfortable with our predilection for atrocity. Arendt, *On Violence*, 59-60.

[321] Beckoff and Pierce, *Animal Justice*, 77.

[322] Bshary, "Social cognition in non-primates," 88.

[323] Beckoff and Pierce, *Animal Justice*, 56.

[324] Beckoff and Pierce, *Animal Justice*, 57.

[325] Beckoff and Pierce, *Animal Justice*, 56.

3.1.4. *Punishment.* Cleaner fish punish their groomed client-fish.[326] Rhesus macaques call when novel foods emerge. Ranking troop members harass finders who fail to call; these sanctions apply only to female troop members.[327] A disrespectful chimpanzee male may be attacked by groups of his cohorts.[328]

3.1.5. *Learned Traditions.* Adult birds mob enemies, teaching young how to treat predators. French grunts (a fish species) learn their daytime schooling sites and migration routes from local grunts. Local songbird dialects inhibit the mate choices of females. Mother cheetahs retrieve live prey for their cubs to practice killing and feeding. White tail ptarmigan mothers teach their fledglings which foods are edible by leading them to foods and pecking edible items. An ant species teaches the location of food sources to unschooled nest-mates by running alongside them until they encounter the source.[329] Fruit bats learn birth technique from unrelated midwife bats, who assist with births.[330]

3.1.6. *Complex Communication.* Honeybees dance informationally. Songbirds build on an innate lyric syntax to establish local dialect songforms. Cetaceans sing dialects and make signature sounds. Dolphins copy the signatures of familiar companions. Primates use vocal and gestural communication.

3.1.7. *Tools.* Elephants scratch themselves with objects. They throw things at other animals. Dolphins use baits in hunting. Gorillas and orangutans use tools in normal foraging. Some herons throw floating objects in the water to lure prey fish. Crows and woodpecker finches lever bugs from bark with twigs. Pavement ants drop soil on predator bees waiting at their entrances. Chimpanzees collect water from tree hollows with leaf sponges and use twigs to capture underground termites. An ant species uses leaves to soak up liquid food which is then carried to the nest. The assassin bug baits termites. The insect captures a termite, sucks it dry, then juts the carcass into the termite mound. Other termites, which consume their dead, seize the corpse, and the assassin bug pulls them from the mound, consumes them, and makes of their corpses fresh bait.[331]

---

[326] Bshary, "Social cognition in non-primates," 88.

[327] Silk, "Empathy, Sympathy, and Prosocial Preferences in Primates," 120.

[328] Silk, "Empathy, Sympathy, and Prosocial Preferences in Primates," 120.

[329] Bshary, "Social cognition in non-primates," 90.

[330] Beckoff and Pierce, *Animal Justice*, 136.

[331] Bshary, "Social Cognition in Non-Primates," 90-91.

3.1.8. *Foresight.* Jumping spiders choose attack paths to prey that remove the prey from their line of sight; the spider recalls the prey site in three dimensions.[332] Other species evidence capabilities that exceed human capacity. Clark's nutcrackers cache around 30,000 food items in 6,000 to 8,000 separate locations, feeding from these caches for a period of six or more winter months.[333]

3.1.9. *Episodic Memory.* Scrub jays recall sequential food caching and recovery events, as well as the social context of each cache. Parasitoid wasps build up to six burrows, then lay an egg and capture a caterpillar host for each larva. They establish a line of egg burrows, each with a larva in different stages of development.

3.1.10. *Imitation.* Japanese quails observe other quail performing a behavior and being rewarded, then imitate the performer to be rewarded themselves.[334] Orangutans mimic one another facially, as do many other primates.

3.1.11. *Decision-Making.* Pigeons exceed human ability to make accurate rapid choices, based upon Hick's test, which measures subject reaction time as choices increase in number.[335]

3.1.12. *Logic.* Pinyon jays, who live in highly stratified social groups, exhibit transitive inference cognition (If A is greater than B, and B is greater than C, the A is greater than C) in ranking experiments.

3.1.13. *Conceptual Categorization.* Alex, the African grey parrot hand-raised by Irene Pepperberg, is trained to discriminate different shapes and colors. Alex can accurately sort objects when asked to select an object of shape A and color C from among many erroneous alternatives. [336]

3.1.14. *Leadership.* Individual barnacle geese exhibit boldness that their flock follows. Researchers speculate that boldness in approaching unfamiliar objects often leads to new food sources. Groups learn to follow leaders whose audacity leads to well-being.[337]

3.1.15. *Culture.* Culture is social transmission of innovation or public knowledge. In nature, researchers have difficulty segregating social transmission of innovation from genetic predispositions, individual learn-

[332] Bshary, "Social Cognition in Non-Primates," 92.

[333] Bshary, "Social Cognition in Non-Primates," 96.

[334] Bshary, "Social Cognition in Non-Primates," 93.

[335] Bshary, "Social Cognition in Non-Primates," 96.

[336] Bshary, "Social Cognition in Non-Primates," 92.

[337] Angier, "Even Among Animals: Leaders, Followers and Schmoozers."

ing, and individual re-engaging behaviors learned long ago but seldom practiced. It is, therefore, likely that many more species engage social transmission of innovations than scientists can readily identify. Convincing evidence for culture exists for chimpanzees, elephants, cetaceans, orangutans, and capuchin monkeys.

3.2. *Specifically Quasi-Moral Animal Behaviors.* Animal researchers may observe behaviors anecdotally or experimentally. Anecdotes, however numerous, do not aggregately constitute data, though they may point to possible fruitful experiments. In interpreting animal behavior, there lies substantial danger of over-interpretation, of projecting human predilection onto animal action. Some find evidence of animal empathy and sympathy, even of animal prosocial[338] behavior in non-human primates, dubious.[339] Other researchers are convinced there exist expansive quasi-moral precursor behaviors in primate actors.[340] Regardless, a great deal of highly suggestive quasi-moral animal behavior has been observed.

3.2.1. *Conflict Resolution.* Not only primates, but also, dolphins, hyenas, goats, sheep, dogs, and cleaner fish reconcile following conflict. Chimpanzees and bonobos console victims of aggressions. Some primates intervene in active conflicts, especially where kin are involved.

3.2.2. *Reciprocity and Altruism.* Grooming trades among primates and impala exhibit a tit-for-tat pattern, with increased grooming frequency among those who have previously groomed one another. Chimpanzees reciprocate food for grooming, even where grooming occurred hours before the food exchange.[341] Reciprocity goes so far as raw altruism. Birds make predator warning calls, putting themselves at risk. Wild dogs will attack cheetahs to protect pups. Male baboons protect the rear of retreating troops. Chimpanzees and gibbons share food. Cetaceans help injured

---

[338]"Prosocial" behaviors are those that benefit another regardless of result for the giver.

[339] Silk, "Empathy, Sympathy, and Prosocial Preferences in Primates," 123. Flack identifies Thomas Huxley, Charles Darwin, and George C. Williams as others who share doubts that cooperation and precursors of moral action inhabit the brains of some non-human large-brained social mammals. Flack, "Any Animal Whatever," 1-2.

[340] Flack and de Waal characterize non-human moral systems as containing "elements of rudimentary moral systems." Flack, "Any Animal Whatever," 2. They argue that core components of human morality predate humanity itself, being inherited by mankind from our mammalian line. Flack, "Any Animal Whatever," 24.

[341] De Waal, *Primates and Philosophers*, 44.

animals survive by pushing them toward the surface to breathe. Wolves show limits in their pack fights, which allows losers to survive.[342]

3.2.3. *Empathy and Sympathy and Compassion.* Experiments indicate that chicken hens empathize with the distress of their chicks.[343] Primates clean wounds, console, and reconcile with other troop mates following conflict.[344] In one experiment, a shocked monkey pressed a lever to stop the stimulus. On seeing another monkey shocked, the subject responded as he had to his own shock. In another experiment, trained macaques pulled a chain for food. When the apparatus was modified so that a macaque in an adjacent cage got a shock when the chain was pulled, the subject macaque stopped pulling the chain.[345] Yet, subjects in chimpanzee experiments show little interest in prosocial action, demonstrating little interest in choosing an option that fed not only the subject, but also a cohort in another cage.[346] CeAnn Lambert reports that one of two baby mice trapped in a garage sink helped his weaker companion to drink, eat, and finally escape.[347] Darwin reports that an aging, blind pelican on a salt lake grew fat, being fed by its companions.[348] Elephants mourn the loss of rhino companions, and linger over ill or dead family members.[349] Knuckles, a captive chimp suffering cerebral palsy, was given special treatment by his group.[350] Behavior that reduces one's likelihood of reproducing in exchange for group benefit (altruism) has been observed widely in the animal kingdom.[351]

---

[342] These latter examples derive from Singer, *The Expanding Circle*, 6-8. Given the animal evidence, Singer concludes, ultimately, that any ethical theory that excludes non-reciprocal altruism categorically must be a false theory. Singer, *The Expanding Circle*, 134 (Chapter 5).

[343] Carolyn Smith, and Sarah Zielinski, "Brainy Bird, 65.

[344] Silk expresses some reservations about these observations, concerned about anthropomorphizing the primate behaviors. Silk, "Empathy, sympathy, and prosocial preferences in primates," 117.

[345] Silk, "Empathy, Sympathy, and Prosocial Preferences in Primates," 118-119. De Waal reports that one of these rhesus monkeys stopped pulling the food chain for five days, another for twelve days, starving themselves to avoid injury to others. De Waal, *Primates and Philosophers*, 29.

[346] Silk, "Empathy, Sympathy, and Prosocial Preferences in Primates," 122-123.

[347] Beckoff and Pierce, *Animal Justice*, 85.

[348] Darwin, *Descent of Man*, 102.

[349] Beckoff and Pierce, *Animal Justice*, 104-105.

[350] Beckoff and Pierce, *Animal Justice*, 96.

[351] Richard Hudson argues that some slime mold cells exhibit altruism when they "elect" to become a part of the slime mold's stalk, which stalk perishes that the aggregate may live to reproduce. See Beckoff and Pierce, *Animal Justice*, 82. I have my doubts that slime molds can be accurately termed

Cruelty exists when an individual inflicts corporal or psychological injury to a social companion with knowledge of the pain created, and often with delight in the result. Cruelty presupposes the shared ability to perceive emotional pain. Since animals express moral precursor behaviors, one should expect that some animals will prove immoral as well. For example, wolves prove immoral when inviting another to play, and then switching to dominance interactions. Jane Goodall's Gombe chimp troop hunted and executed an entire neighboring troop over a period of two years.[352]

3.2.4. *Equity and Justice and Play.* De Waal argues that humans, and all cooperative social mammals, share a sense of social regularity, which sense consists in an expectation about how resources should be divided among comrades and how one and others should be treated. Violations elicit protest by those slighted and repressive action by those benefitted.[353] Capuchin monkeys, trained to exchange tokens for food, received cucumbers, apples, or grapes. Capuchins prefer these foods in reverse order. If a capuchin sees another capuchin receive apple or grape for its token, the observing capuchin will refuse cucumber. Short-changed capuchins sometimes flung their sad cucumbers back at the observers. Observing capuchins also refuse any food if other capuchins receive food without proffering the prescribed token.[354] Chimpanzees were subjects in experiments similar to the capuchin tests. Chimps from troops stable for thirty years delivered tokens without regard to the fruit rewards of other troopmates. But chimps from another troop, stable only for eight years, refused lower value rewards, as had the capuchin monkeys.[355] Unrelated ravens will join in attacks upon food cache raiders even when the raven has not seen the theft.[356]

Play commences only when two animals agree to play, and proves impossible when either violates the rules without rapid apology. Humans, non-human primates, rodents, dogs and wolves, foxes, ungulates, ele-

---

altruistic, though the truncated definition given to the term by some researchers describes slime mold activity.

[352] Beckoff and Pierce, *Animal Justice*, 17-18.

[353] De Waal, *Primates and Philosophers*, 44-45.

[354] Silk, "Empathy, Sympathy, and Prosocial Preferences in Primates," 121. See de Waal, *Primates and Philosophers*, 45-49, for an expanded discussion.

[355] Silk, "Empathy, Sympathy, and Prosocial Preferences in Primates," 121.

[356] Beckoff and Pierce, *Animal Justice*, 10.

phants, and cetaceans play. Even birds and crustacean play.[357] The larger the neocortex, the greater becomes play frequency. Play diminishes the importance of social status and size, at least for the duration of play.[358] In order to maintain the play mood, larger or dominant wolves and dogs self-inhibit the intensity of their bites and undertake role reversal, making themselves vulnerable to injury.[359] Social play is a vignette of morality generally. Some behaviors work for everyone; others do not.

3.2.5. *Grief.* Barbara King attributes human-like animal emotion as the motive for some social separation behavior. Specifically, King finds that many species grieve. She cites examples from bottlenose dolphins, chimpanzees, elephants, giraffes, domestic cats, ducks, dogs, coyotes, rabbits, horses, and birds, which, when they choose one another's company for non-survival reasons, grieve the death of their companion in a manner an observer may recognize.[360]

3.2.6. *Love.* Marc Beckoff, observing coyotes, argues that the love-bond between matriarch and her pups accounts for the pack's grief upon her death.[361] Social member animals, when isolated in zoos or other segregated circumstances, tend toward depression.[362]

One recognizes the propensity in observing non-human behaviors to anthropomorphize these creatures' behaviors. Perhaps what appears to be morality-like action in fact remains something entirely other. We encounter, however, a contrary danger as well. We may well decline to recognize plainly moral action in non-human species to buttress our deep, but often misdirected, conviction of human uniqueness. The evidence convinces that something very much like moral concern motivates many species.

Human morality appears an elaboration of basal quasi-morality inherited from life's chain of being, and necessitated by the structure of social existence.[363] One, whether human or not, trusts, empathizes, sympathizes, salves conflicts, reciprocates, seeks equity, perceives justice, loves, and loses. These events weave themselves into something like morality. The

---

[357] Beckoff and Pierce, *Animal Justice*, 116-117.

[358] Beckoff and Pierce, *Animal Justice*, 121.

[359] Beckoff and Pierce, *Animal Justice*, 124.

[360] King, "When Animals Mourn," 63-67.

[361] King, "When Animals Mourn," 67 (citing Beckoff, *Animals Matter*, 2007).

[362] Beckoff and Pierce, *Animal Justice*, 77.

[363] Paul Bloom argues that the foundations of morality are present in babies at birth, and are acquired by education. Basally, morality derives from human evolution. Bloom, *Just Babies*, 8.

woof of our human social fabric is spun from heritable mammalian quasi-moral capacities. The warp derives from humanity's precocious volume of neo-cortex. The intricate reflective tapestry of human morality results.

> ONE IMAGINES HIMSELF.
>   SUPERMAN IN FLIGHT.
>   HORROR OF OBESITY.
>   JESUS' SIDEKICK.
>   HARBINGER.
>   SAD SACK.
> ONE MISCONSTRUCTS HIMSELF,
> AND, PREGNANTLY, KNOWS IT.
> ALWAYS, STILL,
>   A SAVANNAH HOMININ.

Man evolved. Man shares something-like-morality with the many members of the animal kingdom. The elaborate way humankind chooses, Kate, springs from human brain structure. We are, each of us, a complex neural organ distributed into a human body. Neurally, we are linked with others. Most of these others are human, but some not. We sort the objective physicality of our brain-ness from our subjective experience of person-ness only with marked difficulty. The conceptual problem proves so intractable that most resolve their contraposed self-concepts by predicating an independent substance into which one may project the subjective. Soul or spirit describes reliable aspects of human experience, slathered over a dubious metaphysical construct. The problem, however, is real. It proves difficult to do oneself justice as a moral agent while regarding oneself as three pounds of neural mush plus visceral and motor protrusions. Kate, the agent, requires self-respect, and self-possession, and social standing, just to begin comprehending herself as a human moral agent. Much of this book dwells in the subjectivity of being a human moral agent. This fragment reminds us that we are, at a minimum, brains-in-bodies, despite what we experience subjectively. We hold our enfleshed brain in a feeble grip. Do otherwise.

4. **Brain Evolution.** Human brain architecture evolved under the conditions of the Pleistocene (1.8 million to 10,000 years ago). The Pleistocene geological epoch as it existed in east and south Africa has been called the "environment of evolutionary adaptedness," which means the survival conditions that shaped the human genome.[364]

---

[364] Mameli, "Evolution and Psychology in Philosophical Perspective," 26. John Bowlby coined this term in 1969 in his book, *Attachment and Loss*, Vol. I, *Attachment*.

4.1. *Pleistocene.* The Pleistocene is the sixth of the seven epochs that constitute the Cenozoic Era (65 million years ago to present). The time boundaries of the Pleistocene are disputed. Some argue for the period 1.64 million to 10,000 years ago.[365]

4.1.1. *Hominin Populations.* Around two and one-half million years ago, climate shifted. Hominids diversified in type; populations of hominids grew. Plant eating hominids and omnivore hominins, such as mankind, emerged.[366]

4.1.2. *Temperature Fluctuations.* The climate of the Pleistocene fluctuated with the peaks and valleys of the late Cenozoic Ice Age. Global Pleistocene environments changed dramatically and repeatedly, alternating with the prevailing global mean temperature, which was five to nine degrees Celsius below current mean temperatures during glacial period and zero to two degrees Celsius above current mean temperatures during interglacial periods.[367] Globally, higher latitude landmasses were repeatedly glaciated. Sea levels fell and rose with the expansion and retreat of glaciers as global mean temperatures oscillated.[368] Animals dependent upon African Pleistocene ecologies would have been forced to adapt or change range repeatedly over the course of their species history.[369] Periods of wet or dry climate in Africa occur every 23,000 years, reflecting the 23,000 year cycle of the earth's orbital wobble, which alters the intensity of sunlight fractionally in the area.[370] The fluctuating temperatures, and consequent climate changes, of ice age conditions deeply influenced human evolution.

Ian Tattersall argues that the extreme and repeated aridity of Africa isolated human populations from one another. These climate fluctuations demanded rapid adaptation, and permitted spread of genetic adaptations rapidly through the small populations. Humans emerged from the last of these disruptions with large brains and symbolic thought. Remarkably soon, hominin competitors fell by the evolutionary wayside.[371]

4.1.3. *Land Mass Distribution.* Throughout the Pleistocene epoch, the earth's land masses have been distributed upon the face of the planet in

---

[365] Jones, Martin, Pilbeam, eds, *Human Evolution*, 454.

[366] Jones, *Cambridge Encyclopedia of Human Evolution*, 168.

[367] *Encyclopedia Britannica*, 15th ed., *s.v.*, "geochronology," 19: 897a.

[368] Fagan, *Cro Magnon*, xv.

[369] *Encyclopedia Britannica*, 15th ed., *s.v.*, "geochronology," 19: 903b.

[370] DeMenocal, "Climate Shocks," 51.

[371] Tattersall, "If I Had a Hammer," 58-59.

approximately their current configuration. The presence of a continental land mass at one of the poles is a predisposing factor for ice age climate. The Antarctic land mass draws the planetary climate system into repeated ice ages by serving as an enormous cold sink. The continental ice-clad surface reflects solar radiation, deepening cooling cycles.[372]

4.1.4. *Ocean Levels.* Ocean levels fall as landmass ice accumulates. At the last glacial maximum, ocean levels were 200 to 390 feet lower than present sea level, which exposed land masses that linked regions presently separated by shallow seas.[373] Humans migrated across these land bridges in populating the planet.[374]

4.1.5. *Intersubjective Proto-Humans.* Hrdy argues that though anatomically- and behaviorally-modern humans did not arise until around 200,000 years ago, emotional intersubjectivity (that is, the ability to experience and express empathy, and to care about what others experience) emerged in one or more hominin lines hundreds of thousands of years before talking, creative modern humanity.[375]

4.1.6. *Cooperative Mammals.* Frans de Waal argues, citing Darwin, that, long before humans or their progenitors came on the evolutionary scene, animals that cooperated over time out-prospered others that relied on competition.[376] Collaborative species simply out-breed competitors.

4.2. *Rift Valley and Southern African Pleistocene.* The Pleistocene in east and southern Africa was characterized by harsh climatic conditions. When humans emerged as a distinct species around 200,000 years ago, the climate supported generous food resources and mild conditions. Anatomically (but not behaviorally) modern humans competed with *Homo erectus* and *Homo neanderthalensis* throughout *Homo sapiens'* range.[377] Around 195,000 years ago, the planet entered a period of increased glaciation for seventy thousand years called Marine Isotope Stage 6 (MIS6). African temperatures fell, the African landmass became dry, deserts expanded, and the wealth of foodstuffs on which humans depended bled away. As much of Africa grew inhospitable, human numbers fell from ten thousand to a few hundreds, and humanity teetered at the brink of extinction. Only a few locations could

---

[372] This information derives from (http://www.lakepowell.net/sciencecenter/paleoclomate.htm).

[373] [♪] Wade, *Before the Dawn*, 102.

[374] [♪] Wade, *Before the Dawn*, 116.

[375] Hrdy, *Mothers and Others*, 66, 273-294.

[376] de Waal, *Primates and Philosophers*, 4, 13.

[377] [♪] Wade, *Before the Dawn*, 28.

have supported a viable human population. We have learned from genetic studies that all living humans descend from the one local population who weathered MIS6, possibly located at the tip of what is now South Africa or in the Rift Valley.[378] All living humans descend from this tiny population. The MIS6 withering of human population constituted an evolutionary bottleneck from which mankind might never have emerged.

4.2.1. *Low Population Density.* Throughout the Pleistocene, except for local exceptions attributable to specially fecund circumstances, human populations were sparse. Though difficult to quantify, Hrdy estimates Pleistocene humans had a density on average of one person per square mile. Dense populations would have been several people per square mile. Humans were few, and, hence, endangered.[379]

4.2.2. *Prehistorical Uncertainty.* This general outline leaves many questions unanswered about specific adaptive hurdles faced by human Pleistocene progenitors in the rift Africa, and what psychological mechanisms were available in Pleistocene hominin precursor populations for evolutionary selection.[380]

4.3. *Human Pre-History.* The earliest written records are 5,000 years old. Most archeological artifacts disappear at 15,000 years ago. The first evidence of higher thought among humans begins at approximately 50,000 years ago, as the ancient proto-human tool kit improved. Human history of the intervening 35,000 years remains extraordinarily sketchy. Genetic evidence and inference has begun to fill in some gaps.

4.3.1. *Modern Behavior.* Before 50,000 years ago, anatomically-modern humans developed into behaviorally-modern humans, possibly by virtue of genetic changes that facilitated language.[381] Donald Brown, based on a survey of cultural constants in existing cultures, speculates that one can hypothesize a Universal People's characteristics that may describe the ancestral human population. Families form the basic social unit. Territory defines groups. Men control politics and women submit. Kinship, sex, and age matter for social hierarchy. Mothers and their children are the organizing principle of human troops. Men gain sexual access to a woman by virtue of the father's devotion to mother and child.[382] Members of

---

[378] Marean, "When the Sea Saved Humanity," 55, and [♪] Wade, *Before the Dawn,* 52.

[379] Hrdy, *Mothers and Others,* 29.

[380] Mameli, *Evolution and Psychology in Philosophical Perspective,* 28-29.

[381] [♪] Wade, *Before the Dawn,* 13, 50.

[382] One might wonder, in Brown's analysis, about the role of those women who find "bad boys" attractive, loving them for their non-parental fitness characteristics such as excitement, unpredictability, and ignoring social norms.

troops reciprocate in sentiment, goods, and labor. Troops impose sanctions for rule violations. Supernatural beliefs and confidence in magic are widespread. Foretelling the future is usual, especially in the form of divination. People express themselves in bodily adornment, dress, art, and hair styles. They dance and sing. They build shelters, which are just one example of the broader fabrication of tools.[383] According to Steven Pinker, violence characterized prehistorical behaviorally-modern humans, with raiding and skirmish deaths in some groups reaching thirty percent of the male population.[384] But Pinker may be wrong in his assertions about human prehistorical war.[385]

Hrdy argues that schemes such as Brown's and arguments such as Pinker's project hierarchical and violent tendencies, which trends developed only after sedentism and over-population emerged. Hrdy argues, rather, that the human evolutionary solution to slow-developing human infants with increasingly larger brains was cooperative breeding, with intensive mutual provisioning among tribal members. Others helped mothers to sup-

---

[383] [♪] Wade, *Before the Dawn*, 65-66.

[384] [♪] Pinker, *Better Angels of Our Nature*, 49. Pinker argues that the emergence of states depresses violence among humans. All the tribes Pinker cites derive from information in the historical period. Pinker himself notes that absence of evidence for Pleistocene inter-tribal violence. [♪] Pinker, *Better Angels of Our Nature*, 40. Shermer shares Pinker's perspective, arguing that prehistoric man was massively violent, and has been becoming ever so much more peaceful as time passes. Shermer styles the view that humans are relatively non-violent and lived in relative peace before States emerged as nothing more than an errant myth. Shermer, *The Moral Arc*, 90-102. The problem in these assessments is an abject lack of evidence. Gwynne Dyer (with Shermer and Pinker) acknowledges that we have no evidence about the warlike or peaceable nature of humans communities in the deep past, and further that the evidence available from historical hunter-gatherer peoples is scant and at least somewhat irrelevant. She nevertheless concludes, "the available evidence argues strongly that our ancestors have been fighting wars since long before the rise of civilization." Dyer, *War: The Lethal Custom*, 79. One cannot have it both ways. We possess evidence or we do not. Non-evidence cannot argue strongly for anything. I demur, and note Pinker's and Shermer's dismissive consideration of evidence contrary to their views. Dyer says that prehistorical humans lived in small hunter-gatherer bands that operated by consensus on an egalitarian basis. She further notes that ordinary people tend still to behave in this very same manner. Dyer, *War: The Lethal Custom*, 68-69. Lawrence Keeley argues, from the behaviors of modern hunter-gatherers and the archaeological record that most prehistorical societies warred regularly. Keeley finds that more than ninety percent of known societies war. Keeley, *War Before Civilization*, 28. The last 10,000 years of the archaeological record shows that prehistoric warriors in this time frame were "as ruthlessly violent as any of their more recent counterparts and that prehistoric warfare continued for long periods of time." Keeley, *War Before Civilization*, 38. John Horgan dissents from Pinker, Shermer, Dyer, and Keeley (as does Sarah Hrdy). Examining the archaeological record, Horgan concludes that war is not an innate human behavior. War dates back to 13,000 years ago, not to the emergence of our species. War is a cultural choice made by humans, a choice that we can redirect. Horgan, *The End of War*, 24-26, 58.

[385] Boehm cites Keeley's study of the archaeological record: there is "no definitive evidence of massacres before the Neolithic." Boehm, *Hierarchy in the Forest*, 221, relying upon the research of Lawrence Keeley, *War before Civilization*, probably at page 38.

ply their infants with care and food. Humans did so because, long before our language capabilities emerged, our intersubjectivity (that is, our interest in other's feelings and ability to predict their intentions) evolved.[386] In Hrdy's view, cooperative breeding, not violent struggles with neighbors, drove human evolution.[387] Hrdy argues that violent intertribal contacts emerged only in the last 10,000 years, as need to protect valuable resources, such as children, livestock, wives, and land, from outsider depredations grew with the human population.[388] And this development, she asserts, led to a slide toward patrilocality in social and breeding structure. One needs to stay near brothers and fathers, if one is to take up a weapon in the company of reliable co-defenders.[389] Hrdy wins this debate. The issue is a critical one for which the available evidence is sparse. Is man a naturally violent African predator? Or is man an essentially peace-loving species that spread across the face of the planet to avoid conflicts with neighbors, and adopted war only as a final expedient when migration foundered for lack of new territories? Is man, in his rudiments, a ruthless predator or a reticent self-defender? If man had a choice, would he depredate or cooperate? My equivocal judgment is that humanity is the latter and chooses, where the alternative lies open to him, irenism.[390]

    4.3.2. *Population Spread.* Periodic land connections facilitated the older *Homo* species' movement from Africa into Asia and Europe, and human spread from east Africa to the Arabian peninsula, India, and eventually Australia. Indian populations of modern humans moved into Europe. Asian populations migrated through China to the Americas.[391]

---

[386] Peter Singer notes that, long before our predecessors became human, they were social creatures. Singer, *The Expanding Circle*, 3.

[387] Hrdy, *Mothers and Others*, 30-31.

[388] Wade takes these sorts of assertions to be factually wrong. He sides with Hobbes on human war-making predilection. Wade, *The Faith Instinct*, 49-50.

[389] Hrdy, *Mothers and Others*, 247. John Horgan confirms Hrdy's perspective. He lists all evidence for prehistoric organized human-upon-human predation and finds it ambiguous or misconstrued. The first firm evidence of war emerged only 13,000 years ago, far into overpopulation pressures. Horgan, *The End of War*, 191-195.

[390] "Equivocal" means a concept is subject to more than one interpretation, and hence somewhat indeterminate. "Irenism" is a coinage that provides a word alternative to "peace" and "pacifism," which terms pack political baggage I decline to carry; these forsaken terms also bear connotations of acquiescence and even cowardice. Frans de Waal, a primatologist, concurs that humans, despite their violent potential, are more likely to cooperate than fight. Further, he asserts that our capacity for cooperation accounts for our survival as a species, not our pugilism. Humans cooperate with a frequency and on a scale unrivaled in any other species. De Waal, "One for All," 70-71.

[391] [♪] Wade, *Before the Dawn*, 75, 94.

4.3.3. *Human Types*. Before 50,000 years ago, humans failed to successfully spread outside Africa. One foray into the region of Palestine ended with human populations dying out. It is possible that the other human species, *Homo erectus* and *Homo neanderthalensis*, out-competed the small human population, which shared the tool kit of their *Homo* cousins at the time.[392] After 50,000 years ago, one small group of modern humans crossed the south end of the Red Sea into Arabia, and with their innovative tools and language abilities, began to spread across the planet. The encounter with the more populous Neanderthal lasted some 15,000 years in Europe. The Neanderthals may have interbred with humans, but, ultimately, Neanderthal populations died out.[393] *Homo erectus* died out as well, though their population originally far exceeded that of the burgeoning humans. The ancestral population of humans probably numbered no more than 5,000 in Africa.[394] The humans who survived emigration from Africa numbered as few as 150.[395] Human presence may well have caused the (possibly-intentional) extinction of *Homo erectus* and *Homo neanderthalensis*.[396]

4.3.4. *Hunter-Gatherer Cooperation*.[397] Among ten million terrestrial species, only two engage intentional, male-initiated territorial intrusions to

---

[392] [♪] Wade, *Before the Dawn*, 29.

[393] Wade asserts that there exists no evidence of Neanderthal DNA in the human lineage. [♪] Wade, *Before the Dawn*, 92. Subsequent evidence contradicts Wade's assertion. See Tattersall, *Masters of the Planet*, 166, who asserts that one to four percent of human DNA is of Neanderthal origin, evidencing a modest quantum of inter-species Pleistocene hanky-panky. See also Wilford, "With Science, New Portrait of the Cave Artist," June 14, 2012.

[394] [♪] Wade, *Before the Dawn*, 58.

[395] [♪] Wade, *Before the Dawn*, 75.

[396] The extinctions of these predecessor human species may have proceeded not only by warfare, but also by interbreeding with modern humans. Hammer finds genetic evidence for human hybridizations at multiple locations during time periods overlapping predecessor human species, and argues for interbreeding with local populations in Africa, the Middle East, and southeast Asia. Hammer, "Human Hybrids," 70-71.

[397] Hunting-gathering societies have almost disappeared, despite being the way of life of most humans for the vast majority of human existence. Marjorie Shostak reported her life among Nisa's people, the Zhun/twasi (which means "real people"), beginning in 1961. Nisa was a fifty year old African woman living on the northern edge of the Kalahari desert in Botswana. Shostak found that real people shared all foods, creating an egalitarian economy. The people made decisions by consensus, and constantly adapted. Reciprocal gift-giving and generosity were emphasized in their intense social communalism. The real people lacked chiefs or hierarchies. They worked no more than a few hours a day; women worked more than men. All enjoyed substantial leisure. Women had high standing and substantial influence, but men and women related best within groups of their own sex. The real people's diet was nutritious, but food was seldom stored for long periods. Storytelling, full of hyperbole, was the mainstay of the real people's artistic expression. Life expectancy of real people was about thirty years. Shostak came to believe that Nisa viewed her, despite Shostak's alien ways, as a distant sister. Shostak, *Nisa*, 3-20, 332.

find and kill vulnerable strangers: chimpanzees and humans.[398] Yet, there exists no evidence to support the idea of inter-tribal warfare in the Pleistocene.[399] It is possible that widespread warfare came to exist only after humanity abandoned hunting and gathering in favor of over-populated sedentism. In the Pleistocene, one core survival resource was food sharing within and without groups. We are a cooperatively-breeding species, with alloparents providing at least some of the nutrition required by our young.[400] Sharing mandated social peace, a survival essential. Some call such sharing "reciprocal altruism." Food resources were too unstable for populations to weather without the help of others, and children's need for consistent protein too demanding to permit systemic interruptions such as inter-group skirmishes. As such, scarcity drove conflict-dousing behaviors. Voluminous, willing giving served as social balm and a resource for hard times rumbling just over the horizon.[401] Further, reciprocal altruism, as a base for human relations, requires keeping track of who has given what under which circumstances.[402] Such needs might be an evolutionary impetus to detail recall. The need might explain eventual record-keeping.

4.3.5. *Megafauna Extinctions.* As humans spread planetwide, the megafauna[403] of invaded regions died out. Humans hunted to extinction the large mammals of, first, Australia (45,000 years ago), then Tasmania (41,000 years ago), Japan (30,000 years ago), North America (13,000 years ago), and South America (12,500 years ago). The absence of megafauna grazers affected the continental flora and possibly the methane content of the atmosphere.[404]

---

[398] [♪] Wade, *Before the Dawn*, 149. Comparing chimpanzee to human predatory violence, chimps are 200 times more likely to initiate intra-group aggression. Aggression toward outsiders is roughly equivalent between humans and chimpanzees. Harris, *The Moral Landscape*, 100.

[399] Hrdy, *Mothers and Others*, 19. As Hrdy notes, absence of evidence does not prove no warfare existed. So few were the numbers of humans that such evidence might be excessively sparse, even if substantial intergroup conflicts existed. Horgan offers a timeline of human-on-human violence in an appendix called "A Brief Pre-history of Violence." He argues the oldest unambiguous homicide victim lived 20,000 years ago. Horgan, *The End of War*, 191-195.

[400] Hrdy, *Mothers and Others*, 230.

[401] Hrdy, *Mothers and Others*, 23.

[402] Wright, *The Moral Animal*, 284.

[403] Megafauna are large mammals, usually exceeding 220 pounds. [♪] Wade, *Before the Dawn*, 82.

[404] "Megafauna," at http://en.wikipedia.org/wiki/Megafuana, at page 4-5.

4.3.6. *Sedentism*. The primary human defense to violence was, until 15,000 years ago, mobility. The conflict-resolution rule was: When threatened, move. But sedentism offered advantages: larger population sizes (which created a good defense posture), more expansive cooperation, trade, art, and the simpler accumulation of knowledge and excess foodstuffs. Many psychological traits of hunter-gatherers required change. One had to live with strangers. One had to compensate for the loss of mobility by rules, agreements, and hierarchies. One traded egalitarianism for societal classes.[405] Wade speculates that a genetic change in human aggression was required to accommodate sedentism.[406] Hrdy argues that human cooperative sharing is of much more ancient provenance, distinguishing the human line from its inception.[407] Both might be right. It is likely that, once sedentary, societies required cultural concepts to tamp down human violence. These were slowly invented. The behavioral momentum of 45,000 years of tribal vendetta, if it ever existed, gradually eroded.

4.3.7. *Dogs*. Around 15,000 years ago, dogs joined human society. Wade speculates that dogs domesticated humans as much as humans tamed dogs. Scavenging dogs found humans a ready source of nutritious garbage. Humans profited from dog barking as a predation early-warning system for their nascent settlements. Dogs may also have disrupted the economic communism of hunter-gatherer society. Dogs bond to one master, and so become property of one human. One speculates that the first capitalist may have been a dog-owner.[408] The symbiotic canine-human relationship spread widely. Where humans went, dogs went.[409] They spread over the planet with us. They left the planet before us. The first mammals to survive spaceflight were Russian dogs.

4.3.8. *Agriculture and Animal Domestication*. Humans in settlement developed agriculture. Sedentary social existence predates plant domestication.[410] Drawing upon the paradigm of dogs (possibly), humans began non-systematic adaptation of useful species by controlling their breeding;

---

[405] [♪] Wade, *Before the Dawn*, 101.

[406] [♪] Wade, *Before the Dawn*, 129.

[407] Hrdy, *Mothers and Others*, 23.

[408] [♪] Wade, *Before the Dawn*, 110, restating Colin Renfrew, "Commodification and Institution in Group-Oriented and Individualizing Societies," in *The Origin of Human Social Institutions*, Oxford University Press, 2001, page 114.

[409] [♪] Wade, *Before the Dawn*, 110.

[410] [♪] Wade, *Before the Dawn*, 125.

first, goats and sheep (10,000 years ago), then cattle (10,000 years ago), then the horse (6,000 years ago).

4.3.9. *Animal-Human Disease Vectors.* With the advent of sedentism, infectious disease replaced trauma as the prime cause of human death.[411] Many of humanity's most troublesome diseases emerged only after domestication of animals: poxes, malaria, influenza.

4.3.10. *Starvation and Over-Population.* Once settlements existed, more children survived and technologies for food preservation emerged. This facilitated yet larger populations, necessitating yet better food technologies. This Malthusian dilemma can be detected in the archeology of 15,000 years old Natufian villages;[412] it is still present in world cultures today. At one level, human culture is a race between our inventive capacity and our predilection for ill-considered reproduction. As compared to hunter-gatherers, residents of Neolithic villages were shorter, smaller, had more risk in childbirth, and lived shorter lives. Mobile Neolithic hunter-gatherers enjoyed a twenty-two percent health advantage over their village-bound contemporaries.[413]

4.4. *Human Brains.* Human brains differ in structure from other primates.

4.4.1. *Human Brains.* Human cranial capacity and prefrontal cortex complexity exceed that of other primates.

4.4.1.1. *Human Cranial Capacity.* The volume of the human neocortex (neomammalian) triples that of other modern apes (on a weight adjusted scale). Seventy-five percent of the human brain volume contains neocortex. The human limbic system (old mammalian heritage), the core of emotion processing which lies beneath the neocortex, doubles ape volume. The human brainstem (reptilian heritage, comprising the basal ganglia), which controls autonomic functions, retains its ancient volume. Brain volume alone, even adjusted for weight, is not a sufficient condition for human-like consciousness. The mouse lemur's brain contains three percent of its body weight; human brains are two percent of body weight.[414]

4.4.1.2. *Human Cortical Complexity.* Humans differ from other primates in cortical abilities as well as cranial size. Humans experience complex mental patterns, some of which seem unavailable to non-human mam-

---

[411] [♪] Wells, *Pandora's Seed*, 75.

[412] Natufians of the Middle East settled, but then returned to hunting and gathering during the dry period of the Younger Dryas. [♪] Wade, *Before the Dawn*, 127.

[413] [♪] Wells, *Pandora's Seed*, 23-24.

[414] Deacon, *Primate Brains*, 107.

mals. Humans speak languages with syntax. Nevertheless, fundamental emotional and impulse systems are similar in human and non-human mammals.

4.4.2. *Heightened Cortical Dependency*. The human cerebral neocortex interacts more strongly with limbic and brainstem systems than does the neocortex of rats. If one ablates a rat neocortex, the rodent continues to perform instinctual behaviors. If one ablates a human neocortex, the individual will be paralyzed.[415] The human neocortex performs no discrete functions. The neocortical structure weds deeply with underlying structures to generate human responses to environmental challenges. *Human cognition is best conceived as a loosely-coordinated array of emotionally-active action-oriented responses to sensory and motor input*.[416] This definition, however, fails to capture the essentially social orientation of human neural function.

4.4.3. *Cortical Fragility*. The human cortical abilities are strongly hierarchical, erected upon subcortical foundations. Neocortical functions depend upon brainstem and limbic systems in a non-reciprocal manner. Higher functions cease if lower functions fail; death ensues. Lower functions may persevere despite sore disruption of higher brain function.[417] The plight of vegetative comatose individuals illustrates this possibility.

4.4.4. *Cortical Evolutionary Speculations*. No one at present knows what specific environmental pressures favored heightened cerebral capacity with cortex complexity.[418] Theories abound:

4.4.4.1. *Upright Ambulation*. Human upright posture may have allowed subtle manipulation with the unburdened hands and consequent tool-making. Human cortical capacity may be a hand management adaptation.

4.4.4.2. *Social Vocalization*. African habitat may have favored larger groups, which necessitated more complex vocalization and communication. Human cortical capacity may result from language processing. Robin Dunbar argues that language depends upon the primate propensity for mutual grooming. Primates pick nits; humans gossip.[419]

---

[415] Panksepp, *Affective Neuroscience*, 77.

[416] Barton, "Evolution of the Social Brain," 139.

[417] Panksepp, *Affective Neuroscience*, 79.

[418] Panksepp, *Affective Neuroscience*, 326.

[419] Dunbar, *Grooming, Gossip and the Evolution of Language*, 78.

4.4.4.3. *Cooperative Breeding.* The long gestation of human fetuses and lengthy period of utter infant dependency may have favored social trust and bonding as child care, provisioning with food, and education burdens were shared. This "cooperative breeding" might have driven the human genome toward collaborative social interactions that favored increased human cortical capacity.[420] Sarah Blaffer Hrdy speculates that such cooperative breeding, in which mothers solicit alloparents to shoulder a share of infant care, may have long predated the rise of specifically human primates.

4.4.4.4. *Protein Scarcity.*   Ice Age environmental changes may have thinned early humans' food resources, making organized group hunting and wide resource distribution of great utility. Human cortical capacity may result from processing intense hunting interaction, developing new methods of food storage, and surviving in a harsh climate.[421]

4.4.4.5. *Social Intensity.* Some evolutionary epistemologists theorize that the brain structures underlying human emotion preceded those underlying our intellectual capacities. Increased human cortical capacity, leading to language, may result from managing social complexity caused by the emotional stress of intense social interactions. This is the "social brain hypothesis."[422]

4.4.4.6. *Resource Mapping.* The ability, in times of harsh climatic conditions, to recall where and when viable food sources existed, combined with communicating this information to one's group, may have driven human cortical evolution.[423]

4.4.4.7. *Multi-Species Symbiosis.* Humans, in hunting animals, always depended upon them as a protein and raw materials source. Observation of animals led to control of those animals, and, ultimately, domestication. The lives of the animals that humanity domesticated shaped humanity at the cultural and genetic levels. Humans departed nomadism, to an extent. We grew able to digest lactose. Domestication was bilateral; as humans adapted animals to culture, culture and the human genome conformed to the presence of and opportunities presented by animals. Early human ability to relate to and exploit non-human animals may have driven development of human cortical capacity.[424]

---

[420] Hrdy, *Mothers and Others*, 66.

[421] Panksepp, *Affective Neuroscience*, 328.

[422] Panksepp, *Affective Neuroscience*, 325. See also Dunbar, *How Many Friends*, 22-25.

[423] Marean, "When the Sea Saved Humanity," 61.

[424] Shipman, "The Animal Connection and Human Evolution, 519-538.

4.4.4.8. *Barter*. Exchange of goods and ideas created the dynamic of cultural progress. Cultural exchange of fire starting and cooking technologies enabled more evolutionary investment in brain structures and a relatively reduced expenditure on gut structures. Tool and implement design exchanges again increased efficiency of harvest and predation, freeing time for increased cultural exchanges, which also reduced risk during climatic and other environmental stresses. Economics may have driven the emergence of human cortical capacity.[425] The net effect of barter and increased cortical capacity was collective intelligence and the spread of specialization.

4.4.4.9. *Shared Intentionality*. Michael Tomasello's theory overlaps with several presented above. He argues that human cortical capacities emerged as a result of shared intentionality. Proto-humans made the first step by cooperating in food-gathering with others in their troop. The second step arose as population pressures grew and competition became more prevalent. Language resulted for the purpose of coordinating defensive and productive actions, with the effect that human group life became one big collaborative enterprise. "We" emerged as a plural agent, subsisting in the shared purposes of members. Communal thinking shares three characteristics: a) it searches for objectivity, because members have diverse, sometimes hostile, perspectives on a given matter (objective thinking), b) through individual members, it reflects on itself and makes inferences about members' intentions (reflective thinking), and c) it causes members to evaluate their own intentions and actions in light of the group's intensions and expectations (normative thinking). Human joint intentionality creates a collective perspective, a culture which members believe to be objective (which Tomasello calls the "view from nowhere.") Tomasello styles member mentation after jazz habits, suggesting that individuals improvise from their social position within an interactive cultural cohort.[426]

---

[425] [♪] Ridley, *The Rational Optimist*, 56. Ridley prefers the term "catallaxy" for denominating the idea that barter drove human collective-mindedness. The term was adapted by Friedrich Hayek to replace the word "economy," which he felt implied more goal sharing among participants in an economy than was warranted. The term "catallaxy" derives from a Greek word for reconciling accounts or admitting persons into a community (early Christians used this word to describe the salvific effect of Jesus' death on the cross).

[426] Tomasello, *A Natural History of Human Thinking*, ix, x, 1-5, 84, 93, 120. Stix reports experiments at the Max Plank Institute comparing the cognitive abilities of human toddlers and chimpanzees and orangutans. Intelligence scores for chimps and humans were roughly equal, but the toddlers vastly exceeded chimps in social-cognitive skills. The orangutans lagged behind both other species. The study's authors interpreted these results as demonstrating that human children possess an innate skill set for cultural intelligence that enables them to acquire from other humans learning in a manner that Michael Tomasello calls "shared intentionality." Dissenters dispute that the study ac-

4.5. *Subcortical Survival Strategies.* Human emotional systems evolved in response to typical Pleistocene dangers and opportunities. Affective experiences are patterned responses to survival challenges presented by the human Pleistocene environment indelibly written into our brain structure.[427] The human brainstem and limbic systems represent evolutionary "memory" of workable solutions to common survival challenges. The root brain structures (neocortical, limbic, and brainstem) have different tenors. Were each to speak (only the neocortex has linguistic capability), the primary resonance of the neocortex would be "is," of the limbic would be "ought," and of the brainstem would be "must."

> KNOWING MUCH GENERATES FOG.
> KNOWING LITTLE CONFIRMS CONFUSION.
> ONE KNOWS ENOUGH.
> NO MORE.

4.5.1. *Neocortical Inhibition.* The human neocortex evolved in response to inadequacy of brainstem motivations (hunger, thirst, sexual craving, warmth, etc.) and limbic responses (fear, revulsion, affection, etc.) in competition for scarce resources in the environment of evolutionary adaptedness (EEA). The neocortex modifies, mostly by inhibition, emotional responses and brainstem motivations. As such, the neocortex serves the evolutionarily ancient structures of the brain.[428] All brainstem motivation and limbic emotional output are modified in non-pathological humans by neocortical processing. But subcortical drives and affects potentiate learning; without them, facts would comprise an undifferentiated heap. The human neocortex adds no fundamentally new tools to the social adaptive skills humans share with most higher mammals.[429]

4.5.2. *Cortical Hyper-Valuation.* Individual consciousness *is* the neocortex functioning. As such, cognition[430] may have been dramatically over-

---

curately depicts the extent of social cooperative skills among chimpanzees, perhaps substantially under-estimating those skills. Stix, "The 'IT' Factor," 77, 79.

[427] Panksepp, *Affective Neuroscience,* 39.

[428] Panksepp, *Affective Neuroscience,* 72.

[429] Panksepp. "Prosocial Brain," 153.

[430] "Cognition" is an intellectual brain function that manipulates ideas and perceptions, including such operations as attention, language, reasoning, problem-solving, learning, remembering, and weighing alternatives. Cognition should be distinguished from affection (emotionality) and conation (willing). See footnote 110 above, which describes the differences between cognition, conation, and affection in dictionary parlance.

valued.   The philosophical community has long treated the individual cognition as the "individual."   It may be more accurate to identify the individual as the embodied brain in its total function, most of which functioning is subconscious.   It may advance our self-understanding to relegate consciousness, and its weak but haughty cousins, rationality and analysis, to the subservient position indicated by their evolutionary roots. Rationality is a splinter from the sequoia of consciousness.   Both constitute one tree in the forest of being.

4.5.3. *Role of Ratiocination.*   Elevating cognition to the pinnacle of individuality relegates critical survival functions to second-class status, overestimates the role of cognition in human behavior, and partitions the individual unreasonably.   Humans are not primarily thinking creatures.[431] Humans move, eat and evacuate, sleep, play, reproduce, fabricate, avoid danger, possess, domesticate, and so forth.   Infrequently, human ratiocination improves or innovates with respect to one or more of these functions. More frequently, human thinking wheedles giant conclusions from pygmy facts,[432] leading people to attempt untenable solutions.[433]   In evolution's game of survival, heeding our genetic voices (brainstem drives and limbic affects) points toward safer harbors.   The panoply of behaviors that lies below consciousness is primary among those that make our survival likely.[434]   Human affective responses imbue experience with value, and direct us to what is important among things we might deliberate consciously.[435]

4.5.4. *Dangers of Ratiocination.*   The imperatives of affective drives seldom pass rational muster.   Considered as cost-benefit decisions or linear point-A-to-point-B schemes, the drives of sex, hunger, parenting, relating, fear, anger, or other primal urges disappoint.   A danger of rational deliberation lies in concluding from the apparent rational shortcomings of subconscious imperatives that these imperatives are unimportant, contrary to reason, counter-productive, or even false.[436]   This error underlies rationalism,

---

[431] With typical hyperbolic negativity, Freud declares human intellect a trifle; instincts drive men. However, Freud finds in reason a persistent correction, which gently prods until heeded. [♪] Freud, *The Future of an Illusion*, 87, 96.

[432] Lucretius, *De Rerum Natura*, at a page citation I can no longer identify.

[433] It is so with this book, some allege.

[434] James Griffin argues that our prudential values are plural. Prudence leads one to actions portending well-being. These considerations are many. No one predominates. Griffin, *Well-Being*, 89.

[435] Brooks, "New Humanism."

[436] Ariely, *The Upside of Irrationality*, 294. Wittgenstein argues, following Hume, that no facts imply anything ethical, that one cannot derive ethical imperatives from fact statements. Any appearance that such might occur is a chimera. To say something ethical is to run up against the limitations

asceticism, solipsism, idealism, radical ethical relativism, logical positivism, and views of life that denigrate human affective expression. Rationality plays a role in human survival, but that role falls far short of the exuberances Enlightenment philosophers indulge. Ratiocination presents dangers, as well as opportunities.[437]

4.6. *Distortion Detection, Alternative Exploration.* Higher cortical functions may detect and divert perceptual distortions created by limbic[438] or brainstem[439] responses. Cognition deflects autonomic (brainstem) and limbic/affective scripted behaviors down unexplored avenues, proffering behavioral alternatives among which a member or community may deliberate and choose.[440] This sort of flexibility is a human hallmark, and a powerful evolutionary adaptation.[441]

4.6.1. *Human Conduct.* With choice among cognitive alternatives to limbic affects and brainstem impulses, one arrives at the root of human *conduct*. All animals, including humans, exhibit behaviors. Humans, and some higher mammals, *elect among behavioral alternatives,* which constitutes "conduct." Humans do not elect behaviors without constraints. Humans choose conduct from a delimited set of possible deviations from underlying emotional and impulse imperatives, which emerge from human limbic

---

of language, which enterprise Wittgenstein respects, but finds essentially nonsensical. Wittgenstein, "Lecture on Ethics." Buddhist dogma teaches that reality is illusory, and traps the unwary in their miserable reincarnations. The wise recognize the ephemeral non-existence of "reality," which falls short of the immutability one can imagine. All that is caused crumbles. Recognizing the transient nature of reality, one finds in its stead the bliss of perfect emptiness. [♪] *Dhammapada*, 40, 367. For an evolutionary take on anti-rationalism, Leidloff argues that proto-humans lived without worry until they acquired the ability to think, after which time thought distorted their cultures, issuing in similarly distorted living. One now must create a persistent habit of unthinking, such as meditation. Leidloff, *The Continuum Concept*, 132-133.

[437] Tagore argues that man is greatest where he is unconscious. Tagore, *Nationalism*, unpaginated.

[438] The limbic system is a related set of brain structures (hippocampus, amygdala, dentate gyrus, cingulate gyrus, gyrus fornicatus, the archicortex) in their functional interactions with the hypothalamus, septal area, and medial area of the mesencephalic tegmentum. This group of structures and interconnections influences more primitive behavior by modifying the output of the endocrine and autonomic motor systems. See *Taber's Cyclopedic Medical Dictionary, 17th Edition, s.v.* "limbic system." Arousal of these structures produces the underlying neural correlates of human emotion, which are also called "affective states."

[439] The reptilian brain is an explanatory simplification by Paul McLean of the function of deep brain structures of the brainstem or basal ganglia (also called the striatal complex or corpus striatum), which control biofunctions such as urination and defecation, the pattern of food seeking and inactivity, finding shelter, sexual courtship, and power distribution among members. Panksepp, *Affective Neuroscience*, 70.

[440] Panksepp, *Affective Neuroscience*, 72.

[441] The emergent school of "experimental philosophy" or "x-phi" mines cognitive and neuroanatomical research for insight about the ethical and other philosophical conflicts that humans experience.

and brainstem structures. Apart from impulse and affect, the human cortex, despite its potency, does nothing.[442]

Members and communities exhibit structure consistent with their genetic complement. Environments condition the expression of genes. A primary component of the human environment is human culture, which consists in the collective habits of members. Over habit, members and communities exercise some control, when desiring to do so.[443] The tangle of humanity's evolutionary trajectory creates difficulties (war, overpopulation, obesity, hierarchies, territoriality, as examples). The possibility lies open that, as humans have altered their evolutionary baseline in the past (dwelling in harsh environments, perpetrating less violence, reducing birth rates, as examples), we might cull a course toward a deliberated future.[444]

Not only are we evolved moral animal brains-in-bodies, Kate, but we are brains amidst other brains. In a culture devoted to individual glories, we may lose track of our fundamental togetherness. Alone, none prospers. Alone, we die psychologically, then physically. Solitude, also necessary, is not aloneness, but rather stints of respite from togetherness. Others shape us altogether, transmitting to each member a unique package of self-hood: genes[445], physical bodies, emotional attachment, language, microorganisms, habits, traditions, history, expectations, dreams, capital, and technologies. We wanly differentiate ourselves, a robust hat here, a penchant for baseball trivia there. Mostly, we pare ourselves to remain generally congruent with our social contexts. A few odd birds, whom I call neurodiverse savants, conform less expansively. Their packages are oddly tied; they bring us wonder. We hold our sociality in a sapless grip. Do otherwise.

5. *__Human Sociality__*. Humans are troop primates.

---

[442] Barton, *Evolution of the Social Brain*, 135. Joseph LeDoux says, "Consciousness is a small part of what the brain does, and it's a slave to everything that works beneath it." Cited in Lehrer, *How We Decide*, 23.

[443] Wright, despite his several contrary assertions, acknowledges that even the unspoken evolutionary logic that lies beneath the structure of human consciousness, determining its course, can be deflected by cultural norms. Wright, *The Moral Animal*, 173.

[444] I call that process thanatoid transgenerational deliberation. See below at Section IV. Immanuel Kant reminds us that all such enlightenment of the public can proceed only at a glacial pace (that is, transgenerationally). Rushing deep change in values eradicates one mental despotism only to replace it with another. Kant, *What Is Enlightenment?*, 136.

[445] Gustav Landauer urges that a man is but the most recent instance of the species-spanning community of ancestors. Predecessors are no more dead than we. Our stuff is theirs; theirs ours. We are droplets in the stream of their waters. Landauer, *Through Separation to Community*, 103.

5.1. *Primate Troops.* Most primates are troop animals. Primates breed and forage in relatively small groups that may overlap at territorial margins with other troops. The numbers of members in primate troops are relatively stable, limited by the neural capacity of the individual species, as well as available resources.[446]

5.2. *Niche Construction.* In evolutionary terms, human cerebral capacity and cranial complexity is an "adaptation adaptation." Human bodies lack specialized ecological niche adaptations, such as claws, fur, or echolocation. Human behaviors deviate from primate antecedents in the extent of human capacity for adaptation by culture and tool-making. Humans adapt genetically as well, as do all living creatures. But human adaptivity accelerates in culture. Human technical and cultural adaptations look to a single fact as their source: the ability to store and retrieve knowledge outside our bodies. The emergence of language facilitated useful knowledge stored in other human brains. The technology of writing, books, and now computers facilitate retrieval of knowledge of vast scope and in media more reliable than human memory. Matt Ridley goes so far as to assert that evolution continues apace, not only biologically, but also in the marketplace of ideas. Our minds, considered as cybernetically-interacting complex systems, generate ideas that alter members' survival odds. Genes inhabiting members in communities that generate better adapted ideas are more likely to survive to reproduce themselves. Some evolutionary pressures are, for humans, idea-driven.[447]

> ONE IS BORN OF BODY FROM A KNOWN WOMB,
> A GENETIC FAMILY,
> A GENERAL EDUCATION,
> THE USUAL ATTACHMENTS,
> MASTERY OF UTILITY,
> PEDESTRIAN JOBS,
> AND DEATH IN THE BY-AND-BY.
> ONE IS BORN OF MIND FROM AN UNKNOWN WOMB,
> A FAMILY OF FRIENDS,
> PECULIAR EXCURSIONS,
> OPULENT COMPANIONSHIPS,
> BOOKS LIKE BANK VAULTS,
> OBSESSIONS WITH GODS,
> AND DEATH CONFRONTED DAILY.

---

[446] Zhou, "Social Group Size Organization," 440.

[447] [♪] Ridley, *The Rational Optimist*, 5.

5.3. *Adaptive Alternatives*.   Like many species, humans artificially expand survival niches by means of tools employed as body extensions. Niche construction influences natural selection by modifying environmental selection pressures, increasing the likelihood that the niche constructor may survive.[448]   Humans proliferate because we create quasi-tropical microenvironments by means of clothing and shelters wherever we reside, including underwater, polar, and hard vacuum venues.[449]   These tools and toolmaking strategies are transmitted through generations by culture. Cultures are an evolutionary adaptation of humankind, one purpose of which is to transmit adaptive alternatives.

5.4. *Cultural Critical Mass*.   When lacking sufficient numbers of individuals or sufficient numbers of cultural and trade contacts, cultures regress. Considered aggregately, the human trading and cultural community form a collective mind,[450] and insufficient numbers generate a sort of cultural dementia. Regular infusions of innovation and deviation create a cascade of exchanges that enervate cultural adaptation.

5.5. *Gene-Culture Coevolution*.   Cultures interact strongly with genetic potentials, creating a human cognitive niche as well.[451] Culture may be construed as niche construction seen from a psychological or social viewpoint. Cultures alter the environment in which the human genetic complement unfolds. A single genome[452] may unfold with different phenotypes[453] in response to altered environments. Some argue that human evolution has become a "gene-culture coevolution."[454] Strong evidence indicates that neither nature nor nurture predominate in shaping human behavior. Rather, genes express themselves upon stimulation and learning presented in the

---

[448] Laland, *Niche Construction*, 36-37.

[449] Pilbeam, *What Makes Us Human?*, 2.

[450] [♪] Ridley, *The Rational Optimist*, 80-83. Ridley recounts the "Tasmanian regress," in which the Stone Age immigrants to Tasmania suffered a loss of essential technologies already in their possession due to lack of outside infusion of ideas and insufficient numbers to specialize all the critical skills. The Tasmanians degenerated from fishing and maritime sufficiency to clubbing seals.

[451] Mameli, *Evolution and Psychology in Philosophical Perspective*, 24.

[452] The genes contained in a haploid set of chromosomes. See *Webster's Third New International Dictionary*, s.v. "genome." A haploid set of chromosomes contains one-half the number of chromosomes in a normal body cell (which is a diploid set of chromosomes), and the same number as sexual reproduction cells, which are called gametes.

[453] The physical characteristics of an organism, the observable result of gene-environment interaction. See *Webster's Third New International Dictionary*, s.v. "phenotype."

[454] Mameli, *Evolution and Psychology in Philosophical Perspective*, 31.

member's environment. The primary constituent of a human's environment is its social and cultural, not its physical, components.

5.5.1. *Lactose Tolerance.* An example of gene-culture coevolution is human lactose tolerance, which is a genetic adaptation to domestication of milk-producing ruminants. As domesticated herds made milk products a ready source of nutrition, the milk-abundant environment presented selection pressure favoring lactose tolerant individuals. Human culture has responded to the adaptive lag of a portion of its population with drugs that mimic lactose tolerance.

5.5.2. *Sickle Cells.* Another example of gene-culture coevolution is sickle cell blood characteristics, which confer advantages in malaria-ridden niches created by agriculture.

5.5.3. *Disease Pressures.* Similar changes may be underway in the human genome with respect to AIDS, diabetes, hypertension, alcohol tolerance, carbohydrate tolerance, and obesity.

5.6. *Interpenetration.* Members and the primate troop community interpenetrate. Genetically, member DNA slowly intermixes over time. Physically, members take sustenance from the environment and share foodstuffs with one another. Biologically, the environment hosts the primate community and its members individually; primates in turn host a great number of microscopic and parasitic communities within their bodies, some of which are essential to survival. In humans, bacteria outnumber human cells ten-to-one.[455] Psychologically, members and troops experience intersubjectivity. This dynamic mutualism, in which self-concepts and private experience reciprocally invade and are invaded by group-preference and collective sharing, waxes and wanes in member consciousness.[456] Subconscious neural mechanisms coordinate members' subjective experiences. Psychological affect and actions, through neural mirroring, and ideas and habits, through social learning (culture), slowly conform and synchronize to troop norms. Consciously, many primate activities emerge from pleasure and gain associated with elective grouping.

---

[455] Ackerman, "How Bacteria In Our Bodies Protect Our Health," 38.

[456] "Dynamic mutualism" is my coinage (or I may have forgotten where I stole the words) to describe the role of individual and collective in Hebrew sacred texts, which concept spills over into New Testament ecclesiology, and from there into contemporary Christian theology. See unpublished manuscript: Lancaster, *"Corporate Personality": Sociality in Old Testament Anthropology.* August 1981, and unpublished manuscript: Lancaster, *I-Thou Personalism: An Anthropological Inquiry,* January 1981. The former relies upon works of Peter Berger, Thomas Kuhn, H. Wheeler Robinson, and J. W. Rogerson. The latter relies upon works of B. F. Skinner, Karl Marx, Rene Descartes, Georg W. F. Hegel, John Macmurray, Max Scheler, Soren Kierkegaard, Ludwig Feuerbach, Ferdinand Ebner, Martin Buber, Karl Barth, Emil Brunner, and Dietrich Bonhoeffer. Rousseau argues that human society is a corporate personality that possesses a will distinguishable from that of its particulate members. Rousseau, "A Discourse on Political Economy," 132.

5.7. *Human Interpenetration.* As primates, human members and their social communities interpenetrate in a manner complicated by an overlay of ideas and cultural innovations.

Where healthy, human interpenetration mimics the primate norm.

5.7.1. *Member Porosity.* Language lends deep complexity and great breadth to social mixing. The member's self commingles with others.[457] Others penetrate the self, rendering the borders of individuality indeterminate. De Waal notes that at its root, empathy is direct sharing of bodily states automatically mirrored from an observed other.[458] Self infuses others.[459] The member identity is shaped by the social matrix[460] of groups in which he or she participates. Members' genetic substance, childhood nurture and rearing (and hence attachment, leading to ability to care about others), language and cultural particularities, religious sensitivities, and sense of meaning derive from the member's social community.

5.7.2. *Community Instantiation.* Groups imbibe selves, shaping group identity in response to members of momentary importance.[461] Collectives emerge from social webs of differentiated members. Self and group mingle; they are interdependent. Members instantiate groups, and constitute a collective's physical substance. Groups are the environment into which members are born, educated, and meaningfully occupied. Ultimately, the human group is the context in which each member's contributions aggregate and find appreciation. The conditions of meaningful community demand differentiated selves living within cohesive social groups.[462]

---

[457] Aristotle styles the intimate friend as another self. [♪] Aristotle, *Nichomachean Ethics*, 179 (1170b). Frans de Waal characterizes human empathy as a fundamental "blurring of the line between self and other." De Waal, *The Bonobo and the Atheist*, 33.

[458] De Waal, *The Bonobo and the Atheist*, 131-132. Although the neural mirror matrix is of recent discovery, one finds express discussion of the sociological fact of mirroring in nineteenth century thinker Arthur Schopenhauer. He argues that compassion erodes the distinction between self and other, creating a (weak) identification between the two. "The difference between myself and him is no longer an absolute one. . . . The non-ego to a certain extent [is] identified with the ego," which process Schopenhauer finds fundamentally mysterious. Its scope extends to other animals. Schopenhauer, *The Basis of Morality*, 85-86, 102, 111. From interpenetration springs compassion.

[459] Donald Pfaff suggests a subconscious physiological basis for interpenetration. He argues that altruistic activities emerge from an automatic blending of images of oneself and the other (which he calls cross-excitation). One acts compassionately by doing the act for another as though doing it for oneself. Pfaff, *Altruistic Brain Theory*, 58-59.

[460] A matrix is a context or substance within which something different emerges. *Webster's Third New International Dictionary*, s.v. "matrix" at §2a.

[461] [♪] Freud, *Civilization and Its Discontents*, 136-137 (Chapter 8). Freud speculates on the communal super-ego and its relation to the leading personalities.

[462] See [♪] Buber, *I and Thou*, all. Emmanuel Levinas argues that the idea of being is itself limited and subordinate, and advocates for the metaphysical concept that reality is subjective, interpersonal,

Where defective, human sociality withers, imposing pathologies upon its victims.

5.7.3. *Solipsism.* Solipsistic[463] self-preservation is an evolutionary dead end. The solipsist makes his lone criterion for action his own needs and desires, much to the neglect of his fellows. Contrary to the solipsist, individuals need others.[464] The lone individual remains, despite his contrary self-concept and western culture's support for this individualistic misapprehension, a member of a (massively malfunctioning) community.

5.7.4. *Conformity.* Unfettered coercive socialization[465] is an evolutionary dead end. Human communities need eccentrics. Communities require some differentiated members, that is, members who are tolerated despite their inability or unwillingness to conform to group expectations. Every member, in fact, secrets some incommensurate oddities in herself, aspects of self that cannot be conformed, despite effort to do so. These idiosyn-

---

and pre-eminently "otherwise than being." Levinas, *Otherwise Than Being*, 26. Elsewhere, Levinas argues that time itself emerges from relationship. Levinas, *Time and the Other*, 39. Muhammad reports that wherever men talk, Allah is there as a conversant, adding under-appreciated depth to those exchanges. *Qur'an*, Sura 58:7. See Rahman, *Major Themes of the Qur'an*, 37-38.

[463] A solipsistic individual indulges and defends himself at the expense or abject neglect of others. See *Webster's Third New International Dictionary*, s.v. "solipsism" at §3. Here, though we grant each member's need to survive, we caution that individual survival without group cohesion is itself a threat to members.

[464] Aristotle argues that man is in his essence social. [♪] Aristotle, *Politics*, 13 (Book I, §1253a). See also [♪] Aristotle, *Nichomachean Ethics*, chapters 8-9 on friendship. Cicero argues that the friend is another self. [♪] Cicero, *De Amicitia*, 189 (§80). Human identity emerges from interpenetrating dyads. The pre-eminent such relationship is the divine-human dyad. [♪] Buber, *I and Thou*, 56 (Part I). The deutero-Pauline Epistle to the Ephesians characterizes the existence of the church as one new man in Christ. The early church conceived itself as one person, the body of Christ. *Ephesians* 2:13-22. Dietrich Bonhoeffer's doctorial dissertation argues that sociologically, the church can be conceived as a collective person, and that Christ exists as the church, considered as a collective person. Bonhoeffer, *Sanctorum Communio*, 102. Levinas argues that our encounter with another is primal, preceding all thought, which event renders ethics logically prior to knowledge. One's subjectivity and responsibility emerges from our subjection to the other, the neighbor. See Levinas, *Otherwise than Being*, 46-47 (Exposition 4.a.) Fascist thinkers, such as Gentile (Mussolini's pet philosopher) and Hitler argue that the individual arises from the national collective, which logically precedes all individuality. A citizen owes ultimate loyalty to his *volk*. Hitler mashes the concept of a "people" with that of a "race," which he alleges he can rank. See [♪] Hitler, *Mein Kampf*, 373-385 (Volume II, Chapter I, "Philosophy and Party.") Giovanni Gentile, argues that the individual is truly free only within his collective. The "independent individual" is phantasmal and delimited by the terror of solitude. Humans are collective beings. The State precedes the individual both historically and logically. Individuals emerge because States exist. See [♪] Mussolini, *The Doctrine of Fascism*, 10 (Gentile ghost-wrote this section of Mussolini's work). Gentile, *The Origin and Doctrine of Fascism*, 25-26.

[465] "Socialization" means the activities by which a maturing member is trained for adulthood, learning the habits (language, beliefs, stories, technologies, and so forth) of that member's society. See *Webster's Third New International Dictionary*, s.v. "socialization." Here, the phrase contemplates social schemas in which deviation from norms is strongly punished, seeking unalloyed social conformity.

crasies, most evident in neurodiverse savants, are the wedges by which communities pry themselves loose from stifling sameness, launching explorations of the untried. Communities must remain "loose at the joints," not requiring too strict adherence to community demands.[466] Community conformity and member recalcitrance balance the weal of self and others.[467]

5.8. Communication.

5.8.1. *Non-Verbal Communication.* The most ancient, and more reliable, form of communication is non-verbal (sometimes called gestural). These communication skills developed early in primate evolution, and entail reading faces and gestures, coordinating activities by contextual cues. Non-verbal communication also drives human interaction with domesticated species.

5.8.2. *Oral Communication.* Oral communication in at least some rudimentary form must have accompanied gestural language from early hominin prehistory. Full-blown language would have emerged as the physical glottis, tongue, and neural capacity for framing such interactions emerged in the hominin line. Details of this emergence are likely to be poorly preserved in archeological records. Wade suspects that the emergence of expansive language capabilities may be what distinguishes physically-modern humans (commencing around 100,000 years ago) from behaviorally-modern humans (commencing around 50,000 years ago).[468]

5.8.3. *Graphic Communication.* Writing words that mirror spoken language first emerged around 3200 B.C. in the fertile crescent. Writing numbers preceded that development. Writing may have developed independently in Egypt and China. Writing certainly developed independently in Mexico around 600 B.C. Writing is a form of extra-brain memory, retaining information in a form more durable than one's own or others' individual

---

[466] Christopher Boehm hypothesizes that morality begins in suppressing social deviance. A group has some cooperative purpose, which is derailed by a socially disruptive "wrongdoer." The wrongdoer is punished,. Over millennia, an inner sensitivity evolved to conditions that might lead to such suppression by others—a conscience. Once conscience exists, morality rides onto the human stage. Boehm, *Moral Origins*, 15.

[467] Some overstate the influence of good impulses. Chinese philosopher, Mencius, argued that no man, no matter how evil, has a heart insensitive to people's suffering. *Mencius*, 38 (Book II, Part A.6.) Men are inherently good, though they may be made bad by human means, like splashing water uphill. *Mencius*, 122 (Book VI, Part A,2). Had Mencius no sociopaths? (He did, and addressed them. If cruel men desisted, there would be no failed States or disintegrating families. *Mencius*, 80 (Book IV, Part A,8).) Some overstate the influence of evil impulses. Chinese philosopher, Hsün Tzu, considered human evil ineradicable, blunted only by great effort. Ill-acts proliferate among normal people, who are stupid and undisciplined. [♪] Han Fei Tzu, *Basic Writings*, 93-95 (Section 18: Facing South).

[468] [♪] Wade, *Before the Dawn*, 30-31.

memories. Technologies for extra-brain memory retention have been rapidly evolving in recent centuries. Consider books, printing, digital computers, video, the internet, and other recording and data retention technologies.

5.8.4. *Language-Game Theory.* Ludwig Wittgenstein emphasizes the fluidity of our language capabilities. Lest one think that words mean what dictionaries say, Wittgenstein fashions "language-game" theory of semantics. Words are part of activity. When humans do things, they utter sounds in conjunction. These sounds (words) mean what their role in the activity is. The components of language have no one characteristic, but all the components are related in some way. That is what makes them language. One must look, not suppose.

The word "game" describes many activities, none of which share characteristics with every other game. In the end, concepts overlap to greater and lesser degrees and no one element describes them all. Games share family characteristics. The concept spins many fibers into a thread. No fiber extends the length of the thread. Words are used indeterminately. We can make them rigid, but in normal use they lack frontiers. Some rules apply to some parts of the game; others are left free-floating.

This semantic indeterminacy does not cripple language; it is its nature. Normal descriptions convey meaning. More exact descriptions convey more exact, and slightly different, meanings. Even exact pictures of things described, with myriad details, change the language-game. The game entails semantic indeterminacy. Some would argue that indistinct concepts are useless. Wittgenstein responded that indistinctness is exactly what we need sometimes. We explain games by showing in a general sort of way how they are played; then we play and others join in.[469]

The moral of Wittgenstein's language-game story is this: language is embedded in social interaction; its meaning changes from one use-in-context to the next. To know the meaning of a word, one must observe its use in social context.

5.9. *Friendship.* The human capacity for friendship defines humanity's social parameters. Among chimpanzees, troop outsiders represent threat. Such invaders are killed. There exists no survivable path from outside the chimpanzee troop to inside the troop. Among bonobos, equally as similar to us as chimpanzees, outsiders are cause for concern but are often welcomed. Humans share both capacities. We confront outsiders, sometimes killing.

---

[469] Wittgenstein, *Philosophical Investigations*, 29-29 (Sections 67-71).

We also welcome strangers. The human ability to establish enduring bonds with persons who were originally strangers defines human sociality. Friendship, not family, is the core social bond. Our valuation of families often loses track of the fact that the core of the familial relationship is friendship between a man and woman, and that children remain part of families only to the extent that adult friendship follows a child's maturation. Friendship, conceived as supra-sexual bonding of non-kin members, stands at the root of all human community. As such, friendship is the most essential human predilection and skill.

5.10. *Dyads and families.* Human sexual pairing, as a subspecies of friendship formation, leads to procreation. Where healthy, families resolve into adult friendships as the members mature and take their places in cadres of their own within the human community.

5.11. *Prehistoric Clumping.* Human troop structure persevered until population pressures created competition for resources. Systematic violence, as opposed to occasional opportunistic raiding, erupted. The human response was, until frontiers vanished, to pack up and move from conflict-laden contexts. So, humans spread across all land masses over the course of forty thousand or so years. Migration diminished local population pressures and resource scarcity. When over every hill lay another troop, and empty valleys disappeared, human troops faced unprecedented danger. Troops sought strength in numbers, organizing larger collectives, to bolster resistance to predation by neighbors. Human culture responded with social barriers to cope with anonymous neighbors. Classes, neighborhoods, clubs, gangs, peoples, and sports teams superseded the troop, which shrank, in the end, to the bare nub of nuclear families. That long journey commenced when troops began clumping and building defense works. Hence, hamlets, then towns, then cities, then megalopoli. Each departure exceeded the former, leaving humans mired in anonymity.

5.12. *Pathological Population Growth.* As radical overpopulation spread, community size metastasized, creating bloated collectives beneath which we have struggled for millennia. Where these communities exceed human social capacity (troop size around 1,500), they erode meaning, fail to nurture most members, employ coercive manipulations, do violence, and enforce anonymity. Yet, to survive, people tolerate these alien social structures. For to be altogether alone is to die.

We are, evolutionarily, given to small groups. There, everyone knows everyone. In small groups, concern about reputation and reciprocity precludes the need for laws, armies, defenses, universal gods, and exclusive territories. Humans cooperate and create collaboratively when they are not socially swamped.[470]

Objection 12: Individualism: Some demur that the author now indulges metaphysical inanity. Selves do not interpenetrate. We learn. We care, on good days. We get born. We give and receive. My body is my own, despite being host to myriad bugs. Humans are not members, but individuals. We stand freely, without supports except those we choose. I am grateful to my parents for their care, but I grew up and left home. I may choose a spouse. We may elect to have children. I may drink beer with buddies at my favorite watering hole. But they are not in me, nor I in them. We share friendship, but that is nothing creepy. Monkeys may "interpenetrate." Apes do a lot of things humans do not do. But humans do not walk on all fours, and apes do not use cell phones. I would be sad if all my friends and family died. But I would survive. I am tough. I am an adaptable individual. All this "social interpenetration" talk, if it is not some weird sex lingo, is just religious-sounding, misbegotten leftist flatulence.

Response: Social interpenetration is a weird idea. That I grant. Each stands individually, discrete from every other person. We are separate enough to be identified, whether one calls us members or individuals. There is a tendency, inherent in rational dissection, to deem each subject of attention a separate entity. Then the rational dissecter asks, How do these various entities interact? He names each interaction, and calls the ball of wax an "explanation." I take the objector's self-perception of imperious individuality to be a rational dissection of his social existence. As you may have guessed, I am not enthusiastic about "rational dissection" explanations. Though they work well with machines and simple physical systems, dissections poorly capture the energetic dynamism of complex systems, especially when the system in question is as massively intricate and interactive as primate brains in the company of a troop of primate brains in their home range. What we have learned about complex systems is that they need to be comprehended in their entirety, not just their parts. "Interpenetration" turns one's focus from discrete individuals to the gestalt[471] of their togetherness. Interpenetration, as a concept, captures the interactions of a group of humans in a social setting wholistically.

Members emerge in a stream of life commencing in the deep past, proceeding to the deep future. The member's genetic stuff is the stuff of that history, elementally the detritus of star death, and more recently the DNA of pond scums. In the human time frame, the member emerges from parents, then nurtures children herself, then dies. As a member, she is porous both physically and psychically. The waters of the earth are the same waters in her blood. The pathogens and poisons and nutrients and symbiotes of her home live within and without

---

[470] De Waal argues that big gods (universal gods) became necessary when communities crumbled in the onslaught of overpopulation. Cities need gods with big eyes peering down upon all acts to tamp down free-riding and rapacity. In human-sized communities, one's neighbors did that. De Waal, *The Bonobo and the Atheist*, 219-220.

[471] "Gestalt" is a borrowed German word that denotes the overall feel or function of a combination of structures, ideas, or creatures, which result surpasses the mere combination of those elements. See *Webster's Third New International Dictionary*, s.v. "gestalt."

her. The ideas and habits and gods of her neighbors become, unwittingly, her own. The objector prefers to conceive himself as an intrepid individual, immune to such communal intermingling. He misses that the human is a child of the skein of life, woven to its warp and woof. As for the objector, these rudimentary interconnectivities often elude neurotypical consciousness.

Human relations extend far beyond mere utility ("Get me a beer"). Human relations extend beyond group habits ("We always drink beer on Thursdays.") Human relations extend to meaning ("We live together, and share a history. You affect me, and I you, and that is a rich experience. I cannot imagine life without these friends and family. And, yes, on Thursdays, we drink beer.") Thinking individualistic thoughts amputates whole limbs of human sociality. Individualism is whistling in a desert. Interpenetration is a Viennese symphony.

Not only are we evolved moral and social animal brains-in-bodies, Kate, but our subjective experience of the world (that is, our consciousness) bears an underlying structure different from that we have previously imagined. We are not rational actors taming the beast of unbridled emotion. Rather, we are creatures of assorted fundamental drives, diverted by affective (mostly social) imperatives, which are occasionally deflected from untoward outcomes by conscious inhibition, planning, and perspective. I call this drive-affect-inhibition hierarchy the "coppice of consciousness," which is expressed in multiple semi-independent columns of predispositions to action. This view of the human brain derives from Jaak Panksepp's research into (mostly) rat neurology. Viewing the brain as a tiered hierarchy of competing modules helps explain the many fault lines that dog human decision-making. Our heuristics conflict. We hold our coppice consciousness in an anemic grip. Do otherwise.

6. ***Human Consciousness.*** As a human interacts with her environment, the brain processes internal and external stimulations. Subconscious brain subsystems weed those excitations, eliminating most. Those that portend promise or threat proceed toward consciousness, being adjusted by emotive dispositions. Consciousness consists in neocortical manipulation of those bits of highly-processed subcortical stimulations that mount sufficient intensity to demand attention. Consciousness attends only a tiny fraction of brain subsystem output. The great bulk of neural activity lies below its threshold. This unattended mass of activity is subconscious.[472] The subconscious brain plugs away in anonymity, nurturing the human member in unattended labors: maintaining digestion, cardiac and pulmonary functions, human relations,

---

[472] Timothy Wilson finds consciousness the lesser player in human mental events. Our subconscious minds fabricate our world and roles in it, operating in unappreciated parallel to conscious events. In Wilson's view, conscious efforts, which he calls "story editing" revise subconscious self-narratives. With a revised personal narrative, one may experience new possibilities and impetus. He recommends writing exercises, skilled prompting from professionals, imagining your best self, and starting the good work for which you hope, trusting that your subconscious will straggle along as your habits firm up. Wilson, *Redirect,* 11-17, 27.

Dear Dr. Cohen:

I send you a copy of my recent work. We have not met. I studied Philosophy at UW in 1975-76.
I thought you might enjoy taking a look because of your efforts in sociality and decision-making.
I work now as an attorney in north Seattle.

Thank you for your kindnesses toward others.

Respectfully,

Brad Lancaster

SAINT
GEORGE'S
HILL
PRESS

BRAD LANCASTER
17503 10ᵀᴴ AVE. NE
SHORELINE, WASHINGTON 98155
206-367-3122
brad@lancasterlawoffice.com

June 8, 2017

Marc A. Cohen
Seattle University, Department of Philosophy, Casey 4E
901 12th Avenue. P.O. Box 222000
Seattle, WA 98122-1090

Re: A GIFT OF

Lancaster, Cull: Choosing Well
Lancaster, Cull: Epitomes

sexual cycles, temperature, nutrition, and general homeostasis. The subconscious brain processes sensory input, especially visual input, winnowing it by orders of magnitude. The particular structure of human brain architecture and its history of construction in evolution help explain many conundra about consciousness.

> WITHIN ME FLICKERS A LIGHT, SAYS ONE.
> THE LUMEN WAXES IN CHALLENGE,
>   AT THE NOVEL,
>   IN THE THRALL OF BEAUTY.
> THE FLAME DIMS IN TEDIUM,
>   AT THE USUAL,
>   IN THE GRIP OF THE BANAL.
> MY LIGHT BLAZES MORNINGS,
>   IN THE GLOW OF CHOCOLATE,
>   IN TUTELAGE OF CAREFUL THINKERS.
> MY FLAME SPUTTERS AT NIGHTFALL,
>   IN THE GRIP OF TERRORS,
>   IN THE HACKING OF CHATTERERS.
> WHERE GO I WHEN THE INCONSTANT FLAME WANES?
> I PERSIST, SAYS ONE.
>   IN DARKNESS, I PERSIST.

6.1. *Brain architecture and function.* In gross function, the human brain exhibits hierarchical tri-partite structure: brainstem, overlaid by the limbic system, overlaid by the neocortex. Within individual neurons, signal communication is electrical. Between neurons, which gaps are called synapses, signal communication is chemical. Interneuronal communication emerges from the chemistry of synaptic gaps, determined by a host of bodily processes producing neurotransmitters or their enzyme predecessors and successors. Consciousness emerges from the global function of the human brain, but is only a fraction of the human brain's total activity in sustaining the individual as an organism.[473]

6.1.1. *Physical structure.* Considered in its gross anatomy, the brain evolved as an involution of dermis. The brain is a specialized skin. The intracranial brain has a tri-partite structure.

---

[473] I am asked where the soul resides in all this yammer about brains. Consciousness is one phenomenon (among many) associated with having a brain. No unbrained consciousness exists, so far as I can determine. As Christof Koch put it: "No matter, never mind." Koch, *The Quest for Consciousness*, 17 (footnote 28). Marvin Minsky says, of the insistence of some that humans have a soul-ish core: "A more realistic view would recognize that each human mind that exists today is one result of a process in which decillions of previous creatures on Earth spent their lives reacting, adjusting, adapting, and dying so that some of their descendants might thrive. In that unthinkably vast history, all those creatures contributed to a tremendous set of experiments, each of which may have contributed to giving us slightly more powerful brains." Minsky, *The Emotion Machine*, 342.

6.1.1.1. *Nested Hierarchy*: The human brain comprises a nested hierarchy. Ancient basal structures, located in the **brainstem** and cerebellum, co-ordinate fundamental drives to eat, purge, sleep, breed, and survive. We share these structures with all vertebrates as far back in evolutionary time as amphibians and reptiles. As an evolutionary proposition, these structures have been deeply conserved through all of subsequent evolutionary changes.[474] Mammalian neural developments, located in the several substructures collectively called the **limbic system,** blanket the brainstem. Limbic structures organize affective[475] social nurturance. We share these structures with all mammalian life. The **neocortex**, comprising seventy-five percent of the human brain by volume, over-arches both older structures, integrating strongly with each. Some other mammals with substantial necortical structures are the great apes, dogs, cats, monkeys, bears, and cetaceans.

6.1.1.2. *Behavioral Inhibition*. Evolutionary triune brain architecture[476] follows engineering rules humans would be unlikely to adopt. Only maladaptive structures atrophy; neutral and adaptive structures perse-vere. The brain evolved by adding new adaptive structures atop older brain structures, each integrating with the structures below and inhibit-ing the impulses of older structures. Evolutionarily, emotions represent ancient memory, patterned behaviors responsive to common environ-mental challenges. Affective scripts exhibit greater subtlety and sophis-tication than reptilian activity.[477] Reptilian behavioral scripts diverted by affective concerns become mammalian scripts. The social mammal emerges. Overlying the limbic system, the neocortex rests atop and deeply links to both more ancient structures. Again, the neocortex in-hibits and redirects mammalian and reptilian behavioral scripts, issuing complex higher mammalian behavior. Within this tripartite complexity, one must recall that every brain area has access to every other area by means of some neural pathway. In general, action emerges as drives in the deeper structures commence behaviors that are then modified or in-hibited by the overlying structure(s).[478] Thus, the human literally

---

[474] Panksepp and Biven, *The Archaeology of Mind*, 392.

[475] "Affective" describes things relating to or arising from feelings and emotions. *Webster's Third New International Dictionary*, s.v. "affective."

[476] The concept of the "triune brain" was popularized by Paul McLean. See MacLean, *Triune Brain*, 1990.

[477] Panksepp. "Prosocial Brain," 145-151.

[478] Were the human brain an automobile, all brains would be Ford Model As at root. When better engines emerged, a stronger frame was welded to the Model A and an eight-cylinder engine laid atop

"thinks better" of a course of action when she inhibits impulses or motivations deemed inappropriate under her circumstances.

Behavioral inhibition is not, however, all of a sort. Panksepp argues that drives emerge in columns through affective structures toward the cerebral cortex.[479] Several columns exist. Some support and intensify one another when acting in concert. Others weaken one another when stimulated simultaneously. The interactions are complex.

PAUL LONGS FOR A SEXUAL PARTNER. AT HIS CHURCH, HANNAH SEEMS RIGHT. FRIENDS PROD PAUL. HE AND HANNAH SPEAK AT COFFEE AFTER SERVICE AND ENJOY ONE ANOTHER'S COMPANY. HANNAH INVITES PAUL FOR DINNER AT A LOCAL DINER. MID-MEAL, PAUL BECOMES UNCOMFORTABLE. HE CANNOT SAY WHY. SOMETHING FEELS WRONG, SOMETHING DEEP AND INARTICULABLE. HANNAH APPEARS WELL-SUITED TO PAUL. YET, SOMETHING IS AWRY. THE TWO COMPLETE THEIR MEAL. PAUL THANKS HANNAH FOR HER INVITATION AND COMPANY. THROUGH THE WEEK, PAUL STRUGGLES TO FATHOM HIS FEELINGS, TO NO AVAIL. PAUL DOES NOT SEEK HANNAH'S COMPANY AGAIN.

6.1.1.3. *Self.* The foundational sense of "self" may arise where the brainstem interfaces with elements of the limbic system (specifically, at the mesencephalic periaqueductal gray (MPAG), which is also called the central gray). In these evolutionarily ancient structures, brainstem autonomic functions are overlaid by structures containing primitive affective scripts (fear, anger, sexual impulse, pleasure, pain), creating a sense of the animal presence as an individual located in its environment.[480]

---

the original. Windows, shocks, springs were retrofitted. Eventually an AM radio was stuck to the dash. Finally, yet another frame of aluminum and structural steel was added, and a hydrogen fuel cell engine wedded to the power train. An eight track tape player was installed, followed by a cassette player, a CD player, and digital download music. Finally, web-linked video screens were attached at each seat, and a GPS taped to the Model A gearshift. Throughout the process, mechanics of great skill work to integrate the disparate and time-diverse systems so the vehicle functioned as well as possible, given its design limitations. The analogical vehicle moves by shifting the Model A transmission, engaging the Model A motor, which then stimulates the eight-cylinder engine to purr to life, cuing the fuel cell engine ignition. This latter either puts the car into motion or idles the lower engines. Evolution does not engineer as might human intelligence.

[479] Panksepp, *Affective Neuroscience*, 72-79.

[480] Panksepp, *Affective Neuroscience*, 77. Subsequently, Panksepp has argued that the exact anatomical structures involved in generating the core sense of SELF are indeterminate and his hypothesis controversial. But the MPAG meets the criteria for such functional structures. He further specifies the SCMS/CMS system (a group of related ancient deep midline structures), of which the MPAG is a component, as "the most ancient, and most highly concentrated, emotional convergence zone within the brain," and the "epicenter of the core SELF," which orchestrates the emotional outputs of the human brain. This is to hypothesize a deeply subconscious self (*anoetic*) which serves as a foundation for the conscious self (*noetic*). "The PAG may be the most important location in the brain, because it is richly connected to both higher and lower brain functions. It is a Grand Central Station

This "self" is not the full-blown existential self of ordinary human experience, but rather its foundation, the basement sub-self, oriented in place, time, and context. Humans share the neural structures underlying this sense of "self" with all mammals, and possibly reptiles as well.

6.1.1.4. *Visceral Affective Systems.* The peripheral autonomic nervous system expresses affective (emotional) states in organs of the abdominal cavity. Additionally, there exists a separate visceral nervous system that consists of nerves lining the gastrointestinal and other organ systems. This visceral nervous system feeds responses that influence emotion in the brain.[481] This information is significant in subcortical response to a person's circumstance. Ninety-five percent of a human's neurotransmitter serotonin resides in the gastrointestinal system.[482] These facts may explain the folk admonition to "check your gut."

6.1.2. *Mirror Neurons.* Philosophers and social scientists have long puzzled over the interconnected structure of human cognitive life. Others, and their actions and thoughts, are fundamentally integrated into one's own consciousness. Without others, humans barely exist. Social isolation is a human poison. Our fundamental sociality has been called "intersubjectivity." Intersubjectivity challenges the atomistic individualism of Western cultures.[483] Mirror neurons may be a neurological substrate of inter-subjectivity.[484]

6.1.2.1. *Discovery.* Giacomo Rizzolati, in the 1990s, performed experiments tracking the firing of single neurons in the brains of macaque monkeys. The brain region of interest was in the premotor cortex, which consists in millions of neurons engaged in governing hand actions. The macaque brain region is named F5; the team attached electrodes to single neurons in F5. Their purpose was to study the behavior of the single neurons during grasping tasks to which they put the macaques. An unexpected result emerged. The neurons in question not only fired when the individual macaque grasped or handled an item, but also when the macaque observed another macaque or human grasp or

---

for our affective life, and it is essential for the primal integration of diverse emotional experiences." Panksepp and Biven, *The Archaeology of Mind*, 401-404, 411, 498.

[481] Panksepp, *Affective Neuroscience*, 119.

[482] Panksepp, *Prosocial Brain*, 148.

[483] Iacoboni, *Mirroring People*, 262ff.

[484] Human mirror neurons, as presently understood, are located in three brain regions: Broca's area (an important language center), the parietal lobe, and the presupplementary motor area (located in the frontal lobes). Iacoboni, *Mirroring People*, 55, 91, 146.

handle an object. Over a period of years, the team learned that area F5 in macaques controlled not only macaque grasping, but also mirrored that same activity when another was observed grasping. Over time, they learned that about twenty percent of the neurons in F5 mirrored somatic activity. The remaining eighty percent did not.[485]

6.1.2.2. *Mirror Neuron Function.* Human mirroring takes place on multiple levels: somatic, affective, and complex.

6.1.2.2.1. *Somatic Mirroring.* Human somatic mirroring, as in the macaque monkeys, creates an image of the actions of others in the perceiver's brain. When mirroring, the same neurons fire as when personally performing the action mirrored, but at a reduced firing rate.[486] Somatic mirroring underlies imitation and mimicry. Somatic mirroring undergirds coordinated action, so essential to Pleistocene survival. Somatic mirroring appears also to create our grasp of the intentions of others. When a person mirrors the actions of another in his brain, one grasps, without cognitive analysis, the aim of the mirrored action. The subcortical inference seems to be "If I were doing that, I would be intending such and such." One sees grasping and hand motion toward the mouth. One automatically knows "she wants to eat." Without speech or cognitive analysis, humans infer what transpires in another's skull.

Paula Niedenthal, social psychologist, asked two groups to detect facial expression changes in others. One group was free to imitate. The other group could not do so because they were required to hold a pencil in their teeth, which sorely limits facial expression. Penciled subjects performed poorly in facial recognition. With impaired mimicry, perception of others' expressions and intentions is hobbled.[487] The process of identification of intention by mirroring apparently proceeds as follows: the muscle actions required for an expression are mirrored, after which the limbic system recognizes the emotion associated with those particular facial actions. In other words, somatic mirroring flows directly into affective mirroring.

6.1.2.2.2. *Affective Mirroring.* Mirror neurons undergird empathy. The precursors of empathy are neurologically hardwired into our brains. Humans empathize, directly sharing in the emotions of others. Crying babies make babies cry.[488] Humans laugh, cry, wince, smile, suffer

---

[485] Iacoboni, *Mirroring People*, 8-12.

[486] Iacoboni, *Mirroring People*, 133, 265.

[487] Iacoboni, *Mirroring People*, 111-12.

[488] Gibson, "Mirrored Emotion," page one of article.

embarrassment, discomfort, and express disgust in tandem. Behavioral synchrony is directly correlated to emotional rapport among group members.[489]

6.1.2.2.2.1. Social psychological experiments demonstrate that one is more likely to like a person who imitates one's posture, language, and mannerisms. Maternal empathy is a survival necessity for infants. Mothers' mirror neurons and limbic systems respond strongly to images of their own baby and other babies.[490]

6.1.2.2.2.2. Vision is not required for affective mirroring. Matthew Hertenstein of DePauw University constructed an experiment in which 248 blindfolded students were touched by another student attempting to communicate one of the following: anger, fear, happiness, sadness, disgust, love, gratitude, or sympathy. The chance rate of correct correlation was eleven percent. Accurate identification of the communicated emotion occurred fifty to seventy-eight percent of the time.[491]

6.1.2.2.2.3. Where somatic and affective mirroring remain intact, large scale imitation produces a feedback loop. People imitate, vocalize about it, imitate and transmit the vocalizations, which influences the behaviors of others, which is itself imitated. Cultures emerge. Iacoboni speculates that our capacity to mirror others, and the communal bonds it creates, may be the ground of ethical thought and morality.[492]

6.1.2.2.3. *Complex Mirroring.* In the frontal lobes, a pocket of mirror neurons exists that differs slightly from the Broca's region and parietal mirror webs. Iacoboni calls these mirror nets "super mirrors."[493] "Complex" mirroring involves mimicking human behavior more complex than mere gestures. Ap Dijksterhuis ran a super-mirror test in-

---

[489] Iacoboni, *Mirroring People*, 110, citing Frank Bernieri's studies of young couples. Adam Smith begins his moral work with the words: "How selfish soever man may be supposed, there are evidently some principles in his nature, which interest him in the fortune of others, and render their happiness necessary to him, though he derives nothing from it except the pleasure of seeing it." We also feel other men's pleasures, dangers, passions, and griefs. All humans possess a deep imitative sympathy with others. We feel something like what our companions feel, and either embrace or condemn those feelings. Smith, *The Theory of Moral Sentiments*, 11-14.

[490] Iacoboni, *Mirroring People*, 110, 127.

[491] Bakalar, "Five-Second Touch."

[492] Iacoboni, *Mirroring People*, 271.

[493] Iacoboni, *Mirroring People*, 203.

volving three groups. The first group was asked to think about characteristics of college professors. The second group was asked to think about characteristics of soccer hooligans. A third group was not asked to think about anyone. All three groups were then tested on a series of general knowledge questions. Those who pondered college professors outperformed all. And the control group outperformed the soccer hooligan ponderers. Dijksterhuis concluded that merely thinking about college professors makes one smarter, and ruminating on soccer miscreants makes one less intellectually agile. Mirroring affects the entire timbre of conscious performance.[494] Iacoboni speculates that the super-mirror neurons of the frontal lobe may carve the sense of individuality out of the primal sense of "us" created by more generalized mirroring. Sometimes, the super-mirrors do not respond at all in mirroring circumstances, effectively shutting down classic motor neuron mirroring.[495] This amounts to an executive command, "Do not imitate that."

6.1.2.3. *Conflated Cognition.* From the member's perspective, the mirror system conflates one's first- and third-person experience of behaviors and affects. This conflation may be the basis of empathy.

6.1.2.4. *Mirroring in Time.* The effects of mirroring do not end when a mirrored emotion subsides. In families where a child is hospitalized due to injury, that child's siblings are statistically at higher risk of injury for the following three months.[496]

6.1.3. *Neurochemicals and the Synaptic Environment.* The anatomical structure of the human brain is bathed in cerebrospinal fluid. This liquid bears enzymes, neuropeptides, neurotransmitters, neuroreceptors, and a host of other chemicals occupied in a dance of anabolism (manufacture) and catabolism (destruction). For each, specific sites and purposes exist. Humans share the entirety of this interneuronal chemical structure with other mammals.

6.2. *Functional Neuroanatomy.* Jaak Panksepp extrapolates from rat, sheep, cat, and cow neuroaffective studies to human experience (neuroanatomical homology, which argues that given mammalian brain architecture similarities, what is true of rats may be true of humans as well). Panksepp employs dissection and ablation studies, as well as invasive investigational surger-

---

[494] Iacoboni, *Mirroring People*, 200-01.

[495] Iacoboni, *Mirroring People*, 203.

[496] Klass, "When a Child Gets Hurt, A Sibling May Be At Risk."

ies.[497]   Panksepp argues that the ancient brain structures that generate at least seven brain systems he describes emerge from structures common to all mammalian species, a basic architecture of mammalian neuroanatomy. Granting this premise, it follows that these similar structures (homologous structures) mediate emotional responses common to mammals everywhere. Some, including me, view the sacrifice of animal life to gain this knowledge of brain function a necessary, but ethically troubling, expedient.

So, human consciousness is, structurally, a Swiss army knife.[498]   Tools have emerged to answer environmental challenges, united mostly by the mere fact they are all contained in the interconnected human brain.

A summary of Panksepp's functional neurosystems[499] follows:

6.2.1. *SEEKING System.*   The SEEKING system creates excitement and focus as an individual seeks sustenance for bodily or intellectual needs. Ultimately, the SEEKING system creates meaning for the individual by aggregating causal relations into a larger scheme.   Mythic and theological
ideation emerge.   The SEEKING system governs appetitive effort, the
search for necessary information and resources, as well as the effort to integrate these components into a meaningful whole for the individual.

SEEKING is the neurological fundament of expectation and prediction.   All human predictions, no matter how frequently confirmed, are in-
ductive.   Any future instance may contradict an expectation.   The SEEK-
ING system creates some delusional expectations, because the system
generates perceptions of causation from mere correlation.   Single events
may have many different or multiple causes.   All mammals suffer this
pitfall, all neuro-affectively "jump to conclusions."   We may see the
world in a way that confirms our biases, even when evidence plainly contradicts our view.   Delusional confirmation bias may be the neurological
basis for human superstitious behaviors.   By creating causal expectations,
the SEEKING system manufactures a view of the world in which it is embedded.   That "reality" may then be adopted by individuals similarly situated, resulting in social bonds.   The stress of unrewarded expectation during periods of SEEKING stimulation may result in paranoia.   SEEKING

---

[497] These techniques are ethically impermissible in human subjects. Such interventions in animal subjects disturb one to a lesser degree, though not negligibly. Our willingness to use animal subjects for purposes we deem impermissible for human subjects exhibits speciesism. Consider Singer, *Expanding Circle* and *Animal Liberation*.

[498] Michael Tomasello attributes the "Swiss army knife" metaphor to Tooby and Cosmides in an 1989 article in *Ethology and Sociobiology*. Tomasello, *Natural History of Human Thinking*, 128.

[499] Panksepp and Biven offer their own summary of Panksepp's core emotional neurosystems, which is worth exploring. Panksepp and Biven, *The Archaeology of Mind*, 436-439.

may be the most fundamental of all the emotional systems, serving as a platform of other systems.[500] Creatures must eat before they can relate.

6.2.2. *RAGE System.* The RAGE system activates affective anger, promoting aggressive behaviors. These behaviors are evolutionarily adaptive in the evasion of predators, signaling sexual desirability, self-defense, and competition for scarce resources. In conjunction with human neocortical capacities, the RAGE system may be a component in societal change. The subjective experience of the RAGE system is the urge to initiate violence against someone or something. The associated affect is anger. But all aggressions are not RAGE system products. Panksepp concludes that predatory aggression emerges from the SEEKING system, and inter-male aggression, while interacting strongly with RAGE and SEEKING systems, has its own neurological concourse (that is presently poorly understood).[501] The RAGE system provides motivation for self-defense and increases the likelihood of success in resource competition. The RAGE system may have emerged in evolution as a mammalian prey response. Invigorated response to capture by predators may deter a carnivore, benefiting the angry prey. Frustration may be mild arousal of the RAGE system. Hunger, pain, and competition for scarce resources may also stimulate RAGE circuits. The RAGE system may be diverted or deactivated by other neural systems, such as those controlling sexuality, nurture, and bonding, which control contrary mental and activity predispositions.[502]

6.2.3. *FEAR System.* The FEAR system creates apprehension and anxiety concerning perceived threats, about which a person experiences strong dread and foreboding. An activated FEAR system reduces pain sensitivity. The FEAR system can be distinguished neuroanatomically from other anxiety systems, such as separation distress, panic attacks, post-traumatic stress, and psychiatric disorders inducing anxiety.[503]

The FEAR system, when activated, creates an aversion to threats to the fearful individual's safety, characterized by generalized anxiety (apprehension, jumpiness, excessive vigilance, fidgeting, upset stomach, diarrhea, urination, tachycardia, dry mouth, shallow respiration, perspiration). The FEAR and RAGE systems are intimately associated, each mediating responses to external threats. Mild stimulation of the FEAR sys-

---

[500] Panksepp and Biven, *The Archaeology of Mind*, 399.

[501] Panksepp, *Affective Neuroscience*, 199.

[502] Panksepp, *Affective Neuroscience*, 191.

[503] SM, a middle-aged female whose Urbach-Wiethe disease destroyed both lobes of her amygdala, reported experiencing no fear. Upon testing, her responses are consistent with her reports. Sanders, "Amygdala Gone, She Knows No Fear," 14.

tem induces freezing with intense alertness. Greater stimulations produce physical flight from perceived threats. Humans exhibit innate FEAR responses to many common stimuli: approaching angry faces, dark locations, snakes and spiders, abrupt loud sounds, and heights. Humans also express conditioned FEAR responses based on learning. Simple FEAR responses do not necessarily involve higher cortical function, but more complex stimuli require cortical processing. Some learned anxieties develop without conscious awareness. Elaborations of the FEAR system probably underlie human neuroses.

6.2.4. *LUST System.* The LUST system governs reproductive behaviors, and is differentiated between the human sexes. Male and female sex motivations emerge from different neurological structures within the brain. Homological arguments[504] are less compelling in illuminating the LUST system because, even among our nearest evolutional neighbors, the great apes, there is no consistent pattern of sexual economy. Gibbons mate for life, chimps trade partners freely, gorillas form harems, and orangutans are isolate. Humans may exhibit any, or even all, of these patterns. The LUST system operates in close conjunction with other brain systems controlling social bonding and nurturance.

The LUST system, considered at a species level, propagates humanity. Individually, the LUST system is more indeterminate in its effects. Humans engage sexual activity for purposes other than reproduction. Human sexual identity lies along a spectrum from male to female. Hormonal stimulations at various points in gestation and childhood may produce blends of sexual identity, for example, male minds in male bodies, female minds in female bodies, male minds in female bodies, female minds in male bodies, and blends of orientation of every sort in between.[505] Therefore, since some individually-preferred pairings have no procreative function, not all human sexual behavior propagates humanity directly. The role that homosexuality or bisexuality may play in the genetic conservation of humanity as a breeding population is poorly understood. The LUST system generates the behaviors that precede reproduction. Human reflection produces rich cultural stories about the roles of sexuality in human life, but the bulk of the operation of the LUST system

---

[504] A "homological argument" reasons that cross-species similarities (homologies) in mammalian brain structures render the neurological facts of one species (often rats, cats, primates, or dogs) predictive of the neurologic functions of another species (usually humans). Charles Darwin used homologies among the anatomies of related species to argue for evolutionary adaptation. Darwin, *Origin of Species*, 461-469. .

[505] For an excellent discussion of the details of these hormonal events, see Panksepp, *Affective Neuroscience*, 232-234.

occurs at the fringe of consciousness or subcortically (and therefore below consciousness).

6.2.5. *CARE System.* The CARE system governs nurturance of young and the formation of social bonds. As pregnancy reaches term, components of the CARE system prepare a mother mammal to provide care for her infant(s). Although less responsive to nurture demands than mothers, fathers too learn and provide care, exhibiting their CARE system function. The same system appears to govern generalized social relationship formation. Mothers whose CARE system has been stimulated learn maternal behaviors rapidly. They bond with their offspring, establishing powerful emotional connections. In general social bonding, friendship and openness to social relations appears to derive from the same neural system. Oxytocin elevation created by the CARE system appears to reduce aggression in both males and females, making them more likely to focus on the task of nurturing young or forming enduring friendships.

The CARE system forms the neural substrate of human sociality. It creates the supportive and responsive interactions that provides secure social attachment for infants, and recommends social bonds of friendship with persons who were originally strangers. It is possible that friendship is, at some level, an invitation to provide co-care for offspring, when needed. Friendship is certainly a form of post-parental emotional attachment, especially as friendship pertains to sexual bonding.

Bonding disorders debilitate humans. Where infants suffer insufficient or non-existent nurturance in their first years, attachment disorders may plague adult life. What's more, parental attachment styles tend to govern the attachment style of that person's own children. Apples fall not far from their trees for more than genetic reasons. Emotional patterns propagate. These infant emotional patterns echo through adult life, and into subsequent generations. In the worst of cases, failed attachment may result in death or sociopathy, in which event the ability to bond or share emotions with others fails abjectly.[506]

6.2.6. *PANIC System.* The PANIC system generates social distress responses to social isolation. Its function is most apparent in the distress vocalizations of the young, and in grief responses to death or separation. PANIC system responses decline when the needed person reappears, and are also somewhat attenuated by familiar locations. Marginal stimulation of the PANIC system may be experienced as loneliness. The PANIC system creates response to social absence. It motivates individuals, when possi-

---

[506] [♪] Karen, *Becoming Attached*, 361-393. Attachment theorists and psychoanalysts share a somewhat tortured history of internecine rivalry. See Fonagy, *Attachment Theory and Psychoanalysis.*

ble, to reconnect with co-members. In children, the PANIC system creates distress vocalization, leading to caregiver response.

The PANIC system reveals that humans are fundamentally social creatures. The PANIC system gears our basal affective responses to remedy social separation, and seek the support of needed helpers. Chronic PANIC system arousal may cause depression. When significant social loss occurs (divorce, separation, death), depression grows more likely. Attachment theorists speculate that insecurely-attached children, who grow timid and clingy, evidence different PANIC system capabilities than more securely-attached children.[507]

6.2.7. *PLAY System.* The PLAY system creates the neural precursors of human play. In mammals, rough-and-tumble (RAT) play is universal, teaching a host of integrative skills in coordination, social boundaries, and competition. Play occurs more often in familiar and welcome social circumstances. RAT play diminishes as individuals age.

The PLAY system predisposes mammals to RAT play. Under the influence of cortical structures, play exhibits a startling diversity of form in humans. Play may serve social functions, such as interactive skills, bonding, cooperation, rank and leadership, and effective communication. Play may also serve nonsocial functions, such as physical fitness, increased cognitive flexibility, tool use, and innovation. We frequently associate play with seeking activities, but it appears that the PLAY and SEEKING systems may not be synergistic. Drugs that increase seeking behaviors decrease play behaviors. The PLAY system brings a lighthearted spirit to life, and teaches important physical and social skills. Play may be the waking counterpart of dreaming. Neurophysiologically, play activates many of the same systems as dreaming.

6.3. *The Coppice of Consciousness.* Consciousness is configured by myriad underlying neural systems of which we are seldom aware, some of which organize into systems such as those Panksepp has identified. Consciousness emerges as the end product of competition among columns of coordinated activity among neural micro-systems in the subcortical brain, each potentially the subject of conscious attention. The brain is organized into affective circuits (or columns) which commence in the reptilian brainstem as primal motivations, course up through the subcortical limbic system where they are inhibited for social effect, and then climb toward the neo-cortex, which again inhibits for overall effect and value of given behaviors.[508]

---

[507] Panksepp, *Affective Neuroscience*, 265.

[508] Panksepp asserts we do not yet know how far the emotional subcircuits extend in the brain. Panksepp, *Prosocial Brain*, 147.

Some subcortical affective circuits, detailed above, are FEAR, RAGE, SEEKING, LUST, CARE, PANIC, and PLAY.[509] These terms of art do not indicate the conscious mental states associated with their English words. These (and other) circuits identify subcortical affective columns within brain structure that rise toward the neocortex, mediating the precursors of the emotions and motivations we experience consciously.

Panksepp's research suggests a metaphor: the coppice of consciousness. Imagine a view of the arboreal canopy of a coppice[510] in which a million monkeys play.[511]

> *In the coppice of consciousness, the brainstem roots cling to the soil of basal existence, knotted there with the intertwined roots of a hundred other coppices. Limbic trunks, which are affective columns, rise from the roots, supporting the leafy cerebral canopy. Upon the many emotive trunks of the coppice of consciousness (those trunks being the affective columns of FEAR, RAGE, SEEKING, LUST, CARE, PANIC, and PLAY and others) cavort and squawk the million monkey resources of the brain, in their extravagant competition and interplay. And, atop the coppice canopy, successful climber monkeys pop their heads out into the clear air above the leafy cover. Consciousness consists in the cross-talk of the monkeys topping the coppice. All pay no attention whatsoever to the supportive coppice trunks and roots laboring in darkness below the billowing leaves, or the many unheard monkeys clambering up and down the trunks.*

The subcortical columns and structures that shape consciousness operate simultaneously, creating some of the horde of competing mini-systems that may amalgamate as conscious recognition. Jonathan Haidt captured the complexity of human consciousness memorably: "We assume that there is one person in each body, but in some ways we are each more like a committee whose members have been thrown together to do a job, but who often find themselves working at cross purposes."[512]

Thus, we discover the affective root of human consciousness. Panksepp and Biven call human consciousness, as it proliferates from root

---

[509] Panksepp, *Prosocial Brain*, 146.

[510] I am indebted to Jaak Panksepp for part of this metaphor. His work on affective neuroscience contains his description of consciousness and human emotion as a tree. See Panksepp, *Affective Neuroscience*, 302.

[511] Coppices are any of a number of species of many-trunked trees. Coppices propagate by means of sprouts and root suckers, rather than from seed. Firewood harvesters value coppice trees, because, once cut, a coppice tree sprouts multiple new trunks that can again be harvested. Coppices reproduce themselves locally without husbandry, and become small forests of genetically identical trees.

[512] Haidt, *The Happiness Hypothesis*, 5.

emotive systems into a welter of socially-conditioned cognitive elaboration, the MindBrain or BrainMind. The mind and brain "are really one and the same thing. The MindBrain (or BrainMind) is a unified entity lacking any boundary with the body–it is integral to the physical system [of the brain] as a whole."[513]   Daniel Bor captures the coppice competition of neural resources nicely: "The semi-chaotic activity of our 85 billion neurons undergoes a kind of temporary natural selection every moment of our waking lives, as attention shapes the contents of consciousness. Rival coalitions of neurons compete with one another to be heard the loudest. . . . Every time you have a new thought, that idea has become the dominant clan of our internal world, following a violent battle between jostling, screaming tribes."[514]

6.4. *Fault Lines in the Coppice of Consciousness.* All human decision-making is bounded by limiting factors: available time, degree of difficulty in acquiring reliable information, memory loss, patience and ability of the decision-maker, intelligence or the lack of it, and expense, for example. The human brain employs simple short-cuts (heuristics) to make most decisions. These elementary heuristics frequently lead to decisions as good as or better than standard rational approaches (which rational models prescribe that one should define the goal, collect all available information, rank that data differentially, rank the emergent solutions differentially, and choose the best-ranked alternative for achieving one's goal).[515]   Abundant data may create decisional "noise," rather than clear-headed capture of facts most relevant to decision. Opportunity may be lost, enthusiasm quenched. Each short-cut decisional heuristic may lead to inappropriate decisions when the problem-solving rule and the context in which it is applied match poorly.

Human mental heuristics use as their raw material well-processed data from subconscious neural systems: depth perception, audio mapping, facial recognition, visual tracing, memory, recall, operant conditioning, imitation, social trustworthiness assessments, or mirroring extrapolations. Cognitive heuristics are structural elements of human brains. For purposes of the coppice of consciousness metaphor, these many subsystems are "monkeys" at play in the coppice of consciousness. This work lists several from among

---

[513] Panksepp and Biven, *The Archaeology of Mind*, xiii, 7. Biven goes on to say, "Knowledge of the seven basic emotional systems has begun to revolutionize the practice of psychotherapy because it offers the most comprehensive, data-based brain taxonomy of primary-process emotions that is currently available." Panksepp and Biven, *The Archaeology of Mind*, xiv.

[514] Bor, *The Ravenous Brain*, 122. Bor emphasizes that the human cerebral cortex seeks patterns above all else, and from patterns finds meaning. For information in which to recognize patterns, the human brain is ravenous. Bor, *The Ravenous Brain*, 75-77, 198.

[515] Todd, "Ecological Rationality," 205.

hundreds of identified mini-systems and cognitive heuristics at work, each competing with other systems for influence upon thought and action.

Cognitive heuristics are temperaments or approaches to problems which seem natural or proceed without conscious notice. Both members and communities exhibit cognitive shortcuts. Heuristics may help or harm. Where human thought consistently falls into patterns at odds with circumstantial feedback, our heuristics become potentially life-threatening.[516] Each heuristic was adaptive at some point in the primordial environment of Pleistocene Africa, emerging from evolution's mindless mechanism preserving genes that procreate well. These heuristics and subsystems underlie many dangerous problems in human culture and member psychology.[517] They often constitute fault lines in human cognition. Heuristics prepackage sense data in ways that may have once been perfectly adapted to survival in an environment. But our data packaging may also fundamentally distort what we see and believe. As Derek Parfit said, "The truth is very different from what we are inclined to believe."[518]

This list of interactive systems and their potential conflicts is not intended to be comprehensive or even representative. The text provides examples of cognitive conflicts and subconscious systems sufficient to convince you, Kate, that conceiving your mind as a mostly-unconscious modular organ explains much.

6.4.1. *Default Mode Network*. The brain is constantly active subcortically. One expression of this activity is the default mode network (DMN), which prepares a person for conscious activity or response. The DMN is distributed widely throughout the brain, functioning most noticeably when intense intentional activity has ebbed. The DMN appears to prepare the brain for input and action, coordinating access of various brain systems

---

[516] Robert Nozick argues: "An overturn of our traditional concepts can be disquieting and disconcerting," and "We should expect that many of our evolved concepts will have defects, and we should be prepared to give up reliance upon them, at least in the specialized contexts in which their shortcomings are most evident." Nozick, *Invariances*, 8-9.

[517] Wilson memorably calls these inherited mental conflicts the "Paleolithic Curse." He finds our brains well-adapted to hunter-gatherer life, but less amenable to global and scientific existence. Because of our predilections, we govern ourselves poorly, savor conflict between tribes, and avoid remedies to overpopulation. We care locally, but not globally. Wilson states bluntly that humans are "poorly wired." [♪] Wilson, *The Meaning of Human Existence*, 176-178. Unfortunately, Wilson's prescription for this malady indulges a raw emotion-rationality dualism, advocating for reason in a manner reminiscent of Plato, and deriding sub-factual faiths and ideologies. [♪] Wilson, *The Meaning of Human Existence*, 183-184.

[518] Parfit, *Reasons and Persons*, 281. Jonah Lehrer admonishes: "Why is thinking about thinking so important? First, it helps us steer clear of stupid errors. . . . The mind is full of flaws, but they can be outsmarted." Lehrer, *How We Decide*, 250.

and preventing dysfunctional interferences among the various federated and interwoven brain systems.[519]

6.4.2. *Circadian Rhythms.* Human brain function exhibits several endogenous[520] cyclical behaviors, the most prominent of which are circadian rhythms. These patterns of activity are affected by the suprachiasmatic nuclei (SCN), which region lies above the optic chiasm in the front part of the hypothalamus. The SCN's circadian pattern can be disrupted by shift work or by long distance travel. Two weeks may be required before all the hormone generation elicited by the SCN completes re-coordination after a person changes his sleep-wake pattern by twelve hours (as in traveling half way around the planet). The circadian rhythms derive from deep brain structures. Rapid eye movement (REM) sleep begins deep in the ancient brainstem. Wakefulness emerges from brain structures less ancient than the REM-generator, but evolutionarily older than the structures dominating slow wave sleep.

6.4.2.1. *Wakefulness.* Wakefulness is characterized by low-amplitude, high frequency electroencephalogram (EEG) beta waves. This brain state typifies information processing. The individual experiences high vigilance, as compared to sleep, and responds to environmental challenges.

6.4.2.2. *Slow Wave Sleep.* Sleep follows melatonin production that inhibits SCN function. Multiple systems move the brain deeper and deeper into diminished attention, characterized by EEG delta waves and relative quiescence of the cortex. The brain's firing pattern redistributes, coming to be dominated by thalamic pacemaker neurons and brainstem activity. Some reflexes are inhibited. Slow wave sleep progresses in a sleep period through four stages, each punctuated by REM sleep periods of increasing duration and intensity. Deep slow wave sleep wanes as an individual ages, as does REM sleep.

6.4.2.3. *Dreaming.* REM sleep is a component of neurotypical mammalian sleep during which the emotion-generating areas of the brain are hyperactive, the brain overall is more active than when awake, and the body exhibits inhibition of activity (atonia).[521] Rapid eye movements and other abbreviated bodily actions are typical. Reptiles and fishes have no REM periods. Subjective recollection of REM states, when available, is

---

[519] Raichle, "The Brain's (Dark Energy)," 48-49.

[520] "Endogenous" indicates a phenomenon that arises from the internal function of an organism or system. See *Webster's Third New International Dictionary*, s.v. "endogenous," at section 1b. The relevant antonym is "exogenous."

[521] Panksepp, *Affective Neuroscience*, 128.

reported as "dreaming." Most dreams cannot be recalled during wakefulness.[522] Dreaming may be more ancient than wakefulness, based on the brain locus of its neural generation deep in the brainstem.[523] REM-deprived animals exhibit mania: cortical inhibitions wane, leaving the animal more busy, aggressive, sexual, and motivated. REM-deprivation inhibits production of the neurotransmitter serotonin. Serotonin-deprived individuals dream, lose perceptual and cognitive stability, experience heightened emotional lability,[524] and are at greater risk of suicide.[525]

6.4.3. *Ultradian rhythms.* Ultradian rhythms are periodic behaviors that occur in periods of less than twenty-four hours. Some ultradian rhythms are sleep stages, blinking, pulse changes, hormone release, thermo-regulation, urination, defecation, nostril dilation (including nose picking), facial grooming, and appetite.

6.4.4. *Infradian rhythms.* Infradian rhythms are periodic behaviors that occur in periods longer than twenty-four hours. Some infradian rhythms are menstruation and periodic sodium excretion.

6.4.5. *Sensory Winnowing.* Environmental stimuli constantly bombard humans. The brain automatically edits and structures these inputs, fashioning from them an experience of the world. This winnowing is perhaps easiest to understand with respect to the visual system. Initial stimuli are enormous, with around ten billion bits per second striking the retina. The retina's one million connections output just six million bits per second, and of those only ten thousand bits per second reach the visual cortex. After interpretation by the visual cortex, only one hundred bits per second contribute to conscious visual images.[526]

6.4.6. *Homeostatic Regulation.* The human body maintains its physical well-being by means of a host of regulatory responses that motivate the individual subconsciously, affectively, and cognitively. The acquisition of oxygen, food, water, warmth, micronutrients, and even higher level needs such as sex and companionship, are regulated brain systems seeking homeostasis.

---

[522] Panksepp, *Affective Neuroscience*, 142.

[523] Panksepp, *Affective Neuroscience*, 125.

[524] "Lability" means broad fluctuation of affect. See *Webster's Third New International Dictionary*, s.v. "labile."

[525] Panksepp, *Affective Neuroscience*, 142.

[526] Raichle, "The Brain's (Dark Energy)," 47.

6.4.6.1. *Homeostasis and Pleasure.* Sensations that create equilibrium in bodily homeostasis are perceived as pleasurable. Sensations that disrupt bodily homeostasis are perceived as unpleasant, in proportion to their disruptive effects.[527] Subjective emotional experiences rank sensations and their causes for value to the individual, serving as a homeostatic value-code system for sorting the environment. Pleasure intensity correlates environmental stimuli that may be useful to a mammal with the internal homeostatic needs of that mammal. Ice cream tastes good. It tastes better when hungry. When starving, ice cream becomes ambrosia. Homeostatic displeasure, indicating a lack of utility of the stimulus, may be experienced not only as an affective state, but as feelings of sickness.

6.4.6.2. *Homeostatic Automation.* Most homeostatic operations are wholly subconscious, emerging into consciousness only when obstructed. For example, the suffocation alarm reflex operates only when oxygen depletion grips an individual. The person is filled with anxiety and begins to flail, exhibiting a deep brainstem reflexive response. A full bladder or bowel induces persistent and obsessive urgency to vacate, emerging into consciousness from kidney and intestinal feedback below consciousness. The brain's automatic subcortical modulation of the body's need for energy, micronutrients, sleep, warmth, sex, oxygen, and water constitute genetic memory built into our brain-driven metabolic systems.

6.4.6.3. *Affective Domination.* When homeostatic motivations emerge into consciousness, the emotions they induce change cognition more than cognition changes the emotional motivations. This is a rule in the neurotypical flow of human motivation—affect prevails over cortical response.[528]

6.4.7. *Selecting.* The brain has default rules of thumb used to make repetitive choices among alternatives. These have been styled "fast and frugal" heuristics.[529]

6.4.7.1. *Ignorance Rule.* The ignorance rule guides decision arbitrarily among unknown options, and stops searching at that point. ("I don't know any restaurants in the area, but there is one. Let's go there.")

6.4.7.2. *Recognition Rule.* The recognition rule guides decisions to the more familiar of two alternatives, stopping the search when a recognized

---

[527] Gary Bloom notes the euphoric effects of exercise may prove a counter-example. I would argue that endorphin release during exercise counters the intensely unpleasant effects of physical stress and exercise. Exercise is so necessary and so unpleasant that those with natural narcotics relieving their pain survived more frequently than those lacking the endorphin boost.

[528] Panksepp, *Affective Neuroscience*, 166.

[529] Todd and Gigerenzer, "Mechanisms of ecological rationality," 202.

option emerges. This rule engages humans powerfully. Research indicates that most people are more deeply influenced by an advocate who recommends a lone alternative with which they are familiar than other advocates with more expansive information who recognize several options.[530] ("Let's go to that restaurant. I have been there before.")

6.4.7.3. *One-Reason Rule.* The one-reason rule guides decision to that alternative for which one criterion for preference can be discerned. Options and reasons for preference are examined until one significant difference emerges. ("This restaurant has cheaper entrees. Let's go there.")

6.4.7.4. *The Elimination Rule.* For situations where several options appear simultaneously, the elimination rule selects a relevant criterion, applies that criterion to all options, and eliminates options that fail the criterion. The surviving option is selected. ("All of these restaurants serve tasty fare, but only one serves Greek entrees. Let's go there.")

6.4.7.5. *The Good Enough Rule.* In situations where options appear consecutively, the good enough rule selects one option that meets at least a minimum satisfaction of preference, and terminates the consecutive search at that point. ("All of these local restaurants serve tasty fare. There are several dozen more listed online." "I'm hungry. Let's eat Greek." "There are three Greek restaurants we already know. Which would you prefer?" "Which is closest? Let's go there.")

6.4.8. *Self-Deception.*   Robert Trivers argues that, mostly unconsciously (but sometimes consciously as well) humans distort all information and propagate misrepresentations. Our uptaken information is biased in both perception and encoding. We organize information in false schemas and utilize defective reasoning to bolster it. We forget what we do not prefer, and embellish what we remember. In the end, we project a better self, to ourselves and others, better than the facts (which we distorted) would otherwise indicate.[531] By telling the self-serving fictions, we make ourselves look better to others and feel better about ourselves. The liar augments his reputation in the eyes of others. Because humans lie, lie detection is highly evolved. Self-deception conceals human misrepresentation, even from the liar, making the lie yet more credible by rendering it incapable of de-

---

[530] Todd and Gigerenzer, "Mechanisms of Ecological Rationality," 204.

[531] Trivers, *The Folly of Fools*, 139. Trivers accuses human psychology of "systematic deformation of the truth at each stage of the psychological process." Trivers thinks that self-deception combined with deceit of others is a poor formula for useful society. He argues that fighting one's self-deception improves the self and society. He notes that deceit and self-deception offer "an unending extravaganza of nonsense, comedic and tragic, large and small." Trivers, *The Folly of Fools*, 323, 334.

tection. Subconscious distortions remain invisible to us. Successful subconscious misrepresentation promotes false perceptions of trustworthiness and socially-soothing generosity. The liar's social status is defended or improved. High social status, at least in the primordial African veldt, promoted sexual opportunity and progeny survival.[532]   Because self-deception operates subconsciously, a person cannot reliably report when his assertions are accurate. Hence, human representations of events in the social universe remain equivocal, subject to the veil of self-deception. Where detected deceptions are high, social trust plummets. Self-defense makes transaction costs soar, as people guard against frauds. Where deception succeeds or is avoided altogether, a shared sense of (possibly pretended) fairness reduces transaction costs.[533]   Self-deception offends our sense of identity, veracity, and dependability, creating internal conflicts.

6.4.9. *Status-Seeking.* Humans rank companions subconsciously. Overtly or subtly, we create an hierarchical substructure to social relations. We defer to those deemed superior and disrespect to those deemed inferior. Humans defer naturally to large males and beautiful females, regardless whether those persons show any special competences beyond their appearance. We also equate command of resources (in contemporary cultures, money) with high social rank, and defer accordingly. Human hierarchical impulses run afoul of evaluation of persons by other criteria (for example, competences or loyalties). Status seeking offends our sense of justice and equity, creating internal conflicts.

6.4.10. *Whores and Madonnas.*[534]   Men and women rank women, considered as potential mothers, by the readiness with which they accommodate male sexual advances. Women who resist little gain much popularity among men, but few men wish to make these "easy" women the mother of children in whom those males intend to make high paternal investment. Women who resist sexual advances are subconsciously deemed worthy to bear a male's offspring, and those offspring warrant high male parental investment.[535] The specific expression of the Madonna-Whore perception shifts along a cultural spectrum over time (think Victorian England versus Venice Beach in 1960). The sexes adjust their mating sensitivities as trends mutate, but the categorization of women perseveres.

---

[532] [♪] Pinker, *Better Angel of Our Nature s*, 490-497. See also Wright, *The Moral Animal*, 265-286.

[533] Tierney, "Moral Lessons, Down Aisle 9," *New York Times*, March 24, 2010.

[534] I did not invent this terminology, but, as female friends and feminists of every sex note with many frowns, I repeat it. The language seems, though crude, admirably descriptive.

[535] Wright, *The Moral Animal*, 57-92.

6.4.11. *Causation-Correlation Confusion.* As a survival tool, humans sort experiences for causal relationships. We have a pronounced tendency to confuse events that correlate in time or context for causation. This tendency may be a root of superstition and magical beliefs.

6.4.12. *Happy Violence.* When humans punish someone for perceived injustice, reward centers are activated.[536] We feel good. Yet, we see empirically that punitive coercion invites further injurious response on the part of the punished person, creating a cycle of mutual retributive coercion (vendetta and war), which is, at some level, at least occasionally, enjoyable to both sufferers. The problem lies in that, at least with respect to coercion and violence, humans enjoy what does not work.

Stressed humans may murder. It is the habit of our nearest primate cousins, chimpanzees, to murder intruding individuals without discrimination. Human history is a tale of lethal violence (which, fortunately, is attenuating); human prehistorical evidence of violence is less patent. Nicholas Wade offers evidence that approximately thirty percent of prehistoric tribal males died by murder. Humans spread across the globe in a few thousand years, he theorizes, fleeing potentially lethal conflict with other tribes and members of their own tribes.[537] Others demur.

Some humans murder[538] in the pedestrian sense. They attack members of a society for reasons that persuade them but are not collectively authorized. Almost all non-pathological members avoid murder in their own communities under usual circumstances. Certain unusual circumstances promote murder and intentional assault. In hand to hand conflict, inhibitions against murder weaken if the opponent is denigrated, if sensitivity is dulled by repeated exposure, if one is trained to ignore one's inhibitions, if the context of conflict is alien or unnatural, if the opponent is a stranger who has a different appearance, if one has learned to disparage moral dialogue, if one suffers an emotional implosion of conscious restraint, or if one enters battle ecstasy. Murder also grows more likely where seeking is frustrated, or territoriality expectations are flaunted.

Almost all humans acquiesce in the organized killing of civilians and soldiers during military action, deeming these actions lawful because State agencies authorize the acts. Most allow their funds and social per-

---

[536] de Quervain, "Neural Basis of Altruistic Punishment," 1254-1258.

[537] [♪] Wade, *Before the Dawn,* 74-99. *Contra* Wade's view, the evidence for human pre-agricultural revolution tribal violence appears minimal. It may well be that humans do not indulge predatory violence except when threatened.

[538] "Murder" means an act that intentionally terminates the life of a human being without social warrant. See *Webster's Third New International Dictionary,* s.v. "murder," at §1.

mission to support such lethal conflicts, despite many reservations about the conduct of particular wars. In distance violence (such as bombing), inhibitions against murder weaken because the conflict is imagined but not seen. The murderer is a relatively passive participant in the deed. Responsibility for the distant lethal action is spread among many individuals, especially in hierarchies. Because the ugly precedent of previous distance killings causes moral slippage, future distance murders are often more egregious than those that historically preceded them.[539]

Despite human predilection to murder, we are by far the most cooperative of primates, especially when asked to collaborate with strangers. Many cultural impediments tamp down the urge to murder. Barter requires living traders who are not fearing for their lives. Traders may often be strangers. Strangers pose dangers to self and tribe. Only humans and bonobos among apes (sometimes) resist the urge to kill stranger intruders with any regularity.[540]

Being prone to murder conflicts with our urges to cooperate and to build enduring societies. Hence, internal conflicts run amok.

6.4.13. *Stereotype Threat and Lift.* When tested, if the testee believes that failure on the test will confirm a negative stereotype about a group to which he belongs, he is more likely to fail. This result is the stereotype threat phenomenon. In the stereotype lift phenomenon, if a testee believes succeeding on the test will confirm a positive stereotype of a group to which he belongs, he is more likely to succeed.[541] The effect exceeds stereotyping. Affirmed students perform better on tests than denigrated students.[542] The tester's expressed expectations determine, in part, the testee's performance.

6.4.14. *Memory Revision.* Memory may serve purposes other than recollection. Memory proves significantly unreliable in factual recall. Some have speculated that the primary function of memory is to generate motivating adaptive images of our futures. Thus, events as they occurred are selectively replaced in memory to structure viable images of possible future successes.[543]

---

[539] [♪] Glover, *Humanity*, 47-116.

[540] [♪] Ridley, *The Rational Optimist*, 65. See also [♪] Wade, *Before the Dawn*, 139-148.

[541] Wilson, *Redirect*, 221-222. Wilson reports Claude Steele's experiments (from *Whistling Vivaldi*) in which a standard intelligence test is given, but the instructions are variously diverted, with the result that scores improve or deflate testee performance.

[542] Sharot, "Optimism Bias," 44.

[543] Sharot, "Optimism Bias," 42.

6.4.15. *Time Fluidity.* Subjectively, time proceeds at varied paces, determined by the psychological mood of the perceiver.

6.4.16. *Expectation Confirmation.* Humans tend to endorse evidence that confirms their expectations, and disparage contrary data. When the evidence dismays, it may be ignored. Facts contrary to one's emotional commitments are viewed with suspicion, its bases likely to be challenged, and its author's credentials likely to be criticized.[544]

6.4.17. *Attention Distortion.* We tend to rely excessively in decision-making on one preferred piece of evidence, to the neglect of other more salient data.

6.4.18. *Applause Misconstruction.* We prefer ideas that find wide appeal and are repeated in public discourse confidently, regardless whether such ideas are factual.

6.4.19. *Rational Rubber-Stamping.* Human affective responses emerge much more rapidly than do conscious deliberative thoughts. Much of rationality consists in little more than after-the-fact justifications of pre-existing emotional commitments.[545]

6.4.20. *Framing Flip-flops.* Humans may draw opposite conclusions from identical facts, depending upon the frame into which facts are cast.

6.4.21. *Coin-Toss Fallacy.* People tend to believe that random events are prejudiced by previous outcomes of the random process. Tossing five "heads" in a row may lead the gambler to assume the next toss is more likely to come up "tails."

6.4.22. *Control Presumption.* Humans tend to believe they have more control over circumstances than they in fact do.

6.4.23. *Loss Aversion.* Humans tend to stick with losing strategies longer than evidence warrants, because they are reticent to abandon costs already invested in the losing strategy.

6.4.24. *The Petulant Now.* Most effort must be devoted to immediate needs, if survival conditions are harsh. Scratching one's way into tomorrow dominates consciousness. Yet, in an overcrowded world, tiny deficiencies aggregate into colossal quagmires. Absent deliberate effort, the immediate future dominates all planning and thought.

6.4.25. *Interconnectivity Blindness.* The seat of self in the basal ganglia creates an identity which is inclined to declare that it exists independently of others and of the surrounding environment. Distorted thinking ensues. The individual believes that the environment and others exist to supply his needs. Individual monistic thought misses fundamental features of the

---

[544] Mooney, "Made Up Minds," 48-49.

[545] Mooney, "Made Up Minds," 48-49.

world, which, though patent, are not deeply motivating to individuals. Individual monism distorts human life.

6.4.26. *Mood Contagion.* The affect of a single group-member may, by that person's enthusiasm or reservation, deflect a group from one mood state toward another. Optimistic mood contagion decreases group concern about risks and increases bonding. Pessimistic mood contagion increases concern about risks and impairs bonding.

6.4.27. *Risk Creep.* When a risk is confronted repeatedly with good outcomes, the member or group becomes accustomed to that level of risk, and will tolerate yet greater risks.[546]

6.4.28. *Mounting Trivialities.* We easily dismiss minor failures as negligible. In complex systems, small failures can cascade to become catastrophic collapses. Consider Three Mile Island, the Challenger O-rings, Pan Am 503 at Tenerife, or the Deepwater Horizon explosion.

6.4.29. *Faith in Fallbacks.* Members and communities reliant upon complex systems tend to exhibit unwarranted confidence in safety measures, back-up systems, and fallback protocols. More pedestrians die in crosswalks than jaywalking.

6.4.30. *Conflict Distortions.* Victims tell a tale of unbridled rapacity injuring them irreparably. Perpetrators tell a tale of unavoidable action, wholly justified, inflicting minimal injury.[547]

6.4.31. *Sunshine Bias.* Members and communities prefer good news to bad. Where persistent, bad news is suppressed. Its messengers are shunned. Decisional processes grow biased toward uniform happythink.

6.4.32. *Optimism Bias.* Members and communities tend to believe that the future portends much better outcomes than it probably holds. Given the many downside outcomes that prognostication illuminates, an inherent optimism counterbalance may be an evolutionary necessity. Death's grim prospect demands a rosy rejoinder.[548] Our brains readily encode information that affirms our optimistic hopes. Those same brains encode negative outcomes less reliably. In the end, we hear that fifty percent of marriages fail, but do not believe that our own marriage may collapse.[549]

6.4.33. *Evaluation Boost.* After making a difficult choice, members value their selection more than before deciding and expect the selection to bring

---

[546] David Brooks, "Drilling for Certainty." *New York Times*, 28 May 2010, A19. Brooks ruminates on the failure of complex systems, such as the Deepwater Horizon oil spill (2010).

[547] See Baumeister, *Evil*, 33-59, and [♪] Pinker, *Better Angels of Our Nature*, 488ff.

[548] Sharot, "Optimism Bias," 40-43.

[549] Sharot, "Optimism Bias," 46.

them pleasure. Every choice, even a poor-outcome choice, seems better to the decider than it did before deciding.[550]

6.4.34. *Familiarity Bias.* Estimations of the frequency of events depends upon the ease with which one can recall an example. Therefore, contrary to all statistics, people more greatly fear death by airplane crash than by falling down one's own stairs.[551]

6.4.35. *Particularity and Universality.* Humans find stories about plighted individuals emotionally compelling, but frequently ignore generalized truths (the identifiable victim effect). Paul Slovic calls the psychic numbing in considering more than one sufferer "genocide neglect."[552]

6.4.36. *Trust and Skepticism.* Social openness waxes and wanes with mood states. Oxytocin induces greater social trust. Testosterone induces greater skepticism and scrutiny. Women, at their monthly optimal fertility produce more testosterone, reducing their trust of sexual partners.[553]

6.4.37. *Mysticism and Empiricism.* Deep parts of member consciousness aggregate broad visions of human meaning, visions difficult to rationally articulate. These mysticisms vary in form and content. Buber meets the Eternal Thou.[554] Gandhi prays to be reduced to nothingness that Truth might be all and non-violence (*Ahimsa*) might consume him.[555] And yet, these thinkers, and most mystics, are simultaneously intense observers, given to minute detail in empirical matters. Their empiricism weds poorly with their mysticism. Mystical insight lacks rational warrant, but is not diminished for that deficiency. Mysticism sings limbic symphonies. The rational is not all, or even much, of man's awareness.[556] Mysticism announces a fault line in human consciousness.

---

[550] Sharot, "Optimism Bias," 44, 46.

[551] [♪] Pinker, *Better Angels of Our Nature*, 193.

[552] Slovic's work shows that "setting the story of a single needy person in the context of wider human need reliably diminishes altruism." Harris, *The Moral Landscape*, 69, where Harris cites Slovic's research.

[553] Wade, "She Doesn't Trust You? Blame the Testosterone."

[554] [♪] Buber, *I and Thou*, 123 (Third Part).

[555] Gandhi, *Autobiography*, 504-505.

[556] William James acknowledges in his lively description of mysticism that, once one grants that mystical experiences of some are genuine, and not some odd pretense, then the bases for believing any particular thought are multiplied. We often believe what is more-than or less-than reasonable. Mystical experience enlivens otherwise dry consciousness. James, *The Varieties of Religious Experience*, 418. Michael Shermer would have us believe that rational evidence guides one to moral action. He cites Christopher Hitchens's dictum to the effect that what one believes without evidence can be discarded without evidence. Shermer, *The Moral Arc*, 19. Shermer's is the harsh, monomaniacal view that only what one deems rational is reliable. Shermer neglects other persuasive rudi-

6.4.38. *Attribution Error.* When one has little knowledge of an individual, a person often seizes upon some characteristic of the individual and invests that unknown individual with the attributes of the relevant class (usually negative attributes). The most pernicious among current attribution errors consist in racial or gender or sexual orientation or political preference attributions.

6.4.39. *Unit Completion.* Set a task, most people prefer to complete one unit of that task before stopping. Think of cleaning one's plate or finishing a game.

6.4.40. *In-Group Justification.* People tend to treat members of their own social group better than those outside their group.

6.4.41. *Blame Deflection.* Humans welcome credit for successes, even when one's role was minimal. People tend to deflect blame for failures, blaming external causes.

6.4.42. *Reactive Devaluation.* Most people disparage good ideas if the source of the idea is an opponent.

6.4.43. *System Justification.* In most circumstances, both dominant and subordinate members of a social system justify its existence, submit to its status quo, and seek to stabilize the inequitable system. Social justification, not social revolution, is every culture's norm. This bias causes most people most of the time to view their existing social structure, with its inherent inequities and antinomies, as morally acceptable, desirable, equitable, normal, and possibly unavoidable. [557]

6.4.44. *Identifiable Victim Bias.* We respond differently to a child drowning in a pond and the knowledge that thousands of children are starving to death for lack of resources. Most people will jump in the pond and rescue the flailing child. But we feel less urgency to alleviate the plight of unknown, distant undernourished babies.[558]

6.4.45. One leaves this imprecise list with the hope it proves suggestive in evaluating your thinking, Kate.

A lesson lurks here. The human mind confronts numerous contorted obstacles in the course of evaluating circumstances. We are easily self-deceived, mistaken, or captured by the status quo. We desperately seek to fit into our social context. We frequently not only believe our misconstructions of reality, but "see" only information that supports our erroneous views.

---

ments, such as personal experience, the cogency of a view of life, gut feelings, expectations and hopes, and the chastening role of humility.

[557] Jost, "System Justification Theory," 887-888.

[558] Joshua Greene recounts the tale of Baby Jessica, who fell down a well in Midland, Texas. $700,000 poured in to fund her rescue. Greene, *Moral Tribes*, 262.

Achieving a "finely-elaborated cull of conduct" is no mean feat, but rather the fruit of long inspection of psychic moments, leading one toward global humility and careful observation and counter-contextual explorations.[559] Given the crush of obstacles to constructive deliberation, every thoughtful dissenter is living social treasure.

6.5. *Coppice Conclusions.* Panksepp has identified and offers such experimental evidence as exists in animal studies and human pathology for seven affective neural systems: SEEKING, RAGE, FEAR, LUST, CARE, PANIC, and PLAY. Each represents discrete subcortical systems generating fundamental motivations or emotions that guide human behavior. Panksepp's seven systems are not exhaustive. Others exist. For example, discrete systems may exist for establishing dominance and social ranking. There may be an independent affective substrate that makes pregnancy an appealing prospect to women, and progeny desirable to men, all apart from the sexual drives that create pregnancy and the nurturance drives that motivate parents. Given the prevalence of risky behaviors, thrill-seeking may have independent neural substrate. Laughter and crying, given their adaptability to a multitude of circumstances, may be independent systems. The startle reflex may also be more than mere unexpected alertness. The universality of god-perceptions may indicate that theological insights emerge from some universal neural substructure. Though it is possible that the divine represents a common extrapolation from seeking behaviors, the persistence of this particular conclusion may indicate an independent subcortical origin.

At its root, the coppice of consciousness metaphor teaches that human brains aggregate multitudes of deeply interrelated subcortical microsystems, some of which are organized into larger systems, and most of which remain entirely invisible to the individual in whose brain they operate. From this neural menagerie of impulse and emotion, a tiny fraction of affects and drives rise to consciousness, while the rest perform their evolutionary tasks in the shadows of subconsciousness.[560] Consciousness resembles a symphony. Each note, that is, each neural micro-system (each monkey at play in the coppice), contributes its specific pitch. In the aggregate, the conscious human audits a unity of flowing tonal patterns and meaning.[561]

---

[559] Sam Harris argues: "One of the great tasks of civilization is to create cultural mechanisms that protect us from the moment-to-moment failures of our ethical intuitions." Harris, *The Moral Landscape*, 70.

[560] As Richard Weaver memorably puts it, "sentiment is anterior to reason." Weaver, *Ideas Have Consequences*, 18.

[561] McGregor, "Brain Trust," 68.

Neurally, we are more than we know. Neurally, we are mostly un-known. Human brainstems and limbic structures, draped in neocortex, inte-grate and innovate in ways other mammals do not. But the human brain remains a mammalian brain. We live drives. We deflect our deep motiva-tions by emotional concerns. Occasionally, we may even reflect on them. Most often, we simply live what life neurotypicality proffers.[562]

Objection 13: Sound and Fury: *Some demur that Panksepp's work barely advances consciousness theory. By shredding hordes of cats, rats, cows, and the occasional primate, the professor's work has mapped brain concourses and some behavioral predilections, which may (or may not) analogize to human neu-rology. Capitalizing words for brain modules fails to distinguish those "mod-ules" from the pedestrian experience of the described motivations-emotions. Further, the "coppice of consciousness" metaphor (for which I blame the author of* Cull, *not Dr. Panksepp), describes a consciousness at odds with everyday ex-perience. When I think, that act is my most intimate self interacting with my world. I am not fragmented or conflicted. I am unitary, and differentiated from every other person. Panksepp and coppice talk take us from nowhere to no-where.*

Response: Panksepp's work matters. Panksepp opens a door to treatment of mental illness and comprehension of consciousness that is data-driven and verifiable. Panksepp puts the lie to the myth of unified consciousness by means of hard data. Our many psychological struggles and pathological deviancies gain an interpretive metaphor in the coppice of consciousness. We evaluate the-oretical work by the light it sheds on problems previously deemed intractable. Panksepp's studies illuminate a host of pathologies from autism to sociopathy, and help us flash a light into our ethical quandaries with fresh batteries. I am sure that this objector experiences discomfort thinking of himself as a lightly-organized agglomeration of drives and affects colliding in a skull.[563] I certainly did. But then, the explanatory utility of the metaphor captured me. Be patient with new ideas. Let them germinate in the mind's soil. Do not weed too soon.

---

[562] Leonard Mlodinow is hopeful: "We can use our conscious minds to study, to identify, and to pierce our cognitive illusions. By broadening our perspective to take into account how our minds operate, we can achieve a more enlightened view of who we are. But even as we grow to better un-derstand ourselves, we should maintain our appreciation of the fact that, if our mind's natural view of the world is skewed, it is skewed for a reason." Mlodinow, *Subliminal*, 194.

[563] For an attempt to work out a building block theory of consciousness, see Minsky, *The Society of Mind.* Minsky portrays the many subprocesses of the working brain as "resources" interacting in complex ways. Minsky, *The Emotion Machine*, 2-3. Leonard Mlodinow styles human experience as a two-track affair, the conscious and the unconscious. He argues "that within this two-tier system, it is the unconscious tier that is the more fundamental." Mlodinow, *Subliminal*, 33. Bruce Hood goes farther. He denies the existence of self. The self is "a powerful deception generated by our brains for our own benefit," and it "emerges out of the orchestra of different brain processes like a symphyony of the self." Hood, *The Self Illusion*, ix, xii.

Objection 14: Animal Holocaust: *Another protests that Panksepp's work calls to mind Mengele's. In a time and place less chastened than our own (Nazi Germany), similar work, fundamental to human well-being and scientific understanding, was foisted on human subjects. In a time and place more chastened than our own, Panksepp's work on animals will be similarly scorned.*

Response: Jaak Panksepp finds his use of animal subjects ethically fraught, because of its destruction of animal life to the end of human knowledge. Panksepp is, frankly, speciesist, as, I would guess, are most humans. We prefer and identify with human life in a manner we seldom countenance with non-human species. An exception, perhaps, would be our attitudes toward pets and the young of many species. Panksepp has reasoned, in a manner very prevalent in our culture, that, when unavoidable, human goods must outweigh the welfare of animals. One worries that our animal victims may, in underappreciated fact, be greatly more conscious and suffer much more deeply than we dare admit. Jaak Panksepp shares that concern.[564] We can, if we choose as a culture, elevate non-human species' suffering to parity with human suffering. In my view, there exists no principled distinction between non-human suffering and human suffering. Still, we have not, as a culture, chosen to acknowledge animal suffering as real suffering, except with our pets. Perhaps we should. Perhaps we shall.[565]

Objection 15: Deprecating Reason: *Yet another remonstrates that the author's explanation of human consciousness leaves us with a picture of the human mind fragmented in its purposes, unaware of its own motivations, virtually immune to facts, enslaved to social opinion, driven subconsciously by thousands of hidden programs, given to a host of misconceptions, self-deceived, adrift in mysticisms, laboring under metaphysical miscomprehensions, awash in dubious conclusions, and falling into rationality in only the most unlikely circumstances. Some believe (Lawrence Kohlberg and Peter Singer, for example) that without the ability to reliably reason, humans would be incapable of generalized altruism and might well remain permanently in a state of puerile self-fixation.[566] Michael Shermer goes so far as to attribute all of moral progress to the human capacity for abstract reasoning.[567] The author of* Cull *disparages morality itself by deprecating reason.*

---

[564] Pankseep and Biven note that some research cannot be undertaken in humans for ethical reasons. They also note that some would argue similarly against animal research. Panksepp and Biven conclude that "we have no effective strategy other than to study the corresponding processes in other animals." Panksepp and Biven, further, note that the subject animals must suffer, for otherwise the research itself would be a "fool's errand." The subject animals experience consciousness, in a manner much more similar to our own experience than most like to admit. Subject animals are "sentient beings, and their affective capacities arise from the same type of neural soil as we have." Panksepp calls for "abiding sensitivity, with deep respect and concern for the animals we sacrifice to obtain such knowledge." Panksepp and Biven, *The Archaeology of Mind*, 391, 491-492.

[565] Peter Singer suggests that as a minimal first step, we might cease experimenting where animal suffering serves no direct or urgent purpose, and seek to replace animal experiments with different inquiries that do not involve animal suffering. Singer, *Animal Liberation*, 40.

[566] See Singer, *The Expanding Circle*, 137-138.

[567] Shermer, *The Moral Arc*, 21.

Response: Rationality is rare and inevitably compromised.[568] Normal human mentation is mostly irrational, governed by often-adaptive neural programs of which we remain barely aware. Grand optimism about human reason is but puffing. Rational men do not exist, which is not to say no person ever has a glimmer. Jonah Lehrer puts the matter memorably: "It turns out we weren't designed to be rational creatures. Instead, the mind is composed of a messy network of different areas, many of which are involved in the production of emotion. Whenever someone makes a decision, the brain is awash in feeling, driven by its inexplicable passions. Even when a person tries to be reasonable and restrained, these emotional impulses secretly influence judgment."[569]

Rationality delivers much that we value; it is also the horse on which the internet pedophile and nuclear weapons ride into our midst. Most humans never reach the moral high ground of generalized altruism.[570] Nor do most humans spend any significant portion of their lives doing abstract reasoning. One cause of widespread ethical stunting may be the fitfulness of reason. Reasons, and reasoning itself, just do not matter all that much to the vast majority of humans.

The essential point to fix in mind is this: every person, in every vehement conviction, in every well-grounded opinion, has ample cause for humility.[571]

Objection 16: Unwarranted Exceptionalism: *Still another deprecates the author for writing a book. He disparages thinking. Why, then, does he vent his irrational mind vomiting pointless verbosity?*

Response: Give me a moment. A reason why this book is an exception will come to me.[572]

6.6. Member Consciousness.

6.6.1. *Increased Limited Options.* Members elect among perceived courses of action, aware of the group's view of those choices. Options are not, however, unlimited. Deliberated action cannot deviate from the neurophysiologic concourses of human thought. What cannot be conceived, cannot be chosen.

---

[568] Hobbes bluntly put it: "[F]or the Passions of men, are commonly more potent than their Reason." [♪] Hobbes, *Leviathan*, 131 (Chapter 19).

[569] Lehrer, *How We Decide*, xv. Jonah Lehrer is a neuroscience journalist and author.

[570] Darwin might disagree. Of his wide travels on the vessel *Beagle*, he says the traveler "will discover, how many truly kind-hearted people there are, with whom he never before had, or ever again will have any further communication, who yet are ready to offer him the most disinterested assistance." Darwin, *Voyage of the Beagle*, 487.

[571] Epictetus argues that the true philosopher begins with awareness of his personal weakness in recognizing in life those matters that are of genuine import. Epictetus, *Discourses*, 277 (Book II, Section 11.1).

[572] Richard Weaver complains of the paradox he suffers in writing a book that illuminates the sin of writing. Weaver, *Ideas Have Consequences*, 87.

6.6.2. *Pleistocene Perceptions.* Member consciousness is a product of brain architecture and periconscious[573] competition among brain micro-circuits. The brain evolved to respond to specific challenges of the EEA.[574] Our perceptual systems represent the exterior world, but also have a built-in code of subcortical responses. This fundamental operating system can be considered an "evolutionary epistemology."[575] It predisposes every human to respond to challenges of the contemporary moment with ancient survival strategies, which may be considered a form of genetic recollection. The system emerged in response to conditions of the Pleistocene EEA. The pattern and structure of sense experience derives from brain architecture, which is a product of the EEA. Our environment is much changed, but we perceive with Pleistocene equipment wholly adapted to the EEA.

6.6.3. *Pleistocene Emotions.* Affective systems emerged in mammalian evolution. These emotional systems offered a nuanced response to a mammal's environment, as compared to that of the reptile. The mammalian affective system is subject to social influences, and geared to sustain social relationships. The human affective system, which we share with our mammalian ancestors, constitute pre-programmed responses to typical challenges: predation, hunger, sex, play, and sociality. The emergence of human neocortical capabilities in the Pleistocene period greatly enhanced the subtlety of the responses of human ancestors to the EEA. Still, humanity experiences the world with Pleistocene emotions. Our affective responses to modern environments are Pleistocene responses, sometimes redirected by cultural habits emerging from a carefully deliberated cull of conduct alternatives.

6.6.4. *Inherent Cortical Frustration.* Human cortical capacity creates perspective, the self-reflective knowledge that one perceives from a point of view. One's perspective, however, elaborates underlying limbic and brain stem activity. Neurons of the prefrontal cortex may fire hundreds of times per second. Most limbic neurons may fire only a few times per second. Brainstem (reptilian) neurons may not fire at all unless specific environmental stimuli prompt them to discharge.[576] The pace-of-firing differential between brain regions may create internal stresses, possibly perceived

---

[573]The term "periconscious" is a neuroscience coinage capturing the theory that highly-articulated forms of consciousness evolved from preconscious predecessors, and that most brain activity remains subconscious. Affective (emotional) systems may be the rudiments which underlie the human capacity for ethical thought and valuation. Panksepp, *Affective Neuroscience*, 32.

[574]The Pleistocene period has been called the "environment of evolutionary adaptedness" (EEA).

[575] Panksepp, *Affective Neuroscience*, vii.

[576] Panksepp, *Affective Neuroscience*, 84.

psychologically as frustration with the persistence of one's emotions or compulsions. Metaphorically, the triune brain is a cheetah riding a dog astride a turtle. Brain regions, though interactive, pace the race differently.

6.6.5. *Pure Rationality.*   No non-emotional human experiences (that is, strictly rational experiences, in the positivist's philosophical sense) exist. All human conscious perceptions are limbic-reptilian motivations or responses affected by neocortical diversion or inhibition or elaboration. On a good day, mulling non-excitatory subjects, humans may be, for brief periods, fitfully rational.

6.6.5.1. *Hume's Law.*   David Hume argued that one should exercise caution when deriving an "ought" from an "is," and ought to give a reason explaining how one gets from what exists to what ought to exist.[577] Subsequent interpreters have ossified Hume's caution, asserting baldly that no moral proposition flows from any factual description.[578] Such exaggerations mislead. It is true that states of nature imply no ethical obligation. But, if no strictly non-emotional cognition exists (Hume argues in the same manner), then no merely factual descriptions exist. Behind every "is" lies a motivation and affect that identifies the "is" as important to someone for some reason, most especially to the speaker for his or her own purposes.[579] This is the nature of the scientific endeavor itself. A scientist identifies a testable hypothesis, the answer to which addresses a problem she or others experience. All resulting facts, no matter how objectively stated, lie in the shadow of the initiating affect-impulse. Hume's interpreters believed that since no "ought" can be derived from an "is," all "oughts" are suspect and sub-scientific. The coppice of consciousness metaphor argues conversely. Factual assertions beg unpacking.[580] Every factual declaration is erected upon one or

---

[577] Hume, *A Treatise of Human Nature*, 512ff, especially at 521 (Book III, Part I, Section I).

[578] Patricia Churchland nicely describes Hume's point: "Hume had to make it clear that the sophisticated naturalist has no truck with simple, sloppy inferences going from *what is* to *what ought to be?*" Churchland, *Braintrust*, 5.

[579] Hume himself makes this point. He argues that reason may caution us about the use or hindrance toward which some matter may tend, but to become a moral perception, one requires an underlying sentiment of benevolence, a wish that mankind prosper and avoid ill. Apart from such sentiment, men prove indifferent. Hume, *An Enquiry Concerning the Principles of Morals*, 158 (Appendix 1: Concerning Moral Sentiment).

[580] Jesse Prinz argues that all human moral assertions bear their freight (the rightness or wrongness of the proposition) on the rails of human social approval or disapproval. This approach, which has similarities to Hume's moral theory and Adam Smith's sentimentalist approach, Prinz calls "epistemic emotionism" or "constructivist sentimentalism."   Prinz, *The Emotional Construction of Morals*, 19-21, 49, 307.

more imperatives or feelings. We say what we say, observe what we observe, for some motivating reason. Every "is" implies an "ought," and resides wholly within its shadow.[581] Pure knowledge is a chimera composite. Facticity disguises (or ignores) the foundational oughtness of assertions. Reductionist empiricism merely ignores or denies its motivational imperatives. Empiricism has uses; it corrects some sorts of human error, it offers an investigational methodology. Empirical investigation does not, however, well-describe the humanly-perceived world. Empirical investigation addresses one bucket dipped from the ocean of human experience.[582] Humans seek knowledge for morally-cognizable purposes. We want to know in order to make something or someone, somewhere, somehow better.[583]

6.6.5.2. *Kant's Ethical Rationalism.*   Immanuel Kant asserts that every binding moral idea derives purely from reason, all apart from empirical observations of any sort.[584] Kant imagines himself approaching morality as had he previously analyzed rationality itself—solely by reason reflecting upon itself, in a manner divorced from all sense experience. Coppice consciousness quite directly declares Kant's methodology impossible. Setting oneself the task of deliberating apart from one's empirical setting, free of motivations and emotional priorities, is itself an impulse deflected by an emotion taken up in a thought. Even as Kant imagines himself deliberating *a priori,*[585] he is moved to do so (brain-

---

[581] Frans de Waal agrees. De Waal, *The Bonobo and the Atheist,* 162-165.

[582] James, *Is Life Worth Living?,* 23.

[583] Peter Singer makes a defense of Hume's Law. Singer, *The Expanding Circle,* 72-83. Despite the fact that Singer's book concerns the evolutionary origins of morality, he nevertheless misses the fundamental ought-orientation of human observations. To employ Singer's own terminology in contradicting him, the standpoint of a participant is the only standpoint that exists. The standpoint of an observer is the standpoint of a participant who pretends not to participate. Singer later acknowledges that all reasoning is a scaffold erected upon the foundation of social consciousness that some others are not to be injured. Singer, *The Expanding Circle,* 91. Moral reasoning, in Singer's treatment, becomes a highly-nuanced linguistic form of welcoming lick or irritated growl, but one that may be universalized. Singer, *The Expanding Circle,* 92-93. Hence, moral reasoning emerges. Stephen Asma argues against Hume's Law (which does not derive from Hume). Aristotle and Darwin found facts about human biology relevant to ethical norms. Asma says, "If you want to know what is *good* for human beings, Aristotle thought, you don't study *The Good* (ask Plato tried). Instead, you study *human beings.*" Asma, *Against Fairness,* 45. Polanyi and Prosch argue that even in science, no impersonal objectivity exists. The scientist exercises "dynamic imagination." Science aims not at detachment, but rather at involvement and commitments. Pure objectivity of knowledge in science is a baseless myth. Polyani and Prosch, *Meaning,* 63.

[584] [♪] Kant, *Fundamental Principles of the Metaphysics of Morals,* 169.

[585] Philosophers distinguish *a priori* (Latin: "from before") knowledge (which is usually tautological: "x = x, or definitional " all apples are fruits"), from *a posteriori* (Latin: "from after") knowledge (which requires observation: x = 13, or some apples have maggots).

stem), he wishes to succeed (limbic system). Thus is Kant's agenda derailed before it commences. No de-brained cognition exists.

6.6.5.3. *Aristotle's Divine Shard.* Aristotle styles human intellect a fragment of the divine dwelling in the human mind. One owes this shard his first allegiance. Contemplation is the highest human activity, and a man is well-advised to don the garb of immortality to the extent possible by habituating a life of the intellect.[586] Aristotle goes on to acknowledge the role of feelings and emotions in the structure of human life, but retains purist segregation for the role of intellect. The problem for Aristotle's view remains that, if the coppice metaphor captures the functioning of human consciousness, no such pure intellect exists. Aristotle advocates a phantasm.

6.6.6. *Wholistic Cognition.* If the coppice metaphor well-captures human cognition, then no purely theoretical consciousness exists. Emotionally-charged brainstem drives are central, not peripheral, to cognition. Every impulse is limbically negotiated. Neocortical cognition is a fragment of the entire human organism responding to its changing environments.[587] Every human thought consists in a brainstem urge, redirected by limbic affective imperatives, subsequently refined by neocortical inhibition and expressed by neocortical language. This view of consciousness contravenes several myths we inherit from Greek rationality and Enlightenment optimism about the nature of human cognition.

6.6.6.1. *The Myth of Objectivity.* Plato believed that gifted humans might attain pure objectivity. In Plato's *Republic*, he tells his allegory of the cave.[588] Mankind lies chained in the bottom of a cave near a fire. None can see the fire behind them or the cave shaft, since only the cave wall is visible. The cave shaft extends to the lighted sky above. The fire casts shadows on the wall, which are the perceptions of humans. Some few, philosophers all, break their chains, recognize the fire as derivative, and ascend the shaft to find the blazing sun above. Plato takes the sun to be the Forms, things as they are in themselves, absent the interpretive gloss of phenomenology. This metaphysical vision, in Plato's view, makes of philosophers fit rulers for the chained masses below. Kant styles this observational differentiation "things as perceived" versus "things in themselves."[589] He too believes that humans have some perception of

---

[586] [♪] Aristotle, *Nichomachean Ethics*, 194-196 (1177a-1178a).

[587] Barton, *Evolution of the Social Brain*, 139.

[588] [♪] Plato, *Republic*, 221-223 (Book 7, §514a-517a).

[589] Kant, *Critique of Pure Reason*, 25 (First Section of the Transcendental Aesthetic, §3).

things in themselves through mathematics and carefully delimited reason. Coppice consciousness denies that such cool objectivity exists in human minds. Every concept harbors motive and feeling. Each competes with others, all critical to survival and flourishing. No overarching goal encompasses all human activity.[590] Humanity is a fragmented survival organism.

6.6.6.2. *The Myth of the Impartial Observer.* The scientific community and the legal system, in its forensic mode, promote recourse to the impartial observer. Both communities urge that disinterested parties more accurately perceive circumstances than involved persons. The careful scientific hypothesis fashions controls to inhibit biases. Legal rules exclude or inhibit some testimony and evidence where the possibility of interested manipulation is deemed unacceptably great.[591] Coppice consciousness disputes the possibility of such impartiality. The scientist favors his anticipated result and his focus of attention unconsciously neglects unwanted results. Legal rules of evidence function most often to justify conclusions decision-makers reached before any evidence was submitted. There exist no impartial observers. No controls can exclude weighted conclusions. There are no impartial witnesses, only witnesses.[592]

6.6.6.3. *The Myth of Unified Consciousness.* In his *Phaedrus* dialogue, Plato styles consciousness as uniform rationality troubled by rowdy im-

---

[590] [♪] Dewey, *Human Nature and Conduct*, 229.

[591] Simone de Beauvoir styles objectivity a "vain attempt to be God." Man is just himself. Woman wakes to find herself existing, unclear about what to do. Genuine existence abandons the "dream of human objectivity." Values leap into the world where humans make decisions in "pure contingency." One must decide "whether he wants to live and under what conditions." So, all ethics are ambiguous. No ethics can "forge laws valid for all." Stuck with mere subjectivity, people choose. In choosing, they root themselves in some particular set of circumstances. They choose a perspective and social world. In this way, ethical words (progress, good, bad, success, failure, and so forth) acquire meaning. "To say that [human existence] is ambiguous is to assert that its meaning is never fixed, that it must be constantly won." De Beauvoir, *The Ethics of Ambiguity*, 13-19, 129. De Beauvoir has little, if any, appreciation for the massive substructure of human consciousness that coppice consciousness emphasizes. Humans would seem, from conception, to be launched upon some rudiments of life that are little comprehended and highly resilient. Humans cannot choose to become whatever might strike their fancy. To this extent, Sartre's and de Beauvoir's existentialism misleads. De Beauvoir accepts some internal structure to human existence when she says, "no existence can be validly fulfilled if it is limited to itself. It appeals to the existence of others." De Beauvoir, *The Ethics of Ambiguity*, 67.

[592] Michael Tomasello might object. His account of the evolution of human thinking notes that we think together (that is, share intentionality). Humans believe our collective habits of thought expose what is real. Objectivity is the "view from nowhere," the view of any rational person. From collective thought is born all education (how things work) and morality (what is right, what is wrong). Tomasello, *Natural History of Human Thinking*, 153. Jesse Prinz prefers that our moral judgments be conceived as emotional preferences. In the grip of motivating sentiment, one has a "safeguard against vicious indifference." Prinz, *The Emotional Construction of Morals*, 308.

pulses and emotions.[593] Reason rides the chariot of consciousness pow-
ered by a compliant horse, representing humanity's kinder inclinations,
and an undisciplined steed, representing man's untamed violence and
impulsivity. It falls to the charioteer to break the rowdy steed and take
unchallenged control of his chariot. Royal reason harnesses both steeds
for rational purposes. Bad impulses derive from the earth, and so are
dirty. Good impulses reflect divine light, and so radiate health.

Coppice consciousness finds no charioteer, but rather a sometimes
riotous, but subconscious, competition of inclinations and affects. Consciousness may grow more orderly as age and practice render youthful
excitations equivocal. But consciousness never becomes unified, and
remains a marketplace of drives and emotions, hawked in the coin of
survival import. Rationality, that cranial weakling, diverts impulse and
affect when stirred from its persistent napping. One needs not to stunt
drives and emotions, but to welcome their vital impulses, redirecting
those that injure or confuse. Mankind needs more, not less, impulsivity;
we need a vastly more vital deliberative process to channel the torrent of
human motivations.[594]

6.6.6.4. *The Myth of a Unified and Elegant Reality.* Most physicists posit
that beneath the multiplicity of human experience lie simple and elegant
rules, as yet undiscovered, which explain the universe. Coppice consciousness leads one to question this assumption on a few counts. First,
human consciousness has not proved to be simple or elegant. Would
human rationality, fractured and fleeting, grasp such simplicity if it encountered a founding principle? Second, one wonders whether the conviction of ultimate simplicity does not proceed from the conviction of
the unity of reason. If so, some damage must be done to the belief by
the coppice structure of consciousness. Reason itself is neither unified
nor simple. Third, investigation has not revealed, to date, simple or unified cosmic fundaments. Rather, our best efforts expose a fractured uni-

---

[593] Plato, *Phaedrus*, 471-477 (246A-247E). Cicero shares this common view from Greco-Roman antiquity. See [♪] Cicero, *De Officiis*, 101 (Book I, Section XXVIII). The *Katha Upanishad* from the
Hindu tradition takes up a similar analogy. Atman, one's essential self, rides a chariot, which is a
person's body. Reason is the charioteer and mind is the reins. The bad charioteer lacks understanding and steadiness; his horses are wild. The good charioteer avoids wandering from death to death,
and reaches his journey's end, never to return from the everlasting Spirit. When one abandons sense
experience, he finds mind, then reason, then Spirit, and finally, the Spirit Supreme, Purusha.
Purusha is the end of the road for the good charioteer. [♪] *Upanishads*, 61 (*Katha Upanishad*, Part
3). In another Upanishad, mind's chariot careens behind a wild team of horses. The seer urges one
to tame those horses by silence and rhythmic breathing. [♪] *Upanishads*, 88 (*Svetasvatara Upanishad*, Part 2).

[594] Dewey argues that man needs more, not fewer, passions. Rationality harmonizes our competing
cognitive desires, slowing them, coordinating them. [♪] Dewey, *Human Nature and Conduct*, 196.

verse inhabited by a multitude of subatomic denizens interacting in chaotic patterns that resolve into rules more probable than positive. What's more, it appears that the vast majority of the stuff in the universe has so far utterly eluded human perception (dark matter and dark energy). Belief in unified reality, that is, ultimate simplicity, appears to be little more than a human conceit.[595]

6.6.7. *Sexually-Differentiated Member Consciousness.* Male consciousness, on average, differs in significant respects, on average, from female consciousness.[596] The origin of these differences is primarily biological, which predispositions are confirmed and entrenched by cultural socialization processes.[597] Some sexual differences are:

6.6.7.1. *Physical Structure.* Both male and female share the similar body plans, though there are structural differences between male and female bodies in relative size, reproductive organs, relative strength, longevity, endurance. The male and female brain differ in significant respects, though they share a common basic structure.[598]

6.6.7.2. *Empathy.*[599] Both males and females exhibit ability to predict and manipulate ordered systems and to recognize and respond to the feelings of others (empathy). Most human females exceed males in empathic ability.

---

[595] Gary Bloom finds my use of the word "reality" problematical, noting that is not how physicists express themselves. He wonders if I do not mean to say that unified field theory is proving elusive. I use the word "reality" intentionally. I believe that most scientists accept the myth that, beneath contrary appearances, the universe is fundamentally simple. This is reductionist sentiment. "Reality" is the non-technical word people use to describe their cherished expectations. Scientific experiments and mathematical excursions have not, to date, demonstrated simple commonalities underlying experience. Reality has proved neither simple nor elegant, but rather messy and rife with probabilistic complexities. We describe our world, as Bloom notes, at various levels of abstraction. Humberto Maturana argued that nothing enters the nervous system, but only ruffles one's existing neural state, causing reorganization. I note, however, that this abstract thought does not impede my enjoyment of bourbon. Bloom wonders if sweeping across levels of abstraction, as I do, is not a form of unintentional cheating in my argument. I answer, possibly. With fractured consciousness, how can one decide?

[596] Hobbes doubted men are "the more excellent sex," finding that either sex may, under appropriate circumstances, best the other. Sovereign dominion may root in a man or woman, though more often in men. [♪] Hobbes, *Leviathan*, 139-140 (Chapter 20). Rousseau finds that women are men, except in matters related to sex. Yet, Rousseau explains that sexuality pervades both male and female life, giving to each an appropriate role. Rousseau, *Emile*, 357-358, 363. One wonders if Rousseau would have fallen back on simple equality of the sexes once effective birth control became possible.

[597] Simone de Beauvoir says, "women simply *are not* men." de Beauvoir, *The Second Sex*, xlii.

[598] Lawrence Tancredi notes differences in the size and shape of the corpus callosum and anterior commissure, as well as portions of the cerebral cortex. Tancredi, *Hardwired Behavior*, 86.

[599] Baron-Cohen, "Empathizing and Systemizing," 216-217.

6.6.7.2.1. Boys evidence fifty times more competitive inclination than girls, and girls show twenty times boys' inclination to take turns.

6.6.7.2.2. Boys exceed girls in rough and tumble play (which requires less empathy to engage).

6.6.7.2.3. Female infants one year and older express more sympathetic vocalizations than males. Women report sharing friends' distress, and even that of strangers, more than men.

6.6.7.2.4. At three years of age, females better infer what others are thinking.

6.6.7.2.5. Women score higher on questionnaires measuring empathy. On questionnaires, girls affirm cooperation and value intimacy. Boys are more likely to endorse competition, and value status.

6.6.7.2.6. Males suffer psychopathic personality disorder and conduct disorder much more frequently than females. Three of every four sociopaths are male.

6.6.7.2.7. Neurotypical aggression requires reduced empathy. Males evidence heightened inclination for physical violence, while females evidence relational aggression (gossip, shunning).

6.6.7.2.8. In a study analyzing homicide records of 700 years, males killing males exceeds female killing females by thirty to forty times.

6.6.7.2.9. Males are quicker to form dominance hierarchies.

6.6.7.2.10. The language style of boys is more direct. Girls express opinions by asking questions or accommodating the perspective of the other.

6.6.7.2.11. Women talk more often about emotions than do men.

6.6.7.2.12. Mothers engage children face to face more often than do fathers, and accommodate their language to the abilities of the child more frequently than do fathers.

6.6.7.2.13. Female infants look longer at faces; males look longer at inanimate objects.[600]

6.6.7.2.14. Females may have better language skills than men.

6.6.7.3. *Systemizing.*[601]   "Systemizing" indicates the ability to recognize and manipulate ordered systems, requiring attention to specific detail and conditional thinking. Both males and females exhibit ability to predict and manipulate ordered systems and to recognize and respond to the

---

[600] Thomas Andrews notes that, if this is so, the structure must invert itself in adulthood. Women focus on jewelry and mirrors, while men focus on looking at women. Andrews, in private correspondence, June 5, 2016.

[601] The coinage "systemizing" and this list of characteristics derives from Simon Baron-Cohen. Baron-Cohen, "Empathizing and Systemizing," 218-220.

feelings of others (empathy). Most males exceed females in their ability to systemize.

6.6.7.3.1. Boys prefer mechanical toys.

6.6.7.3.2. Some occupational choices are male-dominated: metalworking, construction, weaponry, musical instrument manufacture, for example.

6.6.7.3.3. Male Scholastic Aptitude Math Test scores are on average fifty points higher. Of those scoring 700 or better, males exceed females thirteen to one.

6.6.7.3.4. Males score better than females on three dimensional assembly tasks, creating structures from two dimensional blueprints, and imagining three dimensional objects from overhead or one-side only views.

6.6.7.3.5. Male children accurately draw water levels more frequently in Piaget's water level test.

6.6.7.3.6. Female visual judgment is more field dependent. Males tend to evaluate each visual variable more independently, and so are less confused by contextual confusions.

6.6.7.3.7. Male attention to relevant detail exceeds female attention.

6.6.7.3.8. Males perform better than females on mental rotation tests.

6.6.7.3.9. Males exceed females in map reading tests.

6.6.7.3.10. Males perform better than females on catching and throwing moving objects and judging which of two objects moves faster.

6.6.7.3.11. Most males systemizing quotients exceed female quotients.

6.6.7.3.12. Male performance on the physical prediction questionnaire (engineering entry examination) exceeds most females.

6.6.7.4. *Hunting and Gathering.* Among tribes that survive without domestication or agriculture, a sexual division of labor exists. Women gather and prepare staples of the tribal diet. Men hunt protein bonanzas. Even where women hunt, they hunt different animals than their men.[602] Both men and women benefit by their specialization, and sexual differentiation in food gathering may have proved a significant advantage in competing for scarce resources in long African droughts.

> *Objection 17: Misogyny: Some demur that the author spouts pure misogyny. The mental and physical differences between human sexes are negligible, absent the cultural inertia of men oppressing women by gender roles. The author seems to prefer broad tolerance, as a social proposition. Yet the author goes on to create an unwarranted "us and them" by belaboring differences between males and females, at least some of which are mere cultural ephemera. The author should desist.*

---

[602][♪] Ridley, *The Rational Optimist*, 61-62.

Response: I am male and gendered. That colors my perspective. To complain of my male perspective is to agree with me about sexual differentiation. Men and women differ in non-trivial respects. All should attempt to get clear as to exactly what differences exist. Men are not women. Women are not men. Neither are hermaphrodites. As a species, we are sexed. Neither sex can survive independently of the other. We dwell in sexual complementarity. Feminist identity politics has bowdlerized all conversation about our sexual dimorphism. That we are sexed seems, to this author, both patent and worth deliberating. That, at the margins, our sexuality and genders are multiple, mixed, and muddled also seems patent. With humans, one size does not fit all. Nor one sex. We should talk about our differences. To fail to do so is both silly and, possibly, dangerous.

6.7. *Community Consciousness: Sociality.*

6.7.1. *Collective Existence.* Participating in community is not voluntary, because human sociality is not elective. All humans exist within (or having been ejected from) one or more communities.

6.7.2. *Member-Dependent.* Communities lack the biological matrix from which collective consciousness might emerge, apart from the biology of their members. Nevertheless, human sociality has been persistently conceived as collective consciousness.[603] The engine of evolution selects adaptive characteristics of groups, as well as members.

6.7.3. *Sociality.* Humans live socially. Members, cut off from the conversation of communities, wither. Human social constructs propagate rules and life structures for members, which in time are deemed as real as physical entities, shape the perceptions of members, and ultimately are hypostatized, becoming divine persons to whom the member is, in some manner, related.

6.7.3.1. *Social Internalization.* Members imbibe social constructs, mostly unconsciously, making of them part and parcel of the member.

6.7.3.2. *Kith Coordination.* Pre-linguistic hominins coordinated community action by subcortical non-verbal gestural language. Modern humans retain signaling, though its operation is complicated by language and the abstraction-overlay of neocortical processes. Trustworthy human peers, not rational argument, frequently guide group decision-making. Those "followed peers", deemed kith,[604] create communal consensus by somat-

---

[603] [♪] Ridley, *The Rational Optimist*, 47-84 (Chapter 2: The Collective Brain). Italian fascist philosopher, Giovanni Gentile (ghost-writer for Benito Mussolini), argued that the State is a corporate personality into which the individual is born and from which he derives identity and meaning. See Gentile, *The Origin and Doctrine of Fascism*, 34. See also Bonhoeffer, *Sanctorum Communio*, *Ephesians* 2:13-16, and the persistent oddity of addressing the nation of Israel as one person in the Old Testament.

[604] "Kith" are social intimates, neighbors and acquaintances, and sometimes those with whom one shares a common culture and locale. See *Webster's Third New International Dictionary*, s.v. "kith."

ic mimickry which evokes empathy and trust, activity that signals interest and enthusiasm, and fluid speech that suggests expertise. This non-
verbal opinion-making activates the primordial habit system of the
mammalian brain; individuals are seldom aware of its operation. The
effect of kith on peers may be called charisma. In groups, the kith charismatic listens intensely, speaks fluidly, and drives conversations with
questions.[605]

6.7.3.3. *Social Hypostatization.* Members hypostatize[606] collectives, making of them "persons" with which members interact as if the collective
were another, encompassing member. In this sense, collectives exist.[607]

6.7.3.4. *Deemed Transcendence.* Hypostatization of collectives, extended
maximally, underlies religious perception. From a sociological perspective, gods can be considered an hypostatized community in its cosmos,
that is, a people in its social and physical environment considered aggregately as a person.[608] Unified godheads are drained of particularities,
coming to represent various components or forces of nature and experience. In monotheism, god becomes all, of whom no specifics can be asserted (*via negativa*), and to whom undivided fealty is owed. Kings (or
presidents or parliaments) bask in divine radiance and do It lip-service.
Imagined connection to the supra-mundane invests values with ultimate
gravity, and shelters values so enshrined from rapid change. Transcendence opens the possibility of response to unanswerable questions. Gods
afford an ultimate attachment figure to replace father and mother as

---

[605] Pentland, "To Signal Is Human," *American Scientist* 98 (June 2010): 204-211.

[606] To "hypostatize" is to conceive an idea as an independent substance or entity, or to presume something insubstantial as a concrete existence, or to reify an idea. *Webster's Third New International Dictionary*, s.v. "hypostatize." John Dewey finds the concept of collective minds a fiction, intending nothing more than the fact that some customs and habits achieve near universality. [♪]
Dewey, *Human Nature and Conduct*, 60.

[607] Law has long hypostatized collectives. Corporations are "persons" in the same sense that people
are persons, for legal purposes. As a matter of constitutional prerogatives, one may question whether there lies any wisdom in making entities into "persons," since such entities never sleep, tend to
have dramatically more money to invest in political process than do individuals, and focus their activities solely on money-mongering. We poor sleeping, loving, defecating sorts of persons have
hardly a chance in head-to-head competition with hypostatized political entities.

[608] Gregory Bateson offers a view of supra-human minds. These transcendent entities remain obscure to human minds, which comprise a part of these super-minds. Major religions mystify this
murk. Bateson believes that using cybernetics, systems theory, ecological concepts, and clinging to
a natural history approach to explanation, we may be able to approach understanding of these massive organizations. Bateson, *Steps To An Ecology of Mind*, 493, and Bateson and Bateson, *Angels
Fear*, 136. Bateson's language calls to mind Aurelius's view of the world as a great spirit or world
animal (Stoicism), and also Hegel's Absolute Spirit, imperiously dragging all us minor minds along
in its wake on its journey of self-realization. See [♪] Aurelius, *To Himself*, and Hegel, *Philosophy of
Right*.

adulthood intervenes and parental health declines. In helpful scenarios, gods invest the effort to create meaningful community with eternal approbation, and permit obedient communities to shelter in the divine penumbra. In gods' names, precocious compassion finds applause. In less helpful scenarios, gods confirm shame and guilt, torment sensitive consciences, and offer ready-made pretense for sociopaths and those concealing their bad faith. In gods' names are the most erosive human impulses summoned and focused. Deemed transcendence offers a wedge by which the manipulative can sunder normal people from community, hearth, and self.

This sociological perception of the divine fails to address a primary theological issue for believers: do gods exist? That issue cannot be approached empirically. The oceans of ink spilled elucidating divine intentions transmit no knowledge, but do evidence the urgency humans feel to find meaning and to anchor ethical deliberation in something more substantial than whim. Of gods, we know nothing at all. Of books men receive from a divine mouth, one doubts. Of arguments concerning the existence and non-existence of gods, one longs to divert conversation to constructive channels.

Cull is an effort to afford ethical deliberation a non-theological fundament.[609] Theological speculation has value, especially when practiced by humble minds intent upon improving human community. This author enjoyed the benefit of a theological education; that long cogitation informs all I think and do. Yet, I depart its frame for what you read here. Of theological ethics, one says: Human minds prune many trees, only some of which bear edible fruit. This book addresses the ethically hungry. It forsakes barren trees in search of sustenance. Those given to theological comprehension should acknowledge that, when we speak of gods, we mumble what we know not.

6.7.3.5. *The* Cul de Sac *of Fascism and Communism.* Fascism proffers a collectivist anthropology similar in some ways to this work's Quad anthropology. Adolf Hitler asserts that mankind finds its highest expression when masses follow a politically-gifted hero, who bears all responsibility and authority for the well-being of his people and nation.[610] Be-

---

[609] Maturana and Varela undertook another such effort. They argue that, since man co-constructs knowledge and reality for himself, one can say little to those outside one's own social universe, regardless how quaint or unhelpful aspects of that alternative construct might seem. Cross-social conflicts cannot be resolved by argument. They are rooted in divergent manners of living and thinking. To resolve such conflicts, one adopts or creates another social universe which the contestants share. Maturana and Varela, *Tree of Knowledge*, 245-246.

[610] [♪] Hitler, *Mein Kampf*, 381.

nito Mussolini's ghost-writer, Giovanni Gentile, argues that human life stands aright only within national collectives. Individualism distorts human existence. A man finds himself in the corporate personality of his nation—doing its tasks, generating its future members, and receiving direction from its dictates. The state controls all. The member obeys.[611] Vladimir Lenin argues that capitalists oppress workers by means of government. Workers must violently wrest control from capitalists, co-opt industrial production to their own purposes, and fundamentally reshape political and economic structures. Government itself will wither and eventually perish. All these events occur under the leadership of revolutionaries with the vision to undertake necessary violence.[612]

Fascist ideology, while grasping the corporate structure of individual existence, careens down roads to nowhere in its commitment to nation-states, totalitarianism, and violence. Nation-states are a ponderous human sociality bloated by over-population, rendered neurotic by perpetual perceived scarcity, and poisoned by incessant coercion. Fascist totalitarianism dismisses the human need for having a say in things. Though humans may for a time tolerate strong intrusion by a collective, all ultimately rankle against compulsions and demand substantial self-expression and self-governance.

Communist ideology shares fascism's commitment to coercion and violence. But communism, like fascism, elevates the corporate aspect of living, gives it due emphasis. Marx urges us that, despite the appearance of indestructibility of society, our habits and corporate existence are malleable and can be refashioned. Leninism teaches that society must serve all, not the few.[613]

Stripped of their commitments to violence and coercion, fascism and communism offer ideas from which the human community can profit, and reinforce the excruciating twentieth century lesson that neurodiverse savants should not be permitted political autonomy. If there must be power, let it fall to plodders. Where revolutionaries hide tyrannical hearts, armed struggle changes nothing but who lounges upon

---

[611] See [♪] Mussolini, *The Doctrine of Fascism,* 10-14 (Giovanni Gentile ghost-wrote the first section of Mussolini's pamphlet).

[612] See Lenin, *The State and Revolution,* 316. Some assert that communism has died. It is not so, despite the fall of the Soviet Union and the capitalization of China. France's Invisible Committee advocates a new communism, one with greater spiritual emphasis than its predecessors. As one would expect, this new communism still weds itself to violence. Invisible Committee, *The Coming Insurrection,* 14-17, 128.

[613] Vladimir Lenin, after his violent communist revolution, sought, at least initially, to replace capitalist wage slavery with a national economy modeled on the post office. All work for the State. All are paid workmen's wages. Lenin, *The State and Revolution,* 308.

the seat of power.   Wollstonecraft says that redistributing tyrannical powers "render[s] the struggle for liberty only a choice of masters."[614]

---

[614] [♪] Wollstonecraft, *A Vindication of the Rights of Men*, 50.

III.   MEMBER CULLING

Think, Kate, *of decisions you will make. I turn from digging philosophical foundations to erecting a superstructure. What might finely-elaborated conduct culling look like in a human life? What attitudes might help people build meaningful community? What choices ought to give pause? What habits help? Which injure? What importance do friends bear? What dangers lurk? Is it even possible to know what course of action may prove better and what may prove worse?[615] I offer thoughts about how to choose, even what to choose. In the end, the choices are yours. I have no concern that you will heed me slavishly. You never do. As it should be.[616]*

7.   *Members Choosing: Simple Rules.*   Meaningful life, so far as this author understands it, emerges from well-deliberated choices fashioned in deeply-connected communities comprising circles of cadres of members. This is Quad sociality. Member relations interpenetrate, as do member-community relations and community-community relations. Each depends reciprocally and essentially upon others. For each member, primal drives wend through emotional deflections, to be restructured cognitively in the coppice of consciousness. For each member, establishing one's own flourishing life entails supporting a flourishing life for her community and the Commons. Members

---

[615] Master Zhuang recounts a discussion between Nie Que and Wang Ni, in which Wang Ni complains: "The way I see it, the rules of benevolence and righteousness and the paths of right and wrong are all hopelessly snarled and jumbled. How could I know anything about such discriminations?" *Zhuangzi*, 41 (in Discussion on Making All Things Equal, Section 2).

[616] Burke said, at the end of his lengthy diatribe against the French Revolution, "I have told you candidly my sentiments. I think they are not likely to alter yours. I do not know that they ought." Burke, *Reflections on the Revolution in France*, 249.

matter; others matter. Every human deliberation is necessarily bi-focal.[617] In what follows, I take up members first (in this section), and then consider communities (in the following section). At every point, one asks the essential question: What set of habits and thoughts, what elements of character, support the meaning-laden communal life of kithdom?

Human consciousness exhibits vast flexibility constrained by the brain's evolutionary heritage. The task in human conduct lies in electing paths to flourishing life consistent with our hard-wired capabilities, while avoiding the pits and sloughs that lie along fault lines in human consciousness. We inherit a tangled trajectory, which, if allowed unfettered play, may result in our extinction, and which currently saddles us with widespread miseries. We also inherit from Pleistocene savannahs the capacity to cull courses of conduct, and to elect a future that substantially, though not wholly, diverges from the habits of humanity's adolescence, within the confines of the genetically possible alternatives.[618] This Section III describes a culled course applicable to most members of most sorts of communities.

Within the human socio-neural matrix, members cull perceived goods from evils. **How are meaning-laden communities built and maintained? What means and outcomes constitute the good that members seek? What possibilities constitute the evils that one should flee? And, critically in collective life, how should one respond to evils that one cannot responsibly flee?**[619]

Members in Quad communities have opportunities and responsibilities to themselves and to one another. Opportunities emerge because every circumstance bears with it possibilities not all perceive. Another sees what you miss. Responsibilities emerge because every member's action tugs some strand of the tapestry of human weal. One cannot act or fail to act without effect. We observe cumulative effects, if we please. Principles emerge from experiments gone well. Principles are not true, once for all, but are well-

---

[617] Bertrand Russell argues that ethics exists in deep duality. The civic does not reduce to the individual. Individuals do not aggregate to community. Two poles must be addressed in every ethical inquiry. Russell, "Individual and Social Ethics," 337.

[618] Tolstoy likens human maturity of his time to an individual's adolescence. Childhood and its rules no longer suffice. Yet manhood and its wisdoms have yet to ripen. In the interim, distractions abound. Tolstoy, *A Letter to a Hindu*, 16 (Chapter VI). Peter Singer argues that our neurobiological knowledge, so recently acquired, opens the possibility that we may deliberately "deflect the tendencies in our genes" from narrow self-interest toward a universalized altruism, impartial and rational, including even non-human species. Singer, *The Expanding Circle*, 169-170.

[619] These questions are ageless and human. The twelfth century Chinese Confucian master, Chu Hsi (also transcribed Zhu Xi), revived a defunct school, the White Deer Hollow Academy, and set out articles of instruction for his students: a) affection between parent and child, b) righteousness between ruler and subject, c) differentiation between husband and wife, d) precedence between elder and younger, and e) trust between friends. Chu Hsi, *Learning to Be a Sage*, 29.

tested hypotheses from which one may commence one's own moral explorations. We all build upon moral foundations, but diversely. Principles respect the hard-won insights of past generations, to erect a new experiment upon them.[620] Never venerate moral principles. Principles comprise the happy guesses of long dead persons, possibly confirmed by experience, but possibly imposed without deliberative warrant. These kithdom rules are not Rules. No god mutters them. These rules may, however, be wise. That means some thought-battered person stammered these rules, and thousands put the rules to the test in real life.[621] In kithdom, thousands of communities will experiment with different formulations of morality, all seeking diverse visions of the same goal. Morality's foundations are deeply-embedded mammalian priorities constraining exuberances to effect community well-being. Empathy, sympathy, mimickry, conformity, equity: these lie beneath our rules. The rules themselves address local concerns and experiments; they are malleable. We adjust these, subject to the constraints of human genetic rudiments.[622]

The words that follow shall certainly enjoin you to do things you already practice. They are likely to advise what seems wrong or incomprehensible. None among these admonitions is facetious. Each seems, to this author, critical. One hopes you find merit in hearing again the familiar, and in digesting propositions you may wish to confute.[623] Please recall that behind these several rules lies a vision of member life in meaningful community, seeking good and fleeing evil, grasping weal available to all, but seizing none that robs others, neither the living nor the yet-to-live. Every morality contains

---

[620] [♪] Dewey, *Human Nature and Conduct*, 240-241.

[621] Michael Shermer waxes widely to convince readers that religion, in general, contributes little to societal well-being. Shermer, *The Moral Arc*, 173. He criticizes biblical morality (which lends itself to parody and ridicule). When Shermer finishes criticizing the Decalogue (the biblical ten commandments), he, oddly, finds it necessary to replace them with ten rules of his own. To my surprise, they are excellent. Shermer's ten principles are the Golden Rule, the Ask First principle, the Happiness principle, the Liberty principle, the Fairness principle, the Reason principle, the Responsibility and Forgiveness principle, the Defend Others Principle, the Expanding Moral Category Principle, and the Biophilia principle (care for all sentient beings and their ecosystems). Shermer's decalogue merits reading. Though Shermer lacks the hoary magnificence of Moses, his Decalogue is more useful. Shermer, *The Moral Arc*, 180-185.

[622] De Waal ably summarizes this view of morality. He finds that morality has bilateral emphases: one-on-one and community concern. All morality is rooted in empathy, desire for harmony, hierarchy, and fear of censure. Morality adjusts between communities, to accommodate their personnel, preferences, and approaches. De Waal, *The Bonobo and the Atheist*, 156-185. Principles that derive from actual living point to depth in human collectivity. If we do not believe the universe expresses purpose, we will be hard pressed to find any adequate purpose in our own lives. See Weaver, *Ideas Have Consequences*, 47.

[623] Anthony Shaftesbury warns with an English saw: "As to what related to private conduct, no one was ever the better for advice." Shaftesbury, *Characteristicks*, 97 (Volume I, Treatise III, Part I, Section I). Shaftesbury proceeds to give himself advice as an author.

within it a vision of justified ends.[624]   The end of this particular vision is flourishing member and community life.

> TO CHATTERERS, COMMOTION IS KNOWING.
> TO ONE, UNDERSTANDING GUIDES UTTERANCE.
>   PRECIOUS LITTLE IS CERTAIN.
>   ONE'S SILENCE IS FREQUENT,
>   HER SPEAKING BARELY AUDIBLE.
>
> TO CHATTERERS, RULES BEG SNUBBING.
> TO ONE, RULES MIRROR CHARACTER.
>   CHOICES ARE FRAUGHT.
>   ONE SIGHS FINDING HANDHOLDS,
>   HIS TREMBLING BARELY SUBDUED.[625]

Marcus Aurelius urges humans to choose simple rules of life that address the rudiments.[626] One finds the emperor wise. Isocrates called people seeking virtuous life to choose an individual as their model of morality, boil that person's decision-making down to precepts, and then exercise oneself upon those maxims as though they were a physical training regime.[627] According to Epicurus, one compresses a thinker's system into a few simple principles, if anything useful is to come of an encounter with that thinker.[628] *Cull* states a simple rule-for-living for each habit advocated, in a manner that addresses the heart of human existence.[629] These are not all the rules, Kate. You and

---

[624] Russell, "Styles in Ethics," 324.

[625] Simmias contradicts Socrates: Where the truth of matters is difficult to ascertain, one must rely either upon divine utterances or upon the best ideas of men. Human ideas, bound together as a raft, provide a rude vessel upon which to brave life's dangerous travels. Lacking reliable human rationality, or undoubted divine instruction, one seeks alternatives. Socrates counters: One must avoid despising all reasonable argument (misology). [♪] Plato, *Phaedo*, Sections 85-89. The simple rules that follow in this book are driftwood from among human conceptions rafted together by frayed strands of culling.

[626] [♪] Aurelius, *To Himself*, 69 (Book IV, Section 3). Likewise, Seneca urges one to choose a norm by which to govern one's entire life, and to persevere with that norm. Seneca, *Epistles 1-65*, 135 (XX, §3). Mencius too would have disciples full of experience they can boil down to essentials. *Mencius*, 90 (Book IV, Part B, Section 15).

[627] Isocrates, *To Demonicus*. 11.

[628] Epicurus, *Letter to Herodotus*, 20.

[629] Emerson dissents. [♪] Emerson, *Conduct of Life*, 1079 (VII): "Although this garrulity of advising is born with us, I confess that life is rather a subject of wonder, than of didactics." Having dissented, Emerson nevertheless makes his own list, by which he ends his essay on the conduct of life: "The secret of culture is to learn, that a few great points steadily reappear, alike in the poverty of the obscurest farm, and in the miscellany of metropolitan life, and that these few are alone to be regarded,—the escape from all false ties; courage to be what we are; and love of what is simple and beauti-

your community will fashion others. Most particularly, these rules bear general application for life within kithdom. You may identify many others that pertain to your idiosyncrasies and uniqueness.

Being young, Kate, you may be disinclined to listen. Stretch your ears. It is better to decide when young how to govern one's life. You are right to assert your independence; do not flex those muscles in a manner that insulates you from sagacity. Wisdom melds thinking, feeling, and willing to the task of flourishing life.[630] There is no need to stumble over known human errors. If you knit together the fabric of wisdom only in your dotage, regret will be all that remains for you.[631]

7.1. *Self-Care.* **Simple Rule: Nurture yourself.** Treat yourself as a lifelong project of caring.[632] One has some measure of influence in shaping one's own thoughts, attitudes, preferences, and habits. A member may shape herself in a manner that benefits both her and her community, leading to an increase of meaning for both. Socrates marveled at the energy that sculptors invested in turning blocks of marble into anatomically perfect humans, and wondered that the sculptors devoted so little effort to sculpting themselves.[633] A member, when she consciously seeks to nurture herself, rudders life by simple rules. Adopt brief axioms that illumine the heart of living. Guide yourself by them.[634]

---

ful; independence, and cheerful relations, these are the essentials,—these, and the wish to serve,—to add somewhat to the well-being of men." [♪] Emerson, *Conduct of Life*, 1096 (VII).

[630] Russell, "The Expanding Mental Universe," 374.

[631] Rousseau, *Reveries of the Solitary Walker*, 47 (Third Walk).

[632] Xenophon says that Socrates taught that each man's dearest friend is the man himself. Xenophon, *Memorabilia*, 39 (Book I, Section II, Number 54). Aristotle teaches that every man ought to love himself, without taking more for himself than is his due. A genuine lover of self acts nobly and sacrifices for the benefit of friends. [♪] Aristotle, *Nichomachean Ethics*, 174-176 (1168a-1169b). Herbert Spencer argues that "egoism comes before altruism. . . . Unless each duly cares for himself, his care for all others is ended by death; and if each thus dies, there remain no others to be care for." Spencer goes on to make clear that the human community is essential, and altruism its engine. Both egoism and altruism are primordial. Spencer, *The Principles of Ethics*, 217, 233.

[633] Diogenes Laertes, *Lives of Eminent Philosophers*, 163 (II 33). The Buddha advises one to fashion oneself as tradesmen manipulate their materials. [♪] *Dhammapada*, 145. Ronald Dworkin urges: "If we manage to lead a good life well, we create something more. We write a subscript to our mortality. We make our lives tiny diamonds in the cosmic sands." Dworkin, *Justice for Hedgehogs*, 423.

[634] See [♪] Aurelius, *To Himself*, 69 (Book IV, 3). This work is more commonly known as Aurelius's *Meditations*. See also [♪] Cicero, *De Officiis*, 275 (Book III, Section II, 5).

Perhaps a metaphor helps. Your character[635] is a vast farm being hewn from wilderness. The territory is uniquely yours. No other can farm your acreage. As you clear brambles from your homestead, you plant what may grow there. Your fields will produce crops similar to those of others, but unique in their combination and flavor. Over decades, your cultivation may become methodical and productive and life-sustaining, or chaotic and tattered and pointless. Most fields of your farm will settle somewhere between these extremes. Be warned: some make of life a conflagration, fatal to them and destructive to others. Your well-conceived efforts and successes encourage neighbors to make something delightful of their own locales. Your failures, when met with resilience, hearten others to persevere, and serve to instruct them and you. With those who share your agricultural philosophy, you may share tools and aspirations and even invitations to assist you in planting or clearing. Always, you pass portions of your farm on to others in the course of life. Counter-intuitively, such generosity enriches others without reducing the acreage of your own fields at all.[636] Happily, your plot borders the similar plots of friends. A robust exchange of ideas and goods enlivens congenial neighboring farms.[637]

One who neglects herself may lose her way. People may not even notice. You may not notice.[638] Spend time with you every day. Put these hours first, not last, on your list of things to do today. You cannot make flourishing life for others if your own languishes. Teach yourself. Work on goals and challenges. Pare hours from labor for self-nurture. Hear yourself whispering to you. Deliberate your life.[639]

7.2. *Self-Knowledge.* **Simple Rule: Observe yourself intently and compassionately.** Learn who you are, and take care of that person.[640] Humans

---

[635] "Character" denotes those features of your physical, mental, and moral presence that combine to distinguish you from others. Cf. *Webster's Third New International Dictionary*, s.v. "character," 2(a)(3)(b).

[636] This metaphor is suggested by an aphorism of [♪] Aurelius, *To Himself*, 71 (Book IV, 3): "retreat into this little plot that is thyself."

[637] [♪] Dewey, *Human Nature and Conduct*, 263. Epictetus believed that one's life is creatively self-adapted, in the manner that a carpenter shapes wood or a sculptor pours bronze. Epictetus, *Discourses*, 105 (Book I, Section 15.2).

[638] So warns Søren Kierkegaard. [♪] Kierkegaard, *The Sickness Unto Death*, 62-64.

[639] Mencius argues that one cannot meet his moral obligations if work demands too much time. *Mencius*, 14 (Book I, Part A, Section 7). Aristotle urges people to pursue self-nurture in intellectual pursuits during non-working hours, and to avoid labor that saps the vitality necessary for contemplation. [♪] Aristotle, *Nichomachean Ethics*, 615-617 (Book X, Chapter vii, Section 6-7).

[640] Heraclitus beckons all to discover themselves, and to pursue that insight with sober responsibility. Heraclitus, Jones translation, *On the Universe*, 106, 107.

possess an immense capacity for self-deception, and an equally prodigious ability to deny the obvious. Resist. Avoid an inflated self-estimation.[641] Your mind, body, beauty, skill, competence, purse, and friendships are what they are, and no more and no less. Don't flatter yourself; your mind is already doing that subconsciously.[642] Don't deprecate yourself; life will make you feel small enough with more-than-sufficient regularity. Practice measured self-observation, to the extent of your abilities. Of desires, some tautologies help: what is, is; what works, works; what you want is what you want. Each of these inanities is a little slap of your sleepy face, enjoining you to note the obvious. Recognize your facts; see first, then evaluate. You may resist your facts, in the exercise of moral rigors. Never begin self-constraint until you have compassionately plumbed how matters stand with you.

You differ from others. Notice those oddities. They are sign posts to your gifts.[643] Report to yourself what you see, even when painful. Ask yourself, as you learn what sort of person you are, what someone might do to help such a person move forward in the project of her person. Do those things for yourself.[644] Do not assume, when you have assembled a perspective on yourself, that you have arrived at a conclusion to self-knowledge. Since one changes, one never does.[645] This task is metaphorical self-trepanation. Bore an imaginary hole in your forehead and peer. Do not expect consistency in what you discover in yourself. You are many people inhabiting a busy skull.[646] Not all the residents are congenial. Some are

---

[641] Muhammad notes that wise Luqman taught his children to avoid arrogance, for God hates boasting. Do not rush. Keep your voice subdued, so you avoid the ugly sound of a braying ass. [♪] Muhammad, Qur'an, 31:18-19.

[642] [♪] Seneca, On Tranquillity of Mind, 40. Trivers asserts that self-deception taints all human consciousness, especially language. Trivers, Folly of Fools, xv. Our self deceptions are so very potent because denial of deception is so very effective in deceiving others. We unconsciously deceive for gain, for good reputation, to praise our social comrades and denigrate outsiders, and construct false historical stories. In short, we unconsciously deceive ourselves, and consciously overlook evidence that confutes our representations. Trivers, Folly of Fools, 15-28.

[643] Lao Tzu asserts that only odd people excel; conformists are negligible. [♪] Lao Tzu, Tao Te Ching, 32 (67).

[644] Seneca, Epistles 1-65, 33 (VI, 7). Befriend yourself. Aristotle concurs. One should be one's own best friend. Love yourself more than any other. [♪] Aristotle, Nichomachean Ethics, 551 (Chapter IX, viii.2).

[645] Heraclitus argues that, despite perpetual intense investigation, one's soul remains forever undiscovered. Heraclitus, Jones translation, On the Universe, 71.

[646] Or so we learn from the coppice of consciousness metaphor, and from hard won experience, carefully dissected.

positively bothersome, in need of redirection, even restraints. Brace yourself, but welcome all of you.[647]

> PUPPIES SCUFFLING, FLIPPED AKIMBO;
> NAPLESS TODDLERS, TILTING IN HASTE;
> DUCKLINGS DISTRACTED, CHASING BUGS.
>   TOOTH IN HAUNCH,
>   SKINNED KNEE,
>   VANISHED MOTHER,
> FRANTIC SCURRY.
>   YELP.
>   SQUALL.
>   SQUEAK.
> SMILES, TEARS, SMILES, TEARS, SMILES, TEARS.
>   CHATTERERS, SAYS ONE.

Friends who love you passionately may possess clarity. A good friend
reports bad news as well as good. Often, friends see that to which one is
blind. Hear friends. Heed them.[648] Then befriend yourself. Most self-
knowledge springs from inward cross-talk. Shackle the wanton liar within
you. Character development is a frank conversation between you and you.
The topic is what sort of person you want to become, and the sorts of steps
you are willing to take to become that person.[649] When aberrant, that conversation can condemn. Be frank with yourself, but never execrate. You
are not detestable. You are never a terrible waste of protoplasm.[650] You are
always, and only, a human in process.

Coming to know yourself is the conversation in which you choose simple rules of life by which to govern yourself.

7.3. *Story Control.* **Simple Rule: Manage your inner narrative.** Silently
and unconsciously, you narrate your world to yourself. You rehearse attitudes and practice thoughts of which you remain either ignorant or barely

---

[647] Lewis Mumford emphasizes that we are complex and in flux. "There are certain aspects of the
human personality that no present system of diagnostic completely embraces, and no future one in
all probability will be able to encompass. For the self is no fixed entity: an essential part of it is revealed only in action through time." Mumford, *The Conduct of Life*, 250.

[648] [♪] Cicero, *De Officiis*, 61 (Book I, Section XVIII, 58), and 93 (Book I, Section XXVI, 91) and
139-141 (Book I, Section XXXVII, 136-137).   See also [♪] Aurelius, *To Himself* (Meditations), 75
(Book IV, Section 12).

[649] Heraclitus notes that the stupid person is not one who lacks native intelligence, but the person
who, though present, is nevertheless absent. Heraclitus, Jones translation, *On the Universe*, 3.

[650] Buddha said that there is no person now, in the past, or in the future who is wholly without value
or wholly to be praised. [♪] *Dhammapada*, 228.

aware. Your self-told story exercises gigantic influence upon your life. Its prophecies are frequently, for good or ill, self-fulfilling. You become what you imagine yourself becoming in your private story.

Tiny edits to one's subliminal story have out-sized effects. One performs better on a test. One finds the courage to do what daunts. One deals with a problem previously intractable. Managing your inner narrative is relatively simple; it amounts to self-therapy. Find something that bothers you. Wait a few days until you can think about the event without getting overwhelmed. Then write about your event, about how you faced it and what your place was in the world as you faced it. Answer why your event occurred. What was your part; what part did others play? Write about your future life, corrected of these aberrations, and exactly what your optimal future life might look like. Do this writing for at least four consecutive days. Your internal narrative will shift. If all else fails, do the good you perceive, even if you cannot make yourself want to do so. You will find that your story line gets dragged along in the direction you prefer. One becomes the good one does.[651]

The point is to access your core story lines, recognize them, and edit them for meaning and purpose. In some lives, core narratives, inherited from family or religion, collapse. Such detritus must be swept away. Substitute a vital personal narrative.[652] If you leave your narrative in the hands of others, even trusted others, deep psychological pressures will drive you toward achieving what they hope for you, rather than what you hope for yourself. Take charge of your personal narrative. Manage who gets to help you shape your story.

7.4. *Habit Formation.* **Simple Rule: Improve your habits**. As you learn what sort of person you are, you will take issue with yourself in some matters. You may wish you behaved otherwise than you do.[653] You will prosper by being blunt in self-evaluation. You are pruning yourself; lop off branches with no future.[654] Some of these self-disputes are remediable; oth-

---

[651] Rousseau, *Emile*, 250. Virtuous acts make one love humanity.

[652] Wilson, *Redirect*, 9-74. Editorial readers have noted that this admonition calls to mind the authenticity advocated in existential thinkers, Zen Buddhism, and the thrust of cognitive behavioral therapy.

[653] The Buddha taught that those who kill, lie, steal, fornicate, or get drunk dig up their own roots. [♪] *Dhammapada*, 246-247. He also taught that you should correct yourself, and put your inner life in order. That is the task to which good monks devote themselves. [♪] *Dhammapada*, 379-380.

[654] Seneca, *Epistles 1-65*, 203 (XXVIII, 10). Confucius also employs the metaphor of pruning one's character. [♪] Confucius, *Analects*, 79 (Book V, Section 22). In an interesting twist, Buddhists believe they lop off bad habits in successive lives, carrying an improved character forward in time. After innumerable reincarnations, one perfects giving, morality, patience, vigor, meditation and wisdom, becoming a Buddha (a person fully enlightened about the nature and meaning of life). [♪]

ers are not.[655] Those matters that can be addressed are usually matters of two sorts: decision-making and habit. We have been addressing decision-making thus far in this work. Consider habits the behavioral residue of repeated decisions you made in the past.[656] You are virtuous only when you have become habitually so. If you suffer habitual ill acts, you will wince indeed. Mishaps pile one upon the next until no path to flourishing remains, glued, as you could become, to that unhappy path by the gooey detritus of habitual foolishness.

You have habits acquired intentionally and accidentally. You have habits you acquired as a result of good or poor decision-making. You have habits that reflect the well- or ill-considered influence of others. You can in some instances select among facets of your actions, keeping habits you value and shedding those for which you have less enthusiasm.[657] In the end, you are changing yourself to become the sort of person you value more than the person you are today. In classical language, you are exercising self-

---

Conze, *Buddhist Scriptures*, 32. The Buddha said to be quick in doing good, and abandon what you do wrongly. If you repeat errors, you give root to desire for wrongs, which desire leads to suffering. One, doing good, develops habits of goodness. These cumulate, bringing in their wake happiness. [♪] *Dhammapada*, 116-118. Han Fei Tzu advises kings about their governments in words that might well apply to individual habits. He warns one not to care about whether there is change or lack of change, but rather retain what works and discard what does not. Do this pruning regardless what others think. These dissenters are timid about incurring the wrath of people stuck in ruts, and such persons are often plainly stupid. [♪] Han Fei Tzu, *Basic Writings*, 93 (§18). David Brooks argues that struggling against oneself in issues of self-improvement is the most important habit one can have. We can emerge victorious from such self-battle. Brooks, *The Road To Character*, 13.

[655] The Buddha urges all to heed their own advice; the self is your slowest student. [♪] *Dhammapada*, 159. Herbert Read warns that one cannot, in shaping herself, plan a life that goes against the grain of our human and personal dispositions. To attempt such brings spiritual death. Read, "What is There Left to Say?" 55. Master Zhuang recounts a story of a sage, Shentu Jai, who had his foot severed. That sage concludes, "To know what you can't do anything about, and to be content with it as you would with fate—only a man of virtue can do that." *Zhuangzi*, 66 (in The Sign of Virtue Complete, Section 5).

[656] The Buddha said that small evils slowly cumulate to great ones, just as small goods cumulate personal goodness, bit by bit. [♪] *Dhammapada* 121-122.

[657] [♪] Emerson, *Conduct of Life*, 1025 (IV): "The mark of a man of the world is absence of pretension. He does not make a speech; he takes a low business-like tone, avoids all brag, is nobody, dresses plainly, promises not at all, performs much, speaks in monosyllables, hugs his fact. He calls his employment by its lowest name, and so takes from evil tongues their sharpest weapon. His conversation clings to the weather and the news, yet he allows himself to be surprised into thought, and the unlocking of his learning and philosophy." Lao Tzu says that the wise person grows wise by treating his defects as defects; each is a matter to be remedied. [♪] Lao Tzu, *Tao Te Ching*, 36 (71). Buddhist sage, Nagasena, in advising King Milinda, advised him to examine his dharmas (which may here mean "mental states"), be rid of the harmful ones, and adopt the helpful ones. [♪] Conze, *Buddhist Scriptures*, 154 (citing *Milindapañha*). The Buddhist *Dhammapada* urges wise persons to tame themselves, as do craftsmen their materials. [♪] *Dhammapada* 80. Muhammad taught that evil deeds encrust a man's heart, making him well-suited to burn in hell. [♪] Muhammad, *Qur'an*, Sura 83:14.

control for the purpose of acquiring virtues that have thus far eluded you. The capacity for self-directed change of one's habits leads to more intimate friendships (including marriage), improved health, greater and more stable wealth, fewer arrests and addictions and unplanned pregnancies, and longer life.[658] So, the stakes here are high.

Inculcating or extinguishing habits begins as voluntary action, cued by a need or event, consciously repeated, until, after a period of approximately two months, the action repeats itself when cued without volitional effort, and comes to be considered normal for the person. [659] Habitual action thereafter appears effortless, betraying the sometimes arduous labor required to engrain a new behavior into one's habitual activities. Habit formation occurs when repeated intentional action forms a behavioral "chunk," which chunk of activity imprints upon several brain regions interacting with one another.[660] Rewarding oneself for successful completion of one repetition of the behavior chunk speeds the process along. Choose a cue for your new habit. Change habits one at a time. More change than that can discourage or distract one. Where there is diligence in addressing desirable habits and quashing ill ones, life is long enough to make of you a deeply nuanced human being.[661]

---

[658] Baumeister, "Conquer Yourself, Conquer the World," 61. It is plain that substance addicted persons cannot control their behaviors. Thoughtful people recommend decriminalizing use of controlled substances, thus opening the door to public access to care for addicted persons. Maté argues that addicted people, to cope with their addictions, need "islands of relief." With care, a place to rest and live, decent food, and unadulterated substances, many may be able to cope with their addictions, and attenuate or eliminate the harm that substances work in their lives. Maté also wishes we many would recognize our own addictions, and face up to the emptiness within that those addictions highlight. Addiction is an attempt to escape from distress. Maté, *In the Realm of Hungry Ghosts*, 35, 317, 354-355.

[659] Habit formation requires sixty-six days on average, with considerable individual variation. Lally, "How Are Habits Formed?" 998-1009. This is old knowledge we are still exploring. Epictetus thought that one does well in establishing a new habit (say, controlling anger) if he has no fits for thirty days, and has done splendidly if still anger-controlled after two or three months. He advises to avoid matters that trigger one's undesirable habit. Epictetus, *Discourses*, 343-345 (Book II, 18.13-14).

[660] Graybiel and Smith argue that intentional repeated acts create a predilection to repeat a behavior involving the infralimbic cortex, striatum, thalamus, sensimotor cortex, and midbrain. After chunking (clumping behaviors to repetitive patterns), the infralimbic cortex determines when the habit should be deployed. Habits, therefore, depend upon cues for initiation. To build a habit, repeat a behavior, then reward yourself. Make the cue for the habit obvious. To extinguish a habit, remove the cue for that chunk. The authors warn that established habits may be suppressed, but perhaps never entirely vanish, but are rather overlaid by subsequent, better-rewarded habits. Graybiel and Smith, "Good Habits, Bad Habits," 43.

[661] Mencius notes that mountain trails, well trodden, become paths, easily followed. If unused, grass grows over them, and they are lost to travel. Of habits, when one begins, his path is clogged with grass. *Mencius*, 161 (Book VII, Part B, Section 21).

Extinguishing habits follows much the same course: one voluntarily, and with considerable effort, redirects undesirable action when it is cued. One perseveres in replacing the habit consciously for a couple of months or so, after which time the replacement habit seems more and more effortless. An error people make in extinguishing habits is to attempt to extinguish without replacement. Let the cue to an unwanted habit cue a new, more constructive behavior. Where possible, remove the cue for an unwanted habit altogether, and replace it with a new, preferable cue.

Mentors help. Imitation lies deep in the human unconscious. Use that tendency to your benefit. Choose a person who lives(d) as you wish you might.[662] Keep that person in mind. Use her as a pattern. Call her to mind when you struggle. Know you will never be that person, for you are you. Use, but do not capitulate to, your mentor's insights. She too struggles, as do you, to restrain and redirect herself.[663] Eventually, your private mentor will retire somewhat from center stage. But early in habit formation, models can help.[664] If your mentor lives and is willing, meet regularly with that person. Talk frankly. Learn that person's deliberative process. Drink in her values. Be critical, but not very critical. There is time enough after you have plumbed a mentor's heart to tweak and edit. Be grateful for a mentor's willingness. We become like those whom we imitate, for good or ill. Your mentor's good (and bad) habits may wriggle their way into your preconscious predilections.[665] So, choose mentors carefully.

Mentors die or move or change. Yet mentors inhabit your inner dialogue. They whisper to you as you go about your business, if you have bothered to know them intimately. Once a mentor dwells in your mental and moral habits, that mentor becomes subject to amendment. Your mentor broadens as you allow the voices of other admired persons to add subtleties to your mentor's perspective. Seek wise counsel. Plumb the works of dead

---

[662] Epictetus advises his students to choose good and excellent persons, compare one's conduct to theirs, and model themselves upon that living or dead person. Epictetus, *Discourses*, 347 (Book II, 18.21). Maimonides, a medieval (twelfth century A.D.) Jewish rabbi, taught: "Man is created in such a way that his character traits and actions are influenced by his neighbors and friends, and he follows the custom of the people in his country. Therefore, a man needs to associate with the just and be with the wise continually in order to learn [from] their actions, and to keep away from the wicked, who walk in darkness, so that he avoids learning from their actions." Maimonides, *Ethical Teachings of Maimonides*, 46 (Laws Concerning Character Traits, Chapter 6).

[663] There is a dynamic tension in profiting from a mentor. Buddha captures this dialectic when he urges disciples to emulate a mentor, a mature person of good acts. He then urges one to avoid following even a wise mentor. Best to go alone. [♪] *Dhammapada*, 328-329. The wise person can hold inconsistent ideas without losing his way. [♪] *Dhammapada*, 411.

[664] Seneca, *Epistles 1-65*, 63-65 (XI, 8-10).

[665] Bargh, "Our Unconscious Mind," 35.

persons, if you suspect wisdom hides in their words. Bother sage persons when you meet them. Buy lunch. Take them some coffee. Ask hard questions. Listen intently to the answers. Give your inner mentor new grist for the habit formation mill. At some level, the inner mentor is a personal metaphor for the broader task of finely-elaborating your cull of conduct. Mentors, inner and otherwise, deflect conduct from impulsive or habitual error toward more adequate solutions.

Character consists in the intricate web of physical and mental and moral habits.[666] Work methodically. Build a better you.[667]

7.4.1. *Neurology of Habit Formation.* Recent studies show that, neurologically, habit formation differs depending upon the nature of the habit acquired or extinguished. Goal-directed habits (for example, walking instead of smoking at morning coffee break) utilize a different pathway through the brainstem (basal ganglia) than does classic stimulus-response habituation (for example, reaching for the phone when it rings). Precise neurologic details of habit formation remain murky for both types of habit formation.[668]

7.4.2. *Habit Selection.* What habits should you acquire or extinguish, Kate? Some habits recommend themselves to all people: regular bathing, talking quietly enough not to break eardrums, and chewing before swallowing, for example. Other habits are idiosyncratic: jazz syncopation, flytying, and hair curling. The canvas of moral virtue has been decorated by

---

[666] In the Buddhist tradition, monks speak of the Four Holy Truths. Life is ill, when one grasps after bodily desires. Ill derives from rebirth due to craving. Ill dies when one stops craving. One stops craving by the eightfold path: right views, right intentions, right speech, right conduct, right livelihood, right effort, right mindfulness, and right concentration. [♪] Conze, *Buddhist Scriptures*, 186-187 (citing Ho-shan's *Memorial*). One restructures the inner self to avoid life's evils, in Buddhist orthodoxy.

[667] Seneca, *Epistles 1-65*, 21 (V, 1). Confucius characterizes habit formation as developing a good root system. Once that is in place, the "Way" blossoms in a man quite naturally. [♪] Confucius, *Analects*, 59 (Book I, Section 2). Mencius suggests that any man can become a moral giant. One lacks not the strength, but the will to undertake the effort required. *Mencius*, 134 (Book VI, Part B, Section 2). Mill says: "It really is of importance, not only what men do, but also what manner of men they are that do it. Among the works of man, which human life is rightly employed in perfecting and beautifying, the first in importance surely is man himself." [♪] Mill, *On Liberty*, 57. Buddhists teach that a holy person treats others tenderly, knowing how they suffer. One must focus on the good; one's mind becomes habituated to its thoughts. So abandon whatever is unwholesome. [♪] Conze, *Buddhist Scriptures*, 109 (*Milindapañha*). The Buddha taught one tames oneself, as a farmer his irrigation water, the fletcher his arrow shafts, and the carpenter his wood. [♪] *Dhammapada*, 145. Maimonides lists desirable traits (slow to anger, abundant loving-kindness, justice, righteous, perfect, powerful, strong) and then says: "A man shall habituate himself in these character traits until they are firmly established in him. . . . He shall repeat them continually until performing them is easy for him and they are not burdensome and these character traits are firmly established in his soul." Maimonides, *Ethical Writings of Maimonides*, 30 (in Laws Concerning Character Traits, Chapter 1).

[668] Yin, "The Role of Basal Ganglia in Habit Formation," 464-476.

many artists, each brushing intellectual hues, literally thousands of them, with distinctive brush and temperament. Quad sociality recommends some habits, and discourages others. You have myriad habits; many are idiosyncratic. *Cull* offers some generally-applicable habits of commission and omission warranted by Quad sociality and validated by some of history's wisest persons.

For each habit, a hundred voices (only a few of which are cited) grumble dissent. Little consensus emerges from the cacophony of human adolescence, which din consumes all of mankind's past. Adulthood, both for members and for humanity, means making choices. I have made mine for myself. In this work, I commend choices to you, Kate, and through you to all humanity. You are choosing, and will continue selecting, your ethical habits, Kate. Which will you advocate for humanity?

John Dewey teaches that character is the matrix of one's many habits interacting.[669] Habits cross-catalyze, and support or defeat one another.[670] Dewey urges people to be loyal to what is best in human life.[671] One should build habits that tend to make one open, concerned about fairness, and full of feeling for others.[672] One supplements Dewey's criteria. Your habits should tend to make you physically healthy, and generally happy. Habits should make one resilient in the face of difficulty and pain. Your habits should support you in doing what you believe is best, and help foster intimacy and collaboration with other people. Your habits ought to make other people's lives better, or at least no worse. Your habits should help you face your challenges squarely, and encourage you to learn from mistakes.[673] Your habits should keep your life balanced, and help you sort what is more important from what is less important. Your habits should guide you when you confront difficult decisions. Ultimately, your habits should help you die with dignified equanimity. Heraclitus issues a succinct warning: character is fate.[674] Habits chart your life's course, for good or ill.

---

[669] [♪] Dewey, *Human Nature and Conduct*, 38.

[670] [♪] Dewey, *Theory of the Moral Life*, 60.

[671] [♪] Dewey, *Human Nature and Conduct*, 21.

[672] [♪] Dewey, *Human Nature and Conduct*, 207.

[673] Bertrand Russell warns that some forms of misguided moralities paralyze intelligence. Russell, "Adaptation: An Autobiographical Epitome," 25.

[674] Heraclitus, Jones translation, *On the Universe*, 121.

7.5. *Action*. **Simple Rule: Act deliberately**. With your habits in process, do things. Humans function best in oscillation between thinking and acting, each mode reciprocally deflecting the other.[675] Act in light of deliberation. Deliberate and adjust your acts.[676] Ping the pong of pragmatism.[677] One should "thact."[678]

Do what makes sense. Note circumstances; address those circumstances.[679] Let your grasp of what makes sense evolve. But act. Epicurus said that the fool has many faults, one of which is preparing to live without ever really living.[680] Take some calculated risks. Better to change course than never to have departed at all. Best is to plan, then begin, then adjust, then succeed. Break complex tasks into sequences of manageable steps. But deliberate. Failing to plan is planning to fail.[681] Entire chains of acts can be rendered pointless by failure to recognize initial conditions or ongoing changes. Pay attention, but get moving. Note well that sometimes the best affirmative act is to do nothing at all. To refrain is not neglect; it is deliberated non-action. Saying nothing can be elegant oratory.[682]

Do not dawdle in facile equivocation. Make decisions; act on them.[683] You are the moral knife that cuts Gordian knots. When one balks at change, having failed to think a circumstance through, she becomes an im-

---

[675] Seneca warns that idleness leads to hating others, hoping they will suffer as do you. Humans naturally move and act, seeking stimulation. [♪] Seneca, *On Tranquillity of Mind*, 34-35.

[676] One knows by doing and does by knowing. To know is to act effectively. Maturana and Varela, *Tree of Knowledge*, 26, 29.

[677] Pragmatism is a school of philosophical thought that directs attention to the connections between theory and practice, and the transitions between these two forms of consciousness.

[678] A mash-up coinage of "think" and "act." Mill said that people do not behave badly from overweening desires, but rather from withered, underutilized consciences. Strong desires are merely human energy at work. [♪] Mill, *On Liberty*, 58. Mumford argues: "To live wisely, each of us must lead a twofold life. We must live once in the actual world, and once more in our minds." Mumford, *The Conduct of Life*, 265.

[679] Martin Buber urges people seeking community to avoid ruts and live in their moment. Such living addresses "the thickets of this pathless hour." Buber, *Paths in Utopia*, 135.

[680] *Epicurea*, Fragment 494 (Usener), as cited by Seneca, *Epistles 1-65*, XIII, 16.

[681] Attributed to Benjamin Franklin, reframed by Winston Churchill.

[682] [♪] Lao Tzu, *Tao Te Ching*, 11 (48), 19 (56), 20 (57), 26 (63).

[683] Rousseau argues that we know men by their acts. Speech hides interiority. Acts reveal what hunkers in a man. Rousseau, *Emile*, 237. This being so, one must note that Rousseau consigned his five infants to a foundling home upon birth. He could see nothing wrong with these decisions. Rousseau, *Confessions*, 333-334. John Paul Lederach says: "Risk means we take a step toward and into the unknown. By definition, risk accepts vulnerability and lets go of the need to a priori control the process or the outcome of human affairs." Lederach, *The Moral Imagination*, 163.

pediment to needful adaptation. Men who resist change rely on the waffling of many for their control. Martin Luther King Jr. complained that white moderates gravely impeded the civil rights movement by agreeing in principle, but disputing tactics of the movement. King felt the tepid agreement of good people injured justice more than the hatred of patent bad faith actors.[684] Jesus rejected lukewarm disciples.[685] Deal with what lies before you, Kate.

Objection 18: Moronic Moralizing: *Some demur that this book suffers a bad turn. It began with didactic[686] excess, and now detours into sententious[687] mazes. Normative moralizing is out of vogue. Full bore life advice leaves a bad taste in one's metaphorical mouth. In a pluralistic world stuffed with perspectives, moral instruction of any sort stinks of religious intolerance and starched underpants. Philosophy should limit itself to questions involving the theoretical preconditions of knowledge (that is, meta-ethics), including the preconditions of moral insight. But actual knowledge proper lies outside the scope of philosophy. This work should be relegated to shelves reserved for theological exhortations and comic books.*

Response: In the long sweep of the history of philosophy, normative moral advice is a staple.[688] Only recently (the last two centuries) have professional philosophers grown obsessed with the preconditions of moral knowledge, to the exclusion of moral knowledge itself. Some suffer the impractical misconception that no moral assertion is factually supportable, following Hume in his error (that no moral assertion can be derived from what exists). Oddly enough, ethics finds renewed scientific scrutiny via the back door of evolutionary biology, rather than through the wide portal of philosophy. I suspect the tide in philosophy

---

[684] [♪] King, *Autobiography*, 195 (from King's "Letter from Birmingham Jail").

[685] *Revelation* 3:15-17 attributes such an attitude to Jesus: "I know not your works: you are neither cold nor hot! So, because you are lukewarm, and neither cold nor hot, I will spew you out of my mouth. For you say, I am rich, I have prospered, and I need nothing; not knowing that you are wretched, pitiable, poor, blind, and naked." It is likely the attribution to Jesus is spurious. See also *Matthew* 5:13, 8:19-22, 10:34-39, 12:30.

[686] "Didactic" denotes a text aimed at teaching, often suffering surplus information and unpleasant presentation, and proposing moral conclusions. See *Webster's Third New International Dictionary*, s.v. "didactic" at sections a, b, and d.2.

[687] "Sententious" means a text replete with overstated moralizing. See *Webster's Third New International Dictionary*, s.v. "sententious" at section 2.b.2.

[688] Consider the Decalogue of the Hebrew people ([♪] *Torah*), the Five Precepts and Eightfold Path of Buddhist traditions ([♪] Conze, *Buddhist Scriptures*), [♪] Cicero's *De Officiis*, the epistles of Paul, the Sermon on the Mount, Mencius, [♪] Confucius's Analects, [♪] Lao Tzu's *Tao Te Ching*, Plutarch's *Moralia*, [♪] Emerson's *Conduct of Life* and other essays, [♪] Thoreau's *On the Duty of Civil Disobedience*, the [♪] *Qur'an*, the *Enchiridion* of Epictetus, [♪] *Mozi*, [♪] Aristotle's *Nichomachean Ethics*, [♪] John Stuart Mill's *On Liberty*, Pascal's *Pensees*, [♪] Hume's *Enquiry Concerning the Principles of Morals*, Seneca's *Epistles*, and even Panksepp's *Affective Neuroscience*. All these constitute the barest sample of philosophical moralizing.

will not long resist its historical moon. Perhaps some will abandon moral agnosticism. One *can* know and reasonably discuss what human habits best serve human ends. One *can* reasonably discuss what human ends best serve human flourishing. In the long view, now seldom adopted, ethical deliberation is the fundamental task of philosophy. Etymologically, philosophy is affection for "*sophos*," which was, to Greeks, practical knowledge and skill in some particular arena of life. William James put the matter bluntly: "For the philosophy which is so important in each of us is not a technical matter; it is our more or less dumb sense of what life honestly and deeply means."[689] What could be more useful than mining the practical knowledge about life choices from history's most eminent journeymen of ethical deliberation? Those who rail against philosophers sorting moral advice advocate that the moral advice we adopt should be poorly vetted and ill-deliberate. Surely, that is foolhardy.

Objection 19: Moral Dissimulation: *Another protests that morality itself is raw pretense. All ethical preening boils down, when stripped of its religious and goody-goody mumbo-jumbo, to hand-wringing about appearances. None wishes to be known as rapacious, despite the universal desire to act corruptly. Morality is self-deception writ large upon human thought. Self-deception is most effective when lies, in fact, deceive the deceiver as well as the deceived. We believe of ourselves what we wish, not what is true. Men prefer indulgence over innocence. Women long for praise more than prudence. Plato's Glaucon pierced human moral dissembling in his dispute with Socrates. Glaucon argues that a ring with power to make a man invisible (the ring of Gyges the Lydian) would explode all moral restraint. That unfettered troglodyte would steal, rape, murder, and befuddle, always certain of impunity. Take way the culprit's ring, and, once again visible, he becomes a saint, full of hymns and sacred sentiments, but secretly cowed by threats of societal censure. Socrates disagreed, arguing that the invisible criminal surrendered to his appetites, and so was enslaved, not free.*[690] *But, as I see things, Glaucon prevailed. Morality is a crock. A lurking miscreant cowers beneath every bridge of social conscience.*[691]

Response: No rings of invisibility exist. Large numbers of humans indulge their corruptions in plain view, so, no rings of Gyges are, apparently, needed. I agree that social approbation motivates humans. Being social, approval necessarily matters to each of us. We look to other's behaviors for nudges motivating our own. Our motivations are, however, far from simple. We do not desire dualistically, electing virtue or vice. We desire in multifarious spires of independ-

---

[689] James, *Pragmatism*, 7-8.

[690] [♪] Plato, *Republic*, 39-41 (§360b-d).

[691] Schopenhauer argues that egoism is the core human motivation. Egoism excavates a trench between a person and every other. Hobbes was right. Absent a punishing State, every man wars with every other. Seeking an adequate hyperbole, Schopenhauer says, "Many a man would be quite capable of killing another, simply to rub his boots over with the victim's fat." He then doubts whether this is an exaggeration at all. Schopenhauer subsequently finds a basis for compassion in identification with others, and argues that one should do no harm (justice), but rather help others (loving-kindness), as one is able. Schopenhauer, *The Basis of Morality*, 77-78, 88.

ent motivations (eating, sleeping, drinking, defecating, seeking, finding, copulating, raging, frolicking, and so forth), deflected by emotional concerns (empathy, sympathy, compassion, mirroring, fidelity, loving, cooperating, collaborating, grooming, and so forth), sometimes inhibited by conscious thought (counting, weighing, alternatives, deciding, inspecting, analyzing, comparing, rationalizing, and so forth). Our inner conflicts are many. Our actions express our largely subconscious heuristics, with a liberal dose of after-the-fact explanation. Men are neither so good as saints, nor so bad as moral cretins. Some human ill-behavior will, I suspect, prove ineradicable. Men may always lust for adventurous trysts and heroic bloodsport. Women may forever pine for babies they can in no conceivable circumstance nurture and indulge vicious gossip. What cannot be changed, one works around. But, among other influences, humans guide aspects of their own fate. *Cull* asks all to seize that tiller, and to do so deliberately and diligently. Glaucon, and Socrates, were wrong.

WHAT IS NEEDFUL?
    AWAITING SUNRISE, NURTURE IN THE COMPANY OF DEAD OTHERS,
    AT DAWN, WALKING WITH ONE'S SWEET DOG,
    NEWS AND OATMEAL,
    A MORNING PLUMB OF CLIENTS' PROBLEMS,
    AND ANSWERING SEEKERS' INQUIRIES,
    MIDDAY SWEAT OR ENCOUNTER WITH FRIENDS OR STOLEN NAPS,
    AFTERNOONS AT LABOR EASING DIFFICULTIES ASSAILING OTHERS,
    AT DAY WANING, RESPONSE TO APPROACHES,
    AND ORGANIZING THE WEAL OF TOWNSHIP,
    DINNER IN THE COMPANY OF INTIMATES AND WINE,
    THEN RELEASE IN RAMBLING OR STERNUM ON ROSEWOOD,
    AS MIND THINS, THE ART OF MANY IN TEXT OR SCREEN,
    IN BED, THE SCENT OF FICTIONS OR ONE'S BELOVED,
    SLEEP ERASES TODAY'S TUMULT, STRAINING TOWARD TOMORROW'S,
    IN FABRICATED SILENCE, ONE TRIMS SAILS AND CONJURES THE ASTROLABE.
        IN ALL, ONE STANDS
        TOGETHER BUT EVER ALONE,
        ALONE BUT EVER TOGETHER.

7.6. *Nurture Other Members.* **Simple Rule: Nurture others.** The other in a community can be teased from the self only with difficulty. Our apparently independent bodies and sense of integration seem to distinguish us from all others, but belie psychological realities. In identity, where I cease and the other commences is hidden.[692] The weal of loved others determines, in

---

[692] See [♪] Buber, *I and Thou*, 62 Aristotle ventures to call the friend another self. In his view, as goodwill finds purchase in common action, intimacy grows between people, and they begin to seek to build for themselves and others what is good and best. [♪] Aristotle, *Nichomachean Ethics*, 169-172 (1166a-1167b). I call that "meaningful community."

large part, one's own well-being. Where a community's other members suffer, their dysfunction bleeds back into the lives of every member, even those members who do not labor under the shortcomings that led to the other members' difficulties. Where one succeeds, all benefit. Our ships ride communal tides. We rise. We fall.[693] To nurture others *is* to nurture oneself.[694]

We imagine that we know what a well-nurtured human looks like. We think those mature humans who have existed in the past are paradigmatic of those to come. I doubt it is so. From the dawn of history, our existence has been beleaguered by scarcity, malevolent predators, human and otherwise, over-population, wanderlust, short lives, high mortality, war, unremediated suffering, and general neglect and deficiency of nurture. We have coerced and murdered and oppressed and ignored others. We have, often from necessity, lived the moment. Mankind descends from cooperative, but occasionally violent, hominins. We have only recently begun to rein in our bloodlust, and barely have we begun to retire coercion as a mode of social existence.

Yet the human future may hold fundamentally different original conditions for unborn children. What would a human think and feel were she nurtured by an attentive team of adults, themselves well-nurtured? If "family" included others not genetically related, but committed to the care of a child, what might be the effect on the child? With eleven "parents," might a child grow wise at an early age? Might such children never discover violence in themselves and make peace? Might such a child feel deep in her bones the futility of excess possessions and financial obesity? Might the child care more about the human future? What if all learning happened with nurturing mentors, forsaking one-size-fits-all tutelage in factories of mass education?[695] What if every child had abundant nutrition every day? What if emotional savagery were rare? What if every child's capabilities were well-assessed, and her peculiar gifts encouraged? What if no human predators struck fear in a child's heart? What if no child lacked a caring parental other to whom to attach? What if the news contained deliberations of

---

[693][♪] Cicero, *De Officiis*, 23 (I, VII, 22). Seneca argues that common life precludes individuals assessing circumstances for personal gain or risk. If one would make his own life worth living, one must devote himself to the well-being of his neighbor. Seneca, *Epistles 1-65*, 315 (XLVIII, 2-3).

[694] Buddhists demur. Friends distract one from meditation and the quiet mind. Friends are a component of samsara and tempt one from meditation to unquiet. Many are fools, praising evil and indulging pettinesses. Travel life alone, seeking placid solitude. From Shantideva, in a poem "*Practices of a Bodhisattva*," as contained in [♪] Conze, *Buddhist Scriptures*, 100-102.

[695] Aristotle recommends individual education; it is superior to any education in common with others. One would not go to his doctor for medical advice with a group of others. [♪] Aristotle, *Nichomachean Ethics*, 202 (1180b).

the human future and well-conceived experiments in living, rather than debacles of human depravity and inanity and collapsed nurture.   What if
apocalypticism found no careless grist in the mill of human experience?

None knows the shape of a world peopled by well-nurtured humans.
To assert otherwise is to insist upon cynicism. To well-nurture a generation
of humans—that is an experiment worth conducting.[696] A few communities
could undertake the task. We would all watch in wonder. Unfortunately,
nurturing seven billion humans exceeds our grasp.

7.7. *Friends*. **Simple Rule: Nurture intimate friendships**. Friendship is the
core habit of human sociality.[697] By friendship, one means intimacy.[698] By
"intimacy," one means a close personal relationship characterized by affection and broad knowledge of one another as each person really is, apart
from pretense or position, and an intermixing of two persons, with deep attention to details.[699] Humans seek amicable intimacy; without it, they languish. Intimates know their friends' interests and capabilities, shortcomings
and injuries. Intimates participate in shaping one another's lives. In times
of need, they intervene. In times of abundance, they share. In fragile times,
intimates nurture and protect, supporting members experiencing disease, in-

---

[696] [♪] Emerson, *Conduct of Life*, 1020 (IV): "We shall one day learn to supersede politics by education." Russell finds institutional education a grinding horror that douses thinking individuals. Russell, "Education," 389. In revised education, lies hope. Russell asserts that a single generation of
women willing to nurture their children differently could redirect the human course, rearing a humanity without fear. Russell, "The Aims of Education," 399, 406.

[697] [♪] Cicero, *De Officiis*, 59 (Book I, Section XVII, 55-57). Life without friends is no life at all.
[♪] Cicero, *De Amicitia*, 189-193 (Section XXII 80 – XXIII 86). Aristotle argues that complete
friendship grows between good people valuing one another for their very goodness. Distance and
lack of communication can dissolve even the best of good intentions between friends, rendering a
friendship moribund. [♪] Aristotle, *Nichomachean Ethics*, 147-149 (1156b-1157b). Aristotle believes that humans are naturally amiable toward strangers. [♪] Aristotle, *Nichomachean Ethics*, 144
(1155a).

[698] To be complete friends, one must have substantial experience of another, and be devoted. It is
not possible to have many friendships based in mutual goodness. [♪] Aristotle, *Nichomachean Ethics*, 150 (1158a). Aristotle argues that friendships emerge from within communities. [♪] Aristotle,
Nichomachean Ethics, 158 (1161b). Socrates, as was his habit, found that, upon deliberation, he had
no idea what friendship was, though he enjoyed it immensely. Plato, *Lysis*, 168. Friendship is a
component of our mammalian heritage. Female baboons with friends outlive and outbreed those
who lack such intimacies. So friendship, or the lack of it, has its evolutionary logic. De Waal, *The
Bonobo and the Atheist*, 161. In intimate friendship, one comes to know and anticipate the other,
just as one is reciprocally known and anticipated. One plumbs the other's history, preferences, habits, relations, turns of phrase, skills, tics, smells, biological functions, dreams, hopes, fascinations, injuries, excellences, weaknesses, family, friends and enemies, and preferred play. One can, with
some accuracy, predict the intimate other's responses. One knows enough to know when to be surprised by the other's choices, and when to intervene in the other's troubles. Reciprocally, one welcomes such interventions by an intimate.

[699] See *Webster's Third New International Dictionary*, s.v. "intimacy" and "intimate."

jury, loss, or other debilitations. With the support of friends, in their affec-tionate embrace, one recovers or passes.[700]

Intimacy knits emotions. It binds, resisting the repulsive force of idio-syncrasy and deformity. One touches the border of intimacy when the oth-er's oddities annoy, alongside the wonder of the other's gifts. Some mis-take revulsion at the other's oddness for a problem in friendship. Intimacy plumbs the other, knowing and being irritated, being known and irritating. Aggravation points the way to the heart of intimacy. When one rankles, one now knows enough to scrape tender psychic flesh upon the granitic core of the other. One adopts the shortcomings of the intimate other as one's own project. One allows the intimate friend access to sacred places and hidden alcoves. One takes the offered hand. Intimacy establishes an affective community of interest. What goodness life grants, it lavishes, for good or ill, upon the togetherness of intimates.[701]

Of all possessions, friendship is most valuable.[702] Spouses, where mar-ital relations are worth retaining, are friendships that blossom into sexual re-lations. Children are friends in the making. Friends become, when nur-tured, another self.[703] To nurture a friend is to care for oneself. The other's well-being becomes one's own. Human sociality, well-conceived, consists in overlapping circles of friends, globally extended.

In Quad sociality, overlapping cadres of intimates form circles. Multi-ple circles of acquaintances form communities. The global community of communities constitutes the Commons. The human social universe ulti-mately roots itself in a rich loam of friendships.

Those among your fellows, who, despite lavish well-wishing and long acquaintance, do not cherish your fears, pains, and aspirations, have yet to become friends. Friends share an identity. Friendship feels like being one

---

[700] Gibson and Pigott, *Personal Safety Nets*, xxvii. Relational intimacy, then, exceeds mere psycho-logical familiarity. Intimacy also includes reciprocal altruistic interventions and chosen commingling and coordination of identities and physical assets with friends on a regular basis. One may remain distant from acquaintances for months or years without injury to relationship. Not so intimates.

[701] Some strands of Buddhism find friends a distraction from meditative emptiness. Friends, barging into one's solitude, disrupt one's stillness. One must practice introversion conscientiously. Friends, like all components of life, are fleeting and impermanent. Relish meditative solitude. Conze, *Bud-dhist Scriptures*, 100-101 (Chapter 2: Meditation, Section 2: The Practice of Introversion).

[702] The Buddha notes that life with childish people is a misery, like living with enemies. There is primordial joy in sharing life with insightful, well-read, truthful friends. [♪] *Dhammapada*, 206-208. Timon, in Lucian's tale, disagrees. Timon proposes a statute for himself declaring that he must al-ways remain solitary and treat every man badly, exercising his core virtues: "testiness, acerbity, rudeness, wrathfulness and inhumanity." Lucian, *Timon, or the Misanthrope*, 373-374 (Sections 42-44).

[703] [♪] Cicero, *De Amicitia*, 199 (XXV, 92). [♪] Cicero, *De Officiis*, 59 (Book I, XVII, 55-56). See also [♪] Aristotle, *Nichomachean Ethics*, 451-575 (Books VIII and IX).

person in two or more skins.[704]   Goods exchange among friends without economic handwringing. Friends are gladly interrupted by another friend's troubles. Friends intervene to keep you whole, because they know your troubles become theirs. They speak, sometimes bluntly, because they care.

7.7.1. *Building Friendships.* Choose friends carefully. Friends ply one's deepest recesses. Less pain attends excluding some inappropriate person than in removing a friend who proves, after a time, unsuitable.[705] Some people will not benefit from your company. Identify them, and find others to befriend.[706]

Some attitudes and habits build friendships. Others do not. To become friends, or to build greater intimacy with a friend, do these things. 1) Actively learn everything about your friend. Inquire and remember. 2) Express your fondness and admiration for your friend. 3) When angered, go to your friend, not away from her. 4) Welcome your friend's suggestions and guidance. Friends' lives are something they do together. 5) Solve those problems between you that can be fixed. Tolerate those that cannot. 6) When you disagree with a friend, keep talking. Do not shut down. 7) Know your friend's dreams and aspirations; help the friend achieve those goals. 8) Build meaning between you and your friend. Know his or her convictions; share your own. Cherish one another's spirituality. 9) Building intimacy takes effort. Do not stint.[707] 10) Spend time with your friend at least weekly, and talk more often than that, if possible. Intimacy can emerge with less frequent contact, but it may take years.[708]

---

[704] [♪] Cicero, *De Amicitia*, 189, 199 (Section XXI, 80-81; Section XXV, 92).

[705] Seneca, *Epistles 1-65,* 11 (III, 2-3).

[706] [♪] Seneca, *On Tranquillity of Mind*, 41.

[707] This advice is adapted from spousal relationship research conducted by John Gottmann at the University of Washington. Gottmann, *The Seven Principles for Making Marriage Work.*

[708] Some ask whether written or electronic communications can suffice to establish intimacy, or, at a minimum, keep an intimate friendship from collapsing altogether upon the shoals of non-contact. Certainly, interpersonal communications have changed dramatically in the last decades. With the advent of cell technology, many correspond with friends and family daily or even more often. I, however, doubt the efficacy of such communications for establishing intimacy or even preserving it for long periods of absence. Verbal (and even video) exchanges step down from face-to-face exchanges, which are jammed with non-verbal cues and content. Email and written epistles step down from voices and images to mere language. All suffer vexing ambiguities and lend themselves to hand-wringing insecurities in the reader. Texts step down from language to snippets. When emoticons arrive, one gags upon empty vessels begging to be filled with whatever ironies or illusions one prefers. The gold standard in human relating is face-to-face contact. Relationships that rely on less dense communication imperil intimacy already kindled. Establishing intimacy electronically may prove impossible, mere stillborn sharing. Cacioppo and Patrick call our truncated electronic communications "single-strand interactions," robbed of the multiple layers that communications fostering social cohesion exhibit. All will forever lack the smells, gestural language, semantics of movements, mimickry, and physical context of face-to-face communications. Cacioppo and Patrick,

11) Share your dreams, history, fears, failings, and skills with friends. Do not hold back. In building friendship, it is as important to talk as to listen. 12) Give friends room to be discouraged with you; tolerate them not liking you occasionally. Oddly enough, liking your friend, though usual, is not essential to intimacy. Mutual respect and persistent content-full dialogue are essential. 13) Intervene in your friend's critical events. When disasters great or small interrupt a friend's well-being, stop what you are doing to attend your friend's needs. If you have special skills, employ them. Go to the hospital. Repair that roof damage. Help find a mechanic. Grieve over lost loved ones. Cook a meal. Feed the dog. Cry together. Sit silently. Intervene. Similarly, when successes occur, cele-brate. Make your friend know that you share his or her life, for good or ill. Be there. Nothing builds intimate trust more readily than attending a friend's critical moments and being supportive at those junctures.[709]

As you can see, intimacy demands time. Make space for friendship, else there will come a moment when you wish to spit out your life.[710] Nothing in human life exceeds the value of intimate friends.[711]

For some, family looms larger than friendship. Family is a cracked mirror of friendship. Family members may become friends. Every parent wishes his child to become an adult friend. Not all do. One becomes family by accidents of history and the bumping of pudenda. Friends are chosen—for their virtue, for their empathy, for their capacity for intimacy and persistence. Family members may lack any such virtues. Where that is so, where family has not or cannot become friends, one's friends must take priority.[712] Friendship defines the boundaries of your well-being. Do not forsake lush intimacy for barren plains of genetic similarity.

Loneliness, 259-260. Putnam offers a compelling analysis of the role of cyber-communications in human communities. He concludes that existing communities may be enhanced by computer-mediated communications, but doubts that computer-mediated communications can create human communities in the first place. Nevertheless, Putnam remains hopeful that internet communications might be bent to the task of "thickening" our social ties, which have grown increasingly frayed. Putnam, *Bowling Alone*, 175-180.

[709] Adam Smith argues: "Society and conversation . are the most powerful remedies for restoring the mind to its tranquility." Smith, The Theory of Moral Sentiments, 28.

[710] [♪] Emerson, *Conduct of Life*, 1046 (V): "Friendship requires more time than poor busy men can usually command."

[711] Confucius argues that men are naturally intimate, but grow isolated by ill habit. [♪] Confucius, *Analects*, 143 (Book XVII, Section 2).

[712] Isocrates argues that a virtuous man cherishes devoted friends more than mere blood relatives. Blood relations are a convention and kinship a matter of compulsion. Friends are natural, chosen for their character. Isocrates, *To Demonicus*, 9.

7.8. *Communication.* **Simple Rule: Talk with friends frankly and frequently.** Intimates feed on conversation. Conversation tills and plants the
soil with friendship.[713]   Talking waters and suns the intimate seedling.
Sharing feeds and weeds the bed.[714]   In healthy social worlds, a member
spends about one-quarter to one-third of her waking time grooming intimates in communication of one sort or another.[715] Friends ask one another
to seek good and flee evil.[716]   Friends awaken one another from moral
slumber.[717] Oddly enough, some dear friends may not be alive, but rather
encountered in their legacy. You can meet dead friends in books or in the
wake of their labors; such acquaintances brim with insight, though they are
generally tight-lipped.[718]

Fear may lead one to tarry, hoping for a propitious moment to speak
one's mind with a friend. Perfect circumstances prove elusive; never wait.
Talk with your friend immediately when you have something that needs to
be spoken. You will want to reflect, insuring that what you have to say to a
friend is not merely some problem in you. But once such precautions are
sorted, approach your friend. One wishes to speak well; do your best, but
do not delay. Procrastination itself injures friendships. Correct your friends
sparingly, only when the matter is unavoidable. But then speak without delay. Show your affection when reproving a friend.[719] Be frank.[720] If you
must be blunt, do so.[721] If you receive corrective communication from a

---

[713] The *Rig Veda*, a core Brahminist text, asserts that wise talking makes one recognize friends. [♪]
Rig Veda 61 (10.71, v. 2). Aristotle notes that intimate friendship requires great draughts of time
and intense familiarity, and so is relatively rare. [♪] Aristotle, *Nichomachean Ethics*, 147 (1156b).

[714] Viktor Frankl said that the meaning of his own life lay in assisting others to find meaning in
theirs. Frankl, *Man's Search for Meaning*, 165.

[715] Dunbar, *Grooming, Gossip, and the Evolution of Language*, 116. Dunbar argues that human language permits grooming of larger groups with more complex interactions than the nit-picking of sub-
linguistic primates. In humans, gossip replaces physical grooming as social glue.

[716] *Mencius*, 96 (Book IV, Part B, Section 30).

[717] *Mencius*, 89 (Book IV, Part B, Section 7).

[718] *Mencius*, 121 (Book V, Part B, Section 8). One can discover intimates long dead, though the intimacy proves one-sided.

[719] [♪] Cicero, *De Officiis*, 139-141 (Book I, Section XXXVIII, 136-137).

[720] [♪] Emerson, *Conduct of Life*, 1049 (V): "In all superior people I have met, I notice directness,
truth spoken more truly, as if everything of obstruction, of malformation, had been trained away."

[721] Emerson advised friends: "Better be a nettle in the side of your friend than his echo." Emerson,
Friendship, 350. Confucius finds that gentlemen agree with a man without being merely an echo,
while small men echo a person without agreeing. [♪] Confucius, *Analects*,122 (Book XIII, Section
23).

friend, heed it.[722] Don't argue; listen. Keep talking until you understand one another.

7.9. *Cooperation.* **Simple Rule: Do constructive tasks with friends**. The genetic origins of friendship, and all human cooperative activity, lie in our cognitive capacity for joint attention. In joint attention, humans attend to a subject and to the response of others simultaneously. Mature joint attention leads to "we-intentionality," the formation of shared goals and coordinated action to achieve those shared goals. Joint attention emerges in human development in infancy. Shared intentionality characterizes all human communities, though the cultural expressions of cooperation vary dramatically. The shared intentionality of humans far outstrips the capacities of even our closest primate relatives. Humans are fundamentally cooperative.[723] Our innate tendency to form cooperative relationships underpins the emergence of friendship. Your friends will emerge from among those with whom you engage some activity collaboratively. If the tasks you jointly undertake address some significant need, then friendship will blossom and you will grow accustomed to doing well by others, an excellent habit.[724]

7.10. *Micro-Communities.* **Simple Rule: Value friendship itself**. Friends form a meaningful micro-community, a cadre in Quad sociality. Friends establish a social bond, augment one another's meaning, undertake constructive activity together, generate a particularized language and mini-culture, and anticipate defending their mutual bond against disruption. In friendship, as in all human relations, identity interpenetrates from one individual to another, and fresh communities emerge. In its essence, a friendship mirrors the structure of meaningful human community generally.[725] As such, friendship is a paradigmatic good. Friendship rivals and frequently exceeds familial bonds in both intensity and durability. Friendship and family are primary local mirrors of the human community generally. Human families endure only where mates are friends and, as children mature, hierarchical child-rearing structures give way to bilateral adult friendship. Human

---

[722] [♪] Cicero, *De Amicitia*, 155-157 (XIII, 44). See also [♪] Emerson, *Conduct of Life*, 1020 (IV): "Good criticism is very rare, and always precious." Confucius urges one not to fear mending his errant ways. [♪] Confucius, *Analects*, 60 (Book I, Section 8).

[723] Wyman, "Human Cooperation," 227.

[724] [♪] Seneca, *On Tranquillity of Mind*, 50-51.

[725] Grayling says that one has "an ethical obligation actively to pursue friendship," and that "friendship as the desired terminus of all relationships . trumps all other relationships." Grayling, *Friendship*, 185. Grayling goes on to opine that one can use the health of friendship as a compass in ethics generally. Whatever injures friendship is wrong. Grayling, *Friendship*, 190.

community, insofar as it is meaningful, is a grand friendship.[726] Disruption of friendship is an evil to flee. Many obstacles thwart friendship. The grandest impediment to friendship lies in your own soul, in your fitful ability to welcome and persistently tolerate the differences of others.

Wealth in friendship occurs when members learn to tolerate differences that do not threaten to disrupt meaningful community. All persons, even the odd and ugly, might become your friend, except that small percentage of the population suffering sociopathy or aggressive narcissism who do harm to others without the normal constraints of conscience.[727] Stay open to people. The deepest problems in human culture trace back to private mental habits of intolerance. We share a world with our friends and neighbors. Others do not share that world with us, and so seem alien. Governments aggregate private prejudices into oppressive policies of discrimination. But the most dangerous intolerances emerge from a majority's social and informal demand for conformity.[728]

Human evolution bequeathed us a sometimes adaptive, but more often problematical, subconscious threat response. One who enters unknown, one who looks different, one who behaves strangely: these trigger our threat subroutine. In chimpanzee troops, such outsiders are often summarily killed. To address evolution's handiwork to the extent threat response hobbles our communities, we need to acquire habits that deflect errant threat assessments, and build communities where the number of those perceived threats is greatly reduced. Threat response agitates people. Agitated people deliberate poorly. The results dismay.

7.11. *Tolerance and Conflict*. **Simple Rule: Tolerate differences in others.** When others deviate from one's experience of the neurotypical, the others' differences threaten to disrupt one's personal equilibrium. The need to maintain psychic equilibrium generates a primal impulse to drive the differentiated person toward behavior or characteristics that conform to one's

---

[726] Every friendship is a component of some community of people. [♪] Aristotle, *Nicomachean Ethics*, 158 (1161b).

[727] Mill argues that no interference with the preferences or actions of another individual are warranted, individually or by government, except when the person threatens injury to another. [♪] Mill, *On Liberty*, 12.

[728] "Society . . . practices a social tyranny more formidable than many kinds of political oppression, since, though not usually upheld by such extreme penalties, it leaves fewer means of escape, penetrating much more deeply into the details of life, and enslaving the soul itself. Protection, therefore, against the tyranny of the magistrate is not enough: there needs protection also against the tyranny of the prevailing opinion and feeling; against the tendency of society to impose, by other means than civil penalties, its own ideas and practices as rules of conduct on those who dissent from them; to fetter the development, and, if possible, prevent the formation, of any individuality not in harmony with its ways, and compels all characters to fashion themselves upon the model of its own." [♪] Mill, *On Liberty*, 8.

sense of the neurotypical. Frequently, offense is mutual, setting the stage for mutual attempts to compel change in the other. Conflicts emerge. Conflicts, unresolved, injure friendship. Sufficient injury dissolves friendship.

We often fail to appreciate the depth of differences among us. We are each born with a differential genetic load of possibilities. We each have childhood history and parental care different from any other. Life deals blows and benefits; of these we may be ignorant, even when they pertain to ourselves. The human spectrum in appearance, behavior, and capability is broad, broader than we can, without effort, begin to comprehend. You are unique. So too is every other. Our tool of grouping unknown members by transient or negligible characteristics betrays the facts. None is exactly like you or any other.[729]

Grouping others by race, religion, sex, nationality, language, or other appreciable characteristics occurs unconsciously. Grouping is one of the functions of intelligence. However, when characteristics are assigned to group members, all apart from knowledge of those members, one frequently errs. Each member is different. Further, one's stereotype injures the other, even where there is no intention to injure. "Stereotype threat" is an emotional state of fear that grips persons against whom the stereotype is projected. Viciously, the fear tends to generate the stereotype anticipated. The psychological effect is widespread and pernicious.[730] Criticize your stereotypes. As to any given individual, stereotypes misrepresent.

To succor friendships, one must learn to tolerate the differences among people.[731] The Japanese have a proverb: Every nail that sticks out shall be driven in. The proverb is true of human propensity, but fatal to friendship-building. Learn to tolerate deviation from your sense of normal, where those differences do not threaten your or others' well-being.[732] Our sensi-

---

[729] The research of behavior geneticist Jerome Kagan makes this point admirably. See Karen's nice summary of Kagan's research. [♪] Karen, *Becoming Attached*, 294-296. These depths of difference reveal the disturbing possibility that, among people, some may prove incapable of understanding the life and motivations of some others. Some gulfs may, despite good faith effort, be too expansive to bridge. Hence, friendship may prove, in unusual circumstances, impossible.

[730] Yong, "Armor Against Prejudice," 76-80.

[731] Maturana and Varela portray conflict as an abrasion of worlds. Conflict cannot be resolved until the combatants find a world to share. When we make room for others to live beside us, when we make room for divergent others, we love. Others, even deeply different others, deserve respect and legitimacy. Hence, broad tolerance is an act of love and maturity. Maturana and Varela, *Tree of Knowledge*, 246-247. De Beauvoir, speculating on greater amity between the sexes, notes: "The fact that we are human beings is infinitely more important than all the peculiarities that distinguish human beings from one another." De Beauvoir, *The Second Sex*, 764.

[732] Leidloff construes intolerance as an imperfection of personality. The damaged persona imagines threat in the eccentricities of his companions. The fulfilled personality, at peace with himself, welcomes the idiosyncrasies of others. Leidloff, *The Continuum Concept*, 147.

tivity to the differentness of others characterizes social mammals generally. We fashion from those often-facile perceptions in-groups and out-groups. Human psychology is scarcely adapted to the demands global membership press upon it. Yet such appears possible for creatures such as us, and is certainly necessary.[733]

We weakly grasp the depth of differentness in others. Our task remains to care for our own differentness, and tolerate that of others.[734]

7.11.1. *Tolerance of Racial Differentiation.*[735] Racial differentiation emerges from the isolation of human populations following the prehistorical diaspora from Africa around 50,000 years ago. African, Asiatic, Australian aboriginal, and European waves of African emigration established relatively isolated breeding populations, resulting in phenotypic deviation over millennia. All humans, despite racial differentiations, form one species and interbreed without genetic complication. The fact of racial differentiation is frequently confused with the need for political recognition of the political equality of every human. As mobile culture has emerged, racial mixing has accelerated, creating of the human planetary population a single breeding group. Racial differentiation is likely to decline sharply in upcoming centuries as the effects of diaspora isolation are erased in global mixing of the human gene pool.

People who disrupt one's equilibrium by looking different may be subjected to all manner of disparagement. Projection and stereotyping control the character imputed to unknown, alien-looking individuals. The unconscious conclusion emerges that "they" are indeed as strange within as they appear without. Visual differentiation underpins much human prejudice. Racism begins in the eyes.

---

[733] De Waal argues that despite our inherited parochialism, we have a remarkable ability to erect new structures upon and in preference to older ones. We troop-lovers may well become global members. De Waal, *The Bonobo and the Atheist*, 235-236.

[734] William James argues that we know our own feelings. Those of others are a mystery, and our judgments about this interiority of others are usually stupid, unjust, and false. When life creates eagerness in a person, that person finds her life significant. Our day-to-day preoccupations deafen us to the variety of worth others experience. One must not judge another's existence to be meaningless. We must, rather, tolerate the life of those who do us no harm. Their life may be incomprehensible to us. But no person knows all of truth and goodness. Our task, so James argues, is to grasp our own possibilities. We must leave those of others to them. James, *On a Certain Blindness in Human Beings*. Martin Buber asserts that vital communities recognize, and even foster, deep differentiation among members, while remaining focused on building intimate connections between them within a community. Buber, *Paths in Utopia*, 145.

[735]Gary Bloom reminds me that "race" is a concept abandoned by physical anthropologists. Racial differentiation notes high points of various physical characteristics in a continuum of ethnic groups. "Race" is a social construct often employed for pernicious purposes. Conjoined with the human fear of differentness, racial intolerance fractures human communities. The very concept tilts us toward prejudices unwarranted by facts plainly before us. Hence, the danger.

7.11.2. *Tolerance of Sexual Differentiation.* Maleness and femaleness represent poles of the human spectrum of sexual development and gender identity. Male and female brains differ in fundamental ways. Female brains coordinate the cerebral hemispheres more globally in language tasks. Males brains rely more heavily on left brain lateralism in speech processing. The larger female corpus callosum (the nerve bundle connecting the two hemispheres) is one component of neuroanatomical differences that explain the divergent cognitive styles of males and females. Male humans have an enlarged lower spinal cord structure, the nucleus of the bulbocavernosus, which affects penile erection and ejaculation.[736] Differences between male and female speech and cognitive outputs can injure friendship.

Humans also sexually differentiate in sexual attraction. In fetal development, an XY chromosome structure may cause male emendations to the basically female structure of all human fetuses, and set the stage, in puberty, for male sexual behaviors. Male fetuses generate carefully timed floods of testosterone, which hormone initiates masculinizing changes in the fetus. If these testosterone incursions fail or are mis-timed, other outcomes occur, including feminized brains in male bodies, masculinzed brains in female bodies, and shades of deviation mediating these polar possibilities. Fetal development influences gender preferences and sexual behavior when, in adolescence, the gonads drive sexual behaviors with bursts of sexual endocrines. The broad spectrum of human sexual activity emerges: male-female, male-male, female-female, male-female alternation, harem preference, asexuality, and trans-sexuality. Sexual differentiation is further volatilized by human choice, cultural expectations, and individual psychology.[737] Although male-female sexuality is the predominant sexual expression among humans, homosexuality and bisexuality emerge from the same fundamental fetal processes, as well as a host of less-frequent alternatives. All are, in the broad scope of human sexuality, normal.

7.11.3. *Tolerance of Bodily Differentiation.* In each of its aspects, the human population spreads itself along a Bell curve. Bodies come in a welter of variations: dwarves, giants, those with deformed or sluggish brains, people with supple brains, people who cannot move, people who cannot stop moving, blind, deaf, vegetative, fat, skinny, deformed of birth or accident. Each repulses, to the extent he or she deviates from typicality. Resist that urge to look away, to neglect the odd.

---

[736] Panksepp, *Affective Neuroscience*, 237.

[737] Panksepp, *Affective Neuroscience*, 237.

Similarly, when a body approximates the average among humans, we find such persons inordinately attractive. Beautiful persons are deemed to have greater potential and finer skills than others less graced, even when facts predominate otherwise. Resist this urge, Kate. Do not gaze fondly upon beautiful people, unless they have proved their worth as must the less-gorgeous of the planet. Discriminating in favor of beauty is a deeply ingrained and utterly unwarranted habit. You will fail to recognize your best friends if you allow the beautiful to enrapture you. In time, your un-beautiful friends shine with a beauty unique to themselves.

Human sexual evolution may lie near the root of our curse of the in-elegant. As a cipher for genetic fitness, human consciousness leans to-ward the tall, the well-proportioned, the symmetrical, the robust. There may have been a time when a woman needed a potent, intimidating male able to kill prey and human threats with testosterone-spitting fierceness. At some point in time, a buxom, well-buttocked mate of flowing hair may have been required to gestate a brute's unending line of vibrant rascals. Perhaps in such a time, the beauty-cipher served mankind well. But, on an overpopulated planet with few surviving environmental threats, beauty mania is specious. A once-adaptive cipher of fitness may have become, in our circumstances, insurance that hulking males will indulge pointless ag-gressions, and preening prom queens will remain juggernauts of endless primping, wedded to their mirrors. Deliberating, humanity must identify habits better fit to futures we imagine for ourselves. Humans cannot free themselves from a preference for beautiful people. We can, however, cri-tique that preference, and establish contravening habits.

7.11.4. *Tolerance of Disease States.* We fear and discriminate against dis-eased individuals. Communicable diseases may warrant measures to limit spread. But human fear of diseased individuals vastly exceeds the dangers imagined. Take appropriate precautions, but avoid hypochondriacal self-quarantine. Every human body contains trillions of bacteria and viruses, any one of which might cause disease under favorable circumstances. Normally, our bodies defend themselves admirably, and with many of these disease vectors establish a stalemate or even symbiosis. Wash your hands regularly. Treat bodily fluids with care. But welcome diseased persons. Resist revulsion.

7.11.5. *Tolerance of Historical Differentiation.* Cultures are niche-adaptations of long-dead predecessors. We inherit a culture, and, though we may adopt others in the course of living, we never rid ourselves of the culture into which we were born. Cultures shape minds, teaching us a first language and dialect. The warp of one's birth culture impresses itself on all subsequent mentation.[738] When we live in bloated anonymous sociality, cultures come to have meanings not immediately evident. Cultures support stereotypes which lend themselves to projection upon milling nameless crowds. Resist such projections. Learn who people are. Maintain deliberate neutrality until evidence rolls in.[739]

Historical differentiation exceeds mere cultural influences. Wealth and poverty ring through generations. Some part of this class structure depends on historical happenstance. Other parts derive from individual initiative and perseverance. Avoid letting a person's poverty or wealth affect the possibility of friendship.

7.11.6. *Tolerance of Religious Differentiation*. Religious faith is a species of historical differentiation. The abundant conflict caused by religious differentiation merits special attention. Perhaps no other cultural feature alienates groups so effectively as religious differentiation.[740] Religions often make of their mutual antipathy points of dogma.[741] Many teach children phobic thoughts about outsiders.[742] Resist such fears, Kate. Every properly theological thought conjures speculation about matters of which humans are wholly ignorant. Some traditions, lacking evidence, elevate writings. Those paragraphs suffer the identical defect. Men know nothing of gods. To make a friend of one who deems you, on the basis of sacred writings, doomed to perdition, requires extraordinary compassion and patience. Undertake such friendship with care. Some people, by virtue of their religious affections, effectively exclude themselves from being your friend. Few, if any, are able to change their religious convictions,

---

[738] None prefers other than his own culture's goods. Tolstoy recounts a Chechen proverb: Dog treats ass to meat; ass treats dog to hay. Both go hungry. Tolstoy, *Hadji Murat*, 91.

[739] Fine education and extraordinary intelligence do not insulate one from ugly intolerance. Note Schopenhauer's anti-semitism, when he laments the "Jewish stench." Schopenhauer, *The Basis of Morality*, 113. This irruption mars Schopenhauer's meditation on compassion. Elsewhere, Schopenhauer disparages American negroes and the uneducated. Schopenhauer, *The Wisdom of Life*, 27-28.

[740] One cannot limit religious thinking to theological communities alone. Many perspectives depend upon faith convictions that have no relation, or a hostile relation, toward gods. De Beauvoir, for example, classes psychoanalysis, Marxism, and Christianity as examples of religions. De Beauvoir, *The Second Sex*, 39.

[741] John Locke advocates for broad religious tolerance among theists, but reserves antipathy and intolerance for atheists, who by banishing gods unwind the skein of society. Locke, *A Letter Concerning Toleration*, 21, 58.

[742] Tolstoy asserts that the most cruel words one man speaks to another are those that portray one's own religion as irrefutable and the other's as moronic. [♪] Tolstoy, *A Confession*, 54 (Chapter XV). Do not trample upon the sacred places of others.

since these, like language, are drunk early in life.[743] Enduring religious
manias in others (or in yourself) may prove your most difficult tolerance
exercise. In tolerating your odd-opinioned friend, you need not white-
wash her views. All ideas are not created equal. In your tolerance, speak
plainly of error, but do so with kindness. Use reasonable arguments, but
take no offense when these are met with dunderhead obstinacy. Many of
religious ilk prove unaccustomed to the accommodations required in difficult conversation.

7.11.7. *Tolerance of Mental Differentiation.* Neurotypicality and neurodiversity matter because it is brain function that most deeply distinguishes
man from the remainder of the animal kingdom, and man from man. The
most complex organization known in the universe is a human brain. Its
trillions of connections exhibit astounding plasticity in response to genetics, injury, environmental stimuli, social input, and inner experience. Giv-
en the statistics of the matter, you never have and never will meet two
people who are neurally identical. That fact promises profound diversity.
It also promises that many will rankle you. There are persons vastly more
supple than you intellectually, more artistic, more humorous, more diligent, better at mathematics, better at social relations, better at –well, you
name it. A welter of others lack the many skills you possess, so deeply so
that it may prove difficult to see an excellence in them of any sort. These
facts can interact with our predilection for hierarchical ranking, leaving
those with fewer and lesser abilities at the bottom of an imagined heap.

Humans are not an intellectual heap. We are each integrated into a
social web where we play some important role. It is useful to presume
that every person plays roles significant to other persons, regardless
whether one knows those persons or those significances. One may, by
this presumption, occasionally err. The fact of sociopathy leads one to
suspect there are persons whose skills are devoted to industry so malevolent that no helpful outcomes can be anticipated. But, if one must err, it
seems a good habit to err on the side of hopeful generosity.

7.11.8. *Tolerance of Moral Differentiation.* Perhaps most difficult, one must
welcome in friendship those one finds morally defective.[744] Such persons

---

[743] Muhammad says to disbelievers that he and they worship different gods. Muhammad will not
change, nor will the unfaithful. Each clings to their religion. [♪] Muhammad, *Qur'an*, Surah 109:1-
6.

[744] Mill argues that society lacks legitimate authority to silence dissenting voices. Mill asserts: "If
all mankind minus one were of one opinion, and only one person were of the contrary opinion, mankind would be no more justified in silencing that one person, than he, if he had the power, would be
justified in silencing mankind. . . . But the particular evil of silencing the expression of an opinion,
is that it is robbing the human race; posterity as well as the existing generation; those who dissent
from the opinion, still more than those who hold it. If the opinion is right, they are deprived of the
opportunity of exchanging error for truth: if wrong, they lose, what is almost as great a benefit, the

as these cannot be merely tolerated. Where one offers the turned head of a social snub or a censorial tut-tut, one chills all dissenters and all their dissents. Social spanking chafes the butt of communion and strangles deliberative dialogue. Where shared sentiment coalesces in a community's rules or laws, the chief effect is that of energizing social stigma against dissenters.[745] Almost the entire power of law rests in informal quashing of deviance. Few find tangible sanction beneath the grinding wheels of judicial machinery. Most compliance leaps from social norms bolstered by law. Stigmatizing dissent drives it underground. Dissenters fume. Schismatics rankle. Heretics hide. One fashions, by crushing deviant opinion, cleaved communities. Dissent enlivens debate; it diverts majorities from comfort to contemplation. People suffer the malady of half-measures; most consider a matter and truncate deliberation at the first supportable argument in its favor. Dissenters deliver the gift of completion; they drive contemplation to thoroughly masticated conclusion.

Where welcomed, dissenters consider compromise. They reconsider the ferment produced, reassess its value. In deliberative community, you will find yourself occasionally the dissenter. Treat every dissenter as you pray to be handled at that juncture.

I advise you to flee evil. Do not believe, however, that beneath every tawdry outfit lies a dark heart. Most perceptions of evil are nothing more than fashion out of time. Discover what lies within a dissenter before rushing off nonplussed. Don his shoes and eyeglasses. Wear them for a time. Most evil consists in misperceived goods. Explore dissenters. Hear their take on goodness; let them criticize yours.[746] Spit the protester out only when you discover a dark adamant recalcitrance within her. Leash your barking pack. Cherish the quack of odd ducks. Among them, if mankind is fortunate, hide neurodiverse savants, from whom human wonders blossom.

7.12. *Structure of Friendship Sociality.* **Simple Rule: Build a wide-ranging group of friendly acquaintances.** Friendship forms tiered concentric circles, as viewed from the member's vantage. The intensity of relationship attenuates as one moves outward from the cadre, to circle, to community, to

---

clearer perception and livelier impression of truth, produced by its collision with error." [♪] Mill, *On Liberty*, 18-19. Henry David Thoreau shares Mill's view, contemplating the possibility that a lone dissenter may exist as a political "majority of one." [♪] Thoreau, *On the Duty of Civil Disobedience*, 259.

[745] [♪] Mill, *On Liberty*, 32.

[746] "[I]t is the privilege and proper condition of a human being, arrived at the maturity of his faculties, to use and interpret experience in his own way. It is for him to find out what part of recorded experience is properly applicable to his own circumstances and character." [♪] Mill, *On Liberty*, 56.

Commons. Three to seven members form an intimate support group, from whom a member seeks advice or help in times of distress. This clutch of intimates is a "cadre." From within this intimate group of friends, members frequently choose sexual partners. Often a person enjoys, beyond the bounds of intimates, twelve to twenty persons with whom the member finds unusual sympathy; the member has special ties of some sort to this group. This larger group may comprise extended family, persons who share common interests, neighbors, or other more exotic connections. This larger group consists in persons who are in the process of becoming intimates or are intimate-candidates. These persons are drawn from a "circle" of around 150 persons with whom a person is well-acquainted; member relations with these other circle members shift over time. One is able to track the many relational convolutions of the members of one's circle. Zhou argues that the circle-size grouping is related to the neocortical capacity of the human brain. At around 150 individuals, which some call "Dunbar's Number," a person begins to lose track of the identities and shifting relationships of the members due to cortical limitations of the human brain.[747] Beyond these personal groupings lies the community, a linguistic and economic unit of 1,000 to 2,000 members, with which the member identifies herself. And beyond the community lies the billion member Commons.[748]

7.13. *Friendship Transitions.* **Simple Rule: Address transitions in intimate friendship directly and compassionately.** All relationships change. Most intimate friendships develop over time, including sexual intimates. Relational changes should be mutually deliberated; frankness must govern those conversations. Negotiate honestly in a relationship in transition. Care for the pain your partner feels. Go slowly enough to allow your friend to adjust to your revised togetherness. Grief often follows relational change; grief has its own schedule for healing. Be patient. Preserve each changed friendship as vigorously as any other. The friend in a changed relationship never

---

[747] Zhou, "Social Group Size Organization," 440. Dunbar argues that groups larger than 150 need to develop a formal hierarchy to remain efficient. Dunbar, *How Many Friends Does One Person Need?: Dunbar's Number and Other Evolutionary Quirks*, 24, 26 (Chapter 3). Robin Dunbar offers an especially helpful detailing of human group-size capabilities in another of his books. See Dunbar, *Grooming, Gossip, and the Evolution of Language*, 69-79.

[748] The concentric structure of kithdom aims to mirror, with liberal concessions to technological existence, the connections and intimacy that were normal to simple human societies through all but the last 15,000 years of humanity's 200,000 year presence on earth. Simple human societies are egalitarian, emphasizing parity among males and disparaging those who seek to become "big men." Coercion is deemed offensive, as is bragging. Leadership is organic and unsystematic. Decisions are made by casual consensus. None exercises authority over others. Member and group demands are balanced by the needs of each. In more complex, sedentary, agricultural societies, groups experience increased male status differentiation, property and possessions and wealth, and social inequality. Social statuses lead to coercive leadership and formal organization, in short, political society. Knauft, "Violence and Sociality in Human Evolution," 395-396.

becomes again a stranger. Your mutual interpenetration of social identities prevents that outcome. Friends, even deceased or absent friends, persevere. They live within you.

7.14. *Friendship Deterioration.* **Simple Rule: Repair strained friendships.** Unnegotiated change in intimate friendship can alienate friends. Delayed or forsaken communication between friends ruptures relationship. Deviance can hobble friendships, especially where a community finds it necessary to censure that deviance. Where one has caused hurt or injury, make repairs. Explain yourself; apologize.[749]   Do so face to face, not by phone or email, unless no alternatives exist. Humans are hard-wired for face to face communication; more significant content is shared in person than by electronic means: facial expression, intonations, gestures, eye talk. And in-person communications are more likely to elicit prosocial emotions than less direct communications. We are inclined to help those who come to us and ask for help.[750]

The Harvard Negotiation Project recommends the following approach for undertaking difficult conversations in strained relationships.

7.14.1. *Three Conversations.* Distinguish three discussions that transpire in every charged conversation: talk about facts, talk about emotions, and talk about meaning and identity. Do not argue or persuade. Listen to your friend's viewpoint. Say his perspective back to him in his own words. Then tell him your perceptions of the problems you are experiencing. Assume you lack information that explains your friend's behavior. Human perceptions are wildly divergent. You do lack critical information.

If, as you contemplate a difficult conversation with a friend, it comes clear to you that the problem lies wholly in you, and not between you, then change the tenor of conversation. Discuss how to help you, not how to improve things between you and your friend. You might also decide to have no conversation with the friend, but a different conversation with someone you believe better able to assist you with your problem.

7.14.2. *Facts.* If you disagree about facts, negotiate a way to ascertain those facts more clearly. Facts are seldom the cause of disputes among friends.

---

[749] Cicero urges apology where one injures another's interests or feelings. Explain yourself. Explain the dilemma in which you found yourself. Use what powers are yours to help your victim, and to demonstrate your regret. [♪] Cicero, *De Officiis*, 243 (Book II, Section XIX, 68). Grayling notes that friends give meaning to our lives. Without friendships, we etch ourselves, and teeter toward nothingness. Grayling, *Friendship*, 202.

[750] Hrdy, *Mothers and Others*, 6.

7.14.3. *Intentions.* Assume you do not know your friend's intention in his acts, and inquire about them.[751] Expect defensiveness from your friend; counter it with reassurance about your affection for him. When you understand your friend's explanation of his behavior, explain to him the impact his behavior had upon you or others. Explain your own motivations in the conversation, and explore with him other possible (usually less-flattering) explanations for your actions. Ask him what other motivations might explain your friend's acts. Assess how each of you contributed to the problems you are experiencing. Laughing helps.

7.14.4. *Emotions.* Discover, evaluate, then share your feelings about what has been happening between you and your friend. Invite him to share similarly. Avoid evaluating these revelations. Just listen to emotion talk. No one exerts voluntary control over their emotions. Emotion can be repressed momentarily, but erupts in subliminal (or not so subliminal) ways later. Acknowledge to your friend the importance of his emotions. Thank him for sharing them.

7.14.5. *Identity.* Every difficult conversation challenges one's personal sense of meaning. One asks, Am I competent? Am I good? Am I lovable? Such questions shake one, and make the difficult conversation more intractable. In your interior self-talk, you can stabilize your identity by avoiding black-and-white thinking, declining to deny your own problems, sidestepping exaggerations, and recalling other facts about yourself besides criticisms. You may need to take a break in the middle of a difficult conversation to regain your equanimity and confidence. Ask for that consideration if you need it. Grant it if sought. Talk about the struggles that the conversation induces in your sense of meaning, if you believe that will help your talking with your friend.

7.14.6. *Learning Conversation.* Direct your talking toward learning about one another and the problem you are addressing. Create a story that includes both friends' perspectives as though it were told by a third person

---

[751] You will encounter bad faith actors, but it is unlikely your friend is one of them. If you find that your friend persists in bad faith acts, harder questions need to be asked. Your friend may suffer narcissistic or sociopathic tendencies. Approximately four percent of the human population harbors sociopathic tendencies, and they wreak much more havoc in the social universe than their numbers would lead you to anticipate. Stout, *The Sociopath Next Door*, 6. You could be in danger. Antisocial personality disorder manifests after fifteen years of age in disregard for and violation of the rights and well-being of others, accompanied by at least three of the following characteristics: disregard for social and legal norms, remorseless lying, impulsivity and lack of planning, irritable aggression, disregard for safety, financial and interpersonal irresponsibility, and indifferent or remorseless rationalizing of ill behavior. See *Diagnostic and Statistical Manual of Mental Disorders* §301.7, fourth edition, text revision (DSM IV-TR). Such psychological difficulties lie beyond the diagnostic or remedial skills of neurotypical laymen. Where a friend may be a narcissist or sociopath, make a professional referral to open a path to help for that person, and quietly walk away from the relationship. Flee evil.

observing your relationship. Help your friend understand you by expressing yourself with clarity, patience, and completeness. Ask your friend to paraphrase to you what you have been telling him. Correct errors of understanding calmly and charitably.

7.14.7. *Problem-Solving.* Solve those problems between you that can be solved. Intractable problems should be frankly acknowledged, and ways to work around them discussed.

Unsolvable problems may weigh so large that the relationship becomes inviable. Not all friendships can be rescued from difficulty. If yours is beyond the pale, acknowledge that gently and respectfully. Talk over what new norms should exist when encountering one another.[752]

When you have completed the process of understanding one another via a series of "difficult conversations," your friendship may still be tattered. Restoring a frayed relationship requires patient, consistent acts of kindness and understanding. John Gottmann calls this process one of bidding and responding. Bids are requests for relatedness, usually small, such as a touch on the shoulder, and inquiring look, a glass of water, listening, or talking. Responses reject, ignore, or welcome bids. A friendship grows where most bids are welcomed and reciprocated. One frustrates bidding by missing the emotional needs of the bidder, persisting in harsh habits, bitter criticism, persisting when a friend is overwhelmed by emotions, and avoiding problem topics. In bidding and responding, you will need to take account of the other person's deep-seated mental habits, their emotional history, and body language and verbal cues. As your friendship recovers, work hard at building shared meaning by supporting one another's aspirations and dreams. Let things between you and your friend be different than they were before your difficulties. Anticipate deep bonding once again.[753]

There will be some friends whose changes preclude further relating. Draw this conclusion only after long effort to re-establish intimacy. The bottom line in friendship remains that both encourage and sustain the life and dreams of the other. Where such mutual succor proves unworkable, terminate the relationship. Do so kindly. Take your time. But be firm. You may love someone with whom you cannot collaborate. You must be yourself, and without the support of your intimates, you cannot achieve that wonder. Permit no friend to hobble you in this grand task. Amputate, as one would a

---

[752] [♪] Stone, Patton, and Heen, *Difficult Conversations.*

[753] [♪] Gottmann and DeClaire, *The Relationship Cure.*

gangrenous limb. One prefers the grief of separation over personal stagnation.[754]

7.15. *Sexual Pairing.* A primal event in human behavior is reproduction. Evolutionary pressures select genetic traits that underlie psychological mechanisms and physical structures that reproduce well. Some argue that all of human behavior can be interpreted as gene transmission strategies.[755] This writer suspects, contrary to reductionist theories, that human choice matters in procreation. This author remain unwilling to deem consciousness a hapless baby-making mechanism.

7.15.1. *Care in Mate Selection.* **Simple Rule: Choose a mate by mature deliberation.** If you cannot yet choose a mate carefully, do not mate. Mate selection determines the structure of vast swaths of one's life. Choose your mate with extraordinary caution and patience. Your mate shapes you, and you your mate. Many believe the mated relationship to be life's most significant.[756] Take time. Be discerning. Ask hard questions. Let experience of candidate mates aggregate through months or years. You may be ready to mate when you no longer say things like "we never fight" or "I would change nothing about him."

7.15.2. *Mate Choice.* **Simple Rule: Attach to and mate with an intimate friend similar to you and your opposite-sex parent.** Never mate with a person who is not your intimate friend. "Love at first sight" merely splashes your hopes across another's blank canvas. Let friendship grow; then consider sex. Across species, breeding male individuals prefer mates similar to the female that reared them. In humans, early childhood imprinting appears to predispose choice of a mate resembling the opposite-sex parent. If rejected during childhood by his mother, a male will be less likely to choose partners resembling that mother. Humans prefer mates that look and smell like their own opposite-sex parent.[757] But less so, if the relationship with that opposite-sex parent is attachment-injured or violent. Most people who suffer divorce view that event as one of life's most

---

[754] Gustav Landauer urges people to form a small community with others who can wish to do so, and to forsake those who, due to their capture in anonymous conformity, cannot grasp the joy of your endeavor. Landauer, *Through Separation to Community*, 107-108.

[755] Robert Wright makes much of the subconscious pressures deflecting human reproduction toward its hidden agenda. Wright does, however, acknowledge the extreme potency of human cultural possibilities in resisting the pressure of genetic selection. Wright, *The Moral Animal*, 261-262.

[756] Mencius finds a man and woman living under the same roof to be life's most important relationship. *Mencius*, 100 (Book V, Part A, Section 2).

[757] Bereczkei, "Parental Impacts," 262-265.

painful and debilitating. A careful, well-deliberated choice at the inception reduces the likelihood of decay of a mated friendship.

The "intimate-friendship-first" rule also insures that you will have copious opportunities to identify your friend-becoming-mate's attachment style. Hazan and Shaver argue that romantic love is an attachment process only slightly dissimilar from the attachment of an infant to its mother. The three broad attachment categories (secure, ambivalent, and avoidant) describe romantic styles as well as infant attachment style, and the models of relating used by adults lovers depend greatly upon the mental model of emotional expectation established in infancy.[758] You will want, once the sound and fury of falling-in-love dissipates and moderate sanity returns from exile, a mate who reliably supports you, knows and cherishes you, and forgives your faults and shortcomings. You will want a partner enthusiastic about you, but one also gripped by a reasonable assessment of your capabilities and shortcomings. Persons who suffer anxious attachment styles, as a result of their inborn temperaments or deficient early parenting, may worship or dazzle you. If they do not, however, stand by you, give you freedom to become what lies within you, and reliably trust and support you, your relationship may sputter senselessly for decades. That an intimate friend suffers anxious attachment of some sort does not preclude mating with that person. It does, however, demand substantial, long-term effort to address and remediate his or her emotional predilections toward anxiety or avoidance in your relationship.[759]

7.15.3. *Commitment*. **Simple Rule: Preserve your mate's trust.** Human sexual pairing includes both the possibility of unrivaled intimacy and a risk of sexual adventure. The thrill of uncommitted sexual encounters threatens the stability of both member and community. Human cultures have historically reinforced human sexual commitment by traditions favoring stable relationships and punishing adventurous trysts.[760] Fidelity to one's mate matters because:

7.15.3.1. Lying to a spouse fractures intimacy and generates deep internal stresses in the prevaricator. Your spouse will view cover-up lies as damning as hidden infidelity. Each evidences un-negotiated change in one's intimate friendship. That disrespect injures an intimate terribly.

---

[758] Hazan and Shaver, "Romantic love conceptualized as an attachment process," 522-524.

[759] See [♪] Karen, *Becoming Attached*. Karen describes the romantic styles of securely-attached, anxiously-attached, and avoidantly-attached lovers at Chapter 25. [♪] Karen, *Becoming Attached*, 379-393.

[760] Marriage, now so frequently disfavored, is one such tradition. The theological baggage of marriage discredits the practice. Marriage, as a sacrament, can safely be discarded. Fidelity to one's mate cannot.

One cannot hide. Non-verbal clues betray your malfeasance. If a mate does not appear to notice infidelity, that is because he or she represses an intuition.

7.15.3.2. Failure of intimacy with your mate injures your children. High stress, elevated death rates of siblings, and the absence of biological fathers induces early sexual readiness in female children and predisposes them to lower-investment parenting strategies with their own offspring.[761]

7.15.3.3. Communities depend on the stability of intimate friendships. Each non-collaborative disintegration of intimacy marginally destabilizes one's community.

7.15.3.4. Long-term stable bonding with your mate makes one healthier and happier. Though marriage suffers a host of legal, theological, and practical debilities, do not let these facts distract you. Married or not, long term social bonding with one's mate makes life better.[762] When the torrent of "being in love" wanes to an emotional trickle, the slow drip benefits of patient partnership wax to flood, inundating life with well-being. Divorce harms people. Nothing you can do (stop smoking, lose weight, exercise, control sugar intake) rivals the health benefits of establishing a stable, long-term bond with your mate.

Nowhere in consciousness is evolutionary logic more apparent than in sexuality. On the surface of consciousness, one game is played. Beneath appearances, another hand governs—the hand of genetic fitness seeking a relentless host of sheep for the evolutionary slaughter. To elbow enough room for choice to govern in matters of breeding, one must recognize that subconsciously all are subtly shoved toward procreation. All, absent deliberation, may create children they do not want. All, absent deliberation, may make babies they harbor no serious intention to nurture.

7.16. *Fecundity.* **Simple Rule: Bear children only if you must.** Runaway human reproduction threatens human well-being. Communities and members, as well as the human species as a whole, suffer from overpopulation. Please grip firmly in mind: your decision whether or not to make babies is the stuff of which our overpopulation problem consists. Curbing human reproduction is a primary challenge. Historical human events have been driven by the scourge of exploding population. In the deep past, dramatically fewer humans strode the planet. But their survival, despite their relative sparseness, lay in peril, for their technologies were primitive. Technology

---

[761] Bereczkei, "Parental Impacts," 259-262.

[762] Putnam, *Bowling Alone*, 333.

has averted apocalypse under the burden of bloated human numbers, but cannot dodge the ultimate debacle.[763]

7.16.1. *Population Numbers.* We lack perspective on overpopulation. Perhaps some numbers help. The entire population of humans on earth derives from a few thousand individuals (perhaps only a few hundred) clinging to the southern tip of South Africa approximately 164 thousand years ago during a terrible global glaciation-induced drought.[764] Before the invention of agriculture, human population growth approximated zero. In 8,000 B.C., there were around 6 million people globally. In 1 A.D., perhaps 250 million persons existed. In 1600 A.D., there were about 500 million persons on earth. In 1800, one billion humans inhabited the planet. In 1930, the population of earth reached two billion; in 1960, three billion; in 1974, four billion; in 1986, five billion; in 1999, six billion; in 2012, seven billion. To the present, the human population has doubled once per millennium on average, but the population more than doubled twice in the last 200 years and once in the last forty years.[765] Numbers, unfortunately, seldom persuade most people of anything whatsoever.

7.16.2. *Population Propositions.* Joel Cohen adds sobering propositions to the statistical circumstance: 1) stopping population growth without coercion will take, at a minimum, decades, 2) if birth rates do not fall, then death rates will inevitably rise, 3) governmental edicts do not work to reduce birth rates (though some forms of government assistance seem to be of some effect), 4) parents cannot on average bear more children than required to replace themselves due to the limited resources of the earth, and 5) the limits of earth's resources to support our present technological and institutional structures will be reached within the next 100 years, barring a dramatic change in human behaviors.[766]

Thomas Malthus, in his famous nineteenth century essay, stated his dour moral assessment that, because food is necessary and sex unavoidable, when sufficient resources exist, men and women will breed heedlessly, until they again lack resources, and are once more mired in misery and

---

[763] Gwynne Dyer notes that overpopulation created the State, government coercion, loss of personal freedoms, poorer life, class distinctions, and seething resentments that permeate modern cultures. She says, "The human race had dug itself a very deep pit, and we would be living in it for a very long time." Dyer, *War: The Lethal Custom*, 145-146.

[764] Marean, "When the Sea Saved Humanity," 55, and [♪] Wade, *Before the Dawn*, 52.

[765] These population numbers derive (with the exception of the estimates of population in 1999 and 2012) from Joel Cohen's definitive work on population. Cohen, *How Many People Can the Earth Support?*, 32, 76-77.

[766] Cohen, *How Many People Can the Earth Support?*, 11, 16.

vice.[767] Malthus certainly underestimated the ingenuity of thoughtful men in avoiding disaster, and has also overstated the compulsive imperative of child-generating sex. Malthus drinks deep nineteenth-century England's putrid class bias and seems convinced that hyperpopulation results from abject dearth of self-restraint in the lower classes. Perhaps we have had enough of blaming the poor for their plight, and so can spit out Malthus's class prejudice in the same gob with his unbridled pessimism. Despite the flaws of Malthus's argument, one still must account for the fact that human coitus appears to have none but the most tenuous nexus with calculations of global well-being.   The horrid net effect of pregnancy in the hyperpopulous twenty-first century is that the birth of this woman's baby insures the death of another woman's baby elsewhere, usually in the Third World. That dark soot besmirches every newborn.

It would appear that women of many cultures, often abysmally poor, are learning that one benefits one's existing children by declining to add to their numbers. One doubts that humans are having less sex. We do seem to be having less sex that leads to pregnancy. That trend corresponds directly with the meaningful education of girls and women.[768] We can augment the trend, creating controlled population deflation without coercion and without famine, plague, or war. Teach women. Offer them and their children better, more stable lives. One can also attempt to teach men, but many among them may prove ineducable.[769]

One draws a conclusion from the statistics and perspectives mentioned above. Future humans will, either by choice or compulsion of circumstance, breed less frequently or expect much less than do earth's present denizens. One way or another, the human population will have zero growth in the near future.[770] We should breed less frequently because we

---

[767] Malthus, *The Principle of Population*, 11, 37.

[768] Cohen, *How Many People Can the Earth Support?*, 65.

[769] An expedient so simple sounds preposterous, when arrayed against a reproductive plight so out of control. Yet, the same conclusion was reached by early feminist author, Charlotte Gilman. In her 1915 utopia, asexual propagation sustains a population comprising only women. These grand creatures, sequestered from masculine depredations, restrain their reproductive impulses by education and reasoned care for the children who do exist and who will come to exist. Gilman, *Herland*, 58-61. Though I find Gilman's sexism unwarranted and hyperbolic, her confidence that women devoted to parenthood will curb natural impulses to insure the well-being of their children and long-term community is heartening. Robert Engelman warns that Africa's population, currently 1.2 billion, could mushroom to 6.1 billion by 2100 A.D. His solution is not coercive government interventions, for in population control, one must push without pushing. He prescribes, rather, a broad program that aims to improve the lot of women, educating them, and offering them the technical means to control family size. Engelman, "Six Billion in Africa," 63. It appears I am not alone in being a population simpleton.

[770] Cohen, *How Many People Can the Earth Support?*, 154.

choose to do so. Humanity should hope for a life ever so much *better* than do our contemporaries. To accomplish this delightful outcome, I ask you, Kate, and every couple undertaking the joy of coitus, to bear children only if you must.

7.16.3. *Moral Decision.*   The conviction that earth is overpopulated with humans is a moral, not mathematical, proposition. Any opinion of the realistic carrying capacity of the planet expresses deeply held values and assumptions.[771] This fact grows clear when one learns that some thoughtful people estimate the optimal human population to be mere millions, while others assert that a possible human population might be one trillion.[772] In determining that number of inhabitants the earth should bear, one deliberates a host of specifically moral considerations that serve to sketch limits to human population.

One weighs, in proposing an optimal population, the following:

7.16.3.1. *Quality of Life.*   For populations over one billion (an equivocal number), population and quality of life are inversely proportional. As population increases, quality of life decreases, and vice versa. One requires sufficient human numbers to maintain redundancy of economic specializations and to weather unanticipated insults to the human community (say, plague or meteor devastations). One wishes at all costs to avoid a global Tasmanian Regress.[773] But beyond mere sufficiency, additional humans degrade quality of life, rendering our existence an unrelenting monotony of outfitting one more member with essentials we just supplied to his predecessor, *ad infinitum.*[774]

---

[771] Cohen offers a helpful analysis of assumptions and issues in assessing earth's human carrying capacity. Cohen, *How Many People Can the Earth Support?*, 261-296.

[772] Cohen, *How Many People Can the Earth Support?*, 177, 212.

[773] [♪] Ridley, *The Rational Optimist*, 80-83. Ridley details the "Tasmanian regress." Tasmania is an island off southern Australia. People walked there during lower Ice Age sea levels, but were marooned when sea levels rose. The Stone Age immigrants to Tasmania suffered a loss of essential technologies already in their possession due to lack of outside infusion of ideas and insufficient numbers to specialize all the critical skills. The Tasmanians degenerated from fishing and maritime sufficiency to clubbing seals.

[774] In hyperpopulation, other endeavors starve (or, at least, should starve). But the arts and sciences live. They prosper by selective attention. We have carved well-being for the fortunate gated cultures of blessed life. In so doing, we have wrongly relegated most of humanity to an impoverished ghetto. We err. This moral error deadens the ethical existence of the blessed, feeding them the false tale that the dying babies of the ghetto are not their problem, or at least not a solvable problem. From the perspective of the ghetto, our morality is sociopathic. Were we less willing to acquiesce to the deaths of millions of outsiders to preventable scourges, over-population would squeeze to the front of civilization's agenda. Albert Weisman proposes that an optimum human population for the planet is the "number of humans who can enjoy a standard of living that the majority of us would find acceptable." That is something like the lifestyle of Europeans. Weisman, *Countdown*, 43.

7.16.3.2. *Non-Human Species.* Non-human species deserve space to prosper and resources to consume. Their ranges support non-human lives, and are savaged by deforestation and plowing. Humans are members of a global biome, and dramatically dependent upon it. No other biome can conserve us, or our vegetable and animal and microbial companions. Conserving our living companions conserves humanity. Further, other species deserve moral status. Our interpersonal relations exceed the merely human, including, analogically, all living things. Human altruism should extend to the weal of our non-human companions.[775] As we expand the list of "isms" we wish to excise from our collective soul, speciesism should go the way of racism.

7.16.3.3. *Other Endeavors.* Surely we shall always invest some effort merely sustaining human biofunctions. What portion of human effort should be directed to that end? To what extent should we be diverted from other efforts? Shall arts and sciences and explorations be abandoned to the extent incompatible with the demands of producing as many persons as possible? Producing sustenance for life is laborious and often boring. Where one labors over nothing but primers, one seldom exults in masterpieces. He who plows seldom sculpts. Excessive sweat of the brow drowns creativity. Life can, and should, consist in more dynamic enterprises than merely insuring that every ill-deliberated birth reaches nurtured adulthood. Do we not seek a human presence that blossoms and flourishes, not merely wilts and goes to seed? For flourishing, one requires liberal leisure and some unassigned resources. Surely, there must exist alternatives other than coercing celibacy or rearing the tiresome fruit of unbridled promiscuity.

One occasionally meets people so ignorant they could not recognize excellent life if it stood before them. None, however, do not want a good life for themselves. Perhaps we should ask everyone politely not to bear children unless they must. We could explain to all exactly what we mean and why we ask. We could even offer every human the tools and procedures that a person might require to avoid bearing unwanted children.

7.16.3.4. *Freedom to Procreate.* According to prevalent views, western "freedoms" reside in individuals and constrain public interventions.

---

[775] Peter Singer would extend moral consideration (and exclude mere instrumental use) to all sentient creatures, those who experience pain or pleasure, and, therefore, have interests. Singer, *The Expanding Circle*, 123. Albert Schweitzer seeks an ethic that reverences all life of whatever sort, with special emphasis on sympathy for animals. Ethical humans, according to Schweitzer, help all life, including leaves, flowers, and insects. They shrink from injuring any living thing. Schweitzer, *The Philosophy of Civilization*, 296-297 (Chapter 25), 310 (Chapter 26).

One possesses freedom from government intrusion into essentially private decisions and life choices. Nothing could be more private than procreative choice, so the story goes. No government should trample such sacred ground. This popular story has such widespread support that its net effect is to forbid discussion of decisions to procreate. Freedom-mongers fear justly; coercive governments regularly intrude wantonly. The meager list of intrusions forbidden to states should be defended. However, "individual freedom" to procreate is a relatively modern invention. Marital fertility did not drop globally until around 1970. The first inklings that factors had conjoined to make family limitation feasible arose in Europe and Japan in the eighteenth century. There exists no predictive socio-economic pattern to family limitation. Generally, family limitation must be socially acceptable, confer an advantage, and be feasible due to fertility reduction techniques.[776] In the end, families make choices about their size, or fail to do so.

Viewed from the vantage of the breadth of human existence, no decision is less private than making babies. Making babies makes the public. Children become members. Each should be entitled to a well-nurtured life of great possibility amidst a meaningful community. This fact alone makes breeding an object of common scrutiny, since it necessarily involves all members in caring and providing.

Every community needs privacy boundaries across which it shrinks to venture. Quad sociality asks members and their cadres to factor the well-being of future humans in today's family calculation. The rule "bear children only if you must" creates ethical family limitation borders for members and for communities. No member should bear children absent strong personal motivation and sufficient resources in her cadre to nurture her child (I include fathers in this "her.") No community should impede a cadre member's natal decision once these questions have been meaningfully answered within that member's cadre.

The cadre of a potential parent consists in that person's closest friends. These have been granted permission to address all of a person's life, to intrude without rebuff, for the lives of friends are shared in common. Friends will be those who are likely to become alloparents to the child, who may provide financial support to the biological parents, who adopt the child as their own when parents perish. It is these persons who deliberate birth-decisions with anticipatory parents. Can the cadre provide needed support? What is the population of the cadre's community and what is its population trend? Are the many communi-

---

[776] Cohen, *How Many People Can the Earth Support?*, 54-63.

ties of earth managing their own population stability? Potential parents and their cadres deliberate, then decide.

Communities must note the natal decisions of their constituent cadres. Are their deliberations meaningful?[777] Are they choosing those persons best able to parent from among persons willing to bear children? Are those parents deeply motivated? Are the cadre's children being deeply nurtured? If not, why not? If not, the community must intervene to remediate the ill-deliberate child-bearing decisions by irenic means. A community may not coerce a cadre or, worse, particular parents into avoiding pregnancy. Neither may a community stand silently by, disapproving.

In the end, in a deeply interpersonal world such as Quad sociality envisions, no member has individual freedom to breed. Nor would any member desire such freedom. For life is shared. Humans, to survive as a species, must reproduce themselves each generation. No person, however, may arrogate to themselves the decision that all must suffer the depredations of hyper-population so that he or she may breed heedlessly.[778] The desire to have a little Tom or Susie who looks "just like you" is the self-indulgent protrusion of a deeply narcissistic iceberg in the ill-deliberate parent's heart.

7.16.3.5. *Transgenerational Horizon.* What planet do we deliver to our descendants, especially our distant-in-time descendants, by the population size we elect? No component of this deliberation about population proportion deserves more attention, and none receives less. Our distant grandchildren will deem us self-absorbed moral midgets for declining to insure their needs. That we do not know their names does not render them less our own. They too are our children. They are the part of us that lives on in our absence, just as we now, for a moment, live on in the absence of progenitors. With respect to delimited resources, our consumption today benefits us, but projects most costs to our descendants. We avoid transgenerational myopia by making the weal of our future

---

[777] A "meaningful deliberation" is one in which those factors that generate meaningful community are embraced, and the erosions that etch meaningful community are eschewed. See Sections 1.12 and 1.13 for a description of more, and less, meaningful communities.

[778] Alan Weisman argues there are four questions that we must answer to evade a hyperpopulation disaster: a) How many people can the earthy really sustain?, b) By what nonviolent means might we convince all the various peoples of the earth that bearing many fewer children is in their best interest?, c) What other species and ecological processes are essential to human survival?, and d) How do we design an economy for a shrinking population, and, ultimately, for a stable, much smaller population? Weisman, *Countdown*, 10-32. I believe that hyperpopulation cannot be addressed without boosting the self-reflective planning capabilities of most of earth's women. That means we must invest dramatically in ending oppression of females, in their education, and in making women players in our cultural decision-making.

offspring a part of present identity. Every human undertaking should express our affection, concern, and commitment to unborn generations of the distant future.[779] When we consider our children's children's children and their descendants to the horizon of human existence, smaller populations appear desirable.

To return to this simple rule, "bear children only if you must," one takes as a provisional waystation the idea that a desirable human population hovers somewhere under one billion members.[780] This number is equivocal. All the functions required to generate meaningful life in Quad communities could be well supported, with cautious redundancies, by a population of that size. This estimate could be wrong. We should calculate carefully, based on our well-deliberated preferences about shared moral values. The benefits would be staggering. We might, by depopulating to mere hundreds of millions, evade our hysterical drama of attempting to produce survival infrastructure for a human population that doubles every handful of years on an accelerating treadmill to nowhere. We might, by dramatically paring our numbers, sidestep debacles of collapsing social systems crushed beneath the terror of starving, diseased billions. But my proposed number should be scrutinized for its adequacy with withering intensity. Humanity needs only that number of members that protects the human legacy into the deep future. Any greater number imperils that legacy at its root.

As a rule for member life, one should bear children only if one is inclined to and able to focus one's attention on nurturing children for the first three to six years of each child's life. What's more, the infant being nurtured needs a mother who is attentive, resilient, and sensitive to the infant's communication and needs. Infatuation with one's infant appears to be necessary for secure attachment of that infant. The bored, distracted, anxious, or unwilling primary caregiver may cause anxious or avoidant attachment in their charge. Mother's absences for work shifts injure very young children. If you lack resources sufficient to enable your constant attention to your infant(s), you should reconsider

---

[779] Cohen details the thought of John O'Neill of University of Sussex, who argues that the earth is a temporal commons, even if none is owned collectively, for future generations depend upon that which we have not presently consumed. To avoid the tragedy of the commons, considered temporally, we must make the chain of generations part of present identity. Cohen, *How Many People Can the Earth Support?*, 259.

[780] Such was the conclusion of H. R. Hulett in 1970. He calculated the optimal population of the earth based on assumptions concerning the desire of many people for lives approximating those enjoyed by First World inhabitants. Though his conclusions are equivocal, they address likely preferences of most: high quality lives in sustainable social structures. Cohen, *How Many People Can the Earth Support?*, 179-183.

making babies. By this, one does not mean that mothers cannot work. The mother's work needs to include her baby, on a hip or back, while mother attends to employment tasks.[781] The workplace can tolerate the interruptions that babies create. There are, after all, matters more important than maximizing efficiency and pecuniary return. If a mother must be absent from her child, then she must provide consistent, responsive, caring alloparents to attend the baby.[782] Absence-injuries to infants ring through life, and injure subsequent generations as well. We are appalled when babies starve. Inattentive or absent nurturance by half-hearted or much-distracted parents starves infants just as surely, and whittles the child's horizons.[783]

Procreation is a calling, not a birthright.[784] Most members lack that vocation, and should avoid pregnancy. Mere possession of ovaries and the propinquity of a willing set of testes are insufficient conditions for parenthood. Parenting well demands substantial social, emotional, psychological, and financial capital. Parenting well demands a wealth of supportive friends committed to alloparenting. Undercapitalized procreation issues those train wrecks of failed attachment and nurturance that plague present societies. Atrocities ensue. Jails flood. Frankly, many children induce great joy in parents, but they also deliver substantial grief and suffering.[785] Children stress one's ability to befriend others, including a spouse. Children impair one's ability to care for oneself. Ill-nurtured children make parental life a living hell. Disabled children may demand unlimited and ultimate devotion. Every instant one spends

---

[781] So, our attitudes toward mothers, babies, and crying in the workplace must shift toward greater tolerance and welcome. The workplace might shift from male task-fixation alone to include a greater measure of female nurturance concern.

[782] Hrdy argues that human babies best prosper when they have *three* secure relationship on which to rely, each of which offers the intense attention and unlimited care provision the infant requires. Hrdy, *Mothers and Others*, 130.

[783] I rely on the results of attachment investigations for this bright-line rule. See [♪] Karen, *Becoming Attached*, Chapters 22-23, pages 313-357.

[784] I am asked who might be voicing such a calling, since god, in my treatment, is a monotone nullity hidden behind an impenetrable metaphysical barrier, and kithdom would seem to permit no enduring human hierarchy. Life calls people. One's circumstances summon a person to her task in life. We perceive our gifts in a matrix of persons and happenstance in which we find ourselves embedded. We recognize, if we look, that purpose for which we were born, the way we fit. One discovers purpose not in asking, What do I want?, but rather in asking, What deep need of others can I meet with my gifts and joy? David Brooks offers a nice discussion of calling. Brooks, *The Road to Character*, 21-26.

[785] Tolstoy offers (perhaps hyperbolic) counterpoint to the child-adulation talk that permeates our (and his) culture. Children torment parents, poisoning parents' relationships, inducing extreme anxieties, and impoverishing many. Tolstoy, *The Kreutzer Sonata*, Chapters XVI-XVIII.

parenting is an instant not otherwise invested. If you well tolerate such efforts, then you may make a good parent. If not, you may prove a lackluster caregiver. Every child deserves more. If you lack a vocation to procreate, devote your energies to an endeavor that thrills you.[786]

Those other endeavors are a second progeny. Man, considered as a member in community, propagates not only by the admixture of genes in children, but also in the creative work of fashioning the communal future and enriching the communal present.[787] Each is critical. We nurture children. We nurture communities. Without either, the human adventure grinds to a halt. Presently, humankind teeters overbalanced. We breed prolifically. Our vision of our own possible futures, however, suffers a ghastly deficit of attention. We are functionally blind to our possibilities. The number of life experiments dared by adventuresome communities wanes to a trickle, throttled by the well-intentioned regulations of coercive governments. Our technologies fascinate us. So thin is the gruel of the life pots in which those technologies stew, that the technologies often appear the stock of culture, rather than a seasoning of it. Human essence is to recognize oneself in the stream of life, awash in human community, wedded in one's genes and culture to all that has come before and all that will come to be. Our many babies mature in a cultural barrens. Enriching the human loam launches experimental creativity. For the possibilities of humanity depend upon the richness and depth of the cultural soil in which each generation is planted.

Our culture, and the host of folkways that have preceded our own, glorify child-bearing. Children, many argue, prove one's health, wealth,

---

[786] Thomas Andrews complains that I have failed to define the critical language of this section: "only if you must." I suggest that some parents are well-positioned to nurture children, and should be encouraged to do so. Others are less well-positioned, and should be discouraged from making babies. I answer Andrews that in this section of *Cull*, I address Kate (and persons positioned like Kate at the inception of adult life). When I consider the circumstances of mankind, which I have described above, I find that few should reproduce. "Only if you must" has, in my mumbling, a subtext that could be put, "Well, if you have considered all I have said about overpopulation and your role in human misery, and you still think it best for you and all the humans yet to be born that you should reproduce, then proceed, you foolish person." Perhaps that overstates my sentiment, but it gives a gist. I value Kate, but stand at the periphery of her cadre. I do not know what is best for her and her intimates. I oppose creating a regime in which parental fitness of members is assessed and ranked. Nor do I hope for a lottery in which everyone, except winners, is compelled to avoid pregnancy. I address Kate. I offer Kate, and the Kates of mankind, reasons not to bear. If, after substantial deliberation, Kate and her cadre find it reasonable for Kate to procreate, I am ill-positioned to gainsay their choice. Our first moral task, after nurturing ourselves, is to nurture earth's babies. In kithdom, there are no ill-nurtured babies, for mankind has put its hand to that plow in a way that now seems impractical or impossible. Andrews, in private correspondence with the author, June 5, 2016.

[787] Gustav Landauer argues for our transgenerational connectivity with past and future. He says that we, despite death, live on in the human community by our children and our deeds. Human nature consists in consensus and community, which is just where the divine lurks. Landauer, *Through Separation to Community*, 104-105.

and normalcy. Children have been deemed the crown of success. Some imagine that, apart from procreation, little else matters. They link child-bearing to family itself, arguing that children make a family.[788] Some ardent proponents claim theological justification for their views.[789] Influential others (Malthus among them) believe that procreative restraint simply lies beyond human capacities, and should.[790]

Given the coercive miseries of our global human adolescence, perhaps it is understandable that parents might project upon their children their hope for simple decencies denied them in their own youths. Given the historical death rate for children, it is perhaps understandable that mates generated the maximum number of offspring, in the hope a few might survive to adulthood. Given the novelty of contraceptive technologies, one grasps that, before 1970, where mates loved, children ensued. These predicates no longer pertain. Contraceptive technologies wait on store shelves. Unwanted pregnancies are terminated. Vasectomy is simple and cheap. Most babies survive. Nurture of each is possible. And one can safely enjoy sex without procreating.[791] So, bear children only if you must.

Behaviors surrounding child-bearing have deep evolutionary roots. You harbor compulsions, of which you may be scarcely aware, to make babies. Making copies of itself is what DNA does. Reproduction carries life forward, and bears the deviations that aggregate into new species. Brain function, some argue, merely regulates behaviors that amplify the frequency of copying one's genes into offspring.[792] This view is unwarranted reductionism. Brain function, at least as evidenced in human consciousness, undertakes tasks other than copulation and the justi-

---

[788] Day, *The Long Loneliness*, 135-136.

[789] For example, *Genesis* 1:28.

[790] Darwin argues that struggle makes man resilient, and ease makes him indolent. "Hence our natural rate of increase, though leading to many and obvious evils, must not be greatly diminished by any means. There should be open competition for all men; and the most able should not be prevented by laws or customs from succeeding best and rearing the largest number of offspring." Darwin, *The Descent of Man*, 618. Perhaps Darwin could not foresee the social mores and technologies that restrain evolutionary culling from its natural operation among humankind. Darwin's over-emphasis on competition, to the neglect of human cooperation, mars his work. In seeing the competitive engine of evolution, Darwin downplayed the tangible result of evolution in humanity: shared parenting and hyper-cooperative eusocial communities.

[791] Singer notes that we have successfully sundered sex from procreation, and so extricated ourselves from the necessity of having children. But the sundering may only be possible because evolution itself has worked indirectly in relating sex and procreation, a fracture we have exploited. Singer, *The Expanding Circle*, 132 (Chapter 5).

[792] Wright, *The Moral Animal*, 53-54.

fication of it. But sexual selection certainly waxes large in human behavior. Let me explain some common features of human child-rearing
from the perspective of evolutionary biologists:

7.16.3.5.1. From a gene's perspective, the goal (though, of course, genes
are subsentient and therefore lack thoughts or purposes) is to propagate into the next generation. Given the likelihood that any gene that
makes its bearer unfit in his environment is likely to result in childlessness or pre-reproductive death, the gene wants to have no impact
or a positive impact. Where a gene renders its bearer even slightly
better adapted to his environment, the gene strikes out on a path to rapid (in a genetic timescale) replacement of individuals lacking the gene
and species-wide replication of itself. Psychological traits of male and
female humans have been evolutionarily selected for their tendency to
maximize fit gene transmission. These psychological traits differ between men and women.

7.16.3.5.2. From a gene's perspective, women must be highly selective in
mate choice. Producing a gene carrier (baby) is an expensive and debilitating event from a female vantage. A woman has a delimited
number of eggs, and a short window of opportunity for using those
eggs to make gene carriers. Female selectivity in choice of mate
drives the evolution of males, since the female bottleneck in reproduction determines the number of opportunities males have for loosing
their abundant sperm. A woman looks for a man who can protect her,
since she will, for several years during pregnancy and while nursing,
be quite vulnerable. A woman looks for a man who can help feed her
and her child. So, a woman looks for a man who will stick around,
who is sympathetic enough to help, and will make substantial paternal
investment in her children.

7.16.3.5.3. From a gene's perspective, men must employ a strategy to
breach the female reticence barrier. One strategy for the male gene to
propagate is to spread itself into every willing ovum, encouraging
copulation as frequently as opportunity permits. This low paternal investment strategy creates many copies of a male's genes, but each carrier (baby) has a relatively low likelihood of survival because of the
father's lack of investment and protection. Another strategy is to capitulate to female sensitivities, to limit oneself to a single female during her reproductive years, and insure, to the extent possible, that the
mother and those offspring prosper to reproduce themselves. This
high paternal investment strategy reduces the number of copies of a
gene effectively transmitted into a child likely to itself breed, but also
dramatically increases the likelihood that any such child will survive
to breed. Men's brains contain periconscious programs that seek

women with breasts adequate to feed babies, and hips wide enough to expel infants without injury. Hence, the hourglass female contour men find so alluring. Men, encountering female selectivity, suffer an evolved psychological mechanism that views a sexual prospect as either Madonna or whore.[793] In courtship, a man assigns a sexual prospect to one category or the other. If the woman surrenders too soon, she does not merit ongoing devotion, after sexual encounter. The woman who expresses reserve, but then embraces a man at just the right moment, becomes to that man a sacred thing.[794] Each category exceeds what the woman's facts warrant, and serves for the male as blinders to keep him on one sexual strategy or the other with regard to a particular female.

7.16.3.5.4. From a gene's perspective, when a man overcomes a woman's wariness, love ensues. Love, from a gene's perspective, is a relatively brief period of infatuation with the sexual partner that insulates the messy, vulnerable, and emotionally stressful business of new coitus from near-term relational collapse. Where the woman once fled, she now clings. Where the man once wandered, he now attends. When infatuation fades, many find themselves linked to partners deeply different than they had imagined. There follows the crucial choice, where one, in a better-deliberated state of mind, elects to persevere with or depart from the now-better-perceived mate.

Evolutionary pressures favored humans with these psychological traits, and extinguished those who lacked them. Our dispositions cumulate the psychological results of such survival pressures in the Pleistocene environment. Considered from the vantage of genes, we are convoluted transmission devices. We live to breed.

Humanity, however, has departed the veldt. In thousands of particulars, we have deflected our Pleistocene psychological traits where they prove disadvantageous, by culture, by thought, by habits. With respect to our breeding habits, deflection is itself a survival trait. If every child matures with the expectation that he or she can and should procreate, it will soon be the case that no family can flourish, without employing deeply self-interested coercion to insure one has sufficient resources for one's own offspring, while others suffer fatal deprivation.[795] So, undeflected

---

[793] Wright, *The Moral Animal*, 72-74.

[794] For an entertaining, if grim, example of this psychological event, see Tolstoy, *The Kreuzer Sonata*.

[795] This unconscionable prospect already pertains on one-half of the planet, which is incomprehensibly neglected by the other, richer half.

procreation demands a stark and ugly rule: kill some babies to preserve others. Repress and deny as we may, this rule governs human procreation at present. Swedish babies survive in vastly greater percentages than those of northern India. American infants survive more often than Malawian. First World babies prosper while Third World babies perish.

We can, with hundreds of millions of members engaged in childless nurture of children (alloparenting), alter and evade this bitter calculus. Humankind's task is to revise its culture of child-bearing, family, and the social scope of parenting. We have no alternative but to celebrate meaningful nurturant childlessness and to support the fecundity of that minority who were born to the task of bearing the next, smaller generation.

To survive, mankind must elect a course at odds with the mechanistic reproductive urgency we inherit from the tangled trajectory imposed by ancestral African savannahs. We must, as we have done so frequently since we abandoned tropical nomadism, cull our own hearts.

7.17. *Parenting.* **Simple Rule: Attach to your young child.**[796] If you elect to bear children, it will be your job to create the team that nurtures your child in his or her first twenty or so years. As a mother or father, you will lead that team of alloparents. Each alloparental team member must, to the extent that person interacts with your child in its first six years, grasp the core relational needs of infants and children. Human member life is an ongoing interaction with other members to acquire the necessities of life and insure that others have them as well. These nurturant interactions commence at conception and end at death. The grand template of one's emotional life commences in the nurturance one experiences before long-term recall commences, in those critical but unremembered first months and years of life.[797] What is the core relational need of young humans?

Children under six years of age need *attentive, enthusiastic, deeply enamored, safety enhancing, emotionally responsive, exploration encouraging, tantrum moderating* interactions with parental adults that are appropriate to the child's age and abilities. These adjectives emphasize that it is the quality of the mother-child relationship, as well as its expanse in time, that generates secure attachment. At every juncture, the prime caregiver provides a secure base of relational safety, from which the child may explore and expand his or her knowledge and competencies. In the most secure re-

---

[796] For the research that supports the assertions of this section, please see [♪] Karen, *Becoming Attached.*

[797] Simon Baron-Cohen, discussing the psychological original of evil, says: "When we fail to nurture young children with parental affection, we deprive them of the most valuable birthright we can give them and damage them almost irreversibly." He recounts John Bowlby's characterization of secure infant attachment as the "internal pot of gold." Baron-Cohen, *The Science of Evil,* 150.

lationships, mothers provide only that assistance the child requires to re-main engaged in exploration.[798] The infant needs constant contact with the mother, either by actual carrying or, as the child ages, by its surrogate, on-going presence, responsiveness, and chatter.[799] The mother intervenes with the young person for guidance and safety, but otherwise lets the child ven-ture at will. As the child ages and matures, alloparents take a more direct role in parenting.

The need for secure attachment is, not merely a human, but more gen-erally a mammalian, urgency. Every mammal is born dependent upon a mother, who shelters, warms, and feeds that infant. This is as true of shrews as of primates. Among half of primate species, infants spend the en-tirety of their first several years clinging to the front of their mother.[800] The primate infant's social world is her mother.

The human primary caregiver from conception to age three is usually the child's mother, but others may, in exigent circumstances, stand in for the mother. These others may not, however, prove adequate replacements. The adult to whom a young infant looks for nurturance is usually only one person, with supportive others backing up that caregiver.[801] For very young children, even high quality care (which is seldom provided by American daycares) fails to suffice. [802] Only as the child ages can he or she be cared for by others over substantial periods without emotional injury. This rule al-so pertains to the child's father. Where a father has, from birth, also nur-

---

[798] [♪] Karen, *Becoming Attached*, 182.

[799] Jean Leidloff offers a compelling version of the infant's need for maternal contact, and the moth-er's correlative need to hold and respond to baby. She portrays a mother-infant relationship some-times quite at odds with the usual practices of Western industrial cultures. In her view, babies' cries and mother's longing to respond constitute a unique language evolution has fashioned between the two. No baby's cry should go unheeded. Crying is not something babies should get over. Rather, annoyance at baby's demands is a feeling mothers must work through for themselves. The infant's cries naturally induce the need to respond in mothers, especially that particular infant's mother. Leidloff, *The Continuum Concept*, 29-75.

[800] Especially among orangutans, chimpanzees, gorillas, rhesus macaques, and savannah baboons. Hrdy, *Mothers and Others*, 68.

[801] Michael Lamb's research showed that during the critical attachment periods between seven and twelve months, infants seek solace from both mothers and fathers, but persistently prefer their moth-ers when both mother and father are present. [♪] Karen, *Becoming Attached*, 198; see also 99.

[802] With professional, attentive care during maternal hospitalizations exceeding ten days, James and Joyce Robertson found that toddlers experienced grave emotional distress at separation from parents, though they bonded eventually to the caregiver, and eventually overcame their consequent insecuri-ty, after a period of months. Robertsons characterized even high-quality substitute care as a hazard for young children merely because it disrupts their primary attachment relationship. [♪] Karen, *Be-coming Attached*, 82-84.

tured the infant, he may stand a close second to the mother.[803] This is not to demote fathers; these words, rather, describe the natural role fathers play in human child-rearing. Fathers are more than sperm-donors. Human males, in the presence of a mother-child pair, undergo endocrine changes and commence behaviors they would not otherwise exhibit. Their prolactin level increases and testosterone levels decrease in proportion to the amount of time they spend with mother and infant, and the amount of time they spend holding the baby. Nursing-mothers-and-babies make alloparental men more maternal, though the means of this hormonal transformation are as yet undetermined.[804] To fathers, the message is simple. Spend a lot of time holding your infant and cherishing its mother. Those simple acts will change you in ways that make you a more supportive parent and ease the burdens of parenting infants.[805]

The mother attaches to the child; the child attaches to the mother.[806] Until the infant can crawl, mothers should hold her baby as much as possible. Take the child on a hip or in a direct-contact carrier wherever you go. Let your instincts guide you, and those of your baby as well. Your interactions are the baby's first language. Your instincts, and those of your baby, crystallize millions of years of primate evolution.[807] The mother endures the child's struggles, and encourages the child to make small forays into unknown experiences. In the first months, these forays consist mostly in recognizing the mother as another person. Then other caregivers enter the

---

[803] Children who establish secure attachment to both parents develop the greatest confidence, competence, and empathy. [♪] Karen, *Becoming Attached*, 199.

[804] Hrdy notes that Fleming's research on parental responsiveness shows that the behavioral changes in fathers are not merely hormonal, rather also depend on prior experience of the male in caregiving. Hrdy, *Mothers and Others*, 170-171.

[805] Though contemporary research confirms attachment of infants to mothers, and subsequently to fathers, the insight is not new. Rousseau complains bitterly of parents who bear but decline to parent. Their children learn to be attached to no one. They pass through the world as though it were composed solely of strangers. Rousseau asks if there exists any person so stupid as not to recognize the links between distant parenting and attachment-injured children. Rousseau, *Emile*, 49.

[806] As Hrdy notes, this process, though natural, is not in humans automatic. In hunter-gatherer societies, mothers examine babies immediately after birth. The baby may be abandoned if deformed, low-weight, neurologically-impaired, or even merely the wrong sex. In !Kung hunter-gatherer societies, about one in one hundred live births was abandoned (with substantial maternal regret). After a mother holds and nurses an infant, bonding overwhelms evaluation of the infant, and the mother protects the child. Hrdy, *Mothers and Others*, 72.

[807] Jean Leidloff argues for a Ye'kuana (Venezuelan rain forest hunter-gatherer tribe) maternal style. The Ye'kuana maintain skin-to-skin contact with infants through much of the child's early years. Infants are carried by the mother on all of her daily tasks, and are handled by many tribe members. Ye'kuana children grow up remarkably well-adjusted, according to Leidoff (who lived with them and other primitive tribes for an extended period), and lack much of the neurotic distress that Western babies suffer. Leidloff, *The Continuum Concept*, 49-56.

child's periphery, and small expeditions ensue, orbiting around the mother. Fathers become outlets for accelerated exploration, and almost-as-good-as-mother secondary sources of attachment. Between age three and six, most children become able to tolerate longer separations from mother and father. The core of this process lies in some one person standing persistently at the ready to guide, comfort, and bond with the child. Where a child receives such care, secure attachment follows for most. The securely attached child knows where to find emotional support, and is therefore prepared for forays of exploration and attempting new activities.[808]

Happily, bonding and attachment occur naturally. Mothers are predisposed to attach to their infants, if they surmount the first seventy-two hours following birth.[809] Infants generate attachment, eliciting care responses from most who encounter them. In tribal circumstances, others (alloparents) provide significant amounts of care for infants (thirty to eighty-five percent of the time).[810] This care exceeds mere holding. Alloparents provide much of the food for the child, including suckling and masticated mushes.[811] Among our great ape cousins, mothers provide one hundred percent of newborn care. What distinguishes human mothers is that they, from the outset, accept assistance from trusted others in supporting the mother and caring for the infant.[812] In most mother-infant relationships, attachment proceeds to secure relationship, to the benefit of both mother and child. Some, even among social researchers, tend to conceive secure attachment as the non-pathological shape of mother-infant "love."[813]

The process is not, however, without perils. In some thirty percent of parent-child relationships, the bond wobbles or collapses.[814] It does so in

---

[808] Stephen Asma argues that early attachment is the foundation of human pro-social behaviors. He warns that we cannot overemphasize non-biased generalized fairness to the extent that it denigrates this critical, deeply-biased infant bonding. Without secure attachment, one may never develop a sense for generalized fairness later in life. That could spell the end of the liberal experiment of Western civilization. Asma, *Against Fairness*, 33.

[809] Hrdy, *Mothers and Others*, 99-100.

[810] Hrdy, *Mothers and Others*, 76-78.

[811] Hrdy, *Mothers and Others*, 79.

[812] Hrdy, *Mothers and Others*, 73.

[813] [♪] Karen, *Becoming Attached*, 90.

[814] Karen reports Sroufe's result that among American middle-class families, children were anxiously attached (ambivalent attachment or avoidant attachment) approximately thirty percent of the time. [♪] Karen, *Becoming Attached*, 220-226. The percentage seems to differ by culture and socio-economic class.

two predictable patterns.[815]   About ten percent of anxiously-attached mother-child pairs experience ambivalent attachment. The mothers in such pairs
tend to be distracted or inconsistent. The infants struggle to learn what behaviors elicit maternal care, and waste time and energy better devoted to
play and exploration in drawing mother into care provision. The result can
be a dependent, insecure, overly-emotional mother-child relationship.
About twenty percent of anxiously-attached mother-child pairs suffer
avoidant attachment. The mothers tend to be frequently unavailable to the
child, starving the child of affection and care. The child withdraws, ceasing
his care-eliciting behaviors.   Such children can appear independent, but
their attitudes betray distress in the mother-child relationship. Anger characterizes avoidant relationships. One observes demanding, even caustic,
exchanges between mother and child. In the early years of a child's development, these injuries can be ameliorated by change in the mother or introduction of another adult better able to serve the child as a locus for secure
attachment. Later interventions prove more difficult, though not impossible, as the emotional patterns imbibed so young settle into established patterns of relationship and emotional expectation.

In a few parent-child relationships, where the mother perceives she
lacks alloparental supports, mothers abandon or kill their infants. Abandonment and infanticide are more prevalent among humans and callitrichids
(marmosets and tamarins), which are the cooperative breeding primates.
This distressing fact illuminates that alloparental care is no novelty, but rather one of humanity's evolutionary characteristics. We breed reliably only
where alloparental care is available in abundance.[816] Hrdy argues that, absent alloparental care, humans would not exist as a species.[817]

Anxious attachments often derive from temperamental mis-match between mother and child. Fussy babies can overwhelm mothers, especially
those mothers who long for persistent positive feedback from their babies.
Depressed mothers, despite best efforts, can sink into non-action. Maternal
listlessness is insufficient to generate secure attachment. Distractions (such

---

[815] I footnote a third pattern: non-attachment. A small percentage of mother-infant pairs fail because
the mother abandons the infant altogether, usually within the first seventy-two hours after birth.
Among primates, only callitrichids (small New World primates like marmosets and tamarins) and
humans among primates demonstrate such a contingent maternal commitment to newborns. Hrdy
argues that this is the downside of cooperative breeding. Mothers expect and need alloparental help
to rear young. If these mothers lack such support, they may abandon the project of child-rearing as
hopeless. Hrdy, *Mothers and Others*, 100-101.

[816] Hrdy notes that the danger of infanticide or abandonment among humans peaks in the first seventy-two hours after birth. Hrdy, *Mothers and Others*, 99-100.

[817] In hunter-gatherer societies, alloparental care reduced the child mortality rate by fifty percent.
Hence, alloparents have enormous evolutionary effect. Hrdy, *Mothers and Others*, 109.

as poverty or maternal relational instabilities or mental illness or mere bad habits) can leave mothers with insufficient concentration to give babies the unbridled attention they need. And unwanted pregnancies can rob mothers of the enthusiasm and affection which infants require, as the baby serves to remind the mother of emotional trauma.

Why does attachment matter? The attachment habits one establishes as an infant set an emotional pattern for future relationships. Bowlby called this template the "internal working model."[818] The developing infant expects others to perform as has his primary caregiver in infancy. These expectations can become self-fulfilling prophecies as persistent distrust poisons otherwise promising relationships, not only in childhood, but also in young adulthood during mating choices. Attachment-deficient familial nurture influences a child's reproductive results and psychological well-being. Anxious attachment may induce: early onset of puberty,[819] decreased ability to form enduring sexual relationships, younger experience of first sexual activity, antisocial and aggressive behaviors, generalized mistrust of others, less-frequent and lower-quality marital communication, negative emotions and depression, more relational distancing behaviors, reduced ability to form friendships, lower emotional and financial investment in their own children, harsher and unsupportive parenting of their own children, transmission of these characteristics to subsequent generations, and an attitude toward others that is opportunistic and ready to take advantage, even occasionally violent.[820] Perhaps most troubling among this recitation of misery is the likelihood that anxiously-attached parents will induce anxious attachment in their own children.[821] The transgenerational emotional echo can be addressed, but only with substantial effort and therapeutic interven-

---

[818] [♪] Karen, *Becoming Attached*, 203.

[819] Early onset menarche in girls is also accelerated by the presence in the family home during their early years (less than five years) of lack of attentive paternal care and the presence of biologically-unrelated males. Belsky, "Childhood Experiences and Reproductive Strategies," 245.

[820] Belsky, "Childhood Experiences and Reproductive Strategies," 243-48. Panksepp and Biven contemplate that severe attachment disorders impair emotional expression and the ability to consciously suppress emotional impulses. Since intense emotionality can attenuate higher cognitive function, impulsivity prevails. So, severe attachment disorders may generate personality disorders Panksepp and Biven, *The Archaeology of Mind*, 419.

[821] [♪] Karen, *Becoming Attached*, 361-378. Alice Miller, a Swiss psychiatrist, focuses attention on child abuse. In psychoanalytic orthodoxy, a patient's claims of abuse are often discounted as wish fulfillment, which Miller chalks up to a poisonous pedagogy in psychoanalytic traditions. Miller credits patient accounts of childhood abuse as historical, and laments the vast expanse of persons who have suffered sexual abuse or assault as children. Miller believes most of society's ills can be laid to repressed child abuse, and its unconscious repetition generation after generation. Miller goes so far as to say that people never mistreat their children unless they have themselves been mistreated. Miller, *Thou Shalt Not Be Aware*, 6.

tion. Hrdy wonders whether humanity might not lose the capacity for empathy, community, and emotional connection if we permit circumstances in which those habits lie unexpressed, just as cave-dwelling fish lose their eyes.[822] That is a frightening prospect indeed.

The bottom line is this: if you are anxiously-attached, work hard on your own emotional repair before you have children,[823] and if you have children, seek members for your alloparental team who can mentor you toward secure attachment behaviors with your infant. If you are securely-attached as a person, let your ancestral inclinations guide you toward that deeply-attentive affection for your baby that will give him or her a secure base from which to operate in the world, both in childhood and in later life. Your baby is drinking you in. Offer security and responsiveness. Keep your child exploring in forays from the safe harbor of his alloparental care team.

Objection 20:   Genetic Determinism: Some demur that the author leans much too heavily on environmental parenting factors in explaining the emotional attachment of children. Genetics produce much of what he mistakes as the effects of parenting. Peter Neubauer studied identical twins separated at birth. In one pair, males, at thirty years of age, shared obsessive-compulsive traits. Both, though they had never met one another and were raised in different countries, were religious, careful dressers, required all clocks to chime simultaneously, and scrubbed their hands fastidiously. Each blamed these traits on his mother. One mother was fanatically well-ordered, while the other's housekeeping was an occasional afterthought. Finnish identical twins, Barbara and Daphne, first met at thirty-nine years of age. They dressed similarly. Each suffered miscarriage in her first pregnancy. Both fell at age fifteen due to weak ankles. Each claims to have met their spouse at age sixteen. They shared height, weight, and mannerisms. Both giggled, managed money carefully (though from homes of different economic circumstances), and preferred privacy. The "Jim twins," studied by Thomas Bouchard, first met at age thirty-nine. Each habitually left little love notes for his spouse. Both were woodworkers. Each built a white round bench circling a tree in his yard. They drove Chevrolets, smoked Salems, and preferred Miller Lite. Both first wives were named Linda. Both were law enforcement deputies. The second wife of each was named Betty. One named his son "James Allan." The other named his child "James Alan."[824] Bouchard's and other's studies of separated identical twins render discussion of en-

---

[822] Hrdy, *Mothers and Others*, 293.

[823] That is, seek a useful therapist to help you get your responses to childhood anxiety in focus, build secure friendships with securely-attached persons, seek a spouse or other alloparent who helps you re-write your internal working model to the extent it impacts your child, make some simple rules, and educate yourself concerning the issues so you recognize your own and your child's behaviors for what they are.

[824] [♪] Karen, *Becoming Attached*, 290-295.

vironmental factors in personality development, even attachment predilections, mostly pointless. So potent do genetic influences appear, after perusing the twin studies, that environmental influences, which may serve as genetic triggers, offer little else to the picture of a child's unfolding personality. Genetics determines (almost) all.

Response: A member's DNA affects much, but determines little. Genes represent a toolbox from which the environment selects needed implements. Certainly, people differ. Some of their difference is genetic. Other parts of differentiation lean upon the member's inputs. Attachment theory argues that some inputs matter massively, such as the affectional bond between an infant and her mother and caregivers. Where this input is absent, no genetic predilection heals the injury. Where the input is defective, no DNA wholly redresses the slight. People develop attachment styles, for good or ill. The research shows that these styles can change, under changed circumstances, most especially while the child in question is quite young. And some flexibility remains throughout life. Were the attachment styles merely a function of temperament and genetic unfolding, such pattern switches would prove impossible. Relationships matter at least as much as genetics in determining a member's weal.[825]

Objection 21:   Presumptuous Parental Puffing. *Another protests that the author is himself childless, and yet presumes to offer parenting advice. One imagines it preferable to have an experience before instructing others about it.*

Response: I am no parent. I have been a step-parent and alloparent to friends' children. As a thoughtful alloparent, I offer a viewpoint that may warrant the attention of some who are engaged in parenting. The unfortunate fact is that bearing children does not guarantee parental insight or the adequate nurture of children. Would that it were so.

7.18. *Childlessness.* **Simple Rule: Nurture children.** You may well avoid breeding. You cannot, however, happily avoid parenting. Every human needs to nurture children.[826] The drive is deep, perhaps deeper than the pressures toward coitus. Simply, human culture stands upon nurture of children. The fine-honed sword of the irenic future is nurture of children. The ineffable, inborn cuteness of babies calls all to care for infants when they have need. We all thrill to attachment's song. The demands of social-

---

[825] Hrdy asserts that attachment style, while influenced by genetic heritage, is not heritable as are other traits. Attachment emerges primarily from the past relationships of the mother or alloparent caring for an infant, and the emotional expectations of the parental figure at the time of giving care. Hrdy, *Mothers and Others*, 291.

[826] Robert Owen, in proposing his improvements upon society (1813), lay society's foundation upon training in good habits from infancy, moral guidance, and rational education (to counter societal prejudices) of the young. Owen calls children "passive and wonderfully contrived compounds" that will take character one teaches them. Society, well-trained, may live without laziness, poverty, crime, or punishment. All persons imbibe their characters from predecessors, largely unawares. Character is given, not won or grown. Owen, *A New View of Society*, 16, 19, 35, 43. Perhaps Owen lacked some appreciation for personality disorders and psychiatric illness.

ization require that all participate in creating habit and custom in minors.[827] Even among adults, friends and strangers teach others habits of thought and action; we call it education.[828] Nurturing others is social cement. Human relations depend on one member recognizing and addressing the needs of another.

Pre-eminent among nurturers stand grandmothers. They teach young mothers, who would often botch their early mothering without grandmaternal instruction, how to care for infants. Grandmothers help pro-vision grandbabies, those of their own daughters and even those of friends and other group members.[829] As we learn to better care for our infants, we can school ourselves in the art of nurture by imbibing the sensitivities of devoted grandmothers.

Please distinguish nurture of children from procreation. Most humans do not need to reproduce and should remain childless. All need sex, or at least crave it. All need to nurture children. But the nexus between coitus and parenting children is equivocal. Not all persons need to make babies, and many are ill-adapted in their temperaments or circumstances to devote themselves to parenting. Genetic transmission may be the ultimate end to which blind evolution puts its DNA fitness machine. Darwin's machine de-livers a host of victims from which to pluck adaptive traits.[830] We may rec-

---

[827] Aristotle complains that, among his contemporaries, only the Spartans show adequate concern for the way people are brought up and what they do with their time. The nurture of children is every member's concern and should be reflected in laws, he argues. Where such concern is neglected in the public sphere, one should undertake to insure the nurture of all children closely associated with oneself. [♪] Aristotle, *Nichomachean Ethics*, 201 (1180a).

[828] I hesitate to use the word "education." The term has become synonymous with the sordid institu-tions of learning we have created. In those grim halls, creativity is quashed and lists of irrelevancies propagated. The education "system" aches to be dismantled, displaced by bare interpersonal and small group mentoring and nurture. At its scarce bright points, the education system leans toward interpersonal intensity, in which nurtured children blossom. In its blight, the education system inoc-ulates children against learning and ensures their failure, abandoning them to the ill-behaviors of the worst-parented children in each school. Bakunin styles education as the "progressive immolation of authority." As the child's intelligence waxes, so authorities of that child are debunked, leaving the student, in the end, perfectly free to choose for herself. Bakunin, *God and the State*, 41 (footnote). I am not so confident of the inherent goodness of unfettered people's choices as is Bakunin. I agree with Aristotle, who argues that individual education exceeds in every way group education, provided Aristotle's sentiment is not misinterpreted to exclude all educative interaction among children. We do not go to doctors in age-restricted huddles, for we require individual attention. [♪] Aristotle, *Nichomachean Ethics*, 202 (1180b). So too children and their minds. If a mentor-driven approach came to dominate our nurture of children, we would still need to negotiate rudimentary standards to share in education. Apart from such agreements, we may rear members incapable of grasping the thought of fellows, which would fundamentally injure our intimacy and affectional ties. See [♪] Walzer, *Spheres of Justice*, 197-226 ("Education").

[829] Hrdy, *Mothers and Others*, 233-272.

[830] Gary Bloom objects that this emphasis on survival, to which environmental challenges put our genetic stuff, is as much politics as science. To parse gene-environment interactions in battle or en-gineering terms amounts to "epistemological anthropomorphism." Bloom notes Richard Lewontin's

ognize and reject its counsel. Many who become parents lack the requisite calling, and neglect their children, to the detriment of all. All such parents should step aside in favor of others who will bond with their child and make themselves persistently available. The primary engine of human misery is ill-nurtured babies reaching adulthood. They wreak their distorted imaginations and ill-formed habits upon friends, neighbors, and milling millions. From train wrecks of parental neglect wander emotional zombies searching for compensatory blood. Human overpopulation and parental neglect strangle human well-being.[831]

Humankind must expand the meaning of family.[832] Friends, nurturing teachers, supportive family members, specially-skilled professionals, neighbors, committed mentors, and others should be invited into one's "family." All, as a team, in conjunction with traditional family support such as grandparents, aunts, and uncles, should nurture a parent's children. These others are alloparents.[833] The quality of the alloparental care team that parents build for their children determines the educational, and possibly survival, success of those children.[834] Hrdy asserts that no mother and father, alone, possess the sufficient resources to rear their child.[835] Supportive others

---

contrarian work on evolutionary theory, who would find my talk of evolution a laughable cartoon. To get nearer accuracy, Lewontin argues, one must consider the entire organism as it exists in its entire environment. Many factors other than fit genes determine survival, such as chance, relationships with others of the species, changes in an environment, and the active manipulation of its environment by a creature. See Gould and Lewontin, "The Spandrels of San Marco and the Panglossian Paradigm." Consider the similar (deeply investigational) arguments of Stephen Jay Gould in *Wonderful Life: The Burgess Shale and the Nature of History.*

[831] In the Pleistocene environment in which man evolved, babies that lacked secure attachment to parents and alloparents simply failed to survive. In today's circumstances, such children regularly survive, opening a Pandora's box of miseries for our bloated societies. See Hrdy, *Mothers and Others,* 290. Mary Wollstonecraft put the matter: "A great proportion of the misery that wanders, in hideous forms, around the world, is allowed to rise from the negligence of parents." [♪] Wollstonecraft, *Vindication of the Rights of Woman,* 246.

[832] Hrdy, *Mothers and Others,* 272.

[833] "Alloparents" are those who nurture a child, sometimes assuming parental roles, though they are not a genetic parent of that child. See Hrdy, *Mothers and Others,* 22. Hrdy reports that arthropods, avian species, and mammalian species practice cooperative breeding, in which non-parental others provision young, including nine percent of bird species and three percent of mammals. Hrdy, *Mothers and Others,* 177.

[834] Hrdy describes the survival benefits of cooperative breeding in species other than humans. Hrdy, *Mothers and Others,* 178-179. Kuhle and his co-authors expressly attribute child survival benefits to alloparental relationships. Kuhle, "Born Both Ways," 308. Panksepp and Biven argue that children deprived of adequate play are more likely to suffer ADHD and pose a sociopathic threat. Further, poor child nurture, especially when conjoined with poor nutrition and aggression in the home and insecure attachment and play-deficiency, portend development of an irritable and aggressive adult. Panksepp and Biven, *The Archaeology of Mind,* 386.

[835] Hrdy, *Mothers and Others,* 166.

should form a care team for children, consult with one another, provide mutual support, in collaboration with a parent or one appointed by a parent. The task of parenting children far exceeds the resources of lone mates. Parents who attempt such isolated parenting exhaust themselves and neglect their children, despite herculean effort and abundant self-sacrifice. The task exceeds one or two persons. Humans are cooperative breeders. The children we bear presuppose alloparental care in their slow big-brained development and in the rapid pace of renewed maternal pregnancy.[836] Were it not for alloparents, there would be no humans.

The nuclear family consists in the sickly nub that remains of a village after one lops off everyone with whom one does not have sex. Such isolation serves corporations, but not your children. And it poorly serves you and your spouse. You will languish and work yourself to death living the life of the western nuclear family. You will feel isolated, exhausted, and ignored. The nuclear family experience will be worse for your children. They will have only two caregivers. In most nuclear families, one of those caregivers is gone all day, every day, working. The other is lonely and often unsupported. Resist this tide. Build an alloparental village of choice around yourself. People it with friends and supportive others. Draft grandmothers. Erect a community to nurture you, your spouse, and your children. Do the same for those others. We are troop primates, no matter how much General Electric might prefer that we be fungible units of mobile production at the ready to be deployed for profit and domination.

Children are the lifeblood of a community, and, as such, belong to that community and the human community at large. Children comprise the Commons at its horizon. Parents hold a special place of responsibility in the nurture of their progeny. Parents do not, however, own their children. The community entrusts its children to broad, supra-genetic families, comprising the many members who nurture those children. Parents, if they possess a vocation for parenting, lead those teams. But parents are two among many collaborators in their children's weal, albeit the chief collaborators, if they are moved to be such.

This perspective proves difficult to imagine from within a culture that so segregates children, so isolates nuclear families, and so erodes suprafamilial nurture of children. Parents fear for their children at the unwelcome intrusions of school boards, and governments, and judges. We all fear the depredations of unrestrained sociopaths and sexual predators. Ours is a family environment of fear. Families lock their doors to, and persistently suspect, outsiders. Where Quad sociality blooms, where children are inten-

---

[836] Hrdy, *Mothers and Others*, 101.

sively nurtured by teams of mentoring adults, such precautions will wither. Sociopaths will be recognized, known, restrained, related to, and watched. The world will be safer. Nurture of children is an alloparental team enterprise, a task for cadres. Nurture of children is an exercise in adult sharing, with children, with one another.

Though emotional components of nurturing attend neurotypical brains, the cognitive components must be learned. We all emerge from a culture deficient in attachment skills and nurturant insight.[837] Invest substantial energy in acquiring skills for attachment to and nurture of children under your care. Failure is fraught.

Humanity reaps the withered harvest of our failure to nurture past generations of children. We are those ill-nurtured children: impaired in our ability to bond to others, steeped in coercion, terrified of scarcity, certain of human rapacity. Some generation will step past its past.[838] Kate, the time is ripe. Till a rich alloparental loam in which to plant your children, if you are called to bear them. Join the alloparental circle of the children of friends.

Objection 22: Sacred Children: Some demur that family is not a subset of friendship. Marital intimacy transcends other relationships.[839] Children are sacred bequests to breeding partners, and not the charge of persons amalgamated to a family or the community at large. Child-bearing fills life with meaning, if it is meaning one seeks. Those who wish to nurture children should make or adopt some of their own, and leave mine alone.

Response: The nuclear family joined humanity only recently. Before the alienating stresses of overpopulation commenced some fifteen to fifty thousand years ago, no father or mother dreamed of rearing children in isolation. Extended family, friends, other mothers and fathers, teachers, leaders, and interested persons joined in the tasks of nurturing children. Classical liberalism invented the nuclear family; even that paltry quantum continues to erode, following liberalism's ceaseless errant elevation of the individual over all collective influences. The "single parent family" reminds one of the Zen koan of meditation upon one hand clapping. A parent's possessive clinging to children betrays the terror one feels at the risks children face in anonymous civilization. It is well that one should find numinous value in children, if one is so inclined. It is also well that

---

[837] I so assert because it has become possible for us to think it unavoidable for millions of children to starve or die of preventable disease in the care of their equally ill-nurtured, uneducated parents. Were every child attached to an alloparental team of nurturing parents and mentors, all themselves well-nurtured, might the human social world right itself before our eyes? Might original sin be unmasked as nothing more than the ill effect of the ignorant, neglectful, isolated parent in his impaired caring for his infant?

[838] [♪] Emerson, *Conduct of Life*, 1067 (VI): "The way to mend the bad world, is to create the right world."

[839] So states the United Nations *Universal Declaration of Human Rights*, Article 16, §3. In my view, the United Nation errs.

parents find their child-rearing activities meaningful. Mentors and involved others are not interlopers upon familial prerogative. They are other faces of family. Welcome them. Much gives life meaning besides children. Perhaps parents in nuclear families find such deep meaning in their children because the rigor of isolated child-rearing robs them of other meaningful endeavors.

Marriage pre-dates all theological speculations about marriage. Friends may become mates. No greater emotional tragedy befalls humans than mating absent the intimacy of friendship. When one marries, all of one's intimates gain a spouse. When one bears, all among one's friends become parents. Ours is a shared existence. To erect life on a less-expansive model is social and psychological self-mutilation.

Objection 23: Nurture Delirium: *Another protests that the author wholly over-estimates the happy results of persistent nurture. "Nurture," in this book, is just education-on-steroids. There is only so much people can do about their impulses and temperaments. After one has been loved, and been taught, and learned skills, we are stuck with ourselves. Humans are flawed. The myth of original sin describes a deep truth about mankind. Man is driven to ill behavior, predisposed to harm himself and loved ones. A globally well-nurtured population portends a vast number of improved conditions for humankind. But nurture is no panacea. Half of everyone's predilection for happiness is inherited from one's parents.*[840] *Some humans lack the neural substrate of conscience. Others fail impulse control. Still another population suffers unbridled, and possibly unbridle-able, intensity of passions. Bad actors will ever dwell among us, and, what's worse, within us.*

Response: I do not foresee a day when no man indulges an ill-deliberated passion. I do not foresee a day when no woman mistakes an evil for good. Human attention, consciousness, and perseverance are delimited. Ill outcomes will forever dog us. We need not, however, encrust this human fact with hoary pessimism. Men are as inclined to good as to evil.[841] No man knows what is possible for humans. None knows what effect persistent global nurture might have upon human experience. We may discover that what some have perceived as a fatal flaw in human plasm may well be nothing more than the transgenerational influence of our rampant neglect of children and one another. There is no ar-

---

[840] Haidt, *The Happiness Hypothesis*, 86.

[841] Dacher Keltner goes farther. Keltner argues that by nature, humans are as much born to do well on behalf of others as to be rapacious. One encourages helpful behaviors, and remediates ill ones. The great human capacity lies not in a genius for murder, but rather in a penchant for cooperation. *Contra* Darwin, Keltner argues for survival of the kindest. Keltner, *Born to Be Good*, 268-269. Donald Pfaff goes farther. He argues that neuroscience demonstrates that mankind's inclinations are toward the good. Healthy humans behave morally quite naturally. Pfaff, *The Altruistic Brain*, 10. If Keltner and Pfaff are right, their thought leads one to serious questions about the culture that results in the torrent of bad faith actions we peruse in our daily news. Christopher Boehm advocates an "ambivalence" theory about humans. People are responsive to and naturally seek hierarchies and domination. But they also resent and resist being dominated. Egalitarian communities, with their relative peacefulness, are, in Boehm's treatment, governed by an insurrection from below. Normal people rally to suppress the ill-behaviors of upstarts and sociopaths, using their numbers and social censure to redirect or overwhelm bad actors. Boehm, *Hierarchy in the Forest*, 157, 237.

chaeological evidence that man, before he overpopulated, indulged the orgies of violence we have suffered in the last fifteen thousand years.[842] We certainly showed a prodigious ability to move, populating the planet in a few thousand years. Perhaps, before self-induced scarcity gripped us, humans sorted irreconcilable differences by migrating over the adjacent hill. This penchant for flight is an irenic, if ultimately flawed, approach to conflict resolution. The theological verdict of "original sin" claims to know all men at all times under all circumstances. No man grasps so much. And gods are mute. We might experiment and seek results. We might offer a sober assessment of human deficiencies, without pessimism. I seek to do so.

Nurture, as I describe it, transcends mere education. The grand twentieth century experiment of mass institutional education has failed. We dump vast resources and waste children's lives propping up such debacles. Many students simply refuse to participate. We call them drop-outs, but they are right. Schools injure as often as they help. Gifted students are tortured, yoked to the slowest learners in their classrooms. Slower students suffer, hapless as fleeter peers breeze past them. At life's most plastic phase, we toss teens into a public forum, leaving them to guide one another. They are ill-equipped. We err. We tear the heart from our most promising talent on the altar of educational equity. We teach algebra at many who cannot learn it, neglecting their skills in repairing machines or teasing food from soil or alloparenting. Educations must be tailored. To accomplish that task, one must know a student intimately. Only the student's parents and friends and mentors could possibly achieve that level of familiarity. Only they can hear the subtle tonalities of their charges' songs. Cadres must mentor their children. Away with factory schools. When we mentor, we teach the skills of Commons dialogue. Our charges learn critical thinking and reading, creativity, active listening, thoughtful speaking, careful writing, fruitful introspection, how to build communities, how to resolve conflicts, and how to work collaboratively.[843] These are the skills that make kithdom percolate.

Sociopathy, impulse-control defects, attachment defects, and irrational exuberance will linger after global nurture. Sad, but true. These maladies may be ameliorated, but they will not be eradicated. We can call these scourges what they are, and avoid despair of salving their negative social impacts. No one knows what persistent effort may achieve. Nurture, indeed, is no panacea. It is, however, an available haven. Shall we despair without exploring its promise?

Objection 24: Non-Parent Parents: *Yet another remonstrates that none should tell others whether they can have children. Such decisions lie at the deepest core of personal identity. None should intrude there. Child-bearing is a human birthright. If you breathe, you may breed. Evolutionarily as a species, and psychologically as individuals, humans are born to reproduce. Our genes, as do those of every species, behave biologically as though they were thinking*

---

[842] Hrdy, *Mothers and Others*, 19. Hrdy asserts that warfare emerged only in the last 10,000 years. Hrdy, *Mothers and Others*, 247.

[843] One finds a useful discussion of the role of dialogue and its benefits in teaching middle and high school students in Copeland, *Socratic Circles*, 7-23.

creatures with a single purpose: replication. This author's admonition to "breed only if you must" denies to most who heed him the simple joy of fulfilling life's most fundamental drive. It is difficult to imagine a simple rule for living more gravely misdirected than his prescription for restraint in reproductive conduct.

Response: Where verdant, empty valleys abound, breed at will. All may flee the results with a day's walk. For more than 100,000 years in mankind's childhood, it was ever so. But no more. Earth's valleys are full or claimed. Walking, one finds none but brimming valleys, awash in humans, or the fences and no-trespassing signs of ownership. No longer can one merely depart the human crush. Like Emerson's giant, it goes with us wherever we go.[844]

Breeding is natural. So, too, are talking, running, urinating, defecating, breathing, nakedness, stinking, complaining, hating, killing, sleeping, and even dying. On all these latter, we demand restraints. Some restraints are mores, others laws, others more subtle, portending sniffs and raised eyebrows. One does not run inside. None yammers during prayer. One pees and poops in designated locations. We breathe inaudibly, neither snoring nor hiccupping. We scrub bacteria from armpits and flatulate discreetly. We sleep timely, not during lectures or dinner. We get naked mostly in private. We murder seldom, and with certainty of stringent disapproval. We delay dying, to accommodate the preferences and convenience of others. All such rules are cultural impositions. All divert human drives. Notably, these critical diversions of natural behavior are not left to choice. One chooses to comply, or one suffers social censure. Why exempt breeding?

Breeding is, for members, natural, but not necessary. Some find joy in offspring. Many (many more than wish to admit it) find child-rearing the unwelcome sequel to ill-deliberated coitus. Many find themselves lured by the myth of child-idylls. They wake from dream to find themselves mired in sleep-deprived chaos, awash in wretched odors. Perfectly attentive parents may discover their children affectionless or sociopathic. Imagining children will become companions for old age, many parents die in isolation, heart-stricken. We could offer realistic images of parenting, images backed by thoughtful research of actual families. We could acknowledge that not all, and possibly not many, stand well-equipped to parent. We could thoroughly-document the stupendous ravages worked by ill-nurtured children, both within the family and in our communities generally. We might adjust our mythologies, or even do away with those that mislead. Maternity suits some, but not most. If one hushes grandparents harping for grandbabies, if one counters sympathetic sighing for those "robbed" of the blessing of children, and if one enlivens possibilities where abject failure of imagination grips people planning their futures, then perhaps one finds that maternity suits few. No one should prevent another from making the babies she wishes to parent. Neither, however, should any entice those ill-suited to attachment and parental care into the emotional and financial trap of child-bearing.

I do not contemplate some telling others they cannot bear children. The Chinese tried breeding coercion; it does not work. I leave every such decision to

---

[844] Emerson, *Self-Reliance*, 278.

anticipatory parents. Most people do as others expect. They seldom launch off on unsanctioned larks. We could tell a different story about child-bearing, a story that asks questions and no longer pretends that we need more children or that children necessarily bring joy. Thus, I offer my simple rule: Bear children only if you must. You decide, Kate. Choose well, being duly informed. Banish insupportable mythologies and unsubstantiated expectations. Ask what child-bearing costs, as well as what it offers. Imagine different paths for your life, and know that life holds insufficient energy and resources to do all one might prefer. Recognize that you need not bear children to nurture children. Then choose.

I anticipate that well-nurtured humanity, dwelling in the bosom of communal kithdoms, carefully informed and pried from the grip of maternal-adulation mythology, will dwindle dramatically in decades, and become manageable in centuries. All without coercion.[845]

7.18.1. *Learning from Children*. **Simple Rule: Learn from children you nurture.** Parents and alloparental mentors teach children skills necessary to prosper in their context, which is one component of a child's education and socialization. This is not, however, a one-sided equation. The needs and abilities of individual children shape parental and mentor socialization efforts. Siblings tend to become more different under the tutelage of their parents and mentors. Global parenting style does not impose a common stripe upon a family's children. Rather, parenting and mentoring adapt to the child's specific orientations and capabilities.[846] Children differ in their temperaments and learning styles. Those temperaments interact strongly with parental and other influences. Parents adapt their efforts to the rhythms and predilections of their individual children. The parent-child triad is massively interactive, and further enriched (or sometimes complicated) by alloparents and social responses from outside the family. One size does not fit all in parenting.[847] Further, nurturing children nurtures

---

[845] Garret Hardin disagrees (perhaps). Hardin, in his classic essay "The Tragedy of the Commons," lays out the effect of self-interested actors on a common resource. Inexorably, the resource is depleted, becoming unavailable. The common good becomes good to none. The decision to bear a child is a decision in the planetary commons. Absent coercion, as Hardin defines it, none will self-restrain, and the global commons shall be sullied or destroyed. Hardin advocates the odd concept of "mutually-agreed coercion," which, in the terms of this book, is not coercion at all, but a deliberated outcome of community consensus. Hardin disputes the effectiveness of appeals to conscience upon those who need to exercise restraint. His presumption is that the appeal derives from strangers in anonymous society, not from friends in one's cadre. Hardin argues that we must soon (he wrote in 1968) abandon procreative liberty, or suffer the tragedy of the commons. Hardin, "The Tragedy of the Commons," 1248.

[846] Bereczkei, "Parental Impacts," 265-268.

[847] See Karen's synopsis of Stella Chess's three decade longitudinal study of temperament in a specific group of children. [♪] Karen, *Becoming Attached*, 269-288. Chess followed 136 infants, evaluating their temperaments for activity level, the reliability of his or her biological rhythms, whether the child favored or disfavored new experiences, how the child adapted to new events over time, the intensity of reaction to discomforts, how intense new experiences have to be before eliciting re-

adults. One learns from children, if one listens. Some argue that the child's mind preserves a simple transparency that adults should emulate.[848]

7.18.2. *Attending Children.* **Simple Rule: Spend copious time with children you nurture.** Western culture distorts childhood and children. Children exist to become good members of a community, not to burnish parental egos. Parents and mentors should follow children's interests, not determine them. Too many "constructive" activities are destructive to children. Children require large spans of time with adult supervision to explore what they wish at their own pace. Parental and mentor involvement of this sort entails reduction of earning capacity for one or both parents and all mentors. Large gulfs of time with children put parents and mentors in position to recognize childhood problems as they sprout.[849] A child's time for educative nurture is relatively limited, given the vast skills and capabilities to be acquired. Make abundant time to communicate that load and support children as they acquire it.

7.18.3. *Evolving Ethos of Childhood.* **Simple Rule: Restrain prepubescents. Collaborate with adolescents. Repair ruptures.** Before the endocrine changes that signal puberty, children need to formulate thoughts and habits that will later serve them well. First among those habits is attachment, to attentive parents and committed mentors, and then to other nurturing adults and peers. Create a stable world for children. Patiently work on habits with children that help them interact constructively with that world. Do not strike or berate your children. Assault builds resentment, not character. Do not compare your children to their siblings or other children, especially when the comparison is unfavorable. The juxtaposition enervates envy and competition, neither of which nurtures your child. Speak with your child of his or her strengths and weaknesses. Guide the child. Make suggestions. Make games of those suggestions. Intervene early when behavioral problems emerge. Restrain a child with as little coercion as possible when his activities threaten his or another's well-being. Beware your own agendas and frustrations. A child does not exist to fulfill your expectations, but rather her own uniqueness.

---

sponse, general mood, distractability, and length of focus on an activity. Chess, from these characteristics, defined four types of temperament: difficult, slow to warm up, easy, and mixed. [♪] Karen, *Becoming Attached*, 274-276.

[848] *Mark* 10:13-16, *Matthew* 19:13-15, *Luke* 18:15-17. Mencius opines that great men are as innocent as infants. *Mencius*, 90 (Book IV, Part B, Section 12).

[849] These admonitions emerge from the advice of 1,200 American adults deemed wise by their peers. See Pillemer, *30 Lessons for Living*, 88-93.

Your frustrations are yours. Take a break. Go for a walk. Let an alloparent care for your child. Keep yourself emotionally refreshed. One cannot build for another a stable nurturant world when one lacks such a world to meet her own needs. Your children need an emotionally resilient parent.

When a girl reaches menarche (usually ten to eleven years) or a boy first ejaculation (usually eleven to twelve years), the nurturant relationship must begin transition as well. Where pre-pubescents accept direction, early teens need to differentiate themselves from parents and mentors. Aim to step alongside teens. The goal is that when they have matured, each will become your adult friend. The transition at pubescence can be wrenching for the child and for parents and alloparents. Note choices and alternatives for a pubescent mentee. Follow up with analysis of results and inquiries about thought-processes. Acknowledge successes; analyze, not lament, failures. Report your own mistakes in your pubescence. Note for your teen the mistakes you have made in guiding them. Stay deeply involved in day-to-day matters, but less visibly so. Give the teen more latitude to make decisions. Intervene only when serious damage may result, and even then gently, when possible. The teen is an adult at the cusp. Let them step over that threshold with your support and participation. Let teens step alongside your adult life with their own, as they are able.

Do not let your relationship with an adolescent rupture. When that dyad fractures, make repairs rapidly. No relational collapse causes more suffering than disintegration between parents or alloparents and their child mentees. The burden of making repair falls wholly on the involved adults. Children are, after all, children. Responsibility for keeping one's relationship with children on an even keel requires the skills of mature adulthood. Prevent rifts; mend those that occur.[850]

7.19. *Resilience.* **Simple Rule: Persevere through difficulties. Help others do so as well.** Seek resilience. The member nurtures resilience in herself, with the knowledge that the community also seeks to act collectively with resilience and promotes resilience in all members.[851] Resilient persons differentiate, recognizing their own needs and challenges and character as distinct from the needs, challenges, and character of others. A resilient member marshals elements within his social universe that support his efforts to persevere in the face of difficulties. Resilient persons know that troubles are more likely to scare than smash us. Terror unnerves one more than most

---

[850] Pillemer, *30 Lessons for Living*, 110-115.

[851] Confucius notes that the gentleman promotes what is good in others, while the small man encourages their vices. [♪] Confucius, *Analects*, 115 (Book XII, Section 16).

predicaments.[852] Specifically, resilient persons weather setbacks, conflicts, difficulties, and disappointments by means of insights gathered in the course of life, independence of thought and feeling, intimate and supportive relationships, taking the initiative, thinking creatively, finding humor in difficulties, and relying on one's moral rules for living.[853] Resilient persons rely on deep reciprocity with others. They negotiate conflicts honestly and actively. Resilient persons practice self-control. Resilient persons discredit disparaging remarks and engage in positive self-talk, making them resistant to psychological wounding. Resilient persons, nevertheless, confront their own weaknesses and accept correction with grace. Resilient persons believe that events have meaning, which meaning can be augmented by purposeful, well-conceived action. Resilient persons construct meaning, undaunted by life's complexities and mixed messages. When resilient persons encounter problems, they believe them manageable.[854] Resilient persons expect improvement, project that expectation into the future, and reject unwarranted pessimism and all cynicism. Resilient persons express compassion for others, and acknowledge the constructive actions of others.

7.20. *Priorities.* **Simple Rule: Do first what matters most.** Some activities matter more than others. One can prioritize demands on one's time. Priority lists assist decision-making. Most people allow trivia to drive life. Keep what is most important first on your agenda. Let less important matters languish until unstructured time affords moments to deal with them. Let more important matters dominate.

7.21. *Generosity.* **Simple Rule: Give.** With friends, give freely. Do not keep score, financially or emotionally.[855] Do not hoard; giving enriches the giver.[856] One must deliberate gifts to determine whether the gift might harm its

---

[852] Seneca, *Epistles 1-65,* 75 (XIII, 4).

[853] Wolin and Wolin, *The Resilient Self,* as cited in Alison Taylor, *Family Dispute Resolution,* 1-52. Buddhists tell the story of the Buddha in a former life being sundered limb from limb by an angry king. The seer endured dismemberment happily, forsaking his body in favor of a grand perception of things as they are (Dharma). [♪] *Buddhist Scriptures,* 26-30. Perhaps the Buddha's patience in the face of this assault was bolstered by his faith conviction that he would be reborn over and over again.

[854] Heraclitus notes that day follows night, summer winter, peace war, plenty famine, gathering scattering, and cold heat,. Everything is in flux. Change is an unavoidable constant of the universe. Now recedes to be replaced by—now. Heraclitus, Haxton translation, *Fragments,* 36, 40, 41.

[855] One might, however, take to heart Timon's complaints about his "friends" who share freely in Timon's wealth, and wandered off when Timon's fortune plunged. Lucian, *Timon, or the Misanthrope,* 335 (Section 8). Choose your friends with care.

[856] [♪] Lao Tzu, *Tao Te Ching,* 31 (81). Elizabeth Dunn and colleagues argue that one receives greater happiness expending funds on others than one derives from spending the same funds on oneself. Dunn, "Spending money on others promotes happiness," 1687-1688.

recipient.[857]   Give a friend what she needs, to the extent your generosity does not injure her self-care. With strangers, give what you are able without injuring your own self-care.   Jesus argued that one should give to strangers without equivocation (but then Jesus thought the world was about to be transformed).[858]   Mo argued that considering the welfare of others as your own combats prejudice within, and so strikes at the root of ugliness in human life.[859] The *Rig Veda* argues that one should give to the hungry person, but more, make him a friend.   John Locke argues that as justice gives you the right to what you produce and what others freely give you, so charity gives every man a right to your surplus property to the extent necessary to relieve that sufferer's extreme want, where those persons cannot otherwise provide for themselves.[860]   Give to any whose need exceeds your own.[861] By so doing, one enriches herself.[862] Aristotle styled the virtue of

---

[857] [♪] Cicero, *De Officiis*, 47 (Book I, Section XIV, 42).

[858] *Matthew* 5:42, *Luke* 6:30. The Buddha taught that no misers become buddhas. Wise people give with gladness. [♪] *Dhammapada*, 177.

[859] [♪] *Mozi*, 42, which comprises a portion of *Universal Love*, Part III, §16.

[860] [♪] Locke, *Second Treatise of Government*, 32 (Book One, Chapter IV, Sections 41-42).

[861] John Rawls argues that any just society structures itself so that those disadvantaged by life benefit from the prosperity of the well-advantaged (the difference principle). He goes so far as to say that our natural gifts, which he calls endowments, are a common asset of our society (though he styles this fact as a kind of agreement among us to treat our gifts as such). One deserves praise for what one does with her gifts, provided that she well-develops them and puts them to purposes that benefit society. [♪] Rawls, *Justice as Fairness: A Restatement*, 75 (§21).
   Nozick dissects Rawls's "difference principle" and asks why Rawls focuses on groups rather than individuals. One is, as an individual, entitled to what one earns, even if the result is unequal, and to make whatever contracts one pleases from that position. This, not some imaginary philosophical daydream (the original position), defines justice. [♪] Nozick, *Anarchy, State, and Utopia*, 105-153, 204. Locke, whom Nozick appreciates, confirms Nozick's thought, but goes on to assert that no man may retain surplus while others, incapable of supplying themselves, exist in terrible deprivation. [♪] Locke, *Second Treatise of Government*, 32 (Book One, Chapter IV, Sections 41-42).
   Peter Singer argues that moral progress consists in a growing expanse of disinterested altruism, extending not only to all humans but to all sentient creatures. A family with excess should give to needy persons until that family with excess, now shorn of its excess, shares the suffering of the needy person. Singer, *The Expanding Circle*, 120-121, 153. Singer's view fixates on egalitarian equity, a sort of fairness allocated freely to all sentient beings: take all sentients, divide by their number, allocate one measure of equity to each.
   Humans are not, however, essentially calculators of disinterested equities. People prefer propinquity. We are unalterably biased. We believe our spouse and children deserve a special measure (as, I am sure, does Singer himself). We believe our friends have a deeper claim upon our loyalty than do others more distant. We prefer our own country and culture over alien ones. And our affection for mankind at large receives from the human heart little more than the occasional platitude (with the exception of a few saintly neurodiverse savants). Stephen Asma argues that Singer's sort of morality is "nemocentric," that is, centered on no one in particular. Asma, *Against Fairness*, 25. Our conceptions of justice and equity are deeply fractured, caught on the horns of the neuroaffective dilemma in which rationality that can conceive of humans impartially, deserving of equal treatment. But human cognition is inextricably conjoined with sentiments dramatically biased toward favoring

magnificence as inclining a person to spend on the well-being of one's community, rather than himself or herself.[863] The Buddha advised one to give to needy others even if poor oneself.[864] It is unlikely that what you can give to others will fundamentally change their lives. That they must do themselves. Where there is choice, give in a manner that enables the receiver to further augment meaning in his or her own life.[865] Teach, more than pity. Actuate, more than contribute. Relate, more than ameliorate. Giving to others affirms one's conviction that social capital counts more than economic capital. And uncalculated giving confirms for needy persons that they do not stand alone. Such convictions matter deeply.[866]

Charity as an institution is a remnant of medieval social class structure. Vested individuals gave to the unvested to prove themselves worthy of vesting.[867] Charity in culled conduct is reciprocal, the hand extended to those with need, the hand taken when personally in need. Beneficence consists not so much in alleviating suffering as in nurturing self-competence in the receiver, leading her to be able to augment the meaning of her own life.[868] The deepest giving transforms the world in which we live into a place where none needs your charity.

7.22. *Peacemaking.* **Simple Rule: Make peace.**[869] Welcome interpersonal conflict. Do not imagine that disputes are fires to be doused. Embrace con-

---

our own at the expense of more relationally-distant others. Asma argues that "it is human to prefer. Love is discriminatory." Asma, *Against Fairness*, 7.

In *Cull's* terminology, this break among ideas concerning justice is a fault line in the coppice of consciousness. Kithdom sates both yearnings. Within the community, one finds ample opportunity to favor and benefit those one loves. Within the Commons, one finds opportunity to accord to all a measure of respect and cooperation.

[862] [♪] *Rig Veda* 69 (10.117, v. 3-6).

[863] [♪] Aristotle, *Nichomachean Ethics*, 67 (1123a).

[864] [♪] *Dhammapada*, 224.

[865] [♪] Dewey, *Human Nature and Conduct*, 293.

[866] Humans imitate one another. As flocks fly in coordination, as schools swim in tandem, so humans unconsciously imitate the postures, thoughts, and ultimately habits of one another. When one practices empathy, others become more compassionate around that person. When one hates, neighbors grow more likely to spew venom. Bargh, "Our Unconscious Mind," 35. When one gives freely, one draws the human penchant for imitation into the service of human weal. Christopher Boehm argues that one's reputation for giving becomes significant in an evolutionary sense, since your fellow members choose to relate (and have sex) with you to the extent they deem you a person of good reputation. Boehm, *Moral Origins*, 293-314.

[867] [♪] Dewey, *Theory of the Moral Life*, 166.

[868] [♪] Dewey, *Human Nature and Conduct*, 294.

[869] Almost every politician speaks as though he prefers peace, just as he votes for war. Cicero, for example, permits war only when one can no longer live with a reasonable expectation of peaceful

flict as that moment when members have finally heard one another well enough to grasp their differences. When humans think of something they wish, they have dreamy, relaxed cogitation. When they encounter something they detest, the full panoply of rational armaments is unleashed upon the offender.[870] Be prepared for a welter of rational-sounding hate-talk. When blame is offered, take it, as an expedient to change the subject to something constructive. Members stressed by conflict re-write history to taste, and flush their potty-mouths. Peacemakers have resilient identities; they don thick skins and sport deep calluses at social rubs.[871]

The habit of making truce, rather than peace, is deeply entrenched in human preferences. Douglas Noll calls truce and stalemate "negative peace." Such "peace" would be war, but for the intervention of some coercive voice. Negative peace is lack of violence, not relational well-being. People who make peace view conflict as an essential and important part of human existence, a facet of everyday life to be managed intelligently.[872]

Our history tells a tale of conflicts buried. Disputants relocate to an adjacent valley. Banked hostility waits to be fanned by an incident, some slight. Then vendetta erupts. Time scabs over unresolved conflict. Time does not, however, heal simmering disputes. Peacemakers tear scabs from festering social wounds. They foster reconciliation. Peacemakers darn the frayed fabric of human sociality.

7.22.1. *Irenism.* Pacifism is the conviction that sufficient means exist to divert human aggressive impulses from violence to creative or, at a minimum, non-destructive channels.[873] Peacemakers recognize that power derives from the acquiescence of those ruled. Peacemakers teach groups to withdraw consent in response to unwanted impositions, thus reducing or destroying the power of overreaching administrators.[874] Peacemakers en-

---

existence, and all doors to discussion have been slammed. [♪] Cicero, *De Officiis*, 37, (Book I, Section XI, 34-35); also 81 (Book I, Section XXIII, 80). Peace-preference talk lacks conviction, and crumbles toward violence when jostled. Indignant peace-preference talk is a staple of pre-war rhetoric.

[870] Thucydides, *Peloponnesian War*, 292 (Book IV, Chapter 8 middle).

[871] One might style *Cull's* irenic kithdom as an attempt at conflict resolution across the human spectrum. By removing many of the usual triggers for violence (for example, scarcity, overcrowding, failure to listen, social ruttedness), the project of building meaningful community inherently tamps down conflict.

[872] Noll, *Peacemaking*, 51, 56. Noll argues that the adversary system that underlies American jurisprudence adopts the "myth of redemptive violence." One achieves order by intervening coercively to end conflict. Noll, *Peacemaking*, 38.

[873] See Herbert Read, "The Truth of a Few Simple Ideas," 39.

[874] Gene Sharp, *The Politics of Nonviolent Action*, Part One, 4.

act what irenic philosophy teaches. Irenism,[875] often called pacifism, claims adherents from the first glimmers of philosophical thought. Irenist tradition is venerable. Irenists disagree among themselves concerning coercion. Some pacifists find that coercion is warranted in exigent circumstances; most reject coercion categorically. Many argue that governments, being by nature coercive, lack legitimacy. Some irenists, therefore, embrace the political philosophy of anarchism.[876]

7.22.2. *Irenist Themes.* Irenism teaches irenic philosophy, which emphasizes rejecting coercion and violence, and opposing all wars, both personal and national. Irenism teaches irenic intervention, which emphasizes ameliorating conflict by peacemaking practices and redressing injustice by irenic opposition, such as marching, occupying, direct civil disobedience, and moral suasion of opponents. At root, irenists wield power by withholding their consent to existing authorities. Without widespread public consent, governments grow hollow and frantic. Eventually, change sweeps regimes.[877] Irenists practice consensus, that is, irenists prefer to negotiate until all involved in an activity concur, or at least decline to dissent. For the alternative is to coerce at least some, which practice is the refuge of imagination-starved strongmen. Irenists prefer injury to oneself

---

[875] I have co-opted the term "irenism" from its Reformation usage, by which theologians distinguished a conciliatory and collaborative approach to theological questions from polemical practices, which encouraged debate and intellectual warfare.

[876] Anarchism teaches that no form of coercive government is warranted or necessary. As Jean Jacques Rousseau says, a well-governed people needs no government at all. Democracies, which Rousseau likens to government without government, require small numbers in which all know all, shared values and habits, relative financial equality among members, and little taste for luxury. [♪] Rousseau, *The Social Contract*, 112-113 (Book III, Chapter 4). Rousseau's "democracy" sounds very much like kithdom. Anarchism, more generally, is a grand bush, in which some branches are pugilist. I reject those branches looking to pick fights, counting them groups driven by the trauma of mass coercion into responsive vendetta. Anarchism embraces all those who find war immoral, statist coercion problematical, economic fixation myopic, and spiritual penury criminal. Some conceive environmental, feminist, anti-war, gay, transgender, neuro-diversity, and other counter-cultural movements as branches of anarchism. So diverse is anarchistic thought that no enduring organization proves possible (as the history of attempts to organize anarchists makes painfully plain). Indeed, anarchists deny the possibility—or the need—for organizational institutions. The term "anarchist institution" is oxymoronic. See Woodcock, *Anarchism*, 228. What all anarchists share is the conviction that the "arche" is unnecessary and dangerous. "Arche," from the Greek ἀρχή, means "beginning or origin," and hence the first, the elemental, or, derivatively, the first power or sovereignty, and, therefore, "empire, realm, magistracy, office, authorities, or magistrates." See Liddell and Scott, *A Greek-English Lexicon*, s.v. ἀρχή. Anarchists are those who doubt the wisdom of suffering arche, and hence are an-archists, those who advocate life without government. As is apparent in *Cull*, Quad kithdom is an attenuated anarchism.

[877] Gene Sharp argues that when peacemakers undertake well-conceived nonviolent resistance, such as refusing cooperation, declining to help, and persistent and loud defiance, governments wither for want of power. All power derives, ultimately, from the consent of the governed. Sharp, *The Politics of Nonviolent Resistance*, Part One, 63-64.

over inflicting injury upon others, which sentiment is bolstered by the irenist conviction that innocent suffering diverts those who inflict such suffering. When third parties injure others, an irenist intervenes by non-violent means. The irenist seeks to preserve life where feasible, including his own. Most irenists oppose capital punishment. Many prefer to avoid slaughter of and cruelty toward animals, and so choose vegetarianism. Some irenists are philosophical anarchists, asserting that the violence and coercive power inherent in states render all states illegitimate; they urge acephalous consensus decision-making.[878] Irenic anarchists rely on strict non-violence and peaceful deliberation of issues; they erect a welter of cooperative organizations and contractual relations as alternatives to violence or coercion by anonymous majorities (democracy).[879]

John Paul Lederach, an experienced peacemaker, argues that peacemaking transcends violence by moral imagination. Moral imagination requires four capacities: a) imagining ourselves in a web of relationships that includes our enemies, b) replacing polar thinking (us-them) with inveterate curiosity about complexity, c) reveling in creating new peaceful situations from shop-worn violent ones, and d) acquiescence in the risks inherent in inventing something new when abandoning violence.[880]

I introduce some core irenists and irenic traditions:

7.22.3. *Prominent Irenists and Irenist Traditions.*

7.22.3.1. *Brahmanic Religions (1500-800 B.C.).* Hinduism and Jainism (as well as Buddhism) teach that *Ahimsa*, which is non-violence and fealty to truth, is a sacred obligation with respect not only to men but to all living creatures.

7.22.3.2. *The Buddha, who was Siddartha Gautama (5ᵗʰ Century B.C.).* The first of Buddha's five precepts obligates the follower to abstain from taking life, by which he means taking any action that terminates human or animal life.[881] Gautama advised to overwhelm wrath with

---

[878] "Acephaly" means "lacking a head," and intends in this context that social relations lack hierarchical power structures, preferring instead contribution from members according to their abilities and skills. See [♪] Taylor, *Community, Anarchy, and Liberty*, §1.5, 33-38, for more on acephalous forms of human society.

[879] Woodcock, *Anarchism*, 16. Tolstoy witnessed an execution by guillotine in Paris in 1857. The Russian novelist asserted that the state is a conspiracy-to-exploit based on stupendous lies. Tolstoy said he would never again serve any government anywhere. Woodcock, *Anarchism*, 187.

[880] Lederach, *The Moral Imagination*, 5, 31-40. Lederach has been involved in peace processes in his local context, and also in Somalia, Northern Ireland, Nicaragua, Columbia, and Nepal.

[881] See also [♪] *Dhammapada* 129, 130, 133.

calm, bad action with good acts, penny-pinching with liberality, and lies with truth.[882]

7.22.3.3. *Mo (5th Century B.C.).* Mo is one among China's Hundred Philosophers. According to Mo, offensive war is crime. When a man murders another, we punish the assailant. When a man murders hundreds, side by side with comrades trained to do the same, we celebrate his martial glory. It is moral confusion to call military murder anything other than homicide.[883] War makes paupers of many, and benefits none.

7.22.3.4. *Socrates (469-399 B.C.).* No Greek thinker eschews violent coercion altogether, especially with respect to inter-polis war. Socrates, however, was frequently attacked and beaten by his detractors. His hair was torn out and opponents scorned him publicly. Diogenes Laertius reports that Socrates declined to exact vengeance in response to these assaults, arguing that if he had been kicked by a donkey, he would not thereafter live by the law of donkeys. [884]

7.22.3.5. *Jesus (4 B.C.-30 A.D.).* The most influential irenist of Western civilization was Jesus, an illiterate Aramaic-speaking Jew. Jesus taught his disciples to turn the other cheek when struck, and to give yet more of their property to thieves who stole from them. According to Jesus, Yahweh, the God of Israel, loves people who make peace where there is human conflict. Jesus submitted to Roman execution for crimes he disputed, rather than contest that outcome violently.[885]

7.22.3.6. *Cathars.* This Catholic sect advocated irenism in southern France. These ascetics rejected violence of all stripes, including war and capital punishment. Cathars adopted vegetarianism to avoid killing sexually-reproducing animals, though they seem to have wavered about fish. Cathar adherents were exterminated in the Albigensian Crusade (1209-1229) mounted by the Roman See under Innocent III.

7.22.3.7. *Anabaptists.* Quakers (from around 1650 A.D.) and Mennonites (from around 1725 A.D.), who are Protestants in the Anabaptist tradition, strongly advocate irenist sentiments. These groups constitute the most persistent voice for irenism in our modern context. Along with many who heed the sayings of Jesus of Nazareth with literal force, both Mennonite and Quaker communities have long practiced non-violence

---

[882] [♪] *Dhammapada*, 224.

[883] [♪] *Mozi*, 53-55 (Part I, §17).

[884] Diogenes Laertius, *Lives of Eminent Philosophers*, 153 (II, 21).

[885] See [♪] Lancaster, *Gethsemane Soliloquy*, in which I epitomize the reliable sayings of Jesus. See also the synoptic gospels (*Matthew*, *Mark*, and *Luke*).

and opposed wars. Both groups are known for anti-war activism, an ethic of non-violence, and seeking conscientious objector status during times of military conscription.

7.22.3.8. *Henry David Thoreau (1817-1862)*.   Thoreau, with Emerson, promoted New England transcendentalism, which emphasized the goodness of man and nature. Thoreau worked as a man of many trades. He taught simple living, abolitionism, civil resistance to governmental wrongs, especially tax resistance to oppose the wrong of slavery, and an incremental anarchism. According to Thoreau, men will have anarchy when they are ready for it. Governments will then stop governing, which is all for the best. In the meantime, Thoreau wants better government.[886] Thoreau's civil disobedience stance became a signal influence upon Mohandas Gandhi and Martin Luther King, Jr.

7.22.3.9. *Te Whiti o Rongomai (1830?-1907)*.   On New Zealand's northern island, this Maori chief abandoned armed resistance to British colonists in favor of non-violent militance. He learned irenism from his New Testament. He tore down farmer's fences, whom he viewed as errant lessees. Te Whiti drove fences across public roads. He and his warriors plowed straight lines right through the soil of immigrant farms. He refused leases to British farmers, but welcomed them as guests. Te Whiti endured substantial incarcerations, and finally won token concessions. His tribe at Parihaka was eventually dispersed.[887]

7.22.3.10. *Immanuel Kant (1724-1804)*.   Kant was a fretful irenist. He owed his professorial occupation to the expansionist Prussian crown, and dwelt in the midst of Europe's eighteenth century bellicose states. Nevertheless, Kant, emerging from a deeply Pietist home, argues for global peace, in typical Kantian manner. Man, for Kant, is deeply torn between, on the one hand, a rationality endlessly fleeting and limited in its competence, and, on the other hand, an inner self ever lured toward the horrid and despicable. So, he wrote, with a little hand-wringing, nine years before his death (at age seventy-one) the essay, *To Eternal Peace*. Kant imagines all the world's nations agreeing to end war. None would retain war materiel. The global treaty includes provisions precluding any acquisition of foreign territory by hostile action or inheritance. Kant prescribes the gradual draw down of standing armies, that states shall not borrow from one another, and none shall intervene in the internal affairs of another. Were war to again erupt, no combatant shall undertake acts that preclude future reconciliation (such as genocide).

---

[886] See [♪] Thoreau, *On the Duty of Civil Disobedience.*

[887] See [♪] Scott, *Ask That Mountain.*

Every state must become a republic, promoting citizen equality and republican legislation, in which legislative powers are segregated from powers of administration. All nations shall unite in a global union of nations for self-governance of the whole of humanity. This global union shall be federal in structure. This encompassing republic will establish world laws guaranteeing all men the right to occupy any spot on the planet. It shall issue eventually in a world constitution. So, ultimately, Kant believed that establishing a universal law, with universal enforcement, will beget universal peace, gradually realized by halting increments. His is a practical plan, aimed at nations as they exist in all their political ferment.

7.22.3.11. *Leo Tolstoy (1828-1910)*. Tolstoy's fame resides in lengthy novels featuring complicated characters in Russian dilemmas. In the 1870s, Tolstoy experienced conversion, adopting an ascetic and idiosyncratic version of Christianity, including adherence to rigorous irenism. His important work, in my view, commenced. In *The Kingdom of God Is Within You*, Tolstoy advocated strict non-violence, and castigated the church for forsaking Jesus' admonitions concerning irenism. In *A Letter to A Hindu*, Tolstoy addresses the editor of Free Hindustan, telling the Indian revolutionary that Britain is able to oppress India only because India forsakes love and indulges violence. Where non-violent resistance prevails, none can enslave others.[888] Tolstoy adopted pacifist anarchism as a political theory, and argued against the legitimacy of all governments due to their use of coercion and violence.[889]

7.22.3.12. *Mohandas Gandhi (1869-1948)*. Gandhi led the Indian nationalist movement against British imperial rule. Gandhi grew up in a home of religious rigor and pacifism. Gandhi studied law in Britain, and began his practice of law in the Indian community of South Africa (1893-1914), where he led challenges to the racial discrimination against Indians he found there. In these formative years, Gandhi was deeply influenced by the examples of Jesus and the Christian non-violent radicalism of Leo Tolstoy. Gandhi returned to India to challenge British rule and re-educate the Indian peoples. He led the Indian National Congress for a time, always advocating nonviolent non-cooperation (*satyagraha*) to British rule. Gandhi advocated spinning and weaving to reduce dependence on British textiles and to generate local employment. Gandhi led a populist march to the sea to gather salt illegally, aiming to break the British monopoly on processed salt. In 1947, the British withdrew,

---

[888] Tolstoy, *A Letter to a Hindu*, 16.

[889] See [♪] Tolstoy, *The Kingdom of God Is Within You*.

leaving India and Pakistan independent. Gandhi is revered in India as the father of the Indian nation. The Indian *Mahatma* (great-souled person) wrote prolifically, but in short snippets. Two compelling compilations of these writings are *Autobiography: The Story of My Experiments with Truth* and *Satyagraha*.[890] Gandhi was assassinated by a Hindu fanatic in 1948.

7.22.3.13. *Martin Luther King, Jr. (1929-1968).* Martin Luther King, Jr., worked as a Baptist preacher in America. King is praised for his non-violent political agitation for racial equality in America. King headed the Southern Christian Leadership Conference, which he helped found, and helped organize the March on Washington in 1963. During that large protest, King delivered his iconic "I Have a Dream" speech from the steps of the Lincoln Memorial. This massive protest influenced passage of the Civil Rights Act of 1964. King taught that ends take the flavor of means used to achieve them, and so destructive means are insupportable.[891] To avoid vendetta, some persons of good sense and moral thoughts must sever the chain of retributive violence and hatred.[892] King practiced non-violence. When his home was bombed during the Montgomery bus boycott, he calmed the angry crowd, and got everyone home intact.[893] Following Thoreau, King's social gospel emphasized that one changes societies to change individuals, and changes individuals to change societies.[894] King was assassinated in 1968.

7.22.3.14. *Tenzin Gyatso, the Dalai Lama of Tibet (1935 -   ).* At age two, Gyatso was recognized as the rebirth of the thirteenth Dalai Lama, the spiritual and political leader of Tibetan Buddhists and Tibet. The Chinese invaded Tibet in 1950. Gyatso attempted to negotiate peacefully, but finally fled to establish a Tibetan government in exile at Dharamshala, India. Gyatso has long taught mutual toleration among believers of various world religions, and non-violent change. Gyatso advocates human rights globally.

---

[890] See [♪] Gandhi, *Satyagraha.*

[891] [♪] King, *Autobiography*, 20. Some blacks disagreed. Malcolm X said: "I would be other than a man to stand up and tell you that the Afro-Americans, the black people who live in these communities and in these conditions, are ready and willing to continue to sit around nonviolently and patiently and peacefully looking for some good will to change the conditions that exist. No! . . . [T]he day of nonviolent resistance is over; . the day of passive resistance is over." Malcolm X, The Harlem "Hate-Gang" Scare, in *Malcolm X Speaks*, 67-68.

[892] [♪] King, *Autobiography*, 63.

[893] [♪] King *Autobiography*, 78-80.

[894] [♪] King, *Autobiography*, 19.

7.22.3.15. *Desmond Tutu (1931 -   )* Tutu served as Anglican Archbishop of Cape Town, South Africa. He opposed that nation's policy of racial segregation, known as apartheid, advocating reconciliation among all parties involved. Tutu has opposed both sides of the apartheid struggle, when either indulged violence or corruption. Tutu focuses his international work on poverty, AIDS treatment, and the abuses of third world dictators. Tutu opposes all who engage war, and has criticized the United States President and British Minister for their armies' actions in the Iraq War. Each leader should be tried for war crimes, according to Tutu.

7.22.4. *Irenist Convictions.* Beneath irenist non-violent action lie principles:

7.22.4.1. *Power.* The irenist sees power (the influence of one person upon another) as inherent among human relations. Power is, for the irenist, diverse, widely spread, and dependent upon the consent or, at a minimum, acquiescence of those influenced. Power is a human penumbra. Hence, the irenist views power as fragile and easily disrupted at its source in the minds of those who are "ruled." The advocate of violence deems power hierarchical and monolithic. Power exists, stable and independent, exuding from powerful individuals in a self-perpetuating emanation. The irenist rallies groups to nonviolent resistance. Those of monolithic perceptions rely upon coercion and violence.[895]

7.22.4.2. *Murder.* Irenists, like most humans, oppose murder. Irenists find solutions other than those that require killing. All great religious traditions forbid intentional killing of humans.[896] Most religious traditions, however, discover exceptions to their rule under various circumstances: war,[897] legal retribution, self-defense. Irenists are, perhaps, less inclined to endorse exceptions. The predominant motive for murder, whether by the State or by individuals, is retribution.[898] Heraclitus notes that the rule of blood-for-blood is like a man, thoroughly muddied, washing

---

[895] This distinction leans heavily upon Gene Sharp, *The Politics of Nonviolent Action*, Part I, 8-10.

[896] Islam: *Quran*, Sura 4:29, Sura 17:33; Hebrew, *Exodus* 20:13; Christian, *Matthew* 5:21-22; Buddhism, the first of the Five Precepts, [♪] *Dhammapada* 129-130; Hindu: *Laws of Manu* 8:345; Confucianism: *Mencius* 83 (Book IV.A.14).

[897] Heraclitus finds war the fundament of human life. It makes of men either gods or humans, free or slave. Heraclitus, Haxton translation, *Fragments* 44.

[898] Other motivations for murder exist. John Brown, in October 1859, faced a Kansas territory careening, with federal assistance and rampant slave-holder intimidation and murder, toward adopting slavery. He and forty-five compatriots seized the federal armory at Harper's Ferry, Virginia, killing some, on behalf of the freedom of black slaves. Brown was besieged and captured. Brown was executed on December 2, 1859. Six other were later hanged. Sistare offers a rationale for accepting violent resistance, under some circumstances, as one strategy in the arsenal of civil disobedience, contrary to the sentiments of most irenist social activists. Sistare, "John Brown's Duties: Obligation, Violence, and 'Natural Duty'," 95-112.

himself in mud.[899] One cannot insure peace by murder, neither institutional murder nor private vendetta.

7.22.4.3. *Coercion.* Most irenists understand coercion, in its many forms, as the precursor to and intellectual progeny of violence.[900] Most agree coercion is undesirable; many, however, make exceptions for some coercive acts. This author is, reluctantly, one such. Until all humans are well-nurtured, and possibly even after such care has been lavished, communities must retain a limited ability to respond to wanton acts.[901] Sociopathy, at a minimum, will persevere as a problem for mankind. The limited place that remains for conscientious coercion is addressed in Section IV of this book.

7.22.4.4. *Building Understanding.* The irenist employs his friend-making skills to build peace where conflicts emerge. Much conflict is imagined, not actual. One dispels misconception, facilitates listening, and frames a neutral story about the conflict in which the participants recognize their contribution to the conflict. Most conflicts subside as understanding grows and parties accept their mutual parts in the source of conflict. Those that do not require what I call the "long conversation." This dialogue spanning months strikes to the heart of opponents' attitudes and orientations, revealing each, and opens the conversational partners to intimate sharing.

7.22.4.5. *Embracing Enemies.* Some conflicts are more deeply entrenched, depending not on momentary fears and confusions, but on convictions a lifetime in the making. Most human conflict occurs when someone ad-

---

[899] Heraclitus, Jones translation, *On the Universe,* 130.

[900] Gandhi argues that Satyagraha can solve the problems of mankind, but only with ongoing effort. What one acquires by truth one retains by ongoing truthful action. What one acquires by violence can only be retained by ongoing acts of violence. Gandhi, *Satyagraha in South Africa,* 306.

[901] A) I distinguish deviant action and differentiated action, which diverge from neurotypical standards, from wanton action and wanton actors. "Wanton" actors disregard the feelings, well-being, and rights of others, even after correction and counsel. The wanton person may indulge cruel brutality without restraint. See *Webster's Third New International Dictionary,* s.v. "wanton" (both considered as an adjective at §5.a., and as a verb at §3). I use the term "wanton member" or "wanton community" to indicate a person or community that has failed to be moved by the needs of others in a manner that injures meaningful life in meaningful community. Wanton members, then, necessitate irenic intervention and possible coercion. See Section IV below. B) Harry Frankfurt identifies "wanton" creatures as those that lack second-order volitions. In first-order volition, one acts upon desire, and wills only that one's strongest desire comes to pass. In second-order volition, one acts upon one's desire to have a different desire than one in fact has. One wishes to be otherwise, and acts to become such. Second-order volitions characterize all "persons," according to Frankfurt. In his view, then, animals, children, and some human adults are not persons. A "wanton" fails to care about his own will; he has no desires deeper or more pressing than the strongest impulse of the moment. A wanton lacks concern about whether or not his desires are desirable. Frankfurt, "Freedom of Will and Concept of a Person," 10-11.

vocates change that another opposes. The primary irenist engine of social change is moral conviction, not coercion. If one wishes to promote change that some adamantly oppose, one defeats his own purposes by coercing the antagonist to conform. Only the antagonist can change himself.[902] The non-violent resister appeals to the oppressor's shame, embraces him despite that flaw, and offers friendship. Attempts to coerce better behavior in others breed recalcitrance. Attempts to exterminate opponents result in vendetta, as well as one's own ethical disfigurement. One needs an opponent's consent to muster effective change. One must convince opponents. To be convinced, an opponent must hear. One changes opponents into proponents by showing human compassion and issuing invitation to friendship to that person.[903] The "long conversation" ensues. The opponent begins to listen, to hear and be heard. One fashions a world of dialogue that opponents may share. One reasons and tolerates and persists, perhaps transgenerationally. Friends heed the admonitions of friends. To end coercion, irenists befriend coercers. Of all weapons, friendship remains the most potent and least ruinous. Only friendship ends conflicts.

7.22.4.6. *Engineering Peace.* All humans behave peacefully some of the time, except a few suffering souls whose broken brains deny them that rest. What is possible to all some of the time could be possible at more or all times. Humanity should explore human peace. It seems likely we can socially engineer a world less prone to violence. Every step away from coercion makes the next act of violence less likely. There is nothing that can be done violently that cannot be accomplished non-violently. The difference is pace. Even if it were the case that the only solution to a conflict lies in the death of opponents, if patient, one finds opponents pass quite naturally, without inflicted violence. Non-violence demands one take the time to win over opponents by making them friends. Peace-making demands time, but not infinite gulfs. One or two devoted generations could make earth peaceful.[904] The task is as simple as this: replace each dying, violence-applauding grandfather with his flourishing irenist grandson.

---

[902] *Mencius,* Book II, Part A, Section 3.

[903] Martin Luther King Jr. said, on the day the Montgomery bus boycott ended after the Alabama bus segregation statute was overturned by the U. S. Supreme Court, that blacks must seek an integration founded in shared respect, and all must return to the buses attempting to make friends of racist opponents. [♪] King, *Autobiography,* 96.

[904] Russell, "The Next Half-Century," 691-692.

7.22.4.7. *Numerical Superiority.* The sheer number of those who wish to preserve peace in the world overwhelmingly exceeds those of violent sentiment. Hidden among the coercive minority are a tiny army of sociopaths and narcissists who lack neurotypical compassion, feeling nothing in the face of others' suffering, and find the prospect of war a winsome entertainment. Unfortunately, these pathological few are often attractive and convincing, and rise, in numbers inconsistent with their small population, to positions of political or military power. Insofar as we occupy democratic regimes, people of peace can demand non-coercion by voting against coercion. The rub is that we then, by governmental machinery, begin coercing the coercive minority into non-coercion. Irenists should expend much effort helping tacit-irenists to recognize their implicit irenism. Non-violent protest turns the passive irenist into an ally, so long as activist irenists refuse violence. Further discussion of irenist resistance to coercive government action is deferred to the next section of this work.

7.22.4.8. *Suffering.* Most irenists view suffering evils as morally superior to inflicting them.[905] When one suffers voluntarily at the hands of another, sympathies, including the emotions of those inflicting the suffering, stir. Humans do violence in only a particular state of mind, one of depersonalization, of moral distance from voluntary action, of disparagement of the victim. Voluntary suffering shatters the violent mindset. A particular person suffers, and makes himself known amicably to the offender. The sufferer is here—he does not flee. The sufferer endures pain to help the afflicting person. Rage and tribal frenzy may collapse toward compassion and care and personal relationship.

7.22.4.9. *Evil as Perverse Good.* Many irenists find evil implausible. They argue that all evils are misperceived goods.[906] Evil's proponents are, to most irenists, confused, not bad. Irenists of this opinion, then, advocate education and compassion as patent remedies for evil. From this prescription emerges an irenist strategy. One addresses the compassionate conscience[907] buried in the mental tombs of violent people, seeking to exhume and revive that corpse. Such irenists may under-estimate the persistence of human recalcitrance and the prevalence of sociopathy.

---

[905] [♪] King, *Autobiography*, 26.

[906] Emerson, while praising the unintended good results of evil acts, says, "there is no moral deformity, but is a good passion out of place; that there is no man who is not indebted to his foibles." Emerson, *The Conduct of Life*, 1086 (VII: Considerations By The Way).

[907] Hobbes calls conscience a thousand witnesses. [♪] Hobbes, *Leviathan*, 48.

7.22.4.10. *Subversive Amity.* Irenism has been often criticized as passive acquiescence in things as they are. Irenists seek needful change as urgently as do proponents of coercion and violence. They do so, however, with moral restraint and immense patience. Irenists wield friendship as a sword. They find opponents to undertake campaigns of subversive affection. Irenists learn opponents, approve their merits, and criticize their defects, just as they do with their other loved ones. Irenists bring skills at tolerance, insight, and argument to bear, as violent people bring rifles and grenades. Irenists bring transgenerational perspective to their battles. If a man cannot win his friend to peace, perhaps his grandson will be able to deflect his friend's grandson. Coercion wins short term gain at the expense of enduring corruption of relationships. Only the irenist stance finally quashes hatred by making friends of enemies. Of all the forces mankind has mustered in his defense, none is so potent as friendship. In the long haul, cooperators defeat coercers.

7.22.4.11. *Prosperity.* One can build tanks or sewer systems, rifles or shovels, prisons or schools, but not both. Every tank depletes school coffers. Every rifle leaves a ditch undug. Every prison squanders human capital in idling and bitterness. Every war or police tax wearies a people to no good effect.[908] Wars are often popular. That measures the acclimation-to-violence of most. Prosperity may be much more popular. We do not know, for America has made war-making a fundament. Give peace a chance, as damnable hippies chant. Take a decade off from war. Let the Pentagon vacation. Divert taxes to social benefit. Then let the people vote. The American public may prefer war-less prosperity more than we suspect. Coercion might become a loser at the polls.

7.22.5. *Cadre Irenism.* Every member is the front line of irenism within his cadre of intimates. Any intimate's conflicts become one's own, for members share a life. One may find wanton behaviors in an intimate, which choices may lead to community censure for the member and cadre. Frankly address intra-cadre conflicts.

If the conflict is yours, Kate, avoid smoothing things over between you and your griped friend. Strive instead toward revised intimacy. Interpersonal conflict is not a bump in the road; it is one *point* of being on the road together. Conflict emerges when, finally, friends get to know one another well enough to be annoyed with the other's habits and comfortable enough to say so. After weathering that squall, intimacy deepens. Post-conflict friendship finds a new, more resonant baseline. Confidence in that friendship burgeons. The great mis-steps in interpersonal conflict

---

[908] So argues Mo. [♪] *Mozi*, 65-67 (Part I, §20).

lie in avoiding it, papering it over, pretending all is well, acting like it never happened, or shouldering more responsibility for the conflict than you actually bear. One knows that intimacy is happening when conflicts surface. We address conflict well when friends plunge through the conflict in a way that strengthens bonds between friends stressed by the changes their togetherness requires. Difficult interpersonal conversations were addressed in Section 7.14.

If the conflict is that of others in your cadre, Kate, you bear a different role. Yours is to mediate. Your cadre is yours. Care for it. Repair its torn roofs and broken hinges. Bear your share of your cadre-mates' dysfunctions. They are part of you, and now experience conflict. At some level, their conflict is yours; you, and your cadre-mates, helped cause it. Tell your friends that you care about them and their conflict. Offer to mediate, to listen, to persevere with their conversation, no matter how long it might take, until their affection for one another makes each willing to change in the ways the relationship demands. Do not think "that crap is their problem." It is your problem. You, by your actions or inactions, contributed to their conflict. You, by your actions or inactions, may help them resolve their conflict.

Here is a blueprint for mediating conflict among intimates.

7.22.5.1. *Reflect, Object, then Listen.* Interpersonal conflicts begin with hints of annoyance. This habit of another bothers; that fact about a friend irritates.

Before three-way dialogue begins, ask your friends to check themselves. Is someone having an off day? Is anyone projecting his unhappiness with a different facet of life onto a friend? Every person's mind, all by itself, is a simmering pot of subliminal discord. Psychological discomfort requires a different remedy than mediated interpersonal conflict. When you grow reasonably clear that a problem *between* others exists, and not merely *within* one or the other, then speak. Ask the parties what happened. Encourage them to begin gently with an expression of annoyance that grants possibilities for his or her experience other than the cadre-mates' idiosyncrasies. Ask your friends not to lie. Encourage them to be forthright. Still, uncertainty about social facts predominates; either could be wrong. Acknowledge doubts. But do not let conversation end with easy agreement about the evident hallucination of one or the other (unless, of course, one is hallucinating). The first defense at the border of every ego is denial. Surmount that.

After speaking, listen. Encourage both to do so actively. The active listener interrupts with questions and seeks clarifications. Be curious. Follow your friends' thoughts. Say their words back to them verbatim.

Then summarize them, and ask for confirmation of your summary's accuracy. Ask your friends to summarize what you said to them. Confirm or disconfirm comprehension. Reaffirm your affection for both.

7.22.5.2. *Resolve Factual Disputes.* In the dispute, factual discrepancies may surface. Resolve those confusions. Agree what information source would resolve the factual question, and consult that source. Where friends cannot agree about sources of information acceptable to both, the dispute is not about facts but about values. Divert the mediated conversation from the facts to the underlying values implicated. Be curious. Explore each puzzling assertion. Listen carefully. Restate and seek confirmation of your understanding. Confirm with each that you have understood accurately.

7.22.5.3. *Express, then Listen.* Having heard the others, probe the conflict's borders. Seldom is an interpersonal annoyance singular. Preceding and surrounding the event under discussion swirl other events, previous irritations that are related, but never rose to consciousness or were previously dismissed as inconsequential. One does not want to drag the kitchen sink and dead cats into the conversation. Neither, however, does one want to let closely-related events go unrecognized or unaddressed. Express the breadth of your concerns; probe their boundaries. Put what should be on the table on the table. It is most helpful, where possible, to do this exploration collaboratively. Such may prove possible if mutual affection is secure, and defensiveness abates. If not, plunge on, expressing the conflict as you see it. Do not be satisfied extinguishing a match when the house is on fire.

After speaking, listen once more. Hear your friends. Audit yourself. If either friend is defensive, listen to him make excuses and denials. Repeat those words to him verbatim, if possible. Turn the conversation again to the conflict issues. Do not be deterred by psychological deflections. Stay on point. Offer to take up the content of each equivocation in a separate, but subsequent, conversation. Recapitulate for both what each has said. Reaffirm affection.

7.22.5.4. *Find a Shared Story; Own Your Responsibility.* From speaking and listening emerges a new story, a fresh tale of the conflict. The characters are your friends (and possibly others). The story line sketches the characters' motivations and faults, how each contributed to the conflict experienced, how the conflict was addressed by the characters, and how the characters changed to alleviate their stresses with one another. If there is no laughing involved in this part of reconciliation, something is awry.

7.22.5.5. *Establish Revised Normalcy.* After reconciliation, both parties need to work toward the new habits suggested by their shared story of conflict.   Conflict is a learning experience; its sequel is conscious amendment of habits. Let your friendship settle into its new concourses. Often, more time together is required. Occasionally recall the conflict; recapitulate lightly. Friends often give seminal conflicts names, to establish a shorthand reference. Some such in my own life are "the asshole conversation," the "abominable boat" dialogue, and the "kimification" epic. If friends do not chuckle when the conflict-epitomizing name is uttered, the conflict remains unreconciled.

7.22.5.6. *Honor Genuine Dissent.* Occasionally, fundamental divergences come to light from interpersonal conflict. Friends may learn characteristics about one another that one or both cannot change, or are unwilling to change. Friendship is a capacious abode, ample to accommodate vast dissents amidst amicable equanimity. The foundation of friendship is not agreement, but affection. Where agreement is absent, friends find much to discuss. Where affection languishes, friendships perish. One's knowledge of all things is fractured and partial. Causes for humility preponderate. Human relations peculiarly merit pronounced circumspection. Friendship is the most complex juxtaposition in the known universe. If you believe otherwise at this point, you need to go back and digest previous materials concerning human consciousness and the brain. One honors a friend by dissenting in a conflict, and waiting patiently with him for insight to dawn on you or him or both.

7.22.5.7. *School for Moral Imagination.*   John Paul Lederach suggests (perhaps as a metaphor that might also apply to interpersonal conflict) that peace might arise from a school for moral imagination of political leaders. They would gather one week per year, friends and enemies alike. The agenda would involve lots of beverages, breaks, garden planting, walks, and conversation, but few lectures or debates. Participants would have one task: tell honestly about your hopes and concerns and fears, and those of your family. All would write poetry or music. Above the exit door would be a small plaque that read: "Reach out to those you fear. Touch the heart of complexity. Imagine beyond what is seen. Risk vulnerability one step at a time."[909]

Objection 24: Pacifistic Yammer: *Some demur that irenists lack substantial resolve to establish peace. A serious pacifist would use coercive violence to bring his vision to pass,*[910] *and to tamp down criminals and other disruptive*

---

[909] Lederach, *The Moral Imagination*, 176-177. See Gottman and DeClaire, *The Relationship Cure.*

[910] Mao, for example, wishes to establish perpetual communist peace, a world without war. That outcome can be achieved only at gunpoint. Coercive violence will, if well utilized, crush the oppressions of human society which cause violent conflict. One wars to end war. [♪] Mao, *Little Red*

forces. When a pacifist faces a gunman, the gunman prevails, regardless the happy entreaties of the irenist. Force must be met with countervailing force. The alternative is subjugation. Only when irenists kill to achieve their ends will their ends become realities. Irenist delicacy about violence betrays character defects. Irenists lack the mettle to enact their visions of the human future. The future springs from the hand of those willing to fashion it coercively. In the end, might makes right.[911] All contrary opinions merely simper.

Response: Many irenists lack gravitas. Most pray peace, but shrink from irenic rigor. I count myself one of these moral weaklings. Tolstoy castigates the Christian church for its flight from irenic suffering.[912] Gandhi said that if the World War II Japanese army had marched into India, Gandhi would have sent several million Satyagrahi to meet them. All of Gandhi's peacemakers would have stood passively as cannon fodder until revulsion at the horrific gore expelled the Japanese, wretching.[913] Jesus went to the cross, wrongly convicted, and castigating his allies for their willingness to ply swords in his defense.[914] Rightly conceived, irenists war against war. Coercers will war until irenists pacify them.[915]

William James noted virtues of warriors—their courage, strength, honor, loyalty, rigor, and general hardiness. James reported that warriors scoff at the prattle of irenists. One cannot slay a scourge with dandy words. People die

---

Book, 61, 63-64. The consistent rationale of every war is that its violence aims to establish or maintain peace. See [♪] Marx, *Communist Manifesto*, 82-86. One ponders starving to establish obesity, or screaming to establish quiet. One must not let bellicose rhetoric distract one from the essential rationale of war: strategic cost-effective killing of humans. See Dyer, *War: The Lethal Custom*, 8.

[911] [♪] Thucydides, *The Peloponnesian War*, 358-366 (Book V, Chapter 7, "The Melian Debate.") Stirner makes a similar, and very Nietzschean-sounding, argument with respect to property. One's property consists in all things that cannot be torn from him by another's superior strength. Stirner, *The Ego and Its Own*, 227. Many view violence as the last means of negotiation. Facts do not support this conclusion. Non-violent resistance is more effective at winning concessions from adamant regimes than responsive violence. Insurgents tend to use violence as the first means of negotiation, even while using last resort propaganda. Chenoweth and Stephan, *Why Civil Resistance Works*, 226-227. Michael Shermer notes that terrorism has a success rate (achieving at least one of its goals) of less than five percent. Shermer, *The Moral Arc*, 85.

[912] See Tolstoi, *The Kingdom of God Is Within You.*

[913] [♪] Gandhi, *Satyagraha*, 377-378 (Section 178). Karl Marlantes blames America's aggressive bellicosity on our code of silence about war. Americans view as impolite discussion of the vast bloodiness and moral compromises that afflict our military engagements. War both thrills and revolts. Without the thrill, we could not seduce our young to engage slaughter. Without revolting extravagances of blood and bounty, disgust would never provoke us to tame our military. Marlantes argues that all experiences of war must be expressed, and the code of silence broken. Then Americans might war wisely (if such is possible), well-apprised that war both beckons and horrifies us. Marlantes, *What It Is Like To Go To War*, 216-219.

[914] *Matthew* 26:52, *Luke* 22:50-51.

[915] Aristophanes tells a ribald tale of the united women of Greece confronting their men's penchant for perpetual inter-city war. The women swear an oath, if young, to forswear sex with their men until they cease fighting, and, if old, to march to the Acropolis and seize the funds for war from the Temple of Athene. As their plot unfolds, Greece's warriors, hobbled by their unrelenting erections, sue for peace with one another, Lysistrata serving as mediator. Aristophanes, *Lysistrata*.

while irenists dawdle. Peace demands a firmer hand and sharper blade than irenists wield, so generals scoff. James calls upon irenists to ferret for themselves a morality commanding the sort of moral hypertrophy that soldiers live and breathe in every battle. Irenists must make of peacemaking the "moral equivalent of war."[916]

Gandhi identifies the gritty realities of effective irenism as: 1) constructive work, which consists in teaching the uneducated, improving hygiene, treating disease, and generally moving the ball of human well-being forward, especially for those who are culturally disadvantaged, 2) benefit refusal, which consists in declining to accept help or reward or accolades or positions from agents of errant institutions, 3) organizing, which consists in marshalling irenist people into effective group action, 4) mentoring, which consists in teaching people inwardness, love of truth, and moral rigor (Gandhi advocated fasting, walking, and spinning thread), 5) civil disobedience, which consists in organizing groups to actively and publicly violate offensive laws, endure prosecution and incarceration and fines, and to promptly repeat the crimes upon release, and 6) dying at the hands of opponents or confused people.[917] Irenism, then, is not really all that peaceful.[918] The same evils that some confront with guns find response. The same longing for rites of passage, for exigent and thrilling action that drives so many misguided young men into military service finds vent. Oddly, the conscientious irenist bleeds and suffers, acts with astonishing courage, and constitutes, for all meaningful purposes, a murderless soldier.

I would augment Gandhi's list. The irenist need not acquiesce in a coercive social construct. One need not control government to divert and ultimately subdue a culture's misdirection. Irenists can build a better world within the rotting shell of nationalism and militarist violence and majoritarian coercion. Irenists can form communities. They can cherish friends, and nurture the coming generation. They can conduct irenic peacemaking. They can address criminals and ill-nurtured persons with fortitude. They can welcome the deformed and crippled and poor and ugly and stupid. They can disdain wealthy elitists, even noisily. They can oppose cultural oppressions and coercions. Ultimately, when coercion has been thoroughly discredited, governments will fall of their own weight or reconfigure themselves as irenic forces for human well-being. That process is, in my view, well under way.

Irenists war against coercion.[919] Surprisingly, irenist sentiments are winning the battle against human violence (despite what one sees on televised

---

[916] See [♪] James, *The Moral Equivalent of War*.

[917] See [♪] Gandhi, *Satyagraha*. By Gandhian standards, I am a wan irenist. *Mea culpa.*

[918] Hence, the rationale for a word other than "pacifism."

[919] Gene Sharp, in this three volume work, offers, first, a theoretical construct explaining the surprising effectiveness of nonviolent action, and, second, a description of the many tools in the irenist mechanic's box as they have been used historically, and, third, a description of how nonviolent action works and what results one may expect from such efforts. An appendix, located at the end of Part Three, lists factors affecting the outcome in nonviolent struggles. Sharp, *The Politics of Nonviolent Action*, Parts One, Two, and Three.

news). The number of wars and war victims falls. The frequency of homicide plummets, on a per capita basis. We have not suffered a global military conflict in more than sixty years.[920] Non-violent resistance is, almost universally, more effective in achieving its aims than its violent correlate.[921] War is, arguably, a bad habit formed when humanity began overpopulating. The archaeological evidence for primordial war is, at best, unconvincing.[922] War is not a natural state for humans.

Objection 26: Abandoning Justice: Another protests that irenism neglects justice. The author proposes reintegrating offenders into the community they injured, refusing death penalties, and minimizing coercion. Pervasive irenism would license sociopaths to run amok, binding the retributive hand behind the social back. Retributive justice, which is responsive coercion, winds deeply into the human essence. Without the conviction that society (and possibly god) rewards good behavior and punishes ill, human community unravels in an epidemic of self-interested rapacity and global distrust. Grisly execution permanently deters the punished criminal. Shocking punishments also give pause to those who contemplate imitation. Fear of retributive consequence restrains the vast majority from evil action. Were we to shift the responsive baseline from proportional coercion to batting eyelashes and shy proposals of friendship, as this misguided author proposes, the beast lurking in the human breast would pillage unfettered. Untold misery would ensue. Humans need retribution.

Response: Rough justice matters. An emotional chord, a resonance deep in human affective life, cries for equity, rages for compensation of wrongs. This is a limbic voice not easily quieted. Capuchin monkeys, happily munching keepers' cucumbers, discard the slices and run riot when they observe others capuchins receiving grapes from keepers.[923] An egalitarian thread is loomed in the fabric of primate consciousness. Yet, in no aspect of life could we be more

---

[920] Please catch up on the last thousand years' statistics on violence. See [♪] Pinker, *Better Angels of Our Nature*. Review the last 200,000 years' pacific developments. See [♪] Wade, *Before the Dawn*. Lack of recent global conflagrations does not mean we have not been plagued by hordes of more local martial nightmares.

[921] Chenoweth and Stephan have analyzed violent and non-violent insurgencies from 1900 to 2006. The nonviolent campaigns were almost twice as likely to partially or completely reach their political purposes. Nonviolent campaigns were more than twice as likely to achieve regime change, and slightly more likely to result in anti-occupation or self-determination changes to political regimes. Further, in some uncategorizable efforts (such as anti-apartheid), only non-violent means worked. Since 2000, the rate of non-violent successes has outstripped violent successes sixfold. Regimes established by nonviolent means prove much more stable and resilient than those begun in violence. Chenoweth and Stephan, *Why Civil Resistance Works*, 7-10. Chenoweth and Stephan argue that nonviolent resistance proves more effective than violent campaigns because high levels of population participation create sustained pressure on a regime, robbing its economic, political, social, and military structures of needed political legitimacy. When a population refuses its consent and collaboration, regimes have little choice but to respond. Chenoweth and Stephan, *Why Civil Resistance Works*, 44, 61.

[922] Horgan, *The End of War*, 58. Consider also Hrdy, *Mothers and Others*, 26-30.

[923] de Waal, *Primates and Philosophers*, 45-49.

bound for disappointment. People are, by nature, unequal. Every member's measure of skill, ability, opportunity, and willingness fills a volume unique to herself. None is equal. Circumstances differ. No human fact could be more patent. Rough justice permits us to overlook the more trivial of these divergences, dismissing them as vagaries of happenstance.

But as to crimes and outrages, victims seek blood for blood. For millennia, justice systems have dampened vengeance retaliation. We have usurped the privilege from victims. We have softened retributive blows. We monetize some outrages, creating bankruptcies in the place of gallows. We install procedural safeguards, hoping to err on the side of caution in assigning retributions. DNA evidence teaches us how flawed are our criminal justice systems. In anonymous society, we frequently never know who perpetrates. The grief of tort victims teaches how inadequate are money damages. Dollars seldom salve years of disruption or pain or grief. And diverting retribution from the affected community to a host of professional strangers licks few wounds. Anger festers into boils of vendetta.

Quad sociality redirects justice from recompense to future weal. Done deeds are done; no new blows relieve old ones. Communities re-integrate offenders and victims, under ordinary circumstances. The perpetrator is a resource, a warning, and a repository of immense communal investment. We need our perpetrators. Evil actors are known in communities; they lack a place to hide. The criminal dwells among his victims, making restitution, building new trust, if he is able.

For that minority whose dysfunctions preclude this possibility, more potent coercive interventions should be employed. I describe such interventions in what follows. For the recalcitrant, transform the prison into a community of recalcitrant offenders. Let them self-govern, feed themselves, help one another exorcise their demons. Hear the voice of criminal communities in the Commons. Show respect. Let those who heal themselves in offender communities rejoin their irenic communities.

No member, no community should allow irredeemable savages to sunder member or community. If one cannot find an irenic path, then one takes what paths remain: flight or combat. Each such non-irenic path betrays collapse of imagination and recurrence to the habits of a dreadful past. One should defend herself and her community, even to the extent of bloodletting. But when one's self-defense comes to crimson streets and corpses, one has failed, even if one survives. Prepare a better defense. Find a principled path skirting recourse to retribution. Begin by rendering no man's life so unpleasant he longs to lash out. Rely on the infinite temperate subtleties of mentored education. Take the ills of others to heart. Help them build communities to their liking; savor their (often ill-deliberate) experiments. Those who refuse to remediate will be compelled to retaliate. Scarcity, in a world of plenty, breeds resentment. Resentment, eventually, boils over. That cauldron contains catastrophe.

Deep beneath this objector's concerns about justice hides the conviction that humans are bent toward evil. Life, so he thinks, must continue as it has. We launch ill-nurtured members, unsupervised, thoughtless, directionless into anonymous society, there they work their feckless confusions. We intervene only *after* atrocity. Quad sociality proposes that none should be so "free." All should be known, meshed in a self-correcting web of friendships. Those who err egregiously should set matters aright, as they are able. The community that failed to recognize the perpetrator's errant steps should reformulate itself for more careful attention. Abusing Orwell's thoughts, we do not need a Big Brother. Every man is Big Brother.[924] Cain should keep Abel. Adam should watch both. Eve should barge in.[925]

Humans are as inclined to do well as ill. Mostly, when we err, we are confused, not wretched. I grant there are exceptions, persons who lack conscience (sociopaths) and indulge wanton impulsivity (narcissists) and export social distress pointlessly (borderlines), working grave injuries. I also grant these dangerous persons are relatively few and generally identifiable, at least to practiced eyes.[926]

Quad irenism does not neglect justice. Irenism wrenches the eyes of justice from yesterday's injury to tomorrow's well-being. Irenism reorients justice.

Objection 27: Violent Urgency: Yet another remonstrates that the author overstates the value of human peace. Peace is quiescence. Where quiet prevails, there change founders. So much needs reformation, in this culture, in every conceivable culture. Those who ask a generation to wait patiently for dubious change, even past their own graves and those of their grandchildren as well, ask too much. Those ask inhuman sacrifice. This author so prescribes; he is wrong to do so. Violence, and the threat of violence, elicit change where reform would otherwise remain elusive. Even vaunted irenists know as much, though they seek to finesse the point. Gandhi's pacifism repeatedly shut down India, and threatened the country's economic ruin. The irenism of Martin Luther King Jr. was persistently underlined by the possibility that King might step back, unleashing scions of black racial hatred to savage white supremacists in bloody street battles. King and Gandhi occasionally acknowledged that one needed to seize the moment, tearing at quiescent stalemate, in order to effect equity. Justice flowers in messy alternation between spasms of coercive violence and consolidating peaces. Endless peace merely sets the status quo in concrete. Deaths dissolve deadlock. Those who disagree self-deceive.

Response: Change is indeed needful. I ask patience, not boundless acquiescence. Irenists do not stand idly by, pleading, with tear-streaked cheeks, for happier outcomes. Irenists demand change. Core issues lie in the means to and

---

[924] Orwell, *1984.*

[925] *Genesis* 4:1-16.

[926] Sociopaths hide. Marquis de Sade's characters Madame de Saint-Ange and Dolmancé entice Eugenie into their sexual oddities. Dolmance says to Eugenie: "We do have something of the treacherous, yes; a touch of the false, you may believe it. But after all, Madame, I have demonstrated to you that this character is indispensable to man in society. . . . The needs for dissimulation and hypocrisy are bequeathed us by society; let us yield to the fact. Allow me for an instant to offer my own example to you, Madame: there is surely no being more corrupt anywhere in the world; well, my contemporaries are deceived in me; ask them what they think of Dolmancé, and they will all tell you I am an honest man, whereas there is not a single crime whereof I have not gleaned the most exquisite delights." De Sade, *Philosophy in the Bedroom*, 279.

pace of change.[927]   The human rule has been coercive violence. From the first wheat field through two world wars, wits and weaponry predominated. The rule for prosperity has been to pillage; the rule for peace has been to win wars. Beleaguered peace hunkered, white-knuckled, in the interstices. As human collaboration spreads toward global cooperation, the sword's role dwindles. Coercive violence wanes not because we have become morally responsive. Violence languishes because it does not work. Violence breeds further violence. Coercion spawns recalcitrance. Ignoring others' needs ensures resentment. Social cauldrons boil over. Blood is spilled; the cycle commences again.

Change proves labyrinthine in bloated societies.   One desiring change stumbles into webs of regulations and laws and interest group opposition and violent threats, all spun by powerful but murky groups committed to personal advantage. Large groups never welcome change. Large groups castrate and eviscerate their lions of change, who still roar reform, but lack the organs to effect it and remain placidly leashed. To experiment, to embrace change, live small. The human brain grasps needful change when it dwells in groups sized to human comprehension. Most towns and cities dwarf human social capabilities. We can, maximally, know 150 persons well enough to recognize them and recite their relations to one another. How big is your town? Your city? Your urban megalopolis? Your nation? Kithdom elects personal existence over anonymous drifting. If one lives large, the reformer has no alternative but to embrace violence and endless frustration. Violence leads nowhere, over and over. On a good day, violence replaces bad rulers with a fresh batch of bad rulers. Universally, their hands are crimson, their swords honed, and their consciences a smoldering ruin.

Irenist strategies douse the spark of violence. Change by agreement, even daring reformations, await smaller communities of friends undertaking winning social experiments. Where viable alternatives exist, communities can deliberate the utility of various approaches. In kithdoms, change grows less threatening, because it happens more frequently and in a non-spasmodic, incremental manner. Change is welcomed because it relieves social stresses, and can be unwound within small communities as easily as it was adopted. Change flourishes because its unintended consequences are limited to the adopting communities, and can be stanched before affecting millions. So, the inherent risks of change dwindle.

The objector romanticizes death. A propitious death may well facilitate some change-of-the-moment. All looks well, until it proves not well at all. Those who welcome such myopic "progress" fail to count the long-term costs of recurring resentment, recalcitrance, and vendetta. Stepping past romantic death-talk, one sees that change-by-death squanders irreplaceable social capital for dubious momentary gains. Violence sunders the trust without which nothing of

---

[927] Edmund Burke says truly, "Political arrangement, as it is a work for social ends, is to be only wrought by social means. There mind must conspire with mind. Time is required to produce that union of minds which alone can produce all the good we aim at. Our patience will atchieve [sic] more than our force." Burke, *Reflections on the Revolution in France*, 172.

enduring social value can be fabricated. Death fails to dissolve deadlock. Blood betrays brotherhood. Those who argue otherwise have not really paid attention.

7.23. *Humility.* **Simple Rule: Correct yourself first; listen humbly.** If one pays attention through a single day, one sees that he mis-hears, mis-sees, and misconceives hundreds of matters, gargantuan and minuscule, in its course. One checks and references constantly, hoping to improve perception. But eyes lie. Ears deceive. Ideas bait. I am in flux, as are you. We inherit a vast gulf of information and opinion; much of it is dross.[928] We rely on its advice to our detriment. Even the "constants" of nature appear to change over time. The universe itself is mutating.[929] So, truth wriggles free, like a puppy at play, too swift for human capture. When we sketch lines of truth, we must ever have at the ready a supple eraser and fresh sheets of paper. Perceptual defects alone warrant humility. But there is more. One's character is incomplete or distorted. One's subconscious imperatives skew consciousness. Defense mechanisms of denial, projection, and self-delusion pester. And one remains certain that other thoughts, yet to occur to one, would change one's view of any matter. Adding it all up, one is driven to listen intently. We are, each of us, less intelligent, beautiful, competent, and wise than we prefer to believe. A wise person corrects himself first, before addressing others.[930] Gandhi magnified his own faults, and diminished those of opponents so that he might, by this intentional distortion, balance scales tipped by his prejudices.[931] Jesus admonished disciples to remove the log in their own eyes before attending to the splinters that obscure others' vision.[932] Mencius called disciples to tremble when in the wrong, though their critic be a dolt.[933] Buddha advised sages to ignore the

---

[928] Confucius said that knowledge turns on saying one knows when he does know and saying he does not know when he does not know. [♪] Confucius, *Analects*, 65 (Book II, §17). Socrates was less generous. Those who say they are wise, aren't. [♪] Plato, *Apologia*, 107 (§29B). An unnamed Hindu sage concurs. Though ignorant, fools deem themselves wise, and bumble about, the blind leading the blind. *Upanishads*, 77 (*Mundaka Upanishad*, Part 1, Chapter 2).

[929] Barrow and Webb, "Inconstant Constants: Do the inner workings of nature change with time?" *Scientific American*, 77. See also Musser, "Where is Here? Our sense of the universe as an orderly expanse where events happen in absolute locations is an illusion," *Scientific American*, 70-73.

[930] The Buddha taught that one sees others' faults readily, but not one's own. We sift the behavior of others, but hide our own. Our disdain and concealments drive us far from right action. [♪] *Dhammapada*, 252-253.

[931] [♪] Gandhi, *Satyagraha*, 75 (Section 24, "A Himalayan Miscalculation.")

[932] *Matthew* 7:3-5, *Luke* 6:41-42.

[933] *Mencius*, 32 (Book II, Part A, Section 2). Mao, who is no one to whom you should look for moral guidance, urged party members to stop excoriating the criticizer and heed his criticism as a warning. [♪] Mao, *Little Red Book*, 260.

shortcomings of others, and focus on what you have done and failed to do.[934] Master Zhuang reports that a disciple dreamed of being a butterfly. When the disciple woke, he was uncertain if he had dreamed he was a butterfly, or he was a butterfly dreaming of being Zhuang's disciple.[935] The big temptation in character development is to abandon one's own field to weed those of others. Be exacting toward yourself; indulge others.[936] If you err, reform yourself now. Do not wait.[937] Defects of perception demand the discipline of humble listening. Good decision-making is collective enterprise. The funniest stories about you are those that report your errors and their consequences with unvarnished bluntness and a wry smile. The funniest stories about others are those that paint them with a broad, sympathetic brush, a portrayal that likely bestows greater kindness on them than they, in strictest justice, deserve.

Quad sociality itself demands humility. Vibrant community rings with laughing listening. Making much of oneself betrays defective attachment and ill-nurture. If you feel the need to trumpet, that would be a good place to begin re-formulating your character.[938] The foundations of human community nestle on bedrock of emotional cognition. We perceive in many modes, modes at least as varied as our fundamental drives. But the glue of community is shared emotion. Humility, considered socially, affirms our need for the perceptions of others.

7.24. *Honesty.* **Simple Rule: Live in candor.** Tell the truth. Tell truth when it helps you; be candid when candor injures you. Tell truth to friends; tell truth to strangers. Don't be embarrassed when candor makes you look the fool. All, except liars, acknowledge occasional foolishness. Never believe you can hide the truth. Your face blathers what cowers within. Humans lie naturally. We lie to others. We lie to ourselves. When we do so, lying makes perfect sense to us. Truth-telling is a habit to wedge deep in your life. One of life's highest compliments is when people find you frank.[939]

---

[934][♪] *Dhammapada*, 50.

[935] *Zhuangzi*, 44 (in Discussion on Making All Things Equal, Section 2).

[936] *Mencius*, 164 (Book VII, Part B, Section 32).

[937] *Mencius*, 71 (Book III, Part B, Section 8).

[938] *Mea culpa.* Augustine said of his teacher, Faustus, who suffered significant limitations: "He was not completely ignorant of his own ignorance. . . . He appealed to me the more for this: more beautiful than all those things I desired to know is the modest mind that admits its own limitations." Augustine, *Confessions*, 121 (Book 5, .Chapter 7, Section 12).

[939] Aristotle argues that the truthful person speaks plain truth, claiming neither more nor less than facts warrant. Such a person tends toward understatement and avoids puffing, not to be seen as a

Generally, truth is difficult to ascertain.[940] We are prone to swallow in-credulities whole, as frogs do flies. Pay attention to evidence and question your conclusions.[941] Truth-telling is a more difficult rule than one might imagine. One must recognize exceptions: a) Tell no truth that inflicts senseless injury.[942] b) Never let truth-telling impair a good joke or anec-dote. Only simpletons fail to cherish hyperbole in story-telling. c) The truth you tell may be sub-factual. You have cause for humility and suffer defective observational skills. Denial and projection overwhelm seeing and remembering in most contexts. The un-true truth you think you know may be the biggest problem you face. Abandon truths and promises that, upon deeper inspection, prove to be morally wrong.[943] Make apologies; set things aright. d) Do not use truth as a weapon. Telling the brutal truth may be neither helpful nor honest, but only thinly-veiled aggression. Exercise discretion. Inspect yourself.

Candor exceeds mere truth-telling. One performs promises.[944] One de-clines to conceal his agenda in negotiations. Candor is good faith. One is what one appears. Bad faith actors proclaim they want one thing, but se-cretly work toward another. In good faith, a woman gives and receives fair-ly. She points out mistakes in her favor. She reports her errors. She pol-ishes the table of trade.[945] Good faith binds people together in trusting soci-ety. Where candor flags, justice proves elusive. Cicero bids his son Marcus

---

boaster. Aristotle warns, however, that suppressing warranted truth about oneself can be its own form of boasting, as when a self-deprecating person deflects all praise. [♪] Aristotle, *Nichomachean Ethics* 76-77 (1127a-b).

[940] Seng-ts'an, a Buddhist monk, finds the entire truth-seeking enterprise fraught with peril. He ad-vises one to stop seeking truth, in favor of the perfect emptiness that attends abandoning intellection and words. [♪] Conze, *Buddhist Scriptures*, 172 (citing "On Believing in Mind").

[941] Cicero warns son Marcus to avoid gullibly adopting speculation as knowledge. [♪] Cicero, *De Officiis*, 19 (Book I, Section VI, 18).

[942] The white lie, a misrepresentation without intent to injure, poses dangers. One seldom knows what becomes of one's words after they are uttered, what others may rely upon them, to what uses they may be put. The white lie presupposes that one knows what one does not know. The white liar bears responsibility for unintended effects of the harmless lie. Rousseau, *Reveries of the Solitary Walker*, 69-71 (Fourth Walk).

[943] [♪] Cicero, *De Officiis*, 373 (Book III, Section XXV, 95).

[944] Mencius notes that in ambitious persons, words ignore deeds and deeds ignore words. *Mencius*, 166 (Book VII, Part B, Section 37). Muhammad argues that God finds hateful people who say they will do things and then fail to do them. [♪] Muhammad, *Qur'an* 61:2.

[945] Donald Pfaff points out that trust is the core element of economic relations. Humans prefer deals with trusted others that benefit both. Pfaff, *Altruistic Brain Theory*, 171.

to wait a while, when he has doubts about an action, since the matter is morally doubtful.[946] Be what you seem; appear as you are.

Strategic deception seduces many. One may profit from deception. The likelihood of deceit rises with decreased likelihood of punishment, where the cost of detection rises, and where others deceive persistently.[947] Deceivers exchange short term gain for long term costs. Those who deceive frequently mislead even themselves. They scramble alluring brambles of words, making worse appear better than it is, re-baptizing evils as evident goods.[948]   Where deceivers prosper, community confidence in justice plummets. The human fabric of good will frays. When no one believes anyone, social relations grind to a halt. That means deception for strategic benefit injures everyone, including the strategic deceiver.

Choose transparent good faith.

7.25. *Affection*. **Simple Rule: Show affection**. We may fail to show what affections we have for others. Non-expression can become habitual. Friends "hear" affection in different modes. Some want words. Some want touching. Many want acts of sympathetic kindness. Some want meaningful help. A few want silence. Find how your friend recognizes affection, and show her yours in that mode.[949] Most of communication is non-verbal. A hug is a sonnet; a kiss, a tome. Dare to touch. Let your face break into smile. Bestow thoughtful gifts. Let your welling heart spill upon others. Enliven your dead face; confute your stoical reservations.

7.26. *Laughter*. **Simple Rule: Laugh.** Laughter is the anthem of friendship. Where comfort waxes to temperatures that simmer intimacy, laughter leaks into conversation. Laugh when you can. If you have wit, make others laugh.[950] Sort laughs. Not every laugh portends friendship. Cruel laughter giggles at another's expense. Stressed rioters may laugh before they murder. Sycophants laugh when their objects signal chuckling. The ninny laughs when caught unprepared. Still, most laughter locates intimacy. Avoid becoming the buffoon. Never make jokes about what people find

---

[946] [♪] Cicero, *De Officiis*, 31 (Book I, Section IX, 30).

[947] David et al., "Receivers Limit the Prevalence of Deception in Humans,"4-5.

[948] So Plato characterizes the young individual of democratic leanings: insolence is called sophistication, lawlessness becomes freedom, extravagance is deemed generosity, and lack of shame is made to seem a semblance of courage. [♪] Plato, *Republic*, 273 (560e).

[949] Bertrand Russell summarizes the good in life as love, conceived as an emotion, guided by knowledge. [♪] Russell, "What I Believe," 349.

[950] Lao Tzu notes that the sage makes people giggle like children. [♪] Lao Tzu, *Tao Te Ching*, 12 (49). Aristotle finds quick-wit a virtue, situated between the extremes of buffoonery and boorishness. [♪] Aristotle, *Nichomachean Ethics*, 78 (1128a).

meaningful; do not poke their sacred spot. Joke about flotsam. Riff about yourself. Twist odd things people say. Juxtapose ill-companioned images. Remember, if you are able, the cadence of jokes that injure none and humor all. Life stages a comedy of errors. If you find nothing amusing, you are not paying attention.

> WHEN CHATTERERS SPEAK, UNSTABLE WINDS BLOW.
> ONE LISTENS, SEEKING COMPREHENSION.
> ONE INTERACTS, SEEKING RECIPROCITY.
> CHATTERERS, OFFENDED, SPIN THEIR TORNADO.
> ONE MURMURS, TITILLATED RABBLE.
> ONE DEPARTS IN SILENCE.

7.27. *Community.* **Simple Rule: Support, but question, others.** You may ask, if we are to live in community by consensus, is not life reduced to a series of half-hearted capitulations to a group's sensitivities? No, one hopes. Your mind is active, Kate. Your gifts must be exercised. All are equal, and yet none are the same. You, Kate, are spread through your friends. You smear into workplaces. A bit of you smudges the larger social structures in which you participate. Assist friends, workplaces, and your community in succeeding. You need them to prosper. They need you to make headway. The alternatives are really quite awful. Consider slums. Consider nuclear arms races and civil wars. Consider depressions, psychological or economic.

But when you have participated and fit in fully, that is not all. Here, we reach a deep trench in the ocean of human consciousness. Humans sail a bifurcated sea, crossing, usually unawares, deep places and deeper places. We are deeply collective. Yet more deeply, you are particular.[951] Communities pray your conformity. Your depths hide two subterrains. One is a deep willing to conform and struggling to do so. The other abyss plunges miles further. You harbor an aspect unconformable, your adamantine oddity.[952] Some style this reliable core as one's "destiny." Perhaps such exuberances overstate. It is sufficient to say of oneself that some things can be changed. Others cannot. Accept both the plastic and the granitic within. Extinguish neither.

---

[951] Emma Goldman argues that the big problem facing humans is how to remain oneself and be simultaneously connected intimately with others. Goldman, "The Tragedy of Woman's Emancipation," in *Anarchism and other Essays*, 100.

[952] Of this incommensurate self, you can read some interesting bombast in Stirner or Nietzsche.

The world around us is governed with decidedly feeble wisdom, Kate.[953] Do not think, when offended, that you misunderstand or lack perspective. Do not rationalize shrinking into shadows. Your incapacities, whatever they may be, do not validate others' inanities. Most people do not know what they are doing most of the time. They guess. Socrates was tempted to advise friends to humble and check friends, not to coddle and flatter them.[954] The most authoritative, gung-ho, towering male with booming diction and testosterone-spewing confidence spouts ill-deliberated drivel in need of a good ethical thrashing.[955] Never submit, Kate.[956] Political power leans heavily upon the willing obedience of people such as you. Without people like you, political power wobbles, then crumbles. If you similarly influence your friends, and they theirs, then erosion of power grows more rapid.[957] So, satisfy yourself. Never acquiesce until you can say "good enough." Ask questions. Inspect evidence. Do so politely, but firmly.[958] Remember: the people in charge, and their predecessors, invented the world you live in. From my perspective, human cultures are not working all that well. Perhaps someone should ask more questions. So, articulate what you see.[959] Listen to the answers, but do not endorse every

---

[953] "Do you not know, my son, with how little wisdom the world is governed?" *"An nescis, mi fili, quantilla prudentia mundus regatur?"* Axel Oxenstierna (1583-1654), Swedish pragmatist statesman, in a letter to his son, Johan, written in 1648, encouraging Johan to hold his own in negotiations for the Peace of Westphalia, which treaty eventually ended the Thirty Years' War.

[954] Plato, *Lysis*, 153 (210e). Socrates always resisted giving advice, preferring difficult questions.

[955] [♪] Emerson, *Conduct of Life*, 1032 (IV): "And the youth must rate as its true mark the inconceivable levity of local opinion. The longer we live, the more we must endure the elementary existence of men and women; and every brave heart must treat society as a child, and never allow it to dictate."

[956] Mencius argues that one cannot improve another by corrupting oneself. *Mencius*, 65 (Book III, Part B, Section 1).

[957] Gene Sharp calls obedience the "heart of political power." Political obedience derives, on the participant's side of matters, from habit, fear of coercion, a sense of moral obligation, self-interested considerations, emotional identification with ruler(s), indifference, and lack of self-confidence in one's contrary views. Sharp, *The Politics of Nonviolent Action*, Part One, 16-24.

[958] "O, it is excellent to have a giant's strength; but it is tyrannous to use it like a giant." Shakespeare, *Measure for Measure*, act 2, scene 2.

[959] Ralph Waldo Emerson urged his reader to tolerate no nonsense: "[S]peak the rude truth in all ways. . . . Your goodness must have some edge to it,—else it is none." [♪] Emerson, *Self-Reliance*, 262. William James opined: "[T]he highest ethical life . . . consists at all times in the breaking of rules which have grown too narrow for the actual case." James, *The Moral Philosopher and the Moral Life*, 183.

scrap of plausible-sounding drivel that tickles your eardrum.[960] Friedrich Nietzsche complained that most people want every man well-leashed and busy as a windmill.[961] Remove your collar, Kate. Bury your lead. Take some time to reflect. Do not fret to find yourself alone in dissent. You may be right anyway. Gandhi said that real men ignore their superiors' immoral commands.[962] Listen, but cherish your own insights over those of others; do not be a reed in the wind, bending this way, then that, in every vacillating breeze.[963] Thoreau said that a person who sees clearly, despite thunderous catcalling, is a majority of one.[964] Lao Tzu noticed that when the inferior man hears the Way, he laughs, for it is the nature of the Way to be denigrated by the foolish many.[965] Mencius argued that only people who refuse to behave poorly accomplish great things.[966] Recognize the best thoughts in each conversation. Honor the speaker of those thoughts, even if the speaker is you.

Fear guides most people. They bow to power. Most duck and cower. Humans bleat when they hunker. Authority renders masses into ruminant herds, slaved to their ram, cowering, obedient.[967] Stand, alone if necessary. Your opinion of you matters most.[968] Speak your piece.[969] Mass hysterics may punish you for dissenting. Emerson argued that all acts of deep conscience are deemed illegal by the communities in which they are fomented.[970] Take their licks. Rise from prostration, smile, and pester the errant with yet more questions.[971]

---

[960] Muhammad enjoins Islamists to avoid being gullible, to see with one's eyes, hear with one's ears, and discern with one's heart, so that, when you act, you know you do what is true and best. [♪] Muhammad, *Qur'an* 17:36.

[961] [♪] Nietzsche, *On the Genealogy of Morals*, 87.

[962] [♪] Gandhi, *Satyagraha*, 53.

[963] *Matthew* 11:7.

[964] [♪] Thoreau, *On the Duty of Civil Disobedience*, 259.

[965] [♪] Lao Tzu, *Tao Te Ching*, 3 (41).

[966] *Mencius*, 90 (Book IV, Part B, Section 8).

[967] Martin Luther King Jr. noted that groups of humans embrace immorality more readily than do individuals. King attributed this insight to Reinhold Niebuhr, a twentieth century neo-orthodox theologian. [♪] King, *Autobiography*, 191.

[968] Seneca, *Epistles 1-65*, 209 (XXIX, 11).

[969] Seneca, *Epistles 1-65*, 239 (XXXIII, 8).

[970] [♪] Emerson, *Conduct of Life*, 1074 (VI): "[F]or the highest virtue is always against the law." Martin Luther King Jr. said that the journey toward freedom often demands travel through jails. [♪] King, *Autobiography*, 113.

Militant irenic anarchists work their subversion of malign norms with the machine gun of persistent inquiry. Pacifists build their armies with emotional intelligence, cementing bonds with loyal, like-minded friends. A better, more human, world waits the midwifery of thoughtful, supportive, inveterate interrogation. Ask questions. When you criticize, offer alternatives.[972] Remember the ease of demolition and the difficulty of creating. Do not let harsh insight outrun planning the good. Make an opponent's task your own; invite him to join you. But question.

If recalcitrance proves immovable, do not shred your life in opposition. Build your community. Depart people of dead habit, tenaciously gripped. Exercise the wisdom of exodus. Wish stuck people well. Leave your door ajar. But move on.

7.28. *Vocation.* **Simple Rule: Work to help others.** Choose vocations in which you contribute to human well-being. Make yourself useful to others; a life of service enriches.[973] Take jobs because they help someone or create something needful, not because of their hefty paychecks.[974] People pay for competent assistance. There are jobs that prey upon human foibles. Do not run a casino. Avoid selling people things no one really needs. Flee trades succoring vanity. Sometimes, what seemed a worthy enterprise turns out to be altogether otherwise. If you have a bad job, find a better one. Make the most of bad jobs, while you are stuck in them. In the long run, seek autonomy in your work. You want to call the shots in your world, so you can stay flexible and adaptive.[975] If you have that ability, others may need you to make decisions for them as well.[976] Find work that suits your peculiar traits and abilities. Take what you know of yourself to the marketplace

---

[971] [♪] Emerson, *Conduct of Life*, 1031 (IV): "Take the shame, the poverty, and the penal solitude, that belong to truth-speaking. Try the rough water as well as the smooth. Rough water can teach lessons worth knowing. When the state is unquiet, personal qualities are more than ever decisive. Fear not a revolution which will constrain you to live five years in one. Don't be so tender at making an enemy now and then."

[972] Mo says that to do otherwise is to fight a flood with water or fire with fire. Such strategies have no meaningful effect. [♪] *Mozi*, 42 (Part III, §16).

[973] Seneca, *Epistles 1-65*, 425 (LX, 4).

[974] Seneca notes that good people decline busy-work, as well as work that lacks intrinsic merit. Seneca, *Epistles 1-65*, 153 (XXII, 8). Heraclitus notes that the exchanges of work are cyclical; one acquires to sell, then sells to acquire. Heraclitus, Haxton translation, *Fragments*, 22. Leaning upon business transactions for one's sense of meaning might dismay. The marrow lies in helpful effect, not profitable antics.

[975] [♪] Russell, "What I Believe," 366.

[976] Heavily adapted from Pillemer, *30 Lessons for Living*, 51-83.

when you seek work. This proves difficult because at the time you must make some vocational decisions, you are young and do not know yourself as well as you will later in life.[977] For idle persons, the future holds a wealth of psychological scab-picking. Make yourself busy doing well for others, both members and communities. You will avoid both boredom and self-recrimination.[978] Insist that your job leaves you sufficient time to nurture yourself, your friends, and to participate in making the planet a better place to live for everyone. The purpose of work is to gain these freedoms.[979] If your boss wants more from you, get a different boss. Take care not to let work consume you. William Godwin thought that, in a world lacking luxuries, war, and over-reaching governments, no more than thirty minutes per day would be required of each human being to meet his fundamental needs.[980] When deciding how much to work, consider what riches you might create during the time you did not work for money.

7.29. *Food.* **Simple Rule: Eat for nutrition.** Eat to keep your body healthy. Eating serves social and entertainment purposes, as well as those of nutrition. In grocery stores, nutrition hovers at the perimeter; fun foods crowd the central aisles. Chronic obesity lurks in the central aisles, at least for most of us.[981] Eat fresh. Eat local, to the extent possible. Eat simply most of the time.[982] Eat meat like your Pleistocene ancestors did—as often as they could, which was not all that often.[983] You can eat fun foods occasionally. Don't let the foods you consume consume you.

---

[977] [♪] Cicero, *De Officiis*, 115-123 (Book I, Section XXXI, 113 – XXXIII, 120).

[978] [♪] Seneca, *On Tranquillity of Mind*, 36.

[979] [♪] Aristotle, *Politics*, 196-197 (Book VIII, Section 3), and [♪] Aristotle, *Nichomachean Ethics*, 6115-617 (Book X, sub vii, sections 6-7).

[980] [♪] Godwin, *Political Justice*, Vol. II, 353 (Book VIII, Chapter VI).

[981] *Mea culpa.*

[982] Seneca, *Epistles 1-65,* 39 (VIII, 5).

[983] Peter Singer reports the extent to which our meat foodstuffs are produced by warrantlessly cruel methods. Higher mammals, and possibly others as well, have interests, and experience pain and suffering. Industrial meat production, egg harvesting, and milking disregard suffering of the animals we later enjoy at our tables. Corporations also use animals for testing, experimentation, and research, all with little regard to the suffering of the subject animals. If one's morality eschews senseless suffering, then one must consider boycotting the industrial products that result from the instrumental use of animals. Singer himself recommends vegetarianism. He draws the line at mollusks. (This line itself seems arbitrary. Mollusks, worms, and plants would also seem to have interests, if one chooses to project human-like mentation upon them. One can see, however, on a sliding scale from gorillas to bacteria, that some entities have a greater claim to sentient suffering than do others.) There are sound mathematical reasons to choose vegetarianism, all apart from moral concern for animal suffering. An ounce of vegetable protein requires less energy and land to produce than an ounce of animal protein. Singer, *Animal Liberation*, 159-183. On a hyperpopulous planet burdened with a dominant species disinclined to pare its numbers, such considerations grow persuasive as re-

7.30. *Sleep.* **Simple Rule: Protect your sleep.** Humans are built to sleep and wake in the cycles of east African diurnalism, nodding off when dark, rising with the sun. Our minds and culture betray us when they tell us we can sleep otherwise. Night shifts, artificial light, early meetings and late, all nighters, and sleep whittled by busy-ness or worry: all nibble sleep, leaving a spindly core. Sleep deprivation leads to increases in car collisions, weight gain, diabetes, heart disease, depression, substance abuse, diminished learning capacity, and mood shifts. Too much sleep can cause many of the same complications.[984] Learn how much sleep you need. Get that much. Cut out disruptive fluff. Avoid unreasonable schedule shifts. Your body works better when sleep and waking arrive at the same time each day. Get some blinds and earplugs, if necessary. Turn off your phone. Tell your friends when your bedtime arrives. Let them go home and respect your sleep. They need their sleep too. Make your bedroom a place to sleep. Keep the room cool, quiet, and very dark. Fresh air is critical. Avoid coffee and alcohol before bed.[985] Crawl into bed, Kate. Sleep enough.

7.31. *Exercise.* **Simple Rule: Stay active.** In Pleistocene Africa, one walked to live. One hunted, gathered, chased children, danced to appease gods, and moved camp as prey migrated. Western culture emphasizes planning and literacy. Neither drives us to move much. Read books, or write books. But do so only before, after, or between bouts of activity.[986] Humans act, then think, then act afresh, then again reflect. Give life a fertile oscillation. Activity informs thought. Thought redirects and enriches action.

7.32. *Flourishing.* **Simple Rule: Flourish.** Find more than mere existence. Choose to flourish. Do not choose barely adequate inner wealth. Never persist for long periods in circumstances that dampen your spirits. Make changes in yourself, and then your circumstances, that let you flourish. Unfurl yourself. Express your uniqueness; utilize your gifts. When you have eaten well, slept adequately, loved your friends, gotten some exercise, and stimulated your brain by learning something new, you should feel good,

---

source utilization climbs toward its maximum. A planet of fifteen billion humans may have little choice but to limit itself to proteins produced by plants.

[984] See online: http://www.sleepfoundation.org/article/how-sleep-works/how-much-sleep-do-we-really-need.

[985] Several of these recommendations derive from Penelope Lewis, *The Secret World of Sleep*, 175-185.

[986] Cicero chides son Marcus never to study with such intensity that he neglects active living. [♪] Cicero, *De Officiis*, 21 (Book I, Section VI, 19). Seneca worries that reading many books distracts and makes one indecisive. He recommends focusing on a few masters. Seneca, *Epistles 1-65*, 7 (II, 2-3).

ready to grapple with life's challenges. If not, you are not flourishing. Change something.

7.33. *Smallness.* **Simple Rule: Keep life simple.** Keep your life bounded and manageable. Avoid letting any portion of your life grow disproportionately. In medicine, such proliferating tissue is cancerous, tending to export itself to unwelcome places (metastasis). Think small but elegant. Choose intensity over extension. Eat to be nourished. Choose clothing that keeps you warm and comfortable. Drink to satisfy thirst. Live in a modest house that meets your simple needs.[987] Avoid clutter. Sidestep obsessions. Prefer adequacy over wonders. Embellish one thing only: your lavish private interior life. Make of Kate a succulent garden. Be an extravagantly wise and nuanced companion. Keep everything else functional and unpretentious.[988]

7.34. *Order.* **Simple Rule: Stay orderly.** Keep things in their place. Keep up on maintenance of your body and living space.[989] Every time you lose something, you waste time better expended otherwise. Every time you reinvent a procedure you previously worked out, you rob yourself of a fragment of life. Keep a calendar. Put things away. Change your vehicle's oil. Make a choice; enact that choice. Never believe people who say they multitask. Human attention barely extends to one task at a time, and that with plentiful distractions and faltering. Make life a continuous string of wellconceived useful acts.

7.35. *Quiet.* **Simple Rule: Keep life quiet.** Technological society and human hyperpopulation stuff living with noise and diversion. Devices make conversation, music, and jabber ubiquitous. Headsets render sounds of choice unobtrusive, and therefore more seductive. The result can be life without silence. Quiet fosters careful deliberation.[990] Silence permits reflection.[991] Even when speaking, do so softly. Subtle thoughts do not survive boisterous emission.[992] In a world ajar with rumbling cacophony, one must constantly suppress noise. Foster quiet in your world.[993] Make time

---

[987] Seneca, *Epistles 1-65,* 39 (VIII, 5).

[988] Seneca, *Epistles 1-65,* 111 (XVII, 5). Great souls prefer modesty. Seneca, *Epistles 1-65,* 261 (XXXIX, 4).

[989] [♪] Cicero, *De Officiis,* 15-17 (Book I, Section IV, 14). Only man, among animals, cares much about order.

[990] Rousseau disagrees. He asserts that those who meditate live against human nature. The meditator is bestial. Rousseau, "A Discourse on the Origin of Inequality," 56.

[991] See Seneca, *Epistles 1-65,* 373-381 (LVI).

[992] Seneca, *Epistles 1-65,* 257 (XXXVIII, 1).

[993] Zen masters advocate structuring one's quiet as meditations (*Zazen*). Sit in quiet place, erect, on a thick cushion. Protrude your abdomen, breathe gently, and enter a concentrated trance (*Samadhi*).

for silent solitude; quietude arms you to brook the onslaught of mass half-baked opinion.[994] Hush.

7.36. *Long-Shots*. **Simple Rule: Season life with difficult tasks.** Quad ethical choices tend to make life simpler and more functional. From that stable place of equilibrium, choose at least some worthwhile enterprises that may not work out. Life tastes better when a bit of uncertainty spices its meat and potatoes. We all differ in our need for the demanding task, for the undertaking that demands all (or more than all) our concentration and effort. But there is some balance right for you, Kate. Do not shy from harsh adventure.[995]   An ascetic muscle lies within you, waiting to be exercised.[996] Pleasure and pain mislead occasionally. Some worthy pursuits bear fruit only when planted in a soil of substantial pain. Unrelenting pleasure dulls the mind. Nevertheless, do not choose harshness for its own sake. Choose at least some harsh paths that lead to great goods. Embrace well-deliberated risks.[997]

7.37. *Exposure*. **Simple Rule: Stay open to novelty.** Go places. Learn new ideas and adopt those that are workable. Stay open to odd experiences. Ask questions of strangers doing weird things. Learn their ways. Keep nourishing yourself with fresh perspectives. When something new emerges, take a taste; spend a moment familiarizing yourself. Prefer "yes" to "no." As Aristophanes said, "What unlooked-for things do happen, to be sure, in a long life!"[998]   Be glad for serendipity. Savor and embrace it, looking on its interruption as masked opportunity.

7.38. *Aging*. **Simple Rule: Embrace, but resist, aging.** As your decades race past, reduce your physical labor, but increase your mental work.[999] Where lived well, the end of life holds delight in existence and brims with

---

To improve one's meditation, read a classic on the subject. An hour of meditation is an hour of being Buddha, they contend. [♪] Conze, *Buddhist Scriptures*, 134-135 (citing Sessan Amakuki, *On Hakuin's Zazen Wasan*, 141-154).

[994] [♪] Emerson, *Conduct of Life*, 1028 (IV).

[995] "Our doubts are traitors, and make us lose the good we oft might win by fearing to attempt." Shakespeare, *Measure for Measure*, act 1, scene 5.

[996] James, *The Varieties of Religious Experience*, 293-94.

[997] Confucius argues that to know what is right to do, and yet to avoid it, is cowardice. [♪] Confucius, *Analects*, 66 (Book II, Section 24).

[998] Aristophanes, *Lysistrata*, 14.

[999] [♪] Cicero, *De Officiis*, 125-127 (Book I, Section XXXIV, 123).

memories of good deeds and glowing moments.[1000] Desirable habits that have long eluded you in your youth fix themselves within you more readily as you age. Lusts subside. The mosaic of your character coalesces in a cascade, just as the final pieces in a jigsaw puzzle find their homes speedily. Your vices struggle with senility, just as your mind crests the summit of its powers. Many win moral battles in old age.[1001] Resist your body's dysfunctions of age; fix what declines. Exercise, learn new things, go places, take reasonable steps to forestall incapacities. When what remains of your life is a scrap, neither surrender it for no good reason nor cling to it tenaciously.[1002] Open your arms to aging. Its depredations are natural, your end certain. Manage your dying: build a care team, make financial arrangements, avoid hospitals and dramatic interventions, take time to help others cope with your approaching absence. Death caps your grandest project— you. Relish the richness of what has come before. Welcome the next, last thing.

7.39. *Illness.* **Simple Rule: Endure illness patiently.** Our bodies consist in a highly coordinated community of more than fifty trillion cells and a vast host of symbiotic micro-organisms. This ride-along menagerie is called the microbiota, a thousand species of bacteria numbering approximately ten times the number of human cells. The microbiota comprise one to three percent of normal body weight. All normally work together to maintain healthy homeostasis.[1003] When you are injured or when a micro-biotic community goes to war with your body, you feel poorly. Energy otherwise available for life activities diverts to defending or healing your body. All this activity transpires unconsciously. Your body requires nothing from you but to wait patiently for it to do its work. Many people worry when sick. They imagine ugly outcomes. They fret. They run to doctors and take meaningless pills. Each moment spent worrying wastes that fragment of your life. You best assist your body as it heals itself by resting, preserving

---

[1000] Cicero, *De Senectute*, 17-19 (Section III, 9). Viktor Frankl notes that old age, in one who has lived well, holds a wealth of fulfilled meanings. The young have a future filled with tenuous possibilities. The old have a past ripe with achieved events. Frankl, *Man's Search for Meaning*, 151.

[1001] Seneca, *Epistles 1-65*, 187 (XXVI, 2). Confucius says that, though he worked at his moral challenges all through life, he did not learn to hew to his own line until his seventies. [♪] Confucius, *Analects*, 63 (Book II, Section 4).

[1002] Cicero, *De Senectute*, 45 (Section XI, 36); 85 (Section XX, 73). See also Seneca, *Epistles 1-65*, 409 (LVIII, 35-37).

[1003] MacDougall, Raymond (13 June 2012). "NIH Human Microbiome Project defines normal bacterial makeup of the body". *NIH*. http://www.nih.gov/news/health/jun2012/nhgri-13.htm. See also, Ackerman, "How Bacteria In Our Bodies Protect Our Health."

healthy optimism, and patiently waiting the matter to run its course. Watch a movie. Take a nap.

7.40. *Perspective.*   **Simple   Rule: Live   from   mortality's   viewpoint.** Thanatoid perspective dampens transitory urgencies.   To decide well, husband a longer view of life, a view from generations after your death, perhaps many generations.   Recognize transience: yesterday, a squirt of semen; tomorrow, nothing but spices and ash.[1004]   Live as though you might die today.   You might.   Thanatoid thinking keeps what matters most at the forefront.[1005]   Look forward to aging; you are growing wiser.   Treat your body like you need it for 100 years.   You may.   Don't worry about dying. Worry wastes life.   You are, then you are not.   Remember: you were not, then you were.[1006]   Death is your personal bookend.   Stay connected to others as you age.   Plan where and how you will live when old.   Do not clutch at life.[1007]   Death interrupts us as naturally as did birth; both arrive without our consent.   You control conduct, not death.   Live well.[1008]

7.41. *Griefs.* **Simple Rule: Be patient with grief.**   Loss strikes all.   Grandparents, parents, pets, siblings, friends, spouse, children, famous people, the infamous, all commoners, even you yourself: all suffer; all eventually die. 130 years from now, every human presently alive on the planet will be dead.   Human bodies often shudder at grief's blows.   Sadness gives way to tear-struck somnolence.   Anger, depression, denial, and bargaining ensue, in widening circles of frustration.   This solemn pattern does not govern all grievers.[1009]   For all, though, over time, the din of anguish wanes.   Acquiescence dawns, only to be drowned in resurgent pain.   After some years, on-

---

[1004] [♪] Aurelius, *To Himself*, 75 (Book IV).   Epictetus says, "Let death and exile and every other thing which appears dreadful be daily before your eyes; but most of all death; and you will never think of anything mean nor will you desire anything extravagantly."   Epictetus, *Enchiridion*, 22 (XXI).

[1005] Cicero admonishes us to be satisfied with whatever time we have to live.   Cicero, *De Senectute*, 81 (Section XIX, 69).

[1006] So Aurelius styles human individual transience.   [♪] Aurelius, *To Himself*, 95 (Book IV, Section 48).

[1007] Seneca, *Epistles 1-65*, 15-17 (IV, 5).

[1008] Seneca, *Epistles 1-65*, 159 (XXII, 17).

[1009] The most common patterns of grief are chronic grief (in which people recover only very slowly, if at all), gradual recovery (where resuming normal life takes substantial time), and resilience (in which the initial shock of loss gives way to rapid resumption of one's life pattern before loss). Bonanno, *The Other Side of Sadness*, 6-7.

going pain squeezes into the subconscious and the rhythm of life is restored. Grief hides, gnawing silently, but a revised equilibrium emerges.[1010]

Grief is one price of human consciousness. One knows that death stands irrevocable. Yet one's bonds to a decedent are inextricable. Social interpenetration crashes into inevitability head on. Agony amputates a limb of one's identity. Grief mangles life. Grief constitutes its own sort of loss. One may grieve grief. Grief surfaces from deeper in our evolutionary history than rationality. Many higher mammals grieve social loss.[1011] Because grief is a limbic recovery, one cannot rationally predict its course. Every grief is idiosyncratic, snatching its mystic program from subconscious depths of affective life. Grief cannot be rushed. Wait for grief to resolve, Kate. Grieve patiently. Do not push yourself to be done with it. Grief exceeds volition. Wait grief's passing, as one does violent thunderstorms. Take a deep breath. Let it out. The hand that brings grief exceeds ours. We bow. Resilience in the face of grief is a door to wisdom.[1012]

7.42. *Faith*. **Simple Rule: Cherish faith.** Recognize your faith.[1013] Most people associate faith with a particular religious hegemony. But one's faith exceeds transitory allegiance to institutions. A man's faith consists in those convictions for which no conclusive evidence exists, but which are nevertheless necessary for his life.[1014] These are convictions of the following sort: I matter; others matter; I am essentially connected to others; life exceeds humanity; life is deeper than our ideas about it;[1015] peace matters more than progress; humans share life with non-human species; mystery engulfs us; unity and diversity are not poles but reflections. No man knows

---

[1010] See Kübler-Ross, *On Death and Dying*. Bonanno disputes Kubler-Ross's "stage" theory of grief as to both its factual basis and its utility. Bonanno, *The Other Side of Sadness*, 22.

[1011] King, "When Animals Mourn," 64.

[1012] Every person has a faith of some sort. Russell, "A Free Man's Worship," 41.

[1013] Bertrand Russell recognizes that man is a believing animal. Men adopt beliefs of some sort. Lacking good foundations upon which to premise faith, man suffices with bad ones. Russell, "An Outline of Intellectual Rubbish," 64.

[1014] Tolstoy, in defining faith, notes that every man, if he is alive, believes in something. [♪] Tolstoy, *A Confession*, 37 (Chapter IX). William James offers a wonderfully cogent defense of believing in matters for which one can offer little evidence. [♪] James, *Will To Believe*. Nicholas Wade asserts that "an instinct for religious behavior is indeed an evolved part of human nature." It gave a survival advantage to people who practiced religious rites. Wade, *The Faith Instinct*, 6.

[1015] Max Weber concludes that even as the philosopher speaks, he knows his words somehow hollow. The deep, existential glimmers of life evade capture in mere nets of ideas. Weber, *The Varieties of Religious Experience*, 446. Several *Upanishads* asserts that ultimate reality exceeds all human thought. See, for example, *Upanishads*, 58 (*Katha Upanishad*, Part 2).

god; most, however, suspect the numen and mana.[1016]   Faith commitments are supra-rational, but not irrational.   Faith finds rationality too sorely hobbled to express faith's perceptions.   Human consciousness exceeds its observations.

One's faith gives life a shape.   Propositions about faith disappoint. Language can never quite capture the deep resonances of conviction.   Faith is more serious than words.   Words are chaff, blown in swirls and piles. Faith sinks its roots deeply into life, providing support and a sense of place. Your faith issues action.   Faith exceeds ideas about faiths.   You will recognize your particular faith commitments in others.   Converse with those who share your faith.   Your faith has nooks and crannies that you have not yet explored, which to others may be familiar.

One can distinguish among faiths of two sorts.[1017]   One species of "faith" asserts that there exists a world beyond this world, a suburb of the cosmos of which knowledge is scarce, but precious.   Of this supra-mundane region, humans know much or little, depending upon the conceits of the speaker.   This first sort of faith insists that meaning burgeons in recognizing the hidden concourse between our life and this superior realm.   Some of this ilk assert that supra-mundane denizens speak or write books, which tomes

---

[1016] "Numen" denotes implicit influences that can be perceived, but not by the senses.   In the Roman usage, numen trended toward suspicions of divine nudging, though some authors use the term to mean "impressive potency."   In sycophantic moments, emperors were applauded for the numen that attended them.   "Mana" derives from Pacific Islander cultures, denoting hidden power resident in all people, objects, and animals.   Some Indian perceptions of the divine are immanent, even psychologized.   The Law Code of Manu (a Brahmanist ancient Indian legal system) concludes: "With a collected mind, a man should see in the self everything, both the existent and the non-existent; for when he sees everything in the self, he will not turn his mind to what is contrary to the Law.   All the deities are simply the self, the whole world abides within the self; for the self gives rise to engagement in action on the part of these embodied beings."   *Law Code of Manu*, 219 (Section 12.118-119).

[1017] There have been persistent (and, to date, unsuccessful) attempts to state a third alternative frame for religious faith.   These efforts seek ecumenical breadth, building on elements common to many existing faiths.   Consider two recent examples.   Karen Armstrong seeks to state an inclusive compassionate faith.   She takes as her rudiment that one should act toward others in the manner one hopes others will act toward oneself.   From this basis, she builds a (mostly secular Buddhist) framework of inclusive compassionate faith, amenable to those of many different faith traditions.   Armstrong, *Twelve Steps to a Compassionate Life*, 144-145.   In a deeply secular way, Joshua Greene seeks to provide a "coherent global moral philosophy" that addresses the shortcomings of humanity's natural preferences, adjusting those with approaches that may resolve disputes among different moral tribes.   This is a utilitarian meta-morality, one that may not always "feel" right, but has the great merit of actually working.   Greene advises that humans should 1) recognize the shortcomings of our moral inclinations, 2) use "rights" language sparingly, since it terminates conversations, 3) find and focus on the facts in disputes, and insist everyone else do so as well, 4) beware of hidden self-serving biases in our preferences, 5) focus on general happiness; choose impartial rules, and 6) give to those who lack.   Greene's approach boils down to qualified restatement of utilitarian priorities, which Greene styles as "deep pragmatism."   Greene, *Moral Tribes*, 14-15, 350-352.

are sacral.[1018]   Others assert that knowledge of the realm lies within, untapped by the dumb masses, but revealed to cognoscenti.[1019]   All versions of this first perspective on faith I call religion.   Religious faith often expresses sordid conceit.   Parishioners say to outsiders, My knowledge of unknowable matters exceeds your knowledge of unknowable matters.[1020]   In this sentiment, religious hatreds find kindling.   After much unjustified murder, religions lose steam.   Over centuries, they congeal into empty formalism and vacant ritual and financial desperation.   Yet within the desert of religious institutions, freshets of sacred life burble unexpectedly, restoring vitality from time to time.[1021]

Another brand of "faith" proves more circumspect.   This second view finds that life demands practical acquiescence in ideas that transcend human observation and rational analysis.   Such believers claim little for these mutating propositions, other than that they seem modestly useful.   This second "faith" lacks revelations and theodictic moments.[1022]   Life exceeds language.   Living greatly exceeds the bounded imagination of rationality.   The

---

[1018] Examples of this sort of god-talk faith are Judaism, Christianity, Islam, Mormonism, and Brahmanism (Hinduism).   Muhammad wrote that the *Qur'an* cannot be changed; he merely speaks what God reveals.   [♪] *Qur'an*, Sura 10:16.   No part of the *Qur'an* can be changed.   [♪] *Qur'an*, Sura 10:64.   Seyyid Qutb turns Qur'anic theodicion into an imagined global culture of Islamic coercion. [♪] Qutb, *Milestones*.   A Christian deutero-Pauline author argues that all scripture (probably meaning the Torah, Writings, and Prophets, as well as the Gospels) is inspired by God, and is profitable to the believer.   *II Timothy* 3:16-17.   God speaks plainly to Moses (*Exodus* 3) and Ezekiel (*Ezekiel* 2).   The Christian scripture, like the later *Qur'an*, cannot change (*Matthew* 5:18-19).   Most Buddhists avoid talking gods, but nonetheless understand themselves to be revealing ultimate truth, unvarnished by human hand.   Brahmanists insist that gods speak in the cacophony of their disparate religious literatures.   Emmanuel Swedenborg claimed that he spoke with angels and saw heaven episodically over a period of thirteen years.   Swedenborg, *Heaven and Hell*, 5 (Section 2).   Joseph Smith claims that an angel spoke to him, directing him to an ancient record, inscribed upon gold tablets, from which the Book of Mormon was subsequently translated by use of "two stones in silver bows" fastened to a breastplate (the Urim and Thummim).   Smith, *The Book of Mormon*, Introduction (Testimony of the Prophet Joseph Smith).

[1019] Examples of this sort of faith are American Transcendentalism, Buddhism, Brahmanism, mysticism, and New Age potpourri spiritualism.   Ibn Khaldûn (Islamic: 1377 A.D.) says: "It should be known that God has chosen certain individuals.   He honoured them by addressing them.   He created them so that they might know Him.   He made them connecting links between Himself and His servants.   There individuals are to acquaint their fellow men with what is good for them and to urge them to let themselves be guided aright.   They are to make it their task to keep their fellow men out of the fire of Hell and to show them the path to salvation."   Ibn Khaldûn, *Muqaddimah*, 70 (Sixth Prefatory Discussion).

[1020] The religious man seeks to make of sacrality a hardened gray concrete, when sacrality is ever a glistening fluid, flowing here, sliding there, elusive of capture.

[1021] Lucian portrays Zeus complaining that Timon must be a philosopher, for philosophers are given to impudence and impious comments about established religions.   Lucian, *Timon, or the Misanthrope*, 333(Section 7).

[1022] To remind the reader, I have coined the term "theodictic" to specify experiences after which one asserts a god has spoken to or through him.

faith you should cherish, Kate, is of this latter, humbler sort.[1023]   Empiricism,[1024] which no man undertakes seriously, truncates human experience,
leading one to disparage faith convictions upon which flourishing life
thrives.[1025] Let your "conviction of things unseen"[1026] be idiosyncratic,
carved to the contours of your inwardness. Russell calls this delimited, su-
pra-institutional faith, a "free man's worship."[1027]

Never allow institutions to convince you that your convictions are sub-
standard. Institutions regurgitate the faith of dead persons, and fill chairs
with mostly uncomprehending adherents, desperate to belong to something,
anything. Religious institutions are ossified bureaucracies, committed to
acts their founders rejected.[1028] All institutions consist in petrified thought
of greater or lesser utility.[1029] The onus lies upon every institution to justify
its continued existence. Where that defense is wanting, communities should
dismantle their offending bureaucracies, religious or secular, in favor of redirected initiatives of action and thought. Retire tottering ideas; surrender
the field to deliberated alternatives. Encourage persistent revision in your
community. Every change discomfits; persistence in errant non-solutions
emasculates a community. Choose perplexity in change over comfortable
petrifaction.[1030]

Some persons claim they lack faith.[1031] If a person has never loved,
never scratched a dog's ear just because the dog relished that touch, never

---

[1023] James, *Is Life Worth Living?*, 25.

[1024] The empiricist asserts that human knowledge consists in sense experience, winnowed by reason. All else is speculation.

[1025] "The greatest empiricists among us are only empiricist on reflection: When left to their instincts, they dogmatize like infallible popes." [♪] James, *Will to Believe*, 44-45.

[1026] *Hebrews* 11:1.

[1027] Russell, "A Free Man's Worship," 44.

[1028] Paraphrased from [♪] Tolstoy, *The Kingdom of God Is Within You*, 43.

[1029] [♪] Dewey, *Human Nature and Conduct*, 331. Herbert Read takes a view more dim. He calls modern institutions megalomaniac, self-perpetuating tyrannies, given to justifying their actions and spreading into every cranny of individual life. See Read, "My Anarchism," 92. One must seek to retain that which builds meaningful community, not that which is old (i.e., ancient, customary, ven-erable, historical, founding, usual, traditional, created by gods, or in accord with the way we have always done things).

[1030] Yevgeny Zamatyin eloquently addresses the dangers of bureaucratic ossification in his dystopian novel, *We*.

[1031] Nicholas Wade argues that human religious sentiment is genetic. Long before we became spe-cifically human, our primate ancestors found survival advantage in togetherness. One answer to the centrifugal force of individual self-interest was the compelling attraction of transcendent ritual and shared ideas about ultimate realities. Wade, *The Faith Instinct*, 39.

savored a dawn, or marveled at a happy juxtaposition of words, never shivered at life's abyssal depths, then he might lack faith. I know no such persons. Persons disavowing faith most often dispute connotations. They cannot stomach the idea that ecclesiastical institutions advocate faiths. And they will have none of that wretched vomit.[1032]   One often hears the theological cynic endorse hyper-restrictive epistemological rules, such as empiricism (which argues that one can know only what one can sense and reproduce for the senses of others) or philosophical skepticism (Socrates argued that one never reliably knows anything).[1033]   Peer past such obfuscations. Faith, in its essence, pertains not to gods or institutions, but to confidence that life transcends our ideas about it.[1034]

One can grasp what cannot be proved. One can act on such convictions. Much in this book reflects faith convictions: theological agnosticism, psychological interpenetration, the dangers of wealth, the non-necessity of child-bearing, anarchistic kithdom, irenism, consensual governance, the critical role of neurodiverse savants, the possibility of thanatoid deliberation, and many of these simple maxims for life. No convincing proof can be offered, though various evidences abound, some of which are cited. Still, lacking certainty, one chooses, or lets life choose by default. Human existence demands choice in the face of irremediable uncertainty. Faith casts a vote in the elections of human conduct.[1035]

Objection 28: Faith is Hubris: *Some demur that faith of any sort, including that personalized wretchedness this author advocates, is raw hubris. One*

[1032] See, for example, Freud's assertion that religion is mere illusion, rampant wish fulfillment projected on the canvas of the universe. Religion is mankind's neurotic obsession. [♪] Freud, *The Future of an Illusion*, 51, 78.

[1033] Jan Oppermann reminds me that Socratic skepticism was a pedogogical tool in the hands of a master teacher. Such skepticism welcomes speculation, which can be life-giving, and breaks the bonds of the usual in favor of exploration and serendipity. Oppermann, in private correspondence with the author, dated October 14, 2015. Sextus Empiricus argues all matters elicit arguments for and against. These are of relatively equal potency. The only answer is the skeptical answer: suspend judgment, avoid asserting anything, and embrace settled tranquility of mind. Sextus Empiricus, *Outlines of Scepticism*, 4-6 (Book I, Section iv, vi). (The English spell skepticism with a "c"; Americans spell it with a "k.")

[1034] [♪] Emerson, *Conduct of Life*, 1056 (VI): "We are born believing. A man bears beliefs, as a tree bears apples. . . . God builds his temple in the heart on the ruins of churches and religions."

[1035] Please note that I have mentioned nothing gods said. That omission is a critical component of useful faith talk. If gods murmur, humans are too deaf to hear. When humans listen for the divine oracle, they hear themselves listening. That said, I note, by way of full disclosure, that I became a Presbyterian of evangelical ilk at age eighteen, and though I departed that tradition with much *sturm und drang* (storm and stress), I remain a theist, often despite myself. I do not advocate theism, since no evidence exists for such opinions (or their alternatives). Still, theism attends me, like an unctuous, sometimes crabby, aunt.

knows little, and of things grand or metaphysical, nothing. Human grasp of truth remains feeble, even in the rigor of massive precautions. The sole hope in acquiring reliable facts lies in empiricism, and its discipline, the scientific method. Knowing one is inclined to believe seven impossible things before breakfast, one creates experiments that isolate some evidence for some hypothesis or other. If the result can be reproduced reliably by others, one has grasped something. Even to such reliable outcomes, the empiricist denies the name of truth, since the results are subject to revision by future investigation and analysis. The empiricist combats, not God, but unwarranted hubris in the believing human, in himself. We know little, but deem our circumstance otherwise. Extrapolating leaps of intuition may be a survival shorthand that permits rapid response to complex situations. These abbreviations find no place, however, in careful thinking. To permit oneself faith is to embrace delusion, to drown newborn doubt in the baptismal font.

Have you read the literature of believers? Sniff its stench wafting across centuries. Brahmanists audit tens of thousands of gods murmuring, one under every stone and happenstance, all mumbling for sacrifices, undercutting divine competitors. Buddhists declare the Brahmanist din a nullity. Men suffer for believing anything. Life's secret is nothingness. Be empty. Embrace nothing. One will then never be disappointed. Taoism advertises non-action. All sins involve commission, none omission. The Taoist Way is wide, difficult to map, and leads nowhere very rapidly. The faith of Israel embraces Yahweh, who launches his nation to genocide of their neighbors, and issues death sentences like parking tickets. Christians reform offensive Judaism, preferring a divinity so universally outraged that he must have the blood of all men, or that of his own son in their stead. Islam imagines god an Arabic-speaking sheriff-sheik, who judges laws narrowly, exacts horrific penalties, and sets his Bedouin hordes to compelling submission of all men at sword-point.[1036] Peoples embracing these assorted books spill much ink scribbling away the odious reek that wafts from their gods. Sadly, in inter-community relations, theologues prefer, if history be the judge, murder. Can you not hear the screech in their sacred words? Do you not detest the grime of their holy intolerance? All men would better prosper were faith utterly abolished from the earth.

Flee faith. Bite the bullet of empiricism. Its thin gruel is the only nourishment available to truth-seeking man.

Response: Much is true in this objector's spewing. Man's greatest crimes have been preached or supported or ignored by his various religions. Organized religions know who is theirs, and who is not. The alienation of men one from

---

[1036] Mustafa Akyol disagrees with this caricature of Islam. He argues, in his nicely-crafted book, that Islam dovetails nicely with an Islamic liberalism, including religious toleration, rationality, and diversity of political viewpoints. Akyol does, however, note that such liberal views are, among Islamists, a minority opinion. Akyol, *Islam Without Extremes*, 296-300. Toshihiko Izutsu offers careful linguistic analysis of the core ethico-religious words of the Qur'an, enlightening the changes to and rejection of pre-Islamic ideas extant in the Arab culture. Izutsu, *Ethico-Religious Concepts in the Qur'an*. Fazlur Rahman wrote a systematic theology of the Qur'an, taking up the scriptural ideas in an orderly fashion, which he calls a "synthetic exposition" of the book that calls itself "guidance for mankind." Rahman, *Major Themes of the Qur'an*, xv,1. Rahman finds in Sura 112, concerning the uniqueness of Allah, the core concept of the Qur'an. Rahman, *Major Themes of the Quran*, 11.

another commences with naming us and them. At such denomination, religions excel. The objector speaks well, also, in delimiting the possibility of reliable human knowledge. Much faith amounts to little more than veneration of antiquity or applause for charismatic personalities. What seems indubitable often proves otherwise. We are, in fact, inclined to erect verities more readily than our epistemological circumstance warrants. And that is, as the objector notes, raw hubris. The plain on which humility could erect its abodes is wide indeed, almost coterminous with consciousness itself. Our penchant for easy and abundant truth injures us.

The objector, however, misses a critical fact in his grim assessment of the influence of religions on human life. Among the grand humans our tenure on earth has produced, one guesses that a majority would be deemed devoted religionists. Some of the best of men adhere to religious institutions. Men have indulged orgies of slaughter in the name of their religions, it is true. But men of faiths often lead while others cower, and make passable, by their compassion and dedication, otherwise intolerable crises. Red-faced, religionists know Calvin burned Michael Servetus in Geneva, atop a pyre of Servetus's much-condemned books, to prove that Calvin was as fanatical for orthodoxy as his Roman inquisitorial counterparts. We also know that Gandhi rallied India, and King marched to Selma. Both were assassinated by reactionaries, and knew that might happen. Roman monks preserved Greek pagan writings. Billions find solace in religious belief of institutional tenor. The verdict on religious institutions is, therefore, decidedly mixed. Their sacred tale is one fraught with the frailties men suffer, and actions women lament. But a canvas of unrelieved black it is not. The panorama of institutional faiths is a splashwork of dabs, each bit a human color, some brilliant, some sullied. To paint this breathtaking landscape monotone with a single brush is to distort.

The objector, in his empiricism, sets a standard to which no human adheres. Human skepticism serves well in ferreting ill-deliberated ideas. Epistemological rigor expresses a frontal lobe shimmer in certain deeply-trained minds. Despite doubts, the remainder of every empiricist's brain perseveres. Empiricism erodes parts of life without which no man can survive. When the objector cuddles his children, he harbors no principled doubts about their existence. When he eats his steak, he never wonders if someone somewhere can verify that experience. When the objector cherishes his friends, he cannot shave them from his heart with Occam's razor.

One cherishes faith when one acknowledges a sober appreciation for the deeper brain functions that make us human: our metabolism, our reproduction, our sociality, our emotions, our cooperation, our compassion, and even our deep, inchoate intuitions that there is more to the world than we may directly perceive with five meager senses and an occasional smattering of rationality.[1037] The meal life sets before us is rich and diverse and satisfying. By faith, we eat. None should subsist on gruel alone, nor ask others to do so.

[1037] Frans de Waal notes that the Dutch call such perspectives "somethingism," betraying an uncategorized taste for personal gods, disdain for organized religions, and a haunting suspicion that things earthly are segregated from those divine by an occasionally permeable membrane. De Waal, *The Bonobo and the Atheist*, 109-110.

Evolution teaches that man's ultimate parent is a tidepool laden with amino acids, now shrouded by three billion winters. In the human imagination, one peels time to regain that puddle. One gazes upon its benighted surface. There, one perceives stars and galaxies reflected from the night sky. In little, we embrace much.

7.43. *Possessions.* **Simple Rule: Keep just enough possessions.** Possessions, and their mathematical cipher, money, can distort life.[1038] The wealth most to be valued arrives in forms other than money or possessions, such as friendship, human wisdom, familial harmony, education, mentoring, interpersonal and societal peace, a sense of well-being, elegant ideas, beauty, and freedom to pursue aspirations consistent with one's uniqueness.[1039] Of money, barely enough suffices. Love of money rots one's moral sensitivity.[1040] Pursuit of money robs one of time necessary for rich existence. Sages warn of money's dangers.[1041]

7.43.1. *Jesus* believed that no man can serve both God and money. Where a man's riches lie, there too lies his heart. One should earn and save possessions that do not rust or rot, and cannot be stolen.[1042] Jesus noted that

---

[1038] Cacioppo and Patrick argue that when money enters consciousness it stifles prosocial behaviors. Money motivates people, but merely thinking about money subliminally makes a person more willing to injure her neighbors. Cacioppo and Patrick, *Loneliness*, 264-265.

[1039] [♪] Emerson, *Conduct of Life*, 1010 (III): "The true thrift is always to spend on the higher plane; to invest and invest, with keener avarice, that he may spend in spiritual creation, not in augmenting animal existence." Michael Walzer argues that the problem with money is not money, but the universalization of money. All things cannot be reduced to or purchased with assets. Possessions, well-acquired, anchor our lives, though the nature of those anchors differs from person to person. Walzer styles things that cannot (or should not) be purchased for money as blocked exchanges, trades that we, as a culture, have decided should not be monetized. Walzer lists (non-exhaustively) these blocked exchanges: humans, political power and influence, criminal justice, freedom of speech, press, religion, assembly, marriage, procreation, the right to emigrate, exemption from public services, political office, police protection, primary and secondary education, trades made from desperation (minimum wages and maximum hours), most prizes and honors, divine approbation, love, friendship, and criminal activity (hiring hitmen). Money, rightly understood, offers exchange in commodities. Many (most?) other values cannot be monetized. Each has an interior logic of its own, and, in a just society, is distributed in accord with its internal logic. [♪] Walzer, *Spheres of Justice*, 99-104.

[1040] [♪] Cicero, *De Officiis*, 245-247 (Book II, Section XX, 71).

[1041] Rousseau hits the mark on possessions. He finds that the poor suffer due to scarcity, but the rich suffer due to surplus. Rousseau, "A Discourse on the Origin of Inequality: Appendix," 119.

[1042] Concerning wealth, Schopenhauer agrees with Jesus (apparently). Schopenhauer argues that wealth little improves happiness, and causes much disturbance. True wealth lies within a man. Schopenhauer, *The Wisdom of Life*, 16.

he had no physical home. If one would be perfect, she must donate her goods to those with greater need.[1043]

7.43.2. *Gandhi* argued that retaining wealth beyond one's needs, narrowly-construed, is theft. Gandhi made a daily point of eating the minimum food possible, since others starve. Human culture must regulate possession of money, and insist on social justice.[1044]

7.43.3. *Confucius* urged people to seek wisdom, not the full belly or comfortable home. Focusing interest on one's salary brings shame. Guard against hoarding.[1045] A gentleman pursues what is moral; the small man chases profit.[1046]

7.43.4. *Socrates* claimed to be nearest to the gods because he had the fewest desires. In the market, Socrates noted the vast number of things he could live without. Wealth and high birth bring upon a man only evil. Of all possessions, leisure is the best, since it can be used to accumulate knowledge and dispel ignorance.[1047] In the *Republic*, Socrates avers that real wealth consists, not in gold, but in what bestows happiness, which is a wise and good life.[1048]

7.43.5. *Lao Tzu* advised the wise man to avoid excess possessions. Giving makes one wealthy.[1049] The worst crime is lust for profit.[1050]

7.43.6. The Hebrew prophet *Isaiah* asserted that worship of Yahweh consists in sharing bread with those who hunger, giving shelter to the homeless, clothing the naked, and relieving the oppressed.[1051]

7.43.7. The Roman statesman *Cicero* warned his son against seeking wealth. Those who love money betray small souls. One must be indifferent toward money. If one acquired funds honestly, use funds to benefit others,

---

[1043] *Matthew* 5:19, 5:24, 8:20, 19:21. Proudhon follows this logic, in an anti-religious vein, with his assertion that property is theft. He says, "Property and society are completely irreconcilable with one another. . . . Either society must perish, or it must destroy property." Proudhon, *What is Property?*, 13, 43.

[1044] [♪] Gandhi, *Satyagraha*, §166.

[1045] [♪] Confucius, *Analects*, 61 (Book I, Section 14); 124 (Book XIV, Section 1); 140 (Book XVI, Section 7).

[1046] [♪] Confucius, *Analects*, 74 (Book IV, Section 16).

[1047] Diogenes Laertius, *Lives of Eminent Philosophers*: 155 (II, 25); 157 (II, 27); 161 (II, 31).

[1048] [♪] Plato, *Republic*, 227 (Book VII, 521a).

[1049] [♪] Lao Tzu, *Tao Te Ching*, 31 (81).

[1050] [♪] Lao Tzu, *Tao Te Ching*, 9 (46).

[1051] *Isaiah* 58:6-7.

and not for mere pleasure.   One should choose a way of life that avoids luxury, and brims with thrift, restraint, simplicity, and deliberate thought.[1052]   The purpose of wealth, if one has it, is to do good for others.[1053]   Love of money may sunder one from friends, which is a terrible outcome.[1054]   Wealth, honestly acquired, benefits one's family and friends, and bolsters one's community.   But there are many immoral paths to wealth, and so much moral danger.[1055]

7.43.8. *Mencius* said that people who aim at wealth cannot be benevolent, and the benevolent never become wealthy.   One must value morality above money.   One improves her heart by reducing desires.[1056]

7.43.9. *Seneca*, a wealthy Roman philosopher, urged his reader to have enough wealth to gain what is necessary and only merely enough.   One need not seek poverty, but should live plainly.[1057]   Nothing causes more misery than possessions to which one's heart grows attached.[1058]   To make a man rich, do not increase his money, but tame his desires.[1059]

7.43.10. *Mozi* urged rulers to avoid the pointless expense of luxuries and musical extravaganzas, and to invest in needed infrastructure.[1060]

7.43.11. *Muhammad* argued that wealth, and even families, can distract one from what matters most: devotion to God.[1061]   To purify herself, one gives her wealth away in a manner that keeps the donation between God and herself.[1062]

7.43.12. *Thoreau* argued that money and virtue are inversely proportional. "Absolutely speaking, the more money, the less virtue."   Money and its pursuit leave only sparse virtue.   Virtue and its acquisition preclude inor-

---

[1052] [♪] Cicero, *De Officiis*, 69 (Book I, Section XX), 97 (Book I, Section XXVI), 107-109 (Book I, Section XXX); 225 (Book II, Section XV).

[1053] [♪] Cicero, *De Officiis*, 237 (Book II, Section XVIII).

[1054] [♪] Cicero, *De Amicitia*, 147 (Section X, 34).

[1055] [♪] Cicero, *De Officiis*, 331-335 (Book III, Section XV).

[1056] *Mencius*, 36 (Book III, Part A, Section 3), 136 (Book VI, Part B, Section 4), 165 (Book VII, Part B, Section 35).

[1057] Seneca, *Epistles 1-65*, 9 (II, 6); 23 (V, 5).

[1058] [♪] Seneca, *On Tranquillity of Mind*, 42; Seneca, *Epistles 1-65*, 123 (XVIII, 13).

[1059] Seneca, *Epistles 1-65*, 145 (XXI, 7).

[1060] [♪] *Mozi*, 67 (Part I, Section 20), 113-119 (Part I, Section 32).

[1061] [♪] Muhammad, *Qur'an*, Sura 9:24.

[1062] [♪] Muhammad, *Qur'an*, Sura 92:17-20.

dinate wealth. Further, Walden's iconoclast asserted that excess money makes one vulnerable to coercive taxation, which turns a man's hand, through his funds, to despicable ends (in Thoreau's case, war and slavery).[1063]

7.43.13. *Aristotle* finds money-making a life of violence. Money is not life's great good. Money has merit only insofar as funds have a particular use in furthering a valued end. One must give to others liberally, avoiding the polar moral defects of prodigality, which is giving too much or to the wrong persons, and stinginess, which is clinging to possessions better donated.[1064] One requires sufficient money to eat and give to others, but more than that hinders virtuous activity. People living a meaningful (eudaemonic) life together may well appear absurd to normal people, for their lives differ from the norm in curious ways.[1065]

7.43.14. *Locke* argues that property begins when a man adds his labor to a natural thing. Where money arises, however, some men gather more than they can use. Land becomes scarce, though still unimproved. He who hoards things he cannot use spoils them. Further, the rich rob others, who, apart from their hoarding, would make beneficial use of what wealthy persons have wrongly taken. The wrong in property consists not in owning much, but rather in wasting any.[1066]

7.43.15. *Bertrand Russell* warns that worship of money launches one down a path that ignores some human essentials (creativity and joy, for example) in favor of activities adapted to acquiring money (repetition and counting, for example). Love of money distorts a man and renders him a parody. When a person has a roof, food, and clothing, everything else is vulgarity.[1067]

7.43.16. *Heraclitus* cautions that one buys her heart's desires in a coin that diminishes the soul.[1068]

7.43.17. *Isocrates* argues that excessive money serves vice, not virtue, in the human soul. It breeds moral license and sloth. Wealth perishes, but sound precepts serve one throughout a long life. Wealth serves only two constructive purposes: meeting life's unexpected reversals, and going to

---

[1063] [♪] Thoreau, *On the Duty of Civil Disobedience*, 261-262.

[1064] [♪] Aristotle, *Nichomachean Ethics*, 15 (1099a), 60 (1119b).

[1065] [♪] Aristotle, *Nichomachean Ethics*, 198-199 (1179a).

[1066] [♪] Locke, *Second Treatise of Government*, 148-150 (Sections 44-47).

[1067] Russell, "Property," 464-465, 467.

[1068] Heraclitus, Jones translation, *On the Universe*, 105.

the aid of worthy friends in need. People who are devoted to making excess money are to be avoided.[1069]

7.43.18. *Godwin* asserts that financial surplus consists of resources hoarded by one person that could be better used by another. Considered in this light, wealth is a moral failing and an anti-social habit. Godwin advises the wealthy to give their surplus to worthy persons or causes, and to live only as all men would live were there no luxury, envy, or overreaching governments.[1070] Godwin argues that eighty percent of potential human happiness evaporates into the depredations of our system of private property.[1071]

7.43.19. *Walzer* finds many spheres of concern and value in human experience, one among which is money and the markets that distribute money. When one sphere (say, money) controls another sphere (say, political power), injustice follows. Money is (or, rather, should be) blocked from purchasing many goods. No human should, for example, be able to buy: humans, political influence, criminal justice, freedom of speech, press, religion, and assembly, marriage and birth, the right to leave, military service, political offices, police protection, secondary schooling, desperate exchanges, prizes and honors, divine grace, love and friendship, or criminal activities. When money can buy elements of different spheres, our collective life grows unjust. Classes, corporations, power, and inheritance distort our culture, denying equality in many spheres to most persons. One must keep money in its proper place, and open the market for all to take risks or seek security. One must redraw the rules and boundaries if any sphere of human endeavor threatens to swallow another.[1072]

7.43.20. *David Hume* notes that, at the deepest theoretical level, property, and its cipher, money, are emblems of scarcity. That which is abundantly available, none claims as property. Only when some commodity or item proves insufficient to supply all of mankind do people make property claims. Beside an abundant river, none claims water. In a desert, men may fight to the death to wet their lips. So, lurking in the bones of property, is a claim over against others that this thing, whatever it may be, is "not yours." You are not close enough to me, not trusted enough, not worthy to share my use of this thing. Depart. Claims to property are at

---

[1069] Isocrates, *To Demonicus*, 5, 7, 21.

[1070] [♪] Godwin, *Political Justice*, Vol. II, 307, 392-394 (Book VIII, Chapter I; Book VIII, Chapter X).

[1071] [♪] Godwin, *Political Justice*, Vol. II, 341 (Book VIII, Chapter III).

[1072] [♪] Walzer, *Spheres of Justice*, 100-103, 116-122.

least a little bit cranky. The systems of thought that govern entitlement to property are a thicket of our own invention. Perhaps mankind should commence some pruning and weeding. Hume argues that justice itself would be without use in a society of persons of capacious minds, brimming with friendship and compassion.[1073]

7.43.21. *Lucian* creates a conversation featuring Timon, who hates people because he gave freely to friends who promptly abandoned him when his fortunes changed. The exchange also includes Zeus, Riches (wealth personified), and Poverty (scarcity personified). Riches bemoans both profligate and miserly people, since both abuse Riches so sorely. Timon credits Poverty with teaching him manliness, strength and wisdom. Timon scorns Riches, for Riches persistently brings friends with him, namely, Folly, Arrogance, and Deceit.[1074]

7.43.22. *Albert Schweitzer* argues that we have settled into a false conception of civilization. We thrill at our burgeoning knowledge and power over things. But we neglect the spiritual components of life, to our detriment. The essence of civilization lies not in stuff or power, but in improving man and his circumstances.[1075]

Some among your friends will devote themselves to possessions. They will relish golden cars and airplanes and mansions and expensive rocks. Humor them gently. Such friends have yet to notice the hollow aftertaste of luxury, lying in wait beneath its short-lived burst of cloying sweetness. Keep your own heart unaffected, Kate. To well-nurtured persons, stuff fails to amaze.[1076] Social, not economic, capital is wealth.[1077] Be warned: what you treasure rules you.[1078]

> **Objection 29: Demeaning Wealth:** *Some demur that wealth accumulation is meaningful activity. Money is an idea, not an evil. Humans obsess when stressed, but, even under stress, their calculative faculties persevere. Markets in goods, and their ciphers in money, are imperfect, yet remarkably supple, mechanisms by which to regulate supply and demand. People may err in their perceptions, but one cannot fault wealth for those misconceptions. Accumulation of money, grand or modest, lacks moral content. As Aristotle argues, moral deci-*

[1073] [♪] Hume, *An Enquiry Concerning the Principles of Morals*, 83-84 (Chapter 3, Sections 4, 6).

[1074] Lucian, *Timon, or the Misanthrope*, 339-371 (Sections 11-40).

[1075] Albert Schweitzer, *The Philosophy of Civilization*, 86 (Chapter 6).

[1076] Mandeville rhymed of his allegorical much-reformed bees: "Those, that remain'd, grown temp'rate, strive, Not how to spend, but how to live." Mandeville, *The Fable of the Bees*, 33.

[1077] Seneca, *Epistles 1-65*, 39 (VIII, 5).

[1078] *Matthew* 6:19-21; *Luke* 12:13-34.

sion emerges when one employs wealth to an end.[1079] *Before it is put to some purpose, money is void of ethical content.*

Response: Wealth accumulates from productive activity. All human conduct is morally cognizable. Wealth, as a product of human conduct, bears moral inquiry.[1080] Where one seeks and receives a fair wage for diligence, one ethically tends his needs and those of his intimates and circle. Where one receives vast sums for his activities, the conduct begs for scrutiny. Substantial fortunes rest on some foundation. Each wealth-generating basis warrants examination. Did a fortune derive from trafficking in human misery? Were workers abused? Did the conduct pander to or prey upon human weakness? Did wealth accumulate by denying health care to the children of the workers who generated the wealth? Did species perish in generating the funds? Did the wealth derive from activity that benefited humanity? Did the employment perpetuate historical disadvantages? Did the profusion well up from a pit of familial neglect? Did the money emerge from market manipulations or distortions? Did the entrepreneur diminish the likelihood of future well-being in acquiring his profit? Did the businessman cumulate capital by concealing crime?[1081]

Praise for capitalist markets lacks warrant. Markets controlled by money-seekers distribute the world's goods in a manner that keeps the money-seekers monied. The price of that system is mass starvation and pointless deaths. Supply and demand boils down to poor people supplying what rich people demand. When supply inevitably mismatches demand, the economy crashes; the poor grow homeless and the rich take a vacation. I value working; so too do most capitalists. Since we agree, we could provide meaningful work for every person. Full employment eludes us because worker desperation fuels the rocket of revenue. Capitalism capitalizes upon the plight of the penniless. I would not coerce devotees of money into other endeavors. Neither would I praise them or pretend their activities are morally inconsequential. I would, however, invite capitalists to explore life more deeply.

Capitalism offers incentives for money-making, but reinforces seeking behaviors that prove counterproductive to the bulk of humanity, and addictive to the money-makers themselves. Greed twists the human spirit. Expending misbegotten funds for laudable purposes fails to rehabilitate the injuries inflicted by the initial money-making. Aristotle did not find wealth lacking in moral content; the stingy person takes money too seriously, exchanging virtue for obsession.[1082] Money misdirects man. Wealth nurtures opulence. Plenitude beckons luxury. Pointless surplus burdens a person. Seek sufficient funds to nurture yourself, care for your social intimates, and participate in global weal. Then

---

[1079] [♪] Aristotle, *Nichomachean Ethics*, 60-61 (1120a).

[1080] [♪] Emerson, *Conduct of Life*, 998 (III).

[1081] Kim Stanley Robinson, acknowledging the dubious origins of wealth, styles the penchant of rich people in that future his novel depicts as "kleptoparasitism." Robinson, *2312*, 428.

[1082] [♪] Aristotle, *Nichomachean Ethics*, 60 (1119b).

stop, Kate. Spare yourself. Spare your children. Spare us all. Make just enough money, then exert yourself amassing social, not financial, capital.

7.44. *Habitations.* **Simple Rule: Choose a small, well-maintained home.** One's home should serve one's needs. Find a house not to impress others, but to assist your activities of life.[1083] Of your house, ask yourself if, were there only one billion humans on the earth, could all live as I do? If so, proceed. If not, reconsider. A house is a complex tool. Maintain it in working order. Keep it simple. Excessively complex homes decimate one's leisure time. What makes a house grand is not its roofline or archways, but rather the moral splendor of its owner, and the wisdom of her friends who visit there.[1084] In the end, a home is a place for mental and social life, for resting and recreating.[1085]

7.45. *Mobility.* **Simple Rule: Live locally.** We live oddly, Kate. Most humans who have ever lived, more than 100 billion of them, never traveled more than a few miles from their place of birth and, when they traveled, walked.[1086] Civilization spins a yarn about the necessity of travel, its freedoms, its seduction. Governments, ever responding to the metastasis of human numbers, scour the earth to install ever more roadways, so ever more people can take ever more stuff to ever larger numbers of locations. Mobility adds to life much weariness. One can spend time talking with friends, or, in the alternative, commuting. One can watch birds, or get his car repaired. One can buy modest vehicles and spend time away from work doing something one loves, or buy lavish conveyances to marginally improve life lived in a cockpit and work yourself to the bone paying for those chariots. Stay out of your car. Read a good book. Take a walk. Visit with a friend.

Mobility tempts one to abandon friends. One rationalizes: "That new job in St. Louis will be fine with its many dollars, and I will keep in touch with my friends where I now live." It does not happen. Friends at a distance freeze; when next you see them, your relationship will have fixated, like a bug in amber. You must relate to friends with great regularity if you wish to develop or maintain intimacy.

[1083] [♪] Cicero, *De Officiis*, 141-143 (Book I, Section XXXIX).

[1084] Cicero calls friends a house's finest furniture. [♪] Cicero, *De Amicitia*, 165 (Section XV).

[1085] [♪] Emerson, *Conduct of Life*, 987 (III): "To build in matter home for mind."

[1086] The Population Reference Bureau (http://www.prb.org) has estimated the number of *homo sapiens* who have lived at 107,603,000,000, assuming a single breeding pair 50,000 years ago, with death and birth rates estimated to the best of their researchers' abilities. This number is likely low, given that the human species is 200,000, not 50,000, years old.

Western economies encourage mobility. Your mobility serves corporate profit interests. Mobility sunders relationships. Such isolation is, to corporations, a job qualification. A lack of roots makes of you a more fungible economic unit, ready to be deployed where profit-taking beckons. And you must, each time you move, spend little buckets of money setting up your new place, and years finding replacement friends for those perfectly fine ones you abandoned.

I am not urging lack of contact with those outside your community. Meet others, across miles and continents, across time and even death. Enliven local life with diverse others. Read excellent books. Parse the Commons conversation. Communicate. But do not abandon home. Make your community rich by your depth and breadth and presence.

Dampen mobility in your life. What matters in the end is not the destinations to which you have traveled, but the person you were during life's journeys.[1087] Live near friends. Find work there. Avoid long commutes. Commuting expends years of your life careening down dangerous highways with people who are barely paying attention. They, too, wish they were elsewhere. Avoid them. Live locally.

7.46. *Education*. **Simple Rule: Manage your learning**. Western democracies, consistent with their economic individualism, drive every person through an educational regime that has plainly failed. Structured, compulsory, universal education fails, not because it is inadequately funded or poorly taught. It fails because ideology blinds it to the persons it serves. All students differ. One size does not fit all. The educational establishment cannot reform itself meaningfully because it would have to abandon principles enshrined in our constitutional heritage—that all people are created equal, that equity means sameness. A maxim politically wise may be educationally absurd. Concerning students, one fact stands bald: all students are not created equal. Some can; others cannot. We salve these savage wounds by lauding rare exceptions—the disadvantaged child who excels despite a poverty-ridden home, neglectful parents, and second-rate education. My point is not to critique the public school system in one paragraph, Kate, but to identify an actor, possibly misguided, in your world. Public education, and all education influenced by it, governs itself with sparse wisdom. Let no fools shape your mind. They would have you sit in a room with people who have no intention to learn, congratulate yourself when you score well in comparison to those non-learners, audit teachers whose primary task is to keep delinquents crimeless for another fifty minutes, and study what was important to someone fifty years ago. Educational institutions

---

[1087] Seneca, *Epistles 1-65*, 199-201 (XXVIII).

will plaster you with diplomas, seducing you to believe you have finished learning.[1088]

Manage your learning, Kate. Teach yourself. Find a mentor, if you prove unable to teach yourself.[1089] Do not surrender to educational orthodoxy. If you need a degree an institution offers, chart a path that gets you that diploma without disrupting your learning. Find what moves you deeply. Learn everything about that sphere. Immerse yourself. Govern yourself. Educate yourself. Keep doing so. Stop when you die.

7.47. *Sociopathy*. **Simple Rule: Identify and flee sociopaths.**[1090] Most sociopaths are not mass murderers. They can be anyone: teachers, dock hands, burger flippers, cops, or dictators. A sociopath may appear utterly normal until one begins interacting persistently with him. Then, one finds: 1) systematic failure to conform to social norms, 2) persistent deceit and manipulation, 3) chartless impulsivity, 4) irritable aggression, 5) reckless disregard for human well-being, including his own, 6) global irresponsibility, and 7) lack of remorse for wrong-doing or injury of others. Few sociopaths share all these characteristics. Psychiatrists find three of seven characteristics sufficient to identify a person suffering anti-social personality disorder. By this definition, some three to four percent of the human population is sociopathic.[1091] Robert Hare notes that these dysfunctions debilitate the sociopath's (he prefers the term "psychopath") emotional and interpersonal world, as well as his more general social interactions, which are characterized by deviance.[1092]

[1088] Bertrand Russell notes, cynically, that some children think, and education aims to heal them of the malady. [♪] Russell, "What I Believe," 357.

[1089] Seneca, *Epistles 1-65*, 185 (XXV, 5).

[1090] Simon Baron-Cohen argues that people who suffer narcissistic personality disorder and borderline personality disorder share the bottom of the empathy Bell curve with sociopaths. People suffering any of these three personality disorders are so absorbed in their own perspectives that they cannot manage to address the perspectives of others. A person suffering borderline personality disorder suffers five or more of these eight signs: unstable and intense interpersonal relationships; impulsivity; extreme mood swings; inability to control anger; suicidal threats or self-mutilation; identity confusions; extreme emptiness; or extreme fear of abandonment. Persons suffering narcissistic personal disorder exhibit five or more of these nine signs: grandiose sense of self-importance; preoccupation with fantasies of success and power, beauty, or ideal love; belief that he is special and should associate with similar people of high status; need for excessive admiration; sense of entitlement; exploiting others; complete lack of empathy; envy of others or a belief others are envious of him; or arrogance. Baron-Cohen, *The Science of Evil*, 45, 169, 197-200. Roy Baumeister asserts: "Evil is socially enacted and constructed. It does not reside in our genes or in our soul, but in the way we relate to other people." Baumeister, *Evil*, 375.

[1091] Stout, *Sociopath Next Door*, 6. These characteristics derive from DSM IV, according to Stout. Patricia Churchland asserts the sociopathy has a 70% heritability factor, which predisposition may be activated by childhood abuse and neglect. Churchland, *Braintrust*, 41.

[1092] Hare, *Without Conscience*, 34-35. Hare cautions that non-professionals are incapable of diagnosing psychopathy in themselves or others. Noting Hare's caution, I nevertheless recommend that

You know a few sociopaths. Turmoil surrounds a sociopath. He entertains himself by creating pointless social drama. Sociopaths find targets, then inflict themselves upon those ill-fated persons. Sociopathy amounts to absence of conscience; the disorder has also been called moral imbecility.[1093] The sociopath recognizes and manipulates, but is sub-responsive to, emotions. The sociopath knows fewer ethical boundaries than most of us, possibly no boundaries at all. You cannot help a sociopath, Kate. Sociopaths are massively resistant to treatment.[1094] Just flee him or her.[1095] Do not explain yourself to a sociopath. All manipulate better than you can imagine. Just walk away.[1096] If you are feeling especially compassionate, make an anonymous psychiatric referral. Recognize sociopaths. Exclude them from your world. Sociopaths are dangerous. The simple rule "identify and flee sociopaths" must be read in conjunction with the next, which concerns addressing resident evils. In Section IV, *Cull* suggests how Quad communities might cope with their sociopaths.

7.48. *Addressing Evil.* **Simple Rule: Address resident evils.** One cannot effectively flee all evils, even sociopathic evil. Some evils reside ineradicably within us. Some dwell in our neighbors and friends. Within your cadre, and within your community, and in the actions of members elsewhere and entire communities, there may dwell some members or communities who cannot or will not participate in good faith human relations.[1097] Such per-

---

you recognize the sociopath in your life and exclude him decisively. Hare agrees. Hare, *Without Conscience*, 205-206.

[1093] Mencius teaches that every man feels others' misery. *Mencius*, 38 (Book II, Part A, Section 6). With respect to sociopaths, Mencius is wrong. Sam Harris says of sociopaths, in refreshing bluntness, "we are free to say that certain opinions do not count." Harris, *The Moral Landscape*, 19. Such intolerance may be uncharitable. It is, however, wise.

[1094] Hare goes farther. There is no treatment for sociopathy, though he entertains some research possibilities. Hare, *Without Conscience*, 193-194.

[1095] Stout, *Sociopath Next Door*, 161.

[1096] [♪] Emerson, *Conduct of Life*, 1092 (VII): "A virulent, aggressive fool taints the reason of a household. . . . But resistance only exasperates the acrid fool, who believes that Nature and gravitation are quite wrong, and he only is right. . . . [W]hen the case is seated and malignant, the only safety is in amputation; . . . [E]xperience teaches little better than our earliest instinct of self-defence, namely, not to engage, not to mix yourself in any manner with them; but let their madness spend itself unopposed;—you are you, and I am I."

[1097] Mencius suggests that apart from cruel men, there would be no war or decimated families. *Mencius*, 80 (Book IV, Part A, Section 8). The Talmud (Lev.R. IV.6) teaches of Numbers 16:22 ("Shall one man sin, and wilt Thou be wroth with all the congregation?"): "It is like a company of men on board a ship. One of them took a drill and began to bore a hole under him. The other passengers said to him, 'What are you doing?' He replied, 'What has that to do with you? Am I not making the hole under my seat?' They retorted, 'But the water will enter and drown us all!'" Abraham Cohen, *Everyman's Talmud*, 184.

sons erode where they could build. You see this in yourself. Etching tendencies scratch your well-being and occasionally spill over onto others.

Where one flees evil (say, a sociopath), one frees that person or group to find new targets. So, flight from evil may offer little moral safety. One prospers in not being savaged. Yet one suffers to see others savaged. With resident evils, fleeing them may merely make them another's problem. All social evils demand that you nurture yourself and others, and develop better habits, both personal and communal. Your identity extends into the members of your circle, and less potently into your entire community. Your well-being hangs upon the weal of others.

Where one cannot flee an evil member or community, one must address them. Ultimately, ethically considered, their evils are your own. Like it or not, many errant humans will make their errors your problem.

When you imagine you confront evil, ask who is injured? Being different portends no evil. Your fear of possible ill-outcomes is no evil. Tangible harm attends evil action. Welcome differentiation. But address resident evils.

I propose an approach to addressing resident evils:

7.48.1. *Acquiesce.* One may address evil by acquiescing in it. No regime of human behavior can alleviate every form of human suffering. Some deficiencies must simply be tolerated. Where the effects are small, where those affected are not especially vulnerable, and where the errant member is not greatly skilled at habit modification, one may choose to acquiesce. Be wary not to let your cowardice don the guise of deliberated acquiescence. Know that evils aggregate. Numerous tolerated peccadilloes can cumulate into constructive resonances that exceed their sum. The urge to correct others contains its own evils: nosiness, busybody interference, self-righteousness, diversion from one's own proper tasks. Jesus and Mencius and Gandhi and Buddha warn of distorted obsessions with the errors of others to the neglect of one's own. Nevertheless, one may, on occasion, shrug one's shoulders and tolerate evils.

7.48.2. *Engage.* Where effects are egregious, acquiescence retires. One acts. Speak with errant members. We tend to segregate or shun deviants. The most potent influence one has on another human being is interpersonal. Engage the problematical person. Inquire. Listen. Confute where necessary. Hear her responses. Keep dialogue open. Persevere. Humans are constructed to mirror friends. Influence deviant members. Befriend them. If possible, work with the member to solve the problem to which the problematical behavior is his solution. Most evils are sorry responses to scarcities of various sorts created by the excesses of others not presently before you. Bear your portion of the wanton member's problem.

7.48.3. *Observe.* When people believe they are being watched, behavior changes.[1098] Be observant. Let members with problems know you are concerned. Do not be intrusive. Neither be oblivious.

7.48.4. *Intervene.* Involve others in speaking with the wanton member. Before doing so, remind yourself about tolerating differentiation. Being different is no evil, even if you are annoyed. It might happen that, in the end of this conversation with the person perceived as evil, you decide to change your behavior and perceptions, belatedly recognizing them as an evil to be avoided. But, after employing the mirror copiously, you may decide to involve others in the problem. Avoid gossip. Honor the wanton member's privacy, but do not let it become his prison.

7.48.5. *Protest.* One may undertake a form of personal suffering, made apparent to the wanton member, for the purpose of highlighting the extent of your concern about his behavior and attitude. For example, skip a meal each day and spend the time with the problem person. Give up one of your favorite activities in favor of influencing your difficult friend. Do not boast or parade. But let the problem person know that his actions have led you to a responsive austerity.[1099]

7.48.6. *Persevere.* Recalcitrance demands patience. Keep chipping away at a member's or community's intransigence. Remember that affection persuades more elegantly than criticism. Make your gentle prodding a persistent drip. Try humor. Let yourself like the errant member. Notice an errant member's good habits and emulate them. Invite reciprocity.

7.48.7. *Restrain.* A community, upon due deliberation and after persistent efforts to persuade irenically, may restrain a member or community coercively, within carefully delineated boundaries. The text addresses collective coercion of errant members and communities in the following section of this book.

7.49. *Goals.* **Simple Rule: Pursue goals.** Deliberating your life leads to plans that exceed a few days' effort. After identifying a goal, break it into component pieces. Set out those pieces on a calendar in an organized fash-

---

[1098] Humans conform their behavior to expected norms when they subconsciously suspect they are being watched. A poster of eyes on the wall causes people to litter less and clean up after themselves. Van der Linden, "How the Illusion of Being Observed Can Make You a Better Person," 1. Mo advocates universal belief in ghosts. He reasons that if ghosts and spirits watch all that people do, even in secret, then behavior improves for fear of ghostly reward or punishment. Even if ghosts do not exist, sacrificing to them offers an opportunity to make friends of neighbors similarly engaged; if ghosts do exist, one feeds one's departed ancestors in addition to making friends. [♪] *Mozi*, 111 (Part III, §31).

[1099] Gandhi would fast in the face of intractable evils, all the while keeping contact with the person whose behavior precipitated the fast. Gandhi thought responsive fasting especially productive within families. [♪] Gandhi, *Satyagraha*, 319-324 (Sections 148, 149, 150). One should imbibe Gandhi sparingly in this regard; he was a devoted ascetic enthusiast.

ion. Keep breaking your goal down into its fractions until you know what to do today to move toward your goal. Goals organize life. Goals keep you investing your time beneficially.

7.49.1. *One year vision.* Your goals may require more than a year to complete. The most important among your goals may require decades. Nevertheless, break your goals into annual segments. Our lives still follow the cycle of seasons. Periodic review helps one keep on track, and affords opportunity to adjust one's heading. Review and adjust your goals at least annually.

7.49.2. *One lifetime vision.* It is difficult to see one's life as a whole. We deeply immerse ourselves in moments. Humans are genetically driven to attend the present, for in the present lies opportunity and threat. Many, however, find a quiet psychological place from which to envisage life from its endpoint. One may determine, in anticipatory hindsight, the sort of person one wishes to be. John Steinbeck urged his readers to live in a manner that, when death comes, no one rejoices in their passing.[1100] To do that, you will have to anticipate outcomes at least one lifetime (yours) in advance.

7.49.3. *1,000 generation vision.* You do not live alone. Humanity commenced 200,000 years in the past. Mankind's future stretches an unknown number of millennia into the future. You, and we all, are here, now. Such is the human condition. Though our collective tenure may span millions of years, our presence always consists entirely in the persons presently alive imagining a future and acting to create it, and interpreting the past and laboring to avoid its errors, with (hopefully) some gratitude for the incomprehensible effort and experimentation our ancestors bequeath us. Look as far into the human future as you can peer. Ask how your actions will change the lives and possibilities of thousands of generations yet unborn. Let those far-flung considerations filter into today's activities and goals. Do nothing that impairs the weal of future generations. Live lightly. Gaze far.

7.50. *Enhancement.* **Simple Rule: Modify your body sparingly.** Human choices affect human and domestic animal evolution. When combined with growing human technical capacity for genetic manipulation, the possibility of eugenic interventions to redress genetic diseases emerges. The door also opens to intentional customizing of human DNA for adaptive, demographic, and even aesthetic purposes. Humans regularly make of themselves what they will, to the extent of their powers. Those powers flower. Human capacity for genetic refabrication of humanity itself will soon advance toward

---

[1100] Steinbeck, *East of Eden*, 412-413.

ends and possibilities at present scarcely imagined. To well-deliberate such sweeping changes, thantoid reflection must govern.[1101]

Aesthetic alteration of one's body and appearance rises from African primordial mists.[1102] Genetic manipulation opens the door to aesthetic, eugenic, and demographic manipulation of the human plasm. Surgical alteration of one's appearance (facelifts or liposuction) and function (RNY gastric bypass or reconstruction) have grown commonplace. Piercings and tattoos, an ancient tradition, surge in a fashion swing. The near future may hold the possibility that one might alter one's body and mind in a deliberated manner. One may wed mechanical devices to the body, or augment one's mind technologically. The long sweep of human history demonstrates a growing human dependence upon mechanical allies. As our tools become themselves intelligent, our collaboration with, and perhaps incorporation into, one another's functioning, may prove a human watershed. Human collaboration with artificial intelligence may shift the baseline premises of human possibilities to date (food scarcity, excessive reproduction, limited lifespan, earth-centrism, memory and mental processing limitations, family structure, psychological aberration, handicap, and so forth).[1103]

Proceed with such technological interventions only after painstaking deliberation, Kate. Fashion, as well as one's preferences and taste, mutate over time. Today's vogue is tomorrow's trash. Publicly-available technologies are usually obsolete by the time they reach market. You must live with your body and mind until the grave. Preserve, and do not mangle, them. Exercising due caution, investigate changes. Go slowly. Be a late adopter.

7.51. *Community.* **Simple Rule: Engage your community.** Humans are inextricably linked, reliant on collaboration with other persons[1104] for their sense of meaning and physical well-being. Population crush dims our communitarian sense. We feel disconnected from society, and often distant even from friends. Anomie is aberrant. It is only because alienation affects the overwhelming majority, that it may seem normal to us. Resist the dis-

---

[1101] See below at Section IV (*Community Culling*) for a discussion of thanatoid transgenerational deliberation.

[1102] [♪] Wade, *Before the Dawn*, 26, 72.

[1103] Jonathan Glover offers a stimulating conversation about the ethical parameters of deciding what sort of creature man may become, given the many onrushing technologies that are, or are about to be, upon us. He argues that, given what we are, we may not be able to solve some of our problems and questions, and yet changing who we are may not be fair to the thousands of generations who will follow us. Glover, *What Sort of People Should There Be?*, 178-187 (Chapter 14).

[1104] Some of these persons are non-human. Pets and other animal companions serve a critical role in human community.

tortions that people-overload creates, Kate. Build friendships. Link those intimates together, forming a cadre. Recognize your circle, and bind cadres of friends and family in acquaintance. Participate in forming a community. Speak in and listen to the Commons. Reach for a smaller, sustainable, deliberated humanity. Relish interpersonal depth.

If you are wondering how you might find time for extensive engagement, the answer is simple. Turn off your television (or computer or phone or tablet or whatever other technology emerges). Television isolates. Emails and texting whittle your companion to a faceless cipher. Broadcast media frequently dumb down difficult issues. They do not teach us to think or express ourselves. Screens with beautiful faces smiling at us make us feel connected when we are not connected. When habituated, we turn toward home and the "show," rather than outward toward a friend or a human dilemma. Simply, television, on the whole, makes us worse people.[1105]

7.52. *Death.* **Simple Rule: Craft a good death.** To die well is one part of living well.[1106] Fortunate people die without planning or effort or pain. They pass in the night of sudden cardiac failure, or collapse after a catastrophic stroke. A substantial (and growing) number of others suffer chronic disease that demands ongoing treatment. These persons can end life voluntarily by declining the life-supporting therapy that sustains them. These persons, effectively, save their "good" disease, the one over which they have a modicum of control. In this manner, they reserve to themselves the manner of life's end. One can skip dialysis or step away from the prescription cabinet or switch off one's respirator.

For many, however, dying proves problematic. Their diseases do not kill rapidly or painlessly. They suffer chronic onslaught upon their well-being, a slow degradation of interaction with others, and erosion of their personal dignity. Their brains fail or their hearts peter out or they become bedridden or they linger in untreatable pain. Because of these latter possibilities, which afflict a substantial portion of the population, one needs to fashion a plan to end life when a member and his cadre deem it no longer worth living.

Life's end, if you live near a modern hospital, hides a trap. Our culture has dramatically improved emergency interventions and intensive care

---

[1105] This is not to condemn all programming. A small fraction enlightens, and much entertains. It is, however, to say that the habit of watching has effects, as does the habit of relating. Cull media for its rich veins, then turn off the device. Be together with someone doing something you both deem important. If you have forgotten how to relate, you could start with telling one another why you turned off your television. For telling analysis of the effects of television on civic participation, see Putnam, *Bowling Alone*, 216-246 (Chapter 13: Technology and Mass Media). Television may be consuming the time with which we would otherwise build communities.

[1106] [♪] Seneca, *On Tranquillity of Mind*, 48.

wards. If your biological systems fail, your local hospital may well have a machine that will support your life functions despite your disease or injury. That is a happy outcome when one survives traumas and insults to live fully again. But as chronic disease takes hold of your body, hospital capabilities and the staff's commitment to preserving life may well make it difficult for you to die. As kidneys fail, you commence dialysis. You get a pacemaker, then aortic pig valves. Your pancreas finds support in regular insulin injections. Your eyes get their cataracts surgically removed and replaced with a plastic chip. Metal hips and knees replace boney joints. Finally, you may outlive your brain. Identity scatters upon time's winds, but your body, tubes erupting from every orifice, may endure. When you are released from the hospital, you may find yourself placed in a nursing home, and your life very safe but very empty.[1107] Our moral convictions about keeping life's end meaningful have failed to keep pace with our commitment to preserve biological function.[1108]

And so, you, dear Kate, may well have to make a choice that our species is ill-equipped to deliberate: when to die. I have some thoughts on this matter. Many will disagree with my views.[1109] That is well enough. Despite what I say, I am not a suicide advocate. I want you to live long, and to address your debilities creatively, finding new outlets for making yourself useful each time your body fails your previous course. Resilience in adversity ranks high in the catalogue of virtues. Yet, despite my applause for resilience, I am unwilling to be chained in a shallow puddle of life by medical administrators' or legislators' fears or values.

When your mind and body near their end, Kate, die well. You and your friends should deliberate how to achieve that purpose. They will support you, knowing you well enough to have an informed opinion concerning your prospects and needs. You may stop treatment or abandon a technology to cause your end. You can call hospice. Palliative care goals differ substantially from those of hospitals. Hospice's mandate is to make the patient's today the best day it can be, even if that shortens life. Hospice cre-

---

[1107] Atul Gawande speaks eloquently of attempts to improve institutional life for very frail persons. Gawande, *Being Mortal*, Chapters 4-5.

[1108] We, as a culture, have proved adept at bodies, which Epictetus called "clay cunningly compounded," but less adroit in dealing with the Emersonian "giant" in each of us. Epictetus, *Discourses*, 11 (Book I, Section 1.11-12). Emerson, *Self-Reliance*, 278. Kübler-Ross details her experiences of caring, as a doctor, for dying patients. She believes that those who meet mortality head on, refusing to divert conversation to happier topics, may suffer "fewer anxieties about their own finality." Kübler-Ross, *On Death and Dying*, 12.

[1109] Aristotle, for example, declares suicide to avoid pain an ignoble act, a form of cowardice. [♪] Aristotle, *Nichomachean Ethics*, 50-51 (1116a).

ates the possibility that one may live to the end with his or her life full of those people and events which give that person's life meaning. For most people, good medical care conjoined with hospice values and insights into the process of dying relieve dying patients of anxieties and make a good death possible.

However, you may be compelled to take a yet more proactive stance. If your pain proves untreatable or your life has been diminished in a manner you find intolerable, you may need to take matters into your own hands. If suicide seems your only alternative, then consider the following thoughts about process.

Apprise all those who will care about your death. Listen to their concerns. Affirm your relationship, but keep your specific plans private, even from your cadre.[1110] Salve the wound your death will inflict in the heart of each of them. Let them address your decision and offer support to the extent you find natural. Leave no appreciation unspoken. When you have loved and been loved, and nothing more that you deem constructive remains within your powers, depart.

Do not rush from life. Painful life may be meaningful life. Life's symphony has interludes and intermissions. Endure harshnesses that appear endless. Even broken bodies and addled minds can find something constructive to do, with a bit of creativity, support, and fortitude. Disease or injury may impair a well spirit, hobbling its customary stride. But the well spirit cherishes utility and marshals resources; you may find a way to limp with great dignity. More service may await than you, even if terribly impaired, dream possible. Give that help, until your imagination founders in the onrushing dysfunction of your plight. Then, find the right moment to cease.

Well in advance, set your affairs in order. Consult with your attorney and physician. Ask about any physician assisted suicide statute in your jurisdiction. Write a Will, directive to physicians, durable power of attorney

---

[1110] I make this latter recommendation to insulate your cadre mates from legal liability. If the legal circumstances grow more accepting of crafting a good death, then it would be appropriate for your cadre to actively participate. In Washington, it is illegal to assist someone in suicide, except in the limited circumstances conforming to the Death with Dignity Act. It is not illegal to commit suicide. Washington has as liberal a physician-assisted suicide statute as exists anywhere in the United States. Under the Washington State regime, I would not permit a friend to help me craft my good death for fear an enterprising prosecutor making a name for herself might target my loved one with baseless accusations under suicide assistance prohibitions. If you must have help ending your life, consider moving to a jurisdiction with less restrictive laws. At present, Switzerland appears to be the jurisdiction of choice, since assisted suicide has long been legal in that country, and the Swiss regime has no residency requirement. To die privately in the manner of one's own choosing is, to the extent one's death injures no strangers, a human right. Naysayers err when they contest the human right to die privately and well by means that injures no others. In kithdom, I would anticipate that cadres would decide the timing of death with their members; these would look to their entire community for support, or, at a minimum, acquiescence.

for health care and finances, and funeral instructions. Die at home, if possible. If you are in a hospital, leave against medical advice, and go home. Two approaches recommend themselves in crafting a good death at your residence. The first is death by barbiturate overdose.[1111] The second is death by inert gas asphyxiation (nitrogen appears to be preferred). You can investigate these approaches on the internet and in books. Check this volume's bibliography under Derek Humphry, *Final Exit*, and Nitschke and Stewart, *The Peaceful Pill Handbook*.

To die well, with a modicum of dignity on one's own terms, tames one of life's terrors. Master Zhuang called such departing "being freed from the bonds of God."[1112] Facing death squarely, with a plan, in the supportive nurture of friends, robs death of its gnawing uncertainty. Such fears can enslave. An intentional plan to die well can effect a psychological emancipation, making one better able to persevere in meaningful life to a time very near one's end. A good plan for death may even induce the freedom never to put that plan into effect. In a long life lived well, we encounter death in grandparents, parents, friends, lovers, even children. We wish all well and thank them for their contributions. We join their ranks, as must every person. As each passes, death scribes that decedent's letter in the book of life, and a brief, but eventful, chapter closes.

Objection 30: Neglecting Rational Deduction: *Some demur that a potpourri of Christian, Hindu, Buddhist, Muslim, Greek, and Stoic precepts, spiced with American proverbs, distracts from the complexities of moral deliberation. Post-theological ethics has one, and only one, course—deduction from universal moral principles. Kant did that (categorical imperatives).[1113] Nietzsche did that (*Übermenschen *consuming herd animals). Even so lowly a creature as the conscientious bureaucrat does that (comply with regulations). Quad sociality's eclectic cherry-picking weakens its deductive rigor, and so wastes what would otherwise have been perfectly good paper.*

[1111] Nitschke and Stewart contemplate that some may wish to seek death by barbiturates, even without compliance with the jurisdiction's Death with Dignity act. They contemplate importation of veterinary grade substances, which process they describe. Nitschke and Stewart, *The Peaceful Pill Handbook*, 168ff and 186ff (Chapter 13-14). I cannot recommend violation of state or federal law to acquire substances for crafting a good death. One can consider visiting a more congenial jurisdiction for help in crafting a good death. Netherlands (*Termination of Life on Request and Assisted Suicide (Review Procedures) Act*) and Switzerland (*Dignitas*) appear to have much more compassionate regimes than are currently available in the United States.

[1112] *Zhuangzi*, 48 (in The Secret of Caring for Life, Section 3).

[1113] Kant warns of abandoning the effort to find a purely rational basis for human conduct. In his view, if one mixes reason with affects and drives, one compels deliberation toward actions that cannot be principled. The result is evil, as often as good. [♪] Kant, *Metaphysics of Morals*, 169.

Response: Human life exceeds our ideas about it. The many cultures of humanity, to the extent we know them, offer wisdom(s). Wisdom is inherently eclectic, since it asks not what fits, but what works. Kant would have every proposition be a rationally-obvious deduction from universal moral principles. Every principle must fit. The monistic mania of reductionists entrances us, but has proved a fragile exuberance. Kant's moral reduction left us the Golden Rule bedecked with German fussiness. In the end, Kantian ethics just do not work at the practical level. Utilitarianism offered a clear admonition: seek the greatest happiness of the greatest number. But its very clarity lopped off evaluation of the means to ends. One may torture the mentally retarded, under a utilitarian regime, if the misery of these few unfortunates makes all of the remainder very happy indeed. Utilitarianism, in its monomania, just does not work. Neither human consciousness, in its modular structure riddled with fault lines, nor human living, driven by a short but potent list of innate drives, permits reduction of deliberated conduct to one or a few precepts. The goal of this book is not deductive rigor, but help in making good decisions. In my view, finely-elaborated culling of conduct draws together many ideas, bringing them to bear on a decisional cusp. Reductionist sentiment impairs well-deliberated conduct.

Objection 31: An Offense of Particularity: Another protests that a host of different principles could substitute for these simple rules of life. The selection proffered is idiosyncratic, revealing more of the author's obsessions and personal defects than a deliberated structure for member life. If one must list life's simple rules, those should be selected by consensus, not by the author of Cull. *I would have no rules at all, rather than his.*

Response: I agree, to an extent. My errant perspectives blind me to truth. Please engage me. Deliberate with me. Excise the idiosyncratic from my list and opinions. Boil this work down to its universal essentials. Add what I have missed. Delete and forget my errors. Drive us all, by the weight of your dissent and the overwhelming intimacy of your friendships, toward consensus. Please improve this work. Continue this effort. Urge your children to put their hands to this plow. So much is at stake in moving mankind out of its lingering adolescence and into a flourishing majority.

This list has direction. I aim not to express mere personal preference, but to recommend actions and attitudes that augment meaningful community amidst a Quad sociality. I advise the nurture of personality that well-situates one for life as a member among intimate associates. The simple rules lie near the enlivening guts of kithdom.

Morality has been mired for millennia in theodictic ethics. The local gods talk; mankind walks.[1114] Human adulthood will abandon neighborhood morality. There will be no Christian, Muslim, secular, Buddhist, or Jewish mystic ethical ghettos, but rather a universal ethic more lively and adaptive than those with which we are now familiar. That ethic is already under collaborative construction. Global communication insures universal dissemination. Insularity has

---

[1114] Wollstonecraft takes divine character as the only reliable rule for morality, which we encounter by means of well-employed human reason. She neglects the role of Christian literatures in her opinion. [♪] Wollstonecraft, *Vindication of the Rights of Woman*, 118.

passed. Those who dream otherwise err. Quad ethics has an empirical basis in brain neurology and evolutionary biology, and so can be studied and clarified. Unlike god-talk ethics, mired in metaphysical goop, Quad sociality's simple rules for living are subject to investigation. One can quantify and count. One can assess subjective responses, if not definitively, then adequately. One can falsify the Quad rules. One anticipates humanity living an experimental, adaptive, goal-driven, provisional morality born of the billion conversations of the deliberative Commons. Decisive, possibly wrong, but always improving: that is the rule for the future.[1115]

You may disagree. That is well. Waffling, however, will not help. Please know that the issues that underlie these simple rules for living will be decided, if not by you, then by others. There will be moral structures in which you dwell. Would you not prefer to participate in their construction? Would you not prefer that our conduct deliberations have some basis more appealable than the murmuring of gods to persons now dead thousands of years? In the elections of morality, every man casts a ballot. In my view, most vote by proxy, deferring to brilliant, but deceased, honorees. What gloried predecessors wrote matters, as this book makes plain. Their thoughts, however, are those of bygone times and places. Ours is another, ripe for review and innovation. One should rely on the insights of previous generations, but not slavishly. Our thoughts are our own; every morning's sun shines afresh. Careful adaptation lies near the human essence.

If you feel aversion to these Quad rules for living, please acknowledge that moral indecision too has its price. For waffling in moral ambiguity, we pay dearly. Some parents cannot say "for sure" that psychoactive drugs are a menace. When adolescents die with needles in their arms, we rationalize. We call vehicular collisions "accidents" because we fear to acknowledge that most have raw negligence at their root. We indulge war, euphemizing like a terrified lawyer before a nonplussed jury, because we lack courage to choose a path with no detours into martial killing. We stand by, hands in pockets and eyes diverted elusively, as children starve.

There are many alternatives to the simple rules I present. That is true. Yet not every whim deserves deliberation. I argue that these simple rules bear broadly upon preferable human conduct. Failure to choose simple rules leaves the squabbling many with indecision and uncertainty. In the end, moral indecision kills and maims. The work of demolition comes easier than that of construction.[1116] Criticize if you must. But make a commitment to correct me (and I you) until we reach consensus on these crucial matters.

[1115] Derek Parfit claims that post-theological ethics (which he calls "Non-Religious Ethics") stands so early in its development, that one cannot at this juncture know whether mankind may, as with mathematics, come to universal agreement about its structure. In non-religious ethics, because of this indeterminacy and startling upside possibilities, one may hope for idyllic outcomes without doubting one's sanity. Parfit, *Reasons and Persons*, 454.

[1116] Thomas Jefferson said, "[I]t is easier to find faults than to amend them." Jefferson, *Writings*, 1397-1398 (*Letter to Samuel Kerecheval*, July 12, 1816).

*Objection 32: **Truncated Individuality:** Yet another remonstrates that these rules (or any rules) create a template for monotone existence. Well-heeded, such lists of simple rules for life erect stifling conformity, issuing in a horde of rule-ridden automata shuffling through life. Mill argues that human life embraces a multitude of patterns. Each person finds his greatest prosperity by choosing his own approach. People differ. They need diverse gardens in which to blossom.*[1117] *Away with lists! Let the wilderness bloom.*

Response: Every person is not neurodiverse; almost none are savants. Odd humans are rare metals, refined by fire. The rest of us are slow cooking in a cool oven. Neurodiverse savants require two things: latitude for oddness, and common ears to sort their rants, obscenities, impieties, and wonders. We must permit upon the tended tree of culture wild sports of strange fruit.

Most, however, find their troubles lie not in securing open prairies to roam unfettered, but in recognizing or erecting fences and corrals to keep them from getting lost in the borderless grasslands. Most people lack wings to soar; we manage to shuffle. Our inclinations tend toward the moderate. We would like good lives. Few of us are clear about how to get such. This culled list of habits to inculcate starts a conversation in which all who have capacity may opine. Where one would deviate, one should deviate. If I am wrong, or if you err, life experimentation will sort us out. We will recognize our errors, if we keep talking to one another. These simple Quad rules offer a pattern from which to commence differentiation and deliberation and toleration.

Wilderness is over-rated. Wild flowers bloom but once or twice each year. Wilderness, from a distance, looms grand. Up close, wilderness brims with carcasses and brambles, impassible rivers and impenetrable bogs. Most of us, confronted with wilderness, appreciate a thoughtfully-constructed map. This I offer.[1118]

*Objection 33: **Praising Death:** Still another deprecates the author for disseminating information on suicide, even helping others plan their sin. God gives life. No man rightly takes life, even his own. Suicide offends God's prerogatives and wisdom. Further, such information assists persons sorely suffering to contemplate an early departure from life, pained by their depressions, losses, or discouragement. To give such advice is to prey upon those weakened by life's depredations just when they are most vulnerable. Shame on this author.*

Response: As to death, the objector knows what is right for every man in every circumstance. I do not. No gods whisper incontrovertible axioms in my ears (though I once believed such events possible, if unlikely). My world suffers equivocal grays between its occasional blacks and whites. The objector knows as little of gods as do I, but puffs otherwise. My advice on the good death could be misused by depressed people or those suffering treatable pain. I trust these persons have friends. All should care for their cadre-mates, and intrude into their friends' lives as needed. No person should suffer depression or

---

[1117] [♪] Mill, *On Liberty*, 65.

[1118] Jan Oppermann reminds me that the wilderness serves its purposes. Life together makes its (quite encompassing) demands, countered by the "wilderness within ourselves." Oppermann, in private correspondence with the author, dated October 14, 2015.

pain without supportive intervention from friends and professionals. To employ some of my advice on the good death, while ignoring other parts, portends poor outcomes. If any person wishes to end his or her life well, please consider my words on the subject as a whole, engaging each step, neglecting none. Involve your friends and doctor and lawyer. I have no medical training; do not take my word alone to guide your plan for ending your life, if such an act proves necessary. I do not extol death. I do, however, believe that, for some persons, some eventualities render life no longer worth living. Every person must sort that morass with their cadre. None, especially those of imperious religious sentiment, should gainsay such perceptions. Coerce no sufferer by law or shame. Our time, at some juncture, ends; death's train idles in every man's precinct. We board, reluctantly, but, for some, at a time chosen. I ask this objector to acquiesce in the private choices I make with my intimates about the life we share. Some of my decisions bear no intrusions from those who are not intimates.

7.53. *The Simple Rules.* To please Marcus Aurelius, so long gone, I aggregate simple rules for living below, for your convenience of reference, Kate:

7.53.1. Nurture yourself.

7.53.2. Observe yourself intently and compassionately.

7.53.3. Manage your inner narrative.

7.53.4. Improve your habits.

7.53.5. Act deliberately.

7.53.6. Nurture others.

7.53.7. Nurture intimate friendships.

7.53.8. Talk with friends frankly and frequently.

7.53.9. Do constructive tasks with friends.

7.53.10. Value friendship itself.

7.53.11. Tolerate differences in others.

7.53.12. Build a wide-ranging group of friendly acquaintances.

7.53.13. Address transitions in intimate friendship directly and compassionately.

7.53.14. Repair strained friendships.

7.53.15. Choose a mate with mature deliberation.

7.53.16. Attach to and mate with an intimate friend similar to you and your opposite-sex parent.

7.53.17. Preserve your mate's trust.

7.53.18. Bear children only if you must.

7.53.19. Attach to your young child.

7.53.20. Nurture children.

7.53.21. Learn from children you nurture.

7.53.22. Spend copious time with children you nurture.

7.53.23. Restrain pre-pubescents. Collaborate with adolescents. Repair ruptures.

7.53.24. Persevere through tough times. Help others do so as well.

7.53.25. Do first what matters most.

7.53.26. Give.

7.53.27. Make peace.

7.53.28. Correct yourself first; listen humbly.

7.53.29. Live in candor.

7.53.30. Show affection.

7.53.31. Laugh.

7.53.32. Support, but question, others.

7.53.33. Work to help others.

7.53.34. Eat for nutrition.

7.53.35. Protect your sleep.

7.53.36. Stay active.

7.53.37. Flourish.

7.53.38. Keep life simple.

7.53.39. Stay orderly.

7.53.40. Keep life quiet.

7.53.41. Season life with difficult tasks.

7.53.42. Stay open to novelty.

7.53.43. Embrace, but resist, aging.

7.53.44. Endure illness patiently.

7.53.45. Live from mortality's viewpoint.

7.53.46. Be patient with grief.

7.53.47. Cherish faith.

7.53.48. Keep just enough possessions.

7.53.49. Choose a small, well-maintained home.

7.53.50. Live locally.

7.53.51. Manage your learning.

7.53.52. Identify and flee sociopaths.

7.53.53. Address resident evils.

7.53.54. Pursue goals.

7.53.55. Modify your body sparingly.

7.53.56. Engage your community.

7.53.57. Craft a good death.[1119]

[1119] I am asked about the absence of patriotism from my list of simple rules. By "patriotism," one means loyalty to one's own group or nation. Surely, members of Quad communities will be loyal to their best friends and neighbors, shaped together as a community. Yet, patriotism's absence is no oversight. For kithdom to prevail, one's loyalty must lie with humanity, not with local instantiations of group loyalty. Patriotism is missing from this list because I doubt that patriotism is a virtue. Patriotism would seem, rather, a fact that has upsides and downsides, and should be addressed with a liberal dose of skepticism. See Singer, *The Expanding Circle*, 51-52. Emma Goldman, an unabashed anarchist, cites Leo Tolstoy for the proposition that patriotism is a way of thinking that justifies training wholesale murderers. Goldman, "Patriotism: A Menace to Liberty," in *Anarchism and Other Essays*, 48. Perhaps Goldman and Tolstoy overstate.

IV. Communal Culling

Think, Kate, *of decisions we make together. I turn from members to communities. As I have said, these interpenetrate. One reflects the other, shaping and evoking feedback in cybernetic loops. It is, however, no thoughtless happenstance that treatment of member conduct precedes deliberation of collective decision-making in this work.[1120] To shape one's community, one must be shaped. A well-shaped community boasts credentials to reflexively shape its members. But communities of grotesque malformation must be ignored and opposed. Ours is a time of grave errors. We wantonly savage ourselves and posterity. Percy Bysshe Shelley argued that the fatal error of modernity lies in extracting ethics from politics.[1121] Morality, as it applies to members, sets the compass for collective action. Communities should deliberate their neurodiverse savants' ravings. Community action should never impair member moral conduct. Rather, community and member action should dovetail like fine joinery.[1122] To deliberate community relations, one must pry free the clenched fist of the usual. What is best may be, at present, unfamiliar.[1123] There was a day, before you*

[1120] Wollstonecraft argues that "private virtue becom[es] the cement of public happiness, an orderly whole is consolidated by the tendency of all the parts towards a common centre." [♪] Wollstonecraft, *Vindication of the Rights of Woman*, 234.

[1121] Shelley, "Letter to Elizabeth Hitchener, January 7, 1812," 167. Cicero concurs. The Roman Senator argues that the morally right and the expedient always concur, except where our comprehension flags. No worse thought ever occurred to men than extracting morality from deliberation of expedience. [♪] Cicero, *On Duties*, 301 (Book III, Section 7). Rousseau opines that people who segregate morals and politics are doomed never to understand anything of either. Rousseau, *Emile*, 235. Machiavelli scoffs. The primary education of a prince is to learn how **not** to be good, but rather how to advantage himself. [♪] Machiavelli, *The Prince*, 53 (Chapter XV).

[1122] E. O. Wilson takes this conflicted duality, member and community, styled in his evolutionary nomenclature as "multilevel selection," to be the primary evolutionary force that created human intelligence and sociality. Wilson argues that gene selection makes of humans selfish individuals but communal altruists, in an ineradicable moral dance to a contrapuntal syncopated melody. [♪] Wilson, *The Meaning of Human Existence*, 33.

[1123] Master Zhuang said, "Words exist because of meaning; once you've gotten the meaning, you can forget the words. Where can I find a man who has forgotten words so I can have a word with him?" *Zhuangzi*, 141 (in External Things, Section 26).

*met your dearest friend, when he was just another stranger. So too ideas.
Be prepared to indulge exotic thoughts, to venture judgments more tasty
than our humdrum porridge. On that mush, modernity gags.*[1124]

8. *Community Choosing: Thanatoid*[1125] *Transgenerational Deliberation.*
Most humans suffer withered imagination.[1126] Only with difficulty do most
picture next week. Next year seldom crosses the mind. Thoughts of the next
generation are limited to substantial hand-wringing about the prosperity of
grandchildren, conjoined to delight in their youthful frolicking. Those who
imagine well, those who prognosticate far into the future, most deem dream-
ers or charlatans. Despite our pervasive failure of imagination, the weal of
mankind depends on probing far into the future, tens of thousands of years
hence. We seek not to predict the future, but to make room for it in our
hearts. Imagination jabs the lazy dog of normalcy, startling the beast, and
takes it for a long, hard run. To flourish, we must peer expectantly toward
distant horizons. To flourish, we must wake the deep aesthetic, slumbering in
every human, which is the art of future-building.

> BUZZING SWARMS THE EARS.
> CHATTERERS WHINE AND SLAP, COMPLAINING, AYYY!
> A SINGLE TRAVELER ALIGHTS ON ONE'S ARM.
> WINGS FLEX, POLLEN CLUMPS, HAIRS BRISTLE.
> THE INSECT RESUMES, VANISHING WITH ITS HORDE.
> BEES, SAYS ONE.
> TENDING WOUNDS AND FEARS, NONE LISTENS.
> WELTS REDDEN.

Thanatoid transgenerational deliberation is culling writ large upon global human conduct. One great obstacle to community culling is the adaptively-

---

[1124] Lewis Mumford warned at the middle of the twentieth century: "Perhaps never before have the
peoples of the world been so close to losing the very core of their humanity. . . . The most generous
dreams of the past have not become immediate practical necessities: a worldwide co-operation of
peoples, a more just distribution of all the goods of life; the use of knowledge and energy for the service of life, and the use of life itself for the extension of the human spirit to provinces where human
values and purposes could not heretofore penetrate. . . . For man existence is a continued process of
self-fabrication and self-transcendence. . . . The main task of our time is to turn man himself, now a
helpless mechanical puppet, into a wakeful and willing creator." Mumford, *The Conduct of Life*, 3-
5. John Paul Lederach takes "moral imagination" to be the primary engine of building a better, more
peaceful, human community. Lederach, *The Moral Imagination*, 21-29.

[1125] The word "thanatoid" denotes something that has the character of death or calls death to mind.
Webster's Third New International Dictionary, s.v. "thanatoid."

[1126] Nassim Nichosas Taleb writes, "Living on our planet, today, requires a lot more imagination
than we are made to have. We lack imagination and repress it in others." Taleb, *Black Swan*, xxxii.
De Beauvoir complains that "our lack of imagination always depopulates the future." De Beauvoir,
The Second Sex,766.

necessary, but unfortunate, human predilection for seeking short-term advantage. Evolutionarily, humans pass their genetic complement to the extent they survive long enough to do so. Transgenerational whispers are inaudible on a stage ringing with the din of breeding hormones and starvation and disease and predators and pestilential humans. In what circumstances might communities deliberate long-term outcomes?

One deliberates the future of the human community in the harsh light of member mortality. Humans spend the vast majority of life in vital deliberation, that is, calculations concerning survival. This preoccupation with the next minute or hour (or at best decade or half-century) distorts community culling.[1127] Humans, when they near their end of days, loosen their grip on the momentary. The aged get happier.[1128] Pride is recognized as a shallow puddle. Flattery and offense loosen their choking grip. Sexual embers wink in the cooling cauldron of copulation. Distractions and desires flag. Personal ambitions pale. Ears open to posterity, and the common good of humanity. One's mind is loosed by death's impending blade from the tangled laces of life's obligations and opportunities. With its bulk in one's past, life in the penumbra of passage blossoms to the human good. In the shadow of death, commonweal, for some, comes clearer.[1129] To subdue life's din, practice death.[1130]

[1127] Lewis Mumford argues: "The great use of life is to spend it for something that outlasts it. No doctrine of ethical conduct that overlooks this wider destiny for person and community has anything but a stopgap value. . . . By entering into purposes that transcend the limits of any single life, sometimes of any historic period, man endows his own limited needs and values with a meaning that outlives their temporary satisfaction or their equally temporary defeat." Mumford, *The Conduct of Life*, 130, 139.

[1128] Gross and Carstensen *et al.*, "Emotion and Aging," 597. Carstensen and her co-authors conclude that older adults show increasing emotional control, by which elders select and enhance positive emotion and, by enhanced emotional control, derail fears, anger, and sadness.

[1129] Divest yourself of passions and personal considerations, undertaking every act as though it were your last. [♪] Aurelius, *To Himself*, 31-35 (Book II, Sections 5 and 11). See also Seneca, *Epistles 1-65* 187-197 (XXVI and XXVII). The man who has learned to die is free from external powers, or, at a minimum, beyond their effective reach. Socrates argues that philosophers practice dying, to clarify their thinking. Dying becomes a habitual viewpoint to the philosopher. [♪] Plato, *Phaedo*, 235 (Section 67E). The Buddha, as a young prince, entered the first trance of his enlightenment when he reflected upon the death of all things, which meditation concentrated his attention and stabilized his mind. His arrogance subsided, along with his youthful, self-centered thoughts, and Buddha rose above local and personal concerns. [♪] Conze, *Buddhist Scriptures*, 42-43. Plato opines that the philosopher kings emerge from men who have reached their maturity, possessed of time to do nothing but philosophy. That occupation renders them able to rule Plato's pustulous city (the luxurious city inflamed and swollen to accommodate humanity's baser desires). [♪] Plato, *Republic* 203 (298b-c).

[1130] Epictetus, a first century A.D. Greek slave, often meditated upon Socrates' habit of practicing death. As a Stoic, Epictetus concluded that one must prepare for life's fatal trials, choose what one will deem good or evil, and having found truths, embrace them with confidence. Epictetus, *Discourses*, 221-223 (Book II, Sections 2.9-14).

Most choices bear transgenerational implications, usually ignored.[1131]
At the horizon of death, communities, and the members who comprise them,
may grasp the corporate stream of human life, its connectedness in biology,
time, and culture to thousands of generations in the future. When gripped by
imminent mortality, individual need and desire wane to extinction. Structuring the web of the future waxes, though our grasp of future specifics remains
ever tenuous.[1132]   To deliberate well as communities, to quiet the jumble of
ephemeral demands for transitory advantage and weal (which is the stuff of
politics), communities must deliberate in the shadow of death. Thanatoid deliberation is not politics, but meta-politics.[1133]   Thanatoid deliberation generates those ideas that clear the path for raucous dialogue. When death's inexorable and universal call is amplified, the weal of the community, which long
survives its members, gains traction in the deliberative mind.[1134]   No human
survives to see the future she created. But as death's embrace tightens, failing
eyes recognize the ephemeral present as flotsam. The yawning ocean of futures engulfs what remains of deliberation.

Although the dying mind provides a metaphorical template for the sort
of deliberation our species requires, all thanatoid deliberation does not transpire in the brains of members nearing the end of life. Some others, not dying, train themselves to existence in death's lee, tamping down denial and

---

[1131] William Godwin argued, in 1796, that the whole of morality may be boiled down to one habit:
calculating future outcomes of present action. [♪] Godwin, *Political Justice*, Vol. II, 69 (Book V,
Chapter IX). Perhaps Godwin is more utilitarian than the world warrants.

[1132] Hannah Arendt argues that death is anti-political. We die alone and powerless. Yet, death impresses upon us that, though we end, our communities endure, perhaps for very long periods indeed.
That inspires dreams of community weal. Arendt, *On Violence*, 67-68.

[1133] Edmund Burke finds society a contract "not only between those who are living, but between
those who are living, those who are dead, and those who are to be born." Burke, *Reflections on the
Revolution in France*, 101.

[1134] Thanatoid deliberation calls to mind John Rawls's "original position," in which all deliberators
of the future of human conditions of justice are robbed of knowledge of their and others' particularities, so that their decisions represent what they honestly and without self-interest believe would benefit mankind. Rawls, *Theory of Justice*, 11, or [♪] Rawls, *Justice as Fairness: A Restatement*, 14-18
(§6). The difference between thantoid deliberation and Rawls's "original position" is that the original position never happens to anyone anywhere, while thanatoid deliberation happens to many
thoughtful people at the end of their days, and to any who might wish to emulate them even before
death. From a thantoid perspective, the screech of political wrangling comes clear as ephemera to be
ignored, and the claims of the future ring louder and louder. Recall Socrates urging his hearers to
practice death. [♪] Plato, *Phaedo*, 235 (67E). Socrates also, in Plato's account, fears that missteps
in transgenerational deliberation (the structure of institutions) would sorely injure his friends, and so
would prefer to have such conversation with his enemies. [♪] Plato, *Republic*, 146 (451a-b). Schopenhauer argues that "as death draws nigh, the thoughts of each individual assume a moral trend,
equally whether he be credulous of religious dogmas, or not; he is manifestly anxious to wind up the
affairs of his life, now verging to its end, entirely from a moral standpoint." Schopenhauer, *The Basis of Morality*, 132.

fear, extending vision. Consider Socrates, Buddha, Aurelius, Seneca, and Kant.[1135] Consider also members who have faced death by suffering serious illness or injury. When time is short, people choose meaning over achievement. Such persons, regardless of age, shift focus from future accomplishments to purposes that are emotionally salient.[1136] That is the nature of thanatoid transgenerational deliberation. It carves a path to the future that retains the emotionally salient essentials of human existence, and deadens the din of momentary urgencies. It hears the basal thrum of meaning, meaning, pulsing beneath life's jostle. Thanatoid transgenerational deliberation insists that present technologies and movements and political tradeoffs countenance the needs of distant generations for meaningful life. Our ideas, choices, and values become tomorrow.[1137]

Most young members face challenges that obstruct thanatoid deliberation. Their hormonal urgencies and breeding pressure, conjoined with dearth of experience of life's harsher moments, may disqualify the young mind from mature transgenerational deliberation. Aristotle denied political education to the juvenile mind, regardless of age. The young (and the careless elder as

---

[1135] *Socrates*: One must, seeing death, flee evil. Evil is so much more fleet of foot than death. *Aurelius*: One must make every decision as though it were one's last, shunting desires and feelings and distractions. *Seneca*: Only vices die in one's senility; life blossoms. Death awaits, so ready yourself every day. To learn to die is to escape slavery. *Kant*: Impose on others those rules you are willing to have imposed on all, including yourself. Kant finds death to the specific and local in the rule of the universal and ideal. *Buddha*: One must abandon anxiety about death, for anxieties obscure the truth that all suffering and death veil karmic reincarnation. One must extinguish empirical thinking. One does so by leaping into death, heedless of body and soul. This is meditation itself. What emerges is not death, but absolute extinction of thought, which blossoms into compassion and enlightenment that surpasses all conscious insight.

[1136] Fung and Christensen, "Goals Change When Life's Fragility is Primed," 248-249. The authors assert that goals are set in a time context, and when the time context is delimited (by age, trauma, disease, social upheaval (SARS or 9-11), attention shifts to concerns more present, more emotionally satisfying, and less utilitarian.

[1137] Taleb warns that we lack the ability to predict the future because we lack the ability to foresee outliers (which I call neurodiverse savants). All we can do, in the end, is adjust to the outlier as he makes himself apparent. Taleb, *Black Swan*, xxiv. I suspect that we detect the outlier in our midst, but ignore him, reassuring ourselves that it is he, not us, who needs adjustment. Perhaps our predictive astigmatism would find help in a finely ground lens focused on identifying and embracing neurodiverse savants. From the perspective of persons who expect sameness, history does not progress, but rather leaps from one point to another. History is a series of lightly-connected disjunctions. Taleb, *Black Swan*, 10-11. The unanticipated bursts upon us. Cultures tend to dismiss their neurodiverse savants as ranting madmen, and their works as despicable. Michel Foucault finds madness a cultural category (which he distinguishes marginally from mental illness) comprising those with whom we no longer speak. Mad members require confinement or exile. He says, "Through madness, a work that seems to drown in the world, to reveal there its non-sense, and to transfigure itself with the features of pathology alone, actually engages within itself the world's time, masters it, and leads it; by the madness which interrupts it, a work of art opens a void, a moment of silence, a question without answer, provokes a breach without reconciliation where the world is forced to question itself." Foucault styles his book an archaeology of the silence between mad and non-mad society. Foucault, *Madness and Civilization*, x-xi, 288.

well) fail of perspective, gripped in the psychological vice of denial. Now is urgent; hither matters little.[1138] The young person, after all, expects (wrongly) an eternity in which to explore and amend errors. Want of experience further abets denial of death. Where one disregards mortality, transgenerational vision dims.[1139]

Communal culling suffers to the extent communities fail to imbibe the fundamental lesson death teaches. Each member's life scribes a letter in the great communal book, nothing more. We scratch our letter; we pass. In community culling, members discern and preserve the sense of that great book written in the hundred billion lives that have passed, protecting the hundreds of billions that may yet lie ahead. The community deliberates distant futures, but does so in the shadow of every member's mortality.

Thanatoid deliberation is one form of neurodiverse savantism. Communities should treat odd members capable of thanatoid deliberation as rich veins of social capital. This we are disinclined to do. We prefer to persecute, to whittle the odd person, to hammer her into conformity.[1140] Thus, the neurodiverse savant dissipates her subtle energies in self-defense, falling exhausted before the best of what she might offer all has been formulated. We waste their gifts in pointless frictions.[1141] Rather, communities should mine neurodiverse savants.[1142] We should refine them. We should use them. One imagines a steady rivulet of thanatoid insight streaming into the virtual Commons. Each community dips from the flow those ideas that it suspects may prove adaptive. Communities experiment. Many adopt strategies that prove adaptive. Others find strategies deemed promising to be unworkable, and reorganize themselves. From community successes and failures, experience-

---

[1138] Not youthful physical vigor, but character, judgment, and careful deliberation deliver great outcomes. [♪] Aristotle, *Nichomachean Ethics*, 9. See also Cicero, *De Senectute*, 27 (VI, 17). The old may be richer in the critical traits.

[1139] Zamyatin disagrees. He finds in children philosophical essence. Children always ask "why?" and "what comes next?" To them, little is predetermined, all remains soft putty. Zamyatin, *We*, 175.

[1140] A Japanese proverb, which I cited earlier, warns odd birds: "The nail that sticks out shall be driven in."

[1141] [♪] Wilde, "The Soul of Man Under Socialism," 134.

[1142] Taleb warns that what we do not know is far more relevant in any circumstance than what we do know. Taleb calls the unexpected, highly-significant event or person a "Black Swan." Of these he says, "A small number of Black Swans explains almost everything in our world, from the success of ideas and religions, to the dynamics of historical events, to elements of our own personal lives. Ever since we left the Pleistocene, some ten millennia ago, the effect of these Black Swans has been increasing." Taleb, *Black Swan*, xxii.

tested thanatoid deliberation seeps into the Commons, guiding many, affecting all.[1143]

Communities, often unknowingly, embrace a Japanese-Buddhist aesthetic: wabi-sabi. To the wabi-sabist, all things are imperfect and transient; in penultimacy lies beauty. From a thanatoid transgenerational perspective, nothing lasts too long, nothing is ever truly finished, and nothing approximates perfection. The aesthetic invites heartfelt longing conjoined with acquiescence in what cannot, under prevailing circumstances, be changed.

Thanatoid deliberation culls failed human experiments from promising ones.[1144] From among the welter of alternative communities whose choices survive scrutiny, communities can chart courses toward a deliberated human future. By structuring collective habits, we can deflect the tangled trajectory that our evolutionary past bequeaths us. Perhaps, as centuries pass, humanity may reach consensus on many matters of moral import. We may reconfigure consciousness, and even affect our genetics, in lightly-guided consensual evolution.[1145]

8.1. *The Technique of Thanatoid Deliberation*.[1146] How does the Commons encourage thanatoid deliberation of the human future, prognosticating without losing focus to the din of short term anxieties? All humans see farther into the future when they set themselves to the task. Some measure of such foresight lies within the powers of reason and the skills of observation of every person. Yet, there exist among us thanatoid savants. We find scarce use for such persons at present. Their skills fill no mouth and erect no bridge. Their books are disjointed and difficult, their voices shrill. Thanatoid deliberation of the human future commences when the Commons

---

[1143] Aristotle recognizes that men differ and so, from town to town, their forms of government differ. Happiness comes to people by various means, and each community must adapt its life to achieve flourishing life for its members. [♪] Aristotle, *Politics*, 177 (1328a.40).

[1144] Bateson lists common ideas that have failed: humans can and should fight to control the environment, humans fight other humans, individualism and parochialisms matter most, resources are essentially unlimited, financial weal is the only fundamentally important endeavor, and all problems with these endeavors shall be resolved technologically. Bateson, *Steps To An Ecology of Mind*, 500.

[1145] Wilson advises otherwise. We should avoid genetic tinkering with the human legacy, and practice what he calls "existential conservatism," preserving the genome as a sacred trust. [♪] Wilson, *The Meaning of Human Existence*, 60.

[1146] John Steinbeck argues that mankind, in its conflicted thoughts, drives, and feelings, is enmeshed, at every conscious and unconscious level, in good and evil. From the first man to the last one, we all live our ethical choices, chained to the good and the bad. All human achievement pales before this ethical fact. Was our life good, or evil? Men want to be good, despite evidence to the contrary. We want to love and be loved. Our cruelties consist mostly in ill-conceived lunges after love. At death, nothing matters but one thing—whether a man loved and was loved. Genius, wealth, and achievement collapse. For the unloved, death becomes a bone-freezing nightmare. We should always choose to think and act in a manner that, when death takes us, none dances for joy. Steinbeck, *East of Eden*, 412-413.

finds use for geniuses of creation, who elaborate futures from the under-whelming present. Communities must encourage people who imagine hu-man futures, support them, and promote their skills. The views of thanatoid seers will be diverse. No single neurodiverse vision should be adopted. Still, in auditing the savant cacophony, one may discern elements of a community's future shape. The many communities comprising the Com-mons can choose their various courses from among the well-culled imagin-ings of neurodiverse savants, creating hundreds of thousands of experiments in member and communal culling. Coercion wanes where communities choose their divergent paths. In every attempt lurks promise for all.

Thanatoid deliberation should be powerless. Power corrupts members, who come, under its influence, to believe themselves exceptions to the well-deliberated prescriptions of their collectives. Aggregation of power in indi-viduals and lone communities should be avoided to the maximum extent possible.[1147] Decentralization promises a verdant future. Centralization sav-ages the garden of man, leaving him with row upon row of well-strangled crops, very tidy, wholly sterile. Communities must hear their deliberative savants, but deny them power.

Power is legitimate authority to coerce. One unilaterally alters the in-centives motivating another to act, diverting choice by means of threats and promises.[1148] Coercion, in Quad sociality, should be rare and utterly excep-tional. Bluntly, there should be little power—anywhere. Communities must choose by consensus; none are coerced. Power, to the extent any is required at all, should devolve to the smallest number of actors with the fewest number of actees in the lowest frequency possible. Power feeds hu-man hierarchical fixation; the dessert to that meal is an oppressive social sludge. Rather, we should encourage persons who engage (suffer?) thanatoid deliberation to influence the human community by disseminating their visions and concerns. The differently-gifted many should listen and deliberate. When they reach consensus in their communities, they should

---

[1147] Kithdom takes one to an order fundamentally different from existing political regimes. Each current regime finds its rudiment in the few governing the many. That is, modern governments con-sist in (mostly) self-appointed (mostly) men, obsessed with the character defect of longing to achieve pre-eminence over others, fashioning coercive rules by which strangers should live, and coercing all to conform. Insanely, we grant to these hobbled persons the power to tax and execute and wage war. Han Fei Tzu styles the State as a king whipping his minions into submission, and then herding the drooling masses. [♪] Han Fei Tzu, *Basic Writings*, 30, 103. Nietzsche and Machiavelli share this view of the measure of society. [♪] Machiavelli, *The Prince*. Nietzsche, *The Genealogy of Morals*. Kithdom asks of all that they take control of life, design and live it with intimates and associates, and surrender no power to strangers. William Godwin calls this attitude "living while we live." [♪] Godwin, *Political Justice*, Vol. II, 383 (Book VIII, Chapter IX).

[1148] [♪] Taylor, *Community, Anarchy and Liberty*, 11-25. Taylor styles persuasion as bilateral alter-ing of attitudes in a transparent manner approved by both parties. *Ibid.*, 20-21.

act and examine the results of their actions. The future of communities emerges from sparked imaginations. Where neurodiverse savants find welcome and support, communities find their visions sharpening.[1149] Adaptive plans evolve. Where savants are silenced or ignored, social ossification induces a crippling arthritis of imagination. So we now suffer.[1150]

8.2. *Distant Futures.* When one peers to the farsight horizon, what does one see? Sometimes one sees no more than a reflection of our present life, seen from great distance, now set in perspective. Other times one gleans an image of a future so different and bracing as to steal the breath. The farsight horizon has a shape that can be discerned. Peer we must, if mankind is to survive to see it firsthand.

8.2.1. *Responsibility to Descendants.* The human Commons bears responsibility to deliver to its descendants meaningful human community. Where we can see needs, our task remains to address those problems constructively and intelligently, with transgenerational concern. The past is a *cul de sac.*[1151] To follow an ancient pattern for no present reason is to repeat error. One culls the past. One strips tradition's blinders from the steed of serendipity.

8.2.2. *Winnowing.* The human Commons has received from its forebearers much of value, as well as a dump of dross. Where matters have come clear, matters that to our ancestors were muddled, our task lies in discarding useless heritage and adorning adaptive habits. Billions now dead devoted their lifeblood to lend us insight, technologies, and attitudes that served them well. Ours is to preserve and transmit adaptive habits, and winnow chaff. That is the essence of culling conduct.

8.2.3. *Incrementalism.* Humans hurry. The more dire our circumstance, the more we justify haste. The farsight horizon, if it portends human weal, is

---

[1149] Hume, in discussing the unity and diversity of moral perceptions among humankind, comes, at the end of *An Enquiry Concerning the Principles of Morals*, to discuss men with "artificial lives." These morally-exemplary men are segregated from the mainstream of mankind. Their world views diverge strongly. He says, "When men depart from the maxims of common reason, and affect these *artificial* lives, . . . no one can answer for what will please or displease them. They are in a different element from the rest of mankind; and the natural principles of their mind play not with the same regularity, as if left to themselves, free from the illusions of religious superstition or philosophical enthusiasm." Hume, *An Enquiry Concerning the Principles of Morals*, 199 (Fifth Appendix, *A Dialogue*, Section 57).

[1150] In the worst of worlds, social ossification cripples the deliberative process itself. Progress awaits the demise of obstructive personalities. The cynical saw goes: "Science progresses, funeral by funeral." Panksepp, *Affective Neuroscience*, 74.

[1151] One must anticipate the unexpected; the way already known is easy and leads nowhere. See Heraclitus, Haxton translation, *Fragments*, 7.

a long journey of innumerable small steps.[1152] Humans little comprehend their sociality. Collectivity has a life of its own, a vital, hunkering animal life, responsive to a logic barely comprehensible. Our togetherness ill-tolerates swift variation. Unduly prodded, humanity rises from ruminative slumber to thunder across the plains of history in a panic. Alarmed, human intelligence collapses into bovine stampede, careening cliffward behind bewildered alpha ruminants.[1153] We are a danger to ourselves. To the extent the farsight horizon holds meaningful community for us, our path demands patient choices. Each builds upon the last. Each comprises a step toward a distant, but not unimaginable, possibility.[1154] There is no goal but that we define. The point of our goals is the journey we undertake to reach them. Dewey argues that we seek control of our lives to augment the intrinsic significance of living.[1155] That is "meaning."

Some would argue for economy of effort. Since all that lies open to us is the next small step, why expend effort bothering to peer to the farsight horizon? The rub comes in this. The steps differ. Actions we take when occupied only with the next moment diverge from those we might choose when peering toward distant centuries. So, outcomes differ. Concern for the farsight horizon transports us to social structures we might never otherwise create.

In their haste, revolutionaries decimate the social infrastructure upon which human weal depends. To the extent social ossification troubles us, those structures need thoughtful dismantling, not frenzied demolition. Building toward a desirable farsight horizon has an ethos. It calls to mind the archeological enterprise, where patient people unearth historical riches

---

[1152] Russell says there are no short cuts to the good life. It is built up, brick by brick, of intelligent choosing, self-control, and sympathetic relationships. One looks to adequate education for help. [♪] Russell, *What I Believe*, 361.

[1153] Kropotkin, in 1920, lamented to Lenin that the Russian Revolution commits atrocities, murders grotesquely, demolishes willy-nilly, and ruins Russia. What shall be done? Kropotkin asks. Kropotkin answers his own question: little or nothing. Revolutions are forces of nature, like earthquakes or violent storms. None controls them. Once one abandons peaceful progress, one can only wait the revolution's wane and the inevitable repressive regime sure to follow. We can do nothing, once revolution emerges, but ameliorate the repressive response. [♪] Kropotkin, *Conquest of Bread*, at letters to Lenin, 259. I answer, contradicting both Kropotkin and Lenin, that we could eschew violence and coercion altogether. What shall be done? Irenic intervention, I answer.

[1154] Martin Luther King, Jr., noted, in a 1952 letter to his wife, Coretta, that only evolutionary change preserved social ethics and sanity. Revolutions are the tools of demented, immoral men. [♪] King, *Autobiography*, 36. He later changed his mind, for in his "I Have a Dream" speech during the March on Washington in 1963, King noted the urgency of now, advocating that one seize the day, rather than cool off or settle for gradualism, which he styled a soporific. [♪] King, *Autobiography*, 224.

[1155] [♪] Dewey, *Human Nature and Conduct*, 267.

from a matrix of detritus with tweezers and whisk brooms. The best artifacts adorn museums, remaining part of our common heritage. Revolutions resemble earthquakes, scenes upended in capricious devastation with no discernible program. Revolution accomplishes too little by attempting too much. Revolutions tend to replace personnel, and little more. Russia replaced the Tzar with Stalin. Mao cast off emperors for regal communism. America replaced Parliament with Congress, and a king with over-reaching presidents. Reject revolution. Embrace carefully deliberated incremental change.[1156] James C. Scott urges that we must take small steps, favor changes that are reversible whenever possible, know that surprises will occur, and rely on the ingenuity of members to address the unexpected.[1157]

For each of us, it is what we are doing now that matters.[1158] A meaningful life undertakes linked productive activities brimming with intrinsic import to the actor.[1159] Imagine a future with your cadre; work toward it. Such purposeful action augments meaning for a member and her community. And that is goodness itself.

8.2.4. *Farsight Horizon.* Modern humans evolved around 200,000 years ago, which, at thirty years per generation,[1160] was approximately 6,700 generations ago. Our challenge is, for the first time in human history, to make no choice that erodes the possibility of meaningful human community for our descendants 1,000 generations (30,000 years) hence. Because no man knows the shape of life thirty thousand years hence, the human community will, with respect to transgenerational impacts, grow conservative, treading lightly in its consumption of non-renewable resources and inculcating a global culture that ensures the farsight future. Still, every community in the Commons will constitute an experiment in deliberated conduct culling, making the Commons a hotbed of deliberated change.

[1156] Despite all the left-leaning language in this book, this incrementalist attitude remains the clarion bugle of traditional conservatism, at least such conservatism before it wedded itself to reactionary religious agendas.

[1157] Scott, *Seeing Like A State*, 345. Scott is not contemplating a structure similar to that proposed by *Cull*, but rather a means of modifying cultures similar to our present one.

[1158] Thoreau said, "As for adopting the ways which the state has provided for remedying the evil, I know not of such ways. They take too much time, and a man's life will be gone. I have other affairs to attend to. I came into this world, not chiefly to make this a good place to live in, but to live in it, be it good or bad." [♪] Thoreau, *On the Duty of Civil Disobedience*, 259.

[1159] [♪] Dewey, *Human Nature and Conduct*, 267-280. Moral goodness consists in intrinsically-meaningful present activity.

[1160] Heraclitus called a generation thirty years, the time required for fathers to bear sons whose wives then bear, or the time required to become a grandfather. Heraclitus, Jones translation, *On the Universe*, 87, 89.

If the Commons is able to achieve this farsight conservative mutualism, we must communicate the habit to the next generation in a compelling and transmissible fashion. And they to theirs. And they to theirs. We may, with effort, become better at living well.

Objection 34: Predictive Astigmatism: *Some demur that insight into the far-flung human future defies human capacity. Our best visions err. All suffer predictive astigmatism, rendering us prospectively blind. Life surprises. None predicts the future or controls it. It matters nothing that one is well-seasoned or gripped with acquiescence in one's own mortality. As an evolutionary proposition, our predictive skills extend to the next full belly or luring coitus. To advocate transgenerational deliberation promises Sisyphean futility. Rousseau said that foresight thrusts us beyond ourselves, and lands us in places we, most likely, shall never visit.[1161] Thanatoid deliberation amounts to nothing more than armchair yammer projected onto the blank screen of uncertainty. Such aimless talk invites small armies of mystagogues and hucksters to opine. And we need their ideological gusts as little as ever.*

Response: Humanity nears the end of adolescence.[1162] We have flexed our muscles. We have proved our overwhelming fecundity. We have poked our heads in every crevice of the planet. Our brains whirl with a billion promising ideas. We now must ask (and answer), *What choices cause human life to flourish?* How can we rid ourselves of humanity's ageless scourges of anomie, scarcity, coercion, denial, neglect, pointless cruelty, violence, and social instability? How must we live together to avoid depleting our planetary resources, and with that depletion, the weal of human posterity? What technologies should we permit, and why? What steps must we take to make room for the well-being of earth's other creatures? These are not merely questions of the moment. They are the inquiries of the ages, deliberations we have been too preoccupied to undertake collectively.

Answers lie in coming to know ourselves as delimited animals evolved in Pleistocene Africa, in structuring human life as a human community believes might prove best, in decentralizing and abandoning the coercive State-theory of human relations in favor of friendship and kithdom, and in mining the minds of those odd persons among us whose strident messages are so frequently censored. Not only is thanatoid deliberation possible, it presently occurs, but in truncated, unsupported, half-baked fashion. Thanatoid deliberation has not yet gotten its task clearly in mind: *What conduct leads to flourishing human life?*

Much of the farsight horizon will always lie beyond human ken. Surprises erupt. That is no cause for despair. Indeterminacy of the farsight horizon will generate a wealth of alternative visions. Those possibilities can be refined. Proposals will course through global deliberation. Communities will choose in-

---

[1161] Rousseau, *Emile*, 82.

[1162] William Godwin calls our current collective psychological state the "present puerility of the human mind," speaking of mankind's current toleration of monopolistic wealth and the miseries it engenders. [♪] Godwin, *Political Justice*, Vol. II, 345 (Book VIII, Chapter IV).

sights by which to structure themselves. Experiments will succeed and fail. The farsight horizon will come clearer, if still blurred by human cognitive astigmatism. Life will improve, and eventually flourish. Do not despair of thanatoid deliberation. Humankind's halting errors in selecting a well-deliberated human future will prove preferable to acquiescence in the willy-nilly outcomes that evolutionary happenstance dumps on our doorstep. As to the "mystagogue" aspersion, neurodiverse savants make easy targets. By definition, they brim with oddities that beg ridicule. Might these few queer ducks, however, see more astutely than we orthodox many?

When we cannot see a horizon, attitudes shape what we believe lies ahead. Where one dwells in factual vacuum, pessimism declares we cannot, without persuasive rationale. Facing the same dearth of data, optimism declares we can, without persuasive rationale. Cynicism declares the human enterprise pointless, and pouts. I understand each vantage. I cast my lot with optimists.

Objection 35: Dissembling Revolution: *Another protests that the author self-deceives when he disclaims revolution. The author's recommendations decimate human society. He would have us choose marital partners differently and artificially enlarge our families. He would have us retire our armies and erase our borders. He would depopulate the planet. He would steal ideas from those who possess them and give them freely to any who can comprehend. He would dismantle our cities and replace them with hovels and hamlets. He would deny us the pleasure of our revenges. He would put patent nutcases in charge of our minds, shutter schools, render money an afterthought, and have us all euthanizing ourselves willy-nilly. Critically, he would have us childless, bereft of life's most fundamental comfort. Though he brandishes no sword or bomb, the author remains a terrorist. The ideas of this book dismantle society as we know it, and launch all upon ill-defined treks fraught with risks barely imaginable. The author would raze all, shackling us with "a ruin instead of an habitation."[1163] Refusing to call this prescription "revolution" is simple bad faith. Conservatism retains present social structures. Liberalism shucks them off with rapidity. Wild-eyed fanaticism contemplates utopias arriving next week on a bullet train.[1164] The author is the latter beast, a revolutionary. Hitler, Stalin, Mao, Qutb, Lancaster. All should vomit this book's fare from the intellectual gut.*

Response: I have terrified this objector. For that, I apologize. The objector is correct in much that he says. I find the societies of mankind ill-conceived and misdirected in many particulars. I would change them in a host of ways, which I specify in this book, as he rightly (though uncharitably) describes. The objector is wrong, though, in his main criticism. I refuse revolution.

If I, by my own hand, had power to effect the changes I deem crucial, I would not. Nor would I applaud others who did so. Coercing change never

---

[1163] So Edmund Burke criticizes the revolutionaries of France, who, in Burke's view, left generations without feeling for one another, and men little more than "the flies of a summer." Burke, *Reflections on the Revolution in France*, 99.

[1164] Burke warns, "Of all things, wisdom is the most terrified with epidemical fanaticism." Burke, *Reflections on the Revolution in France*, 156.

works. Nor is the bludgeon of guns and laws and prisons helpful. All the world needs to achieve flourishing life is some good advice, well-heeded, and adequate time. Where men talk, consensus emerges; where women talk, more rapidly so. Consensus, however, comes not from stupendous argumentation, but from the affection and trust that naturally grow among friends after time living together. Most people have great good sense that they hide, fearing criticism and reprisal. If known and loved, they would cease to cringe. Our conversation, when aimed at important matters, would become content full.

Further, we need no revolution. We trend well. Globally, we are reducing violence.[1165] Despite idiotic increases in global population (the population of humanity has doubled in my lifetime), hunger has diminished and might be extinguished if people of marginal backbone were elected to existing political bodies. Learning may become universalized; deeply intelligent teachers may speak to global student bodies through internet technologies. We soften our deadly grip on national identities and borders as the tide of the migrating poor blasts borders and the necessity of multi-national cooperation and commerce grows ever more apparent. Globally, population increase slows; it should reach maximum this century, and with some well-deliberated advice, the women of earth may reduce the number of their babies such that each infant is substantially nurtured and none starves.

That elements of our existence together lean in desirable directions by no means ensures that we shall continue in those paths. All these hopeful changes need not amount to anything like kithdom. We might endure in our many institutions, suffering armies. We might yet breed ourselves into oblivion. We could go on ignoring the farsight horizon for the lure of the moment. We must share a dream of meaningful human existence, at least in its broad outlines. We must fill in the blanks by hard experimentation and analysis. Mankind can arrive at an image of meaningful life in meaning-laden communities, one that is broadly shared, and adaptable, and hopeful. To achieve this vision of humanity's farsight horizon we must set ourselves the task of sketching its parameters. This book offers thoughts in that regard. I encourage peering forward. Join this task.

Conservatism errs by venerating our heritage without deliberated criticism, and indulging vitriol. Liberalism errs by fracturing societal steps forward into a thousand petty causes, and indulging vitriol. I indulge the conservative by assuring him that none will coerce her contributions to social well-being. I indulge the liberal by embracing deliberated change and opening tens of thousands of experimental communities for attempting those changes. I frustrate the conservative by rejecting petrification or divinization of social norms, and erasing her bludgeon of coercion, the State. I frustrate the liberal by insisting that the pace of change embrace hundreds and thousands of generations and erasing her bludgeon of coercion, the State. I frustrate both by insisting that they exclude murder and incarcerations and wars from their bag of acceptable strategies. In

---

[1165] See [♪] Pinker, *Better Angels of Our Nature*, for a sustained argument of this proposition. I did not believe that violence is waning globally until I read Pinker's book.

my view, conservatism and liberalism are themselves conceptual structures that lack deliberative warrant. Their day has passed.

To call me a terrorist smacks of the silly hyperbole that hobbles so much contemporary political dialogue. Everyone who helps a neighbor or carries a federal gun is not a hero.[1166] Every person who takes up a cause is not a crusader. Every speaker who advocates fundamental change is not a terrorist. Every error is not evil. The sociopaths this objector lists erected bridges to their vision of tomorrow from the bones of opponents and innocents. Their bane is patent. It demeans our ill-judgment of those evil men to speak my name with theirs. I am banal and murderless. I am a typist.

In choosing revolution, one declares her patience exhausted, her imagination fried. If revolution worked, I might participate. We have suffered revolutions. Revolution does not work.

8.3. *Thanatoid Agenda.* Taking a thanatoid perspective, the constituent communities of the Commons might address persistent short-comings.

8.3.1. *Personal Existence.* Man can banish loneliness, anomie, and anonymity. Humankind can revise its social goals, seeking to restructure to small, inter-dependent communities that aim to increase adaptive social experimentation and member identification with the member's community. Quad sociality might spell the end of our already-floundering nation-states. Humans, when gripped with thanatoid perspective, prefer interpersonal richness to impersonal affluence.

8.3.2. *Depopulation.* The human community can guide itself to achieve stable global population at manageable numbers. The necessary technologies already exist. Reaching sustainable populations will entail generations of de-population stresses to reach a number of members the global Commons deems appropriate. One measure of sustainable population is this: Can the human community provide meaningful existence to every child being born?[1167] If not, the sustainable population consists in yet fewer members. Another measure of sustainable population is this: Can the earth's other species, where not inimical to human well being, prosper despite the impact of human communities? If not, there should be fewer humans. Another measure of sustainable population is this: Has scarcity disappeared? Is every person born important, nurtured, and integrated in-

---

[1166] Burke notes (of bishops), "When we talk of the heroic, of course we talk of rare, virtue." Burke, *Reflections on the Revolution in France*, 150.

[1167] Mill said, "The fact itself, of causing the existence of a human being, is one of the most responsible actions in the range of human life. To undertake this responsibility—to bestow a life which may be either a curse or a blessing—unless the being on whom it is to be bestowed will have at least the ordinary chances of a desirable existence, is a crime against that being. And in a country either over-peopled, or threatened with being so, to produce children, beyond a very small number, with the effect of reducing the reward of labour by their competition, is a serious offence against all who live by the remuneration of their labour." [♪] Mill, *On Liberty*, 103.

to a circle in a Quad community? If not, humans need to yet further reduce their numbers, to insure well-being for every child.[1168] One cannot establish a flourishing community where scarcity savages some members. In my view, sustainable human numbers lie somewhere below one billion. My view is equivocal.

8.3.3. *Sustainable Consumables.* The human community can seek technological advances that provide human consumables at much-reduced environmental impact. High on the list of desirable technologies should be high-quality artificial protein. Animal production of protein necessitates the mass killing of animals for human nutrition, and commits humans to employing vast tracts of land to produce those slaughter animals that might otherwise remain wild for native species.[1169] High capacity batteries would change the human energy equation. Higher efficiency solar collectors might charge those batteries. Energy technology should be downsized and decentralized, aiming to supply single communities and each factory individually.

8.3.4. *Condensed Infrastructure.* The human community should concentrate human communities into small, dense centers, leaving most of the planet fallow, for purpose of recovery from overuse and to foster diverse wild species.

8.3.5. *Qualitative Economic Ends.* The human community can revise its economic purposes to aim at improved quality of life, rather than quantity of possessions, thereby reducing economic inequality and environmental degradation. Such change entails a fundamental shift from tangible capital to social capital as the primary measure of prosperity.[1170] We could measure prosperity, not in gold, but in the coin of affectionate intimacy. Misguided wealth produces obscenities of indulgence, which impacts should be mitigated. Communities should cherish egalitarian participa-

---

[1168] [♪] Emerson, *Conduct of Life*, 1081 (VII): "If government knew how, I should like to see it check, not multiply the population. When it reaches its true law of action, every man that is born will be hailed as essential. Away with this hurrah of masses, and let us have the considerate vote of single men spoken on their honor and their conscience."

[1169] Peter Singer notes that we seem incapable of rearing and slaughtering food animals without cruelty and unnecessary animal suffering. Vegetarian cultures (such as Indian Hinduism) prosper without animal meats, as do millions of vegetarians wordide. Singer, *Animal Liberation*, 95-157, 229. I infer that Singer would argue we have no need of artificial animal protein, since vegetable proteins, in combination, provide all the amino acids a human requires.

[1170] Robert Putnam notes that high social capital regions better educate children, and improve child welfare generally. Neighborhoods become safer and more productive. Groups with high social capital are more productive economically. Health and happiness surge. Democracy works better where social capital is high. Putnam, *Bowling Alone*, 285ff.

tion, and elevate human capital over things monetary. Money-hoarders should become objects of moral derision.[1171]

8.3.6. *Irenism.* The human community can restructure its moral values to exclude coercion. We can slow down, emphasizing transgenerational deliberation and patience. Member deviance could be tolerated, except when dangerous. Community deviance should be tolerated, except when impermissibly coercive toward members or other communities. Humans can tame their violent impulses; we have been getting better and better at that for tens of thousands of years. The first line of defense against human aggression is not counter-aggression, but education and nurture and patient opposition. The second line of defense is meta-protest; we intervene with others to remediate the underlying causes of violence. The last, and seldom employed, line of defense lies in collaborating communities employing or combining their martial designees to exercise coercion. When one mulls the human past of extermination, homicide, genocide, species extinctions, feuding, vendettas, raiding, rape, theological murder, cannibalism, and infanticide, one recognizes the urgency of bridling

---

[1171] The Diggers present an instructive tale. Diggers, so named by their detractors, called themselves "True Levellers." Diggers sought, being inspired by the model of first-century Christian communism, to level the economic playing field. They asked that common land be made available to anyone who would till it, and that the law reflect this economic-leveling sentiment. More broadly, Winstanley argued: "And so the Earth that was made a common Treasury for all to live comfortably upon, is become through man's unrighteous actions one over another, to be a place, wherein one torments another." And again, "Those that Buy and Sell Land, and are landlord, have got it either by Oppression, or Murther, or Theft; and all landlords lives in the breach of the Seventh and Eighth Commandements, Thou shalt not steal, nor kill." Winstanley, *True Levelers' Standard Advanced*, 8-9, 14 (original grammar, spelling and punctuation retained). In 1648, at Saint George's Hill, one location where the True Levellers did their vegetable gardening, during a time when food prices had spiked, Gerrard Winstanley published a pamphlet calling for an end to the British aristocracy's perks and privileges. He sought "a just portion [of land] for each man to live, that so none need to beg or steal for want, but everyone may live comfortably." Berens, *The Digger Movement*, 75, citing Winstanley's 1648 pamphlet, *A Light Shining in Buckinghamshire*. Winstanley advocated a classless, agrarian, communist village life, with a strong Quaker theological undertow. The Diggers took up residence on Saint George's Hill, an unoccupied height of Crown land in Surrey near London, planted crops in generally barren land, built huts, and invited all to join them. Winstanley's thought encouraged what we would now call an ecological approach to agriculture, as well as social and economic egalitarianism. Alarmed by the rabble's digging on Saint George's Hill, local landowners complained to the king. A commander of the royal army reviewed the situation and interviewed Winstanley and his co-agitator, William Everard. He found the Diggers doing no harm, and referred the locals to the courts for remedies. The lord of Saint George's Hill took matters into his own hands. He hired gangs to assault the Diggers. Arson consumed the Diggers' communal house. The Diggers were hauled before a court, but not allowed to speak on their own behalf. The Diggers abandoned Saint George's Hill in 1649. The Diggers' concerns have gone unheeded, especially at their hilltop redoubt. Saint George's Hill, now a precinct of Weybridge in Surrey, comprises around 450 mansions, the average selling price of which exceeds three million pounds. Saint George's Hill has become a gated community with twenty-four hour human and electronic security. Saint George's Hill is known for its twenty-eight tennis courts and world-class golf course, and remains one of London's most exclusive residential districts. Saint George's Hill styles itself "Europe's Premier Private Estate," touting its many wealthy residents, proximity to England's most exclusive private schools, and, for those of inordinate wealth, a life simpler than that offered in London proper.

bloodlust. The transgenerational future is an irenic path. Build pacific habits in yourself and your community.

8.3.7. *Interconnectivity.* The human community can restructure its information values to provide free, high-quality information to ordinary members and communities, so that all may nurture sufficient comprehension and intention to participate in the global ethics deliberation.[1172] Human communication is a natural resource; no member should commandeer its course or ration the exchange for profit. Intellectual property is a nullity, violating the fundamental nature of information, which is free to any brain that can comprehend it. Lawyers should deem intellectual property void because it contradicts good public policy. We should collectively compensate creators for their creations, then broadcast their insights freely. We must praise inventive creators, and adopt their ideas and products. We need not, however, grant them license to hide the very information for which we praise them.[1173] Information interconnectivity is the fundament of the Commons. Access to that long conversation about matters essential to every member bears preemptive importance. Ideas coursing in the Commons provide the seed for community innovation. It gives voice to the otherwise persecuted neurodiverse savant. The Commons opens the floodgates of that vast, pent-up reservoir of impermissible innovation, let-

---

[1172] Fledgling steps toward this goal are underway. Gary Bloom finds such attitudes in the Creative Commons. See creativecommons.org.

[1173] As a lawyer, I sense the collective shudder of the intellectual property community. I do not advocate that an inventor or innovator should have no benefit from his labors. I merely urge that information be shared freely so that the uses to which new technologies may be put can be maximally exploited. We must re-balance the public-private balance of use and creation, weighing the public uses more heavily than we have to date. Inventors and innovators can get "paid," to the extent deemed fair, by seeking compensation from those who utilize the information or techniques they created. Intellectual property should flow into the Commons, then out to the global community where it is employed, if useful. One invents or creates. One submits these fruits to the Commons. People utilize the Commons storehouse of human knowledge. Those using such knowledge profitably compensate their benefactors of knowledge with some fair share of profits. We must alter the path to compensation from "invention, sequester, profit, public use" to "invention, public use, profit-sharing." To effect such changes in the United States will require a constitutional amendment. Article I, Section 8 of the United States Constitution provides: "The Congress shall have all power . . . to promote the progress of science and useful arts, by securing for limited times to authors and inventors the exclusive right to their respective writings and discoveries." The constitutional order of values is skewed. Patents and copyrights sequester knowledge until its immediate utility wanes. Patents and copyrights enforce the sad engine of frenzied profit-mongering. These legal institutions injure mankind. Much that private parties would like to seize is the property of all. Corporations seek to patent genes. Publishing houses tie up old texts with a new introduction or translation. Competitors purchase intellectual rights to much-needed inventions to preserve their current market shares. The King estate has turned America's public man into a sequestered money-grubbing corporation. To the contrary, knowledge belongs to all. To sequester is to hoard. Ideas are a cultural commons. Neither they, nor their expression, can be owned. We must value access to knowledge over profit from knowledge. Doing otherwise injures us. Lewis Hyde cited Thomas Jefferson for the proposition, "The field of knowledge is the common property of mankind." Hyde, *Common as Air*, 15.

ting those odd waters flood into the minds of the communities of earth. The Commons provides groundwork for education and nurture of children and adults. All books in the human inventory of tomes should be available to members at no cost.[1174] Every voice should speak. Commonweal emerges from the quality of our collective conversations, and the depth of those topics. Dialogue seeds; communities weed.

8.3.8. *Identity.* The human community can inculcate two identifications: the first, with one's own local community, and, second, with the global human Commons.[1175] The individualist identity promulgated by modern anonymous democracies guts human normalcy. Unbridled differentiation has failed. Humans are members, not individuals. We accomplish nothing important when we trade the coercions of governments for an isolated solipsism. Humans choose together; those with whom we choose are friends. We interpenetrate, shaping one another in cybernetic[1176] reciprocity. Communities can restore the human sense of belonging, without crushing the uniqueness of members. But to do so, our intolerance of the odd must wane. Such an outcome requires nothing more than pointing out our intolerances, and establishing different habits of thoughts.

One might view this list as a starting point for thanatoid deliberation, to be edited and redirected as deeper wisdom possesses mankind.

8.4. *Thanatoid Transition.* Patience and action set the Quad farsight horizon apart from a fool's utopia. Quad sociality will predominate, in humankind's long haul, not because of propaganda or revolutions or coercions of law and custom. Quad sociality will prevail because humans long to cooperate, to survive, to wallow in meaning, and to contribute to the human future. The niggardly acquisitive isolation of many individuals betrays scarcity neurosis, not a corrupt human fundament. Where humans stand well-nurtured, they prove grand collaborators. Fifty thousand years ago, our breeding habits outpaced food production, creating our technological marathon against

---

[1174] John Milton says, "Truth and understanding are not such wares as to be monopolised and traded in by tickets, and statutes, and standards. We must not think to make a staple commodity of all the knowledge in the land, to make and license it like our broadcloth and our woolpacks." Milton, *Areopagitica*, 32. In a feat of self-contradiction, *Cull* is copyrighted, and you have no right to use its language without my permission.

[1175] This list, while heavily adapted to reflect the conclusions of this writer, relies upon Schellnhuber and Molina, *Global Sustainability*, at Chapter 1, Murray Gell-Mann, "Transformations of the twenty-first century: transitions to greater sustainability," 6-7. They call this sort of overview agenda a "crude look at the whole." As an acronym, this is CLAW.

[1176] "Cybernetic" refers to mutual control systems employing feedback loops, in such complex systems as human brains, communication systems, or complex mechanical devices such as computers or thermostats. See *Webster's Third New International Dictionary*, s.v. "cybernetics."

scarcity.[1177] We dwell in the undeliberated result: high technical capability fitfully supporting a dramatically bloated population. The qualitative cost is staggering. We dwell in a monotone rendering that exigency paints on life's canvas, a depiction shorn of much interpersonal depth and meaning-laden brilliance. Some starve. Many wilt. We want more and better.[1178]

After so many confused generations, one hardly expects consensus in Quad sociality to emerge rapidly. Ours is a species in maturation. The welter of human opinion has proved, for millennia, recalcitrant. Life seems divorced from the possibility of meaningful interpersonal opulence. We work, then work, then work, then avoid work, then quit work, exhausted. Then we die. Life drains its effervescence upon humanity's ill-deliberated rat wheel, ever accelerating toward nowhere in particular. We cope with hyperpopulation crises in crescendo. Starvation, then civil war, then pollution, then international police actions, then genocide, then religious fanaticisms, then plagues, then suicide epidemics, then widespread isolation, then men with guns in schools, then economic depression. Relationships fracture in the dissonant assymetry of western culture. What irony to call our present coercive governments and institutions "civilization" and "order," when what they foster is chaos and savage brutality.[1179] Under their tutelage, anomie and epidemic loneliness prosper. Half the planet starves. We sigh, exhausted. Life need not be so. We can cull differently.

[1177] Taylor argues that stateless societies, which he calls "acephalous" (lacking a head) are the human social norm, having been replaced only lately by anonymous, hierarchical states. Taylor argues that even chiefdoms and big-man societies may be anarchic, provided power is not concentrated. Even some peasant communities, dwelling within states, function as quasi-anarchies. They are responsible for regulating their own internal affairs, and do so without formal power or authority. Taylor calls such "closed corporate peasant communities." Intentional community (such as utopian communities, secular family communes, urban non-residential fellowships, and kibbutzim) function in quasi-anarchy, though embedded in a state. [♪] Taylor, *Community, Anarchy, and Liberty*, 33-38.

[1178] Wilson anticipates that, in the course of the twenty-first century, mankind can get well on the way to a functional paradise for humanity and earth's biosphere, but only if we begin to cope with our inherent dysfunctions: anemic mass governance, affection for tribal conflict, addiction to overpopulation, limited horizons, and faith-based ignorances. [♪] Wilson, *The Meaning of Human Existence*, 176-187. In my view, Wilson's schedule is unrealistically optimistic.

[1179] Anselm Bellegarrigue, nineteenth century French revolutionary, argued that government is, in its essence, civil war. When one abandons coercion, and grounds societal structure in the consent of participants, one finds stable order. Any government is, according to Bellegarrigue, too much government. Woodcock, *Anarchism*, 231. Simone de Beauvoir said, "The only public good is that which assures the private good of the citizens; we shall pass judgment on institutions according to their effectiveness in giving concrete opportunities to individuals." De Beauvoir, *The Second Sex*, lviii.

> GUITARS STRETCH GRADED STRINGS;
> PLAYERS TUNE;
> SONGS—HARMONY IN A CONTEXT.
>   COMMUNITIES JUXTAPOSE MEMBER TENSIONS;
>   CULTURES TUNE;
>   MEANING—SYNERGY IN A FRAMEWORK.

One need not wait for mankind to catch up, Kate. Build a Quad community in your life. Start today. Make of yourself a wonder. Deepen friendships. Link friends to one another. Join with other cadres for common tasks. Live near friends. Form a community, if opportunity presents itself, or join one. Help friends recognize their social existence and care about it. Talk about your togetherness, its shape, its possibilities. Mine for yourself, Kate, life's rich veins. Look around yourself carefully; you will see others similarly employed, even if they lack language to pin to their behaviors. Building a cadre with others, that is, making yourself flourish, is not selfish. Fashioning a meaning-laden life is the task to which every member is born. This book offers no one-size-fits-all agenda. For one size does not fit all. *Cull* does not specify how you should create your community, for that cannot be prescribed. Every free community is its own self, as unique as its members individually.[1180] The core technique is something every human can do and longs to do: build friendship, fashion meaning. When you hear of another Quad community, contact them. Share. Build relationships. Invite collaboration. Learn from one another. Redirect the internet to constructive purposes. Divert the din of chatter into deeper, constructive channels, sparking the Commons dialogue. Laugh, but be serious. Life is at stake.[1181]

Within kithdom, you will be called to tolerate experiments by communities other than your own, Kate. Some will adopt forms of life you know lead to no good outcome. Speak to such communities in the Commons dialogue, object, correct, but in the end, tolerate. Life spanks the errant. Oppressed members of those errant communities will recognize better life elsewhere, and depart or dissent. Make sure meaningful existence is visible to them in your life. Trust kithdom. Every human wants what is best for himself or herself. They may not precisely perceive that path for a time,

---

[1180] Since the core structures of Western society (coercive government and global economy) undermine meaningful human community, you will be put to the task of experimenting, then settling upon a solution you deem promising enough to warrant your devotion. Many do likewise, though they are little heralded. They build communes and co-housing and intentional communities, effectively absenting themselves to some degree from their larger urban sprawls as to their fundamental social needs. So Pugh recommends. Pugh, *Biological Origins of Human Values*, 430.

[1181] Chatter is natter splattered with patter.

even for generations. But they will see. Interfere with life in other communities only when they undertake horrors: killing, or class oppressions, or rampant anomie. Let life teach them, as it is teaching you and yours. Life exceeds us, Kate. We are, ever, its humble students. Life is, ever, our faithful parent and instructor.

If you imagine your task to lie in convincing humankind to adopt Quad sociality, you will despair. Most of humanity lingers in adolescent bickering, if they converse at all. The hard work of deliberation daunts. Most humans have yet to become serious about flourishing. Most are consumed with tales of overcoming evil caricatures, ever styling themselves their epic's heroes. Most wander in defensiveness, desperately clawing at every irritant. Many lives cycle from ignorance to denial to anger to depression, then back to ignorance. Listen to the news, Kate. Analogize what you hear to a fairy tale; note the puerile texture of the tale's moral. Most ignore their peril. Most, though social paupers, let toys distract them, and so feel rich. One cannot convince chatterers of their error.[1182] Do not try. Speak to the future. Some of the recalcitrant may waver. But you will certainly persuade hordes of their children and grandchildren of the wisdom of flourishing. Quad sociality dwells in patience. In the human heart lies generosity and empathy, were we but to exclude scarcity and terror. Quad sociality is nothing more than mankind flourishing. And that every person, in the end, wants. For herself. For her loved ones.

9. ***Quad Community Life.*** In the technical sense, this fourth section of *Cull* concerns "politics," but in the Hellenic, even Aristotelian, sense of the word: friends relating within a polis, and relations between polis and polis.[1183] The Greek polis was a town; we might prefer to call them hamlets or villages; often citizens numbered no more than a few thousand.[1184] Aristotle thought the maximum size of a polis was the number of people one could take in in a

---

[1182] Epictetus observes that some people, due to stubbornness of will and intellect, become immune to rational considerations. Such resist what is plain. They are flagrant with facts. There is nothing to be done for such persons. Epictetus, *Discourses*, 37 (Book I, Sections 5.1-3). Christopher Boehm attributes greater significance to chatter. He asserts that moralistic gossip is the spring from which group members imbibe the contents of conscience. Boehm, *Moral Origins*, 33-34.

[1183] In Aristotle's view, the well-constructed polis is the highest good, since such a community includes within its purposes the highest good of every member. [♪] Aristotle, *Nichomachean Ethics*, 4 (1094b).

[1184] For a recollection of relations among Greek cities in war mode, see Thucydides, *Peloponnesian War*. In this Hellenic melee, the cities, each independent, linked by culture of Hellas, form shifting alliances for the ignoble purpose of domination of Hellas by the Attic or Spartan leagues.

glance, and the territory necessary that surveyed in one glance. Even big cities (Athens, for example) were not big by our standards.[1185]

The community, as Quad sociality contemplates it, is not a bellicose Greek polis, but rather a more deeply structured irenic association comprising ten or more circles of 150 or so members each. In this "politics," one does not prescribe for others how they must organize themselves, but suggests ways of associating and relating that may well produce much improved outcomes for people. Community structure and attitudes matter because one fails to deliberate the breadth of human life without considering how groups shape themselves and deal with their common problems.[1186]

Politically, Quad sociality is kithdom.[1187] Communities of friends and associates are the building blocks of human existence for Quad sociality. Communities aggregate circles of cadres into consensus groups. The Commons creates a structure within which communities learn, speak, listen, collaborate, and deliberate. The community, as the prime locus of personal existence and social adaptation, predominates. This work proposes a revised communal agenda that deviates from the common usage of the word "political" and the common practices of existing political institutions. Insofar as it advocates abandoning our anonymous institutional structures altogether, it may not be "politics" at all, in the conventional sense, but rather an "anti-politics."[1188] In kithdom, no States exist.[1189]

[1185] The city, an artifact of Western hyperpopulation, lives to exclude. This is mine; that is yours. These people are mine; those are yours. "Property" is a sign one hangs on his door telling others to keep their hands off. Tagore describes political civilization as a carnivorous weed sprung from European soils overrunning the world, consuming it. Tagore, *Nationalism*, unpaginated. Michael Shermer anticipates that mankind may well choose to dwell in small city-state political communities. Shermer, *The Moral Arc*, 403.

[1186] So Aristotle argues in his transition from *Nichomachean Ethics* to his *Politics*. [♪] Aristotle, *Nichomachean Ethics*, 204 (1181b).

[1187] The term "kithdom" is a coinage from nerd and gamer subcultures. "Kith" means close friends, neighbors and acquaintances, and, at its furthest extension, fellow countrymen. Kith may also reference a group that shares a culture and tends to take mates from within the group. See *Webster's Third New International Dictionary*, s.v. "kith."

[1188] Robert Nisbet (writing in the aftermath of World War II) argues that the quest for community is the most prominent social tendency of that century. The centralized State has so disrupted the core social associations of society that recovering community has become an "ominous preoccupation." Nisbet, *The Quest for Community*, 45, 47.

[1189] I capitalize the word "state" when used to mean a "collective coercive agent" in order to avoid confusion with other meanings of the word.
     Robert Paul Wolff, criticizing all theories of the State, says: "The simple fact is that genuine direct unanimous self-legislation is the foundation of the truly legitimate state, and every other political arrangement is a compromise covertly or overtly designed to aid some interests in society and frustrate others." Wolff, *In Defense of Anarchism*, xxi.

Consider these particular divergences:

9.1. *Delimited Coercion.* Existing political institutions, such as the State, religions, or corporations, are structures for the administration of overt and covert coercions, sometimes violent.[1190] In Quad communities, coercion should be avoided for community purposes, except in exigent circumstances when confronting adamant evils.[1191] Disputes should be settled, not by violence or its threat, but by irenic talking and patience, conjoined with the possibility of further irenic contravening action.[1192] The pace of the Com-

---

Alexis de Tocqueville says of the American and French Revolutions: "A new science of politics is indispensable to a new world." De Tocqueville, *Democracy in America*, xvi. So too, kithdom.

[1190] States successfully claim sole right to violent coercion within a given territory. Weber, *Politics as a Vocation*, 33. Mo reports a Chinese mythology of violent state coercion. In the mythic past, before rulers, every man had an opinion that differed from that of every other man. All thought themselves right. Hatreds brewed, and soon no man would cooperate with another. So the people chose the most benevolent man as Son of Heaven. He created an administration under himself, and required all to report to their superiors and adopt the opinions of their superiors. In this way, order was established. Heaven requires that the people venerate Heaven itself, not just the Son of Heaven. The sage kings devised the five punishments, which were probably tattooing, severing the nose, severing the feet, castration, and death. By these expedients, the Son of Heaven reined in persons who failed to adopt the attitudes and perspectives of superiors. [♪] *Mozi*, 35-39 (Part I, §2). I, for one, am not anxious to suffer the rule of Mo's Son of Heaven.

[1191] Supporters of State coercion say the strangest things in defense of the indefensible. Dante longs for a global kingdom, and argues: "The human race for its best disposition is dependent on unity in wills. But this state of concord is impossible unless one will dominates and guides all others into unity. . . . Nor is this directing will a possibility unless there is one common Prince whose will may dominate and guide the wills of all others." Dante, *De Monarchia*, 61.

[1192] I am an irenist. Quad sociality is a species of attenuated anarchist polity. I wed my version of pacifism with Quad sociality. Pacifism and anarchy are by no means, however, inseparable. Consider violent revolutionists: Marx, Lenin, Mao, Stalin, Stirner, Bakunin, Qutb. Some of the most violent mass murderers of the last two centuries have been anarchists with guns on a mission. Stirner denied the existence of human rights. One gets by force; what one cannot get by force, one lacks. Stirner, *The Ego and Its Own*, 187. Stirner even argues that legitimate human concern never extends beyond one's own personal interests and needs. All other claims to allegiance are forms of enslavement, vehemently to be cast off: parents, friends, one's own conscience. Stirner, *The Ego and Its Own*, 6-14. Stirner truncates human community into a mere aggregation of atomistic egoists. Stirner, *The Ego and Its Own*, 161. For Stirner, the wrongness of the State lies in its willingness (and ability) to coerce him, to despotize the imperious ego. Stirner responds with stern refusal, and a declaration of war. Stirner, *The Ego and Its Own*, 175. The amalgam I seek to foster is equivocal. I call my anarchism attenuated because, in the eyes of most anarchists, my view would not be anarchic at all. I retain the collective, granting it due pre-eminence over the member. Many anarchists advocate extreme individualism, and view themselves as warring with human collectives. Godwin goes so far as to declare the individual all, and society a nullity. [♪] Godwin, *Political Justice*, Vol. II, 128 (Book V, Chapter XX). Most anarchists, in addition to their penchant for advocating violent revolution, seek hasty change for circumstances that they believe constitute emergencies. They demand not merely change, but rapid transformation. Kropotkin wants to violently raze private property, social classes, and existing morality, to achieve a world without government, where men act freely and take initiative. See Kropotkin, *Revolutionary Government*, 2, or [♪] Kropotkin, *Conquest of Bread*, 87 (Chapter VIII). Quad sociality seeks deliberated, transgenerational change over the course of centuries, conserving what works, experimenting to find replacements for approaches that do not work. Woodcock argues that "residual conservatism" lingers in every version of anarchism. Woodcock, *Anarchism*, 404. So, Quad sociality appears the tortoise to anarchy's hare. Hence, I

mons is transgenerational. Thanatoid deliberation admits no implementation by force and needs none. The weight of high-quality transgenerational deliberation crushes short-term urgencies among members educated to thanatoid conversation. When a community deviates, the Commons tolerates, convinced that the outcome will speak for itself. Humans, experiencing urgency, err frequently.[1193] Leisurely deliberation deflects many avoidable missteps.[1194]

9.2. *Obviating Law.*[1195] The handmaid and henchman of political coercion is law.[1196] Laws, and their attendant machinery, lawyers and courts, grind human moral topography to a glassy plain. Law exists to voice society's less subtle demands. Despite the unbridled applause afforded law by its many enthusiasts, law's results, upon inspection, give pause. I do not argue that law should never have existed. I argue that we are positioned at this juncture in human history for law to be superseded by kithdom's mutuality, consensus, and informality.[1197]

---

prefer to style Quad sociality's political theory a kithdom, the dominion of friendship, rather than adopt the term "anarchy," which term describes what its political theory is not, rather than what it is, and which term has been sullied by so many violent, frenetic, ill-deliberate men. Quad sociality, unlike political anarchy, is irenic, paced, deliberative, communal, listening, collaborative, and, one hopes, ultimately natural for members. For a contemporary individualist morality, see Shermer, *The Moral Arc*, 13-14.

[1193] Sarah Conly argues that these many ill-deliberate errors of judgment are inextricable from human decision-making. They justify a dramatic increase in well-intentioned controls, which she calls "coercive paternalism," to keep us from injuring ourselves and making a fundamentally better world impossible. She would have more numerous and more intrusive laws made by democratic processes during our spates of lucid thought. Conly believes, for example, outlawing tobacco and cigarettes would help us all be healthier. (About that, she may be correct.) [♪] Conly, *Against Autonomy*, 32-33.

[1194] See the further discussion of coercion below.

[1195] William Godwin, at the end of the eighteenth century, critiqued law with eloquence. This argument recapitulates portions of Godwin's insights, and adds some twists from a practicing lawyer. [♪] Godwin, *Political Justice*, Vol. II, 288-304 (Book VII, Chapter VIII).

[1196] Cicero would find my characterization of law offensive. Cicero roots law in nature, and argues: "The origin of Justice is to be found in Law, for Law is a natural force; it is the mind and reason of the intelligent man, the standard by which Justice and Injustice are measured." Cicero, *On Laws* (*De Legibus*), 317-319 (Book I, Sections V:19-20). If matters were as Cicero states, I would cherish a kinder opinion of law. Law is what courts and lawyers do. That regularly leaves much to be desired.

[1197] F. A. Hayek disagrees. "When we obey laws, in the sense of general abstract rules laid down irrespective of their application to us, we are not subject to another man's will and are therefore free." Hayek further argues that we stay free from coercive acts by threatening countervailing coercion. Hayek, *The Constitution of Liberty*, 221, 71. Hayek's liberty smells like war. Jared Diamond finds law necessary when living with strangers: "The state's large population also guarantees that most people within a state are strangers to each other. . . . That need for police and laws and moral commandments to be nice to strangers doesn't arise in tiny societies, in which everyone knows everyone else." Diamond, *The World Until Yesterday*, 10-11.

Lawyers, for a living, craft words. Consider America. I am an American lawyer. Some legislators are lawyers. Most judges are lawyers. Almost half of American presidents were lawyers. Confront a lawyer with a problem, and she will give a solution: words. If that lawyer is lucky or well-connected, her solution might become law, when elected lawyers vote to impose that solution upon all. Then another lawyer, a judge, will enforce the lucky lawyer's solution upon those many who are ignorant of the entire process. Where no mechanism for coercing compliance exists, laws lack import. So, for the word "law" one can always substitute the word "coercion." Quad sociality generates lawless society.[1198] This does not mean kithdoms lack rules. Rules in kithdoms are, however, local and directed toward known, consenting friends.[1199] These rules constitute working agreements among intimates, not impositions upon strangers, far and wide, by a doubtfully superior class of strangers.[1200]

Law, as a theory of human relations, has outlived its usefulness, for the following reasons:

9.2.1. *Pessimism.* Law pessimizes. Law perceives society's members as hordes of isolated cretins much inclined to antisocial outrages. Law fashions punishments sufficiently draconian to deter any who dare scoff, including solitary confinement, which inflicts depression and anomie, and death. In its grim, Hobbesian assessment of human sensibilities, law entirely ignores the essential gregariousness and cooperation of humans.

[1198] A "lawless society" would be dysfunctional, in Aristotle's view. One requires law to dissuade normal people, that is those who are neither noble nor habituated to good behavior by an effective intellect, to punish them enough to make compliance with good behavior a persuasive alternative. Where such persuasion proves impossible, one should banish unregenerate evil-doers. [♪] Aristotle, *Nichomachean Ethics*, 200-201 (1179b-1180a). Montesquieu takes law to be a natural sequel to the formation of human societies. First comes society, then inequality, then war. Law emerges to quell the worst of the results of this necessary progression. Montesquieu, *The Spirit of Laws*, 5.

[1199] Lao Tzu painted a picture of ruling according to the Way: "To rule according to the Way is to rule without force: Just and equal give-and-take rules in the community." Lao Tzu, as cited in Rocker, *Nationalism and Culture*, 256. William Morris's Hammond, member of the anarchist society of Nowhere, says: "A tradition or habit of life has been growing on us; and that habit has become a habit of acting on the whole for the best. . . . But when the transgressions occur, everybody, transgressors and all, know them for what they are; the errors of friends, not the habitual actions of persons driven into enmity against society." Morris goes on to report the demise of civil law and courts: "Nobody ever pretended that it was possible to make people act fairly to each other by means of brute force." Morris, *News from Nowhere*, 112.

[1200] David Hume states the contrary view. Because of the disorder of some, all must suffer laws and governments to prevent the specter of global savagery. "Human nature cannot, by any means, subsist, without the association of individuals; and that association never could have place, were no regard paid to the laws of equity and justice." [♪] Hume, *Enquiry Concerning the Principles of Morals*, 99 (Section 4, Number 3). In its best incarnations, law seeks to learn from human experience and remedy our collective potholes and silliness. Oliver Wendell Holmes said, "The life of the law has not been logic; it has been experience." Holmes, *The Common Law*, 5.

When humans gather in numbers, one anticipates remarkable peace and collaboration, often startlingly creative. Law, however, finds no room for celebration. Someone, somewhere in that crowd is likely to err. Law must ferret that person out and stigmatize him or her. Law expresses our fears in their most dark and anxious intrusions. Law's pessimism lies not as a lesion upon its skin, but deep in judicial bones.[1201] Men see themselves, in the mirror of law, not as moral, kind, empathetic, sympathetic, cooperative creatures inclined to help, anxious to create. Rather, the reflection men suffer at law portrays a species whose lives are "solitary, poor, nasty, brutish, and short."[1202] We are, according to law, reluctantly social, and quick to abandon society's needs. Law's mythology of man fixates upon the sociopath (who is definitely a problem to address), to the neglect of society's massively-more-numerous conformers and cooperators. Law is another name for coercion. Mature communities minimize both.

9.2.2. *Volume.* Law grows. Law has metastasized for fifteen thousand years. In a comprehensive law library, millions of pages burden shelves. Each page tells a little tale of coercion. No man knows the law. Law is a lake in a rainy region, shores beyond the horizon, inestimable in volume, flooding by the hour. The lake of law cannot be swallowed, or even adequately tasted. So, law is balkanized. One knows this bay, another that beach. Legal bays are poorly (if at all) coordinated. None knows, even in broad overview, the world's law. American lawyers are selected, by dint of law school admissions and coursework demands, for quick wits and attention to detail. None, however, is smart enough. Lawyers are psychologically and vocationally addicted to laws and coercions. If one complained to a lawyer about law's unmanageable volume, that lawyer might propose a law against further laws.

9.2.3. *Uncertainty and Confusion.* Since none knows the law, due to its avalanching volume, every argument finds support. Uncertainty prevails. Law, one assumes, began thousands of years ago to mitigate ambiguity and lend regularity, but has ended sowing confusion. The virtuous need

---

[1201] Thomas Andrews, a law professor, takes a more positive view of law. He styles much of law as facilitation of relationships among persons, property, and communities. Surely, he is correct. I overstate my case, but, nevertheless, am willing to persevere with that overstatement. Thomas Andrews, in private correspondence with the author, July 2016.

[1202] [♪] Hobbes, *Leviathan*, 107 (Chapter 13). Thomas Jefferson argues that economic desperation, caused by private or public excesses, leads men to be "glad to obtain subsistence by hiring ourselves to rivet their chains on the necks of our fellow-sufferers. . . . Then begins, indeed, the *bellum omnium in omnia*, which some philosophers observing to be so general in this world, have mistaken it for the natural, instead of the abusive state of man." For the government's part in driving men to despair, its primary error is excessive taxation. Jefferson, *Writings*, 1400-1401 (*Letter to Samuel Kercheval*, July 12, 1816).

no laws, the vice-ridden scoff, and the masses muddle along, uncompre-hending, in the shadow of law. If you want to know what is right to do, ask a lawyer. If you disdain that lawyer's answer, ask a different lawyer. Eventually, you will find a lawyer who mumbles the answer you prefer. This uncertainty in law is irremediable. We cannot undertake repairs to make of law a passable rule for living. Circumstances, technologies, peo-ple, social structures, climates, genetics, and divergent values all mutate. Law is perpetually dated, settling questions no longer bearing directly up-on life's cutting edge. So, law asks us to impose dated solutions upon emerging events, leaving us always with a mismatch of varying degrees of severity. That confuses. That renders law unreliable. According to Nozick, none has the moral right to use unreliable procedures of justice to punish another.[1203]

9.2.4. *Categorizing the Unique.* Law abstracts. Law categorizes humans, events, and outcomes. Each such human, event, and outcome is unique, and so defies categorization. Law perseveres undeterred. Law pigeon-holes where no orifice fits, pounding square pegs in round holes on every judicial calendar. Does not justice demand a workable solution to a prob-lem, one tailored to the uniqueness of involved individuals and circum-stances? How, then, can law do justice? Judicial gavels are blunt instru-ments; so too laws.

9.2.5. *Legibility.* Law intrudes. Statutes render citizens, who are multi-form and wild, into lowing, gentle, numbered herds. In this sense, law seeks to make bewildering human oddity legible to administrators.[1204] Bureaucra-cy needs units it can find. Law cuts up the land you live on, and, if you are lucky and diligent, allocates you a chunk. Law tells you where you can and cannot walk. Law specifies what is yours, what is others', and what belongs to governments. In its worst incarnations, law controls your thoughts. Law renders people as one renders fat into useable products— under low, but persistent, heat. Law tells your parents how you must be named. Law assigns you a number. Law cares nothing about knowing you. Law wants to read you as a cipher of yourself.

9.2.6. *Hypertrophy of Procedure.* Lawyers know they get things wrong. At each stumble, pressure grows for reformation. When lawyers reform, they create new procedures or gloss well-worn ones. Procedure grows ever more complex. Forms govern the use of forms, leading one to that form

---

[1203] [♪] Nozick, *Anarchy, State, and Utopia*, 106. Nozick, further, argues that every individual pos-sesses the right to defend himself or herself from justice procedures he deems insufficiently reliable. [♪] Nozick, *Anarchy, State, and Utopia*, 102.

[1204] James Scott styles government an attempt to standardize people and their circumstances for ease of management and control. Scott, *Seeing Like a State*, 2, 183.

preferred for each circumstance. When that approach goes awry, yet more procedures are fashioned. Law becomes a written conundrum metastasizing into a quagmire of endless mazes. Few people believe bumbling through mazes might address their need for guidance and coercion of an opponent. Yet, law has little else to offer.

9.2.7. *Unresponsive.* Law walks backward toward what lies ahead. The judicial eye peers at what has come before, sometimes generations before, only occasionally daring to glance at the future being created. Law calls this penchant for inverted ambulation "precedent." If there were once a case similar to that before a court, the outcome today should follow the solution previously given. So, it is a judge's role to repeat the errors of the past, unless someone rich enough to appeal has convinced a higher court to alter the precedent. Precedent enshrines unwarranted adherence to the choices of now-dead judges in cases long moot. Precedent makes law a bulwark of conservative recalcitrance. One may argue that at least judges deliberate, which activity *Cull* celebrates. And yet one wonders exactly what a judge deliberates.

9.2.8. *Paternalism.* Law presumes normal people, if they have disputes, cannot reasonably shape their own lives. Courts must intervene.[1205] The presumption demeans all, and induces a crippling reliance upon unwieldy (read this as slow, expensive, and emotionally unsatisfying) legal processes for resolving pedestrian conflicts. Poor and middle class people are priced out of dispute resolution, and monied interests nock courts as one arrow from their quiver of financial armaments against competitors and opponents.

9.2.9. *Presumption of Coercion.* Law coerces. The bottom line in every court case is this shrill imperative: do what I want or a judge will compel you to do what I want.[1206] Every law presumes that, once enacted, noncompliance merits penalties. Law gulps the punch bowl of coercion whole. As such, judicial process insures simmering retribution and retaliation, having ended each case in something other than peace. To the coerced litigant, it matters little whether he was strong-armed by an opponent or an impartial judge. The circumstance demands response. The litigated conflict survives its judicial resolution, and flares. Law assumes a

---

[1205] Alternative dispute resolution (mediation, tribal councils, arbitration, collaboration, and so forth) resolves disputes outside the courts. Yet these vibrant options remain "alternative" to primary dispute resolution, judicial determination upon trial.

[1206] Thomas Paine, in his fanciful tale of man's coalescence into societies, imagines that the first public guidance was enforced by nothing more than public finger-wagging. But men discover that considerations of virtue lack sufficient gravity to organize the world, and so government is born for man's freedom and security. Paine, *Common Sense*, 252-253.

command-and-control posture. Having assumed that the persons or entities governed care only about self-interest, law ferrets infractions and punishes offenders. Conversations that might create better-functioning agreements are crushed.[1207]

9.2.10. *Injudicious Judges.* Selecting judges proves problematical. The method of selecting adjudicators has little to do with their wisdom and ability, and much to do with their political savvy, available capital, and connections. Some states elect judges; others appoint.[1208] Election insures judges with familiar names crowd the bench. Appointment favors sychophants and sons-in-law of lame-duck governors. Neither format selects for wisdom or foresight or human empathy.

9.2.11. *Monetization.* Law monetizes non-financial values. Law determines a cash award to compensate for negligent death of a child or spouse. It awards dollars for dreams crushed in breach of contracts. It assesses child support as between parents, which children need attached attention from two or more parents ever so much more than financial clarity. Edmund Burke went so far as to say "The revenue of the state is the state."[1209] Burke confuses means with meaning. Monetization teaches us a rude, untrue lesson: life boils down to money.[1210]

9.2.12. *Vapidity.* Law drones on and on, regulating minutae, missing the momentous. Life exudes vim and mystery. Yet, law drones on. Having lost its feeling, law lionizes mere functioning.[1211] Law, if it were to have value, would brim with humanity's values. Instead, law excises exuberance and pares precocity. Law is a grim aunt, babysitting mankind.

9.2.13. *Lack of Alternatives.* Courts are creatures of States aggregating hordes of anonymous citizens. Impartial laws afford no alternative to cat-

---

[1207] Donald Pfaff notes that some scholars recommend principle-based governance, in which government prescribes outcomes, but leaves means to parties to resolve. Regulators would converse with regulated persons about best approaches, in a reciprocal exchange. Pfaff, *Altruistic Brain Theory*, 172-173.

[1208] Thomas Andrews notes that some jurisdictions appoint judges selected for their pertinent abilities by a citizen commission. Such is the case in England and Wales. Thomas Andrews, in private correspondence with the author, July 2016.

[1209] Burke, *Reflections on the Revolution in France*, 229.

[1210] Chanakya, an Indian teacher whose life bridged the fourth to third centuries B.C., argued that States make happiness. He says that wisdom leads to elder worship, which leads to humility, which leads to control over sense experience, which leads to the State, which leads to wealth, which leads to righteousness, which leads to happiness. Chanakya, *Maxims of Chanakya*, 21-22.

[1211] Schweitzer finds ours a lawless period. Statutes proliferate, but belief in law is a smoking ruin. Law, where vital, is simply humanity codifying itself. Schweitzer, *The Philosophy of Civilization*, 82 (Preface).

egorization and prohibition. Since judges cannot know all litigants, they are prohibited from knowing any. Kithdoms open other possibilities. Small communities might better tailor decisions with members, involving all disputants in collaborative decision-making. The rules of kithdoms might be few, malleable, and aimed at improved social function in the near future. Kithdoms may also prevent many difficulties by addressing conflicts as they emerge (or even before they emerge), rather than years after disputes have hardened into positional controversies.

9.2.14. *Persistent Cooption.* The laws of lands are common tools by which wealthy people oppress the poor. Even where law is ostensibly even-handed, applying to all, one finds that the poor suffer greater penalties and more frequent incarcerations at law. One suspects that, at the edge of pre-history, literate (and hence wealthy) men wrote those first legal codes so that the rich could tell the poor what the poor cannot do without incurring the wrath of aristocrats. Rousseau takes class oppression to be the essence of law.[1212] Because law is the implement of landed people, a disproportionate measure of laws deal with property (that which the landed have and the unlanded lack).[1213]

9.2.15. *Danger of Laws.* Laws aggregate the sentiments and prejudices of legislatures and judges. Laws can be, and are, abused (selective enforcement, overzealous career-mongering, lobbied provisions, and unintended consequences, to mention a few). Abuses, when conjoined with the live possibility of raw bad lawmaking, make law dangerous. Laws intrude. The data collected to enforce laws degrades privacy. Watched intimacy squirms and cools. Being spied and criticized stifles creativity and free-wheeling experimentation. In short, law-driven government threatens human well-being.[1214] Can we not fashion a theory of mutual relation less sorely hobbled?[1215]

[1212] Rousseau, *Emile*, 236. Rousseau finds legal oppression of the poor to be inevitable and universal.

[1213] To dig back toward the origins of law (third millennium B.C.), the Code of Hammurabi would seem to be a long meditation on possession, classes (three: patricians, landless persons, and slaves), and the fate of those who dispossess wrongly. For example, theft from a temple (death: Law 6), robbery (death: Law 22), storing corn of others (one gur per five ka: Law 121), divorce (return the dowry: Law 138), bodily injury (broken bone for broken bone: Law 197), slave insolence (cut off slave's ear: Law 282). *Code of Hammurabi*, 29, 31, 39, 41, 49, 56.

[1214] Oddly, given the sentiment of her book, one finds Sarah Conly agreeing, to a degree. See [♪] Conly, *Against Autonomy*, 148.

[1215] Despite this parade of horribles concerning law, if one grants the existence of too many humans in anonymous societies, no reasonable alternative exists. I find much to admire in law. Intelligent people seek to solve important problems. American constitutional law brims with thoughtful adjustments and careful steps forward. A large number of attorneys appear to be genuinely good hu-

9.3. *Structural Deliberation.* Collective deliberation should replace coercion and violence as the engine of conflict resolution. Conversation has a goal: consensus. Where dissenters obstruct, conversation deepens. The communal structures advocated must be explained clearly; their rationale should be laid bare; their details elaborated. Quad sociality changes our conversation from one of entitlement, rights, self-interest, and freedoms, to talk of a deeper timbre, talk of belonging and gifts and interdependence and social capital.[1216] Association dominates, where once confrontation prevailed.

We humans should make deliberative conversation a cultural mainstay. Human communities must set aside time for deliberation, and invest substantial resources in that conversation, so there is no need to convene groups for emergent discussions. Every person should have her daily half hour reserved for engaging the Commons. Circles should remain small enough that the voices of every cadre can be heard. Communities aggregate the voices of their circles. Since tens of thousands of small communities need to communicate, a deep commitment to universal access to electronic media and unfettered sharing of information must become a shared value. In ideas, a free deliberation with trans-generational patience promises needed adaptivity. As communities experiment with ideas culled from the global conversation, their progress should occupy all. Our gossip and yammer may become more content full. Successes should be replicated, failures discarded in favor of renewed experimentation.[1217] The human community should fail less badly every passing year.[1218]

9.4. *Decentralization.* Centralized authority alienates. The core story line of centralized authority is that a stranger intrudes into one's privacy, making demands. Such interventions rankle humans. Centralized authority treats humans as numbers or ciphers. This is not a bad habit. It is the nature of bloated bureaucracies. These organizations "manage" unmanageable numbers of humans. Personal knowledge of those in bureaucracy's charge exceeds human capacity. So, anonymity defines western existence. We value privacy, not because we wish to be private, but because we do not want

---

mans, for whom I cherish great admiration. That said, we can do better. Law could be better, if better focused on meaningful existence. Law would be best if abandoned in favor of kithdom sociality.

[1216] See [♪] Block, *Community*, 1-7 (Introduction).

[1217] John Stuart Mill says that any government should make of itself a central depository and the primary source of the successful and unsuccessful experiments in living. [♪] Mill, *On Liberty*, 105.

[1218] This idea, in a form directed at the individual, was suggested by David Brooks in an essay I can no longer identify. Bertrand Russell believed that the human dilemma derives primarily from our eagerness to control forces outside ourselves, to the neglect of those pressures inside us. Russell, "Individual and Social Ethics," 343.

strangers barging into our intimacies. We value freedom, not because we wish libertine existence, indulging any whim we fancy, but because we want our life structures to mirror our values, and not the values of someone long dead who lived half a continent or half a world distant.[1219]

In kithdoms, such as Quad communities, decision-makers know one another and live together. Weal and woe are shared. One shapes life with friends in a shared journey of comprehensible proportion. The core story line of Quad sociality is that a friend asks for help, which you, due to affection, give freely. Kithdoms replace political and economic relations with moral exchanges among friends.[1220] Activity adopts a human scale. Decisions have direct consequences for people one loves. The rubber of choice hits the pavement of cooperative living. Choices echo from known voices. Communities expend their own resources for local purposes. Deliberation sidles up to outcome. Practicality prevails.

Centralized authority dehumanizes. Whenever human numbers overwhelm the human ability to interact personally—at around 150 persons—the human ability to cope plummets. *Homo sapiens* is ill-adapted to subpersonal relationships, such as that of massive bureaucracies or modern States. We respond poorly to intruders.[1221] As populations fall to manageable numbers, the door, once slammed, reopens to fundamentally personal social existence. In community life, we are positioned to recognize centralized bureaucracy, intended as a good, for the evil it represents. We have conducted the grand experiment of mass bureaucracy. It proves, as Hannah Arendt called it, the Rule of Nobody.[1222] Its stratified rule is blame-shifting: at lower rungs, minions follow leaders' misbegotten orders; at high rungs, leaders blame berserk minions. Nobody is responsible. Bureaucracy has failed us.

[1219] Even Thomas Jefferson, an architect of the American centralizing political structure, sought to amend the constitution he helped write by creating self-governing "wards" within every county of the nation charged with managing the affairs of their respective neighborhoods. Jefferson, *Writings*, 1399-1400 (Letter to Samuel Kercheval, July12, 1816).

[1220] Woodcock, *Anarchism*, 416. Taylor argues that we can do without the State only if we organize ourselves into small communities, where human relations are personal in the sense that they are direct, multi-sided, reciprocal, characterized by rough economic equality, and interpersonal contact is frequent. [♪] Taylor, *Community, Anarchy, and Liberty*, 2-3.

[1221] Rudolf Rocker, a socialist whose first love is political federalism, said: "No tyranny is more unendurable than that of an all-powerful bureaucracy, which interferes with all the activities of men and leaves it stamp on them. The more unlimited the power of the state over the life of the individual, the more it cripples his creative capacities and weakens the force of his personal will." Rocker thinks that a better future lies "within the framework of a federation of free communes on the basis of social community interests." Rocker, *Nationalism and Culture*, 35, 434.

[1222] See Arendt, *On Violence*, 38-39, 81.

Adapting, we must reduce human numbers (overpopulation, and its attendant non-personal existence, is one premise of centralized bureaucracy), and enliven the human social matrix.[1223]   Humanity's path to meaningful community lies in inter-related communities growing webs of collaborating communities, leading to a global Commons, lacking centralized authority or plutocratic leadership. If all are educated and valued, all may govern themselves locally (kithdoms) and cooperate globally (the Commons).[1224]

9.5. *Adaptive Experimentation*. Adaptive diversity must be welcomed. Communities choose a path. A proliferation of alternatives may erupt. Deliberation recounts the communal learning of these experiments. Life may be reconceived as groups attempting divergent answers to common challenges. Communities adopt successful adaptations of others where they find those adaptations wise. This focus on experimentation reduces human communities' undue reliance on history's ethically-savant geniuses (such as thinkers of the axial age)[1225] or recursion to theological verities (religious traditions

---

[1223] Rabindranath Tagore (India's polymath poet, novelist, composer, philosopher, and friend of Mohandas Gandhi) criticized Western culture for its mechanization of human societies. Mechanized societies are those that are organized on a mechanical template; they produce "neatly compressed bales of humanity." India tried to live a different vision, an organic meditation on peaceful cooperation, but was invaded by the British. Naturally, men live cooperatively. Competition is an aberration introduced by Western mechanical organization of societies. Competition sunders relationships. As people lose their organic connections to one another, meaning drains from their lives. Tagore, *Nationalism*, paragraphs 10-17 (Tagore's text is not paginated).

[1224] In the parlance of philosophical ethics, this is a form of communal pacifist anarchism. Communal anarchism, such as Quad sociality, contemplates no higher organization than that in which relationships remain personal. The Quad community may organize itself as it sees fit, within the consensus of its cadres. In order to maintain its personalist fundament, communities do not, however, form permanent alliances greater than that which exists within a community. Communities confederate cooperatively for discrete projects that exceed the scope of one or a few communities, subject to the advice derived from Commons deliberation. "Anarchy," in the usage of some, connotes chaos. Communal anarchism, and even traditional individualist anarchism (other than its explicitly violent extremists, such as Marx or Bakunin), advocates no socially destabilizing activities. Rather, some anarchists make consent the basis of social existence, rather than coercion, and contract its practice, rather than submission to laws. Absent a bludgeoning State apparatus, human communities can associate freely with those they deem beneficial for purposes they deem worthy. Those who disagree may associate with others they deem preferable for purposes at variance with some communities. Where healthy, non-narcissistic members interact, their interactions are generally anarchic, which is to say those interactions are expressly personal. Human tribes prosper in consensus and creativity, not hierarchy and domination. Hierarchy is what humans do when they have run short of relationships. Domination is what imagination-starved men (and a few women) do when they feel influence waning.

[1225] "Axial age" is a coinage of Karl Jaspers in his tome *The Origin and Goal of History* (1949). Jaspers identifies a fecund period of human history, commencing around 800-200 B.C., during which the foundational thinkers of the world's spiritualities and religions lived and wrote (or are reported). These thinkers include Socrates and Plato, Parsva (of Jainism), Siddartha Gautama (of Buddhism), Confucius, Zoroaster, Lao Tzu, Homer, Parmenides, Heraclitus, Thucydides, Archimedes, Elijah, Isaiah, Jeremiah, and Deutero-Isaiah. One wonders where Jesus and Muhammad fit into Jasper's scheme. Aquinas, Aurelius, Kant, Gandhi, Godwin, and, perhaps, Tutu, as well. Contrary to Jasper's view, I suspect neurodiverse savantism is a perpetual contrapuntal sub-melody in the symphony of human existence, and that all savants build upon what came before them.

parasitizing axial thinkers). If social tolerance means anything, it means that we allow others to conduct their ill-deliberate experiments, and await outcomes.[1226]

> HUNGRY AND THIRSTY, A RAGGED HUNTING TRIBE SLOGS UP A MOUNTAIN. FROM THE GLACIERED PASS, A RIVER VALLEY YAWNS BELOW. A DISTANT GLEN CATCHES ATTENTION. SURVEYING, A SHARP-EYED HUNTER CHARTS A COURSE OVER SCREE AND THROUGH FOREST. TIRED CHATTER AND LAUGHTER OF RELIEF RIPPLE. THE GROUP WALKS, MAKING COURSE ADJUSTMENTS, DIVERTING AROUND AN UNFORESEEN CLIFF. VIGOROUS MEMBERS HELP THE YOUNG AND THE FEEBLE FORD A FEEDER STREAM. AT THE RIVERSIDE MEADOW, ALL DRINK GRATEFULLY. A CHILD DISCOVERS BERRIES. OTHERS HARVEST AND CHEW AND LAUGH. AN OLDER WOMAN ASKS, "WHAT NOW?" CHILDREN, THEIR EYES BRIGHT WITH ANTICIPATION, WATCH. AN ELDER OPENS HIS MOUTH TO SPEAK, "WE ARE TIRED. MAKE CAMP?" ALL CONSIDER, THEN WORDLESSLY START SETTLING. CHATTER RESUMES.

9.6. *Reconstitution.*   Retaining reactionary traditionalisms stifles communities.[1227] Ensuing frustrations enable sociopaths (such as Hitler, Mussolini, Stalin, Mao, Pol Pot), preying upon those dissatisfactions, to torment us. The existential threats that violent psychopaths present necessitate brutal responses, and our violent responses to these wanton members cripple our ethical well-being. At least once each decade, each community may wish to reconstitute itself, adopting the best experiments from the Commons, and shedding ill-adapted fossil structures. Every community should retain the spirit of experiment; none should cherish sameness for its own sake. We do not honor our parents, grandparents, and ancestors by repeating their errors. We do not show faith by adhering to structures that no longer serve constructive purposes. Only that which works deserves loyalty. Structures that work should be reauthorized by formation of a new consensus in support of them. Lacking renewed consensus, moribund structures should be abandoned decadally.[1228]

[1226] Edmund Burke warns of the dangers of social experimentation. "I cannot conceive how any man can have brought himself to that pitch of presumption, to consider his country as nothing but *carte blanche*, upon which he may scribble whatever he pleases. . . . [A] true politician, always considers how he shall make the most of the existing materials of his country. A disposition to preserve, and an ability to improve, taken together, would be my standard of a statesman. Everything else is vulgar in the conception, perilous in the execution." Burke, *Reflections on the Revolution in France*, 161.

[1227] John Dewey argues that permitting variety in the face of organizational rigidity is the essence of political freedom. [♪] Dewey, *Human Nature and Conduct*, 308.

[1228] Thomas Jefferson advocated a similar sentiment in favor of revoking the United States Constitution and all statutes enacted under its umbrella every nineteen years, which he took to be the statistical duration of a generation. A new constitution and statutes could be enacted afresh by the then-

9.7. *Consensus.* Consensus gives a shape to choosing. From diverse intentions, members negotiate a workable togetherness. Members differ. Cadres
differ. Circles differ. Communities differ. The Commons, over time, differs with itself. Dissensus is normal, the product of our biological oddities,
divergent life experiences, and storm-tossed cultures. Will there be room
for these many perceptions and preferences, a few of which some may view
as evil? Consensus exists when collective action lacks dissent. Consensus
becomes possible when a group chooses to confront their dissensus. Consensus does not demand that all agree, which would paralyze communal action. But consensus does imply that none refuses to acquiesce. Many
members who experience reservations find, in their maturity and patience,
that their objections lack sufficient gravity to warrant dissent. Many dissenters may express their reservations, but acquiesce, awaiting outcomes,
maintaining a supportive skepticism. Consensus insures that the community of communities, when it acts collectively, augments meaning for all, not
just the few or even half-plus-one. When consensus proves impossible,
conversation should continue and the community should wait. Members
may have grown fearful. Assuage those fears. Members may loathe one
another. Build bridges; mend fences. Ideas may be garbled. Work on
specificity and detail. Wait for consensus. Build toward it. Let plans settle
and gel. Do not trample roughshod over minority dissent.

Members of a waiting majority need not idle while dissenters dawdle
toward agreement or acquiescence. Dissenters dissent for reasons. Ask.
Listen. Learn. Dissenters suffer the same concatenation of motivational
conflicts as any other person, even if they might pretend singularity of crys-
tal vision in defending their positions. Fathom your dissenting friend. Dissents that impede majorities, especially massive supermajorities (as when a
lone dissenter balks), are invitations to deeper friendship. Plumb your dissenting friend's history, his patterns, his psychology. Ask after his formative relationships. Educate yourself in the classroom of the dissenter's se-
cession. Read together. Think together. In the end, map your friend as
would one a foreign territory. He *is*, at least at this juncture, a foreign territory, landlocked in the midst of your sea of intimacy. Make yourself able to
argue for a dissenting friend's views as well or better than the dissenter
himself, even though you never share his dissent. Draw alongside your reticent friend. If your dissenting friend perseveres, commit to inaction. Then
invert presumptions. Assume the dissenter sees best, and ask him to learn
your views, as you have learned his. Criticize the majority view. Try to
convince yourself that you and the majority err. Ask what unanticipated

---

living generation, if they so chose. Jefferson, *Writings*, 963 (*Thomas Jefferson to James Madison*,
September 6, 1789) and 1402 (*Letter to Samuel Kercheval*, July 12, 1816).

evils may lurk in the majority's apparent good. Consider how to fashion work-arounds, achieving the ends the majority seeks without traveling paths the dissenter eschews. In the end, the dissenter's dissent may persevere. Do not trample him. Do not allow him to acquiesce while he remains certain his dissent is right. His may be the voice of the neurodiverse savant. His words may keep your group from horribly maiming itself. In the face of dissent, do something unobjectionable—or nothing.

Consensus, as a decisional rule, deflects the hatchet of conformity from the tree of life. Bushy diversity advertises political liberty. The forces of social conformity long to prune the odd branch. Human societies may lust to compel compliance. Compulsion nibbles the profuse bush of humanity to a few twigs from which haggard leaves dangle. Consensus emerges slowly. For difficult issues, consensus may require hundreds of years, its pace slower, its results better than majority or autocratic coercion.[1229] One community after another forms, then chooses. When a community chooses an approach to life and making itself useful, those electing that path pursue it, forming a community dedicated to their perspective and choice. Other communities make different elections. Some may choose, for a time, to persevere in the mass urban society we have inherited from humanity's adolescent conquest of the planet.[1230] But their children will not do so, provided communities do their jobs of nurture, education, communication, and deliberation. Those communities, unlike mass society, will cherish every member, will assert peace, will embrace dissenters, will experiment, and will constantly readapt themselves. Adaptation will be possible because communities will be small enough to implement manageable change.[1231]

[1229] Kithdom's aversion to coercion leads some to style kithdom an anarchy. States ground themselves in authoritative decision making. A leader, a bureaucracy, a majority makes decisions and imposes the outcomes upon dissenters. The State distributes society's goods without the consensus of those to whom it distributes. One becomes the willing or unwilling recipient of the State's attentions or inattentions. One's voice falls upon deaf ears. Where voices are heard and honored by patience and continued conversation, no State exists, but rather friendship. Kithdom becomes possible.

[1230] Aristotle argues that, for normal people, one cannot induce change by argument. Their dysfunctional thoughts have grown habitual, and dislodging them proves impossible (or maybe only difficult). One must coerce those who dwell in the grip of their various panics. So, to effect lasting change, one aims at the upbringing of children, preparing the ground for temperance and endurance to root in the young. [♪] Aristotle, *Nichomachean Ethics*, 200 (1179b).

[1231] One imagines no more than 2,000 members in any community, convened as approximately ten circles of approximately 150, and perhaps a maximum of 50,000 to 500,000 communities globally, for a total human population of 150 million to 1.5 billion. Such prognostications are equivocal. The appropriate size of the human population should be determined in thanatoid deliberation over a period of generations. Our conversation has to date determined only one fact: there are too many humans on the planet who are breeding without ethical constraint. Even this patent assertion raises a howl from dissenters.

Communities cooperate for purposes all deem good, and seek to learn from their various individual and cooperative failures and successes.

But all eschew coercion; none chooses force to bring friends and neighbors to their view of matters.[1232] Coercion insures resentment, not consent. To coerce is to declare a little war; discussion ends. To do violence is suicidal: violence kills members, and, if successful, coerces neighbors to acts not freely adopted. Time and bitterness ensure eventual retaliation, and an unmanageable transgenerational spiral of vendetta attacks. Worst, violent compulsion whittles the profusion of human choices to a sickly nub.[1233]

Consensus works in small groups because our brains are hardwired to fit in with our friends. No coercion proves necessary. We fall in line because that seems natural. We fit our opinions and habits to those of our companions. Coercion disrupts this natural tendency in social groups. In coercion, an outsider rides in to compel us to do what seems preferable to that alien. The rider will always be viewed with suspicion and meet rejection. If he succeeds in compulsion, time will bring retribution. No healthy human welcomes coercion.[1234]

9.8. *Delimited Mobility.* A bane of human social stability is the modern penchant for uprooting. Quad sociality presumes that no person stands alone, but rather each integrates into a cadre, circle, and community within the Commons. For a person to move requires that one social universe consents to live without that member, and another consents to adopt the departing member. Surely, such moves will occur regularly, as community's needs and member's skills are matched. Some will move to indulge wanderlust. Others will depart to evade insuperable personality conflicts. Even healthy communities reach points where they need to fission so that their diversity can find new expression. Perhaps most important, the young will survey the field of available communities in the Commons and need to test some, to find themselves, to make a fit. Yet, Quad sociality implies an impedi-

---

[1232] Oddly, for a mass murderer of tens of millions in a demented attempt to coerce revolutionary purity (the Cultural Revolution), Mao shares this sentiment. One builds a society on the basis of respect for its people, and educative persuasion where members dissent. [♪] Mao, *Little Red Book*, 150-151. Gandhi says of majoritarian rule that the idea that the will of a majority binds its minority is immoral and ill-founded in fact. Consent, implicit or explicit, is the only basis for government by the people. [♪] Gandhi, *Satyagraha*, 18, 35.

[1233] I address consensus more fully in what follows.

[1234] Sarah Conly cites Muzafer Sherif's studies of opinion conformity, in which test subjects honestly change their opinions regarding the movement of a light in a room when surrounded by others (many of whom were instructed to lie as part of the experiment) who disagree with the subject's initial assessment. The revised assessment perseveres even when the dissenters leave. [♪] Conly, *Against Autonomy*, 58-59.

ment to changing residence at will, which practice erodes the fabric of communities, and promotes loneliness and solipsistic anomie. Humans need a reliable social context, which structure takes decades of caring to fabricate. None should rend the fabric of friendship glibly.

9.9. *Local Liberty.* Human mettle is tested within human communities. The community is the locus of freedom and restraint for members. In Quad sociality, the community experiments adaptively. It provides for members' needs and nurtures them. The community deliberates its contributions to the Commons. It frames an economic theory as well as industries that express those convictions. The community corrects errors, those of members as well as its own collective mis-steps. One point of Quad sociality is to leave communities unfettered, except by their own learning and the disciplines incumbent in their various experiments.[1235]

One might ask: How shall we feed ourselves? Another answers: Let's deliberate a solution to that. How many husbands may a wife take? Let's talk about that. How many children are sufficient? How shall parents, alloparents, and other mentors relate to children? What means are appropriate for a community to support its constituent cadres of intimates? How should we relate to members who decline to participate in community life? What response is appropriate for those who injure others heedlessly or intentionally? What sort of architecture is appropriate for our needs? What place has art in community? What portion of our weal should be devoted to other communities? How shall we respond to evils in other communities? When is coercion warranted? Who coerces, should we decide force is necessary? Who should lead? What should we expect of leaders? How will families be structured? What role will animals play in our community? How much wilderness is enough? How do we prevent our successful experiments from becoming shackles upon descendants? How much deviance from our community norms is too much deviation? Do we possess neurodiverse savants? Which among the neurodiverse savants of other communities should we heed? What role will their prescriptions play in our daily lives? For what reasons may members relocate? How shall a community nurture members who dissociate themselves from all communities? How much energy should we expend, and how should we generate it? Which technologies support life together, and which do not? When should a technology be adopted, and what safeguards are appropriate? How will we live in a manner that avoids impairing the prospects of our distant de-

---

[1235] To the western conservative, Quad sociality promises slow, deliberate, carefully-conceived change. To the western liberal, Quad sociality promises a path to repetitive structural change and adaptive experimentation of every sort. To both, Quad sociality offers a path out of the box canyon of cultural and governmental gridlock that paralyzes western democracies—a painful solution, but a solution nonetheless.

scendants? How shall we dwell sustainably upon the land? How much collective energy should we devote to creating new technologies? What do we hope humanity might become? When are steps toward that vision appropriate? These inquiries, and the thousand similar questions this author lacks the foresight or experience to articulate, should occupy communities.

In sorting these and other constitutive questions, communities choose for themselves. They will determine what goods and services to produce for trade with others. They will elect to ally with other communities for economic ventures. Communities will decide how to feed themselves, and what to eat. They will decide what role private property should play in their togetherness. They will choose a means of educating their young. Communities will elect social mores, and family structures, and societal norms. Their choices will issue in attitudes and sub-culture, in a definable flavor characteristic of their life together. Communities will choose which savants to heed, and which to avoid. They will set limits to influence over members, and chart paths toward consensus. In short, all the decision-making a human community requires, members will undertake.[1236] The community will be the final word in matters, unless a community should undertake warrantless intrusions upon their own members or other communities.

In their freedom, communities should recognize intrinsic restraints. A community exists to nurture members. All matter. None may be discarded, even those who err egregiously or stink or impose a burden. Within the human Commons, there is no "them." Ideas belong to mankind, not men. Nurture of others is not an infinitely malleable task. Some actions nurture; others do not. *Cull* has described meaningful community at some length, as well as its sad doppelgänger, the eroded community, in which so many humans are trapped. The task before every community is to be the flourishing place it promises, and to avoid erosion of meaning in the community's circles. No community should experiment in a manner incongruent with its members' sense of dynamic mutualism. Some experiments should be avoided for moral reasons. Others exceed tolerable risk limitations. The risks and impediments of every community are the concern of all. The Commons should build as much structure as is consistent with its role as a marketplace of ideas and deliberation, as the mediator of community conflicts, and as the repository of human knowledge, skill, and wisdom. The necessary vestige of coercion that remains in this irenic scheme will be discussed at some length below.

[1236] Thomas Jefferson argues that the United States Constitution should be wholly up for revision every nineteen years. It is a weakness in us to "believe that one generation is not as capable as another of taking care of itself, and of ordering its own affairs." Jefferson, *Writings*, 1401 (*Letter to Samuel Kercheval*, July 12, 1816).

9.10. *Diversity.* Communities are diverse. Failing to embrace diversity is denial. Uniformity by conformity cannot be the organizing principle of communities. People differ. Communities should reject easy conformity in favor of giftedness and the riot of life experiments. Diversity makes us less efficient, but more free. Tolerance evidences communal wisdom. The best community finds ways to live with and benefit from its warts and barnacles.

9.11. *Hints of Asceticism.* In the weave of Quad sociality hides a thread of asceticism. The bugle of western democracy blares profit, profit. Its ethic praises taking; the wallet its mascot. The clarion of medieval Europe sang faith, faith. Its ethic summoned prayer; its mascot god. The trumpet of kithdom blows friend, friend. Its ethic exalts giving; its mascot is service. To the man transitioning from western existence to kithdom, the world feels somewhat constricted; giving depends upon willing self-restraint. Kithdom feels as though a cenobitic[1237] monk has moved into one's garage, with his pared habits, scant bathing, and Spartan simplicity. He begs your company in the garage, which he has swept and organized, thinning junk; he may become a friend.

9.12. *Personal Action.* Kithdoms exist in personal action. No longer does one wait for a disembodied governmental agency thousands of miles distant to rescue one from foolishness. Life in mass society beneath the thumb of usurping authorities dulls natural initiative. Take that back. One bears responsibility, with his circle and community, for the well-being of all friends. Every man is, potentially, such a friend. Make meaningful work. Invent better existence. Create a structure supportive of full-spectrum friendship. Collaborate with other communities. Enrich and benefit from the Commons.

9.13. *Kithdom.* Kithdom is a global society of friends.[1238] Core intimacies (friends, spouses, alloparents, families, colleagues, co-workers) relate in overlapping groups of friends, which are "cadres." When these persons establish norms (of any sort) for themselves, a kithdom commences. Needing to provide for themselves, cadres look for others with whom to cooperate and trade. Those relationships, over time, grow accustomed. As further

---

[1237]The adjective "cenobitic" describes an ascetic tradition in which monks share a common life. See *Webster's Third New International Dictionary, s.v.* "cenobite."

[1238] Apologies to the Quakers, who call themselves formally The Religious Society of Friends. I distinguish "society" from "state" or "people." Society is an organic relationship among humans, emerging among friends and acquaintances. States are coercive regimes that aim to use members for the benefit of rulers, or protect members from themselves, due to the alleged superior wisdom of the governors. A "people" is an artificial designation (and usually a misnomer) in a well-mixed population, intending all those from a common genetic past or origin. Usually, few among a people actually trace their genetic or cultural heritage solely to one people. Humans have, for 200,000 years, been mixing families and cultures, and, according to recent studies, even the genetic pools of human subspecies. See Bernard Wood, "Welcome to the Family," 43-47.

norms emerge, the cadres recognize themselves as a collective, as a circle. Circles should be limited to around 150 members. Groups of greater than 150 exceed human cognitive capacity for remembering names and relationships (Dunbar's number). A circle could, but probably would not choose to, subsist as a community in itself. Instead, most circles will look to associate themselves with other like-minded and complementary-skilled circles for mutual benefit. One anticipates that such collaborations will stabilize at around 1,500 members (ten circles) because that is the size of non-State tribal associations.[1239] Kithdoms elect for themselves structures they deem advantageous: social, economic, ethical. Quad communities may contract with other communities for purposes of common concern. Quad communities report their structural experiments to the Commons, and receive feedback from the constituent communities of the Commons. The world, via the Commons, tracks communal experiments and aggregates knowledge.

9.13.1. *Rationales for States.* Kithdom challenges the theory of States. A host of justifications for coercion of neighbors has long occupied political theory. These theories argue that we legitimately coerce our neighbors because some rationale authorizes us to do so. Some leading coercive rationales are:

9.13.1.1. *Divine Agency.* Theocracy argues that god rules; gods possess inherent divine authority to control and coerce. The deity has designated a human sovereign as his associate to rule during divine absences. As god rules absolutely, so too his king.[1240] This same rationale justifies rule by small groups of co-kings (plutocracy) and larger groups of collaboratively-ruling elites (aristocracy). God himself has so stratified society for the benefit of humanity, often as a reflection of celestial hierarchies. American founding fathers seem to have strained divine sovereignty theory to reach so far as majority rule.[1241]

9.13.1.2. *Social Contract.* Social contract theory asserts that, in times primeval or recent, some ancestors of your line agreed with other such individuals to establish a regime for mutual self-defense and benefit.[1242]

[1239] Zhou, "Social Group Size Organization," 440. Lewis Mumford argues: "The restoration of the human scale is a matter of utmost importance: till that change takes place no effective regeneration can be brought about." Mumford, *The Conduct of Life*, 276.

[1240] Hence, the livid anathema Bakunin and many anarchists pronounce upon institutional religion and even the idea of gods. Religions baptize States, to the detriment of the people. Bakunin, *God and the State*, 12-26.

[1241] See United States' *Declaration of Independence*, references to "Nature's God" and "Sovereign Ruler."

[1242] John Locke offers such a social contract theory of government. A government is a process of decision making and implementation chosen by a people. When that process changes, by either internal or external forces, the government is dissolved. Locke takes laws to be essential to govern-

This ancestral contract obligates current members, who in no way participated in such agreement, to conform to the strictures of the contract, however those obligations may be construed. One's obligation to so perform perseveres even when it is granted that one's own ancestors *in historical fact* concluded no such contract.[1243]

9.13.1.3. *Might*. Many across history have argued that might justifies rule. "Might makes right" asserts that because someone is coercing a people, those coercers have the right to continue coercing that people. This polity infects and mixes with other rationales. We find it in Qutb, Hitler, Mussolini, Mao, Lenin, Stalin, the papacy, Machiavelli, and Han Fei Tsu.[1244]

Majority rule illustrates the primal swagger of might-justification. Since the majority is numerically superior, this majority rule presumes the majority would prevail in armed combat, subduing the dissenting minority. Therefore, skipping the bloody part in favor of foregone concession, majorities prevail. In a less repugnant mode, some justify democratic majoritarian rule as that form of government, from among the many possible forms of rule, that best approximates, though only vaguely approximates, the justice of consent.[1245]

---

ment. "[A] government without laws is, I suppose, a mystery in politics inconceivable to human capacity, and inconsistent with human society." Locke, *Second Treatise of Government*, 233-245 (Sections 197-219).

[1243] See Rousseau, "A Discourse on the Origin of Inequality," 44, where Rousseau admits that he has no special knowledge of what may or may not have been contracted by distant ancestors, asserting that such knowledge is unnecessary. See also Rawls, *A Theory of Justice*, 10, where Rawls expressly disavows any historical reference, placing emphasis, rather, upon the likelihood that all rational persons concerned with their self-interest would likely assent to the terms of a social contract as Rawls conceives it. Rawls calls his social contract the "original position." Rawls, *A Theory of Justice*, 11. Rawls, in his subsequent treatment, styles the original position social contract as hypothetical and nonhistorical. [♪] Rawls, *Justice as Fairness: A Restatement*, 16 (§6). Hence, for Rawls, his social contract conjoins all putatively rational people as a State, who then are authorized to willy-nilly coerce the incoherent rabble. I err by making Rawls's theory sound more coarse than it is. Rawls seeks a transgenerational society of cooperative social intercourse in which every citizen, as an individual, is actually equal and shares similar opportunity, a condition created by sharing of resources presently deemed private property (effected by the difference principle). [♪] Rawls, *Justice as Fairness: A Restatement*, 5-9 (§§2-3), 61-66 (§18). Hobbes finds men driven to the solace of a social contract by their abject terror of one another's depredations. Better an absolute monarch than non-stop aggression from neighbors. [♪] Hobbes, *Leviathan*, 107 (Chapter 13).

[1244] [♪] Han Fei Tsu, *Basic Writings*.

[1245] John Locke falls into this confusion. He argues (persuasively) that conquerors derive, by virtue of their violent conquests, no right to their defeated opponents' property. Nor do victors acquire by conquest a right to rule non-combatants. No oath of loyalty extracted at sword point need be honored. Locke, *Second Treatise of Government*, 226-229 (Sections 183-186). Nevertheless, Locke justifies majority rule in democracies (again persuasively, for Locke is a genuinely persuasive writer) as a necessary coercion to which one owes obedience, because one (not actually, but theoretically) consented to majority rule. Here, Locke omits mention of the unspoken sword point that compels minority acquiescence. Locke, *Second Treatise of Government*, 176-177 (Sections 95-97).

Admixtures pervade the American justification of its democracy. The Declaration of Independence asserts that all just government depends upon the consent of the governed, as God has deemed natural. Yet, God, somewhat confused, proceeds to establish majoritarian coercion of dissenters by means of subsequent Constitution. The Bill of Rights, an afterthought, hardly cures the fundamental coercive mis-step, securing only the right to cling to a minority opinion or religion without facing the guillotine.

9.13.1.4. *Compassion-archy.* Compassion-archy finds many unduly fixated on personal gain. So oblivious are these teeming crowds that their aggregate actions portend possible self-injury and certain depredation of many. Taking matters into the hands of those possessing enlightened sympathies, compassion-archy vests authority in a compassionate ruling elite, who constrain wrong-doers, moral defectives, and free-riders.[1246] Bureaucracies impose regulations necessitating personal moral reform and financial contribution to poor families.[1247] The more-able assist the less-able, on pain of incarceration or fines. Reticent contribution grips society, as taxes, wrenched from resisters' clenched fists, reallocate financial benefit in a manner compassion-archs deem just.[1248]

9.13.1.5. *Min-Archy.* Min-archy laments government of any sort, but admits that some crumb of coercion remains, at least for the present, necessary.[1249] Min-archy, in its various libertarian flavors, frankly acknowl-

---

[1246] Gandhi believes that his non-violent army of spirit-athletes (Satyagrahi) comprise the greatest force imaginable, and they will bring global utopia, rid of all evils, if only they are able to make of one village an ideal template upon which the remainder of humanity may model itself. [♪] Gandhi, *Satyagraha*, 353, 377. The process described in *Cull* seeks just such a template community, though it seems likely to me that many, rather than one, excellent templates will form the backbone of mature and flourishing human society.

[1247] Marx would take from every family its excess, and give to every family what it needs. Marx, *Critique of the Gotha Programme*, 242. Kropotkin concurs with Marx. [♪] Kropotkin, *The Conquest of Bread*, 41-42 (Chapter IV, Section 1) and 87 (Chapter VIII). Rawls, *A Theory of Justice*, would work hard at an inclusive rational majority in establishing societal rules (at page 39), but would define whatever rule emerged as "fair," and impose it upon societal dissenters (at page 12). Rawls is satisfied when an original position scheme comes as close as possible to being voluntary, without actually being unanimous.

[1248] Rawls, *A Theory of Justice*, 13. Rawls casts his proposed regime in a more favorable light, calling his scheme consistent with what rational people would want in a world where many (most?) lack reliable benevolent inclinations, and yet desire a society that cares for all (and is, therefore, "well-ordered").

[1249] Thoreau, conceding that men are ill-prepared for living with no government at all, prays for a regime that seeks to govern as little as possible. If one cannot obtain a tiny regime, then let us at least demand a better one. [♪] Thoreau, *On the Duty of Civil Disobedience*, 251, 252. Gandhi expressly relies on Thoreau's civil disobedience theory in his construction of the non-cooperation, non-violent

edges the injustice of majority coercion, but is equally blunt about the depredations of a few upon the many. Since evil people or States may prey wantonly, all grudgingly permit a sovereign to preclude those, and only those, outcomes. Some min-archists give further leash to their trussed sovereign to organize projects in which a society must collaborate, but only to the minimum extent conceivable.[1250]

9.13.1.6. *Anarchy.* Anarchist theory admits no government whatsoever.[1251] Sovereignty belongs to every individual; no State action may justifiably deflect a citizen from her elected course of action. Coercions of every stripe harm the coerced, and are therefore wrong.[1252] All agents of organized coercion, which include governments, religions, and misdirected institutions, such as money, banks, and private property itself, lack conscientious warrant.[1253] The only justified society is one governed solely by individual preference and agreements among citizens to address shared concerns. States of any sort take property from one citizen to provide protections for another. All are, therefore, inherently redistributionist, constituting nothing more subtle than organized theft.[1254]

9.13.2. *Arguments Favoring Kithdom.* Kithdom minimizes coercion, without licensing sociopathic savagery. Consent governs most human interac-

---

resistance program of Satyagraha, employed in his efforts to free the Indian people from British imperial abuses. [♪] Gandhi, *Satyagraha*, 3 (§1).

[1250] [♪] Nozick, *Anarchy, State, and Utopia*, ix. Nozick, given the difficulties of creating enforceable contracts among citizens without some over-arching adjudicator, grants the necessity of a delimited State, which exists to protect citizens and property, deter con-men, put a bite in contracts, and undertake other carefully limited functions. No State may, according to Nozick, compel one citizen to aid another, or force people to behave reasonably, even for their own good.

[1251] Bakunin, for example, rejects all legislative authority, all licenses, all law, even that consequent to universal suffrage, because, so he argues, all such influences empower an active minority to dominate its lethargic majority. Bakunin permits only learned influence of one man upon another. Bakunin, *God and the State*, 35. Hobbes argues that lack of government is not an identifiable theory of government. [♪] Hobbes, *Leviathan*, 130. Anarchists, of course, disagree. Tagore notes that Nationhood is the greatest evil for any Nation. Nations thrive upon the nutriment of mutilated humanity. Nations whittle man to a moral nub. Tagore, *Nationalism*, unpaginated.

[1252] Bakunin argues that mankind's overweening abilities are thinking and rebelling. He aims the human gun primarily at church and state, both of which should be abolished. If god exists, according to Bakunin, he must be abolished. Bakunin, *God and State*, 1, 9.

[1253] Goldman, *Anarchism and Other Essays*, 3-4. Emma Goldman believed that only when these corrupting institutions are disintegrated can the unity of mankind, including woman-kind, flower. Man, as a species, brims with social proclivities. Unfettered by coercions, man prospers as a living organism of individual-social reciprocity. Bakunin is more blunt than Goldman: destroy all institutions that perpetuate social or economic inequality. Bakunin, *God and the State*, 43 (footnote).

[1254] [♪] Nozick, *Anarchy, State, and Utopia*, 51-52. So Nozick styles objections of the individualist anarchist. This is not, however, Nozick's own position. He prefers what he calls a "minimal state," itself two steps from the anarchist non-state, by way of a transition from the "ultraminimal state."

tions; none is coerced, except in exigent circumstances. No persuasive rationale for government exists other than the express consent of the members presently governed.[1255] Human voluntary associations can collaborate to accomplish needful collective purposes. All impositions, except in response to wanton acts, are illegitimate. Even those delimited coercions must be minimized.

9.13.2.1. *Coercion is Immoral.* Except in self-defense or defense of others, compelling others to one's preferences is illegitimate. Coercion endangers those social ties that our urges to care, bear, nurture, and play establish. Coercion hobbles collaboration, and shatters human unity into its billion fragments. Coercion engenders fear and bad faith prevarication. One never emerges ethically intact from spates of threat or violence, or even grim, jaw-clenching paternalistic interventions. Even when self-preservation or protection of vulnerable others gives warrant, coercive interventions injure coercers. One must return to one's drawing board, reconstructing how one hurtled upon that unhappy coercive crossroads, mapping a path around that intersection's collisions.

9.13.2.2. *Coercion is Ineffective.* Coercion does not work. Forced submission breeds simmering rancor.[1256] Coercion is what one does when peer pressure of a small social group proves ineffective—in groups larger than 150 members.[1257] One may compel compliance, but compulsion insures intent to retaliate. The coercer's resources dribble, then gush, into subsequent repressions, shackling distilled hatred of victims. Retaliations warrant incarcerations, which justify impudence. Ultimately, the cycle of vendetta exhausts all, leaves a bitter social detritus for wiser people to sweep up. The only constructive path open to opponents is to make of one another friends. The conversion of hearts from opposition to joint endeavor opens, rather than slams, doors.

[1255] Thomas Andrews asks, What of new entrants? I respond that new entrants are choosing to join a particular community, and so consent. Andrews continues, What of members who change their minds? I answer that those should depart to participate in a community more to their liking. Further, communities should reconstitute themselves regularly (decadally or more frequently?). Dissenters will have their day to persuade. Thomas Andrews, in private correspondence with the author, July 2016.

[1256] Gandhi asserts that no quantum of earthly power can force a person to acts he refuses. [♪] Gandhi, *Satyagraha*, 347 (§164). One may compel compliance. But the victim's heart lingers recalcitrant.

[1257] Dunbar notes that Hutterites (North American fundamentalist Christian farm communities) fission their groups when the membership reaches 150, because thereafter "they cannot control the behavior of the members by peer pressure alone." Dunbar, *How Many Friends Does One Person Need?*, 28.

9.13.2.3. *Coercion Corrupts.* Where coercion is permitted, coercers abuse such power. When individuals contemplate the possibility of open or hidden circumventions, the inner bifurcation of fraud rots relationships. Where one indulges outright compulsion or violence, one forsakes moral integrity, fragmenting inner deliberations into a thousand instances of weasling. Where one acquiesces in communal coercions, one averts moral eyes, preferring functional self-lobotomy. Some of history's seminal lunatics commenced their wanton depredations under the mantle of legitimized coercion's dripping.[1258]

9.13.2.4. *Consensus Works.* If one adopts consensus as one's rule, one prospers ethically without compelling others, though matters may proceed more slowly than some prefer. Preferences ripen in deliberation, and burrs are smoothed before they wear their joint. Coercers squander vast energy countering the seditions of coerced opponents. Where collaboration springs from consensus, impetus launches unalloyed. Dissenters, acquiescing, cluck and kibitz, but are otherwise supportive. Cooperative ventures zoom where none niggle or squirm. Every venture teeters at failure's brink when a grumbling minority militates. Energy is better spent building consensus than launching long voyages in leaky ships.

9.13.2.5. *Gods Endorse Consent.* This author disfavors natural law arguments. It seems one's god of preference is forever structuring mankind to perform as the believer's locally-dominant religion prefers. So, natural law arguments project on the blank screen of metaphysical uncertainty a local image of virtue. In fact, gods, where theologians are forthcoming, express favor for no particular form of government. Still, it would seem one must indulge "natural law" argument, if only to cajole political philosophers. So be it.

There is nothing natural about coercion in humans. It is true that chimpanzees kill strange chimps on sight. Our primate cousins do not cooperate with strangers. Yet, cooperation with persons outside one's social group is a human hallmark. Killing strangers is pathological human behavior, not natural action.[1259] If any behavior comes instinctually

---

[1258] Consider Mao Zedong. Mao lost (or never possessed) social conscience in the course of his rule of China. Mao considered sacrificing 300 million Chinese to American or Russian nuclear assault. People reproduce, he argued. Mao refused medical treatment of his venereal diseases, though a steady stream of deflowered and infected virgins flowed from his bedroom. Tens of millions "enemies of the people" died in Mao's Cultural Revolution, as Mao re-educated the Chinese intelligentsia to see the world through Mao-colored glasses. Zhisui, *The Private Life of Chairman Mao*, 125, 217, 356-364.

[1259] Military training expends vast sums desensitizing recruits to their natural aversion to coercion and killing. See [♪] Glover, *Humanity*, 47-116 (Part Two: The Moral Psychology of Waging War).

to humans, it is collaborative endeavor. That being so, following the gist of natural law arguments, gods endorse kithdom's consent theory of societal governance, for the divine has fashioned man to cooperate with outsiders, and to make of strangers friends, not corpses.

9.13.2.6. *Kithdom Addresses Deviancy.* Mass society appears incapable of quashing wanton deviancy. Prisons brim, yet crime proliferates.[1260] Anonymity enables deviance. Living with strangers promotes dehumanized interactions. Kithdom enlivens social relations, leaving less psychological room for dangerous deviancy. Quad communities retain a flexible, if perpetually modest, modicum of coercive, even violent, capacity. While dangerous to the community itself, such capability counterbalances the certainty of sociopathic coercion and violence. If, as Stout argues, one in twenty-five persons suffers sociopathy,[1261] every circle contains five sociopaths, every community sixty. Others suffer mental illness or personality disorders. Still others careen wildly, unhinged by circumstantial stresses, especially where childhood nurture collapsed. All these deficiencies prove problematical; not all express violence. Still, some fragment of those lacking moral sensibility, permanently or momentarily, may pursue coercive or violent efforts. No sensible community can permit wanton members to run amok.[1262]

Quad communities address potentially violent (wanton) members, first, by recourse to that member's cadre, where friendship may heal or divert the difficulty. Friends' affection and nurture are most potent social tools. Friendship deflects intimates more readily than confronta-

---

[1260] Dissenters object that violent crime has decreased dramatically in American culture since sweeping incarceration of offenders commenced. This conclusion presumes that the crime within prison walls is not to be counted, since those moral aberrants have been exiled from our midst. It is not so. In prison, criminals continue committing crimes, only now upon one another. Prisons concentrate crime; they produce criminals with better criminal educations and good friends who share their sentiments. Eventually, prisoners are released, and their wanton ways erupt again into society. Even when isolated in prisons, criminals remain members of our communities. Their crimes remain our responsibility for failure of nurture, of intervention, of amelioration. Prisons reflect our failure to care, our tendency to deny responsibility for the accumulating erosions caused by our omissions of affection.

[1261] Four percent of the human population is sociopathic, though not necessarily violent. Of these, three-fourths are male. Stout, *The Sociopath Next Door*, 6-8.

[1262] Gandhi, as a religious axiom, regarded no man as his enemy. Nevertheless, Gandhi militated for sacking British General Reginald Dyer, who authorized the slaughter of hundreds of non-violent protesting Indians at Jalianwala Bagh, firing upon the only exits from the victims' enclosed site for ten minutes. More than 370 died. One cannot, according to Gandhi, grant lunatics power to savage neighbors. [♪] Gandhi, *Satyagraha*, 107 (§45), 155 (§66). For memorable accounts of and justifications for sociopathy run amok, see the Marquis de Sade's bookend novels: *Juliette* and *Justine*. In *Justine*, no good deed or sentiment goes unpunished. In *Juliette*, no depravity or bad faith goes unrewarded. (A warning: de Sade's novels are not for the faint of heart, and may waste your time.)

tions.   Where one's cadre, nevertheless, proves ineffective, the wanton member's circle may intervene, offering support and services to ameliorate the problem.   When neither intervention (cadre or circle) proves adequate to address the problem deviancy, the community must address the wanton member.   Is the member a threat to himself or others?   Do the member's actions erode meaningful community in a manner for which the community cannot reasonably compensate?   If no irenic resolution proves feasible, a community may consider coercive action.   *Cull* describes the course of permissible coercion, when such proves unavoidable, below.

9.13.2.7. *Kithdom Reduces the Risks of Change.*   As communities learn iteratively, they reframe themselves in increments.   Change affects members, but only the members of the iterating community.   In mass society, changes portend disaster.   Tweaks prove difficult.   Millions risk disruption from ill-conceived ventures.   Kithdom insulates the many from improvident change, leaving those jolts to the laboratory of communities.   Proven adaptations are adopted.   Faulty adaptations are discarded.

9.13.2.8. *Kithdom Cooperates with Cooperative Impulses.*   Humans, in small groups, cooperate.   Since all are seen and known, none can afford to free ride, seeking to benefit from communal investment without contributing.   Within man lies a peculiar genius for organizing complex activity to realize shared goals.   Human cooperation can be projected onto large populations, but emerges naturally in communities and circles.   Cooperation falls dramatically where relationships attenuate.   Among strangers, cooperative impulses recede before fear and disgust.   Pattern and habit in large-group tasks may persevere, but the emotional concomitants shrivel.   One, in large groups, may even confront the Hobbesian state of war of all against all, from which "solitary, poor, nasty, brutish, and short" life one flees by appointing an absolute monarch to coerce misbehaved members with such force as may be required [1263] One may also, according to Hobbes, evade the dilemma of coercive neighbors or a coercive sovereign by dwelling in a community of small families with tribal organization. [1264]

[1263] [♪] Hobbes, *Leviathan*, 107 (Chapter 13).

[1264] [♪] Hobbes, *Leviathan*, 108. Hobbes thinks that the concord of such communities depends on "natural lust," and disparages their harmony as something brutish. One may well invert Hobbes's core argument, asking whether it is not the case that sovereigns, and their attendant violent coercions, do not emerge when communal consensus deteriorates, consequent to hyper-population. Leviathan does not, as Hobbes would have it, rescue us from ourselves. Leviathan is the problem from which we flee. For a useful discussion of the idea that the State causes free riding, see [♪] Taylor, *Community, Anarchy, and Liberty*, 56.

9.13.2.9. *Kithdom Embraces Life's Thickness.* Human life harbors labyrinthine complexity. Our relations, our ideas, our very brains brim with interconnection. We are each, quite literally, unique. Kithdom celebrates the intrinsic thickness of the human soup. States, with their incessant thirst to harvest members like farmers milk cows, attenuate humans. States offer thin plans, reflecting anorexic simplifications of the lives they purport to govern. People are not formulae. Nor are they components. We are thick, messy, globs of interconnected biomass. We resist being smashed and trimmed. We resent being addressed as though we were intrinsically one sheet in a sheaf of bleached white paper. We are thick. Kithdom is thick. States cannot simultaneously unitize citizens and honor human thickness.[1265]

9.13.2.10. *Kithdom Unleashes Creativity.* In our current order, most creativity is quashed. Kithdom provides necessities for all, and suppresses wealth aggregation, the need to produce luxury goods, and squandering assets in pointless wars. The net effect of this diversion of activity is to feed, clothe, and house all, leaving a substantial time premium available for constructive leisure. How many Van Goghs have perished in the exhaustion of coal mines? How many Aristotles missed college to feed younger siblings? How many Wrens never designed a building because born to the wrong class? Kithdom promises a cascade of previously-untapped invention, interpretation, and creation. Humanity may, in kithdom, find itself wallowing in deeper meaning than is presently imaginable.[1266]

> **Objection 36: Informal Oppressions:** *Some demur that the autonomy Quad sociality cedes to small communities will re-introduce the worst oppressions of the last 500 years. Racist, Nazi, rich, poor, healthy, drug-addicted, libertine, Puritanical, communist, Irish, soccer-fanatical, fascist, capitalist, abortion-happy, theological, drunk, apocalyptic, abortion-chary, vaccination-free, and even violent communities may emerge. Members trapped in those communities will suffer for lack of nurture and oversight.*

[1265] This metaphor is suggested by language in James Scott, *Seeing Like A State*, 309.

[1266] F. A. Hayek, who would never endorse kithdom, nevertheless, appears to agree with some of kithdom's premises: "We are concerned in this book with that condition of men in which coercion of some by others is reduced as much as is possible in society. . . . The task of a policy of freedom must therefore be to minimize coercion or its harmful effects, even if it cannot eliminate it completely. . . . Coercion, however, cannot be altogether avoided because the only way to prevent it is by the threat of coercion." Hayek, *The Constitution of Liberty*, 57, 59, 71. Men must be free so they will have opportunity to cope with accidents, which are inevitable given human ignorance. From accidents comes serendipity and creativity. Hayek, *The Constitution of Liberty*, 80-81. Oddly, Hayek conceives his overarching task as "improving our institutions" (page 51). Contrary to Hayek's view, I argue that the essential purpose of institutions is to channel or coerce humans.

They might even suffer wanton nurture and oversight. The human penchant for social censure, which coerces conformity by social snub and smack, is a more effective and less pleasant deterrent than rack or noose, or their affectionate cousins, law and judiciary. To leave censure to small group consensus portends unbridled oppression in a thousand varieties. Overall, Quad sociality will injure human well-being. The attic of every righteous household will secret a gagged and hog-tied oddball. People will long for the good old days of anonymous coercion by the IRS, legal code, and helmeted policeman.

Response: Undoubtedly, some communities will emerge that elect evils for themselves. That is one risk of choice. Meaning-erosive choices are a necessary component in creating finely-elaborated conduct culling. One must err, suffer, learn, and adapt. The Commons will exercise non-coercive irenic oversight of all communities as communities critique one another's practices and experiments. No community will stand outside the global deliberative conversation, even those that prefer to opt out. While they err, the remainder of the human Commons will offer perspective and correction, and, if necessary, undertake irenic interventions. We are, after all, in this together.

Global kithdom may lie centuries or millennia in the human future. Habits ingrained over millennia mutate slowly; vestiges will not wither rapidly, absent watershed cusps.[1267] To avoid economic and demographic apocalypse, changes must progress in small quanta. Big changes confuse the many, who find attention difficult to focus and manage habit change chaotically. Any person convinced of Quad sociality looks not to hurry things along, but to deepen the experience of those willing to experiment. When the divide in the social horizon lies not between rich and poor, but between the lonely and the flourishing, much will have been accomplished. One shifts general consciousness in but one way. One makes one's life a beacon. Flourish. Speak deeply with others; broach subjects of import. Share life with others. Invite acquaintances to similarly share. Make your circle a place of wondrous bonding. Set friends to build other associated circles. Imagine communities; link circles to fashion one. Show, more than tell. Know you will fail as well as succeed. That is as it should be.

The objector voices pessimism. Human life, in his view, is inextricably bound to coercive hierarchy. All fear the "stranger," which terror is an insidious disease ever rampant in human consciousness. But the objector understates the upside of community-by-community experimentation in life structures. Our intellectual hoard has been stripped of its more lustrous riches. Habitually, humans have quashed creative initiatives, or co-opted them into the service of normalcy. We have regularly killed or suppressed prophets and social innovators, and crushed their acolytes.

Where humans live with intense nurture and abundant necessities, they have diminished interest in violent, oppressive, and evasive forms of life.

[1267] Carpenter contemplates a long, dwindling run for property, wages, money, and private property, after which dawns a day when only custom, devoid of the odors of coercion, guides men. Edward Carpenter, *Non-Governmental Society*, 28-31. A "cusp" is a point or apex. See *Webster's Third New International Dictionary*, s.v. "cusp." As used here, a cusp is an apex from which one set of circumstances gives way to another.

Communities devoted to aesthetic beauty, to arts, to technical innovation, to contemplation, to peacemaking, community structural planning, to sustainable foodstuff production, to ecological restoration, to astronomical investigations, to ocean husbandry, to ore reclamation, to philosophical exploration: each may emerge. Each community's choice about its focus and lifestyle holds the risk of producing evil. Each community may also create goodness of such abundance as to catch the breath. Each community will inject its voice into the global conversation about human weal. Together, the Commons, and each of its constituent communities, will deliberate.

In twenty-first century America, we use "rights" talk to fend off some intrusive governmental interventions. We use diversity talk to inculcate tolerance in social groups. We outlaw and violently repress wanton dissenters (consider the fate of the KKK, or the Branch Davidians in Waco, Texas). None of these measures are very effective (recall that Timothy McVeigh and friends truck-bombed the Oklahoma City federal building on the second anniversary of, and in retribution for, the Waco firestorm. In retribution, we judicially murdered McVeigh, and incarcerated his sidekick for life). All leave us with a sad culture steeped in anonymity, household-by-household solipsism, and endless simmering pots of retributive bile. Isolation is bad for humans. Humans require social constraints and vital obligations to live well. Normlessness (*anomie*) kindles suicidal depression and antisocial deviance.[1268]

Quad sociality sweeps away half-measures. Quad nurture strikes at the heart of the problem: it creates a social "us" with no "them." Quad sociality deems every man a brother, every woman our mother. Our tribe is a global commons, as well as an intense local matrix of relationships. Local communities reflect global identity, even while seasoning it. Communities-soaking-up-the-structure-of-global-successes is what the Commons is all about. People choose what works, barring institutional impediments.[1269] Parochial silliness stands little chance before the overwhelming fecundity of a Commons serious about deliberation. One must quash the drive for conformity, in oneself, in one's community. One accomplishes that by teaching broad toleration of differences and wading chest-deep into the stream of adaptive community experimentation.

Quad sociality exults in a more humane view of humanity. It cannot, however, drain life of its risks. The likelihood of error is inherent in the human enterprise. Quad sociality relies on errors. From what other source might learning emerge? Other questions seem to me more poignant than handwringing about the evils into which communities might stumble. What wonders might we forego by cowering in ancestral coercions? What marvel might we foster by devotion to communal human flourishing? Just how meaningful might human life become?

[1268] Jonathan Haidt thinks this is the core message of Emile Durkheim's sociology. Haidt, *The Happiness Hypothesis*, 133,175-176.

[1269] Joshua Greene calls this sort of emphasis on what works "deep pragmatism." Greene, *Moral Tribes*, 292.

Objection 37: Big Brother Commons: Another protests that the Quad Commons portends nothing other than global government. Who governs the Commons? Will not some among the earth's communities be more equal than others, as were Orwell's pigs?[1270] Will not some community or handful of cooperating communities seize hegemony over others, especially when they possess critical technology or resources others lack but desire? Humans seek power as do they food and sex.[1271] One cannot excise hierarchical nastiness from the human essence. Coercion is a cudgel to compassion's carrot. To employ this misguided author's terminology, life addresses circumstance by approach or withdrawal. Coercion is the act that creates the response of withdrawal from ill-behavior. Human life, at its core, consists in wars of various sorts aimed to insure the weal of one's own community at the expense of others. That is the nature of the human beast. Interactions among strangers are, for chimps and humans, violent, brief, and ill-tempered.[1272]

Response: The communities of the Commons consensually govern the Commons. The Commons consists in global information exchange and inter-community deliberation. It issues no laws. It has no executive function. It might have a staff. The Commons lacks power to coerce. The Commons, by consensus among member communities, moderates a conversation, giving that complex dialogue direction, order, and etiquette. What minimum coercive capability remains in Quad sociality resides in one member or a few members of each community appointed, in a manner deemed appropriate by that community, to coerce when coercion proves unavoidable. Those member "martials" act only upon community authorization. They join forces with other communities' martials only with Commons consent, which degree of needful acquiescence should be exponential.[1273] The exponential consensus rule makes addressing local problems with coercive force relatively easy, but

---

[1270] According to Orwell, classes emerge naturally, but fraudulently, as gifted individuals manipulate societal rules to advantage for themselves and their progeny, to the woe of loyal, hard-working, but less-talented, neighbors. George Orwell, *Animal Farm*, 123.

[1271] "I put for a general inclination of all mankind a perpetual and restless desire of power after power that ceases only in death." [♪] Hobbes, *Leviathan*, 86.

[1272] "Whatsoever, therefore, is consequent to a time of war where every man is enemy to every man, the same is consequent to the time wherein men live without other security than what their own strength and their own invention shall furnish them withal. In such condition there is no place for industry . . . no arts; no letters no society; and, which is worst of all, continual fear and danger of violent death; and the life of man solitary, poor, nasty, brutish, and short." [♪] Hobbes, *Leviathan*, 107. Rousseau imposes his not unwarranted cynicism on the subject. A man can join the service, during which time he, for sparse compensation, kills others who have done little or no harm. The soldier will be praised because such a fuss is all we are willing to pay him. Rousseau, *Emile*, 456.

[1273] I propose an exponential structure for consensus in employing violent coercion below at proposed Community Policies. Basically, communities require consensus among a number of communities to conjoin their martials into *ad hoc* militias, which number is the integer two to the power of the number of martials proposed to be amalgamated. This rule, as a practical matter, means that one would require the consent of all communities of global kithdom (assuming a global population around one billion) to conjoin twenty-nine or thirty martials into a fighting force.

very difficult for large forces to be amalgamated.   The rule then serves as a check upon the use of violent coercion and especially war.

As to attempts to sequester information, no lasting benefit emerges from permitting property interests in ideas. As mankind has learned of commercial exchange, the upside of free trade overmatches any upside of restraint on trade. The experimental outcome of every idea belongs to all human communities. None should benefit by monopoly or sequestration of concepts or technologies. The urgent need to seek local benefit emerges in human interactions where there exists perceived scarcity. One lacks in comparison to others, and seeks to gain what seems missing. I anticipate, in a world where none lacks life's rudiments and all are, from before birth, valued and cherished, that perceived scarcity will wane. I anticipate, in a world where identity has shifted from nations-money-dirt to humanity-deliberation-flourishing, that human violence will be yet more deeply suppressed. I anticipate, in a world where prestige emanates not from piles of superfluous assets but from accolades for extravagant service to mankind, that hierarchical urgencies will don a more constructive garb.

I do not doubt that, among hundreds of thousands of communities, some will, for a time, exercise more influence than others. Influence, however, constitutes coercion only under a delimited set of circumstances (which I discuss below). Most influence, especially where the influencer lacks ill-intent, cannot be fairly deemed "coercion." Most especially, where no violence or threats exist, claims of coercion are doubtful. Influence of one community upon others: that is a *purpose* of the Commons. The Commons exists to loosen tethers of the past, to gather threads of the future, and to weave a tapestry of earth's one humanity.

Were a community or group of communities to seek hegemony, it lies to the remainder of the Commons to respond with irenic intervention. If all else fails, martial coercion might prove necessary. After such horrors, the Commons should recommence its dialogue. Its first topic should be how the Commons lingered inept while hierarchical and hegemonic fratricide gripped communities. The communities of the Commons should match their coercive capabilities to the hegemonic risks among communities. The first line of defense of a community's security is not arms, but rather promoting a culture of transparent collaboration. The second line of defense is widespread commitment to irenic intervention. The third line of defense is the tactical, but nonviolent, actions of martials in exposing and thwarting hegemonic activity. The final line of defense is responsive coercion. I take up this difficult topic below.

Objection 38: Quagmire of Consensus: *Yet another remonstrates that consensus is an unworkable decisional format. Requiring consensus effectively grants every member a veto over his community's choices. The lone recalcitrant might hobble needful action. Humans cannot function by consensus. Always, a majority drags its minority along in the majority's wake. Majoritarian coercion of minorities best approximates fairness. Majority rule is a hallowed tradition. What gods address this author when he proposes abandoning that deeply-ingrained collective habit?*

Response: I distinguish consensus from unanimity. Consensus welcomes diversity of opinion. Consensus acknowledges the urgency of needful action. Consensus exists when, despite reservations well-expressed, minorities acquiesce in the preferences of majorities. The more needful an action, the more accommodating those with reservations become, and the more compromising do majorities grow. When consensus proves elusive, patient inaction remains a viable alternative.[1274]

Seldom, in any complex deliberation, will a community find itself unanimous. But the world is uncertain. Most "facts" are equivocal. There exists room for any majority or minority to doubt the wisdom of its preferences. Where no pressing circumstance requires decision, conversation may continue, working toward consensus. Where circumstances demand action, opponents also recognize the need to act and reserve their opposition to majority preference. The community acts, with the dissent's opposition lingering in the air, awaiting tangible outcomes to decide the dispute. Some results bolster minority views, which can then take the fore as the majority to a different acquiescing minority.

To act without consensus is to ignore members, to neglect their gifts. There is nothing magical in commanding a majority. That majority, under the usual rules of majoritarian coercion, has utter sway to do as it will, despite having won support from as little as fifty percent plus one. Oscar Wilde called democracy the "bludgeoning of the people by the people for the people."[1275] Coercing a gaggle of dissenters differs little from coercing a lone objector.

Most often, those who object to consensus imagine a cud-chewing redneck obstructing a deliberating majority. Would it were so. As Emma Goldman argues, majorities seldom cogitate; they know nothing of judgment. The mass, characteristically, abandons all independent thought and mewls at the heels of some handsome narcissist. The dissenter's voice is frequently clarion, announcing foresight and courage. Majorities bulldoze dissenters at their peril.[1276]

Consensus as a decisional format asks that a community steel itself to convince its dissenters or be convinced by them. Consensus asks dissenters,

---

[1274] Various intentional communities have adopted consensus as their governing rule. The Aurora Commune, which existed from 1855 to 1883 twenty-five miles south of Portland, Oregon, had its administrative autocrat in its founder, a Prussian pastor named Keil. But crucial changes were determined collectively by the assent of all. Nordhoff, *American Utopias*, 310. At present, communities of the Federation of Egalitarian Communities employ consensus governance, in addition to other forms of decision-making. Such communities are the Acorn Community and Twin Oaks Community, both located in Virginia, the East Wind Community and Sandhill Community and Skyhouse Community, located in Missouri, and the Emma Goldman Finishing School, located in the Beacon Hill neighborhood of Seattle, Washington. See http://www.thefec.org/. It may not be an overstatement to assert that among the planet's eco-villages, communes, kibbutzim, intentional communities, non-residential urban fellowships, and other social experiments, consensus is the dominant decisional rule.

[1275] [♪] Wilde, *The Soul of Man Under Socialism*, 138.

[1276] Goldman, "Majorities and Minorities," 14.

at a minimum, to acquiesce for a time to see how a majority's preference works out in practice, and to keep marshalling arguments aimed to inform and persuade the errant majority. Communal acts do not terminate conversation; communities act in full view of their acquiescing dissenters. Community life is an experiment; all, majority and dissenters alike, stare at outcomes.

There is nothing fair about being coerced. The idea that majorities fairly coerce dissenters is a lie majorities tell themselves to justify their impatience and coercive excesses. A dissenter's dissent is respected only when she comes, after dialogue, to agree or acquiesce. Until dissenters acquiesce, a community should keep talking or wait. Few circumstances demand immediate action. Get comfortable with disputes; learn to engage them respectfully and constructively. Stop sweeping dissenters under carpets. There is nothing sacrosanct in standing among a majority. Where a majority exists, it harvests no divine right to steamroll dissenters. Rather, a majority, by its very existence, publishes the fact that one's community is divided. Existence of a majority privileges one to listen harder to dissenters and to compromise with them or join them. The principle of majority rule erodes meaningful community. To the extent that is so, majoritarian rule is an evil. Consensus is an engine building meaningful community. Consensus enforces a discipline of taking one's friends and companions seriously. Consensus slows human culture down. Consensus prevents missteps and hysterias. Consensus stands near the essence of finely-elaborated conduct culling. Simply, consensus promotes goodness.

Most are wary to adopt consensus governance. Consensus denies majoritarian legitimacy, and so constitutes an American and democratic secular heresy. Consensus rationale supports acephaly, and contradicts hierarchical subordinations, so ubiquitous in western culture. Consensus sounds like, and is, hard work. Consensus presupposes the good faith of minority and majority alike. In our anonymous culture, one imagines that adamant dissent for no particularly pressing reason injures none. The majority rules; dissenters are pushed aside. We are used to being ignored. Still, resentments and retaliations mass, the legacies of strangers behaving badly. Such is the American experience since mid-twentieth century. With those critical of consensus theory, I agree to the extent that consensus is unworkable in institutions premised on anonymity, accustomed to coercive habit, and bloated by overpopulation. One cannot govern the United States by consensus. One cannot even govern an American hamlet by consensus. Where anonymity and its attitudes rule, consensus is unworkable. Ours is a long history of adulation for majoritarian coercions. Majoritarian coercion is enshrined in our Constitution. We pledge ourselves to majoritarian coercion. We mulch up majoritarian coercion as a pablum for our children, indoctrinating them in schools and homes. The right of a majority to coerce its dissenters does not, by its near universal approbation, become right. A lone dissenter, speaking what is true, constitutes a majority of one.[1277] Let the majority learn from its dissenters. Dis-

---

[1277] [♪] Thoreau, *On the Duty of Civil Disobedience*, 259.

senters clog a majority's machine. Let the majority bring the dissenter along in good faith, or let the majority desist.

Dissenters bear grave responsibilities. Petulant dissent, indulging one's hurt or fears, can hobble one's community. Thoughtful adults dissent or consent or acquiesce. When they dissent, members must do so only because they are convinced, after substantial deliberation and conversation, that a grave evil will befall their community should they acquiesce. When matters are uncertain, which describes almost every circumstance, the concerned member should protest in clarion tones, then acquiesce.[1278] All will watch and await the outcome of a majority's choices. The bell of dissent reverberates in the ears of the acting majority. Outcomes tell. More conversation lies ahead.[1279]

Quad sociality presupposes that the relevant decisional group is around 1,500 interactive members. All recognize one another. None wishes to injure corporate life. One's circle, and its well being, are deeply tied to the weal of the deciding community. Pressures different from those that drive anonymous coercive majorities enliven consensus governance in Quad communities. One cannot simultaneously respect and ignore another. None coerces with impunity. Anonymous majorities coerce strangers overtly. That hurt festers frightfully. The social dynamic in consensus decision-making lies in friends choosing a course with friends. Consensus depends upon, and generates, a penumbra of good faith. Consensus exudes an air of well-being, of belonging, of mattering. Those feelings lie somewhere near the enlivening guts of meaningful community.

The objector asks an important question. Just who do I think I am to toss over hundreds of years of the tradition of majority rule? Fair enough. I am one man, a dissenter, deliberating the way we choose to live together. I have objections, which I attempt to state coherently. In my view, the objector's affection for coercive solutions welcomes a decisional strategy inherently flawed, and failing badly. Might we speak together until we agree, or, at a minimum, understand one another and acquiesce in the experiments of the other?

Objection 39: Bridling Corruption: *Still another deprecates Quad sociality for the author's naïve dismissal of human lethargy, envy, laziness, free-riding, greed, jealousy, short-sightedness, and arrogance. Humans, stripped of coercive penalties, lust for havoc. Where law is absent or unenforced, people decline to cooperate, shirk, lie, cheat, steal, indulge cruelty,*

[1278] Bruderhof brothers call acquiescing dissent "consent with a heavy heart." This alternative renders Bruderhof communal unanimity a species of consensus governance. See Zablocki, *The Joyful Community*, 175-176.

[1279] The grave danger in consensus governance lies not in obstinate dissenters but in acquiescing loafers. Where group opinion coalesces, as in Quad communities, pressure to conform increases. Certainly, one temptation would be to "get along by going along." Where such intellectual idling rules, the creativity essential to Quad sociality's benefits attenuates. All suffer. In the Bruderhof movement, a Hutterite communal resuscitation, some who have left the community tell of withholding dissent to avoid group censure. Zablocki, *The Joyful Community*, 174.

and generally, erode human trust.[1280] In shadows beneath every bridge of consciousness hunkers a troll of terror. He would gulp our fine sensitivities, and pick his rotting teeth with our bleached white bones. The privileged, the laboriously educated, and the occasional gentle soul may sport surprising empathy and compassion. We recognize life's Tutus, Kings, and Gandhis. They and their influence hardly suffice. The human ruck hides in its breast blighted characters. Sore parental neglect has convinced these many that no altruist acts truly. All work the long con. A few among the discordant many amount to cancers of the human soul. Such will savage all, if only once does the censorious, coercive communal eye blink.[1281]

Response: I imagine no great nobility in most humans. Would most strove to be better people. I, however, deny to all, beginning with myself (at least on good days), the right to condemn those we have not bothered to nurture.[1282] Hungry people seldom fix creaking systems. Illiterate people do not reform, except in spasms of looting and riot. Sick people aspire to little other than some relief. Quad communities will seem farfetched until we *nurture every child*. Quad communities will appear utopian until every man has a job, a home, sufficient nutrition, a literate mind, and a relatively healthy body. These changes lie within our grasp, were we willing to purchase human capital rather than military escapades. Billions could become better people.

Until they do, we will not know whether human blights incapable of nurture's remediation may remain. Those, if they exist, will prove a difficult challenge indeed. The predatory sociopath, in his coercions and violence, makes himself a nation unto himself. When he kills, he seizes, on his sole initiative, the essence of tyranny. He imperially denies his victims their liberty, seizes their property without warrant, and makes of society a mewling herd, intent, above all else, on safety and eventual reprisal.[1283] Perhaps, even such as these whirlwinds can be calmed. Perhaps not. I leave a slight window, in exigent circumstances, for communities, upon deep deliberation, to coerce errant members and communities. Would there were no need to leave that window ajar.

Most certainly, I do not share the objector's warped view of the human essence. Man is not essentially violent, trembling in barely suppressed rage to dismember his neighbors. The ordinary human sports a semi-universal amity toward strangers, looks for ways to cooperate in shared interests, and considers making of every newcomer a brother. Non-pathological men grow ug-

---

[1280] Shariff and Vohs, "The world without free will," 79.

[1281] Schopenhauer, venting his moral skepticism, says: "The thousands that throng before our eyes, in peaceful intercourse each with the other, can only be regarded as so many tigers and wolves, whose teeth are secured by a strong muzzle. Let us now suppose this muzzle cast off, or, in other words, the power of the state abolished; the contemplation of the spectacle then to be awaited would make all thinking people shudder." Men are born to rapacity, though some few find compassion persuasive. All are unable to change their stripes. Schopenhauer, *The Basis of Morality*, 74, 121.

[1282] So my mouth speaks. My heart occasionally has its own, less generous, view of matters.

[1283] Woodcock so styles the terrorist. Woodcock, *Anarchism*, 256.

ly when ignorant, threatened, starved, or terrorized. We would do well to avoid those predicates. This is the lesson of the twentieth century.

Objection 40: Abandoning States: *Still others disparage kithdom because it encourages humanity to abandon hierarchical mass institutions, especially the State. Contrary to the author's naive regressivism, the State evolved for a specific purpose: to remedy the ills associated with just the sort of tribalism the author mistakes for a panacea. People do not do what one expects. They do what one inspects (and what one demands). The State, as a theory, has purchased for mankind relative peace, material prosperity, a doubled lifespan, the suppression of sociopathic political leaders, a proliferation of life-improving technologies, and a welter of scientific insight. The author would pour sand in the engine of this profusion of well-being, the democratic State. It is true that the State coerces. But most citizens seldom smart under the lash of the State. The brunt of any State's force targets foreign threats without and recalcitrant miscreants within. The author advocates enfeebling government by robbing it of the enthusiasm of its most precious asset: brilliant young minds. One tool, and only one tool, has proved effective in tamping down human violence. That remedy is the State.[1284]*

The State need not metastasize. States are not required to over-reach. The State could be (and sometimes is) the voice of tolerance and prudence amidst the human cacophony. As the author notes (at some length), human perceptions carry inbred distortions. We need more government, not less. People bear children they should not, drink to inebriation, indulge drugs, eat foods that make them fat, fail to save for the future, drive badly, and savage intimate relationships. We need States to generate a coercive paternalism, preventing people, by legal censures, from ill-behavior. Nurturing the population might help, but will not suffice. It is the formal and informal force of law and coercion that makes people behave better than might come to them naturally. Long live the paternal State.[1285]

Response: The objector credits States with more than their due. I do not argue that no State should ever have existed. When violent sociopaths hammer at the door, one fortifies, digs a moat, organizes, finds fatal fury, and, if fortunate, survives. The historical residue of that recurring effort is the State, which, being an institution, lingers generations or centuries after the threat that warranted its creation has faded from memory. The State has played a role in restraining violence. The objector errs, however, when he deems the remedy of the institutional State a lesser evil than the violence it restrained. States coerce; that is, States do intentional violence to those in

---

[1284]Alan Ehrenhalt analyzes America's swing toward choice and against authority. Ehrenhalt doubts the wisdom of people who imagine community without stifling authorities. "There is no easy way to have an orderly world without somebody making the rules by which order is preserved. Every dream we have about re-creating community in the absence of authority will turn out to be a pipe dream in the end." Ehrenhalt, *The Lost City*, 21.

[1285] This last paragraph leans upon the arguments of Sarah Conly in her important book, [♪] *Against Autonomy*, in which she defends coercive state paternalism against objections and misconstructions. Conly believes government can be a force for social good, but also for moral improvement.

their charge. If one grants the objector's premise that States alone can repress miscreant depredations, then humanity's future comes clear. Humanity's tale will ever be one of persistent war, punctuated by the rise and fall of violent men seeking ever more effective means of killing one another.

States govern by corralling human perceptions. States count, name, measure, standardize, make maps, delimit, and explain. Most cannot resist. Minds grow tame, laboring in State-specified ruts. Ultimately, what cannot be controlled cannot be governed. States make legible to State minions the wild brambles of mankind, lopping off those sports, however promising, that cannot be subjected. All must, for the purposes of States, be writable, taxable, assessable, and subject to confiscation. What cannot be so wrangled is deemed "barbarian," by which States mean resistant self-governing, non-subject people. Often, barbarians are bellicose in their refusals. From the State's point of view, *Cull* might be considered a manual for designing barbarians.[1286]

Steven Pinker, whose work I admire, shares some of the objector's sentiment. Pinker finds that the coercive State, when reasonable, creates incentives to peace and punishes aggressive tilting. Peace can become the only reasonable alternative (which does not mean peace will predominate, but makes it more likely so). Pinker also identifies other factors in making the world a generally peaceful place: humanized trade (creating gentle contact among diverse peoples and encouraging specialization), female values (men do most violence; where women have a potent voice, violence declines), sympathy expansion (when we feel, even slightly, the plight of others, we grow less likely to inflict pain upon them), and rationality (reason is sympathy without emotion, giving a motivational boost to the structural changes necessary to creating a pacific society).[1287]

States are a solution as bad as the problem they address.[1288] States are coercions designed to stalemate intruding coercions. In Conly's paternalistic nanny-state, a thoroughly domesticated State fails to savage, and often helps, citizens. I know no such altruistic States. States tend their own habits and needs. The help States offer is most often misdirected and counterproductive. We can do better.

[1286] These ideas were sparked James C. Scott. He describes Zomia, the highland regions of southeast Asia to which fled many tribes seeking refuge from the regimentation of emerging lowland States. The resulting cultural stew Scott calls a "shatter zone." The people of Zomia resisted state legibility until after World War II using their difficult terrain, mobility, swidden agriculture, flexibility, religious dissent, egalitarianism, and oral culture to frustrate would-be rulers. Scott, *The Art of Not Being Governed*, 4-9.

[1287] [♪] Pinker, *Better Angels of Our Nature*, 671-696.

[1288] Such a sentiment is an American staple. Consider Thomas Paine's eighteenth century view: "Society is produced by our wants, and government by our wickedness . . . Society in every state is a blessing, but government even in its best state is but a necessary evil; in its worst state an intolerable one." One should seek, according to Paine, societal security from that form of government that is cheapest and most beneficial. Paine, *Common Sense*, 251. George Orwell, in a tongue-in-cheek mood, wrote: "The secret of rulership is to combine a belief in one's own infallibility with the power to learn from past mistakes." Cited in Mlodinow, *Subliminal*, 196.

I do not advocate regressing to tribalism. Humans were not better off when we were hungry, wandering, flea-bitten troops of hunted veldt primates (Rousseau notwithstanding). Kithdoms are not tribes skating oblivion's razor edge, but rather structured communities of well-nurtured, deeply-educated global members dwelling amongst friends in technology-assisted existence. I believe we are now well-positioned to bootstrap 200,000 years of learning to a new and better status quo. We must step past modernity and the straight-jacket of its thought forms. To do so, we need a different theory. I offer one: Quad irenic kithdom.

> FRIENDS ARE CHOSEN, FAMILY INHERITED.
>   ONE MAKES FRIENDS FAMILY AND FAMILY FRIENDS,
>   SEEKING CONVERGENCE.
> TRIBES ARE CHOSEN, THE PLANET INHERITED.
>   ONE MAKES THE TRIBE PLANETARY AND THE PLANET TRIBAL,
>   SEEKING CONVERGENCE.
> GOODNESS IS CHOSEN, CULTURE INHERITED.
>   ONE MAKES GOODNESS CULTURAL, AND CULTURE GOOD,
>   SEEKING CONVERGENCE.
> CONVERGENCE IS CHOSEN, DIVERGENCE INHERITED.
>   ONE MAKES CONVERGENCE DIVERGE AND DIVERGENCE CONVERGE,
>   SEEKING HARMONY.

9.13.2.11. *Initiative.* None of these Quad sociality transformations will transpire apart from deliberate action on the part of billions of humans. To effect these changes, each must use his or her skills to nurture members, nurture communities, and nurture the Commons. I turn to these topics.

10. **Nurturing Members.** Social capital waxes in intricate interpersonal webs dedicated to meaningful community. No members are individuals in the sense that they stand alone without community support. Human relations cannot be adequately conceived in mere economic terms, nor as aggregations of individuals. Members comprise overlapping webs of relationships. Only within these webs does genuine nurture occur. Communities choose attitudes and habits, as do members. Those collective sentiments aggregate to produce mutual weal or woe.[1289] We either nurture or injure, augment or erode.

Within the social matrix, communities have responsibilities to members and other communities. Some follow:

10.1. *Physical Sustenance.* Humans are tropical animals. We forage fruit, nuts, the occasional kill, and whatever else appears edible in our scaveng-

---

[1289] Mencius asks how murder with a stick differs from murder with a knife. Finding none, Mencius rhetorically asks how murder with a blade differs from murder by misrule. *Mencius*, 7 (Book I, Part A, Section 4).

ing. We have spread to the planetary poles by technological means. Everywhere, we import with us the means to create a marginally subtropical African environment: clothing, houses, fire, winter food sources and storage technologies, water, and so forth. Each community, wherever situated, is obligated to provide for every member a savannah-equivalent environment amenable to life in the community's location. This is not to say that members have no responsibilities in this regard. Communities may and will ask of each member contributions of the sort each is able to provide, and much of that effort will be directed toward creation of sustainable subtropical environments for community members.

10.2. *Meaningful Activity.* Well-nurtured members flourish when collaborating in well-deliberated activities believed to contribute to a community's well-being. Humans find flourishing life meaningful. The task for a community in nurturing members is to integrate each member into the structure of the community's life in a manner consistent with the member's unique capabilities and interests. Communities puzzle a shape of meaning together in a living mosaic of carefully-fitted tiles. Members discover themselves integral to an exquisite canvas of vital art.

10.3. *Productive Activity.* A measure of labor supports any human life. In activity that provides the means of sustenance, the maintenance of health, the quality of environment, the nurture of subsequent generations, all should participate. The grunt portion of labor should be shared by all who benefit. Every member should learn and practice a craft, regardless what other skills and tasks may occupy leisure hours. Members should mentor apprentices in his or her craft, and pass core skills to subsequent generation(s). One point of Quad communities is to cooperate grandly, exploiting the personal familiarity shared among intimates. Communities should broaden their represented skills, and invite mentors from other communities for crafts in which they are deficient. Each community should nurture members to acquire all skills necessary to reproduce the infrastructure of that community, or to form associations with other communities for the same purpose. Communities should reject technical advances without contemporaneous ethical consensus and well-deliberated choices cognizant of the likely needs of future generations.

All should, to the extent possible, choose their labors for the attraction the work holds for the worker. A rump of inextricably dreary labor may remain unchosen; communities should share that unhappy work equitably among all who benefit from it.[1290]

[1290] Godwin, probably unrealistically, estimates this quantum to be one-half hour per day per person. [♪] Godwin, *Political Justice*, Vol. II, 353 (Book VIII, Chapter VI).

10.4. *Leisure Activity.* Life, as we presently live it, is slaved to labor. We work and work. Were unpleasant labors distributed fairly, were war machines never built, were no effort squandered producing luxuries and ill-conceived boondoggles, were none who can work evading toil, then the day's necessary labor would be complete by noon. With the energy and time remaining, every member could find other activity that enriches and expresses that member, and benefits all: painting, drawing, story-telling, writing, thinking, planning, investigating, chronicling, opining, dancing, singing, symphonizing, hiking, swimming, sporting, and all the enriching welter that constructively occupies humans at play and in discovery. A culture flourishes, once its members are fed and housed, in proportion to its well-utilized leisure.

10.5. *Socialization.* The first task of the community is to socialize members. The community's social construct, as well as that of the global Commons, must be taught to its junior members. Each generation must fully preserve and transmit previous generations' insights, wisdom, and technical skills, as well as address the current challenges facing one's community or those of the Commons. The word "education" should be avoided, because the term has become wedded to institutional efforts that have plainly failed in their charge. This book can, from one vantage, be seen as a program to ameliorate the effects of misguided western education.

10.5.1. *Nurturant Mentoring and Member Character.* The character and human relations of members are the primary capital asset of a community. This essential wealth should not be left to institutional muddling or parental neglect, ignorance, and confusion. All anticipatory parents should be instructed in parenting skills and attachment theory. With parents and mentors should lie responsibility for a child's emotional development and education; they should utilize schools as a resource, and never delegate educative responsibility to one or more schools. In addition to parents and schools, every child should live in tutelage of one or more mentors, whose charge lies in: a) recognizing the child's unique abilities and challenges, b) insuring that each child receives appropriate nurture, c) directing, with the child's other intimates, the course of the child's ethical development, and d) guiding the child through his or her social integration. Character must be taught and effective curricula developed in which mentors and parents are expert. The structure of nurturant mentoring should be determined by each community, but the results should be deliberated by all communities.

10.5.2. *Cultural and Moral Socialization.* The global community's socialization curricula should transmit the cultural history of mankind, including its languages, events, ideas, technologies, and deliberations. Social transmission consists in more than technical skills or cultural transmis-

sion. Members need education in conduct; members must learn the results of the global conduct dialogue, and participate in that conversation.
Members must be taught peace and self-restraint, to avoid the worst aspects of human aggression within and among communities.

10.5.3. *Member Morals Curricula*. The content of member conduct socialization evolves in global dialogue about the path along which the human
future may be secured and enriched.   Humanity may no longer trust its
future well-being to the emergence of genius, for good or ill.   Gandhis,
Assissian Francises, and empathic savants emerge; Hitlers, Maos, Stalins,
and sociopathic butchers as well.[1291]   Meaningful communities offer an
evaluation of the human past.   Human morals curricula should include,
among other things, instruction in kindness, compassion, seeing others'
perspectives, self-restraint, and demonstrating affection.   The curriculum
must include exposure to a broad spectrum of cultures and language.   An
evaluation of war and its sources, of megalomania, of interpersonal violence, of sociopathy, of substance abuse, of interpersonal conflict resolution, of decision-making, of irenism, and the many moral issues common
to mankind should be staples.   Whatever changes a community seeks, the
backbone of group reform lies in educating the community's youth out of
their parents' bad habits.[1292]

10.5.4. *Technical Education*.   The global community of communities must
be able to make what it uses and needs.   The community's education of
members should transmit the skills and knowledge necessary to create the
artifacts and systems on which the Commons relies, and to invent and develop future technologies needed.   This technical education should be
globally redundant, to minimize the danger of forgetting critical skills,
and backed up by digital libraries memorializing all such skills and
knowledge in visual and literary formats.   The Commons Library should
be freely available to all via their link to the Commons.

10.6. *Cooperation and Contract*.   Communities emerge from cooperative
friendship of circles.   Communities are too expansive, even at 1,500 members, for intimate personal relationships to govern.   Circles contract[1293] with

---

[1291] See [♪] Glover, *Humanity*.

[1292] [♪] Dewey, *Human Nature and Conduct*, 127.   One ameliorates society's evils by educating
youth out of the group's habits of thought and desire.

[1293] "Contracts" are written or oral agreements among members, cadres, circles, or communities to
collaborate in creating some outcome. We tend to deeply underestimate the power, flexibility, and
breadth of contractual relationships. All we do can, potentially, be governed by contracts. Contracts
memorialize consensus. See [♪] Nozick, *Anarchy, State, and Utopia*, 14. Nozick argues that people
tend to dramatically under-appreciate the manifold possibilities open to them in acting outside state
purview. Instead, most default by inaction, allowing legislatures to determine the boundaries of action. Henry Sumner Maine argued, in his review of the role and development of ancient law, that

one another to form a community of shared interest.   Circle contracts amount to federalism among circles, by means of which communities come to exist.   All members of a community remain familiar, since one interacts constantly with members of various circles, and one's psychological and economic well-being is tied to them.   A community's task, in caring for its members, is to form such contracts between circles and other communities as prove necessary to fabricating meaningful community for members.

10.6.1. *Contracts of Purpose.*   A community, in its survey of opportunities, seeks consensus as to its ethos, values, location, lifestyle, economics, and all significant aspects of community life.   Where there grows consensus among a group of people, communities may take shape.

10.6.2. *Economic Contracts.*   Communities choose how to provide for life's necessities, which services and products to self-produce and which to purchase by contract from other communities.   Economic contracts should be cut to the skills and interests of a community's members and the preferences of its various circles.   A community, for example, might choose to become a manufacturer of plumbing products, having several mechanics and plumbers in its ranks.   Another might become a college for nurses or physicians.   Another may build innovative housing, and broadcast their plans and expertise.   Others may fabricate community contracts of various sorts for other communities and the Commons.   Yet another may design and install water and sewer systems.   Some may choose several such projects.   All will require contracts with other communities to purchase those goods, services, and skills in which a community is deficient.

10.6.3. *Cadre Contracts.*   Cadres form (usually unspoken) contracts.

10.6.3.1. *Forming a Cadre.*   Friendships emerge from all cooperative activities of life.   Over time, especially where members are conscious of their friend-making potentials, friends' intertwined relationships form a cadre, usually quite unintentionally.   Cadres are an image of primal humanity.   Cadres have deep organic roots in human dynamic mutuality.   They happen naturally, like forests, except where cultural arsons savage them.

10.6.3.2. *Participating in a Cadre.*   Cadres bear their own intrinsic rewards.   Meaning emerges from cadre relationships.   We develop a sense of relational place and expectation from our association with intimates.   We know where to turn in dilemmas and disasters.   Caring usually spills over, among friends, into more expressly contractual agreements of greater or lesser import.   These extend from sharing pizzas on Fridays, to joining sports teams together, to forming businesses, and, for some, to

---

"the movement of the progressive societies has hitherto been a movement *from Status to Contract.*" (italics in original) Maine, *Ancient Law*, 165.

enduring sexual partnerships that issue in children and cast the cadre into general alloparental care.

10.6.3.3. *Decision-Making in a Cadre.* Cadre decision-making operates by
consensus. Friends talk. They account for the needs of members. They
chart paths that serve all. *Cull* has discussed consensus and dissent
above.

10.6.3.4. *Departing a Cadre.* Circumstances may require departing a cadre, at least for a time. Education, work, needs of distant loved ones,
medical treatment, and other exigencies may demand one's absence.
Communicate as you are able. Avoid letting the social fascinations of
new circumstances supplant your cadre connections. Return at the first
opportunity.

One may depart a cadre for relational reasons. In my view, departing one's cadre portends serious difficulties. Where intimacy proves
impossible, where conflicts cannot be resolved, where new friendships
require care in different locations, one may consider departing a cadre.
Such departures are social amputations. Leaving injures all. Do so only
with the most deliberate care. Consider alternatives less drastic. If you
must depart, take time to salve your and your cadre members' injury.
Where you can, move to another cadre associated with the same community. You will preserve your identity and your former cadre-mates'
self-concept if you are able to see one another with affection as circumstances permit. And you will avoid the uncertain risk that a new cadre
will be worse than what you seek to avoid. Wherever you go, there you
are. Your warts share your berth. Resolve problems in your home context.

10.6.3.5. *Joining a Cadre.* In joining a cadre, recognize the social structure into which you migrate. Joiners join all members and their intricate
relationships. Undoubtedly, you enjoy a friendship with some cadre
member. Recognize the cadre member you least prefer. Discover if you
can be that person's friend. If so, the door stands ajar. If not, reconsider. A cadre shapes one's life irrevocably. Shared intimacy requires
decades of diligent nurture. Choose carefully.

10.6.3.6. *Forming a Circle.* Cadres naturally overlap. One builds friendships outside cadre intimacy. One meets others with whom one shares
meaning and interests. In building this bridge, one cadre links to another. The bonds are not so intimate as cadres, but nevertheless significant
friendships. By the links of this other cadre, one contacts yet further cadres. If one ponders this interlinkage from a distance, one recognizes a
circle. Most circles presently go unnoticed. You may recognize a circle
by this: you know everyone's name and their core relationships to oth-

ers in the circle. Circles tend to comprise 100-150 persons. The circle too is fluid at its edges, leaking into other circles.

10.6.4. *Circle Contracts*. Circles that intend to be self-supporting seek contracts with other circles for needed goods and services. Circles may also contract to join forces for economic ventures, in order to have sufficient resources to undertake complex endeavors. Circles may also contract to address shared security concerns. Communities should limit their size to around 1,500, which mirrors long-term tribal association size.[1294] This size grows from my presumption that tribal size, when not affected by security threats, reflects some limitation of the human cognitive apparatus—a Dunbar limit aimed not at interpersonal relationships, but rather at inter-circle connectivity.

10.6.4.1. *Forming a Community*. Circles forming a community should engage contracts by consensus. Circles should proceed incrementally. Initial engagement with other circles should be evaluated. One anticipates that beneficial relationships among circles will lead to further agreements among circles, eventually issuing in a relatively stable association among a group of circles. At that point, a community exists.

10.6.4.2. *Participating in a Community*. Communities will establish their own normalcy for member participation in community decision-making. Circles will propose to communities. The community can decide among such initiatives. One should leave the hard work of creating consensus to the intimate relationships of friends in their cadres and circles.

10.6.4.3. *Decision-making in a Community*. All structures for decision-making lie open to communities, in their experiments in living. That communities may choose any structure they please does not mean every structure is a wise choice. I speculate below about communal structures which lack deliberative warrant.

10.6.4.4. *Leaving or Joining a Community*. Some members, in leaving a cadre, may wish to depart a community as well. That is a most serious proposition, since it endangers the member, the community, and the community of communities. The member risks his psychological well-being, since he severs or impairs relationships that required decades of care and financial investment. Given the broad range of member capabilities, some members may be subject to poaching. Communities might seek to lure valuable members from their home communities, to the economic detriment of the community departed. Communities could suffer "brain drain" and social impairment. The Commons, upon community transfers, runs the risk, when members depart communities, of

---

[1294] So Robin Dunbar argues. Dunbar, *How Many Friends Does One Person Need?*, 24-25.

fostering a market in members. High value members might be offered perks, as are employees of businesses in the extant social context. Communities might stratify. Such developments injure the social capital of communities, and distort values in meaning. Humans exhibit a deep fault line in consciousness relating to economic security. We keep our money ducks in a row with difficulty.

Still, a member may leave a community, despite the dangers. Member poaching betrays a community of distorted values. Of that, one complains in the Commons. Members may need to transfer from one community to another to pursue an education, to work in a chosen vocation, to love a mate and her circle, to dwell in a community with sentiments better aligned with the member, to express loyalty to fresh friendships. Undoubtedly, even in communities well-grounded in meaningful existence, member comings and goings will be frequent, as accommodations of member uniqueness.

10.6.4.5. *Community Contracts*. Consideration of contracts among communities is deferred to the section below on nurturing communities.

> ***Objection 41: Absent Intimacies:*** *Some demur that friendships in real life never seem to approach the degree of intimacy the author extols. Friends are dear, even critical to one's well-being, but nevertheless fungible. Friends come; they go. Most often, friends are work-mates. These share ready-made economic relations and community of interest. When the job disappears, so too the friends. Or neighbors become friends. These relationships deteriorate upon the next corporate uprooting to a distant city, or when a house fire evicts friends, who then relocate across town. Babies disrupt friendship. They arrive, their ceaseless demands in tow, rendering an intimate a dull, pre-occupied, sleep-deprived companion. Finally, people's economic manias preclude intimacy. People work and work, stinting time necessary to build intimacy. Friendships founder at the periphery of shared life, waiting upon that IRA contribution or house payment or college tuition or vacation home or fancy car or much-needed vacation. In the end, I am on my own.[1295] My wife is dependable, provided she does not divorce me. My children are friends, unless they crash upon any of life's numberless shoals, or decide, as do so many, that they have not quite just yet tamed adolescent petulance. Quad communities are not possible, because circles are not possible, because cadres are not possible, because friendship is not all that intimate. Thus reads the epitaph on the tombstone of Quad sociality.*
>
> ***Response:*** Some objections are painfully true. This is one. *Cull*, from one perspective, describes a path from abject isolation to meaningful intimacy.

[1295] So Epictetus opines. Men love what serves them. When a friend or daughter or spouse threatens what one prefers, that interferer is likely to be reviled. Affection is a wan sop compared to the dynamo of self-interest. Count on no one but yourself. Epictetus, *Discourses*, 387 (Book II, 22.15).

Intimacy founders in most American relationships. It fails in most marriages. Most children never become their parents' adult friends. Most friends never progress beyond enjoying the things they do together. Many people may not even know what I am talking about in describing intimacy. Intimacy has just never happened to them or their loved ones. They may be at sea in this conversation.

Most intimacy collapses before American profit frenzy. Corporate employers make of workers interchangeable parts, ready to be deployed wherever dollars dangle. Employees, to their detriment, comply, tempted by the error, so essentially American, that money makes a family prosperous. Some people cannot be intimate. Their early nurturers suffered distraction, or their own attachment disorders, or drug-induced lethargy, with the result that the much-neglected child cannot establish deep bonds with others. Such attachment incapacity is epidemic in America. Its specter haunts every mall. Lacking intimacy, buy, buy.[1296]

American friendships are planted in an inclement desert. To husband an intimacy, one must shield that relational seedling from harsh ambient weather. Some of those sprout-withering storms are unfettered mobility, economic monomania, affection for luxuries, distraction, self-indulgence, unwanted children, despair of intimacy, fear of strangers, tight-fisted affection, smile depletion, fear of being touched (haphephobia), and a culture that dismisses collapse of intimacy as an expected cost of human depravity. Overall, America suffers oxytocin deficiency.[1297] Oxytocin floods the parental birth experience. Oxytocin is a hormone that accompanies relaxed thoughts, nurture, and bonding. Intimacy is possible, even in America. Build a windbreak. Buy an umbrella. Stay put. Make time. Dare to care. Have a vision for your friendships. Build toward intimacy, one relational brick at a time.

10.7. *Deviance and Neurodiversity.* Which behaviors should be discouraged? History shows our marked propensity toward over-use of punitive sanctions and over-emphasis on coercing conformity. Frequently, those sanctioned have been merely dissenters, exploring and expressing behaviors different from usual member behavior, but posing no threat to meaningful community. Such a member expresses the neurodiversity inherent among humans, and should be embraced for her uniqueness. No member should be coerced for deviation from behavior deemed normal, except when that per-

---

[1296] Some argue that global capitalism threatens the self directly by sucking attention ever more deeply into cell phones and other electronic devices. This "unholy alliance" of global hucksterism with intrusive technology "hollows out our souls and destroys our imagination." We have not yet plumbed the effects of these new technologies on the human brain, other than to note that they make one dramatically less able to drive attentively. It may be true that the union of global capitalism with cell technologies presents a fundamentally new form of intrusive State, and warrants cautious scrutiny by communities. This note relies upon exchanges with Jan Oppermann, in personal correspondence with the author, dated October 14, 2015.

[1297] See Keltner, *Born To Be Good*, Chapters 10-11.

son's deviation presents a tangible threat to meaningful community. Members who might indulge such extravagances are wanton. Deviation among members should be welcomed, embraced, understood, and put to work for the community's well-being.

10.7.1. *Cherishing Differentiation.* Except where wanton deviation injures meaningful community, communities should tolerate and welcome deeply differentiated persons. One must recognize that, absent a conviction to permit oddities, one endorses coercion of some stripe. The arm-twisting may be so subtle as passing sighs or twitched cheek. Or our coercions may slam the door of solitary confinement and indulge execution. But, where conviction to tolerate fails, responses, at a minimum, wink at coercion.[1298]

10.7.1.1. *Innovation.* Neurodiverse explorations of alternative concepts and lifestyles drive cultural innovation, which enlivens meaningful community, even while simultaneously irritating it. The neurotypical majority should cherish its odd ducks, even if they prove harmless deviants, and recognize that neurodiversity is seldom acknowledged for its fecundity while flowering, but only after it has gone to seed.

10.7.1.2. *Courage of the Neurodiverse.* Neurodiverse members exhibit unusual courage. Little terrifies humans more than social censure. Neurodiverse individuals brave the venom of offended neurotypical members to express their uniqueness. Neurodiverse communities blaze paths that, where adaptive or aesthetically pleasing, will be trodden by future neurotypical communities. In this manner, culture adapts. A certain hardiness nests in the heart of neurodiverse members and communities, a durability to be valued by all.

10.7.1.3. *The Trap of Normalcy.* When convened, human groups self-preserve. They assert, then enforce, their norms. Neurodiverse persons diverge. They opine oddly. They offend, sometimes intentionally. They assert what is, to neurotypicals, insanity. They enact the forbidden, and indulge taboo behaviors. The neurotypical community must recognize, for its own welfare, that in the welter of neurodiverse rants lie seeds of neurotypical adaptation, and ultimately survival.

10.7.1.4. *Committee Non-Creativity.* Committees never innovate. They trend irresistibly toward least-common-denominator solutions, tweaking past habits to limp toward what the committee deems a clearly-

---

[1298] John Stuart Mill asserts that societies, and most especially their governments, lack well-founded warrant to constrain members or citizens, except for the purpose of patent self-defense or protection of others. Rightful coercion does not extend to forcing people to improve themselves, to make themselves happier, to undertake right or wise action. These latter are cause for complaint and negotiation, for remonstrance and pleading. Society should hold its collective tongue except where demonstrable evil threatens members. All else lies beyond justified social control. [♪] Mill, *On Liberty*, 12-13.

envisioned future, justifying themselves by appeal to unwarranted democratic principles and fear of conflict. All futures, from today's vantage, appear muddy, and are usually unanticipated, despite the contrary view of committees. Committee predictive clarity derives from pedantic projection of what was onto what will be. Do not ask committees to accomplish that for which they are ill-suited. Committees play a part. Committees exist to plan and enact what neurodiverse savants imagine and adapting communities adopt.

10.7.1.5. *Neurodiverse Savants.* Oddness, and hence innovation, originates in the neurodiverse member savant. These gifted members seldom fit in well, and so ruminate at the social margins. Communities often disdain neurodiverse savants as odd or insane. Savants stink; they rant; they blurt; they hide. Human communities must identify these persons, and draw them and their thoughts into the core of community, contrary to social sentiment. The neurodiverse savant will resist participation. One must coax her to speak, then deliberate, while the savant hides in the back of the room or the library.[1299] Group sentiment exacerbates social ossification. Without the member savant, social adaptation wanes, heartfelt participation leaks away, meaning languishes, and threats to community weal go unanswered. Communities barely recognize these problems, and when they do, have no adaptive response at hand. Answers lie in member savants. These members innovate, for reasons emerging from their own oddnesses.[1300] They jostle us, keeping our communal joints limber, warding off psychological arthritis. All the innovations we identify as cultural progress aggregated in the minds of neurodiverse savant members.[1301] Neurodiverse savants comprise a core asset of social capital.[1302]

[1299] Though she does not speak of neurodiverse savants, Susan Cain elaborates the different thought system and perceptions of introverted personalities. The introvert needs space. His thought forms need respect. Introversion is not only different, but also another, often more fruitful, way of existing. Susan Cain, *Quiet*, 264-266.

[1300] "In all ages, souls out of time, extraordinary, prophetic, are born, who are rather related to the system of the world, than to their particular age and locality. These announce absolute truths, which, with whatever reverence received, are speedily dragged down into a savage interpretation." [♪] Emerson, *Conduct of Life*, 1057 (VI). "All the feats which make our civility were the thoughts of a few good heads." [♪] Emerson, *Conduct of Life*, 1083 (VII).

[1301] Russell, "Individual and Social Ethics," 337.

[1302] Novelist John Steinbeck argues that only individuals create. Committees and collaborations are fruitless. Groups refine and elaborate what an individual mind fashions. But groups never create. Groups may, however, set themselves to extinguish the creative human mind by stifling, repression, forced educations, drugging, or operant conditioning. This genocidal war on individuality is a sad suicidal spectacle. Its exertions injure that which is most precious. Individual minds should ramble where they will; none should intervene. Steinbeck opposes any State, religion, idea, or system that erodes the individual mind. Social establishments must defend themselves, he understands. Free

10.7.1.6. *Savant Communities.* Communities that welcome and adapt in response to their savants become themselves savant communities. Savant communities must recognize their role in the larger Commons. The savant community is vanguard. The savant community makes itself an experiment in human possibilities. The savant community may prosper or suffer for its efforts. The savant community should open itself to the inspection of all communities. From savant failures, as much as their successes, the Commons adapts itself. Both neurodiverse and neurotypical communities must eschew violence toward one another and their revolutionary or reactionary savant members. Each needs the other deeply.

10.7.1.7. *Persecuting Savants.* Groups tend to kill their prophets, then heed them.[1303] We deem them wanton, for no particularly compelling reason, then hack or burn or strangle them to death. Neurotypical humans relish familiar habits, and imagine those who disrupt custom dangerous.[1304] Neurodiverse savants cannot conform. Some among us cannot run marathons. Some cannot eat wheat. Some, it seems, cannot relish life's goodness, and choose instead to refine traces of gloom from every rainbow. Neurodiverse savants cannot toe the social line. Taking a thanatoid perspective on neurodiverse savants, their wildness serves us. Their odd ideas and habits are a resource to be mined for utility. Ideas that survive scrutiny should be adopted as norms. Short of the fuel of neurodiverse savants, the engine of human cultural adaptation idles, failing to drive us toward adaptive responses.[1305]   Glory in a

---

minds pose grave danger to entrenched systems. Nevertheless, Steinbeck hates and opposes such repressions. Mankind is lost if the creative individual is quenched. Steinbeck, *East of Eden*, 131.

[1303] Heraclitus castigates the Ephesians for their exile of Hermodoros for no greater crime than wishing to be himself. The Ephesians banished Hermodoros because of their vaunted egalitarian prejudices, which Hermodoros transgressed by being an excellent human being in every particular. Heraclitus, Haxton translation, *Fragment* 114.

[1304] Freud would have us believe that communities commence when groups of men join forces to quash the gratifications members would enjoy if not restrained by the collective. [♪] Freud, *Civilization and Its Discontents*, 59.

[1305] John Stuart Mill addresses this matter directly: "Persons of genius, it is true, are, and are always likely to be, a small minority; but in order to have them, it is necessary to preserve the soil in which they grow. Genius can only breathe in an atmosphere of freedom. Persons of genius are, *ex vi termini*, more individual than any other people—less capable, consequently, of fitting themselves, without hurtful compression, into any of the small number of moulds which society provides in order to save its members the trouble of forming their own character. . . . [O]f originality in thought and action, though no one says that it is not a thing to be admired, nearly all, at heart, think that they can do very well without it. Unhappily this is too natural to be wondered at. Originality is the one thing which unoriginal minds cannot feel the use of. They cannot see what it is to do for them: how should they? If they could see what it would do for them, it would not be originality. . . . [A]ll good things which exist are the fruits of originality. . . . In sober truth, whatever homage may be professed, or even paid, to real or supposed mental superiority, the general tendency of things through-

neurotypical person lies in prying open the padlocked door of the usual to embrace a savant.

10.7.1.8. *Outliers.* Some members may seek isolation which exceeds strategic solitude for a limited purpose. A few may choose to live alone. That decision distresses a community from which the member departs. Communities must continue to support their outliers physically and socially, though such support may be scorned. Outliers may suffer untreated mental illness. Attachment disorders may ravage them.

Outliers could become a concern for other communities and the Commons. Outliers may turn to crime to gain sustenance. They may aggregate, forming loose coalitions with other outliers. Such groups could present security issues for communities. Where communities of outliers form, each should be amalgamated to the Commons, if possible. If not, they should be treated as brothers at a distance, whom one visits occasionally, whom one tolerates for love's sake, for whom one demonstrates concern and support.

Regardless, no member or community should be allowed to spin free of the Commons unobserved. Isolated communities present dangers, with which mankind is ever so familiar, to themselves and to others. Their cultures wobble in eccentricity. Outliers are more likely to endorse sociopaths. Historically, outliers murder their own, and indulge war with scant concern. Outliers are then wanton. Until wanton, however, outliers deserve no coercion. They need us, but do not know it. We forgive their error, and support them as they permit.

10.8. *Security.* Communities bear responsibility to generate a meaning-laden collective existence for members. Neurodiverse behavior in members produces important cultural innovation, and so should be widely tolerated. Only when deviance threatens a community's weal should efforts commence to redirect wanton members. Those efforts begin with intensifying friendship with the wanton member. I have described a process by which a cadre might cope with a wanton member. (§7.48, and §10.9.6) I have described steps one may take to reconcile conflicted members by dialogue or mediation (§7.13).

If ever undertaken, coercion of a member should employ the least restrictive alternative available for the minimum time possible. All coercion must have limitations grounded in human dignity, which restriction eliminates the use of demeaning circumstances or solitary confinement or death

---

out the world is to render mediocrity the ascendant power among mankind. . . . The initiation of all wise or noble things comes and must come from individuals; generally at first from some one individual. The honour and glory of the average man is that he is capable of following that initiative; that he can respond internally to wise and noble things, and be led to them with his eyes open." [♪] Mill, *On Liberty*, 62-64.

as permitted forms of coercion.[1306] The primary coercive acts of a community should be persistent observation of the offending wanton member and re-education of him or her. Communities should absorb into themselves the effects of wanton member behavior, and ameliorate the wanton impact for direct victims of the wanton member. The goal must be to re-integrate the wanton member into some role in a circle and to make a constructive place for the wanton member within the community. Wanton members in need of coercion indicate a collapse of the community's social meaning, at least as to the wanton member. Therefore, each instance of necessary coercion offers an opportunity for learning to the afflicted community, as well as the wanton member.

10.9. *Coercion of Members*. Member or community choice consists in freedom from and freedom to: freedom from over-reaching interference with the course one charts for herself, and freedom to receive such benefits from and undertake such obligations to others as one believes will cause her life and those of her intimates to flourish.

Coercion interrupts choice. In so doing, coercion endangers the critical goals that choosing serves. "Freedom from" constrains the interventions of others to those we can deem mere influence, thereby insuring that the member or community influenced charts its own course, possibly over and against well-intentioned advice and concern from others. "Freedom to" beckons the chooser to take up the task of human conduct, to discover for himself or themselves a path honestly assessed to well serve, and to put that choice to the proof in a human community. "Freedom from" entails lack of prohibitive impediment to deliberated courses, and so entails the freedom to fail.[1307] Humility comes in the package.

Not every influence, even when potent, is coercive. Social interactions influence members. When we say "man is a social animal," we mean that most members, most of the time, take cues for appropriate behavior from other members.[1308] Relationships deflect member involvement toward co-

---

[1306] Such a rule, then, excludes retribution from permissible purposes of coercion of wanton members. Collective coercion drives members toward restoration of the *status quo ante*. Retribution will always remain a potent emotion. Humankind has, for 200,000 years, been tamping down recompense frenzy. Like hierarchical fixation and we-them thinking, retribution is one (of many) primal emotions that poorly serve us. We should resist. Restorative justice turns the focus of coercion from what offenders deserve to what victims and societies and perpetrators need. Restoration aims to set matter right. See Shermer, *The Moral Arc*, 371-396.

[1307] Epictetus notes that every person who does evil injures herself and suffers loss. Epictetus, *Discourses*, 273 (Book II, Section 10.19).

[1308] Some characterize human sociality as "obligatory gregariousness." Cacioppo and Patrick, *Loneliness*, 37.

ordination. If conformity failed to beckon the vast majority of member activities, human social existence would crumble as a body without its skeleton. One also influences others by extravagant wisdom well-evidenced, by acts of kindness seeking reciprocity (including offers of help and the promise of cooperative economic enterprise), and by the possibility that one's acts might be condemned categorically, which castigation exceeds mere approval or disapproval by invoking what gods the community reveres. Where one is not materially restrained from acting, as in being jailed or cast out, a member remains free to calculate the relative value of acting in a manner certain to be censured, and, nevertheless, to act in just that manner.[1309] Powerful countervailing considerations do not necessarily constitute coercion. Still, most societies condone some influences over others, and condemn other forms of influence.

Views about coercion diverge, not merely in opinions expressed at taverns and school lunch counters, but also in philosophical deliberations and multi-national conference tables.[1310] What shaping forces constitute permissible influence upon the choosing member, and which pass that evanescent line beyond which lies impermissible coercion? In a culture that vaunts conscientious choosing, when is potent influence upon another warranted? Requiring consensus implies a large quantum of interactive influence among members. What conditions render an instance of influence unacceptably-coercive? The role of and limitations upon coercion are core problems in political philosophy.[1311]

[1309] Taylor asserts that one remains free so long as he retains "pure negative freedom," which term implies that one's action is not rendered impossible by the acts of others. No coercion, in Taylor's view, makes a person unfree. [♪] Taylor, *Community, Anarchy, and Liberty*, 142, 143. In my view, Taylor's position is too strong. Some coercions materially limit the freedom of neurotypical members to act, even though they do not render the contemplated act strictly impossible. The simple fact is that people differ in their ability to resist social censure. Some can tolerate almost none, and so are easily coerced. Others resist with ease, and prove difficult to coerce under any conditions.

[1310] Reidy and Riker find academic consensus that coercions of various sorts are necessary, but substantive theoretical questions about the nature of, limits to, and appropriate agents of coercion persist. In their view, human weal may well await global consensus concerning permissible coercions. Reidy and Riker, *Coercion and the State*, 14. Aristotle takes the strong position that only where the coerced person contributes nothing to an act and the coercer is the sole mover can coercion fairly be said to exist. [♪] Aristotle, *Nichomachean Ethics*, 38 (1110b). Aristotle, however, adds some countervailing considerations in his further discussion.

[1311] Wertheimer accesses philosophical issues concerning coercion by considering examples from legal contexts in contracts, torts, marriage, wills, blackmail, criminal confessions, plea bargaining, and defenses to criminal liability. Wertheimer, *Coercion*, xii (see table of contents at vii-viii). Some thinkers distinguish between interpersonal coercion and institutional or political coercion. See, for example, Reidy and Riker, "Introduction," in *Coercion and the State*, 1. I offer a definition below that seems to cover both sorts of coercion, if in fact two sorts exist. Interpersonal coercion would seem foundational, since, in the end, all coercion, even that by States, is effected by one or more persons influencing one or more other persons. F. A. Hayek, a detester of coercion, offers thoughts on the difficult concept: "Coercion occurs when one man's actions are made to serve another man's will, not for his own but for the other's purpose. . . . Although coerced, it is still I [the coerced per-

10.9.1. *Moral Concept.* At their root, claims of coercion convey a moral perception that the coercer wrongfully imposes his unwelcomed preferences upon another. Despite the inherent immorality of compelling others to unchosen acts, some coercion we commonly deem morally justified. Only some coercive acts do we equivocate or condemn.[1312] For example, most deem forcible restraint of mass murderers justifiable on a community safety rationale. But we deem incarceration of the mass murderer's children unacceptable, even though we fear apples fall not far from their tree. We waffle when deliberating contracts made under substantial financial pressure, especially when the dilemma a person faces has been generated by the person pressuring decision; maybe they coerce, maybe they do not. In each case, we bring to bear subconscious affective responses when making decisions about coercion. Distaste for coercion may be hard-wired into human neurology, as is our penchant for coercing itself. The moral issue lies in the difference between offers, containing as they often do mild subliminal threats,[1313] which most deem morally-acceptable influence, and overt threats that contemplate morally impermissible means or ends.

10.9.2. *Influence-Coercion Spectrum.* In every consideration of the propriety of exercising influence over another, seven nodes affect perceptions of coercion: a) a Chooser with his mental status and moral perceptions, b) Chooser's present activity with its anticipated outcome, c) an Influencer with his mental status and moral perceptions, d) Influencer's preference for Chooser's deviated outcome, e) the pre-existing Relationship between Chooser and Influencer, including the community norms applicable to each, f) the Deflection by which Influencer affects Chooser's activity, and g) the Exigency of the circumstance under which the Deflection occurs. Along each node, a spectrum of possibilities opens. Extremity at any node may render a Deflection, otherwise acceptable, coercive. Less dramatic facts at any node, combined with barely noteworthy conditions in multiple nodes, may aggregate to unacceptable coercion.

10.9.2.1. *Choosers.* Healthy, adult members resist coercion, and may embrace potent influences without surrender. The young or feeble or de-

---

son] who decide which is the least evil [of the alternatives the coercer offers] under the circumstances. . . . Though the coerced still chooses, the alternatives are determined for him by the coercer so that he will choose what the coercer wants." F. A. Hayek, *The Constitution of Liberty*, 199-200.

[1312] Others deem coercion inherently non-moral. These find coercion a fact of nature and human society. One evaluates instances of coercion for means and outcomes, at which point one can assess the morality of coercing under the circumstances. See Reidy and Riker, *Coercion and the State*, 2.

[1313] Taylor calls the offer-threat of interpersonal influence a "throffer." [♪] Taylor, *Community, Anarchy, and Liberty*, 12.

mented resist poorly, and may capitulate with inadequate deliberation to mere suggestion. Coercion deflects a particular person under particular circumstances. Deflection barely influential to a self-possessed person may prove overwhelmingly potent to a less vital Chooser. The relative inequality of bargaining position strongly affects perceptions of coercion.

10.9.2.2. *Chooser's Intentions.* A Chooser acting to reach a clearly-defined, well-conceived goal resists Deflection. Such Choosers may tolerate more intense influence than would a Chooser whose purposes are weakly-sought, ill-defined, or misdirected.

10.9.2.3. *Influencers.* Perceptions of an Influencer's character and capacities affect our decisions about coercion. Tall, fit, decisive men are deemed more likely to coerce than short muddled women. We seem less concerned about the deflections issuing from tall, fit, decisive women than we are those of men. The Deflections of aged doddering pensioners are thought less potent than those of aggressive teens seeking illegal drugs. Some share of perceptions of coercion lies in the degree of influence that an Influencer might, if he chose, bring to bear on a Chooser. Influencers who, due to potent bargaining position, command Chooser compliance, on threat of declining to collaborate with Chooser except upon Influencer's preferred terms, are more readily deemed coercers than those negotiations in which Chooser and Influencer stand as relative equals.[1314]

10.9.2.4. *Influencer's Intentions.* Influencers seek some preferred good which Chooser's path may injure or defeat. Perceptions of coercion emerge more readily when the Influencer's Deflection appears motivated by self-interest or ill-deliberated purposes. Perceptions of coercion are also more likely when Influencer's purpose does not include a potent interest in Chooser's well-being.

10.9.2.5. *Pre-Existing Relationship.* Concerns about coercion diminish where a long term trust exists between Chooser and Influencer. Chooser has selected the Influencer to Deflect him. For example, spouses regularly Deflect one another without claims of coercion, as do parents and children, attorneys and clients, pastors and parishioners, doctors and patients. One's own community exercises Deflections that, were those Deflections initiated by strangers, would constitute coercion. We presume that a strongly influential relationship exists with the consent of, and for

---

[1314] "Contracts of adhesion" are agreements in which the powerfully-situated partner dictates all terms of a deal, even when the less-powerful partner reasonably objects. See *Black's Law Dictionary* s.v. "contract, adhesion contract." At law, contracts of adhesion are presumed substantially nonconsensual, which makes such contracts flawed (consider software licenses, car-purchase contracts, and plea-bargains). Laws frequently protect inferior partners to contracts of adhesion, such as landlord-tenant statutes, consumer protection acts, and employee-protective government agencies.

the mutual benefit of, Chooser and Influencer. For this reason, we deem malicious Deflection by a trusted Influencer (fiduciary breach) especially egregious. For this same reason, we tolerate potent Deflections from persons we know and trust. We claim coercion infrequently where the Influencer is familiar or beloved.

10.9.2.6. *Deflection.* The efficacy of Deflection dominates allegations of coercion. When a Deflection necessarily changes a Chooser's path, as when one places his finger atop another's, forcing that person to pull a gun's trigger, we call that Deflection coercive. As a Deflection's efficacy diminishes, we grow more and more likely to find the Deflection a permissible influence. Weapons are presumptively coercive. A quiet conversation during which Influencer suggests to Chooser reasonable countervailing considerations is a presumptively non-coercive Deflection. Not all Deflections are overt; the equivocations of a self-interested fiduciary that befuddle his ward into ill-deliberate acquiescence may be the darkest of Deflections. In general, potent, self-interested Deflections are deemed more coercive than other-directed restrained Deflections.

10.9.2.7. *Exigency.* When life-threatening dangers or life-preserving opportunities impinge, we tolerate coercion of resistant members more readily, and are inclined to recharacterize such coercions as necessities to which no alternatives existed under the circumstances. Paleolithic life brimmed with dangers from which members frequently needed rescue. Failing to seize opportunity could spell death for a member or community. We may be hard-wired to perceive exigent coercion as necessary and therefore permissible.

10.9.3. *Coercion Defined.* Influencer impermissibly coerces Chooser when Influencer's Deflection becomes the overriding cause of Chooser's unsought change of course, which Deflections, morally-considered, may be exacerbated by Chooser's lack of intimate acquaintance with Influencer, or self-dealing by Influencer, or Chooser's lack of confidence in the good faith of Influencer, and which Deflections may be morally excused when Influencer's Deflection addresses exigent danger to Chooser or risk of loss of opportunities benefiting Chooser.

Coercions with moral taint, some obvious, others less patent, abound. The gunman coerces his victim to empty pockets. The rapist coerces when force makes his victim pliant. The adult grandson coerces when his dying grandmother cannot resist his self-serving demands upon her. The manufacturer coerces when demanding premium prices for shoddy merchandise because the seller holds a functional monopoly. The police officer coerces when demanding citizen compliance at gun point. Religious congregations coerce to salvage the souls of participants. Defalcating fiduciaries coerce when they slant portrayals of likely outcomes so as to induce their beneficiaries to select the fiduciary's preferred course of action, especially when the fiduciary benefits from that choice. Nations coerce when they war or threaten such. Cultures coerce when alternative views and possibilities are proscribed, despite those alternatives posing no threat of harm to any.

Other coercions evade moral condemnation, even though potent. Legislators set the stage for coercion when they promulgate statutes containing punishments for failure to obey. Firemen coerce when ordering a family out of their burning home. Police officers coerce when they turn on lights and siren. Judges coerce when they judge. Nations coerce when they enact trade sanctions, or deploy military assets.[1315] When, if ever, are these coercions warranted? When is what-appears-coercive something other than coercion?

Community action may appear coercive to an outsider. It may not be so, despite effective deflections, because members participate willingly in joint enterprise and restrain their dissents when uncertain of outcomes. Spousal influence can seldom be deemed coercive, despite leaving a partner no alternatives than the preference of the influencing spouse, because marital life is agreed.[1316] Influence among spouses and friends resemble weighing options in a single mind; in intimacy, deliberative tasks are distributed among partners, with tacit agreement to condone one-party preemption of dead-locked issues in necessary give-and-take. All minds, including the collective consciousness that exists in cadres, circles, and communities, are fractured and conflicted. Ample room exists for potent influence and adequate independence to settle side-by-side. In intimacy, as in community, the Influencer's intentions and pre-existing relationships predominate, provided the means of Influence remain irenic.

10.9.4. *Responsibility in Coercion.* We are accustomed, where one is coerced, to deem the intent of the Chooser overborne, and to lay blame for coerced outcomes upon Influencers alone. Influencers do indeed bear special responsibility for the outcomes they over-reach to create. One must, however, recognize simultaneously that Choosers and their commu-

---

[1315] War itself may not be strictly "coercive," since its goal may be extermination of the Chooser, rather than a Deflection of Chooser's actions. Reidy and Riker, *Coercion and the State*, 5, 39-40. Still, wars in fact often serve coercive purposes, their goal being not genocide, but rather extension of negotiation tactics to lethal stratagems. And the idea that the murderer does not coerce his homicide victim waxes strange.

[1316] Thomas Andrews notes that one must have access to effective means by which one may exit an intimate relationship, such as marriage. Lacking such, potent marital influence amounts to coercion. Many other relationships suffer similarly, if no ready exit from that relationship exists. Thomas Andrews, in private correspondence with the author, July 2016.

nities participate in creating circumstances under which coercion prospers. Choosers, in many instances, welcome their Influencers.[1317] They may be wooed by their Influencer in a manner of their own choosing. Choosers may indulge naïve glad-think, looking to others, including their Influencer, for evasion of troublesome facts. Communities also contribute to coercions. Where we tolerate coercive relations, we make them more likely. Where we dismiss coercive damage, or euphemize about it, we swing wide our doors to grasping Influencers. Where we wink at violence, especially where that terror serves purposes we approve, we render all human relations more susceptible to Influencers' depredations and make spiraling cycles of violence more common.

10.9.5. *Ultra-Minimal Coercion.* Humans over-coerce. We are impatient and insistent. Most humans tire rapidly when offering reasons for change, and deal poorly with emotionally-laden conversation portending conflict. So, coercion waits just around every corner.

Coercion, and its sulking brother, violence, create poor outcomes. Coerced members suck a seed of resentment, which they are ready to spit when opportunity presents. Victims of violent coercion plot retaliation, hoping to coerce their coercer at least as violently as the violence suffered.[1318] Counter-counter-violence initiates spirals of vendetta and appeals to allies. War beckons. Coercion, when tolerated, spreads like infectious disease. In our culture, none evades that plague wholly.

Nevertheless, a community's need to counter-coerce cannot be wholly sidestepped.

10.9.6. *Constraining Member Evil: Militant Irenism.* Meaningful communities must secure themselves from wanton evil-doers. Failure to create a reliably safe environment stokes the fires of coercion, making such acts more common and better tolerated. Validating coercion and counter-coercion, we make of ourselves an armed camp. The armed camp is inim-

---

[1317] Epictetus taught that coercion never compels. A man chooses to submit. One of his moral purposes overwhelms another of his moral purposes. Epictetus, *Discourses*, 117 (Book I, Sections 17.25-27).

[1318] *Exodus* 21:23-25, *Deuteronomy* 19:21. The prohibition of *lex talionis*, usually cited as an example of extravagant retribution, in fact limited the counter-violence of victims to that punishment specified by law. The Hebrew practice had been to exact more sweeping vengeance upon the perpetrator and his family than had been inflicted upon the victim and her family, as evidenced at *Genesis* 4:23-24, the Song of the Sword. The priestly dictum of the *lex talionis* pruned vengeance to a maximum of parity. Epictetus spins retaliation differently. He argues that the aggressor who injures another does evil, which necessarily injures the aggressor, as well as his victim. All evil injures its doer. So the victim, when he retaliates, reasons thus: "The aggressor injured himself by injuring me. I, therefore, will injure myself by injuring the aggressor." Epictetus, *Discourses*, 275 (Book II, Section 10.27).

ical to human community. Coercions erode community, and, to the extent they do so, constitute evils.

CAESAR OF SMALLTOWN TAUGHT MARTIAL ARTS. CHILDREN ADORED CAESAR. MEN HEEDED HIM. MOTHERS TRUSTED CAESAR. SLY CAESAR SEDUCED THEIR DAUGHTERS. WHEN DISCOVERED, CAESAR FLED TO A DISTANT LAND WHERE HE KEPT THE COMPANY OF MEN AS TINY AS HIMSELF. CAESAR'S SMALLTOWN LOVER WILTED. HIS IGUANA DIED. SMALLTOWN REMEMBERS CAESAR, NOT FONDLY. CAESARS ARE WEE HERMITS, SELF-BANISHED TO ROCKY ISLANDS, BARREN OF NECESSITIES. IN THE MORNING, CAESARS PADDLE AWAY EMPTY-HANDED. AT DUSK, THEY GLIDE BACK TO HARBOR, CANOES REPLETE WITH DRINK AND FOOD AND EJACULATIONS, THE DAY'S COERCIONS A BONANZA.

IN WHAT COIN DO SCOUNDRELS SECURE THEIR LIVING?
CAESARS MARKET MIRAGES OF MEANING, SAYS ONE.

Some four percent of humans are sociopathic; these members lack neurotypical concern for the well-being of others.[1319] That means in any circle of 150, six sociopaths lurk. Any of these persons, as well as any other person, may perceive evils as goods. Those harboring sociopathic disregard, whether genetic or disease-generated, are much more likely to act on their meaning-eroding impulses. Communities fear these persons, with substantial justification. The impulse to communal coercion of sociopathic wanton members derives from primal motivations: fear, rage, panic. These powerful drives, in a world peopled with others who must be confronted and cannot be avoided, must be diverted, to the maximum extent possible, from their historical outlets: incarceration, expatriation, murder, war, and interpersonal violence.

Where wanton members err, the first line of community defense is the wanton member's friends. Friends act to deter and protect the wanton member and others. *Cull* discussed what friends and circles should do in dialogue about or mediating with respect to another's injurious behavior

---

[1319] Medically, sociopaths (also called psychopaths or anti-social personalities) are unmoved by the needs of others. Onset of this moral blindness often occurs in the mid-teens, and those affected are mostly male. The sociopath causes social turmoil, conflict, and indulges lying, fighting, substance abuse, and sexual impositions. As adults, sociopaths neglect parenting, work inconsistently, and chafe at laws and social restrictions. The cause of sociopathy is not retardation, schizophrenia, or mania. See *Taber's Cyclopedic Medical Dictionary, s.v.* personality, sociopathic, page 1480. See also Stout, *Sociopath Next Door*. Steinbeck complains of monstrosities born of human parents, moral cripples, lacking kindness or the possibility of conscience. Such monsters find normal persons aberrant, and themselves estimable. Steinbeck, *East of Eden*, 71. Donald Pfaff argues that sociopaths are not genetically determined. Rather, dysfunctional social systems interact with a nascent sociopath's genetic heritage to produce a sociopath of greater or lesser severity. One can remediate, at a minimum, the social contexts that impinge upon young sociopaths. Pfaff, *Altruistic Brain Theory*, 209.

above (Section III). When irenic interventions fail, communities must intervene coercively.

Communal coercion must be a last resort.[1320] Where no reliable alternative exists, coercion should preclude re-offense by means that create the lowest impact on the offender and community, both present and future. The cost of providing care for the wanton member is a burden to be borne by all, since we owe care to every member of a community. Those costs, which may at the outset prove tremendous, serve to motivate communities to decriminalize and treat, rather than indulge a regime of retributive criminal segregation.

10.9.6.1. *Scope of Coercive Interventions.* One hopes that in a world replete with deeply-nurtured members, themselves descendants of generations of deeply-nurtured members, community coercion would wither from disuse. None knows the ultimate shape or needs of a deeply-nurtured society.[1321]

Until such irenism roots itself, communities need to remain prepared to intervene coercively when necessary. No member may be permitted to make a community feel or be unsafe. A community must be prepared to respond to reasonably foreseeable threats to safety.

10.9.6.2. *Goal of Coercive Interventions.* The goal for a community is to intervene in troubled circumstances so early and effectively that coercive restraints prove unnecessary. Cadres recognize member problems, and address them. Where cadres fail, circles intervene. Where circles prove ineffective, communities act, seeking to resolve problems irenically.

When coercion proves unavoidable, the goal of all communal coercion should be a twofold restoration of the *status quo ante:* first, for the wanton member's victim(s), one seeks healing and restoration of what has been lost or disrupted, and, second, for the wanton member, one seeks his reintegration as a member in good standing into the human community within which he offended. The affected community must bear the expense of this care and oversight. Wanton members no more ask to be wanton than do neuro-typical members ask to be normal. Care of wanton members measures the maturity of a meaningful community, and its expense is one cost of the task of nurturing social capital and communal meaning.

[1320] Gandhi admits that coercion of wanton members may prove necessary. One cannot, he says, leave lunatics in position to injure others. [♪] Gandhi, *Satyagraha*, 107.

[1321] Godwin expects a general transformation of mankind to self-chosen truth-seeking, if only coercion were reserved solely for dire emergencies. [♪] Godwin, *Political Justice*, Vol. II, 89 (Book V, Chapter XIV).

10.9.6.3. *Review of Proposed Member Coercions.* Each instance of communal coercion should be reported to Commons deliberation before imposition. Others may suggest interventions a community has missed. One global priority should be creating a transparent survey of human coercive acts, both those of wanton members and coercive responses from their communities. All coercions imposed should be assessed for their propriety. Where a community overreacts, the Commons should suggest alternative responses that better address the wanton member's needs. The Commons should urge communities toward similar sanctions for similar misdeeds, even while recognizing that wanton members and their impacts will differ among communities. Every community should empirically evaluate coercions for efficacy, both their own and their neighbors. Effective coercions should be promoted, ineffective ones retired.

10.9.6.4. *Structure of Coercive Interventions.* Coercive interventions, in the rare instances they are undertaken, should follow a course of increasing intensity. All coercions should be determined by the community in which a wanton member acted inappropriately. This fact implies that coercions will differ among communities.

When a member falls into community-erosive action, requiring coercive intervention, the nurturant structures on which he depends need repair. Communities play some role in their wanton members' errors. Where coercion proves necessary, that community must alter its local culture to address underlying problems within the community that contributed to the wanton member's failed nurture and wanton member actions.[1322] Communities must learn or ossify.

An hierarchy of coercive interventions of members follows:

10.9.6.4.1. *Mandatory evaluation and counseling.* The wanton member undergoes physical and mental examination, with reports to his cadre and community. A therapist acts as an assigned friend and monitor, to counsel the wanton member, to assist the wanton member's cadre in caring for their member, and to protect the community from a wanton member's re-offense.

10.9.6.4.2. *Mandatory reconciliation.* The wanton member may be required to listen to his victims, and undergo re-education aimed at teaching the member self-restraint, the needs of others, and the nature of his anti-social impulses. The community may provide, when deemed useful, a structure for ongoing discussions between the wan-

---

[1322] Martin Luther King Jr. said that when one comes upon a beggar, it is not enough to toss him a coin. Our moral responsibility lies in restructuring his society so beggars no longer need charity. [♪] King, *Autobiography*, 340.

ton member and his victim(s) with the purpose of reconciling them to one another.

10.9.6.4.3. *Limitations on freedom of travel and association.* A community may truncate a wanton member's freedom to travel and associate with whom he pleases. One anticipates that a community would assign a cadre-mate to keep track of the wanton member's movements and relationships.

10.9.6.4.4. *Limitations on access to dangerous substances.* Where relevant, a community may limit the wanton member's access to dangerous substances, such as drugs, weapons, vehicles, or explosives.

10.9.6.4.5. *Random monitoring.* Where more limited measures fail, a community may electronically and personally monitor a wanton member's activities by random interruptions and interventions. There is strong evidence that deception and ill-behavior plummet, for subconscious reasons, when one believes others may be observing.

10.9.6.4.6. *Uninterrupted monitoring.* If a wanton member poses substantial ongoing risks, he should be actively monitored, both electronically and personally, until no appreciable risk of re-offense remains. Frequently, one suspects, monitoring might continue for the lifetime of the wanton member.

10.9.6.4.7. *Transfer to a better-suited community.* If such exists, a community better suited to nurturing the wanton member might accept his transfer. The community in which the wanton member offended should remain involved, emotionally and financially, prepared to reintegrate the wanton member if his circumstance improves. No wanton member should be ejected from a community without successful transfer to a better-suited community, for unplanned exile makes of the disgorged wanton member an outlier. From that disconnection, the wanton member becomes a problem for all communities and a danger to nearby communities.

10.9.6.4.8. *Integration into an encapsulated therapeutic community.* Where lesser measures prove inadequate, wanton members may join encapsulated therapeutic communities, formed as are other communities, but for the express purpose of coping with wanton deviance. Encapsulation consists in limited travel freedoms, mandatory therapy, and permanent electronic and personal monitoring. Such communities self-govern and participate in the Commons. Members may transfer to other communities on the same basis as any member transfers from any community. So these encapsulated communities are not prisons. Nor, however, are they entirely normal communities. They are places for wanton members to work on wanton impulses in community with others suffering similar difficulties.[1323]

10.9.6.5. *Welcoming Transferred Wanton Members.* Since communities may effect coercive transfer of wanton members to other communities where a wanton member's prospects appear brighter, every community must welcome such transfers. The financial impact of coerced transfers should be fairly assessed and redressed between communities.

> ***Objection 42: Coercive Paternalism.*** *Some demur that the author's concern about coercion is hyperbolic. The author chooses primarily instances of violence as his exemplars, and so seeks remedy for an ill not nearly so pervasive nor so grave as he imagines. Human consciousness is mostly irrational. We injure ourselves by our poor choices and half-baked ideas. We smoke, we over-eat, we over-breed, we take crazy risks, we war: all these sub-rational propensities must be coercively restrained. The author fears coercion, with some justification. Paternalistic coercion proves difficult in application; it demands hard work and vigilant ferreting of abuses. But widespread coercion is unavoidable. To have a good society, we need not less, but rather much more, coercion. We require highly focused interventions, both legal and moral, to prevent people from harming themselves and others by their impulsive lurching. To coerce less leaves mankind in the grip of personal autonomy, the freedom that Mill vaunted. Autonomy, in the end, means that a tiny fraction of people live at liberty to proceed from success to success, while the vast majority proceed from debacle to debacle, suffering self-inflicted horrors. To disparage coercive paternalism, in effect, applauds the misery of ill-deliberate maiming that people inflict upon themselves. Only sadists advocate cruelty.*[1324]
>
> ***Response:*** To coerce another presumes that one knows in what direction, toward what alternative behavior or lack of behavior, the coerced other should be driven. More, the coercer presumes to know who should decide what "errors" of habit or understanding should be legislatively eradicated. In fact, we know neither what nor whom. Justice Louis Brandeis said: "Experience should teach us to be most on our guard to protect liberty when the Government's purposes are beneficent. . . . The greatest dangers to liberty lurk in insidious encroachment by men of zeal, well meaning but without understanding."[1325]

[1323] Nozick offers thoughts on a society's obligations to compensate members restrained for the purpose of preventing harms they are deemed likely to commit. He thinks such places of confinement would have to be luxurious to adequately compensate the wanton member for collective intrusion upon his liberties. Given the great cost of maintaining such resort institutions, it seems to Nozick unlikely that any society would undertake such a jail, and so none can legitimately restrain others preventively. [♪] Nozick, *Anarchy, State, and Utopia*, 142-146.

[1324] Sarah Conly ably argues her case for coercive paternalism. We must legislate people's private lives, protecting citizens from themselves. Most injure themselves pointlessly, and cause grave harm to others. [♪] Conly, *Against Autonomy: Justifying Coercive Paternalism*, 2-3.

[1325] Brandeis dissent in *Olmstead v. United States*, 277 U.S. 438, at 479 (1928).

Conly, to exemplify her view that society should make it illegal to be unwise, chose a person who is about to drink antifreeze, having mistaken the liquid for a sports drink. Surely, all would apprise the drinker of his error, and intervene to separate the lamebrain from his "beverage," were the dolt so stubborn as to ignore the warning. In Conly's example, one knows what behavior should be prohibited (drinking antifreeze) and who should make the determination to intervene coercively (every person). She (and I) are happy enough coercing mulish idiots bent upon accidental suicide by incomprehension.

One cannot, however, smoothly transition from antifreeze gulpers to the rest of life. Members lack any greatly detailed insight into what people living outside their own community should be doing or avoiding. Communities choose forms of life. These vary as between one another in dramatic ways. Some life-choices prove to be errors. Others prove successes, great or small. Forms of life prove well or ill for communities when tested by actual living. We conceive, attempt, then evaluate. We cannot know preemptively whether such life experiments bode weal or woe, though we will often cherish our suspicions.

Some might mistake my sentiment here for moral relativism. It is not. I do not believe that because you think it, it is true, even true for only you.[1326] Life has structure; outcomes are predictable in many circumstances. Some choices prove more meaningful, others less. My point is this: As a species, we have spent so little time and lavished so few intellectual resources in exploring human possibilities that we possess only the barest sketches of meaningful forms of human living. The book of living can brim with knowledge, if we will do the hard work of making attempts to live meaningfully. To date, most of humanity has been satisfied to rear children upon regurgitated meals cooked up by one long dead savant or another. The fare that issues from our kitchens of meaning is one tuna sandwich, then another tuna sandwich. More and better cuisine awaits.

Within communities, coercion is unnecessary, except in very limited circumstances. Members choose their life together. They amend their common existence as circumstances evolve. Social censure requires no legislative bludgeon to affect members. The often-gentle prick of in-group chiding vastly outpaces the lash of law in redirecting members. Order derives not from a feared punishment, but rather from a predictable, pliant equilibrium among a group's members. The lash breeds recalcitrance, then revolution.

The deep problem with coercive paternalism is compliance. Coerced persons, even when outwardly obedient, secrete recalcitrant bile. That poison spills, when enforcers blink, into consciousness. It poisons the social ma-

---

[1326] Simon Blackburn discredits moral relativism (there is no absolute position from which to judge among human opinions) because it self-refutes. Relativists claim that relativism is an absolute position from which to judge human opinions. Blackburn also discredits moral absolutism because it is difficult to imagine how any command, even a divine command, can make something true. Blackburn, *Truth*, 31, 43.

trix.[1327] Coercion does not work. Have we not learned this lesson? Millions of pages of laws and regulations gather dust in law libraries. We legislate and legislate. To what purpose? Law, as a theory of human relations, has been tried and found wanting. Coercive paternalism: we have been there, done that. The impersonal abstractions of law touch us superficially, if at all, for they are thin. We are persons. We are thick. We respond to persons in webs of meaningful relationships. We nestle in peace only in the bosom of much-loved companions. We rankle at intruders and intrusions. Our togetherness generates a thick stew of familiarity and regularity. This social mass of inter-connection seldom responds deeply to veneers of idea and concept.[1328] It re-sponds to itself, to its own consensus, the fruit of torrents of in-house talk. Coercion is arm-twisting about superficialities.

To improve a member's sordid choices, one needs to teach and model deliberation. Impulsive actors require mentors of patience and intelligence. Wisdom cannot be mandated. Prudence grows within members when their community provides thoughtful, responsive nurture. One cannot arm-twist another into insight. Too much well-meaning intervention crushes or suffo-cates the ill-deliberate. Building a thoughtful adult is bonsai of the soul, lov-ing pruning of one's habits by mentored choosing.

I wish wisdom came more easily; I find no pleasure in these views. If a path so simple as passing some laws could deliver meaningful community, I would gladly advocate that path. The route to meaningful community is a hard path, a trail for gritty adults, a road strewn with lingering pains and star-tling joys and persistent learning.

Coercion erodes community at its root. Avoid it.

11. **Nurturing Communities.** Communities require support. Communities ex-ist in a biological substrate (members); they are best conceived as social enti-ties. A community consists in the congress of member relationships. Yet, a community surpasses its members' many interpenetrations. A community is a gestalt. Its sum exceeds the conjunction of its parts. Human social collec-tivity is a person of sorts.[1329] It suffers hungers and diseases. It rejoices and

---

[1327] Alex Haley reports that Malcolm X said: "Yes, I am an extremist. The black race here in North America is in extremely bad condition. You show me a black man who isn't an extremist and I'll show you one who needs psychiatric attention!" Malcolm X, as recounted in Alex Haley's foreword to *The Autobiography of Malcolm X*, 21. Elie Wiesel reports of himself, after encountering Hungari-an jackboots lashing exhausted Jews to faster travel, "It was from that moment that I began to hate them, and my hate is still the only link between us today." Wiesel, *Night*, 17.

[1328] Sartre's complaints about ontology may boil down to an aversion to the thin-ness of thoughts. Sartre explains the nature of the thinking person: "Consciousness is a being, the nature of which is to be conscious of the nothingness of its being." Sartre, *Being and Nothingness*, 47. If Sartre com-plains of the anorexia of cognition, then his thick book, brimming with obtuse abstractions, may be a prime exemplar of his complaint. At a basal level, Sartre is certainly right. We are self-conscious beings before we begin to be reflective self-conscious beings, that is, before we grasp ourselves as objects in a world of objects.

[1329] See my previous discussion of social interpenetration above at §6. Dietrich Bonhoeffer declares the church to be a *Kollectivperson* in his doctoral dissertation on ecclesiology. Bonhoeffer, *Sancto-*

grieves. It requires attention and affection. It is a member in a larger collective of its own ilk, the human collective. Communities require intentional nurture. The grave danger every community faces lies in its member relations deteriorating into rote repetition, a period during which someone other than the members makes decisions for members.[1330]

Members nurture their communities by:

11.1. *Member Dialogue*. Content-full talking nurtures communities. Some argue that consciousness is a product of language.[1331] Member consciousness, they say, consists in internal cross-talk among modules of the brain. Extrapolating from that model, communities exist in their members' dialogue. A healthy human community brims with conversation. Some chatter life's trivia. Others devote themselves to weightier matters. All move their tongues, jaws, hands, hips, and feet in the dance of dialogue. One nurtures his community by participative talking.

11.2. *Member Affection*. To nurture your community, show you care. The colossal conversation of community has a tenor as well as subject. If talk is the meat of community, its potato is heartfelt affection. Healthy communities hug and laugh. Smiling infects most members. Genuine joy in the presence of other members afflicts most interactions. One nurtures her community by lavishing affection.

11.3. *Frankness*. One nurtures her community by telling it when it is wrong. Communities require frank assessments. The human capacity for denial, projection, studied refusal, self-righteousness, and narrowness afflicts communities as much as members. Some voices pierce those veils. A community must seek and welcome contrarian strains. They balance commonplace distortions, and divert communities from error.

11.4. *Identity*. To nurture your community, let members change you. Communities have identities. Some facets of communal identity are patent; other pieces virtually noumenal. Visibly, a community has habitual locations, the haunts at which its members relate. Communities exhibit aesthetic preferences and collective habits, which amount to sub-cultures. Communities

---

rum Communio, 84, 102. Max Stirner spits this idea out. The state is a spook, not a person. He finds that states, which are not persons, steal the mantle of personhood, as do also gods and tribes. Each then whittles the real persons under its auspices to better accommodate its needs. Individuals suffer. Will dwindles. States prosper, to the detriment of real persons. Stirner, *The Ego and Its Own*, 199, 207.

[1330] Buber, *Paths in Utopia*, 132-133. Buber is concerned that centralization of impersonal power will erode all human community, leaving global governance in the hands of people lusting for power, and community members everywhere conceiving themselves as cogs, not persons.

[1331] Dunbar, *How Many Friends Does One Person Need?*, 22-24. See also Dunbar, *Grooming, Gossip and the Evolution of Language*, 78. Primate grooming has given way, in the human, to servicing important coalitional relationships by language.

exude a "feel," a less-than-descript subjectivity as distinct as human individuality. All identity emerges from perceptions of commonality and diversity. Communities, where they are healthy, recognize themselves as fragments of the larger human whole. They also cherish those features that set
them apart from every other community. One nurtures a community by
embracing that community's ebb and flow of similarity leavened by variation. One does not know a community until he can differentiate it from others.

11.5. *Member Perseverance.* One nurtures a community by staying put. Quad
sociality restrains inter-community mobility. Considerations other than
member desire impinge upon such choices. What the home community
needs and prefers counts. What a receiving community will tolerate also
matters. The net effect of these factors affecting exodus delimits mobility.
The point of reducing residential changes is to induce commitment to communities. Where immature, members may dodge problems by migrating
from them. Some might seek to conceal evils by hiding behind frequent
dislocations. Both injure the member by inhibiting the normal process of
social intervention. But crucially, departures impair community stability.
A departing member, where such leaving is non-consensual, injures his
community's stability and self-assurance. To nurture a community, commit
to persevere.

11.6. *Simplification.* One nurtures her community by keeping life simple.
Quad sociality does away with nation-States and anonymity. Quad sociality
transforms economic relations, eschewing global money-mongering in favor of community-by-community enterprise. Authority, conceived as coercion of strangers by strangers, abates, and, one hopes, vanishes. Life re-
volves not around laws and mass economies, but around the choices of
one's community, the voice of one's cadre in that community, and the life
one's friends and common acquaintances fashion together. Life is simpler
in Quad communities than mass society permits.[1332] Individual liberties,
which protect us from the interferences of anonymous governmental
strangers, resolve into wide-spread reticence among members of a community to senselessly deflect another member's (or another community's) decision-making. An ascetic undertow in Quad sociality drags communal exist-

---

[1332] Anarchist thinkers generally advocate retreat from their own society to a simpler existence. As
anonymous authorities stutter, control of one's life settles back upon primordial social structures:
friendship, acquaintance, community, and loose association with other tribes. For more, see Woodcock, *Anarchism*, 26-28. Murray Bookchin, expressing the optimism of 1960s and 1970s America,
argues that technologies are ending scarcity. Post-scarcity life opens the door to smaller, simpler,
decentralized communities with deeper social commitments to social equity. Bookchin's work is
marred by his affection for Marxist economics, though he gives classical Marxism a negative review.
Bookchin, *Post-Scarcity Anarchism*, 14, 173ff.

ence toward simplicity. Not the voice of god, but rather the voice of self-restraint calls one to live lightly, to make intellectual and physical room, to accommodate. Structural simplicity carves space for deliberative rigor. Toil wanes, in favor of what Aristotle called philosophic leisure.[1333] One works to gain time to mull life carefully. With time and encouragement to think about one's life, days come to be filled with acts expressive of one's uniqueness and gifts and service. Toys and distractions and diversions wane, no longer needed to decompress from stressful labor on behalf of anonymous corporate behemoths and misdirected government wars and programs. So, simplicity proves not merely a wise expedient, but also a spiritual imperative. Simplicity nurtures. The pre-eminent communal task is to nurture oneself, one's community, and humanity itself. None can fulfill this task when harried in a barely-comprehended social morass. To nurture your community, keep things simple.

11.7. *Contracts Among Communities.*[1334] One nurtures communities by forging beneficial agreements between communities. Federative collaboration among communities replaces both the State and the economy.[1335] The thousand interactions presently managed by bloated corporations, over-reaching governments, and moribund bureaucracies must be rejected or replaced. There are goods to deliver, food to transport, standards to determine and maintain, security to provide, and so forth.[1336] If a community desires avo-

---

[1333] [♪] Aristotle, *Politics*, 195 (Book VIII, Section 1), and [♪] Aristotle, *Nichomachean Ethics*, 615 (Book X, sub vii, sections 6-7).

[1334] There exists lively libertarian literature of contract-market approaches to providing the public good of security and contract enforcement. For positive assessment of this possibility, see David Friedman, *The Machinery of Freedom* (Friedman argues for anarcho-capitalism, which holds that society can and should be organized by private property, individual rights, and voluntary cooperation in the absence of government) and Rothbard, *For a New Liberty* (Rothbard endorses Stateless society, arguing that State coercion is immoral, works poorly, and should be ultimately abandoned). For doubt that the market or contract alone or in conjunction might provide adequate security and contract enforcement, see [♪] Taylor, *Community, Anarchy, and Liberty*, 59-65 (Taylor argues that private provision of public goods cannot prevent free riders without some arbiter greater than the individual, which arbiter he believes must be the Stateless human community), and [♪] Nozick, *Anarchy, State, and Utopia*, Chapters 2-3 (Nozick argues that contractual schemes for security and protection of property fail, but nothing more than a minimal State is legitimate).

[1335] Rudolf Rocker calls such federalism an "organic collaboration of all social forces towards a common goal on the basis of covenants freely arrive at." Rocker, *Nationalism and Culture*, 535.

[1336] Akihiko Matsutani writes of economies in shrinking populations, based on the Japanese experience, where population numbers are falling and the citizenry aging. Matsutani argues that Japan will find different approaches and be able maintain its standard of living, by focusing on increase in value-added to products, rather than expansion of markets. Since an older population will be unlikely to sacrifice health care for guns and wars, the remainder of our century may find "geriatric peace" in what Matsutani calls an "abundant society" which is also shrinking in size and planning intensely for further shrinkage. Matsutani anticipates fundamental re-engineering of Japan's socioeconomic systems to accommodate reduced population and economic scale. See Matsutani, *Shrinking-Population Economics: Lessons from Japan*, ix, xi, 155-181, 191.

cados, it will need to grow some or find a community with excess, or establish a market for avocados in which it may participate. Some community may become the grocer for nearby others, sorting the avocado problem for many. Communities will provide what others need. Specialization increases productivity. Trade enlightens and pacifies. The welter of contracts required in kithdom creates opportunity for lively local industry, and thwarts the pressure toward global standardization that diminishes capitalist societies. Local products, reflecting the creativity resident in the producing community, leaven life. They are quirkier, tastier, more nutritious, more useful than one-size-fits-all. One could speculate at length on the structure of inter-community contracts in Quad kithdom. But that would serve little purpose. The first act of a new community might be to schedule a barbeque with a better established community. Contracts erupt from that extended hand. Humans are good at contracting. Even under the hegemony of crippling State usurpations, large swaths of human endeavor are governed by contracts and private agreement, not governments.

All contracts have core elements. Good contracts benefit participants. Good contracts end when benefit ceases, to be replaced by more desirable arrangements. Good faith prevails. Contractees exercise restraint regarding their contract partners, seeing self-interest closely wedded to social harmony. The best contracts are carefully and specifically drawn. They anticipate the contract's end, and provide for an orderly transition at that terminal juncture. The best contracts expel ambiguities, address potential conflicts before they can emerge, provide for a conflict resolution process that countenances the values of the contracting communities.

Ultimately, the Commons itself amounts to a contract among all of humanity. The bare elements of the Commons contract include promises to perform all those collective acts that no reasonable person would reject.[1337]

Every community must answer the question, What might we become together? From a contract perspective, one answers, Anything you can imagine, provided you can create a collaborative alliance with other communities to make that a reality. Communities contracted to one another for longer term projects will become clusters, living in relational, or even physical, proximity. Contracting for goods and services from the global community of communities promises to grant every community access to what it needs,

---

[1337] This "contractualism" mirrors that of Thomas Scanlon. Scanlon argues that such a contractualist theory underlies much of morality, including that of individuals, although morality is "motivationally diverse," and so no one account is likely to encompass all of ethics. Scanlon puts his core concept in this manner: "to treat others only in ways that could be justified to them." Scanlon, *What We Owe to Each Other*, 153, 187, 360.

and give every community the opportunity to make of itself what it will. That is freedom indeed.

11.8. *Self-Expression.* One nurtures her community by projecting oneself into the community's function. When communities eat, bring your best dish and a guitar. When your community works, start five minutes early. Be the last to leave. Never free ride. That another might do your work does not mean you should let them. Participate. Contribute. Pressures toward indolence leap from a culture of overwork, misdirected efforts, and senseless economic oppression. Find a role in your community where you can contribute happily. Make what happens in your community a little bit like you. Mixed with many others doing the same, a remarkable potpourri wafts. Fragrances intermingle over years into that special aroma all savor, the smell of home.

11.9. *Contradicting Communities: Dissent.* One nurtures his community by making its errors patent. Avoid self-doubt. Speak up. Communities, even when virtually unanimous, nevertheless err. Decisions abjectly delusional may well appear to a majority sanity itself. Say so. When you are criticized for your negativity, listen. You might be senselessly pessimistic. Consider that. But if not, dissent. Shut things down, since they need your acquiescence to proceed. Make the group think it through, one step at a time. If, in the end, you see some glimmer that you might be wrong, relent and acquiesce. Watch, and report to all, emerging evidence that your dissent should have prevailed. Watch and report also when emerging evidence convinces you your dissent was mistaken.

A community might decide to ignore your dissent as though its decision were unimpeded. Doing so, the majority violates its own commitment to consensus. The habit of steamrolling dissent is deeply engrained in most cultures of our day. Should this happen to you, find supporters and protest. Stand in some street. Bother someone. Carry a sign and sing badly. There are only 1,200 people in your community. Talk to each politely. Let all know your dissent is serious. You are protecting your community from itself. Be bold.

11.10. *Inviting Influences from the Commons.* One nurtures her community by plumbing the Commons, culling experiments of other communities for those that might enrich your own. In a mature humanity, there would be more than 500,000 communities on the planet. Someone else somewhere is addressing the problems your community faces. Search for them. Find them. Communicate. Exchange ideas. Send someone there. Welcome someone from there. This is the point of Quad sociality. We are getting on the same page with everyone else, the same human page. Every community needs someone who explores the unknown human continent. Venture there. Be that person.

11.11. *Community Policies.* The following policies may (or may not) prove fruitful to communities, but should be considered. Such are the sorts of proposals one might encounter interacting with the Commons.

11.11.1. *Martial Designees.*[1338] It seems likely that every community, given the downside possibilities of sociopathy and failed infant attachment (with consequent solipsism and narcissism), needs a person charged with preventing intentional injury. Such a person is a "martial," marking that this person's duties may lie at the perimeter of war. A martial should be chosen for his or her peacemaking ability, a gift for calming friends, and physical ability to forcibly restrain wanton actors. The human community should agree that weapons designed to kill humans must be relinquished to control of martials, and retained only to the extent a lone martial might need them. None but the martial should learn the skills needed to use these weapons. A martial should take up human-killing weapons only when a human might have to be killed.

At some point, communities may confront a wanton community, one which intentionally injures other communities or its own members. One presumes that nearby communities would undertake all possible irenic steps to deter the wanton community. But what if all peaceful endeavors fail? Under what conditions might communities pool their martial members to coerce wanton communities, effectively creating small militias? An exponential conjunction rule might serve well, as follows: 1) any two communities may combine their martials temporarily, without further consents, to effect necessary coercions within their communities or between their communities; 2) any three communities may combine their three martials upon the consent of eight communities; 3) any four communities may combine their four martials upon the consent of sixteen communities; and so forth. The purpose of this exponential rule is to suppress martial joint action, and to rapidly involve the entire human community in oversight of any war-like activity. Combining thirty martials would require consensus among the entire human population.

11.11.2. *Alienating Excess.* So diverse are human capacities that even rough economic equality appears an impossible goal. Some members work ceaselessly or efficiently, producing more than their measure. Others work little, but creatively, providing that serendipity without which the

---

[1338] I intentionally deviate from the homophone "marshal." The coercer's role is martial, when all levels of conflict resolution have failed. When communities engage evil and require correction, communities collaborate to employ their martial designees individually, or aggregate them to form *ad hoc* militias. All such aggregations should be subjected to Commons deliberation and authorized by exponential consensus.

community cannot flourish. Others underproduce their minimum quantum, and need support. Yet others labor, but do so with bare proficiency. Confiscating the excess of productive members quashes innovation and ambition. Rewarding underproductive members encourages slacking and stokes the fantasies of the free rider. Flourishing life consists in fruitful alternation between deliberation and action; doing nothing satisfies only those burned out by our dysfunctional cultures.

Yet, some of the worst features of current culture project the ambition of ancestors into the bad habits of their successors. Possessing excess without learning the disciplines needed to acquire that excess leads many to habits that injure the possessors and their communities. Western culture has adopted a policy that saddles creditors with the debts of insolvent deceased persons (through the probate creditor claim process), while passing excess assets of members to their genetic progeny or persons of choice. Of necessity, a society that socializes losses but privatizes gains perpetuates class distinctions and fiefdoms. Every community should consider the fundamental unfairness of existing inheritance rules.[1339]

Various social mores produce economic leveling. Family life exists in rough communism, with productive members supplementing less-productive ones. Folkways that require sharing of excess shame some into approximate economic equality. Consider the rush of billionaires to promise to alienate their fortunes for the benefit of mankind. The bottom line is this: kithdoms cannot exist if members have dramatic, transgenerational economic inequality. Economic classes kill kithdom. Rivalries sunder communal bonds.

Avoiding the inherent propensity toward economic inequality might entail four moderate adjustments. Each levels economic disparity over the long haul without quashing initiative and the social benefit of extravagant ambition or watering the weed of self-serving wheedling. First, let a decedent's excess pass to her community, as do a decedent's unpaid obligations.[1340] Let every cadre's children make their own excess, if such they

---

[1339] John Rawls puts matters bluntly. To maintain relative equality among citizens and a generally fair system of government, existing inheritance laws must be changed to benefit the least successful members of society, rather than those selected by the privileged citizens. [♪] Rawls, *Justice as Fairness: A Restatement*, 52-53 (§15). Robert Nozick disagrees. Any such patterned adjustment of economic reality will be defeated by human choices. Once, by any means, we make all equal, those egalitarian folks begin choosing to do this or buy that. Some labor; others luxuriate. Shortly, the egalitarian norm fades in a welter of economic differentiation. [♪] Nozick, *Anarchy, State, and Utopia*, 155-164.

[1340] Robert Nozick offers potent arguments against compulsory contribution to the needs of others (and hence, by implication, against the redistributionist statutes and schemes that permeate American culture). See especially [♪] Nozick, *Anarchy, State, and Utopia*, Chapter 8, pages 232-275. One must, however, question whether holding property grants to one a voice post-death by which to ef-

desire. Second, adopt a social more that the needs of one's neighboring communities are penultimate only to one's own community's needs, and regular transfers of financial excess between communities are expected normal events. Third, communities should not praise those who hoard excess (the wealthy). Some wealth derives from accidental events (e.g., being born with unusual abilities or at a propitious moment or being lucky), and so reflects no merit upon the wealth holder. Other wealth derives from iniquitous behaviors (e.g., crime, unwarranted profit-taking, shady deals, environmental exploitation), and should subject the wealth holder to public censure. Every form of wealth derives from ancestral human labor and ingenuity; our mines, fields, roads, ideas, inventions all stand on structures purchased in blood and sweat by generations now long dead. Our wealth is theirs, devolved to us by virtue of death. Communities should not praise acquisitive behaviors that lead to economic inequality, since that inequality erodes the foundations of the community itself. We could disparage wealth hoarders as persons who retain that to which they have no just claim, despite the injury of their friends and fellow humans. The wealthy suffer psychological dysfunction; we may love them without praising their shortcomings.

Wealth accumulation expresses scarcity neurosis. Having lacked, we hoard excess for future droughts and debacles. In many, accumulation becomes an end in itself, and an obsession. Do not blame the financial hoarder. His exaggerated fears we permitted. By failing to insure that none starve, we insure that many will hoard. By imagining men at odds with one another, we warrant exploitation. By regaling the rich and touting luxury, we insulate the affluent few from the probable corrupt origin of their prosperity. Excess derives from one of two sources: extravagant labor or exploitation of desperate persons. To him who works ceaselessly, one says stop, enjoy your children, walk at sunset with your spouse, and savor that which gives you joy. To him who exploits the neediness of others, one says stop, give employees the fruit of their labors, and retain no more for yourself. Communities, as they move forward in their jour-

---

fectively transmit anything to anyone. Death draws a line. One exists (with property); then one ceases (without property). After passing, no one says or owns anything. Yes, during life one had opinions and intentions. Preference ceases at life's terminus. The legal concept of "testamentary intent" invites scrutiny. Yes, during life one may desire to give to another. But, if that property persists at death untransferred, then the desire to alienate the property was not unambiguous. The gift is unfulfilled by virtue of non-transmission. The testamentary gift contains elements that, during life, one would call an intent not to donate. How can a deceased person both retain and simultaneously alienate property? I argue, to the contrary, that testamentary rights are merely a policy choice. I advocate a different policy, one that preserves the relative egalitarianism necessary to meaningful community. I would not, as might Rawls, use post-death assets to benefit the poor alone. I would vest those post-death assets in the location from which they derived in the first place: a human community in its welter of productive activity. I would leave it to experimenting communities to determine how best to benefit their members.

neys, need not seize from the wealthy their boon. When all are nurtured, exploiters will have none to exploit. When exploiters are nurtured, all lose their need to amass. One addresses wealth inequities, not by coercive redistribution, but by nurturing members and their affection for one another.[1341] Create a culture in which people work in a balanced fashion and exploit none. Then money issues will sort themselves.

Last, communities care for members. We feed, love, bond to, support, caress, and endure those who, due to youth or age or incapacity, contribute less than their keep. Such persons shall always exist. Communities shall ever tend to and integrate needy persons. Communal excess exists to provide for these persons. They are our neighbors, our sick, our children, our elderly, our unlucky. Our possessions are theirs, though these needy members did not produce those possessions. Their claim is human. Wealth belongs, ultimately, to communities, not to individuals of prodigious ambition or fickle luck or shallow morality.[1342]

These four changes amount to mutation in the concept of property. *Cull* does not further rework the idea of property because one does not wish to invade the preserve of communities. Some may choose capitalism, in a modified sense. Others may choose to divide all equally among members, or to each according to need. Others may even elect to maintain the currently prevailing attenuated-socialism, with some ameliorations. Each will be an experiment, subject to change. Every community must recognize that its economic choices are mutable. Property is not ideal and unchanging. Property is what we conceive it to be. Economies are laboratories of invention, engines of needful productions. Make your community's economy flourish.

[1341] In this sentiment, kithdom departs the great debates of the late twentieth century. John Rawls would have us distribute property (coercively) in such a manner that any differences in wealth are permitted only to the extent they benefit the least-well-off of the culture. [♪] Rawls, *Justice as Fairness*. Robert Nozick would have all retain what they are entitled to according to property received or earned justly, regardless the outcome for a culture. [♪] Nozick, *Anarchy, State, and Utopia*. Kithdom would have neither. Let resources flow between friends as needs are perceived and hearts soften. Reserve shame for neurotic money hoarders. And do not let the affections and narcissism of dead people's Wills govern the present. Return hoarded money to the human community at large upon every death.

[1342] So Peter Kropotikin argues. All have a right to well-being. Wealth cumulates from the labor and ingenuity of long-dead generations, not from the lucky or rapacious few who lounge while others sweat. Kropotkin believed all belongs to all. [♪] Kropotkin, *Conquest of Bread*, 18-20. I take this to be a philosophical caution, not a serious economy. All cannot belong to all, since I permit no one else to use my toothbrush. And all cannot effectively utilize all. Still, Kropotkin's point is well-taken. Our property is a trust from previous generations, destined to belong to a series of others who succeed us. We are caretakers and trustees, not owners. Our obligations exceed caring for ourselves and our beloved ones. An economy is a communal lake; it floats all boats.

11.11.3. *Permitting Excess.* While hoarded excess may prove in general a bane of human community, it is nevertheless sometimes a fruit of meaningful self-expression. The human community exists for more purposes than merely to feed, house, and clothe. Meaningful community brims with extravagant expressions of the uniqueness of the members that comprise it. One paints, another has boundless energy for projects of every sort, others read or write or imagine buildings or build tools. Some even build ideas. Such exorbitant gifts may result in aggregating resources in one member or another. One reason to adopt kithdom lies in unleashing the gifts of many that under the present system lie dormant or crushed. Kithdom may well accelerate the propensity to aggregations of excess resources of various sorts. Hoarding expresses fear; still, some excesses may express a core value of human community: meaningful leisure for expressing the creative potential of members.[1343]

11.11.4. *Pruning Sports.*[1344] Humanity has, by technological means, rendered the human environment largely benign. Predators, disease, starvation, human violence, and accident once pruned the human tree. The social environment now determines human fitness. In departing the tangled trajectory of natural fitness eugenics, we take to ourselves responsibility to cull genetic traits that prove detrimental, and to make of the human animal what we will. The ethical conundra of these decisions daunt. They must, however, be deliberated by the human community. We have, by our cultural impetus over the last 200,000 years, left no other effective caretaker of our genetic well-being than ourselves. That task is ours.

11.11.5. *The Generational Reserve.* The existing generation removes some non-renewable resources from its environment. To the extent these cannot be recycled, present generations owe a debt of support to the transgenerational future. Surely, some of this obligation is paid by transmission forward in time of technologies and enduring capital investments, and in preserving the capital, educational, artistic, intellectual, and technical skills of this and previous generations. Some facets of what we consume may not be fungible. Once consumed, it vanishes (for example, oil reserves). Communities may wish to divert some of their resources to ad-

---

[1343] Kropotkin agrees. After meeting basic human needs, society exists to enhance constructive leisure. [♪] Kropotkin, *The Conquest of Bread*, 95 (Chapter IX).

[1344] A "sport" is a genetic mutation leading to a trait different from those of the parent organisms and exceeding the usual gene variation. See *Webster's Third New International Dictionary* s.v. "sport," at definition 2, section 6, page 2206.

dress the encumbrance present consumption presents to future generations.[1345]

11.11.6. *Weighing Dualities.* In constructing communities, some values
come in pairs. Weighting one value in a pair diminishes emphasis on its
paired value. Consider the following:

11.11.6.1. *Communal versus Private Ownership.* Every society provides
for collective ownership of some assets (consider roads, airports, some
land, oceans, air, outer space, the moon, and so forth) and private ownership of other assets (toothbrushes, underwear, some art and sacral objects, burial sites, and so forth). Communalist schemes, such as Quad
sociality, lean toward collective ownership. Libertarian minimal government schemes lean toward private ownership. Both schemes are
necessary in any society. People differ. Their needs and desires differ.
People differ over time, and at different ages. No person or community
is well-positioned to gainsay the desires of others. So, every community
will need to provide a flexible continuum of community and private
ownership.[1346] Private property promotes independence and classes.
Collective property promotes interdependence and equality. No community can long exist without a preponderant component of collective
ownership. No community can long exist without a significant component of private ownership.

[1345] John Rawls proposed "just savings" as an intergenerational tax rendering the well-being of future
generations more likely. Rawls proposes that the appropriate measure of the contribution should be
the sum the current generation wishes previous generations had contributed from the beginning of
human society, and the sum that addresses the likely preferences of those generations yet to be born.
Cull's "generational reserve" concept leans heavily on Rawls's suggestion. [♪] Rawls, *Justice as
Fairness: A Restatement*, 159-160 (§49). I do not, however, adopt Rawls's general program of justice as fairness, since it represents a devoted effort to work out a regime of intergenerational civility
among strangers. To that extent, Rawls's program is misguided. We should, rather, invest our efforts in no longer being strangers to one another.

[1346] I borrow and adapt some of these thoughts from Melvin Spiro's analysis of Kiryat Yedidim, the
pseudonym for a real Jewish kibbutz as it existed in 1951. Kiryat Yedidim was a Marxist farm-
village of some 250 secular Polish-born Jewish immigrants. They honored (worshipped) Soviet
politics, refused to hire any labor (as demeaning of the laborer's inherent independence), eroded
family and marriage in a potent manner, and eked their difficult existence from approximately 2,500
hot agricultural acres near hostile populations. All members aimed to create the New Man of Marxist
imagination by obliterating economic class struggles and private property. Children were commu-
nally raised and educated. Showers and toilets were common facilities. The members believed
themselves to be an embattled, and sometimes ill-appreciated, minority among Israeli Jews. Spiro,
Kibbutz, 10-59. For Spiro's anthropological assessment of the communal experiment of Kiryat
Yedidim, see Spiro, *Kibbutz*, 201-239. I am indebted to my friend Thomas Andrews of the University of Washington School of Law for suggesting that I include some analysis of existing community
life. My reservation in this regard lies in my desire not to pre-empt the experiments that communities are willing to attempt by analysis they have not themselves conducted. I relent because not every person needs to learn by hard experience the turns in a path previously trodden by other intelligent
folk. Still, pain experienced teaches better than pain reported.

11.11.6.2. *Indifference versus Involvement.* Communal social experiments tend to commence with high expectations that communal experience tends to etch over time. Highly-motivated members, especially those to whom ideological commitments matter deeply, tend to become disappointed in members whose attentions trend to other, less-idea-driven, matters (such as working, child-rearing, being in love, arts, literature, story-telling, to name a few). The ideologues view these members as distracted or indifferent. Members not ideologically-driven tend to resent their focused companions, finding them fanatical. Every community needs idea-driven people. Every community needs people to whom ideas seem annoying intrusions upon real caring. One does well to make a place for and value each. In the author's experience, participation rates related to organizational meetings hover, in healthy groups, around fifty percent. When all fail to participate whole-heartedly, then some delegation proves necessary. Those to whom delegation falls acquire proxy powers. Those powers give birth to classes within a group. Classes poison communities. So, communities are forever rebalancing inattention and fanaticism to remain viable.

11.11.6.3. *Old versus Young.* Young persons are often more willing to contemplate dramatic change than are older persons. The young spurt energy and enthusiasm, and have yet to suffer life's moderating lessons. Older members tend to value stability, careers, and material comfort. Older members work less intensely, but more routinely. Young members become old members, changing as decades pass. In doing so, they suffer significant psychological dissonance, gainsaying the changes that occur in their psychologies. Every community needs vital, youthful change, without revolution. Every community needs patient, plodding perspective, without petrifaction. Communities balance age and youth, seeking to stay adaptive without coming unhinged. Every revolutionary, after her storm of change has swept across the social landscape, finds that with which she replaced the old turns out to be quite similar to the old. Revolution is unsustainable. Failure to adapt is fatal. Communities calibrate each, seeking adaptive homeostasis.

11.11.6.4. *Female versus Male.* Though it is feminist heresy to so state, men are not women, and women are not men. So long as women bear children, as some must for the species to persevere, there will be some pressure toward a sexual division of labor in every community. Nursing women need proximity to their babies. Men cannot nurse except by bottle, and always bear the risk, when so doing, of attachment injuries to their infant. Babies need persistent attention, and so some adult will remain in the baby's location to provide that care. Some doubt (this author included) that any but a child's mother can provide such care optimally, at least during the child's first years. Alloparents relieve the mother, but she remains the core. These underlying pressures generate some sexual labor differentiation. Most men are stronger and larger than most women. Where strength matters, many men will be able to do such hard labor more effectively than many women (though the women may work harder). So, the pressures that create a sexually differentiated economic structure appear inherent. Communities must balance male and female needs in their life formulations. For all the work that needs doing must get done, and all the babies anyone creates must be thoroughly and optimally nurtured. I share the feminist objection that work that does not require special strength ought not to be sexually distributed. I also share the conviction that fathers need to parent intently and share household burdens. Every community that has a future finds a workable accommodation of male and female distinctiveness in its formulation of life structures.

11.11.6.5. *Aspiration versus Disillusion.* Every community commences to achieve some purpose, hopefully some good purpose. Every community fails to achieve all it set out to accomplish, except where the community began with underwhelming goals. Of necessity, along each community's path, some member notices and expresses disappointment in her community's outcomes. Disillusion may ensue. Every community lives in a vital tension between its aspirations and disillusionment. The aspirational member lures others along the community's path, inspiring hope and euphoria. He points to progress. The disillusioned member notes the group's shortcomings, inspiring disenchantment and dysphoria. She points to defeats or hypocrisies. Always aspiration and disillusion clash. The threat is that one sort of member might induce his community to banish the other. Both are needed. Aspiration drives us toward purposes we have deemed critical. Disillusion shatters our shackled perceptions, granting fresh eyes. Viable communities make room for both the inspiring and the dispiriting voices of its members. Seldom is one or the other simply "right." Viable communities embrace dreams, but stay grounded in facts.

11.12. *Addressing Community Evil.*[1347] One cannot flee some evils. Some normal and savant community actions enact evil and must, after all noncoercive approaches have been exhausted, be constrained.[1348] Community

---

[1347] Of polygamous communities, Mill said: "I am not aware that any community has a right to force another to be civilized." [♪] Mill, *On Liberty,* 89.

[1348] Gandhi disagrees. Gandhi urged no preparation for depredations from outsiders. If unwanted invasions and abuses occur, Gandhi offers two responses: 1) acquiesce in the invasion, but refuse all cooperation with the invader, or 2) offer non-violent resisters as cannon fodder for the invader, in the

errors merit constraint where an activity precludes formation or nurture of meaningful relationships among members or between communities. Some of the actions that preclude meaningful community are forms of overpopulation, violence, mal- or mis- or non-education of members, intolerance of deviance, social disintegration evidenced in solipsism, loneliness, and aimlessness, failure to recognize harm done to other communities, tolerating member-on-member violence, use of psychoactive substances in a manner that precludes meaningful community, and assertion of member or community self-sufficiency. Where members or communities sink into behavioral quicksands, surrounding members or communities should engage patient irenic intervention. Evil is never apodictic. Intervening members or communities must ask the question whether it is they or the deemed evil-doers (or perhaps both) who err.[1349]

11.12.1. *Prophylaxis.* Coercion is the bane of human communities. It is both over-utilized and insufficiently protective of meaningful community and future weal. Coercion of wanton communities grows violent where long neglect of the ugly impact of wanton deviance renders the need for remediation emergent. To avoid violent coercion of members or communities, communities must adopt a habit of early intervention, diverting negative impacts as they germinate, rather than acting only when destructive deviance blossoms into genuine crisis. Communal intervention must come early and be decisive. Such early interventions will be welcomed only if they arrive in a context of long-shared mutual influence in which the good faith of the other communities is much evidenced. It is the intimate tenor of relationships that makes kithdom possible.

11.12.2. *War.* None should war. All must coercively restrain intercommunity bloodshed.[1350] No war builds meaningful community.[1351]

---

knowledge that even the harshest among them has a heart that can be swayed by innocent suffering. The brave are those who sacrifice themselves non-violently, not those who kill others. [♪] Gandhi *Satyagraha*, 286. F. A. Hayek says grimly. "Coercion, however, cannot be altogether avoided because the only way to prevent it is by the threat of coercion." Hayek, *The Constitution of Liberty*, 57, 59, 71. Sadly, I concur with Hayek.

[1349] Joshua Greene warns that, as between communities of divergent values, "we can't get by with common sense, because our common sense is not as common as we think. Greene, *Moral Tribes*, 295.

[1350] Victory in war is cause for mourning. [♪] Lao Tzu, *Tao Te Ching*, 75 (31). Mencius argues there are no just wars; some are, however, less bad than others. *Mencius*, 157 (Book VII, Part B, Section 2).

[1351] Nicholas Wade might disagree. Wade argues that religious needs and thoughts are innate human features. Religion, especially when conjoined with dancing, music, and song, meld groups into communities. Religion, in Wade's treatment, "evolved as a response to warfare. It enabled groups to commit themselves to a common goal with such intensity that men would unhesitatingly sacrifice their lives in the group's defense." Wade goes on to speculate that perhaps there may exist religion that is not wedded to war. A reformulation, such as that experienced when mankind abandoned

Thus, morally deliberated, every war lacks warrant.[1352]   When the Commons finds itself acquiescing in communities conjoining their martials to restrain the depredations of an errant community, the global Commons must take a step back to ponder the roots of the circumstance.   Such should never arise.   Where the necessity emerges, something is terribly, tragically wrong.   Make repairs.

The daily life of communities is suspended in war.[1353]   Normal processes lurch aside to admit savage considerations.   Once tolerated, the foul breath of that threatened self lingers, long after the crisis evaporates.   We, and our communities, stutter and stumble, rehearsing images of systematic coercion in our minds, like nightmares revisited.

Wars etch the very amiability of man.   Every man, once savaged, builds greater distance between himself and every other man.   Each takes fundamental defensive steps.   Where insecurity endures, men ally themselves, forming larger collectives, for numbers offer some defense. Communities cease fissioning when they ought, for fear that consequent poverty of numbers and resources may make of them prey.   Some communities fuse, creating bloated, but relatively secure, armed camps; every member surrenders her uniqueness to comprehensive compliance.   Neighbors indulge similar steps in anticipatory defensive postures.   Soon, all members live in collectives too populous for interpersonal behavioral controls to function effectively. Community sputters. Anonymity reigns. Hierarchy blossoms.   And the human world slides toward permanent inter-State insecurity, with which structure we have now lived for more than fifteen thousand years.[1354]

---

hunter-gatherer animism, might retain the valuable aspects of religion while distancing itself from self-destructive cultism or nationalist war frenzies. Wade speculates that such a new religion could "touch all the senses and life the mind. It would transcend self." Wade, *The Faith Instinct*, 6, 78, 233-234, 285.

[1352] Stephen Carter argues, in considering the use of just war theory by President Barak Obama, that every war requires an undergirding philosophy of war, without which the military action amounts to nothing more than systematic homicide. Carter, *The Violence of Peace*, xiii. Donald Pfaff argues that war is a relatively recent phenomenon for humans. Warring is not a part of our evolutionary heritage. Pfaff, *Altruistic Brain Theory*, 242. A North Vietnamese soldier, whose pseudonym is Bao Ninh, wrote of his experience of the Vietnam conflict: "War was a world with no home, no roof, no comforts. A miserable journey, of endless drifting. War was a world without real men, without real women, without feeling." Ninh, *The Sorrow of War*, 31.

[1353] Burke says memorably: "Laws are commanded to hold their tongues amongst arms." Burke, *Reflections on the Revolution in France*, 31. Burke himself peers back to Cicero's "*silent enim leges inter arma.*" (Laws are silent in the presence of arms). Cicero in *Pro Milone*, 4.11.

[1354] Taylor so styles the emergence of the state from the acephalous egalitarian communities which are the human norm. [♪] Taylor, *Community, Anarchy, and Liberty*, 58, 129-139.

War is unnatural. Normal people resist killing other humans. Colonel Marshall's investigation of rifleman firing during battle in World War II revealed that only fifteen percent of these soldiers actually fired their weapons at the enemy in battle. If one counts four in one hundred sociopaths as the human norm, adds the likelihood that the infantry may attract more than the population-normal share of sociopaths, and folds in soldiers who fired to defend their comrades from specific threats, it may be the case that almost no soldiers fired their weapons to achieve the stated political purposes of World War II. Subsequent training changes left soldiers in Vietnam shooting to kill the enemy over eighty percent of the time.[1355] Humans can be brainwashed to kill, but ill tolerate the deflection. In World War II, the Army concluded that almost all soldiers break down after 200-240 days of combat. None acclimates to war. The stress savages all.[1356]

11.12.3. *Weapons of War*. Create no weapons of war. Destroy weapons of war when they are discovered. Wars are deteriorated states of relationship, not technological races. One can war with fists, rocks, sticks, and even eyebrows. Where war beckons, arm yourself for painful reconciliation.[1357] Meet that agony with courage. Run onto the field of reconciliation with abandon, as so many before you have run into volleys from gun and mortar. Any who have need should possess such guns, knives, axes, and other implements as are needful for harvesting and controlling the member's environment. No member, with the exception of each community's martial, should possess weapons designed to kill humans. The martial's kit should be defined as the communities of the Commons agree. Innovations in the martial's defensive kit should be viewed as acts of war. Global war ceased seventy years ago. So long as its weapons and sentiments are tolerated, none can say global war will return. Gwynne Dyer

---

[1355] So Gwynne Dyer reports. Dyer, *War: The Lethal Custom*, 54-61. Oddly, despite her acknowledgement that men can be trained or coerced into killing others only with great difficulty, Dyer concludes that war is endemic among humans, historical and prehistorical. She reaches this conclusion despite noting that no pertinent evidence exists. Dyer, *War: The Lethal Custom*, 68-81, critically 79. John Horgan reports that a post World War II study showed ninety-eight percent of soldiers suffered psychiatric symptoms after sixty days of fighting. Two percent did not, and seemed to enjoy it. Horgan concludes that those who enjoyed killing did not go crazy because they were already crazy, suffering aggressive psychopathic personality disorders. Horgan, *The End of War*, 66, 71.

[1356] Dyer, *War: The Lethal Custom*, 23-27.

[1357] Thomas Paine's booklet, *Common Sense*, argues against political reconciliation between Britain and the Americans. He finds in British king and peerage a sufficient cause for separation, and a perpetual fount of corruption and intrigue. Britain's lords and royals are the root cause of war itself. Paine, *Common Sense*, 264-273.

warns that Big War is napping, not gone.[1358] If we let it come, it will wear a nuclear bonnet.[1359] The narcissist, Douglas MacArthur, at the end of his career, testified before Congress. He said, "Sooner or later, if civilization is to survive, . . . war must go."[1360]

11.12.4. *Constraining Community Evil: Militant Irenism.* Communities, given the human capacity for error, may maim themselves. One community may suppress its women or beat its children. Another may neglect mentoring, leaving its members uninformed dolts. Others may be consumed by hatred, initiating physical confrontations with neighbors. Some may form alliances for ignoble purposes. The worst may manufacture weapons and seek hegemony. If nurture of the human population does not improve, the future might hold what the present suffers—nonstop evil from individuals, communities, and nations against one another. Quad irenism makes a demand of such evil-acting members and communities: Stop.

Members constrain communal evil by non-violent activism: early intervention, active listening, non-cooperation, protest, meta-protest, boycott, debate, and appeal to the better sentiments and moral sensitivities of one's community or a deviant community other than one's own. Meaningful response to such constraint should be intense negotiation and efforts to understand, and should be accompanied by exchanges of members to live within the opposed communities. The nonviolence of the communities of communities must be militant, that is, it must intervene to demand peace. If nonviolence is to prevail, its adherents must stand ready, paradoxically, to assert themselves with overwhelming irenic militance. Effective nonviolence fights for peace.[1361] Irenists keep their brothers, as

---

[1358] Dyer, *War: The Lethal Custom*, 1, 5. Dyer says, "War is a huge, multi-faceted, ancient human institution that is deeply entrenched in our societies, our history, and our psyches." Dyer, *War: The Lethal Custom*, 11.

[1359] Dyer memorably says of nuclear war that no one knows how such weapons would work in actual combat. The American assault on Japan used two relatively small weapons. "Strategists discussing nuclear war are like virgins discussing sex." Dyer, *War: The Lethal Custom*, 293.

[1360] Cited in Dyer, *War: The Lethal Custom*, 285.

[1361] See [♪] James, *The Moral Equivalent of War.* James praises martial courage and the comradeship of men in arms, and laments the milk-toast whining of pacifists. For James, if you want peace, you must convince soldiers. To convince soldiers, one must show plain courage and sacrificial exuberance, as do combatants on battlefields. In undertaking militant irenism, one does well to heed the advice of a martial non-pacifist: "If [your battles are] not in the interest of the state, do not act. If you cannot succeed, do not use troops. If you are not in danger, do not fight a war. . . . Therefore, the enlightened ruler is prudent and the good general is warned against rash action." Sun Tzu, *The Art of War*, 50-51.

Cain refused to keep Abel.[1362] Loving peace entails, when warranted, engaging militant irenic action to re-establish peace. The core difference between coercive-culture and irenic-culture lies in the alternatives to and limitations upon coercion.

11.12.4.1. *Comprehension.* One constrains community evil by attempting to understand its sources and proponents. Evil acts erode a community's meaning and affection; such self-mutilation has a source and rationale. Ask. Listen. Where affection is impaired, love takes the form of compassionate attention. Give the wanton community your ear. Bring their concerns to the Commons. Let mankind know their complaints. Grasp their view of matters. Befriend them, to the extent they will permit it. Every human is reticent to purposefully injure friends.

11.12.4.2. *Moral Persuasion.* One constrains community evil, after listening and comprehension, by persuading its adherents to abandon erosive behaviors. Persons possessed of great empathy and wisdom often bridge gulfs between opponents. They broaden the scope of discussions and help antagonists see self-interest in peace. Communities must send these mediating speakers to wanton communities to speak, to reason, to deter, and to convince at least one member to dissent. Then begins discussion within the errant community. That may lead to revised choices.

11.12.4.3. *Immigration.* Where a wanton community declines to listen and lacks voices of dissent, nearby communities should seek immigration to the community for new members willing to make of those others friends. Nearby communities should also invite members of the wanton community to join their own with the purpose of building important relationships that influence those members to see their home community's acts in a less-favorable light. One can wield friendship as a sword. Its edge is keener than steel and reaches farther than bullets.

11.12.4.4. *Protest.* If evil acts persevere, communities should join in protesting the evil community's acts. Block their byways. Bend their ears. Sit around their fires and kibitz. Injure no persons or property. Respect their values. But let none in the evil community believe their actions are approved beyond their hamlet. Nor let them believe they can persevere unimpeded in their acts.

11.12.4.5. *Observation.* Send observers to watch and report to the Commons and nearby communities events in the wanton community. Make observers conspicuous, but silent. Being watched causes humans to quietly question action. Let them know there is no hiding.

[1362] *Genesis* 4:8-10.

11.12.4.6. *Meta-Protest.* Ascertain why, to the extent possible, a community has elected evil. Then remedy the root causes of their choices. Where ignorance proliferates, offer free education. Where women are oppressed, offer cell phones and contraception and educative materials. Where scarcity ravages, help create abundance. Undercut the rationale of evil among community members.

11.12.4.7. *Strike, Boycott, Non-Participation.* If a wanton community perseveres, despite these efforts, neighboring communities should underline their opposition by ceasing to engage the offending community. Such may cause extreme economic hardship to the wanton community, and may injure friendships outside the community permanently. Shunning also exacerbates the sense of scarcity and emergency within the wanton community. So, isolation should commence only when the decision to discorporate the wanton community has been taken with the acquiescence of the Commons.

11.12.4.8. *Discorporation.* Where a community perseveres in wanton acts, after all irenic militance has failed to convince, a community should be discorporated. Nearby communities should convene their martials as a militia, and remove the wanton community members for integration into nearby or distant communities.[1363] Wanton members who have formented a community's evil should be managed by coercive means, until, if ever, they are able to participate constructively in a community.

11.12.4.9. *Reconstruction.* Wanton communities emerge for reasons. The Commons and all communities must dissect such events, that is, wanton community action and discorporations, to identify their origins. Those sources should be quelled and their impacts remediated. All communities participate in the errors of any, even if that shared responsibility is vanishingly small.

> **Objection 43: Irenic Coercion:** *Some demur that covies of communal pacifists flounder hapless before the sordid depredations of Khans, Maos, and Stalins. Within the human breast lies darkness that, left unchecked, extinguishes well-being. Some men (and a few women) are evil in an irredeemable sense. They murder for joy. They rape for sport. They indulge genocide. They succor no regret. One answers such cretins, if one can muster courage to meet them at*

[1363] In the run-up to World War II, Bart. de Ligt listed, at some length, a plan of action in his proposed campaign against war. De Ligt's plan includes: 1) refusal of military service and all work that supports military action, 2) refusal to produce services or goods that directly or indirectly service war, 3) refusal to pay taxes, 4) refusal to provide intellectual justifications for war or war-like mentalities, 5) forming and participating in meetings, studies, arts, parades, demonstrations, and propaganda opposing war, 6) general strikes, 7) sabotage and obstruct (with adequate warning to users) modes of transportation and communications, and 8) destroy munitions, where that can be done without loss of life. Bart. de Ligt, *Conquest of Violence*, 269-285.

all, with equivalent and countervailing force. This is the lesson of Normandy.
Murderous sociopaths cease their harvest not when educated, but when hanged.
This is the lesson of Dahmer and Bundy. Normal people must stand prepared
individually and collectively to wield overwhelming responsive coercion.

Response: One acknowledges the dangers of sociopaths. One further laments the tiny stowaway cowering in every human brain, whose might erupts, when winds of fear and threat and deprivation blow, with coercive furor. A little madman, ranting racial rage and venting violent vagaries, waits to foam at each mouth, absent practiced self-restraint. The free rein given sociopathic predators and genocidal kings is a symptom of impersonal culture. Sociopaths' psychic deformities were apparent from early ages. Where they rampaged, their twist was ignored, as no child's problems should be ignored. Having failed to recognize, soothe, heal, watch, supervise, and redirect them, we made them citizens and gave them anonymity by which to conceal their dark hobbies.[1364] Occasionally, we elect them Chancellor or President, for some sociopaths can be very charming indeed.

Often, when people argue that mankind is a vicious African ape, prone to war and predation, the root of their thought stems from the well-publicized wanton activities of unrestrained violent sociopaths. Humans are not all sociopaths; most recoil at killing and wanton injury of others. Most care and cooperate with abandon. Most value peace. War lies not in the human genome, but rather second among our sordid collective habits (after overpopulating). Change of habits is what the deliberating human does. War may pass, as has burning witches and excising the beating hearts of virgins to sate the bloodlust of deities. Ceasing war will not end human conflict. Ceasing war will, however, make human conflict less lethal.[1365]

One task of any meaningful community is to know its members in their excellences and deficiencies. Healthy, reasonably-proportioned communities can and will know each member. Such communities can and will tailor education to the needs of each. Such communities can and will reduce the number of sociopaths, can and will address their needs, and redirect or constrain those who nevertheless make their home with us.[1366] Crucially, we must never make of the so-

---

[1364] Perhaps the socially-connected life contemplated in kithdom offers a way to control and inhibit the sociopath. Sam Harris says: "The psychopath who lives his entire life in a tiny village must be at a terrible disadvantage. The stability of permanent defection as a strategy would require the defector to be able to find people to fleece who are not yet aware of his terrible reputation." Harris, *The Moral Landscape*, 100.

[1365] Horgan, *The End of War*, 189.

[1366] Bruce Hood tells the story of Jim, who learned that his family held seven murderers in its recent line. Brain scans showed that Jim had the exact lack of activity in the orbital cortex that characterizes sociopathic killers. Jim, who has never murdered, attributes his restraint to parental nurture. He was a special child to his parents, born after four consecutive miscarriages. He received vast attention and affection. Jim, as an adult, does not build strong emotional connections to others, and exhibits little care for others. He acknowledges that he dwells near the borderline of psychopathy. Yet he has not killed. Hood, *The Self Illusion*, 104-105.

ciopathic member a communal martial or task such a person to effect coercive actions.[1367]

I agree that, in some attenuated form, communities must retain the ability, seldom used, to respond in coercive restraint to the challenges of those who would harm wantonly. I concede this necessity reluctantly.

Objection 44: Utopian Blather: *Another protests that Quad sociality suggests yet one more stupid utopia that only fanatics appreciate and idiots undertake. Quad sociality calls one to libertarian messianism. Just do this and that, so the author babbles, and the kingdom of heaven breaks in upon us. Facts point elsewhere. People will never stop being violent with one another. Human collectives will always require standing armies and constables prickling with weapons to forestall the ever-inrushing tide of criminality. Violence lurks within all, a dark, ineradicable stain. Personal corruption defines the human norm. To argue otherwise is fool's yammer.*

Response: I offer no utopia. Utopias consist in thought-structures which some enthusiasts undertake to impose upon groups, usually small, of (mostly) willing participants. These pre-conceived schemes differ little from the institutional structures that presently petrify our social existence. I welcome utopias with no greater enthusiasm than do I stultifying adherence to "the way we have always done things." Each utopia offers a pattern for living not of our own imagination and construction.[1368] *Cull* offers a decisional process in a workable personalist social construct. A vast array of life structures would issue from finely-elaborated conduct culling, as one community after another chooses those experiments in living to which it is willing to commit. The Commons would report those results, for emulation or avoidance by other communities. It is not inherently utopian to reimagine our collective future. Such imagining remains, despite the cynicism of some, an essential human activity. To incrementally improve a wrong-headed culture portends only arriving at destinations no one pre-

---

[1367] Christopher Boehm reports, in his analysis of ethnographic literature, that "bullying recidivistic killers," who are the worst among socially assertive individuals ("upstarts"), are countered within egalitarian groups (subsistence hunter-gatherers and tribes) by assertiveness in censure, and, if necessary, removal. Often, tribes reach an unspoken death sentence, and induce a relative of the bully to assassinate him. Egalitarian communities remain egalitarian only so long as they can mount effective responses, mostly sub-lethal, but if necessary, lethal, to the impositions and terrors of dominating sociopaths. The sanctions Boehm found in the literature were criticism, ridicule, disobedience, ostracism, expulsion, deposition, desertion, and execution. Boehm calls this social control from below "reverse dominance hierarchy." Boehm, *Hierarchy in the Forest*, 64, 66, 81-81, 84.

[1368] Robert Nozick analyzes the conceptual structure of "utopia." He suggests that a utopia is a form of society in which none can imagine a better form of society. (This would seem to entail either very excellent institutions indeed, or an utter collapse of members' imaginative faculties.) In a footnote, Nozick suggests that perhaps the utopian urge represents a principle for evaluating existing institutions, rather than a sketch of *de novo* design of such institutions. [♪] Nozick, *Anarchy, State, and Utopia*, 298. Kithdom offers such an evaluative principle for institutions. Does the institution promote meaningful community? If not, reform or abandon it. Explore possibilities until one shapes a better structure for togetherness. Stay small, so that experiments pose little danger to the broader human community. Stay nimble, so a community's revisions are readily executed, or readily abandoned.

fers more efficiently. Sometimes, we need to pause and start afresh. *Cull* offers a moment for fundamental reappraisal.

The big problems with utopias are three. First, utopias are mappish. In constructing a map, a person focuses on a feature of the world, to the exclusion of others, imagines oneself flying, and records the result. Most ideas are maps of one sort or another. Maps extract relevant information from the living matrix, from which the information is inextricable. In the end, maps present cartoons of life. They amuse. They may prove useful. But maps hardly describe the interlocked intricacy of actual life. If they did, the map would lose utility as it grew as complicated as that which it portrayed. Utopian maps are thin things. Utopias, being maps, winnow all they do not wish to ponder or recognize.[1369] Second, utopias pander to elitist and indolent sentiments. Someone knows enough to restyle society, so the utopian story goes. Others surrender to that superlative vision, glad to be freed from the burdens of observation, deliberation, and choice. In the end, the visionary knows too little, falters, and his minions cannibalize him with the fangs of their never-deeply-submerged passive aggression. Third, there exists the danger that someone might be foolish enough to attempt to enact a handsome utopian map. We have seen this sad spectacle in the march of capitalism triumphal, of Maoist renovation of Sino-Asian society, in Bolsheviks assassinating Tzars, and in the killing fields of Cambodia. Utopias portend terrible danger.[1370] In enacting a mappish revision of society, utopians savage the deep, habit-laden guts of society. We live together by a mass of particularized knowledge, more practical than theoretical, in an interpersonal matrix of inconceivable complexity. The utopian revolutionary takes his bulldozer to this ancient soil, leveling its eccentricities, rendering it barren. He then plants his thin ideological crop, which inevitably withers.

I agree that Quad sociality seems impractical. When one harbors deep reservations about the course of human togetherness, one objects to the very forms of thought that shape what one believes to be "workable." I so object to authoritarian coercion. "Practical" means a scheme that most people perceive as likely to succeed. "Practical" schemes make of the past a preemptive template for future action. To such importation, I object. Our present differs from the past. Our future belongs to us and those who will benefit or suffer from our choices. One must not shackle futures to the failed schemes of now-dead generations. When things change, man adjusts. New conditions pertain. What appears "practical" changes. Quad sociality proposes tectonic shifts in human togetherness. Mankind will adapt as this wisdom seeps into human consciousness. What seems "practical" will mutate.[1371]

You need not consume this meal I have set whole. Investigate. I invite confirmation of theses (both mine and those of others) by analysis and experi-

---

[1369] I credit James C. Scott for these insights. Scott, *Seeing Like A State*, 342-357.

[1370] Burke warns that in revolutionaries "there is nothing of the tender parental solicitude which fears to cut up the infant for the sake of an experiment." Burke, *Reflections on the Revolution in France*, 169.

[1371] For similar thoughts, see [♪] Wilde, "The Soul of Man Under Socialism," 155.

mentation. I offer a process. I offer speculations on the structure of that process. I even imagine possible outcomes of experiments in that deliberative process, and suggest what I take to be a path likely laden with fruits ripe for the plucking. Do well-nurtured, non-coerced humans forsake violence in favor of cooperation? I assert so. Please confirm or disconfirm. Does refusal to coerce others lead all to a more peaceful and fruitful existence, and toward a state of global hyper-cooperation? Test that hypothesis. Conduct experiments. Certainly, all humans possess the capacity for violence. We are animals born of a protein-scarce savannah. We have been predator and prey. But is human violence a capacity that *must* be expressed, or a capability that *might* lie dormant, under appropriate nurturant circumstances? As does sexual activity in faithful celibates. As does breeding in the childless parent. As does fear of incendiary death in experienced firemen. Find out. Is the State an aberrant sociality, born from terror of scarcity and rapine and invasion? The data already exist. Examine them. Are humans in the grip of scarcity more or less likely to behave violently? Does violence wane where nurture and plenty rule? Does violence continue to dwindle where nurture is universal and scarcity extinct? One eliminates scarcity by reducing human population to an optimal size. Humans are, despite the cauldron of overpopulation, reducing violence globally. Steven Pinker argues that for millennia, violence has been declining, and has now become relatively uncommon conduct.[1372] We inhabit the last chapter in the 50,000 year period of human adolescence, during which our numbers have exploded to exceed the carrying capacity of the planet. What seems normal to us is in fact terribly, tragically abnormal. Deliberating humans should explore my theses. The answers will shape our future to the farsight horizon, for good or ill. Violence most certainly dominates recent millennia. Might the future trend otherwise?

We do not see that future at present, though we strain. We shall have to discover it by hard experimentation. Because we know not the shape of the future, we cannot prescribe, but only suggest. Ours cannot be fairly deemed a utopia.[1373] Quad sociality offers a social laboratory, imbued with hope.[1374] To

---

[1372] See [♪] Pinker, *Better Angels of our Nature*. I suspect that Pinker is wrong about the extent of violence in pre-historical communities. Humans avoid, rather than engage, violence, whenever possible. The archaeological record shows violent raiding, with consequent murder, only in the last fifteen thousand years (or so).

[1373] One, however, does acknowledge similarities between Plato's theoretical city and Quad sociality. Plato, by the mouth of Socrates, imagines a small semi-self-sufficient town of a few thousand souls, working their trades, depending upon one another, trading with nearby towns for what they lack. The citizens of this polis make only those children they care to nurture, avoid war, and participate in a manner that avoids poverty. They eat and drink moderately, live in health, and die old. Such, according to Plato, is what justice looks like when lived well. [♪] Plato, *Republic*, 54-55 (371e-372d). The remainder of Plato's *Republic* concerns how to govern a city in which people demand luxuries, independence, and ease, which city Plato thinks is diseased, in that it is essentially unjust. [♪] Plato, *Republic*, 55 (372e).

[1374] Robert Nozick imagines a market in utopias, with communities seeking members that enrich them, and members seeking societies that offer optimal return on investment. [♪] Nozick, *Anarchy, State, and Utopia*, 299-303. Nozick mistakes, as economists and political theorists often do, what matters to people, how they join with other humans for life together. We do not join primarily for perceived economic or ideological advantage. We join to live with friends. We tolerate substantial frustrations and discomfort for that privilege. The human fundament is neither economic nor con-

sweep away these questions, these possibilities, with a swoosh of those great dismissive brooms, utopia and practicality, is lazy or irresponsible. Such "pragmatic" sniffing remains a bastion for complacent cynicism.[1375]

12. *Nurturing the Commons.* The Commons is a conversation of global scope about the weal of humanity that every member follows and to which every cadre contributes. The Commons serves as a global fire pit around which the human tribe gathers to sort itself. A core task of Quad communities is to establish relations among communities that partake the same characteristics of good faith, cooperation, and irenism that govern the internal structure of communities.[1376] The quality of life in each community affects that of every other. Social interpenetration causes the good and ill to leak from each life into that of every other. Our mutuality is inescapable, for we are threads in a common human tapestry. What affects one eventually affects all.[1377] So, nurturing the Commons is no idle exercise or counsel of perfection. Nurturing the Commons lies close by the heart of a kithdom of meaning-laden communities. We keep our brothers and sisters.[1378] Collaborations with other communities create the diverse specialization on which prosperity depends. Ours is a shared humanity. The Commons gives that truth opportunity, a shape, and some procedure.

12.1. *Purposes of the Commons.* At a minimum, the Commons undertakes the following:

12.1.1. *Consensus Against Evil.* Evil communities depend upon their misguided prominences (leaders, theologues, maniacs) for guidance. These will act to injure their own and others, absent potent counter-pressures. The Commons brings that psychological pressure. The Commons gives voice to the sentiments of the vast majority of humans: no war, no slavery, no steamrolling dissenters, no abuse, no meddling intrusions upon intimacies, no economic manias or debacles. The Commons consents to the

---

ceptual, but rather interpersonal. Humans are friend-mongers. Money-mongering and the lure of ideological belonging pale beside this mutualist urge.

[1375] Akash Kapur notes that contemporary reformists so style those who deem intentional communitarians naïve or extreme. Kapur, *Couldn't Be Better*, 67-68..

[1376] Buber so characterizes the critical structural task of Village Communes. Their great temptation and danger lies in isolating communities from one another to avoid annoyance, and in limiting themselves to educative exercises. The task of communities greatly exceeds economics, ritual purity, or education. Where community prospers, it counter-influences anonymous societies, eroding them, opening a path to decentralized and truly personal economies and relationships. Buber, *Paths in Utopia*, 141.

[1377] So Martin Luther King Jr. characterizes the human condition. [♪] King, *Autobiography*, 189.

[1378] Fresh from fratricide, Cain sassed Yahweh, who inquired after Abel's whereabouts, "Am I my brother's keeper?" *Genesis* 4:8-9.

sword of convened community martials. The many of the Commons speak to contravene the deviant few. The twentieth century suffered so because the quiet voice of the irenic many found no microphone. The Commons speaks. Sometimes the Commons must bark.

12.1.2. *Repository of Global Knowledge.* The Commons archives human practical and theoretical knowledge. All skills required to maintain global cultures should be written, enacted for video documentation, and stored. Every book ever written should be stored. Every skill should be demonstrated, from making candles and castrating pigs to rocket engine design and computer programming. The task is massive and unending. To this archive, every human should have unimpeded access by the technology then extant. That technology should provide real time access to Commons dialogue, and have sufficient capacity to download vast amounts of text, video, and pictures.

12.1.3. *Innovation Exchange.* The Commons receives and republishes reports on community innovations, errors, successes. One should be able to follow the course of any of mankind's communities in great detail by access to the Commons. Where relevant, any community should be able to download instructions for needed technologies or skills to effect any of the innovations of any community.

12.1.4. *Global Dialogue.* The Commons hosts the global dialogue on meaningful community. Communities will exchange congratulations, appreciations, criticisms, perspectives, and chatter by means of the Commons exchange. From a twenty-first century perspective, one aspect of the Commons resembles the Internet on steroids with a good purpose. The Commons will structure the etiquette of contribution, recommend time for members to allot to following the Commons deliberation, and put critical questions into a format for response from the global community.

12.1.5. *Recording Contracts.* The myriad contracts among communities will be recorded in the Commons archive. Each should be accessible to all, since it is by these contracts that communities hope to establish their well-being. Others will want to emulate successful experiments. Private contracts should be precluded, since the well-being of all depends upon transparency in what other communities are doing and in making available to all the best practices of each. In kithdom, human relations grow transparent. Record all contracts publicly.[1379] Make them readily available to all.

[1379] Thomas Andrews inquires whether public recording of all contracts would not erode the zone of privacy. I believe public recording would erode privacy. Privacy, however, is not one of the great pillars of kithdom. I assume that life in cadres would course beneath public scrutiny, except when it veers into wantonness. All contracts that are not intimacies, however, should be examined by the members of a community, and by the community of communities, if either so desires. Privacy, in

12.1.6. *Alternatives Bazaar.*   The Commons offers to communities the best alternatives available, and reports the communal experiments that prove the case. The Commons lacks coercive force. Its influence is the affect of each community upon all others. The Commons compels nothing. The force of the Commons lies in its proliferant ideas, culled from all humanity across space and time.

12.1.7. *Commons Agenda.*   Communities will choose how to manage the Commons. Which topics should predominate? How should the archive be structured? What technologies promise deeper meaning within communities?   What information should be retained and what discarded? How will the global dialogue be condensed for general consumption? How will millions of ideas and contributions be communicated to every community's members, without seizing more time from other needful activities than is wise? Communities, reaching consensus, choose. In my view, the Commons should remain unitary, accommodating all. Diverse versions of the Commons could contribute to divisions among communities. All should have to listen to every other if they themselves wish to be heard.

12.2. *Commons versus States.*   The Commons is not a global State.

12.2.1. *States as Over-Population Stopgaps.*   Among works on ethics, discussion of community decision-making and relations among communities is inevitably styled a "political" chapter. But the term "politics" is bloated with connotations absent from my usage. Hence, my aversion to the word "politics." The word "politics" is deeply interwoven with the concept of the State, to such an extent that, for most, politics is nothing other than the subject of the State, its usurpations, and its conduct. When one talks about humans together, most are habitually driven to speak of the State and its numerous sub-agents.

The political State is, however, equivocal. Humans may tolerate States, or they may not, The State emerged in human history as a coercive response to human overpopulation. It replaced tribal structures in which consensus dominated decision-making, and leaders were first among peers.[1380] In the face of scarcity, the strong coerced those unwilling or unable to resist, insuring the strong's prosperity.

---

anonymous society, often constitutes a cloak beneath which dark hobbies prosper. None deserves such shielding.

[1380] So argues Michael Taylor. He conceives the origin of the state as follows: Competent chiefs aggregate supporters. In a threat-filled environment, defensive force would be concentrated under the trusted head. The central chief resists natural communal fissioning (due to overpopulation or conflict), since the departures weaken his domain. But such a chief's defense policies (in keeping a community together when it should fission) weakens community generally, and the communal forces that keep community egalitarian and peaceful erode, being then replaced by centralized force and artificial social controls. Fissioning new communities becomes an unattractive option, since these

Overpopulation occurs at a tipping point between the number of persons harvesting an environment, each laden with their socially-determined expectations of life, and the technology employed to nourish and invest those lives with meaning. When scarcity becomes the human rule due to burgeoning numbers, the State becomes an attractive possibility. Members gamble that they and their young will be among those privileged over others.

The State sunders human members. State laws and institutions favor some, block others. The State ladles gravy on the potatoes of some, and dumps even scraps from the plates of others. The State is a scalpel incising the tumor of overpopulation. States are stopgap expedients addressing our rampant failure to voluntarily restrict our breeding. Lacking the will to limit our numbers, we instead coercively restrict the well-being and meaning of some lives to preserve those features of other lives. As the State has grown habitual for us, humanity has learned to well-tolerate the spectacle of billions living on less than a dollar a day. For many first-worlders, "they" mean nothing to "us." To the compassionless among us, "they" get what they deserve.

In this light, a State is a group of neighbors inclined to coerce or deprive some associates. Rampant coercion delivers a culture not only given to compelling compliance, but one in which the perils of that approach are under-appreciated. Ultimately, political coercion creates an ethos in which violence prospers and is deemed inevitable—the violence of neighbor against neighbor, the violence of State against neighbor, and the violence of State against State. States treat citizens as individuals or units. Individualism and non-personalism, as thought-forms, infect our view of life, and lead us to distorted thinking about ourselves, our families, and our neighbors. In the end, we amount to nothing more than "units" or "collateral damage."

Humans, even when alone, are not individuals or units, but, rather, members.[1381] We prosper and invest life with meaning within small communities. The anonymity of the modern mass State distorts human existence. Our isolation truncates ethical deliberation. Our habit of individu-

---

communities would be weak, and the threats to them increasing. Threats may not only prevent fissioning, but may cause communities to fuse with others to protect themselves. [♪] Taylor, *Community, Anarchy, and Liberty*, 129-137.

[1381] Many philosophical anarchists imagine the individual as imperious. Humans should stand one at a time, consent, and form associations from among those who agree. Consider Wolff, *In Defense of Anarchism*, 12-13. No such humans exist. Even the iconoclastic eremite came from a mother in a tribe, learned a people's ways, and then chose a role within that community, the seldom-sought role of solipsistic recluse.

alism creates stresses that humans are seldom able to bear alone. Our mobility sunders critical human relationships. Our nuclear families, it appears in light of divorce rates, seem inclined to detonate unceremoniously. Loneliness is a cultural plague and public health threat. Western culture, in casting humans as individuals, imagines us as something we are not. We are not lone rangers, renaissance men, or super-heroes. Humans are members.

12.2.2. *The Withering State.* Where humans find meaning, States grow irrelevant. Where adequately nurtured, communities deem States a danger. Meaning-laden communities tamp States down, peacefully, but persistently.[1382] Human circles make decisions by consensus, taking the dissenting voice to heart and adjusting to include that perspective. The dissenter recognizes the need for action, even action he suspects will prove counterproductive, and withholds his veto to let the proposed experiment proceed. Human communities find consensus by long dialogue, eschewing actions for which consensus proves elusive. A global Commons finds consensus by transgenerational conversation seeking the shape of the farsight horizon. None are coerced, for all have been deliberately, thoroughly nurtured. When human numbers fall, and every child is liberally nurtured, the lure of coercion will wane, and the need for instruments of coercive violence will recede. States will atrophy. Free association among affinity groups,[1383] in a proliferant welter, will dominate collective action.

One need not revolt against the State. That is the fatal *cul de sac* into which Bakunin and Most and Marx, by their violence-laden advocacy, led the twentieth century. One needs to choose conduct that obviates State coercion. When we turn our attention from freedom (from State intrusion) to meaning (within our circle and community, coordinated by means of

---

[1382] Marx and Engels imagined that the State would wither as the proletariat completed its usurpation of bourgeois prerogatives, and class conflicts subsided in communist bliss. It would seem communist utopia went astray in the hands of mass murderers like Lenin. See Lenin, *State and Revolution*, Chapter 4, in which the Russian leader scoffs at the possibility of peaceful transition from capitalism to communism, advocates violent revolution, and explains Marx's doctrine of the "withering away" of the State. Marxist theorists uniformly suffer infatuation with violence. I argue that the State withers because it has lost relevance. A scant survey of governments reveals bureaucracies overwhelmed by their need of, but inability to cope with, the billion details required for effective governance. States labor beneath morbid information obesity, slowly being choked to death by their own bloated girth. Smaller communities, enabled by mass communication, promise egalitarian decision-making with information sized to the human brain. See Dyer, *War: The Lethal Custom*, 444.

[1383] The "affinity group" emerged in the FAI's (Iberian Anarchist Federation) self-organization. This organization was part of the Spanish national anarchist labor union, CNT (National Confederation of Labor), which remains to this day influential on the Iberian peninsula in Spanish labor and anarchist sentiment. Affinity groups remained small, to facilitate member intimacy and resist police infiltration. Bookchin, *Post-Scarcity Anarchism*, 221-222.

the Commons), laws and courts and police and States lose momentum. Eventually, those structures, already belabored, atrophy and crumble.

12.2.3. *The Importance of Smallness.* Humans are interpersonal creatures. Members are rankled by impersonal treatment. Our contemporary preoccupation with political equality betrays the fact that we are each concerned that we may matter to no one and exist only as bureaucratic ciphers. People need a few intimate friends with whom they find meaning. Humans need to know the members of their circle of 150. We need to recognize and be familiar with all in our community of 1500 or more. We need to be known by our circles. We need to identify with the community and its purposes in which our circle participates. And we need to know we are recognized and valued by all other members, circles, and communities in the global Commons of humanity.[1384]

One key to each component of meaningful existence is retaining sufficiently small numbers to permit personal knowledge and interaction.[1385] In large numbers, human identity is impaired. Our ethical capacity becomes overwhelmed. In crowds, humans grow inclined to emulate ill-behaviors one might never otherwise contemplate. We fear in a sea of faces, and that terror truncates our fundamental human affability.[1386]

Modern urban society drowns in anonymity. Members, barely known, go berserk, slaughtering neighbors. Gangs fight turf wars, failing to integrate with other circles to form a community with meaningful goals. And States war, employing lethal violence for transient ends, rending the human fabric for generations.

Small is where meaning happens. The historical tendency of mankind toward larger and larger aggregations expresses collective terror of bodily insecurity. Within one's State, one hunkers. Outside that State, massive rapacious predators stalk. Human existence has fallen into less than five hundred aggregates, the nation-states of the world. Each is vastly too large for the human brain to accommodate interpersonally. So, members drift toward anomie. In building the sociality of human maturi-

---

[1384] Rousseau warns of the dangers of societies growing too large. Rousseau, *The Social Contract*, 90-93 (Book II, Chapter 9). John Rawls, who is deeply committed to gigantic anonymous democracies, acknowledges that the conditions that lead to a good and just societies grow more difficult to realize as societies become populous and the social distance between citizens increases. [♪] Rawls, *Justice as Fairness: A Restatement*, 201 (§60).

[1385] Taylor argues that, absent small and stable numbers in a community, social order deteriorates in a manner that makes good faith reciprocity untenable. [♪] Taylor, *Community, Anarchy, and Liberty*, 94.

[1386] I acknowledge my own agoraphobia, usually mild, may color my view of human crowds a gray darker than warranted.

ty, one whittles. No community should contain more members than its denizens can comprehend. Humanity should spin itself into hundreds of thousands of highly-structured dense, but small, communities. Our affable gifts will enrich all.[1387]

Some (Hobbes and Hume, for example) justify the State by noting the incivility of men and their persistent egoism. We live, apart from the coercions of the State, in constant war with all around us. Many adopt this justification for the existence of States. One may ask, however, what part States play in making citizens implacable and self-centered. States crush small communities. Psychologically, communities suffer deep vulnerability to predation by States. The many pick apart small communities, alleging imminent perils for which they, being small, are ill-prepared. Citizens in States practice little altruism, because altruism is not what makes States function. They see little giving, so they express scant contribution. Cooperative ventures emerge stillborn as States insist upon supervision or control. As the State usurps community functions in peace-making, social control, and public goods, fewer and fewer individuals bother personally producing such goods. Functionally, States fashion for citizens lives so paltry that citizens invite the intrusions of State action. States make us chary givers and wary neighbors. It is small wonder, then, that we cannot function as communities. The requisite personal skills and character traits have been stripped from our daily lives by the very State which allegedly exists because of our inadequate social skills.[1388]

Within small communities, human natural diversity finds expression. In mass aggregates, function requires conformity. All must, in masses, trend toward uniformity to keep the anonymous huddle moving, since the wild diversity of human thought and stock cannot be comprehended on so large a scale. Oppression surges, crushing natural initiative. Humans, where healthy, act. All require freedom to conceive, then attempt, imag-

---

[1387] Charles Fourier (1772-1837), an early socialist thinker, contemplated human societies organized in groups of 300-400 families, comprising one male and one female of each of his 800 personality types, for an ideal membership of 1,600 per community (which societies Fourier termed "phylansteries.") These many, released from the oppressions of education, will blossom into remarkable creatures of many astounding capabilities and abundances. Fourier, *The Theory of Four Movements*, 86-87. Fourier's work was taken up by a large number of acolytes who formed phylansteries globally, many in America. Among them was Victor Considerant, who helped found *La Réunion*, a Fourierian utopian community located outside Dallas, Texas, dedicated to harmonious cooperation and gender equality. That community of 400 dwindled over a period of years; it vanished when absorbed into Dallas. See Considerant, *Principles of Socialism*.

[1388] Taylor argues that altruism and cooperation atrophy where potent States exist, but that these characteristics blossom when State intrusion falters. Taylor concludes that one must resist large societies, and any process that aggregates communities. [♪] Taylor, *Anarchy and Cooperation*, 132-135. See also Kropotkin, *Mutual Aid*, 135ff, for a similar argument.

ined goods.[1389]   Human sociality should be structured to accommodate maximal experimentation, to make room for the human need for expression and action.   Mass society cannot nourish this need.   Impersonality has no name.   Overpopulated society makes of every man a number, an impersonal cipher.   Eventually, living amidst anonymous masses truncates one's personhood.

Objection 45: Technical Regression: *Some demur that small is dangerous. By whittling the human population to around one billion, humanity runs the risk of technological retreat. The standard of living could collapse, and the ability to produce the technologies on which we rely might deteriorate. We may precipitate a new stone age, and find life spans returning to the low thirties. Scarcity, presently within reach of being eradicated, might become intractable. We could torpedo all the astonishing gains of the last two hundred years.*

Response: The human population will be reduced.   The planet cannot long support its present human burden.   Malthus has been delayed, not derailed.   Arable land is degrading.   The seas are producing fewer fish.   Insecticides are inducing human cancers.   Population growth is leveling, but more than half of the planet lives in substantial poverty, and one billion straddle survival's razor edge. The question is not *whether* the population will be reduced, but *how* it will be reduced.   A reasoned, value-driven plan of voluntary population reduction may allow humanity time to cope with the pain of economic contraction over ensuing centuries, rather than suffering that change in a few chaotic, excruciating decades.   Indecision in the face of overpopulation may render human existence a stewing cauldron of miseries, boiling over a fire of corpses.

Concentrations of humans grow creative as trade burgeons.   The critical question is why.   Is there some feature of urban density that promotes experimental ideas?   Or does density of communication, whether or not many dwell nearby, loft creativity?   If the latter, then one billion humans, organized in small communities, linked globally with other communities in a vibrant communication Commons, may well suffice.   In tribal cultures, villagers convene in circles around their fire; neighbors sit close enough to share words and objects with one another, to be heard by all.   The Commons must draw our millions so close together, around one fire, a blaze all share.

If technological advances slow, it might be possible for our deliberation of their wisdom to proceed in tandem.   That would solve another problem.

Overheated humanity is hyper-populous, boiling over the planetary cauldron.   Reducing our numbers might settle the human kettle.

[1389] Mill argues that, just as thought should remain at liberty to err, so too action, where it does no others harm, should be free to create experiments in living. [♪] Mill, *On Liberty*, 55.

> ***Objection 46: Hopeless Optimism****: Still another protests the relentless hopefulness of Quad sociality. Moral decadence emerges, like poisonous mushrooms, from the detritus of hysterical optimism.*[1390]
>
> ***Response***:   One declines to apologize for planning desirable outcomes. Culling conduct induces hope.[1391]   I trust (but of this one is never entirely certain) I am not hysterical.

[1390] Richard Weaver so laments "hysterical optimism." To this debility, Weaver attributes the loss of transcendental ideals, and the dominance of moral relativism in modern Western societies. Weaver, *Ideas Have Consequences*, 9ff. Ernst Becker shares the cynical despair that haunts much of psychoanalytic theory and existentialism: "The armor of character was so vital to us that to shed it meant to risk death and madness. If character is a neurotic defense against despair and you shed that defense, you admit the full flood of despair, the full realization of the true human condition. . . . Freud summed it up beautifully when he somewhere remarked that psychoanalysis cured the neurotic misery in order to introduce the patient to the common misery of life. . . . Reality is the misery." Becker, *The Denial of Death*, 57.

[1391] I suspect that some of my hopefulness has been influenced by components of [♪] Ridley, *The Rational Optimist*, and the long meditation on declining violence of [♪] Pinker, *Better Angels of Our Nature*.

V. CULLING FUTURES

Think, **Kate**, *of what lies ahead. Every footfall rattles the future. Some humans loom, steps rumbling through millennia. Others pace quietly, locally. All, however, make their contribution, great or small, good or ill, to the weal of those who come after us. We build more than our own lives and characters. We fashion a heritage in which our descendants dwell. Our choices are fraught with implications for us, but also for billions yet unborn. Do the unborn matter? Can you and I expand our horizons? Can we cherish our defenseless progeny? So far, humans have not done so. We have been sated with the moment, gorged on propinquity. Might we look up from our navels? Might we squint at horizons? Might we recognize ourselves hurtling toward a future we have hardly considered? Peering teaches humility. Peering inspires. Peer, Kate.*

> A CHATTERER MUMBLES: I, FOREVER.
> ONE ANSWERS:
>   UNIVERSAL PINPOINT TO LUMINOSITY TO ENTROPY.
>   KINDLING STAR TO CONSCIOUSNESS TO SUPERNOVA.
>   DUST AGGREGATION TO AWARENESS TO DUST DISPERSAL.
> FEARING DEATH, THE CHATTERER LIES.
>   MOMENTS EVAPORATE INTO FOREVER.
> KNOWING DEATH, ONE LIVES.
>   MOMENTS CONDENSE ETERNITY.

13. *A Thousand Generations.* No member makes a decision, for good or ill, alone. The components of one's thoughts jumped from another's mind into the stream of human deliberation before one existed. The language in which the member expresses her decision, in action or inaction, word or silence, is the language of predecessors. Our very genetic stuff propagates forward in time from events lost in the mists of time's fogbanks. Decision-makers' words and actions also echo forward in time, influencing thousands or millions or billions of other speakers and actors. How much more is this true of communities, whose lifespans cannot be confidently limited to a few decades. When thought rumbles through a community, its thunder shakes the Com-

mons, rattling windows across millennia.[1392]   We mistake our smallness for paucity of influence. Every insight reverberates. Every bitterness impoverishes many whom the injured party will never greet. Every embrace deflects the future toward empathy. Every snarl insures another cycle of coercion. Human predilections ring through generations. Today's pregnant idea is tomorrow's commonplace. Communities exist transgenerationally; only members exist momentarily. All speak and act prospectively. Look forward. If one cannot see into the inchoate future a thousand generations, then squint and peer again. If there is to be a human future, its weal depends upon human identification with and care for unborn people.[1393] We must acquire and heed our thanatoid transgenerational vision of the farsight horizon.

> IN THE PALEOLITHIC, CHATTERERS OUTBRED SUPPLY.
>   ONES SAVED (AND DOOMED) HUMANITY.
>   ONES DELIVERED MARVELS,
>   FIRE AND WHEEL, PLOW AND CANAL,
>   SPEARHEAD AND CITY, BOOKS AND LAW,
>   VOLTS AND BYTES, AND UNIFIED GODHEAD.
> STILL, CHATTERERS BRED.
>   INEXORABLY CAME WAR,
>   DISASTERS, DEHYDRATION, STARVATION,
>   DEPLETION, POLLUTION, FANATICISM,
>   GENOCIDE, DISEASE, AND PSYCHOSIS.
> PRODIGAL MAN RETURNED TO THE PALEOLITHIC,
>   FOR A LONG, DEEP BREATH.
>   ONE RECONSIDERS, AND WAITS.

13.1. *Patient Militance*.[1394]   When a community truncates its horizon to a human lifespan or a generation, the community emits a stench of panic. If a mere eighty or a hundred years lie before a community, during which time a people must achieve its vision for the human future, emergent action seems warranted. Mao Zedong murdered seventy million of China's citizens in

---

[1392] John Stuart Mill said: "To discover to the world something which deeply concerns it, and of which it was previously ignorant; to prove to it that it had been mistaken on some vital point of temporal or spiritual interest, is as important a service as a human being can render to his fellow creatures." [♪] Mill, *On Liberty*, 28.

[1393] Ian Tattersall warns, "Our brains are extraordinary mechanisms, and they have allowed us to accomplish truly amazing things; but we are still only good at anticipating—or at least paying attention to—highly immediate consequences. We are notably bad at assessing risk, especially long-term risk." Tattersall, *Masters of the Planet*, 227.

[1394] Patient militance awaiting change is just the sort of gradualism rejected by most individualist anarchists. The alternative to gradualism is violent revolution and other lesser coercions. A signal lesson of the twentieth century is the futility of violence in changing people or cultures. How many millions need be slaughtered on the altar of coercive ignorance?

his haste to polish the Sino-Asian landscape. America pumps every drop of accessible oil from deep strata to insure travel to fast food stores and vacation extravaganzas. Emergent measures address ill-conceived ends. Our urgencies sprout misdeeds. Were we reproducing sensibly, were our lifestyles modest and luxuries few, were our aspirations aimed more toward human intimacy and less at baubles, toys, and thrills, were our communities lively laboratories in the possibilities of human existence, then our aspirations would grow lengthy, our coercions would wane, and our appreciation of the possibilities of meaning would ripen.

> ONE SCRUTINIZES THIS LANDSCAPE TO ITS HORIZON.
> ONE MAPS A PATH SURMOUNTING THAT TERMINUS.
>   SO REASON FALTERS,
>   SO AFFECT GUIDES,
>   SAYS ONE.

Patience is not acquiescence. Militate.[1395] Act peacefully, but potently. Keep irenic change on the human table. Build conspicuous communities. Convince by doing. Broadcast loud actions. Leave bombast to coercers. Much community building awaits. Do not be seduced into mouthy propagandizing. Let your heart and affection speak for you. Shout down disputants silently. Wield the sword of hugs and kindness. Heartfelt smiles melt frozen souls. Quad sociality convenes people serious about flourishing. And that is work, not chatter.

The human community must consciously extend the human horizon. Doing so, misplaced haste dissipates.[1396] Every community's primary effects are invisibly trans-generational. Our words and acts and ideas and genetics spin forward in time, most often unintentionally, thousands of generations hence. Humility should chasten us. Human members are a sigh in the hurricane of life. A community discovers, then writes, its sentence in mankind's book of legacy. Each of us leaves the remainder of humanity's tome, including the great arc of its story, to unborn authors.

13.2. *Resting in Oneself and Others.* A member's horizon is not humanity's horizon. Humanity will persevere so long as it adapts to changing circum-

---

[1395] Martin Luther King Jr. reminds all white advocates of patience that justice delayed is justice denied. Forbearance-talk slips easily from the tongue of the unoppressed. See King's remarkable "Letter from Birmingham Jail" for eloquent argument to this effect. [♪] King, *Autobiography*, Chapter 18, especially 191-196.

[1396] John Steinbeck argues that hurry impedes success. We rush, neglecting our own purposes. One starts by deliberating the end to be sought. Once satisfied, one focuses all attention on methodically enacting the means chosen. In this manner, one avoids missteps, and blunts errors caused by fear and haste. Few have learned this lesson. Steinbeck, *East of Eden*, 238.

stances. Members perish with comparative predictable rapidity. All of human need is not yours to bear, Kate. Your mix of genes and habits has a role to play in humankind's present and future. Seize your part. Let your activity infuse life around you with depth. Nothing more is required of you than to do your part. If your community is well-structured, doing your part should cause your life to flourish.

> CHATTERERS CHATTER, AS IS THEIR HABIT.
> ONES PONDER, IN CUSTOMARY SILENCE.
> HEAR, CHATTERERS!
> SPEAK, ONES!
> SOW VERDANT FORESTS OF MEANING.

Our lives have reasons bred into them from epochs ancient. Discovering, exercising, and resting in them renders life meaningful.[1397] No one of us bears what humanity needs. But you and I are not all. Some members of the human community are neurodiverse, constantly generating new perceptions and habits, some of which prove adaptive. No lone member need feel responsibility for human weal. We crew a species-spanning ship, sails straining with gusts of life. Collectively, we chart a course. The hand-wringing drone of successive global crises is a din mostly manufactured to keep corporate media profitable. Take a deep breath. Bumps in humanity's road will not break the human axle. There are ample time and sufficient energy to address our problems. Let us cooperate, confident in the human enterprise, squinting at our horizon.[1398]

14. *Answering Kate.* I recur to Kate's question, the inquiry that launched this deliberation. *How does one make good decisions?[1399]* One culls, preferring acts that build meaningful community. One avoids acts that erode a communal sense of purpose with one's friends. Every choice must evidence delicate elaborations deeply attuned to oneself and others. One cleaves to intimacies,

---

[1397] The fourth century B.C. Chinese sage, Master Zhuang, urges us that all things cannot be understood, but may nevertheless be lived. He argues: "The sage embraces things. Ordinary men discriminate among them and parade their discriminations before others. So I say, those who discriminate fail to see. The Great Way is not named; Great Discriminations are not spoken. . . . If the Way is made clear, it is not the Way. . . . Therefore understanding that rests in what it does not understand is the finest." *Zhuangzi*, 39-40 (in the Discussion on Making All Things Equal, Section 2).

[1398] Shermer arrives, despite his persistent empiricism, at a view of the human future very much consonant with that of *Cull*. See Shermer's descriptions of Civilization 2.0. Shermer, *The Moral Arc*, 433.

[1399] Schopenhauer admonishes: "A man cannot say everything in one day, and should not answer more than he is asked." Schopenhauer, *The Basis of Morality*, 144. In this, I have failed you, Kate.

and so fabricates meaning. One invites friendship to import others into one's life, forming circles and communities. One enlivens the social matrix, giving and taking as circumstance dictates. One recognizes oneself as a brain-in-a-body, tied to physicality, yet harboring fractured consciousness, transcendent suspicions, and fitful rationality. One adopts rules for living. One eschews coercion, and seeks consensus. One listens, encourages, confronts. One nurtures children, but bears few or none. One demands the interpersonal over the anonymous. One denies to States unalloyed allegiance. One chooses peace, and fashions it where peace is wanting. One constructs oneself usefully. One succors future generations, embracing those many lives in present imagination and care. One adopts global humanity as family. One savors life and welcomes its bounds. One listens deeply to others, to the Commons. One departs in equanimity. One makes a good decision when that decision generates meaningful life in a meaning-laden society of humans. In the end, dear Kate, you choose well when you dive deep, ask the hard and neglected questions, and undertake breathtaking responses. You choose well, Kate, when you embrace Kate in her expanse and abyss, tied as she is to others in their joys, their pains, their imaginings. There exists much of which we know little, in ourselves, in others. So, experiment. Let that humility appropriate to mankind's limitations nestle in your heart. Discover better approaches. Try them. Revel in them. Every dawn, set yourself to meliorate.[1400]

15. *Conclusion: Meaningful Community*. This book rummages history's attics. It shakes off cobwebs, securing thoughts to mull in culling human conduct, both yours, Kate, and that of mankind at large. We can make better decisions. We can delight ourselves in a meaning-laden global Commons. I have speculated along the way, opining about which changes we might embrace to improve matters as they presently stand. You may agree. You may dissent. All my guesses are equivocal; make your own. Humans seek homeostasis, repetitive approximations of optimal human biological, social, and psychological conditions. Homeostasis has a shape. That shape is meaningful community.

Books are thin stuff. Humans are thick. The best one can hope from a book is gorgeous shimmering within the cerebral cortex, as sheet lightning illuminates turbulent clouds.[1401] On a good day, filigreed thoughts bump trucu-

---

[1400] To "meliorate" is to make things better, to improve circumstances.

[1401] I think better of books than this sentence might convey. I agree with John Milton: "Books are not absolutely dead things, but do contain a potency of life in them to be as active as that soul was whose progeny they are; nay, they do preserve as in a vial the purest efficacy and extraction of that living intellect that bred them. . . . A good book is the precious life-blood of a master spirit, embalmed and treasured up on purpose to a life beyond life." Milton, *Areopagitica*, 5-6. Hence, I of-

lent drives toward preferred outcomes. On a bad day, a good book drives the eyes, but not the heart.[1402]   Always, in choosing well, the heart moves first, then the head. For the heart is deep evolutionary strata that undergird clouds of consciousness: substance beneath evanescence, rock beneath air. "Motivation" means that subconscious depths rumble. The cortex trails along, brilliant, exuberant, but ever late.

Finely elaborating our drives and emotions, by means of intensive nurture and habit-acquisition, humanizes the cull of conduct. Nurturing and attending every human, including our neurodiverse savants and wanton members, promises a wealth of diverse ideas to sort. Carefully fashioning our thanatoid deliberation insures that our own community participates in the great global human venture, the encompassing prosperity of earth-bound humans to the farsight horizon. We cull a course for humanity that departs the tangled trajectory of our evolutionary heritage. Communities persist long after their members. The human community of communities, if it proves wise, has a lifespan limited only by that of the universe itself. We know not what lies ahead, but we squint, we peer. For this meaning, we are born.

Finely-elaborated conduct culling renders human life meaningful. Be a flourishing, beloved member. Build a flourishing, deep community. Deliberate and collaborate with the flourishing, breath-taking Commons. Seize a flourishing future, for yourself, Kate, one flooded with meaning, for your friends, among whom I am one, and for hundreds of billions to come.

Cull. Act. Flourish.

---

fer the several epitomes of *Cull's* second volume, sacrifices to life beyond those authors' own lives. May they touch you as have they me.

[1402] Bernard Gert says: "Moral philosophy should be understandable to the intelligent general reader. A book on moral philosophy understandable only by professional moral philosophers is a bad book on moral philosophy." Gert, *The Moral Rules*, xii.

EPITOME OF
CULL: CHOOSING WELL.[1403]

I.   **Cull.**

The author addresses his young friend, Kate, asking her to think about human conduct. He invites Kate to disagree, and seeks her patience in the sometimes difficult conversation.

1.   *Choosing.* [1]

Consider decision-making. Have you, have we, chosen well? Most would confess not. Our characters disappoint. Our communities suffer. Might we do better? Might you make of yourself a moral wonder? Together, how might we flourish?

When we make a decision to act, we sort better from worse alternatives. That is, we cull. When we choose, our acts make us better, or worse, people. Our communities prosper or suffer. Our lives become meaningful or empty. We flourish or we suffer or we die. Choosing well amounts to a finely-elaborated cull of conduct. In culling, one rehearses for oneself the likely outcomes of an act, and chooses the best among the apparent alternatives. Recognizing the best acts from among the welter of alternatives is what we call wisdom. We have no choice but to act. Even doing nothing is an act. We flourish when we choose and act well.

Choosing happens together as well as alone. In the author's view, we should substantially alter the human social pattern. He proposes revised language for human togetherness. A "cadre" is a group of eight to fifteen intimate friends. A "circle" associates ten or so cadres. A "community" creates a context for ten or so circles. A community is the basic building block of global humanity. The "Commons" gathers the global community of communities for deliberation and reporting and recollection. The Commons is the global fire pit around which the human tribe gathers to share, to talk, to remember, and to choose. The author calls this nested social structure "Quad sociality" (the four "c"s of cadre-circle-community-commons). Quad society is kithdom, that is, a community comprising all of earth's communities of friends.

Choosing well proves difficult. One suffers confusion and ignorance that she needs to dispel. Culling well has a structure: urges are modified by emotions, and both are deflected by thought. To assist in talking about choosing wisely, the author suggests some words to help clear brittle brain brush and tangled confusions. He lists the quagmires. The author describes the parts of this book and suggests reading strategies. Seeking to benefit oneself by making good decisions may seem selfish at first glance. But one lives with others; each of us leaks into others, and they into us. Choosing well enhances the lives of all. That is virtue.

> *Objection 1: Good and Evil.* [12] *An objector criticizes the author's use of the terms "good" and "evil," preferring less loaded language.* The author answers that he rejects the theological baggage of these terms, but finds no adequate alternatives.

[1403] Page numbers for the relevant section of *Cull* are bracketed.

Objection 2: Urban Trajectory. [15] *Another objector criticizes the author's rejection of urban existence; surely, mankind cannot lunge backwards into villages.* The author answers that, though density is helpful, overpopulation crushes mankind. We must reduce human numbers dramatically. The author is, however, unwilling to coerce people into producing fewer babies. The author would nurture every child born, and trust people, well-informed, to voluntarily curb their procreation, except when called to bear the next generation.

Objection 3: Putrescence of Communism. [19] *Yet another objector dislikes using words employed in communist ideology, such as circle and cadre.* The author asks to steal a few terms back from misguided, violent communist thinkers, since we need words to think adequately about choosing and living together.

Objection 4: Identifiable Evil. [21] *Still another objector complains that none can reliably identify evil as it happens. Evil hides and cannot be exposed, until it is too late.* The author responds that evil can be identified if one grasps its structure. Evil erodes meaningful community. None evades what he cannot identify. Every morality specifies what, in its scheme, constitutes evil.

Good acts build meaningful community; evil acts erode it. [23] We constantly employ feedback from our actions to guide future acts. When we do this well, we make better choices. We and our communities prosper. When we cull poorly, all suffer. Humans are predisposed to optimism, which may make us blind to what is not working. Each of us must doubt our rosy optimism. When we discover acts that work well, we make them habits. Our habits, personal and communal, constitute our character. To some habits we are predisposed by our evolution on African plains; we alter these with difficulty. Other habits we invent. These can be changed more readily, but not without effort. Crucially, habits can improve or demolish our lives. So, as we get wiser, we grow cautious about our choices. We deliberate. We have to face the possibility every day that we have chosen poorly and simply missed our errors. Ill-considered habits can savage life, leaving one feeling empty, grumbling that life is meaningless. Evils are habits chosen because they seemed good, but proved otherwise. When this happens, we need to stop and examine how we made that bad decision. Humility helps. Some diseases (sociopathy, for example) and personality problems (narcissism, for example) lead regularly to choosing evils.

Members and communities shape one another. The errors of either become the problems of both. With wonders, it is the same; they spread. Despite the influence communities have on their members, every person hides a kernel that remains unaffected. We are, in deep recesses, unique and resilient.

Humans manufacture meaning for themselves. [35] We do so in the same way we erect buildings or undertake journeys: one brick at a time, one step at a time. We choose habits individually and collectively. These habits become routines. Routines become social structures. We tell supportive stories about our way of doing things, and invent shared tales that put life's difficult moments in perspective. If we forget that we invented our structures and imagined our stories, we may believe gods made them. That can make a community unable to adapt. These are stifling places to live. Some people eventually get fed up with being stuck in the mud. They rebel and establish revised habits. People get hurt and suffer unwanted change. This "invention, ossification, revolution" pattern injures us deeply. We tear up habits that should be retained, and fail to amend other habits that are killing us. We need to get clear on what helps us and what hurts us.

[38] Meaningful human communities: 1) provide shelter and food and care, 2) keep life safe, 3) resist fighting, 4) choose openly how to live together, 5) persevere when problems arise, 6) fit members to jobs that suit them, 7) encourage intimate friendship, 8) tolerate weird and difficult people, 9) make a living by producing something others need, 10) adapt to changes as they occur, 11) revere life and the depth that lies beneath all living things, and 12) seek to cooperate with all human communities.

Objection 5: Trivializing Evil. [47] *An objector argues that evil exists more substantially than mere poor decision-making. Humans are utterly sinful, and Satan induces that horror.* The author rejects personalized evil spirits, arguing that these do not help us make better decisions.

Objection 6: Diversity of Purposes. [48] *Another objector rejects the author's values. Other values exist and may be preferable. We need values diversity.* The author counters that meaningful community encompasses all values. Diverse values, even evil values, may find expression in some communities. Those failures will teach as much as successes.

Objection 7: Existential Death. [49] *Yet another objector asserts that meaning lacks meaning. All ends in death, so meaning is vacuous.* The author answers that none knows what follows life. Humans know life. One can make of life a meaningless hell. Or one can make something substantially better than that. Death is no horror to those who have lived well in the company of friends. Meaning is the final word in ethics.

Objection 8: Authorial Hubris. [50] *Still another objector complains that the author's assertions claim to apply to all humans. No man knows so much. None knows what creates meaning. The author is full of himself.* The author agrees he is arrogant, as are all authors. He hopes speaking his mind helps people make better decisions.

[51] Eroded human communities: a) overpopulate, producing scarcity, then raiding, b) fail to attach to their babies, c) neglect nurture and mentoring, d) imagine life is aimless, e) persecute odd people, f) tolerate selfishness and violence and war, g) coerce members, h) treat animals badly, i) fail to support members, j) tolerate substitutes for meaningful community, such as drug abuse, free-riding isolation, hysterias about global disaster, and rabid pessimism, k) let members feel utterly alone, m) encourage members to doubt the possibility of meaningful community, n) let members get addicted to owning more and more stuff, and o) permit despair that ends in suicide.

Objection 9: Dominating Species. [62] *An objector asserts that overpopulation is not mankind's big problem. Sufficient funds exist, if wars and luxuries were abandoned, to nurture all seven billion humans. Species extinction occurs because humans dominate. That is the natural course of things. Species come; species go. Humans are, frankly, coming.* The author agrees that we could feed all. Mere sustenance will not solve the problem of overpopulation. Without a choice to procreate differently, scarcity will soon return to meet twelve or fifteen billions. Conscientious childlessness and contraception can remedy over-population, and leave room on the planet for animals other than man.

Objection 10: Immoral Morality. [64] *Another objector complains that morality is immoral. Morality makes people compliant with States and religions. Humans are unique, resistant to rules.* The author responds that none stands alone. Every human is social, built for life together. Those who imagine themselves imperious and alone self-delude.

In making decisions, a member sees a problem, checks how she feels about it, thinks it over, asks others, guesses what might happen if she does this or that, takes another hard look, then acts, evaluates the results, makes needed changes, adjusts her habits, then starts again. In making decisions, a community sees a problem, waits, communicates among members and gathers facts, hears and reconciles disputing groups. If the disputing parties cannot be reconciled, they segregate themselves, and eventually fission (split apart) to form new communities. Decision-making seldom follows these lists in any linear fashion, nor should it. Member and community decision-making often occur simultaneously, and cross-influence one another.

Every community, every individual culls. We deliberate, well or poorly. All weigh self-interest against group well-being. Communities and members help one another, expressing very ancient life imperatives. Some decisions prove to be errors, which blossom into evils. None can know for certain when she chooses whether the outcome will be good or evil. One must watch and learn. Where evils take root, neighbors should converse. Where diseased people or communities undertake evil intentionally (the author calls these "wanton" acts), communities must intervene peacefully (which interventions express "irenism," a term the author prefers over "pacifism") to divert the errant member and work reconciliation.

[72] In the history of ethics, schemes at odds with irenic Quad kithdom are plentiful. Some are: virtue ethics (desirable character traits listed), hedonism (raw pleasure), Epicureanism (deferred pleasure), acquiescence ethics (expect less to avoid disappointment), consequence ethics (choose what benefits most), Thou ethics (relationships matter), divine justice ethics (god speaks), legal ethics (human rules), ego ethics (gifted people usurp), duty ethics (reason guides duties). Quad sociality borrows from several of these traditions. No ethical system can be proved. They either help create meaningful life or they do not.

II.   Culling Foundations. [77]

Ancient ideas guide most people's idea of themselves. Better ideas exist, but are ignored. To live better, we must better understand ourselves. To do so, we will need to adopt new ways of thinking.

We weakly grasp what sort of creatures we are. We evolved from mammalian stock in a gyrating climate. Our social world fitted us to survive in moderately-hostile east African plains. Big brains, like humanity's, are a dangerous and unproven gambit in evolution's wandering. We must know what we are, and clear away ensnaring brambles of ideas that clog our self-perception.

2.   Evolution. [79]

Environments are often dangerous places for the creatures that live in them. Tiny differences among creatures' abilities to adapt to circumstances can determine living to breed or dying without breeding. Genes that get passed on to children are called fit. They spread through a species, as individuals lacking those fit genes die off. Evolution has no goals. It does not think. Evolutionary theory describes how and why living systems adapt. For humans, the environment in which our mammalian genes developed was east Africa, between about twenty million and 200,000 years ago. That is when and where some early primates developed into ancestral creatures something like people.

About 50,000 years ago, human behavior changed. Tools improved. Language leapt to the fore. Starting from east Africa, modern humans migrated across the continents, adapting habits to different climates. Humans supplanted the other man-like creatures. Culture grew and diverged. Art began. Man started influencing his own evolution, which influence continues to the present.

> *Objection 11: Fiat Creation.* [83] *An objector criticizes evolutionary theory. He believes that man was created, as the Bible says, by the hand of god. Evolutionists hate god unfairly.* The author answers that evolution is not a value system, though some scientists are confused enough to treat it so. Many people read their sacred texts oddly, in a way they read no other text. The results dismay. We must see man for what he is. Man evolved, as has every animal. Man continues evolving.

3. Non-Human Quasi-Moral Behaviors. [85]

All life seeks what appears helpful, flees what seems harmful. In some animals, that basic process grows much more subtle and accurate. All life culls. Man, as an animal (using skills he shares with many other animals) chooses actions in a complex fashion which we call moral. Humans do things no other animal contemplates (split atoms, build skyscrapers), but share capabilities many other species exhibit. Man shares with animals the ability to cooperate, deceive for tactical purposes, punish others, create cultures, communicate complex information, fashion tools, reconcile fractured relationships, make predictions, remember series of events or things, imitate, choose, deduce, categorize things, and lead.

Animals share specifically moral capabilities as well. Animals resolve conflicts, reciprocate assistance, show empathy and sympathy, evidence concern for their communities, value equity, recognize justice, experience grief and love, and internalize novel norms. Some insist that discussions of animal morality project human experience on dumb animals. The author disagrees. Animal morality resembles our own.

4. Brain Evolution. [94]

Man is a brain distributed into a body. Humans link with other humans and creatures mentally and socially. We generally have a difficult time comprehending that we are brains-in-bodies, sometimes imagining that minds can exist without bodies. It is not so.

The hominin brain evolved in east Africa over the last 1.8 million years. That region suffered harsh conditions and repeated ice ages, which brought temperature changes, droughts, and ocean level fluctuations. Hominins (man-like primates) became cooperative troop animals long before humans became seriously inventive. Around 195,000 years ago, humans almost died out during an extended drought. Around 50,000 years ago, humans spread outside Africa, confronting hominin rivals (*Neanderthal* and *Homo erectus*), with whom humans competed, fought, and interbred. Humans hunted many large mammals on every continent to extinction. Humans were relatively peaceful (though some dispute this) until scarcity due to overpopulation made raiding and war attractive alternatives (arguably beginning before 15,000 years ago, at the horizon of history). Humans stopped most of their migrating and settled. Dogs joined human populations. Man domesticated plants and animals. With close contact to animals, new diseases plagued man. Populations grew, leading to cycles of starvation and increased raiding among groups. Human groups clumped together in hierarchical towns to protect themselves from hungry neighbors. Human life became a technological race to feed people in the face of population growth and pillaging due to scarcity.

The human brain is three-fourths neocortex, by volume. The limbic system (emotion) and basal ganglia (brainstem) make up the remaining one-fourth. Most of what the brain does is subconscious; we are seldom or never aware of it functioning. The part of brain function we know is consciousness. One form of consciousness is thinking. Humans think when the neocortex deflects emotionally-charged impulses toward better outcomes. No one knows why humans developed their abilities to think and speak. Scholars have proposed theories of origin for human mental capabilities: upright walking, group communication, cooperative breeding, protein scarcity leading to cooperative hunting, social complexity, resource mapping over years, working with animals, barter, or generalized shared purposes. The author believes that rationality has been over-emphasized. Most of what humans do proceeds without thinking. Thinking, on a good day, diverts one from rash action to preferable paths. And that event is the deliberation of human conduct, which the author calls "culling."

5.   *Human Sociality.* [110]
Humans live together. We are troop primates. From other humans, living and dead, a person gets his body, genes, emotional security, language, gut bugs, habits, culture, expectations, dreams, technologies, and a vast load of capital. People are mostly similar. Neurodiverse savants (persons of unusual skills, perspective, and personality) may deviate more widely. Humans, using their adaptive skills, build places to live, even in polar regions or outer space, and adapt to those residences. Because man changes his environment so strongly, we influence our own evolution and that of some animals.

Members and their communities shape one another (interpenetration). We feel what others feel, and think their thoughts. We cooperate robustly. We seek friendship, and avoid isolation. We are inclined to conform to group expectations. Our communication is gestural, oral, and written. Our words are fluid and linked to our activities in their meaning. Humans bond powerfully. Friendship governs. We bond to friends, some of whom become sexual partners and co-parents and alloparents (parenting cooperators).

The prehistoric human troop changed when food ran short due to growing population. Raiding supplemented harvesting. Defense became essential to survival. Groups clumped for safety, built defensive ramparts, and hunkered behind their walls. Populations exploded. States formed. About 15,000 years ago (some disagree about the time, arguing the date was as little as 5,000 years ago), history commenced.

> *Objection 12: Individualism.* [119] *An objector rejects the idea of mutual social shaping. The human world consists of individuals standing alone, occasionally cooperating. We do not penetrate into one another.* The author responds that social interpenetration is not obvious. Human groups are complex systems. Such systems exceed their

parts. Humans are porous, physically and socially and psychologically. Human social groupings are the most complex organization known to mankind. Humans make meaning together. That is something lone members cannot accomplish.

6.   *Human Consciousness.* [120]
Structurally, the human brain is a nested hierarchy: brainstem, overlaid by limbic structures, overlaid by neocortex. Brainstem impulses (eat, vacate, sleep, breed, survive) are diverted toward social concerns by the limbic system, and experienced as emotions. The neocortex inhibits both with analytic input. The various types of impulses and diversions cooperate or clash with one another, creating a complex dance. One's sense of self commences in the brainstem. Our brain exceeds the tissue that lies in our skulls; it extends down the spinal column, into the chest and guts, and throughout the body.

Mirror neurons may underlie human cooperative capabilities and our influence upon one another. These mirror centers help members mimic observed behaviors, surmise the intention of others, feel empathy, and bond to one another in our social groups.

[127] Jaak Panksepp, investigating rat brains (rats, being mammals, have brains quite similar to our own), has tracked specific neural pathways that create some behaviors humans share with other mammals. The SEEKING system generates excitement and focus, and recognizes causal sequences. The RAGE system promotes anger and aggression, leading sometimes to violence. It helps a person protect herself. The FEAR system induces anxiety and apprehension, aversion to perceived threats, and reduces pain sensitivity. The LUST system commences sexual behavior, and differs substantially between male and female. The CARE system initiates nurture of young and cements social bonds. It may be the neural basis of friendship. The PANIC system generates aversion to social isolation. This system too may play into friendship. Mild arousal of this system may generate the experience of loneliness; chronic arousal may induce depression. The PLAY system starts rough-and-tumble play, especially among the young. Panksepp discovered a pattern in these seven systems. Action commences in the brainstem, activates one or more of the systems he describes, is deflected by emotion and social concerns, and is then inhibited or redirected by the neocortex. Panksepp's work suggests that consciousness resembles a tree, which metaphor the author expands.

[133] Human consciousness might be imagined as a coppice (a many-trunked tree). Subconsciousness starts in murky drives (like food, warmth, safety, sex) buried among the tree roots. Its hidden life proceeds up many trunks (Panksepp's systems), deflected by social concerns (which are feelings). Subconsciousness spurts into the leafy canopy (which is the neocortex, our big thinking and talking brain). On this great tree play a million monkeys (which are the behavioral programs of our brain). A few of these poke their heads out the canopy and squawk to one another. This cross-talk is our experience of consciousness. Most of our mental life is inaccessible to us, lurking beneath the coppice's leafy canopy, busy but silently so.

Because human conscious is not unified, there exist fault lines between its various components and systems. Humans brains have built-in subconscious short-cuts (called heuristics) to make fast decisions and to cut off interference between the brain's diverse, sometimes conflicting, systems. Some short-cuts are: ignorance (I know nothing, so any choice is fine), recognition (I recognize that, so let's do that), one-reason (I know one reason that is preferable, so let's do that), elimination (I know one reason not to take that option, so let's do one of the others), and good enough (that seems good enough, so let's do it).

Some subconscious systems, in addition to those identified by Panksepp, are: the default mode network (prepares the brain for intentional work), circadian rhythms (sleep and waking), infradian rhythms (such as menstruation), ultradian rhythms (blinking, urination, appetite), sensory winnowing (brain cutting down sensory input to manageable size), and bodily monitoring (homeostasis).

Some observable evidence of fault lines between our subconscious systems follows. Subconscious self-deception reduces stress, and smoothes social relations, but poses a nest of psychological difficulties. We subconsciously seek social status, evaluate women for child-bearing propriety, confuse correlation with causation, and sometimes enjoy violence. We conform to stereotypes, revise our memories, experience time fluidly, prefer evidence that supports our expectations, miss much of what is immediately before us, prefer ideas approved by many, rationalize our emotional predispositions, flip-flop, misconstrue randomness, believe we have control we lack, persevere in losing strategies to avoid losing what has been invested in the losing scheme, focus on now even when later is more pressing, perceive ourselves as alone, adopt the view of the most optimistic or pessimistic person in a group, take greater risks when successful in previous risk-taking, find small failures negligible though they may mount to catastrophic collapses, demonstrate over-confidence in rules and safety measures, tell distorted stories, expect good outcomes, prefer good news, prefer choices we make regardless of their outcomes, prefer the familiar, find stories about one distressed individual more compelling than statistics about thousands of similarly-situated persons, trust when hormonally predisposed to do so, entertain fuzzy mystical and hard-edged rational perceptions side-by-side, impose stereotypes when faced with lack of information, prefer to complete tasks or discrete portions of tasks, prefer our friends, accept credit and deflect blame, and reject opponent's good ideas.

As a neural proposition, we are more than we know, we are mostly unknown, and we remain persistently conflicted.

> *Objection 13: Sound and Fury.* [148] *An objector rejects Panksepp's outcomes because the research subjects are lower animals. The objector claims to be a unified being, not a mash-up of conflicted impulses. Panksepp's work defies common sense, and coppice talk is simple jibberish.* The author responds that Panksepp's work helps us understand the brain and human behavior in its many complexities. The concepts may be new, even disturbing, but they deserve attention.
>
> *Objection 14: Animal Holocaust.* [149] *Another objector scorns Panksepp for using innocent animals as research subjects in lethal procedures.* The author notes that Panksepp has addressed this troubling difficulty in his book; he decided, as have many researchers, that the ethical benefits outweigh the ethical costs.
>
> *Objection 15: Deprecating Reason.* [149] *Yet another objector complains that the coppice concept of consciousness demeans human rationality.* The author acknowledges the depreciation of reason implicit in the coppice of consciousness analogy, but believes it factually warranted. As a moral proposition, coppice consciousness recommends humility to all.

Objection 16: Unwarranted Exceptionalism. [150] *Still another objector castigates a detractor of reason for writing a book.* The author offers no substantial response.

No human can think what his brain will not process. We move to ancient African drives, see with ancient African eyes, and feel ancient African emotions. Pure reason does not exist; rationality is a fitful, passing state that sometimes deflects our more primitive feelings and drives. Philosophers have argued otherwise. Hume's Law argues that no moral assertion can derive from factual description. The author dissents, arguing that all thoughts are drives deflected by emotions deflected by evaluation. So, no non-emotional thinking exists. Behind every "is" lies an "ought" that led the thinker to think in the first place. Kant's ethics lean on pure reason, which does not exist, and so collapse. In the author's view, objectivity, strictly construed, does not exist, nor do impartial observers, or unified human consciousness. One suspects that physicists' search for a unified and elegant theory of everything leans upon a misconstruction of consciousness.

[157] Human consciousness is sexually divided, male and female. Research shows that, as male and female bodies differ, so too consciousness. Females are more empathetic and cooperative. Males play more. Females infer what others are thinking better than males. Males suffer more sociopathy, and are generally more aggressive and prone to violence. Males speak directly and prefer non-personal topics; women speak more frequently about emotions. Female infants like faces; boys prefer objects. Females have better language skills than men. Men better systemize (create ordered systems), and prefer mechanical toys. Men score better than women in math aptitude and three-dimensional rotation tasks. Females better see the field; males catch more details from a field. Most of these differences may relate to evolutionary pressures in ancient east Africa. It is likely a division of labor left the women, all caring for children, gathering foodstuffs near camp, while the men formed teams to hunt protein afar. Each sex evolved skills necessary to their usual tasks.

Objection 17: Misogyny. [160] *An objector argues that most male and female differences exist because of cultural prejudices.* The author responds that he is male and prejudiced. Nevertheless, research indicates that women and men differ substantially.

All humans participate in community, though some communities are sorely eroded. Communities themselves are persons of an odd sort, and are evolutionarily selected as much as individuals. Group habits offer survival benefit. Groups construct themselves, and deem themselves persons. When groups sicken, they may attribute their structure to gods. Then, members identify charismatic leaders and follow them godward. These choices are often destructive, since they obscure the origins of human structures in human choice. As to the existence of gods, no evidence lies at hand. The author, in *Cull*, seeks an ethic untroubled by god-talk, because divine moralities fail to satisfy.

Twentieth-century fascists (such as Hitler and Mussolini) and Statist communists (such as Stalin and Mao) offered a collectivist ethic bearing some resemblance to Quad sociality. All these focused on nations, not communities. Fascist or communist citizens find themselves obeying a State which is, for them, all. Fascism and Statist communism lost themselves in their coercions, horrendous violence, totalitarianism, and hierarchies.   Nothing of value emerged.

III. Member Culling. [165]

7.   Members Choosing: Simple Rules. [165]
What habits and attitudes help a member build meaningful community? What and how should we choose? Each of our decisions is bi-focal: we consider ourselves, and we consider our community amid the community of communities. What member choices lead toward meaningful communal existence? How does one flourish? What ought one to avoid? What ought one to seek? How do we cope with choices that turn out to be evils? One seeks to secure successful experiments, making them into principles and then habits. Even principles may change as experience deepens. Roman emperor Marcus Aurelius advised one to choose rules for life that are brief and address fundamentals. The author does so. He encourages Kate to listen while she is young, since she makes decisions of great import at this time of her life.

[169] *Nurture yourself.* You are your own project. Spend time daily building a flourishing life for yourself. Work less; address your problems; deliberate.

Observe yourself intently and compassionately. Learn yourself. Find perspective; you are what you are, neither more nor less. You have gifts to exercise, and oddnesses to recognize. Let friends help. Listen. Then indulge frank conversation between you and you.

Manage your inner narrative. Beneath consciousness, you tell yourself a private story that shapes you. Take control of this elusive tale. Write repeatedly about disappointing events; get them out onto paper. Gain perspective. Your inner narrative will improve. Let only those who know and love you contribute to your inner narrative.

Improve your habits. Habits change, for good or ill. Manage yours. Diligent conscious alterations of behaviors become routine, then semi-automatic, after a couple of months. A mentor may help early on. Ultimately, you will mentor yourself. Character is all your habits, considered together, in their jostle and swirl. Seek habits that leave you open, fair, and caring for others. Make yourself healthy, resilient, principled, focused, and ready to learn. Heraclitus said that character is fate. He was right.

Act deliberately. Act, then think, then act, then think. Oscillate. Plan, act, adjust. Never dawdle. Do and evaluate. Keep moving.

> *Objection 18:   Moronic Moralizing.* [180]   *An objector criticizes the author's moralizing. People embrace many moralities, often at odds with those of others. In ethics, one should stick to analyzing preconditions of knowledge, and leave moralizing to comic books.* The author responds that moralizing, in the history of ethics, is a philosophical staple. One can discuss what habits best serve humanity. One can mine history for those habits. One should. The author does.
> *Objection 19: Moral Dissimulation.* [188] *Another objector asserts that morality is raw self-deception. Were a person reliably invisible, that person would know no moral bounds. Every person is a creep, except to the extent others watch and censure him.* The author answers that no man is invisible, and each conducts his life in full view of his community. We suffer many psychological

conflicts, but also aspire and deliberate. We must seize the tiller of our boats and chart desirable courses. That is morality.

Nurture others. All are, sometimes invisibly, linked. When one benefits, all benefit. So too suffering. Nurturing others erodes traces of violence in us all. What if all were nurtured? What shape might that world take? None knows. It is an experiment worth undertaking.

Nurture intimate friendships. Humans make friends of one another. We grow intimate, knowing the interests and problems of others. We shape one another, share, and intervene. Intimacy approaches when annoyance blooms. You have trod the sacred ground of that friend and are bothered. Intimates share an identity. Friendship is like wearing one shoe together; there are blisters until you grow accustomed, forgiving, and coordinated. Friends speak bluntly and give freely. Choose friends carefully. Work hard to know them. Set time aside for building intimacy. Family is a subspecies of friendship, a sometimes fractured subspecies.

Talk with friends frankly and frequently. Friends talk. Spend about one-third of your life talking with friends. When you need to say something negative to a friend, do not delay. Procrastination injures friendship. Be frank; be blunt. When your friend confronts you, listen. Seek understanding.

Do constructive tasks with friends. Share goals with your friends, and act on them together. Cooperating in tasks cements friendship.

Value friendship itself. Friendship competes with other forms of human relation: isolation, competition, hatred, cynicism, for example. Choose friendship as your relational theory. In human relations, friendship is the good. Open yourself to friends of all sorts. Odd friends frequently exceed more common ones in commitment and serendipity. Resist intolerance in yourself; it is just an ancient African threat response.

[190] *Tolerate differences in others.* The oddness of others disturbs. We feel put off, unsettled. Since each person is unique, these differences can be great and pervasive. We may stereotype, fear, and even hate the weird other. Each such response is fatal to friendship. Our task is to express our own oddness, and to tolerate that of others. We differ in race, sex, body shape, health, histories and cultures, religions, types and degrees of intelligence, and moral preferences. Each can become a wall dividing one from another. Hidden among the diversities of humanity lie treasures: neurodiverse savants (odd folk with tremendous strange gifts). These gems may prove hardest to tolerate. Every person, even the smelly, foul-mouthed misanthropist, deserves toleration, even affection. One need not agree on much to be friends. And we need to protect the neurodiverse savants among us, for without them, we languish, even perish.

Build a wide-ranging group of friendly acquaintances. All friends are not intimates. One needs three to seven intimates, but also interest groups of various sizes, 150 circle-mates, and 1,500 community members, amidst a billion member Commons.

Address transitions in intimate friendship directly and compassionately. Even intimate friendships may suffer. When intimacy deteriorates, speak directly. Plan a transition, and care for the pain each feels. Do not discard the friendship utterly. Let it transition into something new. Although one is no longer intimate, one should remain friends. Friends continue to live in your consciousness, even if distant socially.

Repair strained friendships. If your friendship is broken, fix it. Speak face to face. When engaging those difficult conversations and planning repairs, speak of what has happened, what you intend, and what you feel. Tell your friend how your fractured relationship affects your self-perception. Learn what has happened to your friend, and discuss how to solve the problems between you. When you have agreed on a plan, be patient. Seek to understand and act with kindness. Approach your injured friend. If rebuffed, forgive, wait a bit, and try again (bidding). Keep at it as long as that makes sense. Friendships may end. If yours does, move on in life. Remain compassionate, but avoid grinding to a halt. You will grieve. Let grief happen; it will eventually pass.

Choose a mate by mature deliberation. Mate well, or do not mate. Much of life takes shape in intimacy with your mate. Take time. Choose well.

Attach to and mate with an intimate friend similar to you and your opposite-sex parent. Mate with an intimate friend. Build intimate friendship first, then explore sex. Sexual mating is a bonding event, very much like infantile attachment. It matters that a man reminds you of your father. It matters that a woman reminds you of your mother. Persons securely-attached to their own parents make more reliable mates. Insecure attachment can be addressed and with effort remediated.

Preserve your mate's trust. Avoid sex outside your mated relationship. Trysts compel lying (which you are unlikely to succeed in hiding), injure your children (because they need a surplus, not a deficiency, of parents), and destabilize your community.

[204] *Bear children only if you must.* Overpopulation threatens the entire human enterprise. Parenting rewards those disposed to parenting well, but tortures those disinclined. Attaching to an infant gulps great swaths of time, energy, and attention. Bearing children brings joy, but also suffering. Most people need not bear children, though all need to parent. If you lack enthusiasm for wretched smells, scarce sleep, incessant wailing, and scant time with your mate, consider doing something other than parenting, something else mankind needs.

Human population in 1800 A.D. was one billion. The last of our seven billion was added in less than forty years. Thomas Malthus argued that population will inevitably exceed food production, leading to global disasters. These nightmares, though delayed by technology, still approach. Not only food, but many resources, are proving inadequate for unrestrained procreation. We foul our nest. Where a community nurtures its women and girls, birth rates fall dramatically.

The optimal number of humans, that number which can sustainably survive, is a moral concept. One weighs quality of life, the survival of non-human species, the value of endeavors surpassing mere survival, and the privacy of procreative choices. To make survivable choices, one must look far to the future and value the humans who will live then. In the author's view, arguably, earth can safely sustain no more than one billion humans. Any greater numbers imperil the transgenerational future of humanity.

Do not bear children unless you are willing to attach to and nurture them. Someone, usually the mother, will need to spend vast expanses of time with her baby during its first years. Separation damages infants and toddlers, risking fundamental emotional insecurity. So, procreation is not a right, but a calling. One needs not only desire for babies, but also appropriate supports and circumstances, to adequately rear children. The demands children make stunt other endeavors, including friendship with one's spouse. There are endeavors in life other than reproducing yourself, grand efforts, deep explorations. Children depend upon many undertaking those other endeavors, those culture-building glories, for their well-being and survivable future.

Some glorify child-bearing. Those attitudes seemed natural when one could not avoid making babies where one loved another. But vasectomy and reliable contraception have arrived. You need not bear children to flourish. The gusts of life blow upon more organs than the uterus alone. Life endorses more activities than mere reproduction. Though human psychology deeply supports procreation, we resist a host of natural drives in living together in modern societies. We do so, in most instances, quite happily. So, bear children only if you must.

You do need, however, to parent. Be an alloparent, supporting the nurture of your friends' or community's children. Procreate only if it is your calling.

Attach to your young child. Young children need age-appropriate interaction with parental adults who are persistently attentive, enthusiastic, enamored, safe, emotionally responsive, exploration-loving, and tantrum-dampening. The big job of biological parents lies in shaping a team of alloparents to support them, nurture their children, and meet the children's diverse needs. A baby's attachment falls first to the primary parent (usually mother), then slowly expands to include father and parent-like others (alloparents). By consistency (regardless of the child's response), create a secure bond between the child, his primary parents, and alloparents. Humans breed cooperatively. Isolated parents are not the human gold standard. Parents lead parental care teams for their children. Failed infant attachment can hobble the attachment-deficient adult and ring through subsequent generations, injuring each tremendously.

> *Objection 20: Genetic Determinism.* [223] *An objector disputes the importance of parental attachment. An infant's genetics determine most outcomes. Separated identical twins share remarkable similarities, despite maturing in different environments.* The author responds that genetics affect much, but determine little. Infant attachment to a primary caregiver is no negligible happenstance. Research shows that mother-infant bonding determines the capacity of the mature infant to bond to and trust others. Genetics matter; so too parental bonding.
>
> *Objection 21: Presumptuous Parental Puffing.* [224] *Another objector complains that the author is childless. What could he know of parenting?* The author responds that he alloparents and step-parents. His viewpoint may have value for some. Given the planetary epidemic of ill-parented children, it is apparent that bearing children does not guarantee insight into nurture of children.

[224] *Nurture children.* Childless adults need to parent. The drive to parent may be as potent as the urge to have sex. Nurturing children matters. If there is to be a future without ceaseless bloodshed, the door to that goodness opens by nurturing every child. Child neglect is a global epidemic. Human misery matches the burgeoning number of ill-nurtured infants. They mature and savage neighbors. Family exceeds genetic relatedness. Invite caring others to join. Make them alloparents. Let them contribute. No father and mother, alone, have sufficient resources to parent a child. Children are the future Commons. It will be as good as they are.

> *Objection 22: Sacred Children.* [228] *An objector asserts that marriage exceeds other intimacies, and children are god-given. No others, especially not communities at large, have an interest. Children give meaning. Make some if you want some.* The author responds that expansive families are the human norm. Alloparents do not intrude, but

rather help. Marriage is but one theory of mating. Quad mating includes others as alloparents.

Objection 23: Nurture Delirium. [229] *Another objector complains that nurture offers less than the author claims. People, even well-loved people, have flaws. Humans behave badly. Nurture cannot fix that.* The author answers that many people succumb to passions. People, however, are as inclined to do well as to do poorly. Quad nurture exceeds mere education, which is hobbled by factory structure and egalitarian theory. Nurture is individualized mentorship by a team of alloparents. Nurture may accomplish wonders. We should try it.

Objection 24: Non-Parent Parents. [230] *Yet another objector complains about advising others not to bear children. We are born to reproduce. Failure to do so frustrates the most basic human drive.* The author suggests that we restrain many impulses voluntarily, and can do so with breeding. Much that is natural we resist. We should speak realistically of the challenges of parenting, and cease telling false tales of its wonders. If informed, people (mostly women) will voluntarily avoid unwanted pregnancy. No mother longs to watch children, hers or others, suffer in hunger or neglect. Non-nurture of children is an all-too-common obscenity.

Learn from children you nurture. As one mentors, she learns from students. Mentors adapt to the child's needs and abilities. Nurturing children teaches adults to nurture themselves and others.

Spend copious time with children you nurture. One cannot rush mentoring. Supervise and enrich your charge's explorations. Do not stint time.

Restrain pre-pubescents. Collaborate with adolescents. Repair ruptures. With young children, foster attachment, coerce lightly without striking, avoid comparisons to others, build good habits in them, and keep yourself refreshed. Set boundaries; enforce them. With adolescents, stand alongside. Advise. Build roots of adult friendship. Offer suggestions and ideas, but let the adolescent act. Follow up on how things worked out. Analyze failures, but avoid lamenting them. Report your own adolescent troubles. Repair ruptures with the adolescent. You are, after all, the adult.

Persevere through difficulties. Help others do so as well. Build resilience in yourself. Recall insights, take initiative, keep some independence, be creative, and find some humor. Rely on your simple rules, be humble, and keep learning. Control yourself. Manage your problems deliberately.

Do first what matters most. Prioritize your time. Leave trivial matters for gaps between critical ones. Let important matters dominate.

Give. Give to friends liberally. Give to strangers wisely. Even if you are poor yourself, give. When possible, make the world a more equitable place.

[237] *Make Peace.* Conflicts emerge when people are getting to know one another. Welcome that. Be prepared to help them care, despite differences. Avoid truces. Truces delay, but fail to resolve, conflicts. Irenism (the author's term for pacifism) values diverting aggression toward understanding, opposes wars, redresses injustice without violence, practices consensus, advocates personal sacrifice, and opposes punishments. Some irenists oppose all killing (including animals) and oppose State coercion of any sort (anarchists), preferring powerless consensual decision-making. Irenists have lived in every historical period. Some prominent irenists and irenist traditions are: Brahmanism (*ahimsa*), Buddha, Mo, Socrates, Jesus, French Cathars, Anabaptists, Thoreau, Te Whiti o Rongomai, Kant, Tolstoy, Gandhi, King, Gyatso (the Dalai

Lama), and Tutu. Irenists oppose murder, and coercion of any sort. They build understanding and embrace enemies. Irenists view peace as a social structure to be erected, like a brick building. Most people are of waffling irenist sentiment. Oddly, irenism fails to guide our politics or temper our military ventures. Irenists prefer suffering themselves when others suffer, hoping to shame perpetrators. Irenists know that affection subverts anger, and that one cannot both war and prosper.

Within cadres, peacemakers build deeper intimacies when conflicts emerge. To mediate one listens to disputants, resolves factual discrepancies, and probes. Then a mediator suggests a story concerning the conflict that the parties share, and a path toward revised normalcy between the parties. Some conflicts cannot be resolved; these should be recognized and honored by both parties. Their conversations can proceed, now without fisticuffs.

> *Objection 25: Pacifistic Yammer.* [252] *An objector complains that irenists are never so proactive as the author suggests. Irenists lose when guns deploy. They lack the fortitude to die for their convictions.* The author notes lack of gravitas in some irenists, including himself. Others, however, war against war, demonstrating military hardiness in the face of conflicts. Consider, Jesus, Gandhi, and King. The irenist war exceeds military conflict. Irenists build a just world without coercion. Irenists may, in fact, be winning that war.

> *Objection 26: Abandoning Justice.* [255] *Another objector asserts that irenists neglect justice. The author would have communities reintegrate offenders, which licenses sociopaths to prey again and again. One must punish, even execute. To deter, mankind must retribute.* The author agrees that humans need rough justice. Yet, for millennia, we have whipped and hung, to no avail. Justice systems now pass out money, but offer little solace to victims. Our thirst for vengeance should be diverted to improving the circumstances that led to crime. Criminals warn us that we have paid too little attention, ignored ongoing problems. Criminals, even sociopaths, do evil when we stand by, hands in pockets, doing nothing. Irenism reorients justice toward the future, and retributive fury toward nurture.

> *Objection 27: Violent Urgency.* [257] *Yet another objector disputes the value of peace. Peaceful cultures stagnate. No one can fairly ask people to wait generations for change. Justice lives in the cracks between violent opposition and consolidating peace. Death moves the societal ball forward.* The author disputes that irenism leads to quiet stagnation. Violence fails to improve circumstances. Stagnation derives from overpopulated anonymous States, not irenism. Who can change large groups? None. Meaningful communities, ripe for change, await kithdom. Deaths change nothing. Sons of violent martyrs mature, indulging vendettas.

Correct yourself first; listen humbly. Humans have serious perceptual error built into their brains. We perceive poorly. Worst, we doubt we misperceive and ache to fix the perceptions of others. Cause for humility abounds. Fix yourself; listen to others intently. They may well be right.

Live in candor. Tell truth in word and action. Truth-telling proves difficult. Inflict no senseless injury. Perform your promises. Never deceive tactically; it shreds the fabric of trust. Act in good faith.

Show affection. We express less affection than we feel. Learn how a friend prefers to have affection expressed toward her. Give her that.

Laugh. If friendship has a sound, it is laughter. Avoid cruelty, at which some laugh. Some laughing is not funny at all. Make jokes about yourself. Life is funny; if you disagree, pay better attention.

[263] *Support, but question, others.* One prospers when others prosper. So, support their endeavors. Every person conforms. Yet, in their depths, no person can conform utterly. This uncomfortable duality cannot, should not, be resolved. All are both conformist and recalcitrant. Fools run much of the world. Speak up. Ask questions. Be polite, but firm. Do not be shamed or shushed into silence. You might be the majority of one who saves the mewling crowd from itself. Irenists wield sharp questions as do soldiers their swords. If you are utterly ignored, drop the matter. Move on, but leave your door open a crack. Keep your dissent a live, if neglected, issue.

Work to help others. Choose a job that helps people. Service to human well-being makes life meaningful. Ask about service first, money second. Find work that suits your oddities. Avoid overwork. Well-utilized leisure makes life worth living.

Eat for nutrition. Make your body healthy. Many of us are fat and diseased. Food is a factor. Eat well and simply.

Protect your sleep. Sleep is biologically determined. You can ignore your internal clock, but at a price in disease and misery. Retire and wake regularly. Protect those hours.

Stay active. Human ancestors walked to live. We read. Alternate sitting with moving.

Flourish. Exceed mere existing. Grow your inner life. Expand into other people. If you do not feel good most of the time, ready to cope, then you are not flourishing. Adjust.

Keep life simple. Stay small. Choose elegant understatement. Get fancy only with your exuberant inner life. Otherwise, be merely functional.

Stay orderly. Time spent finding your keys is wasted. Keep a calendar, put things away. Stay focused.

Keep life quiet. Noise abounds, and brings in its wake distraction. Find and foster quiet.

Season life with difficult tasks. Choose some tasks that exceed you. Learn your way into them. Do no fool's errands, but neither stay simply safe. Some risks merit the effort.

Stay open to novelty. Seek odd places and things. Talk with people of strange perceptions. Welcome serendipity in the midst of your well-managed existence.

Embrace, but resist, aging. You are aging. As decades slide past, reduce physical labor and increase mental work. Good habits grow easier as you get older. Keep your body in good shape. When the time comes, manage your dying well.

Endure illness patiently. When sick, be patient. Rest, and let your body heal itself. Do quiet tasks that require little. Avoid worry.

Live from mortality's viewpoint. Survey your life from its end. One need not welcome death; neither clutch at life.

Be patient with grief. People pass. Humans grieve loss. Grief has a course to run. Let it. Grief is not rational; do not ask it to be reasonable or stay on schedule.

Cherish faith. [273] Know it or not, you have faith. You may avoid religious institutions, but still have faith. Much that is crucial to meaningful life cannot be proved; some matters even elude lucid description. Those are articles of faith. Some people of faith accept that gods speak to men, leaving literatures or insights. Another sort of faith pretends less. Its core is the conviction that life exceeds our ideas about it. Keep your faith, whatever its shape, safe.

> *Objection 28: Faith is Hubris.* [277] *An objector spits out the author's view of faith. None knows gods. One barely knows what can be observed. We know what we can prove by controlled experiment. All else is dreck. Religious literatures offer nothing of value.* The author answers that, despite the failings of institutional religions and literatures, much good and many good people have emerged religious institutions. This does not excuse the evils perpetrated by religious institutions, but is another fact about religious institutions. Empiricism too is an unworkable life theory. None doubts his wife's existence. None is satisfied with raw fact; we yearn for meaning. Faith embraces not what is irrational, but what may be supra-rational.

[280] *Keep just enough possessions.* Stuff confuses us. What matters most has no monetary value: friendship, wisdom, harmony, knowledge, peace, cooperation, well-being, beauty, justice, equity. Nevertheless, many adore money. Sages advise against wealth: Jesus, Gandhi, Confucius, Socrates, Lao Tzu, Isaiah, Cicero, Mencius, Seneca, Mozi, Muhammad, Thoreau, Aristotle, Russell, Heraclitus, Isocrates, Godwin, and Walzer concur. Friends devoted to money should be loved, but cajoled about their obsession with wealth. Ill-gotten wealth brings shame in its wake.

> *Objection 29: Demeaning Wealth.* [285] *An objector argues that money is not a moral topic; its uses are. Wealth too has no meaning. What matters is how one employs wealth.* The author counters that wealth comes from activity, and so can be considered morally. Most wealth begs scrutiny. Wealth twists its possessors. Make just enough money.

Choose a small, well-maintained home. Residences are complex tools supporting life. They are grand when filled with the remarkable friends of a wise resident. Make your home a place for mental and social excellences. Avoid the grand or fancy.

Live locally. Choose a neighborhood peopled by friends and live there. Our bloated cities demand long commutes and endless dashing about. Avoid mobility. Put down roots. Work near home.

Manage your learning. Mass education fails us. Students differ; how could all sit in one classroom with one teacher? Someone is being missed. Educate yourself, with your mentors' help. Use schools when they serve your education. Never surrender your learning. Your education is your lifelong duty and privilege.

Identify and flee sociopaths. Sociopaths cannot care what happens to others. Messes and debacles cascade around sociopaths. You cannot help sociopaths. Perhaps no one can. Make a professional referral, then flee.

Address resident evils. Some evil one cannot flee. Evils may lie within us or our community. We build and create, but we also etch and erode. If you identify evil, question yourself. Then be bold. To address local evils, one can acquiesce, engage, observe, intervene, protest, persevere, or, in emergencies, restrain.

Pursue goals. Set goals, then break them into daily tasks. Decide what to do this year. Decide what you hope to accomplish in your lifetime. Think about how you want human life to be long after your own death; work to make your existence contribute to that outcome.

Modify your body sparingly. Customizing appearance is an ancient human tradition. We fluff, cut, tattoo, eye-line, style, gloss, and upgrade appearance. We may soon be able to wed devices to ourselves or shift our genetics. Fashion is fickle. Alter yourself with care, Kate. Adopt innovations late.

Engage your community. Population overload makes humans withdraw. Resist. Build a cadre and community. Work toward a smaller, deliberated humanity.

[295] *Craft a good death.* You may be so lucky as to die without working at it. Some, however, have to plan death because ceasing proves elusive. Life can grow so bounded that it proves no longer worth living. Keep living, despite pain, so long as you can do something meaningful for your community. When meaning fails you, you may need a plan. Shape your plan by talking with your doctor, your attorney, and your friends. Many plans are possible; two appear preferable. First, one may die by barbiturate overdose with physician assistance (in some locations). Second, one may die by nitrogen gas asphyxiation. Avoid involving your friends in preparations. Tell them. Comfort and love them. But prepare alone. Having a plan may help you, even if you choose not to enact it.

>   *Objection 30: Neglecting Rational Deduction.* [298] *An objector dismisses the author's eclectic approach to morality. All ethics should proceed by rational deduction from universal principles.* The author responds that rationality is too sandy a foundation for life. Kantian duty ethics and utilitarianism both disappoint. Broad review of wisdom offers help in making good decisions.

>   *Objection 31: An Offense of Particularity.* [299] *Another objector complains that other moral rules could have been chosen. The author's "simple rules" reflect the author, not humanity.* The author answers that he most happily entertains alternative rules. We all should work on improving the simple rules together. Persisting in moral indecision injures just as pursuing a misguided principle might. We should work toward consensus on these basic matters.

>   *Objection 32: Truncated Individuality.* [301] *Yet another objector fears that any set of rules creates bland conformity. Rules stifle individuals.* The author rejoins that the odd duck needs vast latitude to be himself, but not so most people. Most appreciate thoughtfully drawn recommendations. The simple rules are that.

>   *Objection 33: Praising Death.* [301] *Still another objector depreciates the author for telling people how to kill themselves. Suicide offends god. Depressed people may fall prey to this advice.* The author counters that he knows nothing of god's view of death. He offers some advice, and asks for some privacy for those contemplating a good, planned death.

[302] The author lists the simple rules, for convenience.

IV. Communal Culling. [305]

> 8. *Communities Choosing: Thanatoid Transgenerational Deliberation.*
> [309]
> Members and communities affect one another, but members take the moral lead. Thinking about how to shape communities requires free thinking. The way we presently structure life together needs extensive revision. We drown in ill-wisdom.
> Thanatoid transgenerational deliberation envisions life thousands of years into the future. We cannot see; we squint. We see better when we take the perspective of people near life's end (thanatoid perspective). We see better when we recognize that though we die after a few decades, the human community may persevere for hundreds of thousands, even millions, of years (transgenerational perspective). All those involved in such deliberation may not be old; all will, however, be mature. We deliberate, when we cull, promising community experiments from failures and extrapolate (deliberative perspective). We look for thanatoid savants, people with special gifts for imagining our future. We grant such people no power, since we prefer that no person exercise power to coerce. When one peers forward in time, one sees that we can deliver meaningful community to our descendants, that we must cast off useless structures and ideas for fresh ones, that we must go slowly and choose with care, and that we need to be able to see how meaningful community can persevere at least 30,000 years from now.

> > *Objection 34: Predictive Astigmatism. [316] An objector complains that the distant future is invisible. We can neither see nor predict so far. Humans plan tomorrow, not next week. Talk of 30,000 years hence lets nutcases project hallucinations on a blank screen.* The author counters that man is changing, maturing. We are positioned to choose how to flourish. We see our impacts and deficiencies. We are African primates with attendant wonders and flaws. Where the future blurs, alternative visions arise. We can experiment with those. Peering, we will see further. Critically, we must stop crushing our seers, and start mining them. Optimism is warranted.

> > *Objection 35: Dissembling Revolution. [317] Another objector spits out the author for preaching revolution, then denying he does so. When one changes marriage, education, economics, family life, nation-states, the military, and death wholesale, that is revolution. The author is dangerous; he is utopian. He shares views of the worst of recent mass murderers. Ignore him.* The author apologizes for scaring the objector. Much should change. Change will be painful. But the author seeks no revolution. Nor do we need revolution. Society trends toward kithdom, unawares. The author asks the objector to avoid wild hyperbole in criticisms. Such is the bane of our day, truncating every conversation. The author declines revolution; it betrays poverty of patience.

Society suffers misdirections. These we should correct. We should link people together in friendship. We should depopulate. We should consume only sustainable products, and direct inventive energy toward needful technologies. We should fashion dense communities of limited footprint, to make room for other species. We should shift values from money to relationships, from financial to social capital. We should stop warring and build a wealth of conflict-resolution resources. We should limit coercive activities to emergencies, and then to designated martials only (the author promises explanation below). We should open virtual connectivity to all and freely offer every form of knowledge, which the Commons holds in trust. We should amend human identification from nations and land and football teams to communities and the Commons. These topics might serve as kindling for the Commons thanatoid transgenerational deliberation.

Humanity will transition to kithdom slowly. It may take centuries or millennia. Our self-inflicted injuries have cumulated for millennia. None need wait for the dawdling many to adopt kithdom. Deepen intimacies. Form a cadre, then a circle. If others nearby have done likewise, commence a community, an economy, an alternative to anonymous conformity within States. Put the technology wizard among you to the task of building an infrastructure for the Commons dialogue. Do it whatever way works for you. There is no template. Tell your grandchildren to keep encouraging chatterers to get serious about flourishing. But most, flourish yourself. Do it for you and those you love, Kate.

9.   *Quad Community Life*. [326]

Quad communities shape themselves: cadre, circle, community, commons. They also reshape politics itself. Perhaps, Quad communities practice anti-politics. For in kithdom, no States exist.

Quad communities differ from States by virtually eliminating coercion, abandoning law as a theory of human relations, putting discussion of human structures and futures on the table every day, shifting decision-making from distant experts to small communities, encouraging communities to adopt social experiments and report results to the Commons, and suggesting periodic reshaping of each community to adopt the best recent ideas. Kithdom also differs from States in demanding the discipline of consensus, refusing majoritarian coercion, discouraging mobility and changes of residence, addressing fundamental moral and ethical questions, making choices in these debates community by community, cherishing diversity, tasting a bit of asceticism, relying on local action, and relishing the global community of communities in Quad sociality.

States have rationales, which the author reviews. Some argue gods authorize States; god chooses a king or noble class (kingdom, aristocracy, plutocracy, timocracy). Others support social contract theories; ancestors agreed, so we must as well (Rousseau, Hobbes, Hume, Locke, Kant). Many have argued that might makes right; those who can compel have a right to do so (Nietzsche, Han Fei Tsu, Hitler, most majoritarian democracies). Some believe that enlightened bureaucracies should rule, imposing a system of compassionate order (Confucius, Mencius, Rawls). A few believe that governments should be as small as possible (Nozick, Thoreau). Some dispute the validity of any government whatsoever (Gandhi, Bakunin, Godwin).

Strong reasons exist for adopting kithdom. Kithdom admits no coercion, except in emergency circumstances, and, so, respects persons. Consent rules; consensus is the norm. Coercion is immoral; it engenders bad faith, fear, and retaliation. Coercion is ineffective; coerced people comply until their first opportunity to resist or rebel. Coercion corrupts; the moral sense of those charged with coercing erodes, leading to power-mongering. Consensus works; all are valued and heard. Gods endorse consensus (the author makes a tongue-in-cheek natural law argument for kithdom). Kithdom effectively addresses wanton deviancy by supervised reintegration of offenders into their communities. Communities retain a truncated, but effective, degree of coercive capability in their martials. Kithdom supports the cooperative impulses in humans. And kithdom unleashes creativity that is presently suppressed.

Objection 36: Informal Oppressions. [354] *An objector fears Quad sociality will open the door to oppressions eradicated with great effort over the last 500 years. Hosts of half-baked ideas may dominate communities. If we seek wisdom, the collective insight to date has been that anonymous bureaucratic States are much preferred over wacky oppressive hamlets.* The author responds that some communities will undoubtedly err. One learns by error. Centuries of slow, deliberate change may pass before kithdom predominates. Communities of remarkable wonder may also emerge. Our "rights and freedoms" culture of coercion serves us poorly. We can live in a more deeply humane manner.

Objection 37: Big Brother Commons. [357] *Another objector complains that the Commons is global government. Will not some communities prosper while other languish? We need coercion; it smacks those that need smacking.* The author clarifies that the Commons is governed by consensus among human communities. The Commons helps keep mankind working toward good purposes. Only martials coerce, and they do so seldom and with grave limitations. Information and dialogue are tasks of the Commons. The Commons exists so that some communities can influence others. It might prove necessary to restrain a community. If that happens, the Commons should determine how it missed that glaring problem.

Objection 38: Quagmire of Consensus. [358] *Yet another objector asserts consensus will not work. Consensus grants dissenters a veto, which will hobble communities. No alternatives to majoritarian coercion exist.* The author answers that consensus is not unanimity. Consensus includes acquiescing dissenters. Communities act, awaiting outcomes. Majorities need their dissenters to clarify decisions. Never ignore them. Convince them to acquiesce, or revise proposals, or wait. Consensus cannot work in bloated institutions of strangers accustomed to coercing. Consensus requires interpersonal relationships, and their attendant preference for accommodation. Coercion alienates. We presently cook in the cauldron of coercion's incivilities. Can we agree to respect one another and try something new?

Objection 39: Bridling Corruption. [361] *Still another objector complains that the author understates the human inclination to ill-behaviors. Without coercion, society turns ugly. We need potent oversight, with penalties in tow.* The author agrees that many presently suffer moral collapse. Matters improve as nurture improves. When global nurture prevails, we may still find that some remain rapacious. We might have to coerce them. But, generally, humans are as inclined to good as evil.

Objection 40: Abandoning States. [363] *Yet still another objector asserts that States solve problems, not create them. Look. Life spans have doubled, relative peace prevails, crimes decline, technologies proliferate, wealth grows, and science marches. Who can gainsay that track record?* The author replies that the objector whitewashes States. State solutions are as bad as the problems they address. Several factors have improved the world, not just the State.

Kithdom is not tribalism resuscitated. Kithdom's members stand deeply educated, thoroughly nurtured global participants in a high technical culture. We can dispense with coercions, for the most part.

10.   Nurturing Members. [365]
Communities nurture members by insuring members find physical sustenance (shelter, clothing, food, water), meaningful activity, well-fitted productive activity, constructive leisure, and deep socialization by means of mentoring and technical training. Communities nurture members by supporting well-structured cooperative contracts for forming, sustaining, and living within cadres, circles, and communities.

> *Objection 41: Absent Intimacies.* [372] *An objector notes that intimacy is not nearly so intense as the author represents. Friends can be replaced. Even spouses and children neglect one. Quad sociality will not work, because friendship is not all that intimate.* The author recognizes that intimacy is an endangered species in America. Many cultural demands wither intimacy. To find intimacy, one must shelter portions of life from that inimical heat. One works at intimacy. It cannot be purchased off the shelf.

We tend to overcoerce. Dissenters, the odd person, people of flighty talk, bad breath, or infrequent bathing: all get coerced. Coercion and nurture work poorly together. People who are different deserve a place at our common table. They bring value. Neurodiverse people innovate, exhibit admirable courage, are not captured by normalcy, and gainsay committees. Among the ranks of the neurodiverse stand savants, upon whom our weal and future lean. Neurodiverse savants inoculate members against crippling arthritis of mind; they rattle chains of conformity; they birth tomorrow. Not only individuals, but also communities under the influence of neurodiverse savants, may become savant. These open vistas neurotypical communities never consider. We injure ourselves when we persecute neurodiverse savants.

Even outliers, who spit out their communities in favor of isolation, deserve nurture. We should relate to and support them, to the extent they permit. For, despite their prickly personas, they remain members.

Communities nurture members by keeping them secure. Where all irenic interventions have failed to prevent community injury, communities may coerce wanton members. These maximally-minimal coercions aim to use the least force possible on the smallest number of persons for the minimum time necessary. Every intervention, even where potent, is not coercive. Coercion occurs where someone making a choice is effectively deflected from that preference by another, where the other is not a trusted friend acting in good faith, or where an emergency exists threatening the chooser's well-being or prospects. Choosers bear some responsibility for the coercions they suffer.

[386] When coercion of a member proves necessary, the militance of irenism reveals itself. A priority in meaningful community is creating a safe environment within which to live and experiment. Wanton actors fail to care about outcomes for others. Coercion within kithdom commences with a wanton actor's friends. They do the irenic work of caring for and convincing a member to desist. When they fail, community coercion steps up. Coercion aims to address the problem behaviors and reintegrate the wanton actor into his community. In coercions, communities should seek Commons input. Others may have faced similar difficulties. Coercions occur in an ascending order of

severity: mandatory evaluation and counseling, mandatory reconciliation efforts, travel and association limitations, prohibitions on dangerous substances, random monitoring, uninterrupted monitoring, transfer to preferable community, and transfer to an encapsulated therapeutic community. Because of coerced transfers, every community may need to welcome wanton transferees.

> *Objection 42: Coercive Paternalism.* [389] *An objector argues that people make such poor decisions that wiser heads must intervene to protect them from themselves. We must legislate people's personal choices if we are ever to have a semblance of sanity in our societies.* The author answers that no one knows what errors should be quashed or who should choose. Communities must experiment with meaning and observe results. Humanity does not presently know what forms of life may prove best. So, we guess and hope. Many look to the past, to geniuses long dead, and call their rote formulae good enough. Coercion does not create compliance, but rather recalcitrance. To make members wise, we must mentor them to be such.

11.   Nurturing Communities. [391]

Communities exceed their members and require nurture. One nurtures her community by content-full talking, demonstrative affection, frank assessments, linking one's identity to her community, enduring with a community, keeping one's life simple, forging necessary contracts with other communities, expressing oneself into the community's life, dissenting from a community's erroneous decisions, and discovering useful exemplars and advice from the Commons.

Communities should consider, but need not adopt, the following policies. First, a martial designee may be needed. Such a person is a peacemaker, and controls the instruments designed to kill humans in a community. Communities may need to pool their martial designees to form temporary militias. The author endorses an exponential consent rule, in which the number of consenting communities endorsing formation of a militia is the integer two to the power of the number of martials to be joined. Second, the concept of property should be amended, since economic inequality poisons communities. Property held at the time of death passes to one's community. Regular transfers of excess to struggling communities should be expected. The origins of wealth are suspect. Wealth should be an embarrassment, not cause for praise. Excess should support less-productive members. That said, communities should not forbid wealth to its maker. People differ. Some lives generate excess. Wealth may derive from a person's essence. Third, communities need to discuss and care for human genetic fitness. Given our control of our environment, we no longer can rely on hostile circumstances to keep the human genome adaptive. We must prune ourselves. Fourth, our culture consumes resources that cannot be regenerated. Communities should consider setting aside a generational reserve to help descendants address the depletions our current consumption and overpopulation creates. Communities, when structuring themselves, weigh dualities of competing interests: communal versus private ownership, indifference versus involvement, old versus young, female versus male, and aspiration versus disillusion.

[404] Communities may adopt evils. One hopes sister communities will intervene early, preventing the eruption of ill-deliberate communal acts. Regardless, war must be avoided. If war occurs, the Commons should stop to reevaluate its function. Weapons of war should not be manufactured, except to

provision martials. If an erring community proves recalcitrant, neighboring communities should address the difficulty with militant non-violent activism in an approach of increasingly invasive intervention. Neighbors should inquire and listen, seek to persuade, immigrate into the community to create a dissenting voice, protest visibly and persistently, station observers with recording devices, meta-protest (which consists in alleviating the root causes of a community's evil acts), boycott and decline to collaborate, and, finally, discorporate the wanton community. If such occurs, the Commons should deliberate causes, and remediate as needed. For the Commons has, under such coercive circumstances, plainly gone astray.

> *Objection 43: Irenic Coercion.* [410] *An objector asserts that pacifists lack gumption. The sociopath is serious; he does damage for its entertainment value. To address the wanton community, one brings overwhelming responsive coercion, or nothing at all.* The author agrees that sociopaths present dangers. So too our own prejudices and blindnesses. All must intervene with others as needed. Sociopaths were once children, not leaders of wanton communities. A host of errors over decades promoted the sociopath to leadership and power. We must coerce under such circumstances. We should do so with restraint, in a manner that expresses our values.
> *Objection 44: Utopian Blather.* [412] *Another objector finds irenic kithdom silly. Violence demands perpetual armed vigilance.* The author insists his is no utopia, but rather a decisional scheme for improving matters. Practicality describes the usual. *Cull* contemplates a degree of change that departs the usual. The author could be wrong. Experiment. Report. Prove your point. Will the objector confess if experiments prove him wrong?

12.   Nurturing the Commons. [415]

The Commons conducts a global conversation about human life. The Commons serves as a global fire pit around which the human tribe gathers to sort itself.

The Commons has tasks. At a minimum they include the following: maintaining an accessible repository of global knowledge, facilitating innovation exchanges between communities, structuring the global dialogue about human weal and the farsight horizon, recording contracts, presenting alternative community structures for consideration, and creating an agenda and format for Commons participation.

The Commons is not a global State. Though deeply influential, the Commons lacks power to coerce. States exist because overpopulation creates scarcity that leads to pillaging. States sunder human relationships. States privilege some by depriving many. The State withers, as a theory. Persistent war, plagues, starvation, obscenities of wealth maldistribution, and so forth: the list goes on and on. Vital communities find States a threat. One need not revolt. Build a community. Create the Commons. Let States atrophy. Lavish indifference upon them.

To prevail, communities must remain small. Humans have limited abilities. Do not overwhelm members socially by letting numbers bloat. That leads to threat and States. Keep everyone known and valued. Permit no anonymity. Small grows meaningful. States pare member life, slashing the intimacy members require, subverting their communities. Resist. Nurture your community and yourself. Deny the State your loyalty or attention.

Objection 45: Technical Regression. [422] *An objector fears that reducing human population to one billion might cause technical regression in which humanity loses core technologies on which we depend. We might plummet back into the stone age.* The author counters that population will plummet one way or another. We stress the planet and ourselves. We decide not whether to reduce population, but only *how* it will be reduced. Technical innovations might slow; that might allow our moral deliberations to keep pace.

Objection 46: Hopeless Optimism. [423] *Another objector complains that Quad sociality is hysterical in its optimism.* The author declines to apologize for being hopeful, and hopes he is not hysterical.

V.   Culling Futures. [425]

13.   A Thousand Generations. [425]

We choose together. We choose in the ongoing stream of humanity, launched from a deep African past, hurtling toward we know not what. So we guess and hope. Despite our fragility and evanescence, our thoughts and choices ring forward millennia. We boom transgenerationally. Let us take care with our legacy.

A desirable future commences today. Militate, but be patient. Act potently, knowing we do not well envision the distant impacts our choices generate. Leave big talk to chatterers. Devote yourself to irenic change. Love your community, your friends. See as far as you are able.

Communities persist long after their members. The human community of communities, if it proves wise, has a lifespan limited only by that of the universe itself. You are yourself, nothing more. Give what you can. Build what you are able. Humanity is more than you and me. We crew a species-spanning ship, sails filled with gusts of life. We do our part, then die, confident in others to chart a constructive course. As have we.

14.   Answering Kate. [428]

One makes good decisions by culling conduct well. Good decisions build meaningful community. Bad decisions erode meaningful community. Recognize your nature. See where it leads and the weaknesses it entails. Choose rules for yourself that promise well-being for you and your friends and community. Make peace, nurture children, learn how to agree with others, work meaningfully, and die well. Keep unborn generations near the front of your mind. Be devoted to flourishing. With such attitudes deeply-rooted in yourself, you will make good decisions, Kate.

15.   Conclusion: Meaningful Community. [429]

Humanity can make better decisions. Books are thin, while humans are thick. Still, a good book is not nothing, if one lets it in. We can create meaning-laden lives in a meaning-laden Commons. Finely-elaborate your culling, Kate. Peer forward. Cull. Act. Flourish.

BIBLIOGRAPHY

Ackerman, Jennifer, "How Bacteria In Our Bodies Protect Our Health," *Scientific American* 306, Issue 6 (June 2012): 37-43.

Akyol, Mustafa. *Islam Without Extremes: A Muslim Case for Liberty*. New York: W. W. Norton & Company, 2011, 2013.

Alighieri, Dante. *De Monarchia*. Translated by Aurelia Henry. San Bernadino, California: Veritatis Splendor Publications, 2012.

Angier, Natalie, "Even Among Animals: Leaders, Followers and Schmoozers," *New York Times* (April 6, 2010).

Appiah, Kwame Anthony. *Experiments in Ethics*. Cambridge, Massachusetts: Harvard University Press, 2008.

Aquinas, Thomas. *Aquinas's Shorter Summa: St. Thomas Aquinas's Own Concise Version of His Summa Theologica*. Translator unknown. Manchester, New Hampshire, 2002.

Arendt, Hannah. *Eichmann in Jerusalem: A Report on the Banality of Evil*. New York: Penguin Books, 1992.

Arendt, Hannah. *The Human Condition*. Chicago, Illinois: The University of Chicago Press, 1958.

Arendt, Hannah. *On Violence*. New York: Harcourt, Inc., 1969.

Ariely, Daniel. *The Upside of Irrationality: The Unexpected Benefits of Defying Logic at Work and at Home*. New York: HarperCollins Publishers, 2010.

Aristophanes. *Lysistrata*. Translator unknown. New York: Dover Publications, 1994.

Aristotle. *Eudemian Ethics*. Translated by H. Rackham. Cambridge, Massachusetts: Harvard University Press, 1952.

Aristotle. *Nichomachean Ethics*. Translated by H. Rackham. Cambridge, Massachusetts: Harvard University Press, 1975.

Aristotle. *The Politics and The Constitution of Athens*. Translated by Jonathan Barnes, relying upon the Jowett translation. Edited by Stephen Everson.. Cambridge: Cambridge University Press, 2010.

Armstrong, Karen. *Twelve Steps to a Compassionate Life*. New York: Anchor Books, 2010.

Asma, Stephen T. *Against Fairness*. Chicago, Illinois: University of Chicago Press, 2013.

Augustine. *The Confessions of St. Augustine*. Translated by John K. Ryan. Garden City, New York: Image Books, 1960.

Aurelius, Marcus. *Marcus Aurelius Antoninus, Emperor, To Himself*. Translated by C. R. Haines. Cambridge, Massachusetts: Harvard University Press (2003).

Backman, Frederik. *A Man Called Ove*. Translated by Henning Koch. New York: Washington Square Press, 2014.

Bakalar, Nicholas, "Five-Second Touch Can Convey Specific Emotion, Study Finds," *New York Times* (August 11, 2009).

Bakunin, Michael. *God and the State*. New York: Dover Publications, 1970.

Bargh, John A. "Our Unconscious Mind," *Scientific American* 310, Number 1 (January 2014), 30-37.

Baron-Cohen, Simon, "The Evolution of Empathizing and Systemizing: Assortative Mating of Two Strong Systemizers and the Cause of Autism," in *Oxford Handbook of Evolutionary Psychology*. Eds., R. I. M. Dunbar and Louise Barrett. (Oxford: Oxford University Press, 2007), 213-226.

Baron-Cohen, Simon. *The Science of Evil: On Empathy and the Origins of Cruelty*. New York: Basic Books, 2011.

Barrow, John D. and John K. Webb, "Inconstant Constants: Do the inner workings of nature change with time?" *Scientific American*, Volume 21, No. 1, Spring 2012, 70-77.

Barton, Robert A., "Evolution of the Social Brain as a Distributed Neural System," in *Oxford Handbook of Evolutionary Psychology*. Eds., R. I. M. Dunbar and Louise Barrett. (Oxford: Oxford University Press, 2007), 129-144.

Bateson, Gregory. *Steps To An Ecology of Mind*. Chicago Illinois: University of Chicago Press, 1972.

Bateson, Gregory and Mary Catherine Bateson. *Angels Fear: Toward an Epistemology of the Sacred*. Creskill, New Jersey: Hampton Press, Inc., 2005.

Baumeister, Roy F., "Conquer Yourself, Conquer the World," *Scientific American* 312 No. 4 (April 2015): 60-65.

Baumeister, Roy F. *Evil: Inside Human Violence and Cruelty*. New York: Henry Holt and Company, 1999.

Becker, Ernest. *The Denial of Death*. New York: The Free Press, 1973.

Beckoff, Marc and Jessica Pierce. *Wild Justice: The Moral Lives of Animals*. Chicago: University of Chicago Press, 2010.

Begley, Sharon, "Sins of the Grandfathers: What happens in Vegas could affect your offspring. How early-life experiences could cause permanent changes in sperm and eggs," *Science* (November 8, 2010): 48-50.

Belsky, Jay, "Childhood Experiences and Reproductive Strategies," in *Oxford Handbook of Evolutionary Psychology*. Eds., R. I. M. Dunbar and Louise Barrett. (Oxford: Oxford University Press, 2007), 237-254.

Bender, Frederick L., "Historical and Theoretical Backgrounds of the Communist Manifesto," which introduces Marx, Karl. *The Communist Manifesto*. Edited by Frederick L. Bender. New York: W. W. Norton & Company, 1988.

Benjamin, Walter. *Critique of Violence*, in *Reflections: Essays, Aphorisms, Autobiogrpahical Writings*. Translated by Edmund Jephcott. New York: Schocken Books, 1986.

Bentham, Jeremy. *An Introduction to The Principles of Morals and Legislation*. New York: Hafner Press, 1948.

Bereczkei, Tamas, "Parental Impacts on Development: How Proximate Factors Mediate Adaptive Plans," in *Oxford Handbook of Evolutionary Psychology*. Eds., R. I. M. Dunbar and Louise Barrett. (Oxford: Oxford University Press, 2007), 255-272.

Berens, Lewis H. *The Digger Movement: Radical Communalism in the English Civil War*. St. Petersburg, Florida: Red and Black Publishers, 1906.

Berger, Peter. *The Sacred Canopy: Elements of a Sociological Theory of Religion*. Garden City, New York, Anchor Books, 1969.

Berger, Peter and Thomas Luckmann. *The Social Construction of Reality: A Treatise in the Sociology of Knowledge*. Garden City, New York: Anchor Books, 1966.

Bergson, Henri. *The Two Sources of Morality and Religion*. Translated by R. Ashley Audra and Cloudesley Brereton. Notre Dame, Indiana: University of Notre Dame Press, 1977.

Bhagavad Gita. Translated by Laurie L. Patton. New York: Penguin Classics, 2008.

Bible. Revised Standard Version. Camden, New Jersey: Thomas Nelson & Sons, 1952.

Bishop, Michael A. *The Good Life: Unifying the Philosophy and Psychology of Well-Being*. Oxford: Oxford University Press, 2015.

Blackburn, Simon. *Truth*. Oxford, Great Britain: Oxford University Press, 2005.

Black's Law Dictionary, Seventh Edition. Edited by Bryan A. Garner. St. Paul, Minnesota: West Group, 1999.

Block, Peter. *Community: The Structure of Belonging*. San Francisco, California: Berett-Koehler Publishers, Inc., 2008.

Bloom, Paul. *Just Babies: The Origin of Good and Evil*. New York: Crown Publishers, 2013.

Boehm, Christopher. *Hierarchy in the Forest: The Evolution of Egalitarian Behavior*. Cambridge, Massachusetts: Harvard University Press, 1999.

Boehm, Christopher. *Moral Origins: The Evolution of Virtue, Altruism, and Shame*. New York: Basic Books, 2012.

Bonanno, George A. *The Other Side of Sadness: What the New Science of Bereavement Tells Us About Life After Loss*. New York: Basic Books, 2009.

Bonhoeffer, Dietrich. *The Communion of Saints: A Dogmatic Inquiry into the Sociology of the Church*. Translated by R. Gregor Smith. New York: Harper & Row, Publishers, 1963.

Bookchin, Murray. *Post-Scarcity Anarchism*. Berkeley, California: Ramparts Press, 1971.

Bor, Daniel. *The Ravenous Brain: How the New Science of Consciousness Explains Our Insatiable Search for Meaning*. New York: Basic Books, 2012.

Brooks, David, "Drilling for Certainty," *New York Times*, 28 May 2010.

Brooks, David, "The New Humanism," *New York Times*, 9 March 2011.

Brooks, David. *The Road to Character*. New York: Random House, 2015.

Brooks, David. *The Social Animal: The Hidden Sources of Love, Character, and Achievement*. New York: Random House, 2011.

Bshary, Redouan, Lucie H. Salwiczek, and Wolfgang Wickler, "Social Cognition in Non-Primates," in *Oxford Handbook of Evolutionary Psychology*. Eds., R. I. M. Dunbar and Louise Barrett. (Oxford: Oxford University Press, 2007), 83-102.

Buber, Martin. *I and Thou*. Translated by Walter Kaufmann. New York: Charles Scribner's Sons, 1970.

Buber, Martin. *Paths in Utopia*. Syracuse, New York: Syracuse University Press, 1996.

Buddhist Scriptures. Selected and translated by Edward Conze. London: Penguin Books, 1959.

Bunney, Sarah, Steven Jones, Robert Martin, and David Pilbeam, eds. *The Cambridge Encyclopedia of Human Evolution*. Cambridge University Press, 1994.

Burke, Edmund. *Reflections on the Revolution in France*. Edited by Iaian Hampsher-Monk. New York: Cambridge University Press, 2014.

Cabrera, Isabel, "Is God Evil?", 17-26, in *Rethinking Evil: Contemporary Perspectives*. Edited by María Pía Lara. Berkeley, California: University of California Press, 2001.

Cacioppo, John T. and William Patrick. *Loneliness: Human Nature and the Need for Social Connection*. New York: W. W. Norton & Company, 2008.

Cain, Susan. *Quiet: The Power of Introverts in a World That Can't Stop Talking*. New York: Crown Publishers, 2012.

Calvin, John. *Institutes of the Christian Religion*. Translated by Henry Beveridge. Grand Rapids, Michigan: Wm. B. Eerdmans Publishing Company, 1993.

Cameron, William Bruce. *Informal Sociology: A Casual Introduction to Sociological Thinking*. New York: Random House, 1963.

Carpenter, Edward. *Non-Governmental Society*. Published as an independent work; previously published as chapter six of *Prisons, Police and Punishment* by Edward Carpenter. London: A. D. Fifield, 1911.

Carter, Stephen L. *The Violence of Peace: America's Wars in the Age of Obama*. New York: Beast Books, 2011.

Chanakya. *Maxims of Chanakya*. Translated by V. K. Subramanian. New Delhi, India: Abhinav Publications, 2000.

Chenoweth, Erica and Maria J. Stephan. *Why Civil Resistance Works: The Strategic Logic of Nonviolent Conflict*. New York: Columbia University Press, 2011.

Churchland, Patricia S. *Braintrust: What Neuroscience Tells Us About Morality*. Princeton, New Jersey: Princeton University Press, 2011.

Chu Hsi. *Learning to Be a Sage*. Translated by Daniel K. Gardner. Berkeley, California: University of California Press, 1990.

Cicero. *De Amicitia*. Translated by William Armistead Falconer. Cambridge, Massachusetts: Harvard University Press, 2001.

Cicero. *De Legibus*. Translated by Clinton Walker Keyes. Cambridge, Massachusetts: Harvard University Press, 1988.

Cicero. *De Officiis*. Translated by Walter Miller. Cambridge, Massachusetts: Harvard University Press, 2001.

Cicero. *De Senectute*. Translated by William Armistead Falconer. Cambridge, Massachusetts: Harvard University Press, 2001.

Code of Hammurabi. Translated by L. W. King. San Bernadino, California: publisher not identified, 2015.

Cohen, Abraham. *Everyman's Talmud: The Major Teachings of the Rabbinic Sages*. New York: Schocken Books, 1949.

Cohen, Joel E. *How Many People Can the Earth Support?* New York: W. W. Norton & Company, 1995.

Confucius. *Analects*. Translated by D. C. Lau. London: Penguin Books, 1979.

Conly, Sarah. *Against Autonomy: Justifying coercive paternalism*. New York: Cambridge University Press, 2013.

Considerant, Victor. *Principles of Socialism: Manifesto of 19th Century Democracy*. Translated by Joan Roelofs. Washington, D.C.: Maisonneuve Press, 2006.

Copeland, Matt. *Socratic Circles: Fostering Critical and Creative Thinking in Middle and High School*. Portland, Maine: Stenhouse Publishers, 2005.

Dalai Lama. *How to Practice: The Way to a Meaningful Life*. Translated by Jeffrey Hopkins. New York: Atria Books, 2002.

Darwin, Charles. *The Descent of Man and Selection in Relation to Sex*. United States: Benediction Classics, 2009 (1871).

Darwin, Charles. *The Origin of Species: By Means of Natural Selection or The Preservation of Favored Races in the Struggle for Life*. New York: The Modern Library, 1993.

Darwin, Charles. *The Voyage of the Beagle*. New York: E.P. Dutton & Co., Inc., 1906.

David, G.K., C. H. Condon, C.L. Bywater, D. Ortiz-Barrientos, and R.W. Wilson, "Receivers Limit the Prevalence of Deception in Humans: Evidence from Diving Behaviour in Soccer Players," PLoS ONE 6(10): e26017. Doi: 10.1371/journal.pone.0026017.

Day, Dorothy. *The Long Loneliness: The Autobiography of the Legendary Catholic Social Activist.* New York: Harper & Row, Publishers, Inc., 1952.

Deacon, Terrence W., "Primate Brains and Senses," in *The Cambridge Encyclopedia of Human Evolution.* Sarah Bunney, Steve Jones, Robert Martin, David Pilbeam, eds. Cambridge University Press, 1994.

de Beauvoir, Simone. *The Ethics of Ambiguity.* Translated by Bernard Frechtman. New York: Citadel Press, 1948.

de Beauvoir, Simone. *The Second Sex.* Translated by H. M. Parshley. New York: Alfred A. Knopf, Inc., 1952.

de Ligt, Bart. *The Conquest of Violence: An Essay on War and Revolution.* London: George Routledge & Sons, Ltd., 1937.

de Menocal, Peter B., "Climate Shocks," *Scientific American* 311 No. 3 (September 2014): 48-53.

de Quervain, Dominique J.-F., et al., "The Neural Basis of Altruistic Punishment," *Science* 305 No. 5688 (August 27, 2004): 1254-1258.

de Sade, The Marquis. *Juliette.* Translated by Austryn Wainhouse. New York: Grove Press, 1968.

de Sade, The Marquis. *Justine, Philosophy in the Bedroom, and other writings.* Translated by Richard Seaver and Austryn Wainhouse. New York: Grove Weidenfeld, 1965.

de Tocqueville, Alexis. *Democracy in America.* Translated by Henry Reeve. New York: Adlard and Sanders, 1838.

de Waal, Frans, "One for All: Our ability to cooperate in large societies has deep evolutionary roots in the animal kingdom," *Scientific American* 311 No. 3 (September 2014): 69-71.

de Waal, Frans. *Primates and Philosophers: How Morality Evolved.* Princeton, New Jersey: Princeton University Press, 2006.

de Waal, Frans. *The Bonobo and the Atheist: In Search of Humanism Among the Primates.* New York: W. W. Norton & Company, Inc., 2013.

Dewey, John. *How We Think.* Mineola, New York: Dover Publications, 1997.

Dewey, John. *Human Nature and Conduct.* New York: Henry Holt and Company, 1922.

Dewey, John. *Theory of the Moral Life.* New York: Holt, Rinehart and Winston, 1932.

Dhammapada. Translated by John Ross Carter and Mahinda Palihawadana. Oxford: Oxford University Press, 1987.

Diamond, Jared. *Collapse: How Societies Choose to Fail or Succeed.* New York: Penguin Books, 2005.

Diamond, Jared. *The World Until Yesterday.* New York: Viking, 2012.

Diogenes Laertius. *Lives of Eminent Philosophers.* Loeb Classical Library, Volume 184. Translated by R.D. Hicks. Jeffrey Henderson, ed. Cambridge, Massachusetts: Harvard University Press, 1972.

Dunbar, Robin I. M. *Grooming, Gossip, and the Evolution of Language.* Cambridge, Massachusetts: Harvard University Press, 1996.

Dunbar, Robin I. M. *How Many Friends Does One Person Need?: Dunbar's Number and Other Evolutionary Quirks.* Cambridge, Massachusetts: Harvard University Press, 2010.

Dunn, Elizabeth W., L. B. Aknin, and M. I. Norton. "Spending money on others promotes happiness," *Science* 319 (March 21, 2008): 1687-1688.

Dworkin, Ronald. *Justice for Hedgehogs.* Cambridge, Massachusetts: The Belknap Press, 2011.

Dyer, Gwynne. *War: The Lethal Custom.* New York: Carroll & Graf Publishers, 2004.

Ehrenhalt, Alan. *The Lost City: The Forgotten Virtues of Community in America.* New York: BasicBooks, 1995.

Emerson, Ralph Waldo. *The Conduct of Life.* In *Ralph Waldo Emerson: Essays and Lectures.* Edited by Joel Porte. New York: Literary Classics of the United States, 1983, pages 257-282.

Emerson, Ralph Waldo. *Friendship.* In *Ralph Waldo Emerson: Essays and Lectures.* Edited by Joel Porte. New York: Literary Classics of the United States, 1983, pages 339-354.

Emerson, Ralph Waldo. *Self-Reliance.* In *Ralph Waldo Emerson: Essays and Lectures.* Edited by Joel Porte. New York: Literary Classics of the United States, 1983, pages 257-282.

Empiricus, Sextus. *Outlines of Scepticism.* Edited by Julia Annas and Jonathan Barnes. Cambridge, United Kingdom: Cambridge University Press, 2004.

Encyclopædia Britannica, The New. 15th Ed. Chicago: Encyclopædia Britannica, Inc., 1987.

Engleman, Robert, "Six Billion in Africa: Population projections for the continent are alarming. The solution: empower women," *Scientific American* 314, No. 2 (February 2016): 56-63.

Epictetus. *Enchiridion.* Translated by George Long. Amherst, New York: Prometheus Books, 1991.

Epictetus. *The Discourses As Reported by Arrian.* Translated by W. A. Oldfather. Cambridge, Massachusetts: Harvard University Press, 2000.

Epicurus. *The Essential Epicurus: Letters, Principal Doctrines, Vatican Sayings, and Fragments.* Translated by Eugene O'Connor. Amherst, New York: Prometheus Books, 1993.

Fagan, Brian. *Cro-Magnon: How the Ice Age Gave Birth to the First Modern Humans.* New York: Bloomsbury Press, 2010.

Fanon, Franz. *Concerning Violence.* Translated by Constance Farrington. London: Penguin Books, 1965.

Feyerabend, Paul. *Against Method.* Third Edition. New York: Verso, 1988.

Flack, J. C. and F.B. M. de Waal, "Any Animal Whatever," *Journal of Consciousness Studies* 7 No. 1-2 (2000): 1-29.

Fonagy, Peter. *Attachment Theory and Psychoanalysis.* New York: Other Press LLC, 2001.

Foucault, Michel. *Madness and Civilization: A History of Insanity in the Age of Reason.* Translated by Richard Howard. New York: Random House, 1965.

Fourier, Charles. *The Theory of the Four Movements.* Translated by Ian Patterson. Edited by Gareth Stedman Jones and Ian Patterson. Cambridge, United Kingdom: Cambridge University Press, 1996.

Frankfurt, Harry G., "Freedom of the Will and the Concept of a Person," *The Journal of Philosophy* 68, No. 1 (January 14, 1971): 5-20.

Frankl, Viktor. *Man's Search for Meaning.* Part I translated by Ilse Lasch. Boston, Massachusetts: Beacon Press, 2006.

Freud, Sigmund. *Civilization and Its Discontents.* Translated by Joan Riviere. London: Hogarth Press LTD, 1953.

Freud, Sigmund. *The Future of an Illusion.* Translated by W. D. Robson-Scott. New York: Doubleday Anchor Books, 1953.

Friedman, David. *The Machinery of Freedom: Guide to a Radical Capitalism.* La Salle, Illinois: Open Court Publishing Company, 1995.

Fung, Helene H., and Laura L. Christensen, "Goals Change When Life's Fragility is Primed: Lessons Learned from Older Adults, the September11 Attacks and SARS," *Social Cognition* 24, No 3 (2006): 248-278.

Gandhi, Mohandas K. *An Autobiography: The Story of My Experiments with Truth.* Translated by Mahadev Desai. Boston, Massachusetts: Beacon Press, 1957.

Gandhi, Mohandas K. *Non-Violent Resistance (Satyagraha).* Mineola, New York: Dover Publications, Inc., 2001.

Gandhi, Mohandas K. *Satyagraha in South Africa.* Translated by Valji Govindji Desai. Ahmedabad, Pakistan: Navajivan Publishing House, 1928.

Gawande, Atul. *Being Mortal: Medicine and What Matters in the End.* New York: Henry Holt and Company, 2014.

Gazzaniga, Michael S. *The Ethical Brain: The Science of Our Moral Dilemmas.* New York: HarperCollins Publishers, 2005.

Gell-Mann, Murray. *The Quark and the Jaguar.* New York: Henry Holt and Company, LLC, 1994.

Gert, Bernard. *The Moral Rules: A New Rational Foundation for Morality.* New York: Harper Torchbooks, 1973.

Gibson, Lydialyle. "Mirrored Emotion," *University of Chicago Magazine* 98, Issue 4 (April 2006), at http://magazine.uchicago.edu/0604/features/emotion.shtml.

Gibson, John and Judy Pigott. *Personal Safety Nets: Getting Ready for Life's Inevitable Changes and Challenges.* Seattle, Washington: Classic Day Publishing, 2007.

Glover, Jonathan. *Humanity: A Moral History of theTwentieth Century.* New Haven, Connecticut: Yale University Press, 1999.

Glover, Jonathan. *What Sort of People Should There Be?* New York: Penguin Books, 1984.

Godwin, William. *Enquiry Concerning Political Justice and Its Influence on Morals and Happiness.* Philadelphia, Pennsylvania: Bioren and Madan, 1796.

Goldman, Emma. *Anarchism and Other Essays.* Boston, Massachussetts: IndyPublish.com, 2005.

Goldstein, Rebecca Newberger. *Plato at the Googleplex.* New York: Pantheon Books, 2014.

Gottmann, John M., and Joan DeClaire. *The Relationship Cure: A 5 Step Guide to Strengthening Your Marriage, Family, and Friendships.* New York: Three Rivers Press, 2001.

Gottmann, John, and Nan Silver. *The Seven Principles for Making Marriage Work: A Practical Guide from the Country's Foremost Relationship Expert.* New York: Three Rivers Press, 1999.

Gould, Stephen Jay. *Wonderful Life: The Burgess Shale and the Nature of History.* New York: W. W. Norton, 1989.

Gould, Stephen Jay and Richard C. Lewontin, "The Spandrels of San Marco and the Panglossian Paradigm: A Critique of the Adaptationist Programme," *Proceedings of the Royal Society of London* 205 (September 21, 1979): 581-598.

Graybiel, Ann M. and Kyle S. Smith, "Good Habits, Bad Habits: Researchers are pinpointing the brain circuits that can help us form good habits and break bad ones," *Scientific American* 310, Number 6 (June 2014): 38-43.

Grayling, A. C. *Friendship.* New Haven, Connecticut: Yale University Press, 2013.

Greene, Joshua. *Moral Tribes: Emotion, Reason, and the Gap Between Us and Them.* New York: The Penguin Press, 2013.

Griffin, James. *Well-Being: Its Meaning, Measurement and Moral Importance.* Oxford: Oxford University Press, 1986.

Gross, James J., and Laura Carstensen *et al.*, "Emotion and Aging: Experience, Expression, and Control," *Psychology and Aging* 12, No. 4 (1997): 590-599.

Haidt, Jonathan. *The Happiness Hypothesis: Finding Modern Truth in Ancient Wisdom.* New York: Basic Books, 2006.

Hammer, Michael F, "Human Hybrids: DNA Analyses find that Early *Homo sapiens* mated with other human species and hint that such interbreeding played a key role in the triumph of our kind," *Scientific American* 308, Number 5 (May 2013): 66-71.

Han Fei Tzu. *Basic Writings.* Translated by Burton Watson. New York: Columbia University Press, 1964.

Hardin, Garrett, "The Tragedy of the Commons," *Science* 162, Number 3859 (December 13, 1968): 1243-1248.

Hare, Robert D. *Without Conscience: The Disturbing World of the Psychopaths Among Us.* New York: The Guilford Press, 1993.

Harmon, Amy. "Neurodiversity Forever; The Disability Movement Turns to Brains," *New York Times*, May 9, 2004.

Harmon, Katherine, "Shattered Ancestry: New fossil discoveries complicate the already devilish task of identifying our most ancient progenitors," *Scientific American* 308, Number 2 (February 2013): 42-49.

Harris, Sam. *The Moral Landscape: How Science Can Determine Human Values.* New York: Free Press, 2010.

Hazan, Cindy and Phillip Shaver, "Romantic love conceptualized as an attachment process," *Journal of Personality and Social Psychology* 52(3) (March 1987): 511-524.

Heraclitus. *Fragments: The Collected Wisdom of Heraclitus.* Translated by Brooks Haxton. New York: Penguin Group, 2001.

Heracleitus. *On the Universe.* Translated by W. H. S. Jones. Cambridge, Massachusetts: Harvard University Press, 1931. [This text, which translates the same text as the previous entry in this bibliography, is contained as the last portion of Volume IV of the Loeb Classical Library, and is bundled with Hippocrates, whose name stands first in notation of this text, as Hippocrates's words fill the greater portion of the volume.]

Hitler, Adolf. *Mein Kampf.* Translated by Ralph Manheim. New York: Houghton Mifflin Company, 1971.

Hobbes, Thomas. *Leviathan, or The Mattere, Forme, & Power of a Common-Wealth Ecclesiasticall and Civill.* Cambridge, United Kingdom: Cambridge University Press, 2014.

Holmes, Oliver Wendell. *The Common Law.* Boston, Massachusetts: Little, Brown and Company, 1963.

Hood, Bruce. *The Self Illusion: How the Social Brain Creates Identity.* Oxford, Great Britain: Oxford University Press, 2012.

Horgan, John. *The End of War.* San Francisco: McSweeney's, 2014.

Horrox, James. *A Living Revolution: Anarchism in the Kibbutz Movement.* Oakland, California: AK Press, 2009.

Hrdy, Sarah Glaffer. *Mothers and Others: The Evolutionary Origins of Mutual Understanding.* Cambridge, Massachusetts: Harvard University Press, 2009.

Hsün Tzu. Translated by Burton Watson. New York: Columbia University Press, 1996.

Hume, David. *A Treatise of Human Nature.* Edited by Ernest C. Mossner. New York: Penguin Books, 1984.

Hume, David. *An Enquiry Concerning the Principles of Morals.* Edited by Tom L. Beauchamp. Oxford, England: Oxford University Press, 1998.

Humphry, Derek. *Final Exit: The Practicalities of Self-Deliverance and Assisted Suicide for the Dying.* Eugene, Oregon: The Hemlock Society, 1991.

Hyde, Lewis. *Common as Air: Revolution, Art, and Ownership.* New York: Farrar, Straus and Giroux, 2010.

Iacoboni, Marco. *Mirroring People: The New Science of How We Connect with Others.* New York: Farrar, Straus and Giroux, 2008.

Ibn Khaldûn. *Muqaddimah: An Introduction to History.* Translated by Franz Rosenthal. Edited by N. J. Dawood. Princeton, New Jersey: Princeton University Press, 2005.

Isocrates. Volume I. *To Demonicus.* Translated by Geroge Norlin. Cambridge, Massachusetts: Harvard University Press, 1928.

Invisible Committee. *The Coming Insurrection.* Translator unknown. Los Angeles: Semiotext(e), 2009.

Izutsu, Toshihiko. *Ethico-Religious Concepts in the Qur'an.* Montreal, Canada: McGill-Queen's University Press, 2007.

James, William. *Essays of Faith and Morals,* "Is Life Worth Living?" Edited by Ralph Barton Perry. Cleveland, Ohio: The World Publishing Company, 1962.

James, William. *Essays of Faith and Morals,* "On a Certain Blindness in Human Beings." Edited by Ralph Barton Perry. Cleveland, Ohio: The World Publishing Company, 1962.

James, William. *The Varieties of Religious Experience: A Study in Human Nature.* New York: The Modern Library, 1902.

James, William. *Essays of Faith and Morals,* "The Will to Believe." Edited by Ralph Barton Perry. Cleveland, Ohio: The World Publishing Company, 1962.

James, William. *Pragmatism.* Minneapolis, Minnesota: Filiquarian Publishing, LLC, 2007.

James, William. *The Will to Believe.* "The Moral Philosopher and the Moral Life." New York: Elibron Classics, 2005.

Jefferson, Thomas. *Writings.* Edited by Merrill D. Peterson. New York: Literary Classics of the United States, Inc., 1984.

Jones, Steve, Robert Martin and David Pilbeam. *The Cambridge Encyclopedia of Human Evolution.* Cambridge, Great Britain: Cambridge University Press, 1992.

Jost, John, T., Mahzarin R. Banaji, and Brian A. Nosek, "A Decade of System Justification Theory: Accumulated Evidence of Conscious and Unconscious Bolstering of the Status Quo," *Political Psychology* 26, No. 6 (2004): 881-919.

Junger, Sebastian. *Tribe: On Homecoming and Belonging.* New York: Twelve, 2016.

Kant, Immanuel. *Fundamental Principles of the Metaphysics of Morals.* Translated by Thomas K. Abbott. In *Basic Writings of Kant,* Allen W. Wood, ed. New York: The Modern Library, 2001.

Kant, Immanuel. *Idea for a Universal History with Cosmopolitan Intent.* Translated by Carl J. Friedrich. In *Basic Writings of Kant,* Allen W. Wood, ed. New York: The Modern Library, 2001.

Kant, Immanuel. *What is Enlightenment?* Translated by Thomas K. Abbott. In *Basic Writings of Kant,* Allen W. Wood, ed. New York: The Modern Library, 2001.

Kant, Immanuel. *To Eternal Peace.* Translated by Carl J. Friedrich. In *Basic Writings of Kant,* Allen W. Wood, ed. New York: The Modern Library, 2001.

Kapur, Akash, "Couldn't Be Better: The Return of the Utopians," *New Yorker* XCII, No. 31 (October 3, 2016): 66-71.

Karen, Robert. *Becoming Attached: First Relationships and How They Shape Our Capacity to Love.* Oxford: Oxford University Press, 1998.

Kautilya. *The Arthashastra.* Translated by L.N. Rangarajan. New Delhi, India: Penguin Books, 1992.

Keeley, Lawrence H. *War Before Civilization: The Myth of the Peaceful Savage.* New York: Oxford University Press, 1996.

Kelly, "Navigating Past Nihilism," *New York Times, Opinionator Blogs,* 6 December 2010. http://opinionator.blogs.nytimes.com/2010/12/05/nativating-past-nihilism/

Keltner, Dacher. *Born to Be Good: The Science of a Meaningful Life*. New York: W. W. Norton & Company: 2009.

Kierkegaard, Søren. *The Sickness Unto Death*. Translated by Alastair Hannay. London: Penguin Books, 2004.

King, Barbara J. "When Animals Mourn: Mounting evidence from species as diverse as cats and dolphins indicates that humans are not the only species that grieves over the loss of loved ones," *Scientific American*, 309, Number 1 (July 2013): 62-67.

King, Jr., Martin Luther. *The Autobiography of Martin Luther King, Jr.* New York: Grand Central Publishing, 1998.

Klass, Perri, "When a Child Gets Hurt, A Sibling May Be At Risk," *New York Times*, June 7, 2010.

Knauft, Bruce M. "Violence and Sociality in Human Evolution," *Current Anthropology* 32, Number 4 (August-October 1991): 391-428.

Koch, Christof. *The Quest for Consciousness: A Neurobiological Approach*. Englewood, Colorado: Roberts and Company Publishers, 2004.

Kraut, Richard. *What is Good And Why: The Ethics of Well-Being*. Cambridge, Massachusetts: Harvard University Press, 2007.

Kropotkin, Peter. *Revolutionary Government*. Translator unknown. Van Nuys, California: Srafprint Co-op, 1970.

Kropotkin, Peter. *Mutual Aid: A Factor of Evolution*. Translator unknown. St. Louis, Missouri: Dialectics, 2013.

Kropotkin, Peter. *The Conquest of Bread and Other Writings*. Translator unknown. Edited by Marshall Shatz. Cambridge: Cambridge University Press, 2005.

Kübler-Ross, Elisabeth. *On Death and Dying*. New York: Touchstone, 1969.

Kuhle, Barry X. and Sarah Radtke, "Born Both Ways: The Alloparenting Hypothesis for Sexual Fluidity in Women," *Evolutionary Psychology* 11(2) 2013: 304-323.

Kuhn, Thomas S. *The Structure of Scientific Revolutions*. Chicago, Illinois: University of Chicago Press, 1970.

Laland, Kevin N., "Niche Construction, Human Behavioural Ecology and Evolutionary Psychology," in *Oxford Handbook of Evolutionary Psychology*. Eds., R. I. M. Dunbar and Louise Barrett. (Oxford: Oxford University Press, 2007), 35-48.

Lally, Phillippa, Cornelia H. M. van Jaarsveld, Henry W.W. Potts, and Jane Wardle, "How Are Habits Formed: Modeling Habit Formation in the Real World," *European Journal of Social Psychology* 40, Issue Six (October 2010): 998-1009.

Lancaster, Brad. *"Corporate Personality": Sociality in Old Testament Anthropology*. Pasadena, California: Ph.D. diss. (incomplete), Fuller Theological Seminary, August 1981.

Lancaster, Brad. *I-Thou Personalism: An Anthropological Inquiry*. Pasadena, California: Ph.D. diss. (incomplete), Fuller Theological Seminary, January 1981.

Landauer, Gustav. *For Socialism*. Translated by David J. Parent. St. Louis, Missouri: Telos Press, 1978.

Landauer, Gustav. *Through Separation to Community*, in *Revolution and Other Writings: A Political Reader*. Edited and translated by Gabriel Kuhn. Pontypool, Wales: The Merline Press Ltd., 2010.

Landauer, Gustav. *Revolution*, in *Revolution and Other Writings: A Political Reader*. Edited and translated by Gabriel Kuhn. Pontypool, Wales: The Merline Press Ltd., 2010.

Lanphear, Fred. *Songaia: An Unfolding Dream*. Bothell, Washington: Songaia Press, 2014.

Lao Tzu. *Tao Te Ching*. Translated by Victor H. Mair from the Ma-Wang-Tui manuscripts. New York: Bantam Books, 1990.

Law Code of Manu. Translated by Patrick Olivelle. Oxford, Great Britain: Oxford University Press, 2004.

Lederach, John Paul. *The Moral Imagination: The Art and Soul of Building Peace*. New York: Oxford University Press, 2005.

LeGuin, Ursula. *The Dispossessed: An Unambiguous Utopia*. New York: Harper Voyager, 1974.

Lehrer, Jonah. *How We Decide*. New York: Houghton Mifflin Harcourt, 2009.

Leidloff, Jean. *The Continuum Concept: In Search of Lost Happiness*. New York: Da Capo Press, 1975.

Lelyveld, Joseph. *Great Soul: Mahatma Gandhi and His Struggle with India*. New York: Alfred A. Knopf, 2011.

Lenin, V. I. *Essential Works of Lenin.* Edited by Henry M. Christman. New York: Dover Publications, Inc., 1987.

Lesher, J. H. *Xenophanes of Colophon: Fragments.* Toronto: University of Toronto Press, 1992.

Levinas, Emmanuel. *Otherwise Than Being.* Translated by Alphonso Lingis. Pittsburgh, Pennsylvania: Duquesne University Press, 1998.

Levinas, Emmanuel. *Time and the Other.* Translated by Richard A. Cohen. Pittsburgh, Pennsylvania: Duquesne University Press, 1987.

Lewin, Roger. *Bones of Contention.* New York: Simon & Schuster, 1987.

Lewis, Penelope. *The Secret World of Sleep: The Surprising Science of the Mind at Rest.* New York: Palgrave MacMillan, 2013.

Liddell, H. G. and Robert Scott. *Greek-English Lexicon.* Oxford: Oxford University Press, 1935.

Locke, John. *A Letter Concerning Toleration.* Roslyn, New York: Walter J. Black, Inc., 1947.

Locke, John. *Two Treatises of Government.* Norwalk, Connecticut: The Easton Press, 1991.

Lucian. *Timon, or the Misanthrope.* Translated by A. M. Harmon. Cambridge, Massachusetts: Harvard University Press, 1915.

Lucretius. *De Rerum Natura* (The Nature of Things). Translated by Charles E. Bennett. Roslyn, New York: Walter J. Black, Inc., 1946.

Machiavelli, Niccoló. *The Prince.* Translated by Peter Bondanella. Oxford, England: Oxford University Press, 2005.

MacIntyre, Alasdair. *After Virtue.* Notre Dame, Indiana: University of Notre Dame Press, 2002.

MacLean, Paul. *The Triune Brain in Evolution.* New York: Plenum Press (1990).

Maimonides. *Ethical Writings of Maimonides.* Translated by Raymond L. Weiss. New York: Dover Publications, Inc., 1975.

Maine, Henry Sumner. *Ancient Law: Its Connection with the Early History of Society, and Its Relation to Modern Ideas.* Tucson, Arizona: University of Arizona Press, 1986.

Malcolm X. *Malcolm X Speaks: Selected Speeches and Statements.* New York: Grove Press, 1965.

Malcolm X. *The Autobiography of Malcolm X.* London: Penguin Books, 1965.

Malthus, Thomas. *An Essay on the Principle of Population, as it Affects the Future Improvement of Society, with Remarks on the Speculations of Mr. Godwin, M. Condorcet, and Other Writers.* London: J. Johnson, 1798.

Mameli, Matteo. "Evolution and Psychology in Philosophical Perspective," in *Oxford Handbook of Evolutionary Psychology.* Eds., R. I. M. Dunbar and Louise Barrett. (Oxford: Oxford University Press, 2007), 21-34.

Mandeville, Bernard. *The Fable of the Bees and Other Writings.* Edited by E. J. Hundert. Indianapolis, Indiana: Hackett Publishing Company, 1997.

Mao Zedong. *On New Democracy.* Translator unknown. Peking: People's Publishing House, 1954.

Mao Zedong. *Quotations from Chairman Mao Tsetung,* which work is also known as the *"Little Red Book."* Translator unknown. Peking: Foreign Languages Press, 1972.

Marean, Curtis W., "The Most Invasive Species of All," *Scientific American,* Vol. 313, Number 2 (August 2015): 32-39.

Marean, Curtis W., "When the Sea Saved Humanity," *Scientific American,* Vol. 303, Number 2 (August 2010): 54-61.

Maritain, Jacques. *The Person and the Common Good.* Translated by John J.Fitzgerald. Notre Dame, Indiana: University of Notre Dame Press, 1966.

Marlantes, Karl. *What It Is Like To Go To War.* New York: Grove Press, 2011.

Marx, Karl. *The Communist Manifesto.* Edited by Frederick L. Bender. New York: W. W. Norton & Company, 1988.

Marx, Karl. "Critique of the Gotha Programme," in *Essential Writings of Karl Marx.* Translator unknown. Edited by Red and Black Publishers. St. Petersburg, Florida: Red and Black Publishers, 2010.

Maté, Gabor. *In the Realm of Hungry Ghosts: Close Encounters with Addiction.* Berkeley, California: North Atlantic Books, 2010.

Maturana, Humberto R. and Francisco J.Varela. *The Tree of Knowledge: The Biological Roots of Human Understanding.* Translated by Robert Paolucci. London: Shambahala, 1998.

McElreath, Richard and Joseph Henrich, "Modelling cultural evolution," in *Oxford Handbook of Evolutionary Psychology.* Eds., R. I. M. Dunbar and Louise Barrett. (Oxford: Oxford University Press, 2007), 571-585.

McGregor, Michael, "Brain Trust: Music, Memory, and Mistakes: Top Neuroscientists Explain How the Mind Copes in a Chaotic World," *Discover* (March 2009): 66-70.

McKnight, John and Peter Block. *The Abundant Community: Awakening the Power of Families and Neighborhoods.* San Francisco, California: Berrett-Koehler Publishers, Inc., 2010.

Mencius. Translated by D. C. Lau. London: Penguin Books, 2003.

Mill, John Stuart. *On Liberty.* London: Random House, 1992.

Miller, Alice. *Thou Shalt Not Be Aware: Society's Betrayal of the Child.* Translated by Hildegarde and Hunter Hannum. New York: Farrar, Straus and Giroux, 1981.

Milton, John. *Areopagitica and Of Education.* Wheeling, Illinois: Harlan Davidson, Inc.,1951.

Minsky, Marvin. *The Emotional Mind.* New York: Simon & Schuster, 2006.

Minsky, Marvin. *The Society of Mind.* New York: Simon & Schuster, 1985.

Mlodinow, Leonard. *Subliminal: How Your Unconscious Mind Rules Your Behavior.* New York, Pantheon Books, 2012.

Muhammad. *The Qur'an.* Translated by M.A.S. Abdel Haleem. Oxford: Oxford University Press, 2010.

Montesquieu, Baron de. *The Spirit of the Laws.* Translated by Thomas Nugent. New York: Hafner Press, 1949.

Mooney, Chris. "Made-up Minds," *This Week* (May 20, 2011), 48-49.

Moore, G. E. *Principia Ethica.* New York: University of Cambridge Press, 1903.

Morris, William. *News from Nowhere and other Writings.* New York: Penguin Books, 1993.

Most, Johann. *Science of Revolutionary Warfare.* Translator unknown. El Dorado, Arizona: Desert Publications, 1978.

Mozi. Translated by Burton Watson. New York: Columbia University Press, 2003.

Mumford, Lewis. *The Conduct of Life.* New York: Harcourt Brace Jovanovich, Inc., 1970.

Musser, George. "Where is Here? Our sense of the universe as an orderly expanse where events happen in absolute location is an illusion," *Scientific American* 313, Number 5 (November 2015): 70-73.

Mussolini, Benito. *The Doctrine of Fascism.* Translator unknown. New York: Howard Fertig, 1935.

Nieman, Susan. *Evil in Modern Thought: An Alternative History of Philosophy.* Princeton, New Jersey: Princeton University Press, 2002.

Nietzsche, Friedrich. *Beyond Good and Evil, (Jenseits von Gut und Bose).* Translated by Walter Kaufmann. New York: Modern Library, 1992.

Nietzsche, Friedrich. *On the Genealogy of Morals: A Polemic. By way of clarification and supplement to my last book,* Beyond Good and Evil. *(Zur Genealogie der Moral).* Translated by Douglas Smith. Oxford: Oxford University Press, 1996.

Ninh, Bao. *The Sorrow of War.* Translated by Phan Thanh Hao. New York: Riverhead Books, 1993.

Nisbett, Richard E. and Timothy DeCamp Wilson. "Telling More Than We Can Know: Verbal Reports on Mental Processes," *Psychological Review* 84, Number 3 (May 1977): 231-259.

Nisbet, Robert A. *The Quest for Community.* New York: Oxford University Press, 1953.

Nitschke, Philip and Fiona Stewart. *The Peaceful Pill Handbook.* Bellingham, Washington: Exit International US, 2014 (Revised May 15, 2014).

Noll, Douglas. *Peacemaking: Practicing at the Intersection of Law and Human Conflict.* Telford, Pennsylvania: Cascadia Publishing House, 2003.

Nordhoff, Charles. *American Utopias.* Originally published in 1875 under the title *The Communistic Societies of the United States.* Stockingbridge, Massachusetts: Berkshire House Publishers, 1993.

Nowak, Martin A., "Why We Help," *Scientific American,* July 2012, 34-39.

Nozick, Robert. *Invariances: The Structure of the Objective World.* Cambridge, Massachusetts: Harvard University Press, 2001.

Nozick, Robert. *Anarchy, State, and Utopia.* New York: Basic Books, Inc., Publishers,1974.

Orwell, George. *1984.* New York: Signet Classics, 1949.

Orwell, George. *Animal Farm.* New York: Harcourt Brace Jovanovich, Inc., 1946.

Owen, Robert. *A New View of Society, and Other Writings.* Edited by Gregory Claeys. New York: Penguin Books, 1991.

Paine, Thomas. *Common Sense.* New York: Alfred A. Knopf, 1994.

Panksepp, Jaak. *Affective Neuroscience: The Foundations of Human and Animal Emotions*. Oxford University Press, 1998.

Panksepp, Jaak, and Lucy Biven. *The Archaeology of Mind: Neuroevolutionary Origins of Human Emotions*. New York: W. W. Norton & Company, 2012.

Panksepp, Jaak. "The Neuroevolutionary and Neuroaffective Psychobiology of the Prosocial Brain," in *Oxford Handbook of Evolutionary Psychology*. Eds., R. I. M. Dunbar and Louise Barrett. (Oxford: Oxford University Press, 2007), 145-162.

Parfit, Derek. *Reasons and Persons*. Oxford: Clarendon Press, 1984.

Paschal, Blaise. *Pensées*. Franklin Center, Pennsylvania: The Franklin Library, 1979.

Pentland, Alex (Sandy). "To Signal Is Human," *American Scientist* 98 (June 2010): 204-211.

Pfaff, Donald W. *The Altruistic Brain: How We Are Naturally Good*. New York: Oxford University Press, 2015.

Pilbeam, David, "What Makes Us Human?," in *The Cambridge Encyclopedia of Human Evolution*. Sarah Bunney, Steve Jones, Robert Martin, David Pilbeam, eds. Cambridge University Press, 1994.

Pillemer, Karl. *30 Lessons for Living: Tried and True Advice from the Wisest Americans*. New York: Hudson Street Press: 2011.

Pinker, Steven. *The Better Angels of Our Nature*. New York: Penguin Group, 2011.

Plato. *Apologia*. Translated by Harold North Fowler. In *Plato I*, Loeb Classical Library. Cambridge, Massachusetts: Harvard University Press, 1960.

Plato. *Lysis*. Translated by J. Wright. In the *Collected Dialogues of Plato*, 145-168. Edited by Edith Hamilton and Huntington Cairns. New York: Bollingen Foundation, 1966.

Plato. *Phaedo*. Translated by Harold North Fowler. In *Plato I*, Loeb Classical Library. Cambridge, Massachusetts: Harvard University Press, 1960.

Plato. *Phaedrus*. Translated by Harold North Fowler. In *Plato I*, Loeb Classical Library. Cambridge, Massachusetts: Harvard University Press, 1960

Plato. *The Republic*. Translated by Tom Griffith. Edited by G. R.F. Ferrari. Cambridge: Cambridge University Press, 2000.

Polyani, Michael and Harry Prosch. *Meaning*. Chicago, Illinois: University of Chicago Press, 1975.

Prinz, Jesse J. *The Emotional Construction of Morals*. Oxford, England: Oxford University Press, 2007.

Proudhon, Pierre-Joseph. *What is Property?* Translated by Donald R. Kelley and Bonnie G. Smith. Cambridge, England: Cambridge University Press, 1993.

Pugh, George Edwin. *The Biological Origin of Human Values*. New York: Basic Books, 1977.

Putnam, Robert D. *Bowling Alone: The Collapse and Revival of American Community*. New York: Simon & Schuster, 2000.

Qutb, Seyyid. *Milestones*. Translator unknown. Damascus, Syria: Dar al-Ilm, publication date unstated.

Rahman, Fazlur. *Major Themes of the Qur'an*. Chicago, Illinois: The University of Chicago Press, 1980.

Raichle, Marcus E., "The Brain's (Dark Energy)," *Scientific American*, March 2010.

Rawls, John. *Justice as Fairness: A Restatement*. Cambridge, Massachusetts: Harvard University Press, 2001.

Read, Herbert. "My Anarchism," in *The Cult of Sincerity*. New York: Horizon Press, 1968.

Read, Herbert. "The Truth of a Few Simple Ideas," in *The Cult of Sincerity*. New York: Horizon Press, 1968.

Read, Herbert. "What is There Left to Say?" in *The Cult of Sincerity*. New York: Horizon Press, 1968.

Reidy, David A. and Walter J. Riker, eds. *Coercion and the State*. Dordrecht, Netherlands: Springer Science+ Business Media B.V., 2008.

Ridley, Matt. *The Rational Optimist: How Prosperity Evolves*. New York: HarperCollins Publishers, 2010.

Rig Veda. Translated and edited by Wendy Doniger O'Flaherty. New York: Penguin Books, 1981.

Rizzolatti, Giacomo and Leonardo Fogassi, "Mirror Neurons and Social Cognition," in *Oxford Handbook of Evolutionary Psychology*. Eds., R. I. M. Dunbar and Louise Barrett. (Oxford: Oxford University Press, 2007), 179-196.

Robinson, Kim Stanley. *2312*. New York: Hachette Book Group, 2012.

Rocker, Rudolf. *Nationalism and Culture*. Translated by Ray E.Chase. Los Angeles: Rocker Publications Committee, 1937.

Roosevelt, Franklin D. *Jefferson Day Speech*. http://www.presidency.ucsb.edu/ws/?pid=16602.
Rothbard, Murray N. *For a New Liberty: The Libertarian Manifesto*. Auburn, Alabama: Ludwig vonMises Institute, 1978.
Rousseau, Jean-Jacques. *The Confessions of Jean-Jacques Rousseau*. Translated by J. M. Cohen. New York: Penguin Books, 1953.
Rousseau, Jean-Jacques. "A Discourse on the Arts and Sciences," in *The Social Contract and the Discourses*. Translated by G. D. H. Cole. New York: Alfred A. Knopf, 1992.
Rousseau, Jean-Jacques. "A Discourse on the Origin of Inequality," in *The Social Contract and the Discourses*. Translated by G. D. H. Cole. New York: Alfred A. Knopf, 1992.
Rousseau, Jean-Jacques. "A Discourse on Political Economy," in *The Social Contract and the Discourses*. Translated by G. D. H. Cole. New York: Alfred A. Knopf, 1992.
Rousseau, Jean-Jacques. *Emile, or On Education*. Translated by Allan Bloom. United States: Basic Books, 1979.
Rousseau, Jean-Jacques. *Reveries of the Solitary Walker*. Translated by Peter France. London: Penguin Books, 1979.
Rousseau, Jean-Jacques. *The Social Contract*. Translated by Maurice Cranston. New York: Penguin Books, 1968.
Royce, Josiah. *The Philosophy of Loyalty*. New York: The McMillan Company, 1908.
Russell, Bertrand. "Adaptation: An Autobiographical Epitome," in *The Basic Writings of Bertrand Russell*. London: Routledge, 2009.
Russell, Bertrand. "The Aims of Education," in *The Basic Writings of Bertrand Russell*. London: Routledge, 2009.
Russell, Bertrand. "Education," in *The Basic Writings of Bertrand Russell*. London: Routledge, 2009.
Russell, Bertrand. "The Expanding Mental Universe," in *The Basic Writings of Bertrand Russell*. London: Routledge, 2009.
Russell, Bertrand. "A Free Man's Worship," in *The Basic Writings of Bertrand Russell*. London: Routledge, 2009.
Russell, Bertrand. "Individual and Social Ethics," in *The Basic Writings of Bertrand Russell*. London: Routledge, 2009.
Russell, Bertrand. "The Next Half-Century," in *The Basic Writings of Bertrand Russell*. London: Routledge, 2009.
Russell, Bertrand. "An Outline of Intellectual Rubbish," in *The Basic Writings of Bertrand Russell*. London: Routledge, 2009.
Russell, Bertrand. "Property," in *The Basic Writings of Bertrand Russell*. London: Routledge, 2009.
Russell, Bertrand. "Styles in Ethics," in *The Basic Writings of Bertrand Russell*. London: Routledge, 2009.
Russell, Bertrand. "What I Believe," in *The Basic Writings of Bertrand Russell*. London: Routledge, 2009.
Sanders, Laura, "Amygdala gone, she knows no fear," *Science News*, January 15, 2011 (reporting on a study published December 16, 2010, online in *Current Biology*).
Sartre, Jean Paul. *Being and Nothingness*. Translated by Hazel E. Barnes. New York: Philosophical Library, Inc., 1956.
Sartre, Jean Paul. *Existentialism and Human Emotions*. Translated by Bernard Frechtman. New York: Kensington Publishing Corp., 1957.
Sartre, Jean Paul. *Nausea*. Translated by Lloyd Alexander. New York: New Directions Books, 1964.
Sartre, Jean Paul. *No Exit*. Translated by S. Gilbert. New York: Alfred A. Knopf, 1976.
Scanlon, Thomas. *What We Owe To Each Other*. Cambridge, Massachusetts: Harvard University Press, 1998.
Schellnhuber, Hans Joachim and Mario Molina, *Global Sustainability: A Nobel Cause*. New York: Cambridge University Press, 2010. (Chapter 1 authored by Murray Gell-Mann, "Transformations of the twenty-first century: transitions to greater sustainability.")
Schopenhauer, Albert. *The Basis of Morality*. Translated by Arthur Brodrick Bullock. Mineola, New York: Dover Publications, Inc., 2005.
Schopenhauer, Albert. *The Wisdom of Life* and *Counsels and Maxims*. Translated by T. Bailey Saunders. Amherst, New York: Prometheus Books, 1995.

Schopenhauer, Albert. *The World as Will and Representation*. Translated by E. F. J. Payne. New York: Dover Publications, Inc., 1958.

Schweitzer, Albert. *Out of My Life and Thought: An Autobiography*. Norwalk, Connecticut: The Easton Press, 1933.

Schweitzer, Albert. *The Philosophy of Civilization*. Translated by C. T. Campion. New York: Prometheus Books, 1987.

Scott, Dick. *Ask That Mountain: The Story of Parihaka*. Auckland, New Zealand: Reed Books, 1975.

Scott, James D. *The Art of Not Being Governed: An Anarchist History of Upland Southeast Asia*. New Haven, Connecticut: Yale University Press, 2009.

Scott, James C. *Seeing Like A State: How certain schemes to improve the human condition have failed*. New Haven, Connecticut: Yale University Press, 1998.

Seneca. *Epistles 1-65*. Translated by Richard M. Gummere. Cambridge, Massachusetts: Harvard University Press: 2002.

Seneca. "On Tranquillity of Mind," in *Dialogues and Letters*. Translated by C. D. N. Costa. London: Penguin Books, 1997.

Shaftesbury, Anthony. *Characteristicks of Men, Manners, Opinions, Times*. Indianapolis, Indiana: Liberty Fund, 2001.

Shakespeare, William. *Measure for Measure. The Complete Works of William Shakespeare, Vol. I: Comedies*. Roslyn, New York: Walter J. Black, Inc., 1937.

Shariff, Azin, F. and Kathleen D.Vohs," The world without free will: What happens to a society that believes people have no conscious control over their actions?" *Scientific American* 310, Number 6 (June 2014): 76-79.

Sharot, Tali. "The Optimism Bias," *Time* (June 6, 2011): 40-46.

Sharp, Gene. *The Politics of Nonviolent Action. Part One: Power and Struggle*. Boston: Porter Sargent Publishers, 1973.

Sharp, Gene. *The Politics of Nonviolent Action. Part Two: The Methods of Nonviolent Action*. Boston: Porter Sargent Publishers, 1973.

Sharp, Gene. *The Politics of Nonviolent Action. Part Three: The Dynamics of Nonviolent Action*. Boston: Porter Sargent Publishers, 1973.

Shermer, Michael. *The Moral Arc: How Science and Reason Lead Humanity Toward Truth, Justice, and Freedom*. New York: Henry Holt and Company, 2015.

Sidgwick, Henry. *The Methods of Ethics*. Indianapolis, Indiana: Hackett Publishing Company, 1981.

Shipman, Pat, "The Animal Connection and Human Evolution," *Current Anthropology* 51 (August 2010): 519-538.

Shostak, Marjorie. *Nisa: The Life and Words of a !Kung Woman*. Cambridge, Massachusetts: Harvard University Press, 1981.

Silk, Joan B., "Empathy, Sympathy, and Prosocial Preferences in Primates," in *Oxford Handbook of Evolutionary Psychology*. Eds., R. I. M. Dunbar and Louise Barrett. (Oxford: Oxford University Press, 2007), 115-126.

Singer, Peter. *Animal Liberation: The Definitive Classic of the Animal Movement*. New York: HarperCollins Publishers, 2009.

Singer, Peter. *The Expanding Circle: Ethics, Evolution, and Moral Progress*. Princeton, New Jersey: Princeton University Press, 1981.

Sistare, Christian T. "John Brown's Duties: Obligation, Violence, and 'Natural Duty'," in *Coercion and the State*. Edited by David A. Reidy and Walter J. Riker. Dordrecht, Netherlands: Springer Science+ Business Media B.V., 2008, 95-112.

Skinner, B. G. *Beyond Freedom and Dignity*. Indianapolis, Indiana: Hackett Publishing Company, Inc., 1971.

Smith, Adam. *The Theory of Moral Sentiments*. Cambridge, United Kingdom: Press Syndicate of the University of Cambridge, 2002.

Smith, Carolynn "K-Lynn" L. and Sarah L. Zielinski, "Brainy Bird: Chicken are smart and they understand their world, which raises troubling question about how they are treated on factory farms," *Scientific American* 310, No. 2 (February 2014): 60-65.

Smith, Joseph. *The Book of Mormon: An Account Written by the Hand of Mormon Upon Plates Taken from the Plates of Nephi*. Salt Lake City, Utah: The Church of Jesus Christ of Latter-day Saints, 1981.

Sorel, Georges. *Reflections on Violence*. Translated by T. E. Hulme. New York: B. W. Heubsch, 1912.

Spencer, Herbert. *The Principles of Ethics.* Two volumes. Indianapolis, Indiana: Liberty Fund, 1978.

Spinoza, Benedict de. *Ethics.* Translated by W. H. White. Ware, Great Britain: Wordsworth Editions Limited, 2001.

Spiro, Melvin. *Kibbutz: Venture in Utopia.* New York: Schocken Books, 1963.

Steinbeck, John. *East of Eden.* New York: Penguin Group Inc., 1980.

Stirner, Max. *The Ego and Its Own.* Translated by Steven Tracy Byington. David Leopold, ed. Cambridge: Cambridge University Press, 1995.

Stix, Gary, "The 'IT' Factor," *Scientific American*, Volume 311, Number 3 (September 2104): 72-79.

Stone, Douglas, Bruce Patton, and Sheila Heen. *Difficult Conversations: How To Discuss What Matters Most.* New York: Penguin Books, 1999.

Stout, Martha. *The Sociopath Next Door.* New York: Three Rivers Press, 2005.

Sun Tzu. *The Art of War.* Translated by Yuan Shibing. Wordsworth Editions Limited, 1998.

Swedenborg, Emanuel. *Heaven and Hell.* Translated by George F. Dole. West Chester, Pennsylvania: Swedenborg Foundation, Inc., 2008.

Taber's Cyclopedic Medical Dictionary. Edited by Clayton Thomas. Philadelphia, Pennsylvania: F. A. David Company, 1989.

Tagore, Rabindranath. *Nationalism.* Lexington, Kentucky: unidentified publisher, 2013.

Taleb, Nassim Nicholas. *The Black Swan: The Impact of the Highly Improbable.* New York: Random House, 2010.

Tancredi, Lawrence. *Hardwired Behavior: What Neuroscience Reveals About Morality.* New York: Cambridge University Press, 2005.

Tarkan, Laurie, "For Parents on NICU, Trauma May Last," *New York Times* (August 25, 2009).

Tattersall, Ian, "If I Had a Hammer: A radical new take on human evolution adds a large dose of luck to the usual story emphasizing the importance of our forebears' ability to make tools," *Scientific American* 311 No. 3 (September 2014): 54-59.

Tattersall, Ian. *Masters of the Planet: The Search for Our Human Origins.* New York: Palgrave MacMillan, 2012.

Taylor, Alison. *The Handbook of Family Dispute Resolution: Mediation Theory and Practice.* San Francisco, California: Jossey-Bass, 2002.

Taylor, Michael. *Community, Anarchy, and Liberty.* Cambridge: Press Syndicate of the University of Cambridge, 1982.

Taylor, Michael. *Anarchy and Cooperation.* Bath, Great Britain: John Wiley & Sons Ltd., 1976.

Thomas, Clayton L., ed. *Taber's Cyclopedic Medical Dictionary*, 17th ed. Philadelphia, Pennsylvania: F.A. Davis Company, 1993.

Thoreau, Henry David. *On the Duty of Civil Disobedience.* In *Walden and Civil Disobedience.* New York: Harper & Row, Publishers: 1965.

Thucydides. *The Peloponnesian War.* Translated by Rex Warner. Suffolk, Great Britain: Penguin Books, 1959.

Tierney, John, "Moral Lessons, Down Aisle 9," *New York Times*, March 24, 2010.

Todd, Peter M. and Gerg Gigerenzer, "Mechanisms of Ecological Rationality: Heuristics and Environments that Make Us Smart," in *Oxford Handbook of Evolutionary Psychology.* Eds., R. I. M. Dunbar and Louise Barrett. (Oxford: Oxford University Press, 2007), 197-210.

Tolstoy, Leo. *A Confession.* Translated by L. and A. Maude. San Bernadino, California: WLC Books, 2009.

Tolstoy, Leo. *The Kingdom of God Is Within You: Christianity Not as a Mystic Religion But as a New Theory of Life.* Translated by Constance Garnett. Breinigsville, Pennsylvania: Watchmaker Publishing, 1951.

Tolstoy, Leo. *A Letter to a Hindu.* Unknown translator. Introduction by Mohandas K. Gandhi. Lexington, Kentucky: Create Space Independent Publishing Platform, 2013.

Tolstoy, Leo. *The Kreutzer Sonata.* New York: Dover Publications, Inc., 1993.

Tolstoy, Leo. *A Letter to a Hindu.* Lexington, Kentucky: CreateSpace Independent Publishing Platform, 2013.

Tolstoy, Leo. *Hadji Murat.* Translated by Richard Pevear and Larissa Volokhonsky. New York: Vintage Books, 2012.

Tomasello, Michael. *A Natural History of Human Thinking.* Cambridge, Massachusetts: Harvard University Press, 2014.

Treffert, Darold A., "Accidental Genius," *Scientific American* 311 No. 2 (August 2014): 52-57.

Trivers, Robert. *The Folly of Fools: The Logic of Deceit and Self-Deception in Human Life.* New York: Basic Books, 2011.

Upanishads. Translated by Juan Mascaró. New York: Penguin Books, 1977.

Van der Linden, Sander, "How the Illusion of Being Observed Can Make You a Better Person," *Scientific American* online, at http://www.scientificamerican.com/article/how-the-illusion-of-being-observed-can-make-you-better-person/.

Wade, Nicholas. *Before the Dawn: Recovering the Lost History of Our Ancestors.* New York: Penguin Books, 2006.

Wade, Nicholas. *The Faith Instinct: How Religion Evolved and Why It Endures.* New York: Penguin Books, 2009.

Wade, Nicholas, "She Doesn't Trust You? Blame the Testosterone," *New York Times,* June 7, 2010.

Walzer, Michael. *Spheres of Justice: A Defense of Pluralism and Equality.* Lexington, Kentucky: Basic Books, 1983.

Watzlawick, Paul, ed. *The Invented Reality: How Do We Know What We Believe We Know? Contributions to Constructivism.* New York: W. W. Norton & Company, 1984.

Watzlawick, Paul, Janet Beavin Bavelas, and Don D. Jackson. *Pragmatics of Human Communication: A Study of Interactional Patterns, Pathologies, and Paradoxes.* New York: W. W. Norton & Company, Inc., 1967.

Wayland, Francis. *The Elements of Moral Science.* Cambridge, Massachusetts: Belknap Press, 1963.

Weaver, Richard M. *Ideas Have Consequences.* Chicago, Illinois: University of Chicago Press, 2013.

Weber, Max. *The Vocation Lectures*: "Politics as a Vocation." Edited by David Owen and Tracy B. Strong. Translated by Rodney Livingstone. Cambridge, Massachusetts: Hackett Publishing Company, 2004.

Weisman, Albert. *Countdown: Our Last, Best Hope for a Future on Earth?* New York: Little, Brown and Company, 2013.

Wells, H. G. *Men Like Gods.* Rockville, Maryland: Wildside Press, 1923.

Wells, Spencer. *Pandora's Seed: The Unforeseen Cost of Civilization.* New York: Random House, 2010.

Wertheimer, Alan. *Coercion.* Princeton, New Jersey: Princeton University Press, 1987.

Wiesel, Elie. *Night.* Translated by Stella Rodway. New York: Bantam Books, 1960.

Wilde, Oscar. "The Soul of Man Under Socialism," in *The Soul of Man Under Socialism & Selected Critical Prose.* London: Penguin Books, 2001.

Wilson, David Sloan, "Group-Level Evolutionary Processes," in *Oxford Handbook of Evolutionary Psychology.* Eds., R. I. M. Dunbar and Louise Barrett. (Oxford: Oxford University Press, 2007), 49-56.

Wilson, Edward O. *The Meaning of Human Existence.* New York: Liveright Publishing Corporation, 2014.

Wilson, Timothy D. *Redirect: The Surprising New Science of Psychological Change.* New York: Little, Brown and Company, 2011.

Winstanley, Gerrard. *The True Levellers' Standard Advanced.* Introduction by Will Jonson. San Bernadino, California: unknown press, 2016.

Wittgenstein, Ludwig, "Lecture on Ethics," delivered November 17, 1929, to the Heretics Society at Cambridge University. For critical text, see Wittgenstein, Ludwig. *Lecture on Ethics.* Edited by Eduardo Zamuner et. al. West Sussex, United Kingdom: John Wiley & Sons, Ltd: 2014.

Wittgenstein, Ludwig. *Philosophical Investigations.* Translated by G. E. M. Anscombe. Malden, Massachusetts: Blackwell Publishing Ltd., 2001.

Wittgenstein, Ludwig. *Tractatus Logico-Philosophicus.* Translated by C. K. Ogden. Mineola, New York: Dover Publications, Inc.: 1922.

Wolff, Robert Paul. *In Defense of Anarchism.* Los Angeles, California: University of California Press, 1998.

Wolin, S.J., and S. Wolin. *The Resilient Self: How Survivors of Troubled Families Rise Above Adversity.* New York: Villard, 1993.

Wollstonecraft, Mary. *A Vindication of the Rights of Men* with *A Vindication of the Rights of Woman* and *Hints.* Edited by Sylvana Tomaselli. Cambridge, United Kingdom: Cambridge University Press, 1995.

Wood, Bernard, "Welcome to the Family: The latest molecular analyses and fossil finds suggest that the story of human evolution is far more complex—and more interesting—than anyone imagined." *Scientific American* 311 No. 3 (September 2014): 42-47.

Woodcock, George. *Anarchism: A History of Libertarian Ideas and Movements.* North York, Ontario, Canada: University of Toronto Press, 2009.

Wright, Robert. *The Moral Animal: The New Science of Evolutionary Psychology.* New York: Vintage Books, 1994.

Wyman, Emily, and Michael Tomasello, "The Ontogenetic Origins of Human Cooperation," in *Oxford Handbook of Evolutionary Psychology.* Eds., R. I. M. Dunbar and Louise Barrett. (Oxford: Oxford University Press, 2007), 227-236.

Xenophon. *Memorabilia.* Translated by E. C. Marchant. Cambridge, Massachusetts: Harvard University Press, 1923.

Yin, Henry H., and Barbara J. Knowlton, "The Role of Basal Ganglia in Habit Formation," *Nature* 7 (June 2006): 464-476.

Yong, Ed, "Armor Against Prejudice: even subtle reminders of prejudice against one's sex, race or religion can hinder performance in school, work and athletics. Researchers have found new ways to reverse and prevent this effect," *Scientific American*, 308, Number 6 (June 2013): 76-80.

Zablocki, Benjamin. *The Joyful Community: An Account of the Bruderhof, a Communal Movement Now in its Third Generation.* Chicago, Illinois: The University of Chicago Press, 1980.

Zamyatin, Yevgeny. *We.* Translated by Mirra Ginsburg. New York: Harper Collins Publishers, 1972.

Zhisui, Li. *The Private Life of Chairman Mao: The Memoirs of Mao's Personal Physician.* Transalte by Tai Hung-Chao. New York: Random House, 1994.

Zhou, W.-X., R. A. Hill, and R. I. M. Dunbar, "Discrete Hierarchical Organization of Social Group Sizes," *Proceedings of the Royal Society B* 272 (February 17, 2005): 439-444.

Zhuangzi: Basic Writings. Translated by Burton Watson. New York: Columbia University Press, 2003.

Zimbardo, Philip. *The Lucifer Effect: Understanding How Good People Turn Evil.* New York: Random House, 2007.

INDEX

ACKNOWLEDGEMENTS

Many, living and dead, have contributed to this work. I thank each, though some of those best deserving gratitude hear no more.

Of my spouse, who perseveres, no superlatives of appreciation suffice.

My friends, who are always treasure, have proved rich support and loving editors. The members of the Witless Protection Program, a weekly Saturday morning reading cadre that convenes for adult conversation about difficult topics, deserve special praise. They recognize many streams of our fifteen year dialogue in these pages. Witless is an author of this book, if we count typing for nothing. *Cull*'s flaws are mine alone, since the Witless folk are perfect (or so they seem to me).

Last, I thank you, who have bothered to read this work. I smile, knowing you steal precious hours from tasks others deem more pressing to appraise our collective hurtle, to inquire where in the world we, willy-nilly, hasten. I trust these pages have rewarded your impudence.

SAINT GEORGE'S HILL PRESS

On St. George's Hill (southwest of London), in 1648, poor people, under the influence of Gerrard Winstanley, tilled and built shacks on public land to feed themselves, when food prices soared during the English Civil War. They called themselves True Levellers, and sought reduction of the financial chasm between the poor and the wealthy. The king sent a representative, who found the group doing no appreciable harm. A local lord felt otherwise, and commissioned thugs to assault the True Levellers. Some were beaten. Their common meal house was burned. Leaders were tried; the judge refused to let them speak in their defense. The True Levellers, dubbed Diggers by opponents, abandoned their plots for less hostile locations. In the twenty-first century, St. George's Hill is home to an exclusive gated and closely-guarded community, consisting in 450 mansions with tennis club and golf course amenities. St. George's Hill claims to be the premier private residential estate in Europe, close to London and Britain's most desirable private preparatory schools. The median price of a residence on St. George's Hill exceeds £3,000,000. St. George's Hill, then, is the dirt upon which clash desperate diggers and entrenched elites, a metaphor barely metaphorical.

Made in the USA
San Bernardino, CA
07 May 2017